P9-DFX-514

fundamentals of Management

ESSENTIAL CONCEPTS AND APPLICATIONS

Canadian Second Edition

STEPHEN P. ROBBINS
San Diego State University

DAVID A. DE CENZO
Towson State University

ROBIN STUART-KOTZE
Oxford University

Prentice Hall Canada
Scarborough, Ontario

Canadian Cataloguing in Publication Data

Robbins, Stephen P., 1943–
    Fundamentals of management: essential concepts and applications

Canadian 2nd ed.
ISBN 0-13-649377-7

1. Management.   I. DeCenzo, David A.   II. Stuart-Kotze, Robin.   III. Title

HD31.R5643   1999   658   C97-932696-6

© 1999, 1996 Prentice-Hall Canada Inc., Scarborough, Ontario
A Division of Simon & Schuster/A Viacom Company

ALL RIGHTS RESERVED

No part of this book may be reproduced in any form without permission in writing from the publisher.

Prentice-Hall, Inc., Upper Saddle River, New Jersey
Prentice-Hall International (UK) Limited, London
Prentice-Hall of Australia, Pty. Limited, Sydney
Prentice-Hall Hispanoamericana, S.A., Mexico City
Prentice-Hall of India Private Limited, New Delhi
Prentice-Hall of Japan, Inc., Tokyo
PEARSON EDUCATION ASIA PTE. LTD., SINGAPORE
Editora Prentice-Hall do Brasil, Ltda., Rio de Janeiro

ISBN 0-13-649377-7

Publisher: Patrick Ferrier
Acquisitions Editor: Mike Ryan
Developmental Editor: Amber Wallace
Senior Marketing Manager: Ann Byford
Copy Editor: Allyson Latta
Production Editor: Melanie M. Meharchand
Production Coordinator: Jane Schell
Photo Research: Karen Taylor & Alene McNeill
Permissions: Susan Wallace-Cox
Cover Design: Sarah Battersby
Cover Image: Image Bank/Michel Tcherevkoff Ltd.
Page Layout: Heather Brunton/ArtPlus Limited

Original edition published by Prentice Hall Inc. A Division of Simon & Schuster.
Upper Saddle River, New Jersey. Copyright © 1998, 1995 by Prentice-Hall, Inc.

    3 4 5   CC   03 02 01 00 99

Printed and bound in the United States of America.

Visit the Prentice Hall Canada Web site! Send us your comments, browse our catalogues, and more.
www.phcanada.com Or reach us through e-mail at **phcinfo_pubcanada@ prenhall.com**

Brief Contents

Contents

Contents

PART II PLANNING 59

CHAPTER 3
Foundations of Planning 59

CHAPTER 4
Planning Tools and Techniques 88

CHAPTER 7
Organization Design for the Twenty-first Century *171*

CHAPTER 8
Human Resource Management *208*

CHAPTER 9
Managing Change and Innovation 239

PART IV LEADING 264

CHAPTER 10
Foundations of Behaviour 264

CHAPTER 13
Leadership and Supervision   336

CHAPTER 14
Communication and Conflict Management   364

PART V CONTROLLING *392*

CHAPTER 15
Foundations of Controlling *392*

CHAPTER 16
Control Tools and Techniques *417*

Preface to Canadian Second Edition

To the Instructor

In the first edition of this book we said that we thought there was a market for a "different" kind of management textbook. Not different just for the sake of being different, but a book that was truly reflective of the "reengineering" efforts in the world of business. To us, that meant a book that focused on the foundations of management—one that covered the essential concepts of management, provided a sound foundation for understanding the key issues, had a strong practical focus, and yet also covered the latest research studies in the field. In short, a textbook that would provide a student with a solid understanding of managing in Canada and in the global economy. Also, a textbook that would be possible to teach in a one-term course. Perhaps most important, a book that provided significant value both in relevance and in cost to its readers. Our first edition sought to fill that need. This revision continues that tradition.

Assumptions

Every author who sits down to write a book has a set of assumptions—either explicit or implied—that guide what is included and what is excluded. We want to state ours up front.

Management is an exciting field. The subject matter encompassed in an introductory management text is inherently exciting. We're talking about the real world. We're talking about how a company like Hummingbird Communications can achieve five-year profit growth of 228 per cent; how small start-ups, such as Oasis Technology in Toronto, can achieve staggering growth in sales (114 per cent in five years); how companies such as Bombardier and Magna can become major players on the world stage; how to redesign an entire company to cut waste, control costs, and increase productivity; and techniques that can make a university more efficient and responsive to its students. A good management text should reflect this. For nowhere is it written that a textbook has to be dry and boring! It should include lots of examples and visual stimuli to make concepts come alive, capture the excitement of the field, and convey this to the reader.

It is our belief that management should not be studied solely from the perspective of "top management" or "billion-dollar corporations." The subject matter in management encompasses everyone from a supervisor to a chief executive officer. The content should give as much attention to the challenges and opportunities in supervising 15 clerical workers as to those in directing a staff of vice-presidents. Similarly, not everyone wants to work for a large company. Readers who are interested in working in small businesses or not-for-profit organizations should find the descriptions of management concepts applicable to their needs.

Content should emphasize relevance. Before authors commit something to paper and include it in their text, they should administer the "So what?" test. Why would someone need to know this fact or that? If the relevance isn't overtly clear, either the item should be omitted or its relevance should be directly explained.

Content must also be timely. We live in dynamic times. Changes are taking place at an unprecedented pace. A textbook in a dynamic field like management must reflect this fact by including the latest concepts and practices.

To reflect these changes occurring around us, we have built this book around the four functions of management supplemented with material on current issues affecting the field. For example, we take the reader through the changing world managers face (Chapter 2), look at organization designs for the twenty-first century (Chapter 7), and integrate throughout the text such relevant topics as reengineering, empowerment, work teams, and total quality management. The text is divided into five parts: Part I: Introduction; Part II: Planning; Part III: Organizing; Part IV: Leading; and Part V: Controlling. There are a total of 16 chapters; plus an appendix that describes the evolution of management thought.

Bringing an introductory management text in at 16 chapters required us to make some difficult decisions regarding the cutting and reshaping of material. After a lot of review and considerable discussion, we believe we've identified the essential elements students need in an introductory management course. Of course, the choice of "right topics" is a judgment call. We ask you, however, to take a look at our Table of Contents. We think you'll find included the critical issues that you typically expect in an introductory management text.

Important Features in the Book

Classic research studies   Achieving our goal of writing a "lean and mean" version of the 800-page hardback texts required some major changes. In addition to cutting material that we considered to be marginally relevant to introductory students, we concluded that much of the research that is covered in the "big books" was not as critical for introductory students. In fact, we cut through the theory where possible and emphasized a more practical approach to discussing management. But we respect the fact that there are classic studies that most authors include as part of the body of the text and that many instructors want their students to know about. Unfortunately, most students aren't as interested as text authors and instructors in the details behind these classics. In response, we've created boxed vignettes called Details on a Management Classic. Although the research implications are discussed in the body of the text, the background on the research is reserved for the Details boxes. For example, in Chapter 6, in our discussion of authority and power, conclusions based on Milgram's obedience study are presented. In an accompanying box, we provide details on how Milgram got his results. This approach allows you—the instructor—a choice of emphasizing research findings or leaving them out; whichever best facilitates your course objectives.

Management skills   We recognize that today's student is unlikely to end up as a CEO featured in *Report on Business Magazine*'s "Power Book." Rather, she is likely to be an entrepreneur, a senior executive in a small business, a manager in a not-for-profit organization, or a mid-level manager in a large company. Success in these jobs will require practical skills. Therefore, we have included skill boxes throughout the text, which provide a step-by-step basis for handling a particular facet of managing. We call these Developing Management Skills.

Ethics   Business educators now recognize the importance of including a study of ethics in all key business areas. Consistent with that, we have included Ethical Dilemmas in Management boxes. To increase student awareness of the broad range of ethical issues managers face, we pose ethical dilemmas for students to address.

Practical applications   Our experience has led us to conclude that students like to see and read about people who have had a significant influence on their organization's performance. Consequently, we have included Managers Who Made a Difference boxes. These sections feature managers—often prominent in the Canadian business world, sometimes very effective managers of small businesses—who have achieved such success. We have also added Young Canadians boxes that introduce students to the success stories of entrepreneurs under age 40.

Encouraging Understanding with In-text Learning Aids

Just what do students need to facilitate their learning? We began to answer that question by pondering some fundamental issues: could we make this book both "fun" to read and pedagogically sound—a book that motivates students to read on and that helps them to learn? Our conclusion was that an effective textbook should teach as well as present ideas. Toward that end, we designed this book to be a quality learning tool. Let us specifically point out some pedagogical features that we included to help students better assimilate the material presented.

Headings designed around questions   We have introduced major topic areas with main headings in each chapter. But within these headings are a series of questions to guide the reader in his learning. How many times have you had a student approach you and say that he is reading the material, but still not performing well on tests? From our experience, we have come to believe a lot of students confuse reading with understanding. We know they're not the same. To help students improve their understanding, we have created subheadings that read as questions. This allows readers to identify what important concept they should be looking for in a particular section.

Learning objectives   Before you start a trip, it's valuable to know where you're headed. That way, you can minimize detours. The same holds true in reading a text. To make learning more efficient, each chapter of this book opens with a list of learning objectives that describe what the student should be able to do after reading the chapter. These objectives will focus students' attention on the major issues within each chapter.

 Weblinks   Exciting and useful Internet sites are integrated throughout the text and are easily identifiable by the Weblinks icon shown here in the margin.

Chapter summaries   Just as objectives clarify where one is going, chapter summaries remind you where you've been. Each chapter of this book concludes with a concise summary organized around the opening learning objectives.

Review and discussion questions   Every chapter ends with a set of eight to 10 review and discussion questions. If students have read and understood the contents of a chapter, they should be able to answer the review questions. These review questions are drawn directly from the material in the chapter.

The discussion questions go beyond the content of the chapter. They require the reader to integrate, synthesize, or apply management concepts. The discussion questions will allow students to demonstrate that they not only know the facts in the chapter, but also can use those facts to deal with more complex issues.

Testing Your Comprehension questions Built-in self-tests at the end of each chapter allow students to assess their comprehension of issues and concepts in the text.

Self-assessment exercises Our experience is that students like to get feedback about themselves that they then can use in their development. Toward this end, we have included a self-assessment in each chapter. These self-assessments will focus on some managerial aspect from the chapter in which they are contained.

Class exercises Today's students are tomorrow's employees, who will undoubtedly work in teams. To help facilitate teamwork, we've included a number of in-class group exercises, which are also tied to content in their respective chapters.

Case applications Each chapter contains a recent, realistic, and—in most instances—an actual case of an organization that has experienced some dilemma. These end-of-chapter cases give students an opportunity to use one or more concepts discussed in the chapter, and apply them to actual problems faced by managers.

Video cases New video cases are featured at the end of each Part. These are based on episodes from the CBC *Venture* series. The write-ups of these video cases could also be used as stand-alone case applications for teachers not wanting to show the video.

Supplements Package

Fundamentals of Management, Canadian second edition, is accompanied by a complete supplements package.

Instructor's resource manual with video guide The guide contains both a brief and a comprehensive lecture outline for each chapter; answers to review and discussion questions; suggestions for discussing boxed material; discussion of both the self-assessment and class exercises; as well as answers to the case applications and video case questions, and video case notes.

Test item file The file contains more than 1,600 multiple-choice, true/false, and short essay questions. Each question is rated by level of difficulty and includes a text page reference. It is available in both printed and electronic formats.

Prentice Hall custom test The Prentice Hall custom test merges the test item file with a powerful software package in the Windows platform. With the Prentice Hall custom test's user-friendly test-creating abilities, you can create tailor-made, error-free tests quickly and easily. The custom test allows you to create an exam, administer it traditionally or online, and evaluate and track students' results—all with the click of a mouse.

Transparency resource package More than 150 transparency masters, including figures, graphs, and key concepts featured in the text, are available in printed format and electronically in PowerPoint 4.0.

Prentice Hall Canada/CBC Video Library Prentice Hall Canada and the CBC have worked together to bring you 10 segments from the CBC series *Venture*. These programs have extremely high production quality and have been chosen to relate directly to chapter content. Please contact your Prentice Hall Canada sales representative for details.

Companion Web site For a multitude of practice questions, key terms and concepts, Weblinks to related sites, newsgroups, CBC video updates, a syllabus builder, and more, check out the *Fundamentals of Management*, C/2/e, companion Web site at **www.prenticehall.ca/robbins_fom.**

Acknowledgments

Producing a textbook requires the skill and hard work of a number of people whose names never appear on the cover. We'd like to thank some of them here.

The people at Prentice Hall Canada Inc. deserve all of our gratitude. First and foremost, thanks go to Pat Ferrier, Publisher, the linchpin of an incredible staff. None of this could have been produced without him. Our gratitude goes out to Maurice Esses for his work on the previous edition. Amber Wallace, Developmental Editor: Our thanks for overseeing all facets of this book, from conception to birth—no small task. And for calmly and politely enforcing deadlines; diplomacy is a rare gift. Production Editor Melanie Meharchand, who came into the project in the middle of its chaos and calmly and dexterously dealt with all the problems, little and large. Leslie Mann, whose work on the last edition and on this one was superb. It has never been anything less than a true pleasure to work with Leslie; her patience, acumen, and professionalism have been greatly appreciated. We're certain that she will continue to excel in her new position as Senior Developmental Editor, and we'll miss working with her directly. Allyson Latta, Freelance Editor extraordinaire. Thank you for all your suffering in the trenches of incessant complications—and for never once complaining. At Prentice Hall in the U.S., Natalie Anderson and Judy Leale.

In addition to these people, we would also like to show our appreciation to the following for all their help: Jim Boyd, Lisamarie Brassini, Mary Helen Fitzgerald, Stephanie Johnson, Bill Oldsey, Margo Quinto, Crissy Statuto, Sandy Steiner, Teri Stratford. We gratefully acknowledge the contributions of the following reviewers: Ross Gowan, Fanshawe College; Beverly Linnell, Southern Alberta Institute of Technology; Norman Smith, Georgian College; Rae Verity, Southern Alberta Institute of Technology; and Monica Diochon, St. Francis Xavier University. Our apologies to anyone we may have inadvertently missed.

Finally we'd like to add personal notes. Each of us has some special people we'd like to recognize.

From Steve's corner: I thank my bride, Laura. You are making great strides in helping me balance my life. Every day is better because you're in it.

From Dave's: I'd like to recognize my family. Through thick and thin, they're always there. To Teri, my lovely wife, here's hoping that all our dreams are fulfilled. To Mark, Meredith, Gabriella, Natalie—and the dog and the cat—thanks. You've always been my inspiration and ever so special to me. Always remember that I am there—even if it is in my office "playing" on my computer.

From Robin's: I'd like to thank my wonderful son, Gavin, of whom I am inordinately proud, for all his help and ideas, and for his continuous mastery of the challenges of working with a father who travels over 160,000 kilometres a year. This one's for you Gavin.

To the Students

Now that our writing chores are over, we can put our feet up on the table and offer a few brief comments to those of you who will be reading and studying this book. First, this text exposes you to the fundamentals of management. As you'll see in our first chapter, fundamentals implies coverage of the basic functions of management. We've made every effort to give you the essential information a student will need to solidly build a knowledge foundation about this dynamic, exciting, and often chaotic field. A knowledge base, however, is not easily attained unless you have a text that is straightforward, timely, and interesting to read. We have made every effort to achieve these goals with a writing style that tries to capture the conversational tone that you would get if you were personally attending one of our lectures. That means logical reasoning, clear explanations, and lots of examples to illustrate concepts.

A book, in addition to being "enjoyable" to read and understand, should help you learn. Reading for reading's sake, without comprehension or understanding of what you've just read, is a waste of your time and effort. So we've developed a structure for this text that should serve as a learning aid. We've introduced major topic headings in each chapter. These number-one heads, as they are called, provide exposure to a broad management concept. Most of these number-one heads are followed by questions. Each of these "question" headings was carefully chosen to reinforce understanding of very specific information. Accordingly, as you read each of these sections, material presented will address the question posed. Thus, after reading a chapter (or a section for that matter), you should be able to return to these headings and "respond" to the question. If you can, congratulations. You've added to your knowledge base. If you can't, or are unsure of your response, you'll know exactly what sections need to be reread or reviewed, or where more of your effort needs to be placed. All in all, this format provides a self-check on your reading comprehension.

We've also added other checkpoints that you should find useful. Our review and discussion questions are designed to reinforce the chapter learning objectives from two perspectives. First, review questions focus on material covered in the chapter. These are another way to reinforce the important concepts in the chapter. The discussion questions require you to go one step further. Rather than requiring you to recite facts, discussion questions make you integrate, synthesize, or apply a management concept. True understanding of the material is revealed when you can deal with these more complex issues.

There is another element of this text that we hope you'll share our excitement about. These are our Developing Management Skills boxes. Practising management today requires sound competencies; competencies that can be translated into specific skills. In chapters 2-16, we've taken a major concept and developed a series of specific steps (skills) that if followed (and mastered), can make you more effective as a manager. We hope that you carefully review each of these, focus on the central behaviours we are explaining, and keep these handy for later reference in your career.

Good luck this semester—and we hope you enjoy reading this book as much as we enjoyed writing it.

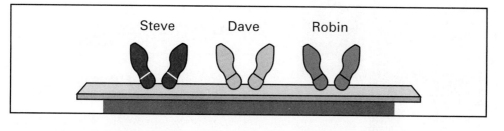

Steve Robbins   Dave De Cenzo   Robin Stuart-Kotze

companion Website...

Your Internet companion to the most exciting, state-of-the-art educational tools on the Web!

The Prentice Hall Canada Companion Website is easy to navigate and is organized to correspond to the chapters in this textbook. The Companion Website is comprised of four distinct, functional features:

1) **Customized Online Resources**

2) **Online Study Guide**

3) **Reference Material**

4) **Communication**

Explore the four areas in this Companion Website. Students and distance learners will discover resources for indepth study, research and communication, empowering them in their quest for greater knowledge and maximizing their potential for success in the course.

A NEW WAY TO DELIVER EDUCATIONAL CONTENT

1) Customized Online Resources

Our Companion Websites provide instructors and students with a range of options to access, view, and exchange content.

- **Syllabus Builder** provides *instructors* with the option to create online classes and construct an online syllabus linked to specific modules in the Companion Website.

- **Mailing lists** enable *instructors* and *students* to receive customized promotional literature.

- **Preferences** enable *students* to customize the sending of results to various recipients, and also to customize how the material is sent, e.g., as html, text, or as an attachment.

- **Help** includes an evaluation of the user's system and a tune-up area that makes updating browsers and plug-ins easier. This new feature will enhance the user's experience with Companion Websites.

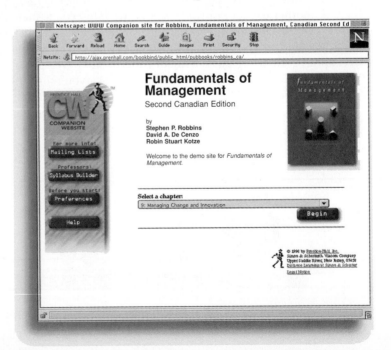

www.prenticehall.ca/

2) Online Study Guide

Interactive Study Guide modules form the core of the student learning experience in the Companion Website. These modules are categorized according to their functionality:

• True-False   • Multiple Choice   • Essay questions

The True-False and Multiple Choice modules provide students with the ability to send answers to our grader and receive instant feedback on their progress through our Results Reporter. Coaching comments and references back to the textbook ensure that students take advantage of all resources available to enhance their learning experience.

3) Reference Material

Reference material broadens text coverage with up-to-date resources for learning. **Web Destinations** provides a directory of Web sites relevant to the subject matter in each chapter. **NetNews (Internet Newsgroups)** are a fundamental source of information about a discipline, containing a wealth of brief, opinionated postings. **NetSearch** simplifies key term search using Internet search engines.

4) Communication

Companion Websites contain the communication tools necessary to deliver courses in a **Distance Learning** environment. **Message Board** allows users to post messages and check back periodically for responses. **Live Chat** allows users to discuss course topics in real time, and enables professors to host online classes.

Communication facilities of Companion Websites provide a key element for distributed learning environments. There are two types of communication facilities currently in use in Companion Websites:

• **Message Board** – this module takes advantage of browser technology providing the users of each Companion Website with a national newsgroup to post and reply to relevant course topics.

• **Live Chat** – enables instructor-led group activities in real time. Using our chat client, instructors can display Website content while students participate in the discussion.

Companion Websites are currently available for:
• Starke: Contemporary Management in Canada
• Kotler: Principles of Marketing
• Evans: Marketing Essentials
• Horngren: Cost Accounting
• Horngren: Introduction to Financial Accounting

Note: CW '99 content will vary slightly from site to site depending on discipline requirements.

The Companion Websites can be found at:

www.prenticehall.ca/robbins_fom

PRENTICE HALL CANADA

1870 Birchmount Road
Scarborough, Ontario M1P 2J7

To order:
Call: 1-800-567-3800
Fax: 1-800-263-7733

For samples:
Call: 1-800-850-5813
Fax: (416) 299-2539

E-mail: phcinfo_pubcanada@prenhall.com

chapter 1

Managers and Management

Learning Objectives

What will I be able to do after I finish this chapter?

1 • Differentiate managers from operatives.

2 • Define management.

3 • Distinguish between efficiency and effectiveness.

4 • Identify the roles performed by managers.

5 • Differentiate the activities of successful managers from effective ones.

6 • Explain whether the manager's job is generic.

7 • Explain the value of studying management.

8 • Distinguish among the process, systems, and contingency approaches.

The old adage that "only the strong survive" is especially true in the world of business. Here, survival means being better than the competition and doing things that others can't. In today's fiercely competitive markets, survival requires organizations to produce quality products and services in order to ensure that they meet customers' expectations. But how does an organization achieve these ends? The answer is through a vision created and implemented by individuals committed to the organization.[1]

These individuals are called managers, and they come from all walks of life. They differ in terms of shape, colour, age, and gender, but they have this in common: they work to produce a profit or to achieve some social good. But managers don't accomplish those goals by themselves. Rather, their goals are completed through the efforts of others.

Frank Stronach is one such manager. Stronach is the founder and chairman of Magna International Inc., an auto parts manufacturer based in Markham, Ontario. Magna is one of Canada's great success stories on the international scene. The company supplies parts and systems to such clients as Honda, G.M., Ford, Chrysler, Daimler-Benz, B.M.W., Volkswagen, and Toyota. Yearly revenue is more than $7 billion, and the company operates 128 manufacturing centres in 12 countries, with 30 years experience behind it.

Stronach accounts this success to Magna's management and labour, who operate in what he calls a "fair enterprise system." All employees at Magna benefit from a profit and equity participation plan, giving them a greater sense of commitment to the organization. Managers and labour are also given a good deal of decision-making authority, whereby their contributions to the organization are felt on a more personal level. Stronach himself has stated, "The system is stronger than any one person or group of people." Still, an organization needs strong leadership to guide its course, and in this capacity Frank Stronach excels.

Magna has managed to stay ahead of industry trends by understanding where the automotive industry is going and adjusting the organization to fit these changes. The large global automobile manufacturers are now demanding more from their suppliers; instead of dealing with many suppliers, they want to deal with a few to make their operations more efficient. Therefore, suppliers must have versatile manufacturing systems to produce a wide variety of parts to satisfy auto makers. Magna moved into this type of manufacturing long ago, anticipating the coming changes.

MAGNA INTERNATIONAL INC.
www.magnaint.com/

Frank Stronach controls one of Canada's top 25 corporations and is one of this country's most powerful businesspeople. You will read about many more Canadians who have achieved such staggering success and who manage billion-dollar organizations, but these people do not represent management as a whole. Managers can be found from under age 18 to over 80. Nowadays, they are as frequently women as they are men.[2] They manage large corporations, but also small businesses, government agencies, hospitals, museums, schools, and such nontraditional organizations as cooperatives. Some hold positions at the top of their organizations, while others are first-line supervisors. These people can also be found doing their managerial work in every country.

This book is about the work activities that Frank Stronach and the tens of millions of other managers like him do. In this chapter, we want to introduce you to managers and management by answering, or at least beginning to answer, these questions: Who are managers and where do they work? What is management and what do managers do? And why should you spend your time studying management?

Who Are Managers and Where Do They Work?

Managers work in an organization. Therefore, before we can identify who managers are, it is important to clarify what we mean by the term organization.

An **organization** is a systematic arrangement of people that accomplishes some specific purpose. Your college or university is an organization. So are fraternities, government agencies, churches, Canadian Tire Corporation, your neighbourhood gas station, the Canadian Medical Association, the Montreal Expos baseball team, and the United Way. These are all organizations because they all have three common characteristics.

organization
A systematic arrangement of people that accomplishes some specific purpose.

What Common Characteristics Do All Organizations Have?

First, each organization has a distinct purpose. This purpose is typically expressed in terms of a goal or set of goals. Second, each is composed of people. Third, all organizations develop a systematic structure that defines and limits the behaviour of its members. This would include, for example, creating rules and regulations, identifying some members as managers and giving them authority over other members, or writing job descriptions so that members know what they are supposed to do. The term organization therefore refers to an entity that has a distinct purpose, includes people or members, and has a systematic structure.

How does an organization like the 1997 world champions, Team Canada, become successful? By having a systematic arrangement of quality people all focused on achieving a goal.

How Are Managers Different from Operative Employees?

operatives
People who work directly on a job or task and have no responsibility for overseeing the work of others.

managers
Individuals in an organization who direct the activities of others.

Managers work in organizations, but not everyone in an organization is a manager. For simplicity's sake, we can divide organizational members into two categories: **operatives** or managers. Operatives are people who work directly on a job or task and have no responsibility for overseeing the work of others. The people who attach fenders in an automobile assembly line, serve your coffee at a Second Cup, or process your licence renewal application at the motor vehicles office are all operatives. In contrast, **managers** direct the activities of other people. They are shown in the coloured areas in Exhibit 1-1. Managers may also have some operative responsibilities; for example, an insurance claims supervisor may also have basic responsibilities to process insurance claims in addition to overseeing the activities of the other claims clerks in the department. However, our definition presumes that a manager has subordinates. Also, as shown in Exhibit 1-1, we typically classify managers as either first-line, middle, or top.

**Exhibit 1-1
Organizational Levels**

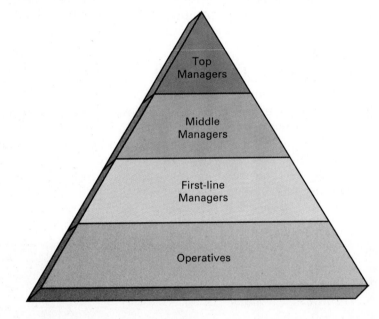

Top
Managers

Middle
Managers

First-line
Managers

Operatives

How Are Managers Classified?

first-line managers
Supervisors; the lowest level of management.

Identifying exactly who the managers are in an organization is often not a difficult task, although you should be aware that managers come packaged in a variety of titles. **First-line managers** are usually called supervisors. They are responsible for directing the day-to-day activities of operative employees. Middle managers may have titles such as department or agency head, project leader, unit chief, district manager, dean, bishop, or division manager. These individuals manage other managers (like a first-line supervisor) and are responsible for translating the goals set by top management into specific details that other managers can perform. At or near the top of an organization, managers typically have titles such as vice-president, president, chancellor, managing director, chief operating officer, chief executive officer, or chairperson of the board. These people are responsible for establishing the direction of the organization.

What Is Management and What Do Managers Do?

Just as organizations have common characteristics, so do managers. In spite of the fact that their titles vary widely, there are common characteristics to their jobs—regardless of whether the manager is a supervisor in the mail room at Alcan who oversees a staff of seven or the chairperson of the board of Barrick Resources. In this section, we define management, present the classical functions of management, review recent research on managerial roles, and consider the universal applicability of managerial concepts.

How Do We Define Management?

Management refers to the process of getting activities completed efficiently with and through other people. The process represents the functions or primary activities engaged in by managers. These functions are typically labelled planning, organizing, leading, and controlling. We elaborate on these functions in the next section.

Efficiency, a vital part of management, means doing the thing right. It refers to the relationship between inputs and outputs. For instance, if you get more output for a given input, you have increased efficiency. Since managers deal with input resources that are scarce—money, people, equipment—they are concerned with the efficient use of these resources. Management, therefore, is concerned with minimizing resource costs.

It is not enough simply to be efficient. Management is also concerned with getting activities completed; that is, it seeks **effectiveness**. Effectiveness, then, is doing the right thing. In an organization, this means achieving organizational goals (see Exhibit 1-2).

Efficiency and effectiveness are interrelated. For instance, it is easier to be effective if one ignores efficiency. Seiko could produce more accurate and attractive timepieces if it disregarded labour and material input costs. Some federal agencies have been regularly attacked on the grounds that they are reasonably effective but extremely inefficient; that is, they get their jobs done but at a very high cost. Management is therefore concerned not only with getting activities completed (effectiveness), but also with doing so as efficiently as possible.

Can organizations be efficient and yet not be effective? Yes, by doing the wrong things well! A number of colleges and universities have become highly efficient in processing students. Through the use of computer-assisted learning, large classes, and heavy reliance on part-time faculty, the administrators have significantly cut the cost of educating each student. Yet some of these colleges have been criticized by students, alumni, and accrediting agencies for failing to educate students properly. Of course, high efficiency is associated more typically with high effectiveness. And poor management is most often due to both inefficiency and ineffectiveness, or to effectiveness achieved through inefficiency.

management
The process of getting activities completed efficiently with and through other people.

efficiency
Doing the thing right. Concerned with the relationship between inputs and outputs; seeks to minimize resource costs.

effectiveness
Doing the right thing. Goal attainment.

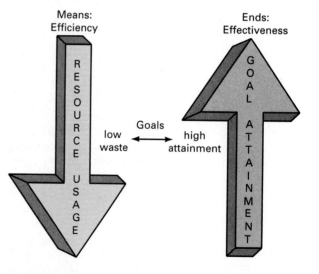

Means:
Efficiency

Ends:
Effectiveness

RESOURCE USAGE

GOAL ATTAINMENT

Goals

low waste ← → high attainment

**Exhibit 1-2
Management Seeks Efficiency and Effectiveness**

What Are the Four Functions of Management?

In the early part of this century, a French industrialist named Henri Fayol wrote that all managers perform five management functions: They plan, organize, command, coordinate, and control.[3] In the mid-1950s, two professors at UCLA used the functions of planning, organizing, staffing, directing, and controlling as the framework for a textbook on management that for 20 years was unquestionably the most widely sold text on the subject.[4] The most popular textbooks still continue to be organized around **management functions**, though these have generally been condensed to the basic four: planning, organizing, leading, and controlling (see Exhibit 1-3). Let's briefly define what each of these functions encompasses. Although we'll look at each as an independent function, keep in mind that managers must be able to perform all four functions simultaneously and that one function has an effect on the others. That is, these functions are interrelated and interdependent.

If you don't have any particular destination in mind, any road will get you there. Since organizations exist to achieve some purpose, someone has to define that purpose and the means for its achievement. Management is that someone. The **planning** function encompasses defining an organization's goals, establishing an overall strategy for achieving these goals, and developing a comprehensive hierarchy of plans to integrate and coordinate activities. Like Frank Stronach, good managers set goals to keep the work to be done in proper focus.

Managers are also responsible for designing an organization's structure. We call this function **organizing**. It includes determining what tasks are to be done, who is to do them, how the tasks are to be grouped, who reports to whom, and where decisions are to be made.

Every organization contains people, and it is management's job to direct and coordinate these people. This is the **leading** function. When managers motivate employees, direct the activities of others, select the most effective communication channel, or resolve conflicts among members, they are engaging in leading.

The final function managers perform is **controlling**. After the goals are set, the plans formulated, the structural arrangements delineated, and the people hired, trained, and motivated, something may still go amiss. To ensure that things are going as they should, management must monitor the organization's performance. Actual performance must be compared with the previously set goals. If there are any significant deviations, it is management's job to get the organization back on track. This process of monitoring, comparing, and correcting is what we mean when we refer to the controlling function.

The continued popularity of the functional approach is a tribute to its clarity and simplicity. But is it an accurate description of what managers actually do?[5] Following the functional approach, it is easy to answer the question, What do managers do? They plan, organize, lead, and control. But is this really true of all managers? Fayol's original functions were not derived from a careful survey of thousands of managers in hundreds of organizations. Rather, they merely represented observations based on his experience in the French mining industry.

---

management functions
Planning, organizing, leading, and controlling.

planning
Includes defining goals, establishing strategy, and developing plans to coordinate activities.

organizing
Determining what tasks are to be done, who is to do them, how the tasks are to be grouped, who reports to whom, and where decisions are to be made.

leading
Includes motivating employees, directing others, selecting the most effective communication channels, and resolving conflicts.

controlling
Monitoring activities to ensure that they are being accomplished as planned, and correcting any significant deviations.

Planning	Organizing	Leading	Controlling	Lead to	Achieving the organization's stated purpose
Defining goals, establishing strategy, and developing subplans to coordinate activities	Determining what needs to be done, how it will be done, and who is to do it	Directing and motivating all involved parties and resolving conflicts	Monitoring activities to ensure that they are accomplished as planned		

Exhibit 1-3
Management
Functions

YOUNG CANADIANS

Sarah Jane Baxter: SJB Enterprises

Following through on a great idea is not often all happiness and success. To make an idea work, one has to pay in the form of some anxiety and stress. Sarah Jane Baxter took a shot at following through on her idea of making Odd Noggins, kits designed to add some flair to boring bicycle helmets. Her company, SJB Enterprises in Toronto, began with Baxter producing all the kits herself. She quickly discovered that one of the first major obstacles a company faces is growing pains. After many headaches and sleepless nights, Baxter now contracts out production and focuses on other aspects such as marketing. A recent contract with Sea World in Florida has SJB making Odd Noggins kits with a likeness of Shamu the killer whale—quite a step from using her kitchen as a manufacturing centre.

What Are Management Roles?

In the late 1960s, Henry Mintzberg undertook a careful study of five chief executives at work.[6] What he discovered challenged several long-held notions about the manager's job. For instance, in contrast to the predominant views at the time that managers were reflective thinkers who carefully and systematically processed information before making decisions, Mintzberg found that his managers engaged in a large number of varied, unpatterned, and short-duration activities. There was little time for reflective thinking because the managers encountered constant interruptions. Half of these managers' activities lasted less than nine minutes. But in addition to these insights, Mintzberg provided a categorization scheme for defining what managers do based on actual managers on the job.

management roles
Specific categories of
managerial behaviour.

Mintzberg concluded that managers perform 10 different but highly interrelated roles. The term **management roles** refers to specific categories of managerial behaviour. These 10 roles, as shown in Exhibit 1-4, can be grouped under three primary headings—concerned with interpersonal relationships, the transfer of information, and decision making.

ROLE	DESCRIPTION	IDENTIFIABLE ACTIVITIES
Interpersonal		
Figurehead	Symbolic head; obliged to perform a number of routine duties of a legal or social nature	Greeting visitors; signing legal documents
Leader	Responsible for the motivation and activation of subordinates; responsible for staffing, training, and associated duties	Performing virtually all activities that involve subordinates
Liaison	Maintains self-developed network of outside contacts and informers who provide favours and information	Acknowledging mail; doing external board work; performing other activities that involve outsiders
Informational		
Monitor	Seeks and receives wide variety of special information (much of it current) to develop thorough understanding of organization and environment; emerges as nerve centre of internal and external information about the organization	Reading periodicals and reports; maintaining personal contacts
Disseminator	Transmits information received from other subordinates to members of the organization—some information is factual, some involves interpretation and integration of diverse value positions of organizational influencers	Holding informational meetings; making phone calls to relay information
Spokesperson	Transmits information to outsiders on organization's plans, policies, actions, results, etc.; serves as expert on organization's industry	Holding board meetings; giving information to the media
Decisional		
Entrepreneur	Searches organization and its environment for opportunities and initiates "improvement projects" to bring about change; supervises design of certain projects as well	Organizing strategy and review sessions to develop new programs
Disturbance handler	Responsible for corrective action when organization faces important, unexpected disturbances	Organizing strategy and review sessions that involve disturbances and crises
Resource allocator	Responsible for the allocation of organizational resources of all kinds—in effect, the making or approval of all significant organizational decisions	Scheduling; requesting authorization; performing any activity that involves budgeting and the programming of subordinates' work
Negotiator	Responsible for representing the organization at major negotiations	Participating in union contract negotiations

**Exhibit 1-4
Mintzberg's
Managerial Roles**

Source: Henry Mintzberg, *The Nature of Managerial Work* (New York: Harper & Row, 1973), pp. 93–94. Copyright © 1973 by Henry Mintzberg. Reprinted by permission of Harper & Row, Publishers, Inc.

How Are These Roles Evident in Managers' Jobs?

All managers are required to perform duties that are ceremonial and symbolic in nature, which are **interpersonal roles**. When the president of a college hands out diplomas at commencement or a factory supervisor gives a group of high school students a tour of the plant, she is acting in a *figurehead* role. All managers have a role as a *leader*. This role includes hiring, training, motivating, and disciplining employees. The third role within the interpersonal grouping is the *liaison* role. Mintzberg described this activity as contacting external sources who provide the manager with information. These sources are individuals or groups outside the manager's unit and may be inside or outside the organization. The sales manager who obtains information from the personnel manager in his same company has an internal liaison relationship. When that sales manager has contacts with other sales executives through a marketing trade association, he has an outside liaison relationship.

All managers will, to some degree, receive and collect information from organizations and institutions outside their own. Performing these activities is part of **informational roles**. Typically, this is done through reading magazines and talking with others to learn of changes in the public's tastes, what competitors may be planning, and the like. Mintzberg called this the *monitor* role. Managers also act as a conduit to transmit information to organizational members. This is the *disseminator* role. When they represent the organization to outsiders, managers also perform a *spokesperson* role.

Finally, Mintzberg identified four roles that revolve around the making of choices—**decisional roles**. As *entrepreneurs*, managers initiate and oversee new projects that will improve their organization's performance. As *disturbance handlers*, managers take corrective action in response to previously unforeseen problems. As *resource allocators*, managers are responsible for allocating human, physical, and monetary resources. Last, managers perform as *negotiators* when they discuss and bargain with other groups to gain advantages for their own units. (If you want to learn more about managers' roles, see Details on a Management Classic.)

interpersonal roles
Roles that include figurehead, leader, and liaison activities.

informational roles
Roles that include monitor, disseminator, and spokesperson activities.

decisional roles
Roles that include those of entrepreneur, disturbance handler, resource allocator, and negotiator.

Whenever a manager, like Maureen Kempston Darkes, CEO of General Motors Canada, represents the company to the community, that individual is performing what Mintzberg called the spokesperson role.

Are Effective Managers Also Successful Managers?

Fred Luthans and his associates looked at the issue of what managers do from a somewhat different perspective.[7] They asked the question, Do managers who advance most quickly in an organization do the same activities and with the same emphasis as managers who do the best job? You would tend to think that managers who were the most effective in their jobs would also be the ones who were promoted the fastest. But that's not what appears to happen.

Luthans and his associates studied more than 450 managers. What they found was that these managers all engaged in four managerial activities.

▶ **1.** *Traditional management:* Decision making, planning, and controlling
▶ **2.** *Communication:* Exchanging routine information and processing paperwork
▶ **3.** *Human resource management:* Motivating, disciplining, managing conflict, staffing, and training
▶ **4.** *Networking:* Socializing, politicking, and interacting with outsiders

Managers studied spent 32 per cent of their time in traditional management activities, 29 per cent communicating, 20 per cent in human resource management activities, and 19 per cent networking. However, the amount of time and effort that different managers spent on these four activities varied a great deal. Specifically, as shown in Exhibit 1-5, managers who were successful (defined in terms of the speed of promotion within their organization) had a very different emphasis from managers who were effective (defined in terms of the quantity and quality of their performances and the satisfaction and commitment of their subordinates). Networking made the biggest relative contribution to manager success, while human resource management activities made the least relative contribution. Among effective managers, communication made the largest relative contribution and networking the least.

This study adds important insights to our knowledge of what managers do. On average, managers spend approximately 20 to 30 per cent of their time on each of the four activities of traditional management, communication, human resource management, and networking. However, successful managers don't give the same emphasis to activities as do effective managers. In fact, they do almost the opposite. This challenges the historical assumption that promotions are based on performance, vividly illustrating the importance that social and political skills play in getting ahead in organizations.

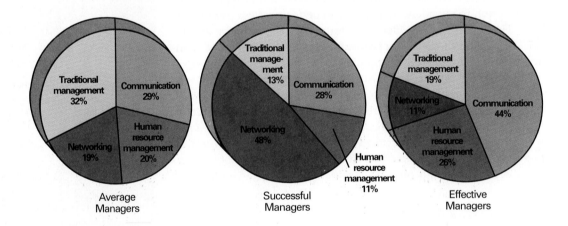

Exhibit 1-5   Distribution of Time per Activity by Average, Successful, and Effective Managers

Source: Based on Fred Luthans, Richard M. Hodgetts, and Stuart A. Rosenkrantz, *Real Managers* (Cambridge, Mass.: Ballinger Publishing, 1988).

Is the Manager's Job Universal?

We have previously mentioned the universal application of management. To this point, we have discussed management as if it were generic; that is, a manager is a manager regardless of where she manages. If management is truly a generic discipline, then what a manager does should be essentially the same regardless of whether he is a top-level executive or a first-line supervisor; in a business firm or a government agency; in a large corporation or a small business; or located in London, England, or London, Ontario. Let's take a closer look at the generic issue.

DETAILS ON A MANAGEMENT CLASSIC

Mintzberg's Roles

A number of follow-up studies have tested the validity of Mintzberg's role categories across different types of organizations and at different levels within given organizations.[8] The evidence generally supports the idea that managers—regardless of the type of organization or level in the organization—perform similar roles. However, the emphasis that managers give to the various roles seems to change with hierarchical level.[9] Specifically, the roles of disseminator, figurehead, negotiator, liaison, and spokesperson are more important at the higher levels than at the lower ones. Conversely, the leader role is more important for lower-level managers than it is for either middle- or top-level managers.

Have these 10 roles, which are derived from actual observations of managerial work, invalidated the more traditional functions of planning, organizing, leading, and controlling? Do they diminish the importance placed on these functions or negate the reasons we study them? No! First, the functional approach still represents the most useful way of conceptualizing the manager's job. "The classical functions provide clear and discrete methods of classifying the thousands of activities that managers carry out and the techniques they use in terms of the functions they perform for the achievement of organizational goals."[10] Second, although Mintzberg may offer a more detailed and elaborate classification scheme of what managers do, these roles are substantially reconcilable with the four functions.[11] Many of Mintzberg's roles align smoothly with one or more of the functions. Resource allocation is part of planning, as is the entrepreneurial role. All three of the interpersonal roles are part of the leading function. Most of the other roles fit into one or more of the four functions, but not all of them do. The difference is substantially explained by Mintzberg's intermixing management activities and pure managerial work.[12]

All managers do some work that is not purely managerial. The fact that Mintzberg's executives spent time in public relations or raising money attests to the precision of Mintzberg's observational methods, but shows that not everything a manager does is necessarily an essential part of the manager's job. This may have resulted in some activities being included in Mintzberg's schema that should not have been.

Do the comments above mean that Mintzberg's role categories are invalid? Not at all. Mintzberg has clearly offered new insights into what managers do. The attention his work has received is evidence of the importance attributed to defining management roles. Future research comparing and integrating Mintzberg's roles with the four functions will continue to expand our understanding of the manager's job.▼

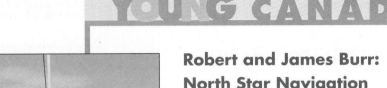

YOUNG CANADIANS

Robert and James Burr:
North Star Navigation

These brothers faced the first major organizational challenge for their small Quebec company when they took on a contract from Bell Canada to transport 117 repair vans to flooded areas in California. Hiring trucks, picking up vans throughout Ontario and Quebec, and having them delivered within 48 hours, these two proved they had the managerial ability to handle a crisis.

www.bell.ca/

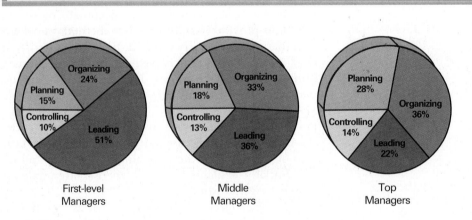

Exhibit 1-6 Distribution of Time per Function by Organizational Level

Source: Adapted from T.A. Mahoney, T.H. Jerdee, and S.J. Carroll, "The Job(s) of Management," *Industrial Relations*, Vol. 4, No. 2 (1965), p. 103.

We have already acknowledged that the importance of managerial roles varies depending on the manager's level in the organization. But the fact that a supervisor in a research laboratory at Northern Telecom doesn't do exactly the same things as the president of Northern Telecom should not be interpreted to mean that their jobs are inherently different. The differences are of degree and emphasis, but not of function.

In functional terms, as managers move up the organization, they do more planning and less direct supervising. This is visually depicted in Exhibit 1-6. All managers, regardless of level, make decisions. They perform planning, organizing, leading, and controlling functions. But the amount of time they give to each function is not necessarily constant. Also, the content of the managerial functions changes with the manager's level. For example, as we'll demonstrate in Chapter 7, top managers are concerned with designing the overall organization, while lower-level managers focus on designing the jobs of individuals and work groups.

Even though we recognize that all managers perform, to some degree, the four basic functions of management, a more crucial question becomes, What critical skills are related to managerial competence? In the 1970s, management researcher Robert L. Katz attempted to answer that question.[13] What Katz and others have found is that managers must possess four critical skills: conceptual, human, technical, and political.

Conceptual skills refer to one's mental ability to coordinate all of the organization's interests and activities. **Human skills** address the manager's ability to work with, understand, and motivate other people. **Technical skills** require one to use the tools, procedures, and techniques of a specialized field. Finally, **political skills** refer to one's ability to enhance one's power, build a power base, and establish the "right" connections. Undoubtedly, as we are becoming more skills-oriented in our pursuit of organizational goals, it becomes crystal clear that possessing and demonstrating these skills are important to one's success as a manager.

conceptual skills
A manager's ability to coordinate the organization's interests and activities.

human skills
A manager's ability to work with, understand, and motivate people.

technical skills
A manager's ability to use procedures and techniques of a specialized field.

political skills
A manager's ability to build a power base.

Is Managing the Same in Profit and Not-for-profit Organizations?

Does a manager who works for Revenue Canada or a public library do the same things as a manager in a business firm? Put another way, is the manager's job the same in both profit and not-for-profit organizations? The answer is, For the most part, yes.[14] Regardless of the type of organization a manager works in, there are commonalities to her job. All make decisions, set objectives, create workable organization structures, hire and motivate employees, secure legitimacy for their organization's existence, and develop internal political support to implement programs. Of course, there are some noteworthy differences. The most important is measuring performance. Profit, or the "bottom line," acts as an unambiguous measure of the effectiveness of a business organization. There is no such universal measure in not-for-profit organizations. Measuring the performance of schools, museums, government agencies, or charitable organizations, therefore, is made considerably more difficult. Managers in these organizations generally don't face the market test for performance.

Our conclusion is that while there are distinctions between the management of profit and not-for-profit organizations, the two are far more alike than they are different. Both are similarly concerned with studying the role of decision makers as they plan, organize, lead, and control.

Is the Manager's Job Any Different in a Small Organization Than in a Large One?

This question is best answered by looking at the job of managers in small business firms in terms of our previous discussion of managerial roles. First, however, let's define small business and the part it plays in our society.

There is no commonly agreed-upon definition of a small business because of different criteria used to define "small"—for example, number of employees, annual sales, or total assets. For our

Micheline Charest, founder of Montreal-based CINAR Films Inc., has taken her company (which produces and distributes nonviolent children's television programs) from its beginnings in the early '80s to revenue of more than $40 million a year in the late '90s.

small business
An independently owned and operated profit-seeking enterprise having fewer than 500 employees.

purposes, we'll call a **small business** any independently owned and operated, profit-seeking enterprise that has fewer than 500 employees.

Small businesses may be little, but they have a very large impact on our society. Small businesses in Canada far outnumber large ones, and account for most of our job creation; they employ more than 60 per cent of the private workforce; they dominate such industries as retailing and construction; and they will generate a significant majority of all new jobs during the next decade.

Now to the question at hand: Is the job of managing a small business different from that of managing a large one? A study comparing the two found that the importance of roles differed significantly.[15] As illustrated in Exhibit 1-7, the small business manager's most important role is that of spokesperson. The small business manager spends a large amount of time doing such outwardly directed things as meeting with customers, arranging financing with bankers, searching for new opportunities, and stimulating change. In contrast, the most important concerns of a manager in a large organization are directed internally—toward deciding which organizational units get what available resources and how much of them. According to this study, the entrepreneurial role—looking for business opportunities and planning activities for performance improvement—is least important to managers in large firms.

Compared with a manager in a large organization, a small business manager is more likely to be a generalist. His job will combine the activities of a large corporation's chief executive with many of the day-to-day activities undertaken by a first-line supervisor. Moreover, the structure and formality that characterize a manager's job in a large organization tend to give way to informality in small firms. Planning is less likely to be a carefully orchestrated ritual. The organization's design will be less complex and structured. And control in the small business will rely more on direct observation than on sophisticated computerized monitoring systems.[16]

Exhibit 1-7 Importance of Managerial Roles in Small and Large Firms
Source: Adapted from Joseph G.P. Paolillo, "The Manager's Self Assessments of Managerial Roles: Small vs. Large Firms," *American Journal of Small Business*, January-March 1984, pp. 61–62.

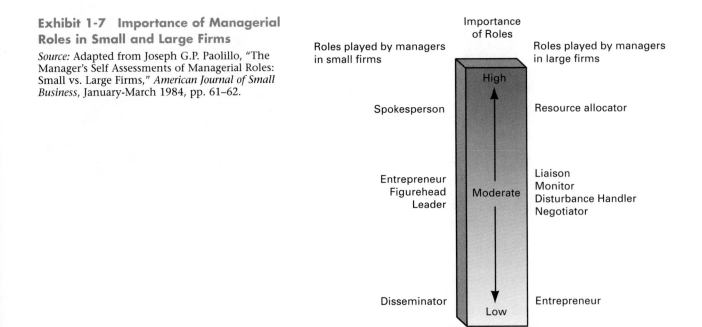

Again, as with organizational level, we see differences in degree and emphasis, but not in function. Managers in both small and large organizations perform essentially the same activities; what is different is how they go about them and the proportion of time they spend on each.

Are Management Concepts Transferable Across National Borders?

If managerial concepts were completely generic, they would apply universally, regardless of economic, social, political, or cultural differences. Studies that have compared managerial practices between countries have not generally supported the universality of management concepts. In Chapter 2, we'll examine some specific differences among countries. At this point, it is sufficient to say that most of the concepts we'll be discussing in future chapters apply to Canada, the United States, Great Britain, Australia, and other English-speaking democracies. However, we would have to modify these concepts if we wanted to apply them in India, China, Chile, or any other country whose economic, political, social, or cultural environment differs greatly from that of the so-called free-market democracies.

How Much Importance Does the Marketplace Put on Managers?

Good managers can turn straw to gold. Poor managers can do the reverse. This realization has not been lost on those who design compensation systems for organizations. Managers tend to be more highly paid than operatives. As a manager's authority and responsibility expand, so typically does her pay. Moreover, many organizations willingly offer extremely lucrative compensation packages to get and keep good managers.

If you were privy to the compensation paid to employees at such large public accounting firms as Price Waterhouse and Arthur Andersen, you would discover an interesting fact. Their best accounting specialists rarely earn more than $75,000 a year. In contrast, the annual income of their senior managing partners is rarely less than $125,000 and, in some cases, may exceed $750,000. The fact that these firms pay their managers considerably more than their nonmanagers is a measure of the importance placed on effective management skills. What is true at these accounting firms is true in most organizations. Good managerial skills are a scarce commodity, and compensation packages are one measure of the value that organizations place on them.

Do All Managers Make Six-figure Incomes?

All managers don't make six-figure incomes. Such salaries are usually reserved for senior executives. What could you expect to earn as a manager? The answer to this question depends on your level in the organization, your education and experience, the type of business the organization is in, comparable pay standards in the community, and how effective a manager you are. Most first-line supervisors earn between $25,000 and $45,000 a year. Middle managers start near $35,000 and top out at around $90,000. Senior managers in large corporations can earn $1 million a year or more. For instance *Report On Business Magazine*'s 1997 Power Book list of Canadian CEOs' salaries listed Laurent Beaudoin of Bombardier with a salary and bonus take of more than $19 million, Michael Brown of Thomson Corp. at more than $11 million, and Gerald Schwartz of Onex Corp. taking in more than $8 million.

Thomson Corp.
www.thomcorp.com/

Francesco Bellini was ranked third in the 1997 pay ranking in Canada compiled by *R.O.B.* magazine. His combined salary and bonus for the previous year was $9,993,104.

However, while the average cash compensation for the top 25 chief executives was roughly $6 million in 1996, this figure is not indicative of the Canadian business world as a whole.

However, while the average cash compensation (salary plus bonus) for chief executives at the 200 largest publicly held corporations was $3.2 million in 1992, Canadian executives are generally compensated on a much lower scale. Management salaries reflect the market forces of supply and demand. Management superstars, like superstar athletes in professional sports, are wooed with signing bonuses, interest-free loans, performance incentive packages, and guaranteed contracts.

Why Study Management?

The first reason for studying management is that we all have a vested interest in improving the way organizations are managed. Why? Because we interact with them every day of our lives. Does it frustrate you when you have to spend three hours in a department of motor vehicles' office to get your driver's licence renewed? Are you perplexed when none of the salespeople in a department store seem interested in helping you? Are you angered when you call an airline three times and its representatives quote you three different prices for the same trip? These are all examples of problems caused by poor management. Organizations that are well managed—including McCain Foods, Hummingbird Communications, Motorola, Bank of Nova Scotia, and Canadian Tire—develop a loyal constituency, grow, and prosper. Those that had been poorly managed—for example, General Motors or IBM—found themselves with a declining customer base and reduced revenues. Eventually, the survival of poorly managed organizations becomes threatened. Thirty years ago, Canadian Breweries, IAC, and Massey-Ferguson were thriving corporations. They employed tens of thousands of people and provided goods and services on a daily basis to hundreds of thousands of customers. But weak management did them in. These companies no longer exist.

The second reason for studying management is the reality that once you graduate and begin your career, you will either manage or be managed. For those who plan on careers in management, an understanding of the management process forms the foundation upon which to build their management skills. But it would be naive to assume that everyone who studies management is planning a career in management. A course in management may only be a requirement for a degree you want, but that needn't make the study of management irrelevant. Assuming that you will have to work for a living, and recognizing that you will almost certainly work in an organization, you will be a manager and/or work for a manager. If you plan on working for a manager, you can gain a great deal of insight into the way your boss behaves and the internal workings of organizations by studying management. The point is that you needn't aspire to be a manager to gain something valuable from a course in management.

How Do We Study Management?

www.moneys.com/

Prior to the mid-twentieth century, a number of diversified approaches to management were suggested (see Appendix, p. 450). In recent years, however, we have witnessed the establishment of a framework for integrating the various approaches to organizing the subject matter of management. These are the process, systems, and contingency approaches.

MANAGERS WHO MADE A DIFFERENCE

Len Bykowski: Money's Mushrooms

Money's Mushrooms was originally set up as a cooperative of mushroom farmers in British Columbia. It was devised by W.T. Money back in 1931 as a way to collectively market B.C.'s white mushrooms. Money's handled the marketing and distribution of the farmers' mushroom output. But problems arose in the late 1980s. The market in western Canada began to shrink substantially, but Money's management could do nothing to rectify the situation. The problem lay in the fact that as a cooperative, all of the 65 farmers involved had equal say in the operational decisions at Money's— effectively tieing the hands of the general manager (the organization went through nine managers in 12 years previous to Bykowski).[17]

When Bykowski took over the job of managing Money's, he was immediately hit with a desperate situation. The bank was threatening to cut off Money's line of credit, since the marketing organization was losing $1 million per year. Things looked bleak. Without the bank's support, operating expenses could not be met and Money's employees (150 of them) could not be paid. Bykowski was not aware going into the job that the situation was so dire. But he accepted the challenge. The bank was convinced to give Money's a stay of execution until Bykowski could come up with a solid business plan to save the organization.

The first move was to turn Money's into a corporation, thereby giving Bykowski and the management team he would select more decision-making authority. The farmers agreed to the idea, realizing that something major had to be done. Len Bykowski was then CEO of Money's Mushrooms Ltd., a newly formed corporation in drastic need of overhaul.

Bykowski formed a management team and the turnaround began. Money's convinced farmers to move into new products for new markets, both domestic and foreign. Focusing heavily on U.S. and Asian markets, Money's has now shifted 45 per cent of production to export. If Bykowski has his way, that figure will heavily increase. All told, Bykowski's turnaround has been rapid and successful. Within five years Money's had doubled its sales volume, and losses of $1 million annually have turned into profit. The future looks promising for Len Bykowski and his creation, Money's Mushrooms Ltd. ▼

What Is the Process Approach?

In December 1961, Professor Harold Koontz published an article in which he carefully detailed the diversity of approaches to the study of management and concluded that there existed a "management theory jungle."[18] Koontz conceded that each of the diverse approaches had something to offer management theory but then proceeded to demonstrate that (1) the human resources and quantitative approaches were not equivalent to the field of management, but rather were tools to be used by managers, and (2) a process approach could encompass and synthesize the diversity of the day. The **process approach**, originally introduced by Henri Fayol, is based on the management functions we discussed earlier. The performance of these functions—planning, organizing, leading, and controlling—is seen as circular and continuous (see Exhibit 1-3, page 7).

Although Koontz's article stimulated considerable debate, most management teachers and practitioners held fast to their own individual perspectives.[19] But Koontz had made a mark. The fact that most current management textbooks follow the process approach is evidence that it continues to be a viable integrative framework.

How Can a Systems Approach Integrate Management Concepts?

The mid-1960s began a decade in which the idea that organizations could be analysed in a systems framework gained a strong following. The **systems approach** defines a system as a set of interrelated and interdependent parts arranged in a manner that produces a unified whole. Societies are systems, and so too are automobiles, animals, and human bodies. The systems perspective, for instance, has been used by physiologists to explain how animals maintain an equilibrium state by taking in inputs and generating outputs.

There are two basic types of systems: closed systems and open systems. **Closed systems** are not influenced by and do not interact with their environment. In contrast, an **open systems** approach recognizes the dynamic interaction of the system with its environment (see Exhibit 1-8). Today when we talk of organizations as systems, we mean open systems; that is, we acknowledge the organization's constant interaction with its environment.

An organization (and its management) is a system that interacts with and depends upon both its specific and general environments (closed and open systems). Exhibit 1-8 shows a diagram of this perspective. For a business firm, inputs would be material, labour, and capital. The transformation process would turn these inputs into finished products or services. The system's success depends on successful interactions with its environment; that is, those groups or institutions upon which it depends. These might include suppliers, labour unions, financial institutions, government

process approach
Management performs the functions of planning, organizing, leading, and controlling.

systems approach
A theory that sees an organization as a set of interrelated and interdependent parts.

closed systems
Systems that are neither influenced by nor interacting with their environment.

open systems
Dynamic systems that interact with and respond to their environment.

**Exhibit 1-8
The Organization and Its Environment**

agencies, and customers. The sale of outputs generates revenue, which can be used to pay wages and taxes, buy inputs, repay loans, and generate profits for stockholders. If revenues are not large enough to satisfy environmental demands, the organization shrinks or dies. Management must understand its environment and the constraints that environment imposes.

What's a Contingency Approach to Management?

Management, like life itself, is not based on simplistic principles. Insurance companies know that everyone doesn't have the same probability of being in an auto accident. Factors such as age, gender, past driving record, and number of miles driven per year are contingencies that influence accident rates. Similarly, you can't say that students always learn more in small classes than in large ones. An extensive body of research tells us that contingency factors such as course content and the teaching style of the instructor influence the relationship between class size and learning effectiveness. It's not just a coincidence that university courses in introductory psychology are often taught in mass lectures—the course content lends itself well to the straight lecture format. The **contingency approach** (sometimes called the situational approach) has been used in recent years to replace simplistic principles of management and to integrate much of management theory.[20]

> **contingency approach**
> Recognizing and responding to situational variables as they arise.

A contingency approach to the study of management is intuitively logical. Since organizations are diverse—in size, objectives, tasks being done, and the like—it would be surprising to find universally applicable principles that would work in all situations. But, of course, it is one thing to say, "It all depends," and another to say what it depends upon. Management researchers, therefore, have been trying to identify these "what" variables. Exhibit 1-9 describes four popular contingency variables. This list is not comprehensive—at least 100 different variables have been identified—but it represents those most widely in use and gives you an idea of what we mean by the term contingency variable.

Organization Size The number of people in an organization is a major influence on what managers do. As size increases, so do the problems of coordination. For instance, the type of organization structure appropriate for an organization of 50,000 employees is likely to be inefficient for an organization of 50 employees.

Routineness of Task Technology In order for an organization to achieve its purpose, it uses technology; that is, it engages in the process of transforming inputs into outputs. Routine technologies require organizational structures, leadership styles, and control systems that differ from those required by customized or nonroutine technologies.

Environmental Uncertainty The degree of uncertainty caused by political, technological, sociocultural, and economic changes influences the management process. What works best in a stable and predictable environment may be totally inappropriate in a rapidly changing and unpredictable environment.

Individual Differences Individuals differ in terms of their desire for growth, autonomy, tolerance for ambiguity, and expectations. These and other individual differences are particularly important when managers select motivation techniques, leadership styles, and job designs.

Exhibit 1-9
Popular Contingency Variables

Summary

This summary is organized by the chapter Learning Objectives found on page 1.

1. Managers are individuals in an organization who direct the activities of others. They have such titles as supervisor, department head, dean, division manager, vice-president, president, and chief executive officer. Operatives are nonmanagerial personnel. They work directly on a job or task and have no responsibility for overseeing the work of others.

2. Management refers to the process of getting activities completed efficiently with and through other people. The process represents the functions or primary activities of planning, organizing, leading, and controlling.

3. Effectiveness is concerned with getting activities completed—that is, goal attainment. Efficiency is concerned with minimizing resource costs in the completion of those activities.

4. Henry Mintzberg concluded from his study of five chief executives that managers perform 10 different roles or behaviours. He classified them into three sets. One set is concerned with interpersonal relationships (figurehead, leader, liaison). The second set relates to the transfer of information (monitor, disseminator, spokesperson). The third set deals with decision making (entrepreneur, disturbance handler, resource allocator, negotiator).

5. Fred Luthans and his associates found that successful managers—those who got promoted most quickly—emphasized networking activities. In contrast, effective managers—those who performed best—emphasized communication. This suggests the importance of social and political skills in getting ahead in organizations.

6. Management has several generic properties. Regardless of level in an organization, all managers perform the same four functions; however, the emphasis given to each function varies with the manager's position in the hierarchy. Similarly, for the most part, the manager's job is the same regardless of the type of organization she is in. The generic properties of management are found mainly in the world's English-speaking democracies, and it is therefore dangerous to assume that they are universally transferable outside so-called free-market democracies.

7. People in all walks of life have come to recognize the important role that good management plays in our society. The study of management, for those who aspire to managerial positions, provides the body of knowledge that will help them to be more effective managers. For those who do not plan on careers in management, the study of management provides a great deal of insight into the way their bosses behave and into the internal activities of organizations.

8. A unifying framework for management began to be developed in earnest in the early 1960s. The process approach was proposed as a way to synthesize the diversity. Managers plan, organize, lead, and control according to the process approach. The systems approach recognizes the interdependency of internal activities in the organization and between the organization and its external environment. The contingency approach isolates situational variables that affect managerial actions and organizational performance.

Review and Discussion Questions

1. What is an organization? Why are managers important to an organization's success?

2. Are all effective organizations also efficient? Discuss.

3. What four common functions do all managers perform? Briefly describe them.

4. Contrast the four functions with Mintzberg's 10 roles.

5. What are the four managerial activities identified by Luthans? Contrast the emphasis placed on these four activities by average, successful, and effective managers.

6. How does a manager's job change with his or her level in the organization?

7. Is your instructor a manager? Discuss in terms of both Fayol's managerial functions and Mintzberg's managerial roles.

8. In what ways would the mayor's job in a large city and the president's job in a large corporation be similar? In what ways would they be different?

9. Some so-called managers oversee only assembly line robots or a room full of computers. Can they really be managers if they have no subordinates?

10. How might the job of an owner-manager of a small business compare with the job of president of a large corporation?

11. How is the process approach integrative?

12. Explain how practising managers can benefit by using the contingency approach.

Testing Your Comprehension

Circle the correct answer, then check yourself on page 471.

1. An organization is commonly considered a
   a) systematic arrangement of people to sell goods or services
   b) structural grouping of people to accomplish a set of objectives
   c) structural grouping of managers and subordinates to attempt to increase profits
   d) systematic grouping of people to establish procedures, rules, and regulations

2. Operatives can BEST be described as
   a) those who actually do the tasks of an organization
   b) those who work anonymously behind the scenes
   c) manual labourers
   d) those who supervise others

3. Which one of the following titles is usually associated with a middle manager position?
   a) receptionist/typist
   b) chairperson of the board
   c) dean of students at a university
   d) chief financial officer

4. Management is BEST described as the process of
   a) personally completing tasks in an efficient manner
   b) efficiently completing tasks with the help of others
   c) using scarce resources to minimize output
   d) organizing activities over a long period of time

5. When managers perform management functions such as organizing and planning, they are applying the teachings of
   a) Henry Mintzberg
   b) Henri Fayol
   c) Frank Stronach
   d) Len Bykowski

6. The managerial concept that focuses on task completion is
   a) efficiency
   b) of little concern to first-line managers
   c) mostly the job of top managers
   d) effectiveness

7. Which one of the following BEST demonstrates the concept of efficient management?
   a) getting activities completed
   b) maximizing output
   c) maintaining output with fewer resources
   d) increasing output and input

8. When a manager fails to complete the department's tasks but has used the resources sparingly and wisely, the results are said to be
   a) efficient and effective
   b) efficient and ineffective
   c) inefficient and effective
   d) inefficient and ineffective

9. The planning function of management includes
   a) directing the activities of others
   b) monitoring an organization's performance
   c) comparing actual results with plans
   d) establishing an organization's goals

10. The organizing function of management includes
   a) how tasks are to be grouped
   b) conflict resolution among subordinates
   c) comparison of actual results with a budget
   d) definition of an organization's goals

11. The activities of motivating employees, directing others, selecting the most effective communication channels, and resolving conflicts refer to which management function?
   a) planning
   b) organizing
   c) leading
   d) controlling

12. When a famous speaker, such as the prime minister of Canada, addresses a university graduating class, he is exhibiting Mintzberg's role of
   a) liaison
   b) disturbance handler
   c) disseminator
   d) figurehead

13. When Lisa Wilson, the sales manager of Acme Corporation, reviews actual sales and compares them with the annual forecast, she is demonstrating the management function of
    a) planning
    b) leading
    c) controlling
    d) organizing

14. Concerning Mintzberg's managerial roles, which of the following statements is MOST accurate?
    a) Managers perform essentially different roles in different types of organizations.
    b) Managers perform essentially different roles at different levels of an organization.
    c) The emphasis managers place on the various roles differs according to organizational level
    d) Roles of figurehead, disseminator, and liaison seem to be most appropriate for first-line managers.

15. Which of the following statements is MOST correct?
    a) Decisions in public organizations reflect political considerations, whereas business decisions are politically neutral.
    b) Both public and business organizations have essentially the same managerial functions.
    c) Managers in public organizations are constrained by procedures, but business decision makers rarely are.
    d) Compared with their business counterparts, public employees are more security-driven than they are involved with their work.

16. Which of the following statements is LEAST accurate?
    a) Regardless of the organizational level, managers perform essentially the same functions.
    b) Most managerial functions are the same throughout the world.
    c) Small and large organizations perform essentially the same functions.
    d) The entrepreneurial role is more prevalent in small organizations than in large ones.

17. Which of the following would not be considered stakeholders of an organization?
    a) retired employees of an organization
    b) customers
    c) fluctuations of the Canadian dollar
    d) public pressure groups

18. The view that management involves recognizing and responding to variables as they arise is known as the
    a) systems approach
    b) functional approach
    c) process approach
    d) contingency approach

Self-Assessment Exercise

How Strong Is Your Motivation to Manage in a Large Organization?

The following questions evaluate your motivation to manage in large and complex organizations. They are based on seven established role dimensions in the manager's job. For each question, circle the number that best describes the strength of your motivation.

	Weak						Strong
1. I have a desire to build positive relationships with my superiors.	1	2	3	4	5	6	7
2. I have a desire to compete with peers in games and sports.	1	2	3	4	5	6	7
3. I have a desire to compete with peers in work-related activities.	1	2	3	4	5	6	7
4. I have a desire to behave in an active and assertive manner.	1	2	3	4	5	6	7
5. I have a desire to tell others what to do and to impose sanctions in influencing others.	1	2	3	4	5	6	7
6. I have a desire to stand out from the group in a unique and highly visible fashion.	1	2	3	4	5	6	7
7. I have a desire to carry out the routine duties often associated with managerial work.	1	2	3	4	5	6	7

Turn to page 463 for scoring directions and key.

Source: Based on John B. Miner and Norman R. Smith, "Decline and Stabilization of Managerial Motivation Over a 20-Year Period," *Journal of Applied Psychology*, June 1982, p. 298.

Class Exercise

Class Expectations

One of the more unnerving aspects of beginning a new semester is gaining an understanding of what is expected in each class. By now, your instructor has probably provided you with a course syllabus that gives you some necessary information about how the class will function. Understandably, this information is important to you. Yet, there is another component—giving your instructor some indication of what you want/expect from the class. Specifically, there are some data that can be useful for providing insight. To help collect these data, you'll need to answer some questions. First, take out a piece of paper and place your name at the top; then respond to the following:

1. What do I want from this course?
2. Why is this important to me?
3. How does this course fit into my career plans?
4. How do I like an instructor to "run" the class?
5. What is my greatest challenge in taking this class?

When you have finished answering these questions, pair up with another class member (preferably someone you do not already know) and exchange papers. Get to know one another (using the information on these sheets as a starting point). Prepare an introduction of your partner, and share your partner's responses to the five questions with the class and your instructor.

Source: The idea for this exercise was derived from Barbara K. Goza, "Graffiti Needs Assessment: Involving Students in the First Class Session," *Journal of Management Education*, Vol. 17, No. 1 [February 1993], pp. 99–106.

Case Application

TSI Soccer Scores

Evan Jones started his company, TSI Soccer Corporation, because he felt there was room in the marketplace for a well-managed soccer equipment mail-order company. After devising a business plan and enticing investors, Jones rented space in a warehouse. Jones hires and trains each employee personally, stressing efficiency and customer satisfaction. Although he doesn't require employees to be soccer players, Jones encourages them to keep on top of the sport by reading *Soccer America*.[21] Jones wants everyone in the organization to know what is "hot" in the sport and how the business may have to transform itself to reflect changing trends. For example, Jones feels that a mail-order business alone is not good enough to be successful in the future. He believes TSI must expand into retail stores. Jones has already opened four stores and wants to have 20 in the next two years. This transition from a mail-order business to a retail chain with projected revenues of $40 million will make TSI the number one soccer retailer in North America.

Questions

1. Describe how Evan Jones performs the four functions of management.
2. What management roles did Evan Jones perform in starting TSI Soccer Corp.? Would any of these roles likely have changed over time?
3. Describe the management competencies Evan Jones must possess in order to become North America's number one soccer retailer.

c h a p t e r

2

The Changing Face of Management

Learning Objectives

What will I be able to do after I finish this chapter?

1 • Explain the importance of viewing management from a global perspective.

2 • Contrast multinational and transnational corporations.

3 • Describe why corporations downsize.

4 • Explain why small business concepts are being found in large companies.

5 • Describe the workforce of 2005.

6 • Identify the five primary components of TQM.

7 • Define social responsibility and social responsiveness.

8 • Differentiate between incremental change and quantum change.

9 • Explain the increased popularity of managers performing a coaching role.

10 • Define ethics.

11 • Describe why managers are concerned with stimulating innovation and change.

12 • Explain the workforce diversity implications for managers.

The emergence of the global marketplace has been one of the defining aspects of the 1990s. Trade barriers have been coming down, communications have taken massive strides forward, and businesses are increasingly looking to foreign markets for new opportunities. The year 1997 saw the third national trade mission overseas, the event that includes the prime minister, provincial premiers, and businesspeople who make up what has now been dubbed "Team Canada." The success of this trip was heavily touted by the federal government, which took credit for having lead the first trips of this kind. And, indeed, the trade mission was a coup for Canadian industry. Companies on the tour (which went through the Philippines, Korea, and Thailand) took in a total of $874 million in contracts, along with a further $1.25 billion worth of possible future business.

Doing business in foreign nations often differs greatly from doing business domestically. Canadian companies must be aware of the different customs of foreign nations. The advantages of the Team Canada approach are numerous. The involvement of the Canadian government can make foreign companies and governments feel more secure, and therefore more comfortable in their business dealings. Moreover, in Asian nations a personal approach toward business is more common than in North America. Before a deal is made, personal relationships must be formed, and this requires a third-party introduction. Then, as trust is fostered, business can follow. The Team Canada approach is very conducive to introductions of this sort. In cultures where official ceremonies are of extreme importance, the official aspect surrounding the prime minister and the premiers provides a good atmosphere for business introductions.

The prime minister and the premiers show that under some circumstances even they can work together for a common goal.

Succeeding in today's business environment is difficult at best. Faced with global competition, a need for better quality products and services, diversity in the workforce, and concerns for better treatment of the environment, managers have had to make sweeping changes in the way they do business. For companies that do, this results in both higher quality output and improved productivity from employees—and, ultimately, increased profitability. In the current dynamic business environment, managers need to rethink many of their old and established practices.

A generation ago, successful managers valued stability, predictability, and efficiency achieved through economies of scale. But many of yesterday's stars have faded. For instance, in Exhibit 2-1, we have identified a number of industries, the 1960s star, and the current leader in the market.

What common factors characterize today's stars? They're lean, fast, and flexible. They are dedicated to quality, work around teams, and minimize hierarchical overhead. Furthermore, employees in these organizations understand the right thing to do, as many of these companies stress the importance of managing the business in an ethical manner.

In this chapter, we'll establish a foundation for understanding this changing world of work. No successful organization can operate without understanding and dealing with the dynamic environment that surrounds it.

The Increasingly Dynamic Environment

As our 1960s stars in Exhibit 2-1 demonstrate, organizations that remain stagnant and highly bureaucratic are increasingly fading from the limelight. Why? Because one of the biggest problems in managing an enterprise today is trying to hold on to the past. Our world has changed, resulting in concerns for dealing with an international market, restructuring of our companies, and more emphasis being placed on the small business and entrepreneur. And if that isn't enough, our workforce has changed drastically over the past two decades. In this section, we'll explore some of the more important forces that are making the environment, in which managers must operate, more challenging.

INDUSTRY	1960s STAR	1990s STAR
Automobiles	General Motors	Toyota
Brewing	Canadian Breweries	Labatt
Broadcasting	CBS	CNN
Cameras	Bell & Howell	Minolta
Computers	IBM	Gateway 2000
Cosmetics	Revlon	L'Oreal
Film	Eastman Kodak	Fuji
Food	Dominion Stores	Loblaws
General Retailing	Sears	Wal-Mart

Exhibit 2-1
Corporate Stars:
1960s versus 1990s

What Is the Environment?

The recognition that no organization is an island unto itself was a major contribution of the systems approach to management (see Chapter 1). Anyone who questions the impact of the external environment on managing should consider the following:

▶ The bankruptcy of Eaton's meant heavy losses for many suppliers. Adorable Junior Garment of Montreal was owed roughly a million dollars for a shipment of spring clothes. Luckily, a U.S. vulture fund purchased the debt at 80 per cent—but the nearly 15 per cent of Adorable's business that Eaton's accounted for was suddenly up in the air. The company was forced to refocus its efforts on new U.S. markets.[1]

▶ Peerless Clothing of Montreal was faced with a major change in its business when the Free Trade Agreement was implemented between Canada and the U.S. One would assume that competition from the U.S. would pose a great threat, but, in fact, Free Trade was the saving grace for Peerless. The company had been losing money for years, but suddenly it changed its focus to south of the Canadian border. A lower tariff in Canada on European wool meant Peerless could produce its suits more cheaply than American manufacturers. Today Peerless is the largest producer of men's wool suits in North America. Sales in 1997 were more than $140 million.[2]

▶ When rebels deposed Zairian dictator Mobutu Sese Seko in May 1997, rebel leader Laurent Kabila assumed power. Suddenly Canadian mining company Tenke did not know whether its agreement with the former dictator over developing a copper-cobalt mine would remain valid under the new government. The whole project, including a $50-million (U.S.) down payment made by Tenke, was no longer secure.

environment
Outside institutions or
forces that potentially
affect an organization's
performance.

The measure of a company's
transnationality is based on the percentage of that company's foreign
business as compared to its domestic business. In the United Nations'
rankings of companies with at least
(U.S.) $4.5 billion in foreign assets,
Canadian-owned Thomson Corp.
(deputy chairman Michael Brown
pictured here) was the *most* transnational company in the world.

NORANDA
www.noranda.com/

**SPEEDY MUFFLER
KING**
www.speedy.com/

global village
The production and
marketing of goods and
services worldwide.

As these examples show, there are forces in the environment that play a major role in shaping managers' actions. The term **environment** refers to institutions or forces that are outside the organization and affect the organization's performance. As one writer put it, "Just take the universe, subtract from it the subset that represents the organization, and the remainder is environment."[3] But it's really not that simple.

To help make some sense of this quotation, let's consider an organization's environment as consisting of two areas: the general and the specific environments (see Exhibit 2-2).

The general environment includes everything outside the organization, such as economic factors, political conditions, the social environment, and technological factors. It encompasses conditions that may affect the organization but whose immediate effect is not clear. The specific environment, on the other hand, is the part of the environment that is directly relevant to the achievement of an organization's goals. It consists of the critical components that can positively or negatively influence an organization's effectiveness. The specific environment, then, is unique to each organization and may change with conditions.

The environmental factors that one organization is dependent upon and that have a critical bearing on its performance may not be relevant to another organization at all, even though both may appear at first glance to be in the same type of business. For example, Humber College and the University of Toronto are both institutions of higher education, but they do substantially different things and appeal to different segments of the higher education market. Subsequently, the administrators in each institution face different constituencies in their specific environments. What's the point of this defining of the environment? The elements in the environment are undergoing rapid change and are imposing new demands on organizations. As such, managers must respond—or see their organization decline or even go bankrupt.

Is There a Global Village?

Part of the rapidly changing environment managers face is the globalization of business. Management is no longer constrained by national borders. Noranda, Pan-Alberta Gas, Avenor, and Stone-Consolidated are examples of major Canadian companies that receive more than 70 per cent of their sales through exports. New Brunswick's McCain Foods, the world's largest french-fry producer, does business in places such as Argentina, Brazil, and even India. Bombardier sells Ski-Doos in Russia and has none other than Canada's old hockey nemesis, Vladislav Tretiak, selling them. Toronto-based Speedy Muffler King operates nearly 400 muffler shops in France. Similarly, many of the products and services we use are produced by foreign nations. Many of the companies we view as inherently Canadian are, in fact, owned by foreign interests. The TDL Group Ltd. (operators of Tim Hortons), for instance, is owned by Wendy's International, Inc., the American fast-food organization. And many Americans would be surprised to discover that Burger King is, in fact, owned by the British brewing company Guinness. The world has undoubtedly become a **global village**, and statistics such as those showing that 60 per cent of Canadian manufac-

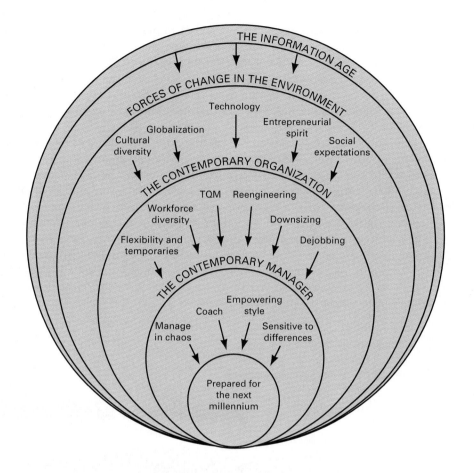

Exhibit 2-2
General versus
Specific Environments

tured goods were exported in 1996, compared to 30 per cent in 1988, make it clear that we have become a part of this phenomenon. In 1997, various international surveys ranked Canada as third in the world for countries expected to have the best business environment going into the new millenium; fourth in international competitiveness; and third in overall quality of corporate management. Also, a study found that Canada has 23 companies among the fastest-growing 200 in the world—with three companies in the top 15—while the U.S. did not have one in the top 25. Canadians can certainly compete in the global village. The world is changing rapidly, and successful businesses must change with it. To be effective, managers today need to adapt to cultures, systems, and techniques that are different from their own.[4]

In the 1960s, Pierre Trudeau described Canada's proximity to the United States as analogous to sleeping with an elephant: "You feel every twitch the animal makes." In the 1990s, we can generalize this analogy to the entire world. A rise in interest rates in Germany instantly affects managers and organizations around the globe. The fall of communism in Eastern Europe and the collapse of the Soviet Union, as well as the opening up of markets in places such as China, have created vast new opportunities for business firms throughout the world. The World Trade Organization, made up of nearly 70 countries, has begun to play a major role in shaping global business. A worldwide agreement on telecommunications, for example, was ratified in February 1997, allowing for substantially more freedom of competition. Canadian industry should benefit significantly from this easier access to world markets, because we are

WORLD TRADE
ORGANIZATION
www.wto.org/

leaders in the telecommunications field.[5] Another example that illustrates the point happened to Hershell Ezrin, CEO of Toronto-based Speedy Muffler King, while on a recent trip to Paris. Speedy operates nearly 400 muffler shops in France, and Ezrin was searching for a new Speedy billboard along a major thoroughfare in Paris. When Ezrin asked his cab driver if he knew the exact whereabouts of the sign, the driver immediately answered that he did, and that his country was "very proud of this French company."[6]

International businesses have been with us for a long time. Siemens, Remington, and Singer, for instance, were selling their products in many countries in the nineteenth century. By the 1920s, some companies, including Fiat, Ford, Unilever, and Royal Dutch/Shell, had gone multinational. But it wasn't until the mid-1960s that **multinational corporations (MNCs)** became commonplace. These corporations—which maintain significant operations in two or more countries simultaneously, but are based in one home country—initiated the rapid growth in international trade.

multinational corporations (MNCs)
Companies that maintain significant operations in more than one country simultaneously but manage them all from one base in a home country.

One way to grasp the changing nature of the global environment is to consider the country of origin for ownership of some familiar companies. Take a look at the following list and check which ones you think are Canadian owned. Write down the name of the country where the primary owners reside.

1. Nestlé (food)
2. Jaguar (automobiles)
3. Beatrice (foods)
4. Canada Dry Beverages (soft drinks)
5. Shell Oil (oil & gas)
6. Alcan (aluminum)
7. Union Gas (natural gas)
8. Rothmans Inc. (tobacco)
9. Husky Oil (oil & gas)
10. Connaught Laboratories Ltd. (pharmaceuticals)

transnational corporation (TNC)
A company that maintains significant operations in more than one country simultaneously and decentralizes decision making in each operation to the local country.

The global village is extending the reach and goals of MNCs to create an even more generic organization—the **transnational corporation (TNC)**. This type of organization doesn't seek to replicate its domestic successes by managing foreign operations from home. Rather, decision making in TNCs takes place at the local level. Nationals typically are hired to run operations in each country. And the products and marketing strategies for each country are uniquely tailored to that country's culture. Nestlé, for example, is a transnational. With operations in almost every country on the globe, it is the world's largest food company, yet its managers match their products to their consumers. Thus, Nestlé (which is a Swiss company) sells in parts of Europe, for instance, products that aren't available in Canada or Latin America.

We should point out that while managers of multinational and transnational organizations have become increasingly global in their perspectives and accept the reality that national borders no longer define corporations, politicians and the public have been slower to accept this fact. The United States has had a love/hate relationship with Japan for years. During the 1992 recession, the cry was "Buy American." The

---

There are only two Canadian-owned companies on the list: Alcan and Union Gas. Connaught Laboratories—France; Husky Oil—Hong Kong; Nestlé—Switzerland; Shell—Netherlands; Canada Dry—United States; Beatrice—Italy; Jaguar—United States (it's owned by Ford); Rothmans—The Netherlands.

irony is that many of the so-called Japanese products that critics were attacking were made in the United States. As a case in point, Honda employs more than 10,000 Americans at four plants in central Ohio and is now actually exporting Accords to Japan. Moreover, a number of those so-called American cars sitting in Chrysler show-rooms—cars with Dodge and Plymouth insignias—were made by Japanese workers employed by Mitsubishi Motors Corporation. Similarly, most Sony televisions sold in the United States are made in California, while "American" manufacturer Zenith's TVs are made in Mexico. The message from these examples should be obvious: A com-pany's national origin is no longer a very good gauge of where it does business or of the national origin of its employees.

Just a few years ago, international competition would be described in terms of country against country: the United States versus Japan, France versus Germany, Mexico versus Canada. In the 1990s, global competition is being reshaped by the cre-ation of regional cooperation agreements. The most notable of these are the 16-nation European Union, and the North American Free Trade Agreement (NAFTA). These regional cooperative arrangements among countries are essentially designed to stim-ulate trade among members by removing tariffs and other barriers. We have summa-rized these alliances in Exhibit 2-3.

		Exhibit 2-3
The European Union	The formation of the 16-nation European Union (Belgium, Denmark, France, Greece, Ireland, Italy, Luxembourg, Netherlands, Portugal, Spain, the United Kingdom, Austria, Sweden, Finland, Norway, and Germany) united 330 million people. By combining into a single market, the European Union is now one of the world's single richest markets.	**Trading Alliances**
North American Free Trade Agreement (NAFTA)	With the passage of NAFTA, a free trade zone from the Yukon to the Yucatan has been created. Encompassing Canada, the United States, and Mexico, NAFTA consolidates 360 million consumers into a $6-trillion market.	

Furthermore, with the Cold War over, communism is on the retreat, and capi-talism is spreading throughout the world. In the last several years, Germany has been reunited; countries such as Poland and Romania have introduced democratic govern-ments; and the former Soviet Union has become a set of independent states trying to implement market-based reforms. Even in Cuba, capitalism is becoming increasingly prevalent. The world is opening up to free markets and profit-seeking enterprises.

In terms of the changing global environment, the spread of capitalism makes the world a smaller place. Business has new markets to conquer. Additionally, well-trained and reliable workers in such countries as Hungary, Slovakia, and the Czech Republic provide a rich source of low-cost labour. The implementation of free markets in Eastern Europe further underscores the growing interdependence between coun-tries of the world and the potential for goods, labour, and capital to move easily across national borders. These changes should be of great benefit to Canada, because we are in an excellent position to take advantage of the new global business climate. In 1997

Canada was ranked by an international survey as having the fourth most competitive economy in the world.[7]

A boundary-free world introduces new challenges for managers. One specific challenge is managing in a different national culture. You know that your environment will differ from the one at home, but how? What should you look for?

cultural environments
The attitudes and perspectives shared by individuals from a specific culture, or country, that shape their behaviour and the way they see the world.

Anyone who finds herself in a strange country faces new challenges. These result from the legal-political, economic, and **cultural environments**. It is beyond the scope of this book to go into detail on these environments. Suffice it to say, using an old adage—When in Rome, do as the Romans! That is, whenever you go to another country, you must understand its legal, political, economic, and cultural systems. Not doing so may result in failure for that assignment—or worse, even death! A businessman in Vietnam was sentenced to face a firing squad in 1997 after being convicted of fraud, and laws enforcing such white-collar crime are set to become even more stringent.[8]

One definitive study of the differences among cultural environments was conducted by Geert Hofstede.[9] By analysing various dimensions of a country's culture, Hofstede was able to provide a framework for insight into what one might find when one goes to work in the global village (see Details on a Management Classic).

Why Are the Big Guys Laying Off?

downsizing
An activity in an organization designed to create a more efficient operation through extensive layoffs.

AIR CANADA
www.aircanada.ca/

Pick up any recent newspaper and you're almost assured of finding a common story in the business section—organizations are laying off workers, an action called **downsizing**. In the year leading up to 1997, 50,000 public sector workers across Canada were laid off. We have seen company after company—including major firms such as Air Canada, the major Canadian banks, Southam Inc, Sears Canada, Cape Breton Development Corp., and Canadian National Railways—all cutting staff by the thousands. But this phenomenon is not limited to Canada. Jobs are being eliminated in almost all industrialized nations. For example, Peugot (France) has cut nearly 10 per cent of its workforce in the last five years; AT&T (U.S.) has cut 80,000 positions; and Volkswagen (Germany) is eliminating about 30,000 jobs. Why? Because to maintain some flexibility to deal with the changes around them, companies had to create flatter structures and redesign the way work has traditionally been carried out. This means fewer levels of management between employees and senior management. Downsizing also promotes greater use of outside firms for providing necessary products and services (**outsourcing**), and redesign of work processes to increase productivity. Are we implying that big companies are disappearing? Absolutely not! But how they operate has changed.

outsourcing
An organization's use of outside firms for necessary products and services.

CANADIAN TIRE
www.canadiantire.com/

rightsizing
Linking staffing levels to organizational goals.

Big isn't necessarily inefficient. Companies such as Corel, Bombardier, and Northern Telecom have managed to blend large size with agility. But they typically divide their organization into smaller, more flexible units. Few managers today accept the notion that large organizations should automatically produce at lower cost because of economies of scale. Moreover, not every large corporation is laying off. Many are, in fact, increasing their workforces. Canadian Tire, for example, saw its workforce grow by roughly 30 per cent between 1993 and 1997. If adding staff in certain departments adds to the value of the organization as a whole, then this is the route to pursue. The objective is to link staffing levels to organizational goals, which is called **rightsizing**. In the steel industry, for example, many of Nucor's minimills are 20 to 60 per cent more efficient than the larger plants of Dofasco and Stelco.

Hofstede's Cultural Variables

individualism
A cultural dimension in which people are supposed to look after their own interests or those of their immediate families.

collectivism
A cultural dimension in which people expect others in their group to look after them and protect them when they are in trouble.

power distance
A cultural measure of the extent to which society accepts the unequal distribution of power in institutions and organizations.

uncertainty avoidance
A cultural measure of the degree to which people tolerate risk and unconventional behaviour.

quality of life
A national cultural attribute that reflects the emphasis placed upon relationships and concern for others.

quantity of life
A national cultural attribute describing the extent to which societal values are characterized by assertiveness and materialism.

To date, the most valuable framework to help managers better understand differences between national cultures has been developed by Geert Hofstede.[10] He surveyed over 116,000 employees in 40 countries who worked for a single multinational corporation. What did he find? His huge database indicated that national culture had a major impact on employees' work-related values and attitudes. More important, Hofstede found that managers and employees vary on four dimensions of national culture: (1) individualism versus collectivism, (2) power distance, (3) uncertainty avoidance, and (4) quantity versus quality of life.[11]

Individualism refers to a loosely knit social framework in which people are supposed to look after their own interests and those of their immediate family. This is made possible because of the large amount of freedom that such a society allows individuals. Its opposite is **collectivism**, which is characterized by a tight social framework in which people expect others in groups of which they are a part (such as a family or an organization) to look after them and protect them when they are in trouble. In exchange for this, they feel they owe absolute loyalty to the group.

Power distance is a measure of the extent to which a society accepts the fact that power in institutions and organizations is distributed unequally. A high power distance society accepts wide differences in power in organizations. Employees show a great deal of respect for those in authority. Titles, rank, and status carry a lot of weight. In contrast, a low power distance society plays down inequalities as much as possible. Superiors still have authority, but employees are not fearful or in awe of the boss.

A society that is high in **uncertainty avoidance** is characterized by an increased level of anxiety among its people, which manifests itself in greater nervousness, stress, and aggressiveness. Because people feel threatened by uncertainty and ambiguity in these societies, mechanisms are created to provide security and reduce risk. Their organizations are likely to have more formal rules, there will be less tolerance for deviant ideas and behaviours, and members will strive to believe in absolute truths. Not surprisingly, in organizations in countries with high uncertainty avoidance, employees demonstrate relatively low job mobility, and lifetime employment is a widely practised policy.

Quantity versus **quality of life**, like individualism and collectivism, represents a dichotomy. Some cultures emphasize the **quantity of life** and value things like assertiveness and the acquisition of money and material goods. Other cultures emphasize the quality of life, the importance of relationships, and show sensitivity and concern for the welfare of others.

Into which countries are Canadian managers likely to fit best? Which are likely to create the biggest adjustment problems? All we have to do is identify those countries that are most and least like Canada on the four dimensions.

Canada is strongly individualistic but low on power distance. This same pattern was exhibited by Great Britain, Australia, the U.S., the Netherlands, and New Zealand. Those least similar to Canada on these dimensions were Venezuela, Colombia, Pakistan, Singapore, and the Philippines.

Canada scored low on uncertainty avoidance and high on quantity of life. This same pattern was shown by Ireland, Great Britain, the Philippines, the U.S., New Zealand, Australia, India, and South Africa. Those least similar to Canada on these dimensions were Chile and Portugal.

These results empirically support part of what many of us suspected—that the American manager transferred to London, New York, Melbourne, or a similar Anglo city would have to make the fewest adjustments. In addition, the results further identify the countries in which "culture shock" is likely to be greatest and the need to modify one's managerial style most imperative. ▼

Once, when you had a job with CN, you had it for life. But difficult times have forced the company to take some Draconian measures, including the laying off of thousands of employees.

entrepreneurs
A manager who is confident in his abilities, seizes innovative opportunities, and capitalizes on surprises.

As noted above, management is cutting layers out of their organizations and widening the number of employees reporting to each manager. At Avcorp Industries in British Columbia, employees are involved in teams that span several functions and departments. Through this system, products are developed with input from a wide field of expertise. These teams are involved in various functional activities from production to engineering to marketing. The 1,500 Eastman Kodak employees who make black-and-white film are now organized horizontally. This means that these employees don't work in departments but in what they call "the flow." A 25-member leadership team watches the flow. Within the flow are "streams" defined by customers. And within these streams, most employees work in semiautonomous teams.

Why Is the Future of Business with Small Business?

In Chapter 1, we introduced the small business in terms of differences in managing a small business versus a large one. Although some differences were noted, the issue before us is one of size. As more and more companies downsize, the trend is for them to emulate the small business. Why? Generally speaking, small businesses are faster to respond to a changing environment. Because the owner/manager is involved in the day-to-day operations, that individual is usually closer to the customer.

The small business also has several other attributes that are welcomed in today's larger organizations. First, the owner/manager is usually the main decision maker, and all employees report to her. Accordingly, this is a flat organization containing very few, if any, layers of hierarchy. Second, individuals who manage these businesses often possess unique characteristics. They are independent workers who tend to take calculated risk, while at the same time tend to accept the fact that mistakes occur.[12]

In business, people who demonstrate these characteristics are often called **entrepreneurs**. Some organizations today have witnessed the benefits of having managers who possess these characteristics because it has helped increase the speed at which work gets done. Does this imply, then, that entrepreneurs can exist in large, established organizations? The answer to that question depends on one's definition of entrepreneur. The noted management guru Peter Drucker, for instance, argues that they can.[13] He describes an entrepreneurial manager as someone who is confident in his abilities, who seizes opportunities for innovation, and who not only expects surprises but capitalizes on them. He contrasts that with the traditional manager who feels threatened by change, is bothered by uncertainty, prefers predictability, and is inclined to maintain the status quo.

Drucker's use of the term entrepreneurial, however, is misleading. By almost any definition of good management, his entrepreneurial type would be preferred over the traditional type. Moreover, the term **intrapreneurship** is now widely used to describe the effort to create the entrepreneurial spirit in a large organization.[14] Yet intrapreneurship can never capture the autonomy and riskiness inherent in true entrepreneurship. This is because intrapreneurship takes place within a larger organization; all financial risks are carried by the parent company; rules, policies, and other constraints are imposed by the parent company; intrapreneurs have bosses to report to; and the payoff for success is not financial independence but, rather, career advancement.[15] We'll come back to entrepreneurs in the next chapter.

intrapreneurship
Creating the entrepreneurial spirit in a large organization.

YOUNG CANADIANS

Chris Griffiths: Griffiths Guitar Works

Chris Griffiths of St. John's, Newfoundland, took his first guitar apart at the age of 12. After that his career choice was a fait accompli. He opened his own custom guitar shop (doing repairs and selling custom-mades) at the age of 19. On the way he learned how to deal with bureaucracy trying to collect start-up capital, as well as all the difficulties of starting a new business. But it worked. Five years later Griffiths Guitar Works has seven employees and $370,000 in sales a year. Next on the agenda: a rock music camp operating year-round and, in the future, a plant to manufacture guitars on a large scale using cutting-edge technology.

What Will the Workforce of 2005 Look Like?

The bulk of the pre-1980s' workforce in North America consisted of male Caucasians, working full time to support a nonemployed wife and school-aged children. Such employees are now true minorities in organizations. Today's organizations are characterized by **workforce diversity**—that is, workers are more heterogeneous in terms of gender, race, and ethnicity. But diversity includes anyone who is different: the physically disabled, gays and lesbians, the elderly, and even those who are significantly overweight.

Until very recently, we took a "melting pot" approach to differences in organizations. We assumed that people who were different would somehow automatically want to assimilate. But we now recognize that employees don't set aside their cultural values and lifestyle preferences when they come to work. The challenge for managers, therefore, is to make their organizations more accommodating to diverse groups of people by addressing different lifestyles, family needs, and work styles. The "melting pot" assumption is being replaced by the recognition and celebration of differences.[16]

workforce diversity
Employees in organizations are heterogeneous in terms of gender, race, ethnicity, or other characteristics.

Why the Increased Concern with Quality?

total quality management (TQM)
A philosophy of management that is driven by customer needs and expectations.

There is a quality revolution taking place in both business and the public sector.[17] The generic term that has evolved to describe this revolution is **total quality management**, or TQM for short. It was inspired by a small group of quality experts, the most prominent of them being the late W. Edwards Deming.

An American, Deming found few managers in the United States interested in his ideas. Consequently, in 1950, he went to Japan and began advising many top Japanese managers on how to improve their production effectiveness. Central to his management methods was the use of statistics to analyse variability in production processes. A well-managed organization, according to Deming, was one in which statistical control reduced variability and resulted in uniform quality and predictable quantity of output. Deming developed a 14-point program for transforming organizations. (We'll look closer at this program in Chapter 16 when we discuss control techniques.)

**Exhibit 2-4
What Is Total Quality
Management?**

▶ **1.** Intense focus on the *customer*. The customer includes not only outsiders who buy the organization's products or services, but also internal customers (such as shipping or accounts payable personnel) who interact with and serve others in the organization.

▶ **2.** Concern for *continual improvement*. TQM is a commitment to never being satisfied. "Very good" is not good enough. Quality can always be improved.

▶ **3.** Improvement in the *quality of everything* the organization does. TQM uses a very broad definition of quality. It relates not only to the final product but also to how the organization handles deliveries, how rapidly it responds to complaints, how politely the phones are answered, and the like.

▶ **4.** Accurate *measurement*. TQM uses statistical techniques to measure every critical variable in the organization's operations. These are compared against standards or benchmarks to identify problems, trace them to their roots, and eliminate their causes.

▶ **5.** *Empowerment of employees*. TQM involves the people on the line in the improvement process. Teams are widely used in TQM programs as empowerment vehicles for finding and solving problems.

Today, Deming's original program has been expanded into TQM—a philosophy of management that is driven by customer needs and expectations[18] (see Exhibit 2-4). Importantly, however, the term "customer" in TQM is expanded beyond the traditional definition to include everyone who interacts with the organization's product or service, either internally or externally. So TQM encompasses employees and suppliers, as well as the people who buy the organization's products or services. The objective is to create an organization committed to continuous improvement.

TQM represents a counterpoint to earlier management theories that said low costs were the only road to increased productivity. The automobile industry, in fact, represents a classic case of what can go wrong when attention is focused solely on trying to keep costs down. Throughout the 1970s and 1980s, companies such as GM, Ford, and Chrysler ended up building products that a large part of the car-buying public rejected. Moreover, when the costs of rejects, repairing shoddy work, recalls, and

Who is singlehandedly regarded as the individual who helped build the quality into Japanese products? It's W. Edwards Deming, an American professor whose ideas on quality were originally rejected by American businessmen. Some 50 years later, however, Deming's concepts began to catch on and quickly spread in American corporate cultures. Before his death in December 1993, Deming gained the respect in America that he had held for half a century in Japan.

expensive controls to identify quality problems were factored in, the North American manufacturers actually were less productive than many foreign competitors. The Japanese demonstrated that it was possible for the highest-quality manufacturers also to be among the lowest-cost producers. Only recently have North American auto manufacturers realized the importance of TQM and implemented many of its basic components, such as quality control groups, process improvement, teamwork, improved supplier relations, and improved customer relations. TQM—or at least the recognition that continuous improvement in quality is necessary for an organization to compete effectively—is not just a fad. It is here to stay!

What Responsibility, If Any, Do Managers Have to the Larger Society?

The issue of corporate **social responsibility** drew little attention before the 1960s when the activist movement began questioning the singular economic objective of business. For instance, were large corporations irresponsible because they discriminated against women and minorities, as shown by the obvious absence of female and minority managers at that time? Was the Canadian pulp and paper industry ignoring its social responsibilities by clear-cutting areas of British Columbia forest large enough to be seen by the naked eye from the space shuttle?

Before the 1960s, few people asked such questions. Even today, there are good arguments that can be made for both sides of this issue (see Exhibit 2-5). Arguments aside, times have changed. Managers are now regularly confronted with decisions that have a dimension of social responsibility—some of the more obvious are philanthropy, pricing, employee relations, resource conservation, product quality, and operations in countries with oppressive governments. To help managers make such decisions, let's begin by defining social responsibility.

Few terms have been defined in as many different ways as has social responsibility. Some of the more popular meanings include "profit making only," "going beyond profit making," "voluntary activities," "concern for the broader social system," and "social responsiveness."[19] Most of the debate has focused at the extremes. On one side, there is the classical—or purely economic—view that management's

social responsibility
An obligation, beyond that required by the law and economics, for a firm to pursue long-term goals that are good for society.

CANADIAN
PACIFIC HOTELS
& RESORTS
www.cphotels.ca

only social responsibility is to maximize profits. On the other side stands the socioe-conomic position, which holds that management's responsibility goes well beyond making profits to include protecting and improving society's welfare.

Canadian Pacific Hotels & Resorts began an environmental program in 1990 for its hotels across the nation. At the time it was seen as groundbreaking. An employee survey found that more than 80 per cent of workers at CP would volunteer free time to environmental improvement. Since then the chain has cut institutional waste by 50 per cent, put blue boxes in the rooms, switched to energy-saving light bulbs, and introduced a host of other environmentally friendly reforms. As a result, CP's efforts have been adopted by hotels around the world, and CP has won more than 20 awards for environmental achievement, including the 1996 Green Hotelier of the Year Award from the International Hotel Association.[20]

How Can an Organization Go from Obligations to Responsiveness? Now it's time to narrow in on precisely what we mean when we talk about social responsibility. It is a business firm's obligation, beyond that required by the law and economics, to pursue long-term goals that are good for society.[21] Note that this definition assumes that business obeys the law and pursues economic interests. We take as a given that all business firms—those that are socially responsible and those that aren't—will obey all laws that society imposes. Also note that this definition views business as a moral agent. In its effort to do good for society, it must differentiate between right and wrong.

We can understand social responsibility better if we compare it with two similar concepts: social obligation and social responsiveness.[22] **Social obligation** is the foundation of business's social involvement. A business has fulfilled its social obligation when it meets its economic and legal responsibilities and no more. It does the minimum that the law requires. A firm pursues social goals only to the extent that they contribute to its economic goals. In contrast to social obligation, both social responsibility and social responsiveness go beyond merely meeting basic economic and legal standards.

Social responsibility adds an ethical imperative to do things that make society better, and not to do those that could make it worse. **Social responsiveness** refers to the capacity of a firm to adapt to changing societal conditions.[23]

As Exhibit 2-6 (page 42) describes, social responsibility requires business to determine what is right or wrong and thus seek fundamental ethical truths. Social responsiveness is guided by social norms. The value of social norms is that they can provide managers, such as Marlene Conway (see Managers Who Made a Difference), with a more meaningful guide for decision making. The following makes the distinction clearer.

When a company meets pollution control standards established by the federal government or doesn't discriminate against employees over the age of 40 in promotion decisions, it is meeting its social obligation and nothing more. The law says that the company may not pollute or practise age discrimination. Public opinion and changing social values shape social responsiveness in organizations. The government of Prince Edward Island's pledge to institute a province-wide waste management system by the year 2000 is a socially responsive measure. The desire of individual municipalities

social obligation
The obligation of a business to meet its economic and legal responsibilities.

social responsiveness
The capacity of a firm to adapt to changing societal conditions.

Exhibit 2-5 Arguments for and against Social Responsibility
Source: Based on R. Joseph Monsen, Jr., "The Social Attitudes of Management," in Joseph M. McGuire, ed. *Contemporary Management: Issues and Views* (Englewood Cliffs, N.J.: Prentice-Hall, Inc., 1974), p. 616; and Keith Davis and William Frederick, *Business and Society: Management, Public Policy, Ethics*, 5th ed. (New York: McGraw Hill, Inc., 1984), pp. 28–41.

▶

The major arguments supporting the assumption of social responsibilities by business are:

▶ **1. Public expectations.** Social expectations of business have increased dramatically since the 1960s. Public opinion in support of business pursuing social as well as economic goals is now well solidified.

▶ **2. Long-run profits.** Socially responsible businesses tend to have more secure long-run profits. This is the normal result of the better community relations and improved business image that responsible behaviour brings.

▶ **3. Ethical obligation.** A business firm can and should have a conscience. Business should be socially responsible because responsible actions are right for their own sake.

▶ **4. Public image.** Firms seek to enhance their public image to gain more customers, better employees, access to money markets, and other benefits. Since the public considers social goals to be important, business can create a favourable public image by pursuing social goals.

▶ **5. Better environment.** Involvement by business can solve difficult social problems, thus creating a better quality of life and a more desirable community in which to attract and hold skilled employees.

▶ **6. Discouragement of further government regulation.** Government regulation adds economic costs and restricts management's decision flexibility. By becoming socially responsible, business can expect less government regulation.

▶ **7. Balance of responsibility and power.** Business has a large amount of power in society. An equally large amount of responsibility is required to balance it. When power is significantly greater than responsibility, the imbalance encourages irresponsible behaviour that works against the public good.

▶ **8. Stockholder interests.** Social responsibility will improve the price of a business's stock in the long run. The stock market will view the socially responsible company as less risky and open to public attack. Therefore, it will award its stock a higher price-earnings ratio.

▶ **9. Possession of resources.** Business has the financial resources, technical experts, and managerial talent to provide support to public and charitable projects that need assistance.

▶ **10. Superiority of prevention over cures.** Social problems must be dealt with at some time. Business should act on them before they become more serious and costly to correct and take management's energy away from accomplishing its goal of producing goods and services.

The major arguments against business assuming social responsibility are:

▶ **1. Violation of profit maximization.** This is the essence of the classical viewpoint. Business is most socially responsible when it attends strictly to its economic interests and leaves other activities to other institutions.

▶ **2. Dilution of purpose.** The pursuit of social goals dilutes business's primary purpose: economic productivity. Society may suffer as both economic and social goals are poorly accomplished.

▶ **3. Costs.** Many socially responsible activities don't pay their own way. Someone has to pay these costs. Business must absorb these costs or pass them on to consumers in higher prices.

▶ **4. Too much power.** Business is already one of the most powerful institutions in our society. If it pursued social goals, it would have even more power. Society has given business enough power.

▶ **5. Lack of skills.** The outlook and abilities of business leaders are oriented primarily toward economics. Business people are poorly qualified to cope with social issues.

▶ **6. Lack of accountability.** Political representatives pursue social goals and are held accountable for their actions. Such is not the case with business leaders. There are no direct lines of social accountability from the business sector to the public.

▶ **7. Lack of broad public support.** There is no broad mandate from society for business to become involved in social issues. The public is divided on the issue. In fact, it is a topic that rarely fails to generate a heated debate. Actions taken under such divided support are likely to fail.

for the creation of a provincial system that will use recyclables and compost materials, and reduce landfill waste by half, has forced the government to act. If the government of P.E.I. had taken this action a decade ago, it would have been characterized as socially responsible.[24]

How Is Social Responsibility Extended to Women in the Workplace?

What about an organization's responsibility to its employees—especially women? Over the past few years there has been a major concern over the issue of sexual harassment in our organizations. How did this come about?

Professor Anita Hill's widely publicized allegations of sexual harassment against the U.S. Supreme Court nominee Clarence Thomas in the fall of 1991 singlehandedly moved the topic of sexual harassment to the top of many organizations' education agendas.[25]

sexual harassment
Behaviour marked by sexually suggestive remarks, unwanted touching and sexual advances, requests for sexual favours, or other verbal or physical conduct of a sexual nature.

Sexual harassment that is work related has been defined by the Violence Against Women Survey conducted by Statistics Canada[26] as the following unwelcome actions by co-workers, bosses, customers, patients, or students:

▶ making a woman uncomfortable by commenting inappropriately about her body or sex life;
▶ making her uncomfortable by repeatedly asking for a date and refusing to take no for an answer;
▶ leaning over her unnecessarily, getting too close, or cornering her;
▶ hinting that she could lose her job, or that her employment situation might suffer, if she is unwilling to have a sexual relationship.

The Statistics Canada survey was the first national survey of its kind to be conducted anywhere in the world. It reported that almost 25 per cent of Canadian women over 18 have been sexually harassed on the job. The most frequent assailants were coworkers and bosses. The least severe forms of harassment were the most prevalent, with 77 per cent of the women who reported being harrassed saying that a man had made inappropriate comments about their body or sex life, while 18 per cent reported being pressured to have sex under the threat that their job might suffer. The more severe forms of sexual harassment, such as unwanted sexual touching and being forced into having sex, were reported by 5 per cent and 1 per cent of the respondents respectively.[27]

**Exhibit 2-6
Social Responsibility
versus Social
Responsiveness**

Source: Adapted from Steven L. Wartick and Philip L. Cochran, "The Evolution of the Corporate Social Performance Model," *Academy of Management Review*, October 1985, p. 766.

	SOCIAL RESPONSIBILITY	SOCIAL RESPONSIVENESS
Major consideration	Ethical	Pragmatic
Focus	Ends	Means
Emphasis	Obligation	Responses
Decision framework	Long-term	Medium- and short-term

Marlene Conway at Envirolutions

Ten years ago Marlene Conway was climbing the ranks at C.I.B.C., enjoying her work and living a very settled life, when everything began to change. Conway suddenly found herself having to raise her two children and shoulder the burden of debt on her own. Faced with this situation she decided to take control of her life, but in order to do this she had to be willing to enter a world that was wholly unfamiliar to her.[28]

For some time Marlene Conway had been thinking about the vast amounts of disposable diapers her children were going through. Conway had been considering the possibility of recycling, and had been researching the problem in her spare time. Suddenly this became more than an idea in the back of her mind—it became her future. Conway quit her job at the bank and devoted herself to Knowaste, the company she formed and dedicated to the challenge of turning diapers into a renewable resource. Familiarizing herself with the scientific understanding involved was Conway's first task, along with raising $1 million to begin research and development. Conway achieved both tasks within a year and a half, and had landed some free space to set up her lab. From there Knowaste formed strategic partnerships with some major companies such as Procter & Gamble and DuPont. Eventually Knowaste developed a process, which they patented, that allows wood pulp to be separated from the diaper's super-absorbent polymer. This allows the two substances to be recycled. This is cutting-edge technology, and the potential for its use is enormous. Five million tonnes of diapers are disposed of each year in North America. Knowaste today is controlled by Caithness Resources Inc., which had become the major investor in the company. Under Caithness' guidance, Knowaste has set up contracts with nearly 400 hospitals and day-cares. They have also begun to test a "pink bag" program that would run alongside blue box operations in residential areas. Knowaste's plans for expansion are huge—including the construction of 21 plants worldwide in the next decade.

Marlene Conway remains the second-largest shareholder in Knowaste, and stands to become very wealthy as a result of the technology she pioneered, but today she is more concerned with her new projects. Under the moniker Envirolutions, Conway has begun a new company dedicated to environmental concerns. Some of the projects she and her team are working on include turning zebra mussels into fertilizer, producing bricks from materials culled from carpeting, developing an industrial-waste water treatment process, and creating another process for recycling medical waste. Not bad for someone without much scientific or managerial experience.

DEVELOPING MANAGEMENT SKILLS

▼ GUIDELINES TO PROTECT A COMPANY FROM SEXUAL HARASSMENT CHARGES ▲

▶ **1.** Issue a sexual harassment policy describing what constitutes sexual harassment and what is inappropriate behaviour.

▶ **2.** Institute a procedure (or link to an existing one) to investigate sexual harassment charges.

▶ **3.** Inform all employees of the sexual harassment policy. Educate these employees about the policy and how it will be enforced.

▶ **4.** Train all supervisory personnel how to deal with sexual harassment charges and what responsibility they have to the individual and the organization.

▶ **5.** Investigate all sexual harassment charges immediately.

▶ **6.** Take corrective action as necessary. Discipline those doing the harassing, and "make whole" the harassed individual.

▶ **7.** Continue to follow up on the matter to ensure that no further sexual harassment occurs or that retaliation does not occur.

▶ **8.** Periodically review turnover situations to determine if a potential problem may be arising.

▶ **9.** Don't forget to privately recognize individuals who bring these matters forward. Without their courageous effort, the organization might have been faced with a serious liability.

Sources: Adapted from Clifford M. Keon, Jr., "Sexual Harassment Claims Stem from a Hostile Work Environment," *Personnel Journal*, August 1990, pp. 97–98; Martha E. Eller, "Sexual Harassment: Prevention, Not Protection," *The Cornell H.R.A. Quarterly*, February 1990, p. 87; Maureen P. Woods and Walter J. Flynn, "Heading Off Sexual Harassment," *Personnel*, November 1989, p. 48; and Jacqueline F. Strayer and Sandra E. Rapoport, "Sexual Harassment: Limiting Corporate Liability," *Personnel*, April 1986, pp. 32–33; Sharon Nelton, "Sexual Harassment: Reducing the Risks," *Nation's Business*, March 1995, pp. 24-26; Rebecca A. Thacker, "Innovative Steps to Take in Sexual Harassment Prevention," *Business Horizons*, January-February 1994, pp. 29-32.

From management's standpoint, harassment is a concern not only because of moral issues, but because it intimidates employees, interferes with job performance, and exposes the organization to legal liability. On this last point, the rulings of human rights cases in Canada have made it clear that if the employee who is guilty of the sexual harassment is a supervisor or agent for an organization, then the organization is liable for sexual harassment, regardless of whether the act was forbidden by the organization or even whether the organization knew of the act.

Management must establish a clear and strong policy against harassment, coupled with regular discussion sessions among employees, in order to avoid these situations.

Why Must Managers Think in Terms of Quantum Change Rather than Incremental Change?

Although TQM is a positive start in many of our organizations, it focuses on continuous improvement or ongoing incremental change. Such action is intuitively appealing—the constant and permanent search to make things better. Many of our companies, however, live in a time of rapid and dynamic change. And as the elements around them change quickly, a continuous improvement process may keep them behind the times.

The problem with continuous improvement is that it provides a false sense of security. It makes managers feel like they're actively doing something positive, which is only somewhat true. Unfortunately, ongoing incremental change can obscure the possibility that what the organization may really need is radical or quantum change,

The roller skate versus the in-line skate. Which is more representative of reengineering? Although the roller skate may be improved, the in-line skate reveals a start-from-scratch approach to manufacturing a "better" product.

commonly referred to as **reengineering**.[29] Continuous change may make managers feel like they're taking progressive action, while at the same time avoiding implementing quantum changes that will threaten organizational members. The incremental approach in continuous improvement, then, may be the 1990s version of rearranging the deck chairs on the Titanic.

reengineering
Radical, quantum change in the organization.

If you've been reading this chapter closely up until now, you may be asking yourself, Aren't these authors contradicting what they said a few pages ago about TQM? On the surface, it may appear so, but consider this. While TQM is important for organizations and can often lead to improvements, TQM may not always be the right thing initially. For example, if what you are producing is outdated, a new improved version of the product may not be helpful to the company. Rather, in a number of instances major change is required. After that has occurred, then continually improving it (TQM) can have its rightful place. Let's see how this may be so.

Assume you are the manager responsible for implementing some type of change in your roller skate manufacturing process. If you took the continuous improvement approach, your frame of reference would be a high-top leather shoe on top of a steel carriage, with four wooden wheels. Your continuous improvement program may lead you to focus on things like using a different grade of cowhide for the shoe, adding speed laces to the uppers, or using a different type of ballbearing in the wheels. Of course, your skate may be better than you previously made, but is that enough? Compare your action to that of a competitor who reengineers the process.

To begin, your competitor poses the following question: How does she design a skate that is safe, fun, fast, and provides greater mobility? Starting from scratch, and not being constrained by her current manufacturing process (à la reengineering), she completes her redesign with something that looks like today's popular in-line skates. Instead of leather and metal skates, you are now competing against a moulded boot, similar to that used in skiing. Your competitor's skate is better than one made from leather—and has no laces to tie. Additionally, it uses four to six high-durability plastic wheels, which are placed in line for greater speed and mobility.

In this contrived example, both companies made progress. But which do you believe made the most progress given the dynamic environment they face? It's a moot point, but it clearly reinforces why large organizations such as Imperial Oil, Canadian National Railways, and even the United Nations, as well as smaller ones such as Clearly Canadian Beverage Corp., have opted for reengineering as opposed to incremental change. It is imperative in today's business environment for all managers to consider the challenge of reengineering their organizational processes. Why? Because reengineering can lead to "major gains in cost, service, or time."[30] And these kinds of gains will take organizations well into the twenty-first century.

New Challenges for Managers

If you stop for a moment and digest what you've been reading in this chapter, you've got to be thinking that managers as we described them in Chapter 1 no longer exist. That is, it may no longer be appropriate to accept the status quo and manage the company from a traditional, hierarchical position. The fact is that managers, too, must change with the times. In this section, we'll explore some of the implications of these changes on managers.

How Do Managers Change from Bosses into Coaches?

Frederick Taylor, the "father of scientific management" (see Appendix), argued for the division of work and responsibility between management and workers. He wanted managers to do the planning and thinking. Workers were just to do what they were told. That prescription might have been good advice at the turn of the century, but today's workers are far better educated and trained than they were in Taylor's day. In fact, because of the complexity of many jobs, today's workers are often considerably more knowledgeable than their managers about how best to do their jobs. This fact has not been ignored by management. Managers are transforming themselves from bosses into team leaders. Instead of telling people what to do, an increasing number of managers are finding that they become more effective when they focus on motivating, coaching, and cheerleading. Managers also recognize that they can often improve quality, productivity, and employee commitment by redesigning jobs to increase the decision-making discretion of workers. We call this process empowering employees.[31]

empowerment
Increasing the decision-making discretion of workers.

    Empowerment builds on ideas originally conceived by early management writers who promoted the well-being of employees. For many years, a lot of organizations stifled the capabilities of their workforce. They overspecialized jobs and demotivated employees by treating them like unthinking machines. Recent successes at empowering employees in companies across Canada suggest that the future lies in expanding the worker's role in his job rather than in practising Taylor's segmentation of responsibility.

    The empowerment movement is being driven by two forces. First is the need for quick decisions by people who are most knowledgeable about the issues. That requires moving decisions to lower levels. If organizations are to successfully compete in a global village, they have to be able to make decisions and implement changes quickly. Second is the reality that the large layoffs in the middle-management ranks during the late 1980s and early 1990s have left many managers with considerably more people to supervise than they had a decade earlier. The same manager who today oversees a staff of 35 can't micromanage in the ways that were possible when she supervised 10 people. The letting go and stretching process required to manage extended groups of people can be likened to that used by a sports team **coach**.

coach
A manager who motivates, empowers, and encourages her employees.

    Consider the job of head coach of a football team. This individual is the one who establishes the game plan for an upcoming game and readies the players for the task. Even though the plans and the players are prepared, the fact remains that the coach cannot go out on Saturday and play the game. Instead, it is the players who execute the game plan. So what does the coach do during the game? It depends on how well the plan is working. When the competition is doing something that is counter to the game plan, new plans are quickly formulated to give the players another competitive advantage. Thus, the coach deals with the exceptions. And regardless of the game's outcome, as the players play the game, the coach becomes one of the major cheerleaders—recognizing outstanding performance in fulfilling the plan, and boosting player morale. So, too, must today's managers!

How Do Managers Motivate Today's Workers?

As recently as 20 years ago there were plenty of semi-skilled jobs in the steel, automobile, rubber, and similar manufacturing industries that paid solid middle-class wages. A young man in Hamilton, for example, could graduate from high school and immediately get a relatively high-paying and secure job in a local steel plant. That job would allow him to buy a home, finance a car or two, support a family, and enjoy other lifestyle choices that come with a middle-class income. But that's ancient history.[32] A good portion of those manufacturing jobs in first-world industrialized countries are gone—either replaced by automated equipment, reconstituted into jobs requiring considerably higher technical skill, or taken by workers in other countries who will do the same work for a fraction of the wage. What's left can best be described as a **bi-modal workforce**—where employees tend to perform either low-skilled service jobs for near-minimum wages or high-skilled jobs that provide the means to maintain a middle-class or upper-class lifestyle.

bi-modal workforce
Employees tend to perform either low-skilled service jobs for near-minimum wage or high-skilled, well-paying jobs.

At wages of $4.50 to $7.50 per hour, today's low-skilled workers can't come close to moving into the middle class. Moreover, their promotion opportunities are limited. This leads to a major challenge for managers: How do you motivate individuals who are making very low wages and have little opportunity to increase their pay significantly either in their current jobs or through promotions? Can effective leadership make a difference? Can these employees' jobs be redesigned (empowered) to make them more challenging? Does management have an ethical responsibility to raise these wages so they can provide employees with an adequate income? Should management target these jobs for elimination? Until 20 years ago, managers didn't have to concern themselves with such questions. Today, however, they may lead to answers that are long overdue. (We'll come back to motivation in Chapter 12.)

Jon Slangerup, president of Federal Express Canada Ltd., based in Mississauga, Ontario, knows what it is like to take on the role of coach. In the early 1990s, Slangerup formed a team of his employees from across the organization and gave them the challenge of formulating a new strategy for the company—in only six weeks. The team decided to temporarily refocus the company's business away from the Canadian domestic market, with its high price sensitivity and competition, to shipping from Canada to the U.S. Thanks to their efforts FedEx in Canada is today a profitable and growing division of FedEx worldwide.

How Do Managers Improve Their Ethics?

Many observers believe that we are currently suffering an ethics crisis. Behaviours that were once thought reprehensible—lying, cheating, misrepresenting, covering up mistakes—have become, in many people's eyes, acceptable or necessary practices. Managers profit from illegal use of insider information.

Concern over this perceived decline in ethical standards is being addressed at two levels. First, ethics education is being widely expanded in college and university curriculums. For instance, the primary accrediting agency for business schools now requires all its member programs to integrate ethical issues throughout their business curricula. Second, organizations themselves are creating codes of ethics and introducing ethics training programs. Let's look more closely at this issue of ethics.

Is it ethical for a salesperson to offer an expensive gift to a purchasing agent as an inducement to buy? What if the gift comes out of the salesperson's commission? Does that make it any different? Is it ethical for someone to understate her educational qualifications to get a job during hard times if that person would ordinarily be considered overqualified for the job? Is it ethical for someone to use company gasoline for private use? How about using the company telephone for personal long-distance calls? Is it ethical to ask a company employee to type personal letters?[33]

ethics
Rules and principles that define right and wrong conduct.

Ethics commonly refers to the rules or principles that define right and wrong conduct.[34] But understanding ethics may be difficult, depending on the view one holds on the topic. We have presented the three views of ethical standards[35] in Exhibit 2-7.

Regardless of one's view of ethics, whether a manager acts ethically or unethically will depend on a number of factors. These factors include one's morality, individual differences, the organization's culture, and the issue that is being called into question.[36] People who lack a strong moral sense are much less likely to do the wrong things if they are constrained by rules, policies, job descriptions, or strong cultural norms that frown on such behaviours. Conversely, moral people can be corrupted by an organizational structure and culture that permits or encourages unethical practices. For example, you are in a class where a copy of the final exam is being sold for $50. Rumours abound in the department, but nothing is done. Do you buy a copy because without it you'll be disadvantaged, or do you do without it and try your best? If the faculty member suspects a copy is floating and does nothing and then gives no curve on the exam because the grades are so high (mainly due to those who had a copy of the exam), the professor is doing little to dissuade cheating. In that case, you may rationalize getting a copy for yourself.

The example above illustrates how ambiguity about what is ethical can be a problem for employees. Codes of ethics are an increasingly popular response for reducing that ambiguity.[37] Such ambiguity can lead to serious dilemmas in the workplace. Codes of ethics are an increasingly popular response. A recent survey found that 90 per cent of Canadian companies with revenue over $1 billion have a stated code of ethics. In 1997, a coalition of Canadian corporations also began promoting a code of ethics for doing business internationally. Many Canadian corporations have committed to the code, which defines ethical business practices while operating overseas.[38] A **code of ethics** is a formal document that states an organization's primary values and the ethical rules it expects employees to follow. It has been suggested that codes should be specific enough to guide employees in making decisions, for example—yet loose enough to allow for freedom of judgment.[39]

code of ethics
A formal statement of an organization's primary values and the ethical rules it expects its employees to follow.

What's More Important: Stability or Flexibility?

The organizational world that existed when early management theorists wrote no longer exists. Managers now confront an environment in which change is taking place at an unprecedented rate; new competitors spring up overnight and old ones disappear through mergers, acquisitions, or failure to keep up with the changing marketplace. Constant innovations in computer and telecommunications technologies combined with the globalization of product and financial markets have created chaos. As a result, many of the past "principles of management" guidelines—created for a world that was far more stable and predictable—no longer apply. The successful organizations of the next century will be flexible, able to respond quickly, and led by managers who can effectively enact massive and revolutionary changes.

As you'll see in later chapters of this book, the need for innovation and change is requiring many organizations to reinvent themselves. Managers are restructuring their organizations by eliminating unnecessary levels of overhead, cutting redundant functions, and eliminating low-performing units.

YOUNG CANADIANS

Lenna Bradburn: Chief of Police

Lenna Bradburn has been a force for change in her position as chief of police in Guelph, Ontario. Bradburn forged a strong link between the citizenry and its police force, keeping the town informed concerning police matters, and even keeping in touch with public opinion by means of questionnaires delivered in the mail. Efforts such as these and others have led to a more efficient police force. As Bradburn says, "As long as I can change things for the better, then I'm happy."

How Do We Make People in Organizations More Sensitive to Cultural Diversity?

Recognizing that the workforce of 2005 will be considerably different from that of two decades ago, management must implement programs to create more sensitivity to cultural diversity. In doing so, managers must recognize that workforce diversity will carry with it important implications for their practice. They will have to shift their philosophy from treating everyone alike to recognizing differences and responding to these differences in ways that will ensure employee retention and greater productivity. At the same time, they must not illegally discriminate against their employees.

A number of organizations are providing sophisticated diversity training programs for their managers to help them better communicate, motivate, and lead. These

Exhibit 2-7 Three Views of Ethics

Utilitarian View of Ethics	Refers to a situation in which decisions are made solely on the basis of their outcomes or consequences. The goal of utilitarianism is to provide the greatest good for the greatest number. On one side, utilitarianism encourages efficiency and productivity and is consistent with the goal of profit maximization. On the other side, however, it can result in biased allocations of resources, especially when some of those affected lack representation or voice.
Rights View of Ethics	Refers to a situation in which the individual is concerned with respecting and protecting individual liberties and privileges, including the rights to privacy, freedom of conscience, free speech, and due process. The positive side of the rights perspective is that it protects individuals' freedom and privacy. But it has a negative side in organizations: It can present obstacles to high productivity and efficiency by creating an overly legalistic work climate.
Theory of Justice View of Ethics	Refers to a situation in which an individual imposes and enforces rules fairly and impartially. A manager would be using a theory of justice perspective in deciding to pay a new entry-level employee $1.50 an hour over the minimum wage because that manager believes that the minimum wage is inadequate to allow employees to meet their basic financial commitments. Imposing standards of justice also comes with pluses and minuses. It protects the interests of those stakeholders who may be underrepresented or lack power; but it can encourage a sense of entitlement that reduces risk taking, innovation, and productivity.

Source: Gerald F. Cavanaugh, Dennis J. Moberg, and Manual Valasquez, "The Ethics of Organizational Politics," *Academy of Management Journal*, June 1981, pp. 363–74.

training programs are designed to raise diversity consciousness among current employees, and to address racial, ethnic, and gender stereotypes. In addition, a number of companies have instituted special mentoring programs to deal with the reality that lower-level females and minorities have few role models with whom to identify.

**Exhibit 2-8
Canadian Managers'
10 Most Important
Issues of Ethical Risk**

1. Integrity of books and records
2. Worker health and safety
3. Security of internal communications
4. Quality and safety of products and services
5. Receipt of inappropriate gifts, favours, entertainment, and bribes
6. Security and use of proprietary knowledge and intellectual property
7. Discrimination on the basis of sex, race, or religion
8. Privacy, confidentiality, appropriate use of employee records
9. Sexual harassment
10. Reports of fraud or compliance failures

Source: The Globe and Mail, February 21, 1997, p. B11.

Summary

This summary is organized by the chapter Learning Objectives found on page 27.

1. Competitors are no longer defined within national borders. New competition can suddenly appear anytime, from anywhere in the world. Managers must think globally if their organizations are to succeed over the long term.

2. Multinational corporations have significant operations functioning in two or more countries simultaneously, but primary decision making and control is based in the company's home country. Transnationals also have significant operations in multiple countries, but decision making is decentralized to the local level.

3. Corporate downsizing in North America has occurred in response to global competition. Downsizing was an attempt to make the companies more responsive to customers and more efficient in operating.

4. Small business concepts are being used in larger companies to help them respond faster to a changing environment.

5. The workforce of 2005 will witness heterogeneity of gender, race, and ethnicity. It will also include the physically disabled, gays and lesbians, the elderly, and those who are significantly overweight.

6. TQM focuses on the customer, seeks continual improvement, strives to improve the quality of work, seeks accurate measurement, and empowers employees.

7. Social responsibility refers to an obligation, beyond that required by law and economics, for a firm to pursue long-term goals that are good for society. Social responsiveness is the capacity of the firm to adapt to changing societal conditions.

8. Incremental change refers to change that is constant and continuous. Quantum change, or reengineering, is radical change in determining new processes for the organization.

9. Managers today can no longer manage in the classic sense. Through downsizing, managers are supervising more and more employees. Thus, managers must allow these employees freedom to act within the confines of the overall unit's goals. The coach, then, provides the structure for the employees and encourages employees to succeed.

10. Ethics refers to rules or principles that define right or wrong conduct.

11. Managers have become increasingly concerned with stimulating innovation and change because the environment in which organizations exist has become dynamic. Successful organizations will be flexible, able to respond quickly, and led by managers who can effectively enact massive and revolutionary changes.

12. Because of workforce diversity, managers will have to shift their philosophy from treating everyone alike to recognizing differences and responding to these differences in ways that will ensure employee retention and greater productivity.

Review and Discussion Questions

1. Why must managers pay attention to the global village?

2. What is the difference between a multinational corporation and a transnational corporation?

3. "Corporate downsizing for better customer service and more efficiency was just a ruse by large companies to reduce their payrolls and increase their profits." Do you agree or disagree with this statement? Explain.

4. Given that different kinds of people will make up tomorrow's organizations, what are the managerial implications?

5. "TQM includes contributions from all management approaches." Do you agree or disagree with this statement? Discuss.

6. In what ways do you think the face of management has changed or will change the way in which a company selects and trains managers?

7. "Coaching will never replace traditional managers. There's too much at stake to be left up to coaching techniques." Do you agree or disagree with this statement? Explain.

8. Would you prefer to work in a company that offers a good salary but no reward for your performance or one in which your base salary is lower but you have an opportunity to more than double your yearly earnings based on your performance? Discuss.

9. Over the past 20 years, has business become less willing to accept its societal responsibility? Explain.

10. While Playboy Enterprises has a female president, the magazine it publishes contains photographs and stories that may be regarded as exploitive. With this in mind, discuss the following: "Companies that promote women are acting ethically, but those that exploit women are acting unethically." Could Playboy be both?

Testing Your Comprehension

Circle the correct answer, then check yourself on page 471.

1. When we find organizations with employees who are heterogeneous in terms of gender, race, ethnicity, sexual preference, or other characteristics,
   a) it indicates that successful hiring practices exist in the organization
   b) we have workforce diversity
   c) we have an example of the contingency approach in hiring in the global village
   d) it indicates that the teachings of Geert Hofstede are being followed

2. In terms of total quality management (TQM), the customer is
   a) always right
   b) the party actually using the good or service
   c) any internal or external party who interacts with the organization
   d) the party who buys an organization's products or services

3. Institutions and forces outside an organization that affect its performance
   a) are collectively called environmental forces
   b) create an organization's culture
   c) have a minor impact on management's options
   d) define an organization's structure

4. Which of the following statements demonstrates that the world is becoming a global village?
   a) The family is becoming more important throughout the world.
   b) With the fall of communism, capitalism is becoming more widespread as an economic system.
   c) Companies are no longer constrained by national borders.
   d) Students are being required to learn foreign languages in schools.

5. In his work, Hofstede attempted to
   a) encourage the fall of communism and replace it with a more "pro-business" system
   b) stabilize international exchange rates to encourage easy money transfers
   c) establish foreign trade zones to facilitate regional cooperation
   d) provide a framework for analysing cultural differences

6. Organizations today are gaining more flexibility by eliminating layers of hierarchy. This de-layering is best reflective of
   a) reengineering
   b) controlling the environment
   c) downsizing
   d) none of the above

7. Which of the following statements is TRUE about reengineering?
   a) Reengineering focuses on incremental change.
   b) Reengineering is the new TQM buzz word.
   c) Reengineering implies major changes.
   d) Reengineering provides a false sense of security.

8. A code of ethics is NOT
   a) formal
   b) an increasingly popular response
   c) aimed at encapsulating an organization's primary values
   d) required by law

9. Which of the following is FALSE regarding contemporary managers?
   a) Many managers are transforming themselves from bosses into coaches.
   b) Managers must be considerably more knowledgeable than their employees about how the employees' jobs should be done.
   c) Technological improvements are making the manager's job more complex in terms of dealing with employees.
   d) Managers must be prepared to make opportunities out of chaos.

10. Which of the following is NOT an attribute associated with entrepreneurial spirit?

    a) taking risks

    b) learning from mistakes

    c) controlling one's own destiny

    d) accepting the status quo

11. Which of the following individuals is BEST associated with fostering a total quality management (TQM) environment in organizations?

    a) Edwards Deming

    b) Alvin Toffler

    c) Geert Hofstede

    d) Marlene Conway

12. Which of the following is NOT a characteristic associated with TQM?

    a) continuous improvement

    b) predictability

    c) customer focus

    d) accurate measurement

13. Which of the following statements is TRUE?

    a) Multinational corporations are based in several countries.

    b) Multinational corporations gained popularity in the 1980s.

    c) Transnational corporations encourage major decisions to be made at the local site.

    d) Transnational corporations often do not hire locally.

14. Which of the following statements about social responsibility is TRUE?

    a) Social responsibility often lacks broad public support.

    b) Social responsibility involves doing things to make society better and not to harm it.

    c) Social responsibility refers to the capacity of a firm to respond to social pressures.

    d) Social responsibility and an organization's social obligations are the same thing.

15. The use of outside firms for providing necessary products and services to an organization is called

    a) outsourcing

    b) reengineering

    c) de-layering

    d) total quality management

Self-Assessment Exercise

What Are Your Personal Value Preferences?

Listed below are 18 values. Indicate their importance to you by rank—ordering them from one to 18. Place a "1" next to the value that has the greatest importance as a guiding principle in your life, a "2" next to the one with the second-highest importance, and so forth.

Values	Rank	Values	Rank
ambitious (hard-working, aspiring)	_____	imaginative (daring, creative)	_____
broadminded (open-minded)	_____	independent (self-reliant, self-sufficient)	_____
capable (competent, effective)	_____	intellectual (intelligent, reflective)	_____
cheerful (light-hearted, joyful)	_____	logical (consistent, rational)	_____
clean (neat, tidy)	_____	loving (affectionate, tender)	_____
courageous (standing up for your beliefs)	_____	obedient (dutiful, respectful)	_____
forgiving (willing to pardon others)	_____	polite (courteous, well-mannered)	_____
helpful (working for the welfare of others)	_____	responsible (dependable, reliable)	_____
honest (sincere, truthful)	_____	self-controlled (restrained, self-disciplined)	_____

Turn to page 463 for scoring directions and key.

Source: Based on William C. Frederick and James Weber, "The Values of Corporate Managers and Their Critics: An Empirical Description and Normative Implications," in W.C. Frederick and L.E. Preston, eds. *Business Ethics: Research Issues and Empirical Studies* (Greenwich, Conn.: JAI Press, 1990), pp. 123–44.

Class Exercise

The International Culture Quiz

How knowledgeable are you about customs, practices, and facts regarding other countries? The following multiple-choice quiz will provide you with some feedback on this question. First, take the test by yourself. Then in groups of four to five class members, discuss your answers. Did your group develop any consensus on the questions? If so, what? After seeing the correct responses, what has this exercise taught you about international culture? What might this indicate for anyone considering work abroad? How about for individuals who will stay in Canada but work with people from other countries?

1. In which country would Ramadan (a month of fasting) be celebrated by the majority of people?
   - **a.** Saudi Arabia
   - **b.** India
   - **c.** Singapore
   - **d.** Korea
   - **e.** All of the above

2. On first meeting your prospective Korean business partner, Lo Kim Chee, it would be best to address him as:
   - **a.** Mr. Kim
   - **b.** Mr. Lo
   - **c.** Mr. Chee
   - **d.** Bud
   - **e.** Any of the above are acceptable

3. In Brazil, your promotional material should be translated into what language?
   - **a.** French
   - **b.** Italian
   - **c.** Spanish
   - **d.** No need to translate it
   - **e.** None of the above

4. In Japan, it is important to:
   - **a.** Present your business card only after you have developed a relationship with your Japanese host
   - **b.** Present your business card with both hands
   - **c.** Put your company name on the card, but never your position or title

d. All of the above

e. None of the above

5. Which one of the following sports is the most popular worldwide?
   - **a.** Basketball **d.** Soccer
   - **b.** Baseball **e.** Golf
   - **c.** Tennis

6. For a Canadian businessperson, touching a foreign businessperson would be least acceptable in which one of the following countries?
   - **a.** Japan **d.** Venezuela
   - **b.** Italy **e.** France
   - **c.** Slovenia

7. Which of the following would be an appropriate gift?
   - **a.** A clock in China
   - **b.** A bottle of liquor in Egypt
   - **c.** A set of knives in Argentina

d. A banquet in China

e. None of the above would be appropriate

8. Which one of the following countries has the most rigid social hierarchy?
   - **a.** United Kingdom **d.** India
   - **b.** United States **e.** Germany
   - **c.** Japan

9. Traditional western banking is difficult in which of the following countries because its law forbids both the giving and taking of interest payments?
   - **a.** Brazil **d.** India
   - **b.** Saudi Arabia **e.** Greece
   - **c.** Mongolia

10. The capital of Germany is:
    - **a.** Berlin **d.** Cologne
    - **b.** Bonn **e.** Munich
    - **c.** Frankfurt

Turn to page 464 for scoring key only after your group has reached consensus.

Source: Professor David Hopkins, University of Denver, 1991. With permission.

Case Application

What Is Going on at General Electric?

Jack Welch, CEO of General Electric, is one of the most powerful and revered managers in the world, but his tenure at GE has not all been wine and roses. Over the past two decades GE has been involved in half a dozen major scandals. In 1995, GE pleaded guilty for overcharging the U.S. Air Force for the Minuteman missile contract. In 1989, GE paid $3.5 million as a penalty for falsifying time cards on a government contract, and $30 million for other fraudulent practices involved in Defense Department contracts. In 1992 the organization had to pay out $69 million for inappropriate practices involving the sale of jet engines to Israel—a sale that involved employee bribes.[40]

Maybe Welch's greatest embarrassment came from GE's Kidder Peabody investment subsidiary. K.P.'s chief government bond trader was allegedly involved in a scheme that produced roughly $350 million in phony profits. Top managers at K.P. apparently disregarded standard operating procedures, allowing the trader's actions to go unnoticed for some time.

Welch commissioned an investigation of the scandal and forced the resignations of several senior managers. GE also took a $210-million charge against profits to absorb the loss created by the false profit results.

Questions

1. Do you think GE's goal of being number one in every one of its markets had any influence on the Kidder Peabody scandal?

2. Do you think that Jack Welch handled the K.P. scandal ethically?

3. How can a corporate leader who heads such a huge organization prevent scandals or other unethical practices from occurring in his organization? Do you think that Jack Welch is ultimately responsible for what happens in his organization?

4. General Electric has a code of ethics in place, but it doesn't seem to be working. What do you think might be the reasons?

Shuttlecraft

The things that you will be reading about in this book—the aspects of business that constitute the fundamentals of management—are well illustrated by the situations that Shuttlecraft is and will be facing in its bid to become, well. . . a profitable company. The three founders and partners in the Saskatchewan company are prime examples of the entrepreneurial spirit—a subject that will be touched on throughout this text. The first managerial task the three had to face was planning. Deciding to develop this product and bring it to market were the first steps in their organization's growth, but it is essential for them to have both specific and directional (general) plans concerning the growth of Shuttlecraft. Setting a target of "$200 million" in sales, as the partners stated in the *Venture* program, is a directional plan, but to achieve that goal, specific plans must be in place to guide the company.

Shuttlecraft management will face many of the challenges detailed in the upcoming chapters, such as management of human resources, change, communication and conflict, and control tools and techniques.

With Trevor Hewison managing production, Dan Bolak managing administration and finance, and Wayne Washington managing sales and marketing, the three seem to have operations under control at this stage, given the uncertainty that inevitably comes with starting a new business. But as Shuttlecraft takes off, these partners will find a myriad of new challenges and obstacles facing them. They will have to plan, organize, lead, motivate, communicate, schedule, and control, and more, in order to turn their organization into a successful one.

Questions

1. Is formal training in management necessary for success in business? If you were starting a business like Shuttlecraft, what sorts of skills would you want to develop? List the 10 most important things you feel you would need to know about, or skills you would like to have.

2. Looking at Mintzberg's roles, which would you think are the most important ones for these three partners to master while (a) starting up Shuttlecraft, and (b) running the business?

3. What characteristics do you need to possess to be a successful manager? List what you feel are the five most important ones and explain your choices.

Video Resource: "Shuttlecraft," *Venture* 614 (October 27, 1996).

The Woes of the Software Game

Braindead 13, Readysoft's computer game, has been sitting snugly on shelves in computer software stores for some time since the production of this *Venture* program. After numerous setbacks, the final product made it to market. The story of how this product was developed is a testament to just how difficult it can be to follow through on a set plan, especially in a business with as many contingencies as the software industry.

One major setback for Readysoft was the loss of programmers. Chris Gray (who is one of this textbook's featured Young Canadians) has said that, "Finding people to create the programming is the toughest part of the business. If we could find as many talented people as we could put to work, we would easily be twice or three times the size we are right now." Keeping staff after hiring them is yet another challenge.

The nature of the business makes it difficult for companies to follow strict planning schedules. Creating a game can easily take longer than expected, and it is always possible to add new and valid refinements, making it difficult to know when a product is really "ready." It is easy to see how different divisions in a firm, such as the marketing and production divisions at Readysoft, can have trouble coordinating their efforts. When a product is scheduled to hit the market on a specific date, it is essential that people managing each aspect of the business are aware of what people in other areas are doing. When timing is of the essence, planning is imperative. If Readysoft can learn from the headaches that beset this venture, the company will be better organized and prepared to face future difficulties.

Questions

1. Do you think it is possible to devise a plan that would take care of the problem of recruiting enough talented workers in the field of programming? What solutions can you come up with? What kinds of contingency plans might be useful for a company such as Readysoft with regard to the loss of programmers?

2. How could planning be used to coordinate operations at Readysoft?

3. What role would specific plans play in the creation of Braindead 13? What about the role of directional plans?

Video Resource: "Braindead 13," *Venture* 561 (October 8, 1995).

Additional Sources: Justin Smallbridge, "Masters of the Game," *Canadian Business*, July 1995, pp. 18–24.

chapter

3

Foundations of Planning

Learning Objectives

What will I be able to do after I finish this chapter?

1 • Define planning.

2 • Explain the potential benefits of planning.

3 • Distinguish between strategic and operational plans.

4 • State when directional plans are preferred over specific plans.

5 • Identify four contingency factors in planning.

6 • Explain the commitment concept.

7 • Define management by objectives and identify its common elements.

8 • Explain the importance of strategic planning.

9 • Outline the steps in the strategic management process.

10 • Explain SWOT analysis.

11 • Compare how entrepreneurs and bureaucratic managers approach strategy.

s planning really worth the time it takes? We made the point in Chapter 2 that business needs to think in terms of quantum changes. How does this fit with the slow and deliberate concept of planning? An analogy is taking a trip. First, you need to know where you want to end up; then you figure out how to get there. You may wish to go the quickest way, the most interesting way, the safest way, the cheapest way, etc. In fact, you have to *plan* the trip. And if it's a trip across town, for instance, it's a good idea to take a number of factors—like traffic flows, construction, and accidents—into account. Just going the same way every time may not be best—a lesson some large companies have learned the hard way.

One of the best examples of the power of planning is the largest consumer electronics company in the world—Matsushita. Like many successful companies, Matsushita began with an idea. In 1918, when Konosuke Matsushita started in business, most houses with electricity in Japan only had one ceiling outlet. Matsushita developed a double-ended socket that allowed for extension cords, and, more importantly, meant that electric devices other than lighting could be used. The company developed an electric iron that, by 1929, had gained a 50-per-cent market share. It also developed radios and other electric-powered devices for the rapidly growing market, and in the 1950s moved into TV sets, stereos, tape recorders, and so on.

Thirty years ago the market for television sets was dominated by domestic giants such as RCA, GE, and Zenith. Today Matsushita, the largest manufacturer of television sets in the world, dominates the North American market.

One of the elements in the success of Matsushita is planning. On May 5, 1932, Konosuke Matsushita announced a 250-year plan. Yes, 250 years—but broken into 25-year segments. "I, myself and you assembled here," he told his employees, "are to carry out the first 25 years. Our successors will carry on exactly the same for another 25 years, and so on." In the early 1950s, Matsushita established a goal to dominate the U.S. television market. Over the 25-year period, every one of his U.S. competitors retired from the business—either bankrupt or acquired by foreign interests.

On the other hand, many dynasties have crumbled after growing complacent, failing to change with the times and look to the future. From the store Timothy Eaton founded in 1869, Eaton's grew not only into a retailing giant, but into a Canadian cultural institution. The winter of 1997 saw this giant stumble, filing for bankruptcy protection. The Canadian press was quick to point out that the writing had been on the wall for some time, that within the organization there had been no foresight, no planning, no adaptation to changing times. Through the everyday stagnation of "business as usual," time caught up to Eaton's. By the time the organization looked in the mirror and saw how old it had become, it was too feeble to change.

Poor planning led to the downfall of Eaton's, which had to file for bankruptcy protection in 1997.

EATON'S
www.eatons.com/

MATSUSHITA
www.mei.co.jp/

This chapter presents the basics of planning. In the following pages, you'll learn the difference between formal and informal planning, why managers plan, the various types of plans that managers use, the key contingency factors that influence the types of plans that managers use in different situations, and the important role that strategic planning plays in promoting better organizational performance.

Planning Defined

As we stated in Chapter 1, planning encompasses defining the organization's objectives or goals, establishing an overall strategy for achieving these goals, and developing a comprehensive hierarchy of plans to integrate and coordinate activities. It is concerned, then, with ends (*what* is to be done) as well as with means (*how* it is to be done).

Planning can be further defined in terms of whether it is informal or formal. All managers engage in planning, but it might only be the informal variety. In informal planning, nothing is written down, and there is little or no sharing of objectives with others in the organization. This describes planning in many small businesses; the owner-manager has a vision of where she wants to go and how she expects to get there. The planning is general and lacks continuity. Of course, informal planning exists in some large organizations, and some small businesses have very sophisticated formal plans.

When we use the term planning in this book, we are implying formal planning. Specific objectives are formulated, covering a period of years. These objectives are written down and made available to organization members. Finally, specific action programs exist for achieving these objectives; that is, management clearly defines the path it wants to take to get from where it is to where it wants to be (see Managers Who Made a Difference).

Purpose of Planning

Managers should engage in planning because it gives direction, reduces the impact of change, minimizes waste and redundancy, and sets the standards to facilitate control.

Planning establishes coordinated effort. It gives direction to managers and non-managers alike. When all concerned know where the organization is going and what they must contribute to reach the objective, they can begin to coordinate their activities, cooperate with each other, and work in teams. A lack of planning can foster "zigzagging" and thus prevent an organization from moving efficiently toward its objectives.

By forcing managers to look ahead, anticipate change, consider the impact of change, and develop appropriate responses, planning reduces uncertainty. It also clarifies the consequences of the actions managers might take in response to change.

Planning also reduces overlapping and wasteful activities. Coordination before the fact is likely to uncover waste and redundancy. Further, when means and ends are clear, inefficiencies become obvious.

Finally, planning establishes objectives or standards that facilitate control. If we are unsure of what we are trying to achieve, how can we determine whether we have achieved it? In planning, we develop the objectives. In the controlling function, we compare actual performance against the objectives, identify any significant deviations, and take the necessary corrective action. Without planning, there can be no control.

MANAGERS WHO MADE A DIFFERENCE

Dr. Margaret Kerr: Northern Telecom

**NORTHERN
TELECOM**
www.nortel.com/

Dr. Margaret Kerr is senior vice-president of human resources and environment for Northern Telecom, the biggest equipment manufacturer in the Canadian telecommunications field. Dr. Kerr is a strong proponent of the ideas of total quality management, but she has adapted TQM's ideals to her specific area of expertise: environmental management. Dr. Kerr joined Northern Telecom in 1987, and for more than a decade has devoted her efforts to developing and implementing new manufacturing processes that do not harm the environment. Her strategy is to attack problems at the root. "The quality movement taught businesses to shift from counting defects to designing processes that prevented defects," she says.[1]

To this effect, Dr. Kerr first tackled NorTel's massive use of chlorofluorocarbons (CFCs). The company was using solvents loaded with CFCs in the production of circuit boards. Dr. Kerr did not simply attempt to remedy the situation by replacing the solvents—this would probably result in switching one poison for another. Instead, she developed an alternative to the manufacturing process itself—one in which no solvents whatsoever would be used. A pleasant side-benefit to this new process would be a significant reduction in manufacturing costs. The company gladly instituted the changes. By doing so, NorTel became the first multinational telecommunications company to remove CFCs from its production process, doing so nine years before an international agreement was to take effect banning the substances.

Dr. Kerr then developed an environmental life-cycle program at NorTel, the mandate of which is to reduce waste in every area of the manufacturing process. In true TQM fashion, Kerr's team now works with NorTel's employees, suppliers, and customers to achieve its goals. And changes have been taken beyond the manufacturing processes to the design stage, where engineers now take environmental issues into account in the design of new products, such as a lead-free phone developed in 1997.

Dr. Kerr's influence on Northern Telecom has been enormous. And luckily for the rest of the world, she has helped to found a group with other manufacturers known as the International Cooperative for Ozone Layer Protection. Through this organization, Northern Telecom's environmental advances are shared with other companies, and governments, such as China's and Brazil's, are given training on environmental issues. ▼

Planning and Performance

Do managers and organizations that plan outperform those that don't? Intuitively, you would expect the answer to be a resounding yes. Reviews of the evidence are generally affirmative, but that shouldn't be interpreted as a blanket endorsement of formal planning. We cannot say that organizations that formally plan always outperform those that don't.

Dozens of studies have been undertaken to test the relationship between planning and performance.[2] They allow us to draw the following conclusions. First, generally speaking, formal planning is associated with higher profits, higher return on assets, and other positive financial results. Second, the quality of the planning process and the appropriate implementation of the plans probably contribute more to high performance than does the extent of planning. Finally, in studies in which formal planning hasn't led to higher performance, the environment is typically the culprit. When government regulations, powerful labour unions, and similar environmental forces constrain management's options, planning will have less of an impact on an organization's performance. Why? Because management will have fewer choices for which planning can propose viable alternatives. For example, planning might suggest that a manufacturing firm produce a number of its key parts in Asia in order to compete effectively against low-cost foreign competitors.

Types of Plans

The most popular ways to describe plans are by their breadth (strategic versus operational), time frame (short- versus long-term), and specificity (specific versus directional). However, these planning classifications are not independent of one another. For instance, there is a close relationship between the short- and long-term categories and the strategic and operational categories. Exhibit 3-1 lists these types of plans according to category.

CATEGORIZED BY	TYPES
Breadth	• Strategic
	• Operational
Time Frame	• Short-term
	• Long-term
Specificity	• Specific
	• Directional

Exhibit 3-1
Types of Plans

How Does Strategic Planning Differ from Operational Planning?

Plans that apply to the entire organization, that establish the organization's overall objectives, and that seek to position the organization in terms of its environment are called **strategic plans**. Plans that specify the details of how the overall objectives are

strategic plans
Plans that are organizationwide, establish overall objectives, and position an organization in terms of its environment.

operational plans
Plans that specify details on how overall objectives are to be achieved.

to be achieved are called **operational plans**. Strategic and operational plans differ in their time frame, their scope, and whether they include a known set of organizational objectives.[3] Operational plans tend to cover shorter periods of time. For instance, an organization's monthly, weekly, and day-to-day plans are almost all operational. Strategic plans tend to include an extended time period—usually five years or more. They also cover a broader area and deal less with specifics. Finally, strategic plans include the formulation of objectives, whereas operational plans assume the existence of objectives. Operational plans offer ways of attaining these objectives.

In What Time Frame Do Plans Exist?

Financial analysts traditionally describe investment returns as short and long term. The short term covers less than one year. Any time frame beyond five years is classified as long term. Managers have adopted the same terminology to describe plans. For clarity, we'll emphasize **short-term plans** and **long-term plans** in future discussions.

short-term plans
Plans that cover less than one year.

long-term plans
Plans that extend beyond five years.

What's the Difference Between Specific and Directional Plans?

specific plans
Plans that are clearly defined and leave no room for interpretation.

It seems intuitively correct that specific plans are always preferable to directional, or loosely guided, plans. **Specific plans** have clearly defined objectives. There is no ambiguity, no potential for misunderstandings. For example, a manager who seeks to increase his firm's sales by 18 per cent over a given 12-month period might establish specific procedures, budget allocations, and schedules of activities to reach that objective. These represent specific plans.

directional plans
Flexible plans that set out general guidelines.

However, specific plans are not without drawbacks. They require clarity and a sense of predictability that often does not exist. When uncertainty is high, which requires management to maintain flexibility in order to respond to unexpected changes, directional plans are preferable.[4] **Directional plans** identify general guidelines. They provide focus but do not lock management into specific objectives or specific courses of action. Instead of a manager following a specific plan to cut costs by 8 per cent and increase revenues by 5 per cent in the next six months, a directional plan might aim at improving corporate profits by 6 to 12 per cent during the next six months. The flexibility inherent in directional plans is obvious. This advantage must be weighed against the loss in clarity provided by specific plans.

Contingency Factors Affecting Planning

In some cases, long-term plans make sense, in others they do not. Similarly, in some situations, directional plans are more effective than specific ones. What are these situations? In this section, we identify several contingency factors that affect planning.[5]

Does Planning Differ According to One's Level in the Organization?

Exhibit 3-2 illustrates the general relationship between managerial level in an organization and the type of planning that is done. For the most part, operational planning dominates the planning activities of lower-level managers. As managers rise in the hierarchy, their planning role becomes more strategy oriented. The planning effort by the top executives in large organizations is essentially strategic. In a small business, of course, the owner-manager needs to do both.

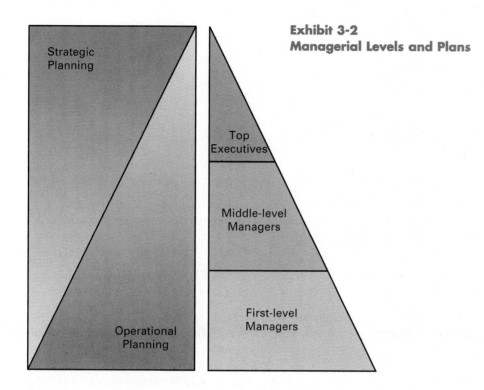

**Exhibit 3-2
Managerial Levels and Plans**

How Are Plans and the Life Cycle of the Organization Related?

Organizations go through a life cycle. Beginning with the formative stage, organizations then grow, mature, and eventually decline. Planning is not homogeneous across these stages. As Exhibit 3-3 depicts, the length and specificity of plans should be adjusted at each stage. If all things were equal, management would undoubtedly benefit most by developing and using specific plans. Not only would this provide the clearest direction, but it would also establish the most detailed benchmarks against which to compare actual performance. However, all things aren't equal.

When an organization is mature, predictability is greatest. It is at this stage in the life cycle, therefore, that specific plans are most appropriate. Managers should rely more heavily on directional plans in an organization's infancy. It is at precisely this time that high flexibility is desired. Objectives are tentative, resource availability is more uncertain, and the identification of clients or customers is more in doubt. Directional plans, at this stage, allow managers to make changes as necessary. During the growth stage, plans become more specific as objectives become more definite, resources more committed, and loyalty of clients or customers more developed. The pattern reverses itself on the downward swing of the cycle. From maturity to decline, plans need to move from specific to directional as objectives are reconsidered, resources reallocated, and other adjustments made.

**Exhibit 3-3
Plans and the
Organization
Life Cycle**

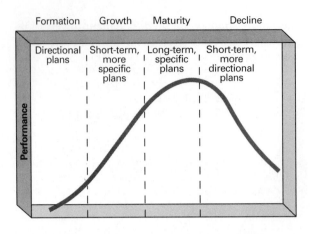

The length of planning should also be related to the life cycle. Short-term plans offer the greatest flexibility and therefore should be more prevalent during the formative and decline stages. Maturity is the time when stability is greatest and long-term plans can pay the biggest dividends.

How Does the Degree of Environmental Uncertainty Affect Planning?

The greater the environmental uncertainty, the more plans should be directional and emphasis placed on the short term. If rapid or important technological, social, economic, legal, or other changes are taking place, well-defined and precisely chartered routes are more likely to hinder than to aid an organization's performance. When environmental uncertainty is high, specific plans have to be altered to accommodate the changes—often at high cost and decreased efficiency. For example, in the late 1980s, when intense rate wars were raging among airlines on major cross-country routes, the airlines should have moved to more directional plans concerning price setting, number and size of aircraft allocated to routes, and operating budgets. Moreover, the greater the change, the less likely plans are to be accurate. For example, one study found that one-year revenue plans tended to achieve 99-per-cent accuracy in comparison to 84 per cent for five-year plans.[6] Therefore, if an organization faces rapidly changing environments, management should seek flexibility.

What Effect Does the Length of Future Commitments Have on Planning?

The final contingency factor again relates to the time frame of plans. The more that current plans affect future commitments, the longer the time frame for which management should plan. This **commitment concept** means that plans should extend far enough to see through commitments made today. Planning for too long or for too short a period is inefficient.

commitment concept
Plans should extend far enough to see through current commitments.

Managers are not planning for future decisions. Rather, they are planning for the future impact of the decisions that they are currently making. Decisions made today become a commitment to some future action or expenditure. Tenure decisions in universities provide an excellent illustration of how the commitment concept should work.

When a university gives tenure to a faculty member, it is making a commitment to provide life-long employment for that individual. The tenure decision must therefore reflect an assessment by the university administration that there will be a need for that faculty member's teaching expertise through her lifetime. If a university awards tenure to a 30-year-old sociology instructor, it should have a plan that covers at least the 30 or more years this instructor could be teaching in that institution. Most important, the plan should demonstrate the need for a permanent sociology instructor through that time period.

Clive Beddoe has achieved unprecedented growth for Westjet Airlines in western Canada by successfully employing directional plans.

Management by Objectives

At Husky Injection Molding Systems in Bolton, Ontario, employees define specific, quantifiable objectives for which they are responsible. CEO Robert Schad uses an objective-setting program that specifies exactly what his managers and employees are expected to accomplish—a program designed to motivate rather than to intimidate. It is a system of participatory objective setting.

Robert Schad is using **management by objectives (MBO)**, a system in which specific performance objectives are jointly determined by subordinates and their superiors, progress toward objectives is periodically reviewed, and rewards are allocated on the basis of this progress. Rather than using goals to control, MBO uses them to motivate.

management by objectives (MBO)
A system in which specific performance objectives are jointly determined by subordinates and their superiors, progress toward objectives is periodically reviewed, and rewards are allocated on the basis of this progress.

What Is MBO?

Management by objectives is not new. The concept goes back 40 years.[7] Its appeal lies in its emphasis on converting overall objectives into specific objectives for organizational units and individual members.

Exhibit 3-4
Cascading of
Objectives

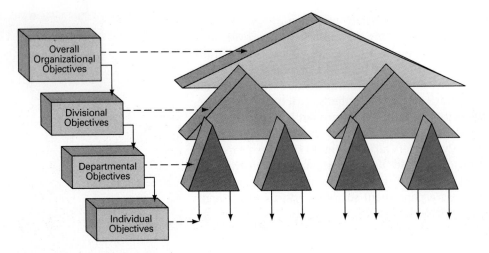

MBO makes objectives operational by devising a process by which they cascade down through the organization. As depicted in Exhibit 3-4, the organization's overall objectives are translated into specific objectives for each succeeding level—divisional, departmental, individual—in the organization. Because lower-unit managers jointly participate in setting their own goals, MBO works from the "bottom up" as well as from the "top down." The result is a hierarchy that links objectives at one level to those at the next level. For the individual employee, MBO provides specific personal performance objectives. Each person, therefore, has an identified specific contribution to make to his unit's performance. If all the individuals achieve their goals, then their unit's goals will be attained, and the organization's overall objectives will become a reality.

Are There Common Elements to an MBO Program?

There are four ingredients common to MBO programs: goal specificity, participative decision making, an explicit time period, and performance feedback.

The objectives in MBO should be concise statements of expected accomplishments. It's not adequate, for example, merely to state a desire to cut costs, improve service, or increase quality. Such desires have to be converted into tangible objectives that can be measured and evaluated. To cut departmental costs by 7 per cent, to improve service by ensuring that all telephone orders are processed within 24 hours of receipt, or to increase quality by keeping returns to less than 1 per cent of sales, are examples of specific objectives.

In MBO, the objectives are not unilaterally set by the boss and assigned to subordinates, as is characteristic of traditional objective setting. MBO replaces these imposed goals with participatively determined goals. The manager and employee jointly choose the goals and agree on how they will be achieved (see also Details on a Management Classic).

Each objective has a concise time period in which it is to be completed. Typically, the time period is three months, six months, or a year.

The final ingredient in an MBO program is feedback on performance. MBO seeks to give continuous feedback on progress toward goals. Ideally, this is accomplished by giving ongoing feedback to individuals so they can monitor and correct their own actions. This is supplemented by periodic formal appraisal meetings in which superiors and subordinates can review progress toward goals and further feedback can be provided. MBO is used, in a variety of forms, by many organizations in Canada, from government departments to charities, from manufacturers to marketing companies.

DETAILS ON A MANAGEMENT CLASSIC

Peter Drucker's Management by Objectives

Several decades ago, management professor Peter Drucker developed a system called management by objectives. Often the main question raised about MBO is, Does it work? Assessing the effectiveness of MBO is a complex task. Let's briefly review a growing body of literature on the relationship between goals and performance.[8] If factors such as a person's ability and acceptance of goals are held constant, evidence demonstrates that more difficult goals lead to higher performance. Although individuals with very difficult goals achieve them far less often than those with very easy goals, they nevertheless perform at a consistently higher level.

Moreover, studies consistently support the finding that specific hard goals produce a higher level of output than do no goals, or generalized goals such as "do your best." Feedback also favourably affects performance. Feedback lets a person know whether her level of effort is sufficient or needs to be increased. It can induce a person to raise his goal level after attaining a previous goal, and can inform a person of ways to improve his performance.

The results cited above are all consistent with MBO's stress on specific goals and feedback. MBO implies, rather than explicitly states, that goals must be perceived as feasible. Research on goal setting indicates that MBO is most effective if the goals are difficult enough to require the person to do some stretching.

But what about participation? MBO strongly advocates that goals be set participatively. Does the research demonstrate that participatively set goals lead to higher performance than those assigned by a superior? Interestingly, the research comparing participatively set and assigned goals on performance has not shown any strong or consistent relationships.[9] When goal difficulty has been held constant, assigned goals frequently do as well as participatively determined goals, contrary to MBO ideology. Therefore, it is not possible to argue for the superiority of participation as MBO proponents advocate. One major benefit of participation, however, is that it appears to induce individuals to establish more difficult goals.[10] Thus, participation may have a positive impact on performance by increasing one's goal-aspiration level.

Studies of actual MBO programs confirm that MBO effectively increases employee performance and organizational productivity. A review of 70 programs, for example, found organizational productivity gains in 68 of them.[11] This same review also identified top management commitment and involvement as important conditions needed for MBO to reach its potential. When top management had a high commitment to MBO and was personally involved in its implementation, the average gain in productivity was found to be 56 per cent. When commitment and involvement were low, the average gain in productivity dropped to only 6 per cent. ▼

The Importance of an Organizational Strategy

Before the early 1970s, managers who made long-range plans generally assumed that better times lay ahead. Plans for the future were merely extensions of where the organization had been in the past. However, the energy crisis, deregulation, accelerating technological change, and increasing global competition, as well as the other environmental shocks of the 1970s and 1980s, undermined this approach to long-range planning.[12] These changes in the rules of the game forced managers to develop a systematic means of analysing the environment, assessing their organization's strengths and weaknesses, and identifying opportunities where the organization could have a competitive advantage. The value of strategic planning began to be recognized.

A recent survey of business owners found that 69 per cent had strategic plans, and, among those owners, 89 per cent responded that they had found their plans to be effective.[13] They cited, for example, that strategic planning gave them specific goals and provided their staffs with a unified vision. Today, strategic planning has moved beyond the private sector to include government agencies, hospitals, and educational institutions. For example, the skyrocketing costs of a university education, cutbacks in federal aid for students and research, and the decline in the absolute number of high school graduates have led many university administrators to assess their organizations' aspirations and identify a market niche in which they can survive and prosper.[14]

The Strategic Management Process

strategic management process
A nine-step process encompassing strategic planning, implementation, and evaluation.

When an organization attempts to develop its strategy, senior management goes through an activity called the **strategic management process**. The strategic management process, as illustrated in Exhibit 3-5, is a nine-step process that involves strategic planning, implementation, and evaluation. While strategic planning encompasses the first seven steps, even the best strategies can go awry if management fails either to implement them properly or to evaluate results. Let's look at the various steps in the strategic management process.

These senior Data Point managers spend considerable time each year setting the strategy for their software design company, establishing goals, and planning their future direction.

How Does the Strategic Management Process Operate?

mission
The purpose of an organization.

The first step for organizational members is to identify the organization's current mission, objectives, and strategies. Every organization has a **mission** that defines its purpose and answers the question, What business or businesses are we in? Defining the

Exhibit 3-5   The Strategic Management Process

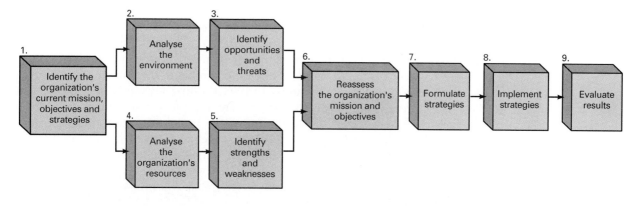

1. Identify the organization's current mission, objectives and strategies

2. Analyse the environment

3. Identify opportunities and threats

4. Analyse the organization's resources

5. Identify strengths and weaknesses

6. Reassess the organization's mission and objectives

7. Formulate strategies

8. Implement strategies

9. Evaluate results

organization's mission forces management to carefully identify the scope of its products or services. It has been argued, for instance, that the decline of the railways was due to their misdefining the business they were in. During the 1930s and 1940s, if the railways had considered themselves to be in the transportation business instead of the railway business, their fate might have been quite different.

Determining the nature of one's business is as important for not-for-profit organizations as it is for business firms. Hospitals, government agencies, and universities must also identify their missions. For example, is a university training students for the professions, training students for particular jobs, or educating students through a well-rounded, liberal education? Is it seeking students from the top 5 per cent of high school graduates, students with low academic grades but high aptitude test scores, or students in the vast middle ground? Answers to questions such as these clarify the organization's current purpose (see Class Exercise). Once classified, the organization can begin to look outside the company to ensure that its strategy aligns well with the environment.[15] As a case in point, take Eddy Match Co. of Pembroke, Ontario. Eddy is the major producer of matches in Canada, and we have all handled its products at some point. But what business is Eddy in? Eddy found itself asking that question, and discovered that it was, in fact, in the advertising business. Personalized matchbooks for individual bars and restaurants, as well as many other businesses, was where Eddy's market existed. Once Eddy realized this, the company could focus on its objectives and strategies as an advertising medium, not simply as a match producer.

Management of every organization needs to analyse its environment (step 2). It needs to know, for instance, what its competition is up to, what pending legislation might affect the organization, and what the supply of labour is like in locations where the organization operates. Step 2 of the strategy process is complete when management has an accurate grasp of what is taking place in its environment, and is aware of important trends that might affect its operations.

An organization like Corel must continually strive to understand the technological and social changes it faces in order to produce products customers want and need.

What Are the Primary Steps in the Strategic Management Process?

After analysing the environment, management needs to evaluate what it has learned in terms of opportunities that the organization can exploit and threats that the organization faces (step 3).[16] Keep in mind that the same environment can present opportunities to one organization and pose threats to another in the same industry because of the organizations' different resources. In 1993, the long recession had created a weak Canadian economy. Business bankruptcies were at postdepression highs (see Ethical Dilemmas in Management). Especially hurt were businesses—like home-furnishing retailers—that sold large-ticket items whose purchase could be easily postponed. However, several large, prosperous, and well-managed chains of home-furnishing retailers saw this situation as an opportunity. They were able to buy inventories of former competitors at bargain prices and to selectively take over these competitors' better locations. The result—a consolidation among the larger and more prosperous furniture retailers. So what an organization considers an opportunity or a threat depends on the resources that it controls.

Next, in step 4, we move from looking outside the organization to looking inside. That is, we are evaluating our internal resources. What skills and abilities do the organization's employees have? What is the organization's cash position? Has it been successful at developing new and innovative products? How does the public perceive the organization and the quality of its products or services?

This fourth step forces management to recognize that every organization, no matter how large and powerful, is constrained in some way by the resources and skills it has available. A smaller automobile manufacturer, like Alfa Romeo, isn't able to move into making minivans simply because management sees opportunities there. Alfa Romeo doesn't have the resources to successfully enter the minivan market against the likes of Chrysler, Ford, Toyota, and Nissan.

The analysis in step 4 should lead to a clear assessment of the organization's strengths and weaknesses (step 5). Management can then identify the organization's **distinctive competence**, or the unique skills and resources that determine the organization's competitive weapons. Black & Decker, for instance, bought General Electric's small appliances division—which made coffeemakers, toasters, irons, and the like—renamed them, and capitalized on Black & Decker's reputation for quality and durability to make these appliances far more profitable than they had been under the GE name.

An understanding of the organization's culture and the strengths and liabilities it offers management is a crucial part of step 5 that has only recently been getting the attention it deserves.[17] Specifically, managers should be aware that strong and weak cultures have different effects on strategy and that the content of a culture has a major effect on the content of the strategy.

In a strong culture, for instance, almost all employees will have a clear understanding of what the organization is about. This should make it easier for management to convey to new employees the organization's distinctive competence. A hotel chain like C.P. Hotels & Resorts, which has a very strong culture that embraces service and customer satisfaction, should be able to instil its cultural values in new employees in a much shorter time than can a competitor with a weak culture. The negative side of a strong culture, of course, is that it is more difficult to change. A strong culture may act as a significant barrier to acceptance of a change in the organization's strategies. In fact, the strong culture at Wang Labs undoubtedly kept top management

distinctive competence
The unique skills and resources that determine the organization's competitive weapons.

ETHICAL DILEMMAS IN MANAGEMENT

▼ IS "GOING BANKRUPT" AN UNETHICAL STRATEGY? ▲

Dow Corning, the company that developed and marketed silicone breast implants, has a list of 19,000 lawsuits facing it, with the litigants including some 10,000 Canadian women. Dow and the other two large producers of the implants negotiated a $4.2-billion (U.S.) fund to settle world claims. Dow's share was $2 billion over 30 years. However, it became clear that this amount would not be enough to cover all the claims being made against the company, and on May 15, 1995, it sought bankruptcy protection under Chapter 11 of the U.S. Bankruptcy Code. The effect of this action is to freeze all lawsuits and turn the claimants into creditors who will be asked to negotiate a settlement as part of the company's efforts to restructure its finances. Canadian women have been outraged by the action.

But the law of the U.S. allows companies to use Chapter 11 to nurse themselves back to financial health, continuing operations and keeping managers and staff employed—whether they are bankrupt or not. In other words, a company can file for reorganization without being bankrupt, and Chapter 11 has become a strategic option. The discretionary nature of the law has allowed organizations, almost at will, to escape from undesirable financial obligations.

In Canada, also, bankruptcy protection is often used as a strategic option. In our country, companies have the Companies' Creditors Arrangement Act (CCAA), which gives companies court-ordered protection from their creditors, while they develop a restructuring plan. Major corporations such as Dylex and Eaton's have taken this route in the '90s.

Is it wrong for managers to use bankruptcy as a strategy? It does allow the company to continue to operate and thus save employees' jobs. It can, in the longer term, even create enhanced value for stockholders. But it can place an undue hardship on creditors and other claimants. Creditors may have to settle claims for just a few cents on the dollar. Landlords may be left with broken leases, and unions may be left with unenforceable labour agreements. And innocent customers who endured pain, suffering, or even death as a result of a company's negligence may be unable to achieve anything near an equitable financial settlement. When bankruptcy is used to evade responsibility and liability, is management acting unethically?

from perceiving the need to adopt a new corporate strategy in the 1980s in response to changes in the computer industry. Successful organizations with strong cultures can become prisoners of their own past successes.

DOW CHEMICAL CO.
www.dow.com/

How Do You Reassess the Organization's Mission and Objectives?

A merging of steps 3 and 5 results in an assessment of the organization's opportunities (step 6) (see Exhibit 3-6, page 75). This is frequently called SWOT analysis because it brings together the organization's strengths, weaknesses, opportunities, and threats in order to identify a niche that the organization can exploit.

In light of the SWOT analysis and identification of the organization's opportunities, management needs to reevaluate its mission and objectives. Are they realistic? Do they need modification? If changes are needed in the organization's overall direction, this is where they are likely to originate. On the other hand, if no changes are necessary, management is ready to begin the actual formulation of strategies.

YOUNG CANADIANS

Alnoor Sheriff:
Shikatronics

Shikatronics in La Prairie, Quebec, has set itself apart from its competition by offering unparalleled customer service, including speedy delivery, quality product, and on-site client support. This helped Alnoor Sheriff's creation become the second-fastest growing company in Canada in 1997.

SHIKATRONICS
www.shikatronics.ca/
frame3.html

cost-leadership strategy
The strategy an organization follows when it wants to be the lowest-cost producer in its industry.

differentiation strategy
The strategy a firm follows when it wants to be unique in its industry along dimensions widely valued by buyers.

How Do You Formulate Strategies?

Strategies need to be set for all levels in the organization (step 7). Management needs to develop and evaluate alternative strategies and then select a set that is compatible at each level and will allow the organization to best capitalize on its resources and the opportunities available in the environment.

This seventh step is complete when management has developed a set of strategies that will give the organization a competitive advantage. That is, management will seek to position the organization so that it can gain a relative advantage over its rivals. This requires a careful evaluation of the competitive forces that dictate the rules of competition within the industry in which the organization operates.

One of the leading researchers into strategy formulation is Michael Porter of Harvard's Graduate School of Business.[18] His competitive strategies framework demonstrates that managers can choose among three generic strategies (see Details on a Management Classic). According to Michael Porter, no firm can successfully perform at an above-average level by trying to be all things to all people. Rather, Porter proposed that management must select a strategy that will give its organization a competitive advantage. Management can choose from among three strategies: **cost-leadership** (low-cost production), **differentiation** (uniqueness in a broad market), and focus (uniqueness in a narrow market). Which strategy management chooses depends on the organization's strengths and its competitors' weaknesses. As such, management should avoid a position in which it has to slug it out with everybody in the industry. Rather, the organization should put its strength where the competition isn't. Success, then, depends on selecting the right strategy—the one that fits the complete picture of the organization and the industry of which it is a part. This will enable organizations to gain the most favourable competitive advantage.

**Exhibit 3-6
Identifying an
Organization's
Opportunities**

Big Rock Brewery of Calgary has been successful, in a marketplace dominated by Labatt and Molson, by offering distinctive products.

How Do You Implement the Strategic Management Process?

The next-to-last step in the strategic management process is implementation (step 8). No matter how effective strategic planning has been, it cannot succeed if it is not implemented properly. Top management leadership is a necessary ingredient in a successful strategy. So, too, is a motivated group of middle- and lower-level managers to carry out senior management's specific plans. And finally, results must be evaluated (step 9). How effective have our strategies been? What adjustments, if any, are necessary? In Chapter 15, we'll review the control process. The concepts and techniques that we introduce in that chapter can be used to assess the results of strategies and to correct significant deviations.

DETAILS ON A MANAGEMENT CLASSIC

Michael Porter's Generic Strategies

According to Michael Porter, when an organization sets out to be the low-cost producer in its industry, it is following a cost-leadership strategy. Success with this strategy requires that the organization be the cost leader and not merely one of the contenders for that position. Additionally, the product or service being offered must be perceived as comparable to that offered by rivals, or at least acceptable to buyers.

How does a firm gain such a cost advantage? Typical means include efficiency of operations, economies of scale, technological innovation, low-cost labour, or preferential access to raw materials. Examples of firms that have used these strategies include Chapters bookstores, Tim Hortons, and Irving Oil.

The firm that seeks to be unique in its industry in ways that are widely valued by buyers is following a differentiation strategy. It might emphasize high quality, extraordinary service, innovative design, technological capability, or an unusually positive brand image. The key is that the attribute chosen must be different from those offered by rivals and significant enough to justify a price premium that exceeds the cost of differentiating. There is no shortage of firms that have found at least one attribute that allows them to differentiate themselves from competitors. Terra Boots (quality), The Real Canadian Superstore (selection and price), Lenscrafters (service), and Bombardier (innovation) are some examples.

The first two strategies sought a competitive advantage in a broad range of industry segments. The **focus strategy** aims at a cost advantage (cost focus) or differentiation advantage (differentiation focus) in a narrow segment. That is, management will select a segment or group of segments in an industry (such as product variety, type of end buyer, distribution channel, or geographic location of buyers) and tailor the strategy to serve them to the exclusion of others. The goal is to exploit a narrow segment of a market. Of course, the feasibility of a focus strategy depends on the size of a segment and whether it can support the additional cost of focusing. GDT Softworks of Burnaby, B.C., has created its niche by developing technology that allows Macintosh computer users to become compatible with DOS-based printers.[19] For businesses, being able to use a single printer for work on both Macs and PCs saves on costs. GDT has been working on a form of wireless telecommunications that will allow users to connect to the Internet or e-mail on their laptops or hand-held computers. Mountain Equipment CO-OP, headquartered in Vancouver, has close to a million members, broke $100 million in revenue in 1996, and has increased sales by 285 per cent over the past five years.[20] One of the primary reasons for this is the company's vast selection of products—everything that might be desired by anyone stepping into the great outdoors.

focus strategy
The strategy a company follows when it pursues a cost or differentiation advantage in a narrow industry segment.

MOUNTAIN EQUIPMENT CO-OP
www.karo.com/karo/
services/2101.htm

Strategy Is Part of Every Manager's Job

Have you ever attended a symphony or watched a play? Did you ever give much thought to what made the event successful? One of the key ingredients is that all members must work together in harmony. So, too, must organizational members.

Strategies in an organization provide that direction. These goals indicate to all members where the organization is going and what it takes to be successful. Furthermore, strategic planning serves as a catalyst that drives every other activity in the organization. For example, when a company sets its goals, it identifies which specific human resources are needed to accomplish its objectives (see Developing Management Skills). Therefore, employees are selected (either internally or recruited from the outside) based on their possession of the required skills, knowledge, and abilities necessary to successfully complete the jobs. As such, a major focus of hiring should be the fulfilment of company goals.

There is another important aspect of strategic planning that must be recognized—its filtering-down effect. When senior managers set the strategic direction for the company, they establish the overall goals for the corporation. But it is not at this level that the actual work takes place. Thus, these goals must be pushed downward. In essence, corporate goals are achieved through the collective activities in each division or department. By translating these strategic goals into more specific plans, each successive level in management, in turn, will identify specific work activities of the unit's employees. And finally, strategy aids all managers in their decision-making process. Any decisions made should be supportive of the company's objectives.

DEVELOPING MANAGEMENT SKILLS

▼

STEPS IN GOAL SETTING

▲

▶ **1. Identify an employee's key job tasks.** Goal setting begins by defining what it is that you want your employees to accomplish. The best source for this information is each employee's job description.

▶ **2. Establish specific and challenging goals for each key task.** Identify the level of performance expected of each employee. Specify the target for the employee to hit.

▶ **3. Specify the deadlines for each goal.** Putting deadlines on each goal reduces ambigu-

ity. Deadlines, however, should not be set arbitrarily. Rather, they need to be realistic given the tasks to be completed.

▶ **4. Allow the employee to actively participate.** Allowing employees to participate increases their acceptance of the goals. However, employees must perceive that you are truly seeking their input, not just going through the motions.

▶ **5. Prioritize goals.** When someone is given more than one goal, it is important for you to rank the goals in order of importance. The purpose of prioritizing is to encourage the employee to take action and expend effort on each goal in proportion to its importance.

▶ **6. Rate goals for difficulty and importance.** Goal set-

ting should not encourage people to choose easy goals. Instead, goals should be rated for their difficulty and importance. In doing so, individuals can be given credit for trying difficult goals, even if they don't fully achieve them.

▶ **7. Build in feedback mechanisms to assess goal progress.** Feedback lets employees know whether their level of effort is sufficient to attain the goal. Feedback should be both self generated and supervisor generated. In either case, feedback should be frequent and recurring.

▶ **8. Link rewards to goal attainment.** It's natural for employees to ask, "What's in it for me?" Linking rewards to the achievement of goals will help to answer that question.

TQM as a Strategic Weapon

An increasing number of organizations are applying Total Quality Management as a way to build a competitive advantage. As we discussed in Chapter 2, TQM focuses on quality and continuous improvement. To the degree that an organization can satisfy a customer's need for quality, it can differentiate itself from the competition and attract and hold a loyal customer base. Moreover, constant improvement in the quality and reliability of an organization's products or services can result in a competitive advantage others can't steal.[21] Product innovations, for example, offer little opportunity for sustained competitive advantage. Why? Because usually they can be quickly copied by rivals. But incremental improvement, which is an essential element of TQM, is something that becomes an integrated part of an organization's operations and can develop into a considerable cumulative advantage. To illustrate how TQM can be used as a strategic tool, let's look at four companies—AMP of Canada Ltd., Cargill Limited, Pratt & Whitney Canada Ltd., and Steelcase Canada Limited.[22]

AMP, a manufacturer and distributor of electric and electronic connecting products to original equipment manufacturers of computers and telecommunications equipment, has created an environment that is organized around processes rather than functions, and it has done this by not filling staff vacancies as they arise in the company. This forces people to wear more than one hat and to focus their activities on what the customer wants rather than what the function wants. A cross-functional team that exemplifies this flexibility and customer focus is the "on-time delivery" team, made up of people from quality, inside sales, warehouse, and inventory control departments. They have achieved 98- to 99-per-cent delivery "as promised."

Pratt & Whitney Canada, a manufacturer of small gas turbines for corporate aircraft, commuter aircraft, and helicopters, and auxiliary power units for jumbo jets, has integrated the efforts of marketing, engineering, manufacturing, procurement, customer support, and finance to cut the product development cycle from five years to two-and-a-half years.

Steelcase Canada is a manufacturer and distributor of office furniture and equipment. Its "focus factories," which integrate all functions in production, inventory, ordering, procurement, and production scheduling, have cut cycle times of eight to 10 weeks down to four weeks and decreased inventory by 50 per cent in two manufacturing areas. Their Quick Ship program ensures delivery of items in 12 days or less.

Cargill is a diversified agricultural company with operations across Canada in grain, fertilizers, and farm chemicals, livestock and feed and seed. By linking a computer to the finished goods scanning system to tell the meat fabrication line when orders from sales for any given cut of meat have been filled, a 15- to 20-per-cent improvement in production accuracy has been achieved.

However, the record of TQM attempts has not been good overall. A *Canadian Business Review* article in the winter of 1992 documents a U.S. survey showing that only 13 per cent of CEOs reported that TQM efforts resulted in higher profits or operating income. A British study showed that in the U.K. 80 per cent of TQM efforts fail. A Canadian study showed that while 80 per cent of Canadian companies are making some effort at implementing total quality programs, only a third have achieved tangible positive results.

Entrepreneurship: A Special Case of Strategic Planning

Stories of businesses bootstrapping (surviving with very little capital) to success are always popular news fodder, and if you read the business section of your local newspaper today you will probably find a story of such entrepreneurship. As full-time, satisfying careers in the large corporations become less prevalent, Canadians are embarking on their own business projects more and more often. The following examples are typical of this entrepreneurial spirit.

Linda Stober and Shawn Feinstein began SLS Personnel Inc. (in Montreal) in 1993, because of dissatisfaction with the large health-care personnel agency at which they were managers.[23] To quote Shawn Feinstein, "In the ladies' room of our office this company was born." The two women believed they could offer better service than anyone else serving the marketplace for private nursing care. And it has paid off. Steadily growing revenues (after a couple of hard years) have brought SLS up to the level of $1 million projected for 1999. Offering comprehensive and sensitive health care should allow the two to continue to prosper, as the population in Canada ages.

This is how Hector Jacques describes the beginnings of his partnership with fellow engineer Michael Whitford: "There were 5,000 bucks and there were two of us."[24] That was in 1972 when Jacques Whitford Group Ltd. was formed in Dartmouth, Nova Scotia. Today revenues are in the $40-million range, reflecting double-digit growth for every year in operation. The company has diversified into many areas of engineering, from construction of buildings and bridges to waste-management systems, and in doing so has never suffered from a lack of contracts. "Look where the market is going and get there first," Jacques advises.

Dorothy Spence sums up her definition of entrepreneurship as follows: "You see this opportunity, and you put everything on the line for it.[25] Then it actually starts to work and you think 'Oh my God, I'm going to be rich.'" This is pretty much the ideal definition of entrepreneurship, but for Spence and partner Linda Weaver, it is wholly accurate. The two formed TecKnowledge Healthcare Systems Inc. in Halifax, back in 1993. Three years later they sold half of the company for a six-figure amount. Their beginning was very much how most people envision entrepreneurs making their start: the two women using their houses as collateral on a $50,000 loan, and setting up in Weaver's basement. TecKnowledge sells telemedicine systems (systems that allow medical professionals in various parts of the world to communicate live with each other, exchanging expertise). The company's growth has been astounding, with annual sales of more than $4 million. Since the two founders have held on to 50 per cent of the company, Spence may soon have to adjust her definition to "*very rich.*"

Strategic planning carries a "big business" bias. It implies a formalization and structure that fits well with large, established organizations that have abundant resources. But the primary interest of many students is not in managing large and established organizations. Like Daniel Langlois of Montreal's Softimage (which has merged with Microsoft), Fred Smith of Federal Express, or Michael and Aaron Serruya of Markham, Ontario's franchising sensation Yogen Fruz, they're excited about the idea of starting their own businesses from scratch—an action that is called entrepreneurship.

Karl Brackhaus is an example of somebody who did just that. He finished a PhD in engineering physics at the University of British Columbia in 1976 and started a firm to help companies apply programmable industrial-control technology. Three years later he produced a colour graphics display system, called the Grafix Terminal, which was quickly bought by breweries, mines, and sawmills, principally in British Columbia. Brackhaus's company, Dynapro Systems Inc., was off and running.

Except for one hitch. Allen-Bradley, a subsidiary of the giant Rockwell International, became interested in entering the field. Instead of trying to compete head-to-head with Allen-Bradley, Karl Brackhaus did a deal with them whereby Allen-Bradley bought 50 per cent of Dynapro Systems, and became its major customer. Sales have risen an average of 50 per cent per year since 1983, surpassing the $40-million mark in 1994.[26]

What Is Entrepreneurship?

entrepreneurship
A process by which individuals pursue opportunities, fulfilling needs and wants through innovation, without regard to the resources they currently control.

There is no shortage of definitions of **entrepreneurship**.[27] Some, for example, apply it to the creation of any new business. Others focus on intentions, claiming that entrepreneurs seek to create wealth, which is different from starting businesses merely as a means of income substitution (that is, working for yourself rather than working for someone else). When most people describe entrepreneurs, they use adjectives such as bold, innovative, venturesome, and risk taking. They also tend to associate entrepreneurs with small businesses. We'll define entrepreneurship as a process by which individuals pursue opportunities, fulfilling needs and wants through innovation, without regard to the resources they currently control.[28]

It's important not to confuse managing a small business with entrepreneurship. Why? Because not all small business managers are entrepreneurs.[29] Many don't innovate. A great many managers of small businesses are merely scaled-down versions of the conservative, conforming bureaucrats who staff many large corporations and public agencies.

Do All Entrepreneurs Possess Similar Characteristics?

One of the most researched topics in entrepreneurship has been the search to determine what, if any, psychological characteristics entrepreneurs have in common. A number of these characteristics have been found. These include willingness to work hard, self-confidence, optimism, determination, and a high energy level.[30] But three factors regularly sit on the top of most lists that profile the entrepreneurial personality. Entrepreneurs have a high need for achievement, believe strongly that they can control their own destinies, and take only moderate risks.[31]

The research allows us to draw a general description of entrepreneurs. They tend to be independent types who prefer to be personally responsible for solving problems, for setting goals, and for reaching these goals by their own efforts. They value independence and don't like being controlled by others. While they're not afraid of taking chances, they're not wild risk takers. They prefer to take calculated risks when they feel that they can control the outcome.

The evidence on entrepreneurial personalities leads us to two obvious conclusions. First, people with this personality makeup are not likely to be contented, productive employees in the typical large corporation or government agency. The rules, regulations, and controls that these bureaucracies impose on their members frustrate entrepreneurs. Second, the challenges and conditions inherent in starting one's own business mesh well with the entrepreneurial personality. Starting a new venture, which they control, appeals to their willingness to take risks and determine their own destinies. But because entrepreneurs believe that their future is fully in their own hands, the risk they perceive as moderate is often seen as high by nonentrepreneurs.

YOUNG CANADIANS

Jennifer Corson:
The Renovator's Resource

After having studied architecture, and being aware of the amount of construction and demolition material going to landfill sites, Jennifer Corson found herself scavenging in old buildings in Halifax when she hit upon a business idea. Under the moniker of the Renovator's Resource Inc., she makes bids to remove from demolition sites flooring, fixtures, and even entire buildings, which her company then resells. Founded in 1994, estimated annual revenues in 1997 were $500,000. Meanwhile Corson's business efforts include a television show, an architecture practice, and a new enterprise involving disassembling soon-to-be-destroyed buildings and shipping them to appreciative buyers.

	TRADITIONAL MANAGERS	ENTREPRENEURS
Primary motivation	Promotion and other traditional corporate rewards such as office, staff, and power	Independence, opportunity to create, financial gain
Time orientation	Achievement of short-term goals	Achievement of five- to ten-year growth of business
Activity	Delegation and supervision	Direct involvement
Risk propensity	Low	Moderate
View toward failures and mistakes	Avoidance	Acceptance

Exhibit 3-7 Comparing Entrepreneurs and Traditional Managers
Source: Based on Robert D. Hisrich, "Entrepreneurship/Intrapreneurship," *American Psychologist,* February 1990, p. 218.

How Do Entrepreneurs Compare to Traditional Managers?

Exhibit 3-7 summarizes some key differences between entrepreneurs and traditional bureaucratic managers. While the latter tend to be more custodial, entrepreneurs actively seek change by exploiting opportunities. When searching for these opportunities, entrepreneurs often put their personal financial security at risk. The hierarchy in large organizations typically insulates traditional managers from these financial wagers and rewards them for minimizing risks and avoiding failures.

Summary

This summary is organized by the chapter Learning Objectives found on page 59.

1. Planning is the process of determining objectives and assessing the way these objectives can best be achieved.

2. Planning gives direction, reduces the impact of change, minimizes waste and redundancy, and sets the standards to facilitate controlling.

3. Strategic plans cover an extensive time period (usually five or more years), cover broad issues, and include the formulation of objectives. Operational plans cover shorter periods of time, focus on specifics, and assume that objectives are already known.

4. Directional plans are preferred over specific plans when uncertainty is high and when the organization is in the formative and decline stages of its life cycle.

5. Four contingency factors in planning include a manager's level in the organization, the life stage of the organization, the degree of environmental uncertainty, and the length of future commitments.

6. A manager should plan just far enough ahead to see through commitments she makes today.

7. Management by objectives is a system in which specific performance objectives are jointly determined by employees and their bosses, progress toward objectives is periodically reviewed, and rewards are allocated on the basis of the progress. The four ingredients common to MBO programs are goal specificity, participative decision making, explicit time periods, and performance feedback.

8. In a dynamic and uncertain environment, strategic planning is important because it can provide managers with a systematic and comprehensive means for analysing the environment, assessing their organization's strengths and weaknesses, and identifying opportunities in which their organization could have a competitive advantage.

9. The strategic management process is made up of nine steps: (1) identifying the organization's current mission, objectives, and strategies; (2) analysing the environment; (3) identifying opportunities and threats in the environment; (4) analysing the organization's resources; (5) identifying the organization's strengths and weaknesses; (6) reassessing the organization's mission and objectives based on its strengths, weaknesses, opportunities, and threats; (7) formulating strategies; (8) implementing its strategies; and (9) evaluating results.

10. SWOT analysis refers to analysing the organization's internal strengths and weaknesses, as well as external opportunities and threats, in order to identify a niche that the organization can exploit.

11. Entrepreneurs approach strategy by first seeking out opportunities that they can exploit. Bureaucratic managers approach strategy by first determining the availability of their resources.

Review and Discussion Questions

1. Contrast formal with informal planning.

2. How does planning affect an organization in terms of performance?

3. Describe the six different types of plans discussed in this chapter.

4. How does the planning done by a top executive differ from that performed by a supervisor?

5. How does environmental uncertainty affect planning?

6. Compare an organization's mission with its objectives.

7. Describe the nine-step strategic management process.

8. What is a SWOT analysis?

9. How would you describe Wal-Mart's competitive advantage in its industry?

10. All managers are involved in the strategic planning process. Describe how this happens.

11. How can TQM provide a competitive advantage?

12. Are all small-business managers entrepreneurs? Explain your answer.

Testing Your Comprehension

Circle the correct answer, then check yourself on page 471.

1. The term *planning* implies all of the following EXCEPT
   a) defining an organization's goals and objectives
   b) establishing an overall strategy for goal achievement
   c) providing directions for ethical behaviours
   d) developing a series of plans to coordinate activities

2. A lack of planning can
   a) foster cooperation among employees
   b) reduce wasteful activities
   c) ensure the coordination of activities
   d) none of the above

3. A manager once quipped, "Though I hate it, formulating the annual business plan forces me to think through every single aspect of my business in advance." This BEST illustrates which benefit of planning?
   a) reduction of overlapping and wasteful activities
   b) establishment of standards to facilitate control
   c) reduction of uncertainty by anticipating change
   d) establishment of coordinated effort

4. Which of the following statements is MOST accurate?

   a) Many studies confirm the positive relationship between planning and performance.

   b) All organizations that plan extensively outperform those that plan less formally.

   c) All organizations that plan outperform those that do not.

   d) Many studies confirm that planning does not lead to greater performance because labour unions are weak.

5. Plans that determine specific details about organizational objectives that are to be achieved are called

   a) strategic plans

   b) tactical plans

   c) long-term plans

   d) detailed plans

6. Plans are commonly described according to all of the following EXCEPT

   a) breadth

   b) time frame

   c) length

   d) specificity

7. Which of the following statements is NOT a criticism of planning?

   a) Planning creates rigidity.

   b) Planning assists in dealing with changes in a dynamic environment.

   c) Planning reinforces success.

   d) Planning focuses managers' attention on today's competition, not on tomorrow's survival.

8. Management by objectives

   a) uses a top-down goal-setting process

   b) uses goals that indicate the general direction desired

   c) has a hierarchy of objectives that are closely linked between organizational levels

   d) was first proposed in the late 1970s

9. According to the philosophy of MBO,

   a) feedback occurs at the annual performance review

   b) goals follow a top-down approach

   c) goals typically are broad, general statements of intent

   d) constant feedback is provided

10. MBO assists in answering the question "What's in it for me as an employee?" by
    a) linking rewards to goal attainment
    b) identifying employees' key job tasks
    c) allowing employees to participate actively
    d) prioritizing goals

11. The mission of a nonprofit organization is MOST accurately described by which of the following phrases?
    a) the set of traditions in an organization
    b) a physical location remote from the main operation
    c) a statement of what business the organization operates
    d) a detailed plan of expected resources for a set time period

12. When an organization seeks to identify environmental opportunities and match them with its strength, it is
    a) seeking to develop its mission statement
    b) determining its distinctive competence
    c) identifying environmental uncertainties
    d) creating a multinational corporation

13. SWOT analysis
    a) matches the organization's competencies with its environmental forces
    b) sometimes involves industrial espionage tactics
    c) occurs during the mission statement formulation
    d) is most useful for helping an organization sustain its competitive advantage

14. According to Michael Porter, the goal of the focus strategy is to
    a) exploit a narrow segment of the market
    b) seek competitive advantages in large market segments
    c) use technological innovation to more accurately target customers
    d) bring suppliers and distributors together to combine efforts

15. Which of the following is NOT a strategic implication of TQM?
    a) TQM can assist an organization in differentiating itself from the competition.
    b) TQM can assist an organization in forecasting product sales in the global village.
    c) TQM can assist an organization in attracting and holding a loyal customer base.
    d) TQM can assist an organization in sustaining its competitive advantage.

16. Which of the following is a characteristic associated with an entrepreneur?
    a) focuses on the opportunity to create
    b) refuses to accept failure and mistakes
    c) emphasizes direct supervision of employees
    d) emphasizes achievement of short-term goals

Self-Assessment Exercise

Are You a Good Planner?

Instructions: Answer either Yes or No to each of the following eight questions:

	Yes	No
1. My personal objectives are clearly spelled out in writing.	_____	_____
2. Most of my days are hectic and disorderly.	_____	_____
3. I seldom make any snap decisions and usually study a problem carefully before acting.	_____	_____
4. I keep a desk calendar or appointment book as an aid.	_____	_____

	Yes	No
5. I make use of "action" and "deferred action" files.	_____	_____
6. I generally establish starting dates and deadlines for all my projects.	_____	_____
7. I often ask others for advice.	_____	_____
8. I believe that all problems have to be solved immediately.	_____	_____

Turn to page 464 for scoring directions and key.

Source: Ted Pollack, "Are You a Good Planner," *Supervision*, January 1980, pp. 26–27; "How Good a Planner Are You?" *Supervision*, July 1983, p. 24; and "How to Be a Good Planner," *Supervision*, April 1984, pp. 25–26. Reprinted by permission of © National Research Bureau, P.O. Box 1, Burlington, Iowa 52601-0001.

Class Exercise

Your School's Mission

Often we lose sight of our university's goals and objectives as we pay more attention to our studies. Even so, your school must also be prepared to carve out its niche in an effort to provide something of value to its students. For this exercise, your professor will put you into small groups. The charge of each small group is to prepare responses to the following questions and present its findings to the class.

1. What do you think is your school's mission?
2. How would you describe your school's environment?
3. What are the strengths and weaknesses of your school? Its competitive advantage?
4. What resources does your school have that support its mission?
5. Given your perception of your school, what strategic suggestions would you make?

Case Application

Setting Strategies at Drypers Corp.

Years ago, companies such as Procter & Gamble and Kimberly-Clark dominated the market for disposable diapers. Their big-brand sellers, Pampers and Huggies, were the heavyweights in the marketplace. Today, however, competition is getting fierce, and Dave Pitassi and Wally Kemp hope to take a large part of the market share. The two partners thought up their business idea while they were students. They developed a business plan to become a low-cost producer of quality disposable diapers. Although they ran into many roadblocks along the way, the two persevered. Pitassi and Kemp's main thrust was to use materials from local businesses in their production. This approach enabled them to manufacture a cheap but good-quality diaper. With long-term planning and successful marketing, Drypers sales reached $35 million in just three years. With a careful analysis, Drypers has expanded its market share, acquiring two regional diaper manufacturers. Today, sales are more than $150 million.[32]

Questions

1. What type of grand strategy is Drypers pursuing?

2. Michael Porter identified three generic strategies that companies can follow to develop a competitive advantage. Which one do you think Drypers has used? Discuss and support your choice.

3. How would you recommend Drypers exploit its competitive advantage?

chapter 4

Planning Tools
and Techniques

Learning Objectives

What will I be able to do after I finish
this chapter?

1 • Describe techniques for scanning the environment.

2 • Contrast quantitative and qualitative forecasting.

3 • Explain why budgets are popular.

4 • List two approaches to budgeting.

5 • Differentiate Gantt and load charts.

6 • Identify the steps in a PERT network.

7 • State the factors that determine a product's break-even point.

8 • Describe the requirements for using linear programming.

9 • Discuss how queuing theory can be a planning tool.

Allen Fracassi likes to keep things in perspective. This is what he has said about the company he founded with his brother: "I was just trying to pay off my mortgage when I started." That company, Philip Services Corp. (formerly Philip Environmental Inc., until the summer of 1997), is now the largest industrial waste-management company on the continent. Allen (president) and his brother Philip (vice-president) founded the company in Hamilton in 1980 as a waste-disposal business. At that point they had two trucks, and to minimize tipping fees at landfills they would take whatever could be salvaged out of the waste before dumping. While hauling sand from local steel plants, they developed a method for separating the steel from the sand, and then resold both. It did not take long before the Fracassis had decided that recycling was the direction in which their company needed to go.[1]

At the time, this focus on recycling was unique in the industry. Growth came rapidly. The company's revenues grew 50 times larger between 1989 and 1994. At that point, Allen Fracassi had definitely developed a plan. Philip earned revenues of $650 million in 1995, $800 million in 1996; with a projected $2 billion in 1997, and a projected $3 billion in 1998. This phenomenal growth can largely be attributed to Philip's continual acquisitions. In 1996 and 1997, Philip purchased more than 15 companies, including a $540-million (U.S.) acquisition—

Allwaste Inc. in Houston. Allen Fracassi believes that the industry is consolidating, and that the hundreds of companies that operate in the field today will disappear, leaving only about 10 major companies. To remain at the top of its field, Philip must continue to grow, and Fracassi predicts that the company will continue to acquire firms at a fast rate until about the year 2002. Philip is careful, however, not to lose control of operations during this period of growth. Philip buys only companies that produce services useful to the existing client base. As Allen Fracassi has said, "We're not out on an acquisition binge just to grow revenue. This is a well thought out strategic plan."

The Fracassis carefully plan every step they take in the growth of their company.

In this chapter, we'll discuss a number of basic planning tools and techniques. We'll begin by looking at three planning techniques to assist managers in assessing their environment: environmental scanning, forecasting, and benchmarking. We'll review the most popular planning tool used by managers: budgets. We'll then discuss scheduling, break-even analysis, and other operational planning tools. Finally, we'll conclude this chapter by offering some ideas to help you in your personal, day-to-day planning.

Assessing the Environment

In our last chapter, we introduced planning and the strategic management process. In this section, we want to review several techniques that have been developed to help managers with one of the most challenging aspects of this process: assessing their organization's environment. Twenty years ago, environmental analysis was an infor-

Where does Goodyear look to see what its biggest competitor is doing next? It scans Michelin's operations in France and Japan because their products typically show up shortly in Canada.

MICHELIN
www.michelin.com/
us/eng/home.htm

mal endeavour based on intuitive judgments. Today, using structured techniques such as environmental scanning, forecasting, and benchmarking, a manager's ability to accurately analyse an organization's environment has improved measurably.

What Is Environmental Scanning?

Poco Petroleums, of Calgary, Alberta, has developed from a small producer and marketer of gas to one of the top three non-aggregator exporters to the United States, along with Shell and Mobil (non-aggregators principally sell the gas they produce; aggregators sell gas they acquire). It accomplished this by carefully scanning the environment and recognizing the changes needed to survive and prosper. By understanding the changes taking place in the market, the regulation changes affecting pipelines, the evolving relationships with customers, and the opportunities to buy and sell gas in either the Canadian or U.S. market wherever prices warranted, Poco has developed a strong customer base, and knowledge and relationships within the exceedingly complex world of gas marketing that now make it very difficult for competitors to catch up.

Managers, like Bobbie Gaunt (see Managers Who Made a Difference), in both small and large organizations, are increasingly turning to environmental scanning to anticipate and interpret changes in their environment.[2] The term, as we'll use it, refers to screening large amounts of information to detect emerging trends and create a set of scenarios.

The importance of environmental scanning was first recognized (outside of the national security establishment) by firms in the life insurance industry in the late 1970s.[3] Life insurance companies found that the demand for their product was declining. Yet all the key environmental signals they were receiving strongly favoured the sale of life insurance. The economy and population were growing. Baby boomers were finishing school, entering the labour force, and taking on family responsibilities. The market for life insurance should have been expanding, but it wasn't. What the insurance companies had failed to recognize was a fundamental change in family structure in Canada.

Young families, who represented the primary group of buyers of new insurance policies, tended to be dual-career couples who were increasingly choosing to remain childless. The life insurance needs of a family with one income, a dependent spouse, and a houseful of kids are much greater than those of a two-income family with few, if any, children. That a multibillion-dollar industry could overlook such a fundamental social trend underscored the need to develop techniques for monitoring important environmental developments.

competitor intelligence
Environmental scanning activity that seeks to identify who competitors are, what they're doing, and how their actions will affect the focus organization.

How Does Competitive Intelligence Help?

One of the fastest-growing areas of environmental scanning is **competitor intelligence**.[4] It seeks basic information about competitors: Who are they? What are they doing? How will what they're doing affect us? Accurate information on the competition can allow managers to anticipate competitor actions rather than merely react to them.

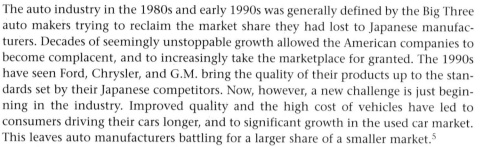

MANAGERS WHO MADE A DIFFERENCE

Bobbie Gaunt: Ford Canada

**FORD
CANADA**
www.ford.ca/

The auto industry in the 1980s and early 1990s was generally defined by the Big Three auto makers trying to reclaim the market share they had lost to Japanese manufacturers. Decades of seemingly unstoppable growth allowed the American companies to become complacent, and to increasingly take the marketplace for granted. The 1990s have seen Ford, Chrysler, and G.M. bring the quality of their products up to the standards set by their Japanese competitors. Now, however, a new challenge is just beginning in the industry. Improved quality and the high cost of vehicles have led to consumers driving their cars longer, and to significant growth in the used car market. This leaves auto manufacturers battling for a larger share of a smaller market.[5]

So, how is this battle going to be fought? Ford made its strategy fairly explicit when in April 1997 it appointed Bobbie Gaunt as CEO of Ford Canada. Gaunt comes from a marketing background, and has a very specific view of how to handle the new trends emerging in the industry. As she states, "Ford has been a mass marketer for years, and it worked wonderfully. But when your industry becomes saturated and doesn't have a lot of natural growth, the only way you're going to find a way to grow in a profitable way is being smarter about the customer than anybody else."

Gaunt has been with Ford since 1972, when she joined the company with plans to enroll in its management training program (Chrysler and G.M., at the time, refused to allow women into their executive ranks). In 1979 Gaunt helped form a women's marketing committee (unheard of among the Big Three at the time) to address the needs of female drivers. Management at Ford eventually took notice, and had the good sense to encourage the development of marketing directed toward women. By 1990, women accounted for 42 per cent of car purchases—a giant leap from a decade earlier when men were the overwhelming consumer force. Today women purchase at least half the cars bought in North America. Gaunt, the first woman to head up Ford Canada, came to her new position after handling sales and marketing for Ford in the U.S. Her predecessor at Ford Canada, Mark Hutchins, also concentrated on marketing through the

company's dealerships. Hutchins has left Ford Canada in good shape, with vehicle sales up 22 per cent from 1995, as well as increases in both lease market share and customer satisfaction every year for the past five years. Now it is time for Bobbie Gaunt to build on Ford's new success.

Gaunt's appointment as CEO is a watershed for Ford Canada. Gaunt will be steering the company through a time of major changes in the industry. The plans that are put in place now will determine how Ford copes with these changes. As Gaunt says, ". . . it's about how this product fits the customer, not how the customer fits the product." The new car market will become more competitive, and executives like Bobbie Gaunt will have to be prepared for the shifts in consumer tastes.▼

One expert on competitive intelligence emphasizes that 95 per cent of the competitor-related information an organization needs to make crucial strategic decisions is available and accessible to the public.[6] In other words, competitive intelligence isn't organizational espionage. Advertisements, promotional materials, Web sites, patent applications, press releases, reports filed with government agencies, annual reports, want ads, newspaper reports, and industry studies are examples of readily accessible sources of information. Trade shows and the debriefing of your own sales staff can be other good sources of information on competitors. Many companies even regularly buy competitors' products and have their own employees evaluate them to learn about new technical innovations.

But sometimes these practices escalate and upset the parties involved. In the mid-1990s, a mini-war of words erupted between Future Shop, an international retailer of electronic equipment and computers with 53 stores in Canada and 10 in the U.S., and A & B Sound, a regional electronics and music retailer with eight stores in British Columbia and three in Alberta. A & B accused Future Shop of sending their staff into A & B's stores to disrupt service and occupy their sales staff's time. Future Shop did not deny having its staff check pricing and sales at A & B. Peter de Verteuil, Future Shop's manager of advertising, says, "Shopping the competition is a common practice in all parts of the retail industry. In the end it's good for the customer." Bob Hitchcock, director of marketing for A & B Sound, says, "It's retail terrorism. Everybody likes to know what is going on on the sales floor of their competitors. But if they are disrupting business, it's not fair." Where is the line between gathering competitive intelligence and guerilla-style tactics?[7] Mind you, this example is a far cry from competitive intelligence practices in many other nations. The French government, for instance, supports a major commercial intelligence program—to the extent that Air France reportedly bugged first-class seats and employed state intelligence operatives to pose as crew members in the early 1990s, to glean information from executives on board flights.[8]

Though in countries such as Japan and Sweden many organizations have their own competitive intelligence departments, Canada's CI industry just began to seriously emerge at the end of the 1990s. Membership in the Society of Competitive Intelligence Professionals started to grow by leaps and bounds from 1995 to 1999.

Is There Any Way to Help Predict the Future?

scenario
A consistent view of what the future is likely to be.

A **scenario** is a consistent view of what the future is likely to be. If, for instance, scanning uncovers increasing interest in Manitoba's provincial legislature for raising the minimum wage, Wendy's could create a multiple set of scenarios to assess the possible consequences of such an action. It would then be better prepared to initiate changes in its strategy to gain and hold a competitive advantage.

What Are the Different Types of Forecasts?

Environmental scanning creates the foundation for forecasts. Information obtained through scanning is used to form scenarios. These, in turn, establish premises for forecasts, which are predictions of future outcomes. Probably the two most popular outcomes for which management is likely to seek forecasts are future revenues and new technological breakthroughs. However, virtually any component in the organization's general and specific environment can receive forecasting attention.

Sara Lee's sales level drives purchasing requirements, production goals, employment needs, inventories, and numerous other decisions. Similarly, BCIT's income from tuition and government grants will determine course offerings, staffing needs, salary increases for faculty, and the like. Both of these examples illustrate that predicting future revenues—**revenue forecasting**—is a critical element of planning for both profit and not-for-profit organizations.

revenue forecasting
Predicting future revenues.

YOUNG CANADIANS

Bruce Poon Tip:
The Great Adventure People

In 1990, at the age of 23, Bruce Poon Tip was working with a travel company when he found a market that was being ignored: tours focusing on the cultural aspects of exotic locations. Founding The Great Adventure People, Poon Tip grew his company up to more than $4 million in revenues by 1996.

Where Does Management Get the Data for Developing Revenue Forecasts?
Typically, management obtains data for developing revenue forecasts by reviewing historical revenue figures. For example, what were last year's revenues? This figure can then be adjusted for trends. What revenue patterns have evolved over recent years? What changes in social, economic, or other factors in the general environment might alter the pattern in the future? In the specific environment, what actions can we expect from our competitors? Answers to questions like these provide the basis for revenue forecasts.

What Is Technological Forecasting? Technological forecasting attempts to predict changes in technology and the time frame in which new technologies are likely to be economically feasible. The rapid pace of technological change has seen innovations in lasers, biotechnology, robotics, and data communications dramatically change surgery practices, pharmaceutical offerings, the processes used for manufacturing almost every mass-produced product, and the practicality of cellular telephones. Few organizations are exempt from the possibility that technological innovation might dramatically change the demand for their current products or services. The environmental scanning techniques discussed in the previous section can provide data on potential technological innovations.

We are by now all used to the convenience of paying by Interac at our local grocery store. A few years ago, however, this was not such a common phenomenon. The

SAFEWAY
www.safeway.com/

quantitative forecasting
Applies a set of mathematical rules to a series of past data to predict future outcomes.

qualitative forecasting
Uses the judgment and opinions of knowledgeable individuals to predict future outcomes.

benchmarking
The search for the best practices among competitors or noncompetitors that lead to their superior performance.

grocery chains had to make a decision to embrace this technology as an inevitable change in their business process. The large stores such as IGA, Sobey's, and Safeway used technological forecasting to prepare themselves for the change. A decade ago this technology, although certainly possible, was not considered economically feasible. Today chances are that even a small mom-and-pop store will have this capability.

What Are the Different Types of Forecasting Techniques? Forecasting techniques fall into two categories: quantitative and qualitative. **Quantitative forecasting** applies a set of mathematical rules to a series of past data to predict future outcomes. These techniques are preferred when management has sufficient "hard" data from which to work. **Qualitative forecasting**, on the other hand, uses the judgment and opinions of knowledgeable individuals. Qualitative techniques typically are used when precise data are scarce or difficult to obtain.

Exhibit 4-1 lists some of the better-known quantitative and qualitative forecasting techniques.

How Can Benchmarking Help?

Another planning tool is **benchmarking**. This is the search for the best practices among competitors or noncompetitors that lead to their superior performance.[9] The basic idea underlying benchmarking is that management can improve quality by analysing and then copying the methods of the leaders in various fields. As such, benchmarking is a very specific form of environmental scanning (see Ethical Dilemmas in Management).

TECHNIQUES	DESCRIPTION	APPLICATION
Quantitative		
Time-series analysis	Fits a trend line to a mathematical equation and projects into the future by means of this equation	Predicting next quarter's sales based on four years of previous sales data
Regression models	Predicts one variable on the basis of known or assumed other variables	Seeking factors that will predict a certain level of sales (for example, price, advertising expenditures)
Econometric models	Uses a set of regression equations to simulate segments of the economy	Predicting change in car sales as a result of changes in tax laws
Economic indicators	Uses one or more economic indicators to predict a future state of the economy	Using change in GNP to predict discretionary income
Substitution-effect	Uses a mathematical formulation to predict how, when, and under what circumstances a new product or technology will replace an existing one	Predicting the effect of microwave ovens on the sale of conventional ovens
Qualitative		
Jury of opinion	Combines and averages the opinions of experts	Polling all the company's personnel managers to predict next year's university recruitment needs
Sales-force composition	Combines estimates from field sales personnel of customers' expected purchases	Predicting next year's sales of industrial lasers
Customer evaluation	Combines estimates from established customers of expected purchases	Surveying of major dealers by a car manufacturer to determine types and quantities of products desired

Exhibit 4-1   Forecasting Techniques

ETHICAL DILEMMAS IN MANAGEMENT

▼

WHEN DOES COMPETITIVE INTELLIGENCE BECOME ESPIONAGE?

▲

Boeing, the Seattle-based aerospace giant, not too long ago hired several engineers from its rival north of the border, Bombardier. While these engineers were undoubtedly well-qualified, so were many other candidates. Was having a knowledge of Bombardier's development plans a major factor in the hiring of these engineers? Was it unethical for Boeing to have hired these people? Would it be acceptable to hire them away from Bombardier with the lure of more money, but unacceptable to question them concerning Bombardier's operations?

The vice-president at a major book publishing company encourages one of her editors to interview for an editorial vacancy at a competing book publisher. The editor isn't interested in the position. The sole purpose of the interview will be to gain as much information as possible on the competitor's near-term publishing list and relay that information back to the vice-president. Is going to such an interview unethical? Is asking a subordinate to engage in this intelligence mission unethical?

Neither of these situations involves obtaining publicly available information. Yet tactics like these are practised by organizations in a number of highly competitive businesses. When does competitive intelligence become espionage? Does any effort to conceal one's real motives when attempting to gather information automatically brand that action as unethical? What do you think?

Xerox undertook what is widely regarded as the first benchmarking effort in North America in 1979. Up until then, the Japanese had been aggressively copying the successes of others by travelling around, watching what others were doing, and then applying their new knowledge to improve their products and processes. Xerox's management couldn't figure out how Japanese manufacturers could sell mid-size copiers for considerably less than Xerox's production costs. So the company's head of manufacturing took a team to Japan to make a detailed study of their competition's costs and processes. They got most of their information from Xerox's own joint venture, Fuji-Xerox, which knew its competition well. What the team found was shocking. Their Japanese rivals were light-years ahead of Xerox in efficiency. Benchmarking those efficiencies marked the beginning of Xerox's recovery in the copier field. Today, in addition to Xerox, companies such as Magna, Bombardier, Ford, and Motorola use benchmarking as a standard tool in their quest for quality improvement.

To illustrate its use in practice, let's look at its application at Ford Motor Company. Ford used benchmarking in the early 1980s in developing its highly successful Taurus. The company compiled a list of some 400 features its customers said were the most important and then set about finding the car with the best of each. Then it tried to match or top the best of the competition. When the Taurus was updated in 1992, Ford benchmarked all over again. For instance, the door handles on the latest Taurus were benchmarked against the Chevrolet Lumina, the easy-to-change taillight bulbs against the Nissan Maxima, and the tilt steering wheel against the Honda Accord.

The Waterford hospital in St. John's began its plan to become a leading psychiatric hospital in Canada by looking at all of its departments and processes, then identifying which hospital in Canada had the best example of these departments or processes, visiting each hospital to find out what they were doing and how they were doing it, identifying the elements that contributed to being the best, and then focus-

BOEING
www.boeing.com/

BOMBARDIER
www.bombardier.com/

These German autoworkers, producers of Volkswagens, will benchmark their product lines against the industry leaders in an effort to regain their world-class standing.

ing on doing these things as well, or, in most cases, better than they were being done elsewhere. Benchmarking allows an organization to take established best practices and develop them further.

Budgets

budget
A numerical plan for allocating resources to specific activities.

Few of us are unfamiliar with budgets. Most of us learned about them at an early age, when we discovered that unless we allocated our "revenues" carefully, we would consume our weekly allowance before half the week was out. A **budget** is a numerical plan for allocating resources to specific activities. Managers typically prepare budgets for revenues, expenses, and such capital expenditures as machinery and equipment. It's not unusual, though, for budgets to be used for improving time, space, and the use of material resources. These latter types of budgets substitute nondollar numbers for dollar terms. Such items as person-hours, capacity utilization, or units of production can be budgeted for daily, weekly, or monthly activities. However, we'll emphasize dollar-based budgets.

Why Are Budgets So Popular?

Budgets are popular probably because they are applicable to a wide variety of organizations and units within an organization. We live in a world in which almost everything is expressed in monetary units. Dollars, pesos, francs, yen, and the like are used as a common denominator within a country. Even human life has a monetary value. Insurance actuaries regularly compute the value of a lost eye, arm, or leg. While most people argue that life is priceless, Canadian insurance companies and juries regularly convert the loss of human body parts or life itself into dollars and cents. It seems logical, then, that monetary budgets make a useful common denominator for directing activities in such diverse departments as production and marketing research or at various levels in an organization. Budgets are one planning device that most managers, regardless of their level in the organization, help to formulate.

What Are the Primary Types of Budgets?

There is no shortage of items or areas for which budgets can be used. The following—revenue budgets, expense budgets, profit budgets, cash budgets, capital expenditure budgets, fixed and variable budgets—represent the ones managers are most likely to use. Exhibit 4-2 provides an overview of each.

incremental budget
A budget that allocates funds to departments according to allocations in the previous period.

How Do Incremental Budgets Differ from Zero-based Budgets? There are essentially two approaches managers can take to budgeting. By far the most popular approach is the incremental or traditional budget. But in recent years, managers in some organizations have been trying to make budgets more effective by experimenting with the zero-based budget. Let's look at each of these approaches.

The **incremental** (or traditional) **budget** has two identifying characteristics. First, funds are allocated to departments or organizational units. The managers of these units then allocate funds to activities as they see fit. Second, an incremental budget develops out of the previous budget. Each period's budget begins by using the

Revenue Budget:	A budget that projects future sales.
Expense Budget:	A budget that lists the primary activities undertaken by a unit and allocates a dollar amount to each.
Profit Budget:	A budget used by separate units of an organization that combines revenue and expense budgets to determine the units.
Cash Budget:	A budget that forecasts how much cash an organization will have on hand and how much it will need to meet expenses.
Capital Expenditure Budget:	A budget that forecasts investments in property, buildings, and major equipment.
Fixed Budget:	A budget that assumes a fixed level of sales or production.
Variable Budget:	A budget that takes into account those costs that vary with volume.

**Exhibit 4-2
Types of Budgets**

last period as a reference point. Only incremental changes in the budget request are reviewed. Each of these characteristics, however, creates a problem.

When funds are allocated to organizational units, it becomes difficult to differentiate activities within units. Why? Because organizational units typically have a multiple set of goals and hence engage in a number of activities. Incremental budgets don't take this diversity of activities into consideration. They focus on providing funds for units rather than for activities within the units. Given that units have multiple goals, it seems reasonable to conclude that (1) some goals are more important than others, and (2) unit managers have varying degrees of success in achieving these multiple goals. Incremental budgets throw everything into the same pot. Thus, as planning devices they lack sufficient focus and specificity.

Zero-based budgeting (ZBB), originally developed by Texas Instruments, requires managers to justify their budget requests in detail from scratch, regardless of previous appropriations.[10] It's designed to attack the second drawback we mentioned in incremental budgets: activities that have a way of becoming immortal. Once established, organizational activities can take on lives of their own. This is especially true in public organizations.

ZBB shifts the burden of proof to the manager to justify why her unit should get any budget at all. The ZBB process reevaluates all organizational activities to see which should be eliminated, funded at a reduced level, funded at the current level, or increased (see Details on a Management Classic).

zero-based budgeting (ZBB)
A system in which budget requests start from scratch, regardless of previous appropriations.

Why Isn't Zero-based Budgeting Appropriate for All Organizations? The difficulty and expense of implementing ZBB suggest that it is not for every organization.

The politics of large organizations often undermine any potential gain that ZBB might produce. It is possibly most effective in smaller public organizations, in supporting staff units in business firms, or in declining organizations. For example, because the resource requirements of staff units in business firms, which include areas like market research and human resource management, are rarely related directly to the firm's output, it's difficult to determine whether their budgets are realistic or denote efficient operation. Thus, for this type of unit, ZBB may be a valuable planning and control device. Also, ZBB is compatible with managing declining resources.[11] When organizations face cutbacks and financial restraints, their managers look for devices that effectively allocate limited resources. ZBB can be just such a device.

DETAILS ON A MANAGEMENT CLASSIC

Texas Instrument's Zero-Based Budgeting Technique

When Texas Instruments was developing its budgeting system, the company decided on a three-part process:

▶ **1.** Each discrete departmental activity is broken down into a decision package.
▶ **2.** The individual decision packages are ranked according to their benefit to the organization during the budget period.
▶ **3.** Budget resources are allocated to the individual packages according to preferential rank in the organization[12] (see Exhibit 4-3).

The decision package is a document that identifies and describes a specific activity. Usually prepared by operating managers, it includes a statement of the expected result or purpose of the activity, its costs, personnel requirements, measures of performance, alternative courses of action, and an evaluation of the benefits from performance and consequences of nonperformance from an organization-wide perspective. In more specific terms, each package lists a number of alternative methods of performing the activity, recommends one of these alternatives, and delineates effort levels. These effort levels identify spending targets—for instance, how the activity would be completed at 70, 90, and 110 per cent of the current budget level. Any large organization that adopts ZBB will have literally thousands of these packages.

Once departmental managers have completed the decision packages, the packages are forwarded to the top executive group, which determines how much to spend and where to spend it. This is done by ascertaining the total amount to be spent by the organization and then by ranking all packages in order of decreasing benefits to the organization. Packages are accepted down to the spending level. When properly executed, the ZBB process carefully evaluates every organizational activity, assigns it a priority, and results in either the continuation, modification, or termination of the activity.

ZBB is no panacea. Like incremental budgeting, it has its own set of drawbacks.[13] It increases paperwork and requires time to prepare; the important activities that managers want funded tend to have inflated benefits; and the eventual outcome rarely differs much from that of an incremental budget.▼

Operational Planning Tools

What Is Scheduling?

scheduling
A listing of necessary activities, their order of accomplishment, who is to do each, and time needed to complete them.

If you were to observe a group of supervisors or department managers for a few days, you would see them regularly detailing what activities have to be done, the order in which they are to be done, who is to do each, and when they are to be completed. The managers are doing what we call **scheduling**. In the material that follows, we will review some useful scheduling devices.

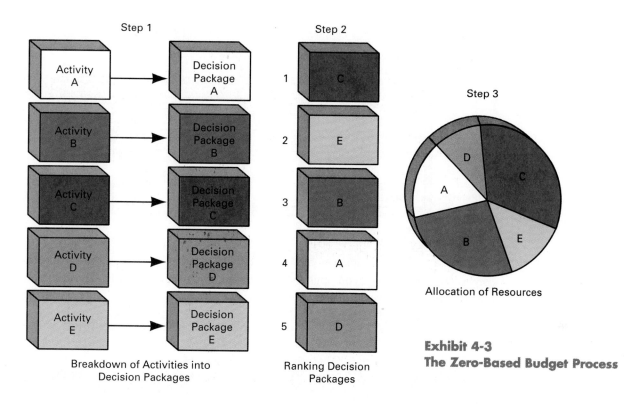

Exhibit 4-3
The Zero-Based Budget Process

How Do You Use a Gantt Chart?

The **Gantt chart** was developed around the turn of the century by Henry Gantt (see Appendix), a protégé of Frederick Taylor. The idea is inherently simple. It is essentially a bar graph with time on the horizontal axis and the activities to be scheduled on the vertical axis. The bars show output, both planned and actual, over a period of time. The Gantt chart visually shows when tasks are supposed to be done and compares that to the actual progress on each. It is a simple but important device that allows managers to detail easily what has yet to be done to complete a job or project, and to assess whether it is ahead of, behind, or on schedule.

A modified version of the Gantt chart is called a **load chart**. Instead of listing activities on the vertical axis, load charts list either whole departments or specific resources. This allows managers to plan and control for capacity utilization. In other words, load charts schedule capacity by work stations. An example of a load chart for six production editors from the same firm is shown in Exhibit 4-4.

> **Gantt chart**
> A graphic bar chart that shows the relationship between work planned and completed on one axis and time elapsed on the other.

> **load chart**
> A modified Gantt chart that schedules capacity by work stations.

What Is a PERT Network Analysis?

Gantt and load charts are helpful as long as the activities or projects being scheduled are few in number and independent of each other. But what if a manager had to plan a large project such as a reorganization, the launch of a cost-reduction campaign, or the development of a new product that required coordinating inputs from marketing, production, and product design personnel? Such projects require coordinating hundreds or thousands of activities, some of which must be done simultaneously and some of which cannot begin until earlier activities have been completed. If you're

Exhibit 4-4
An Example of a
Load Chart

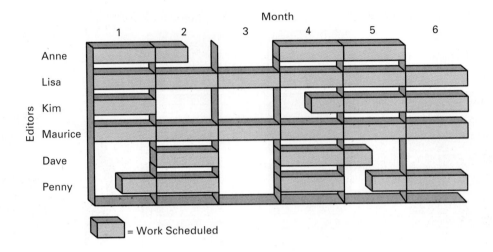

= Work Scheduled

constructing a building, you obviously can't start erecting walls until the foundation is laid. How, then, can you schedule such a complex project? You could use the Program Evaluation and Review Technique.

The **Program Evaluation and Review Technique**—usually just called PERT or PERT network analysis—was originally developed in the late 1950s for coordinating the more than 3,000 contractors and agencies working on the Polaris submarine weapon system.[14] This project was incredibly complicated, with hundreds of thousands of activities that had to be coordinated. PERT is reported to have cut two years off the completion date for the Polaris project.

A **PERT network** is a flowchart-like diagram that depicts the sequence of activities needed to complete a project and the time or costs associated with each activity. With a PERT network, a project manager must think through what has to be done, determine which events depend on one another, and identify potential trouble spots (see Exhibit 4-5). PERT also makes it easy to compare the effects that alternative actions will have on scheduling and costs. Thus, PERT allows managers to monitor a project's progress, identify possible bottlenecks, and shift resources as necessary to keep the project on schedule.

What Are the Key Components of PERT? To understand how to construct a PERT network, you need to know three terms: events, activities, and critical path. Let's define these terms, outline the steps in the PERT process, and then develop an example.

Events are end points that represent the completion of major activities. Sometimes called milestones, events indicate that something significant has happened (such as receipt of purchased items) or an important component is finished. In PERT, events represent a point in time. **Activities**, on the other hand, are the actions that take place. Activities consume time, which represents the time or resources required to progress from one event to another. The **critical path** is the longest or most time-consuming sequence of events and activities required to complete the project in the shortest amount of time. Let's work through a simplified example.

Assume that you are the superintendent for a residential home builder. You have been assigned to oversee the construction of a custom home. Because time really is money in your business, you must determine how long it will take to put up the house. You have carefully dissected the entire project into activities and events.

Program Evaluation and Review Technique (PERT)
A technique for scheduling complicated projects comprising many activities, some of which are interdependent.

PERT network
A flowchart-like diagram showing the sequence of activities needed to complete a project and the time or costs associated with each.

events
End points that represent the completion of major activities in a PERT network.

activities
The time or resources needed to progress from one event to another in a PERT network.

critical path
The longest sequence of activities in a PERT network.

Exhibit 4-6 outlines the major events in the construction project and your estimate of the expected time required to complete each activity. Exhibit 4-7 depicts the PERT network based on the data in Exhibit 4-6.

To coordinate some 3,000-plus subcontractors in the building of this submarine, a PERT chart was used. In doing so, two years were cut off the completion date for the project.

Developing a PERT network requires the manager to identify all key activities needed to complete a project, rank them in order of dependence, and estimate each activity's completion time. This can be translated into five specific steps:

▶ **1.** Identify every significant activity that must be achieved for a project to be completed. The accomplishment of each activity results in a set of events or outcomes.

▶ **2.** Ascertain the order in which these events must be completed.

▶ **3.** Diagram the flow of activities from start to finish, identifying each activity and its relationship to all other activities. Use circles to indicate events and arrows to represent activities. This results in a flowchart diagram that we call the PERT network.

▶ **4.** Compute a time estimate for completing each activity. This is done with a weighted average that employs an optimistic time estimate (t_o) of how long the activity would take under ideal conditions, a most-likely estimate (t_m) of the time the activity normally should take, and a pessimistic estimate (t_p) that represents the time that an activity should take under the worst possible conditions. The formula for calculating the expected time (t_e) is then

$$t_e = \frac{t_o + 4t_m + t_p}{6}$$

▶ **5.** Finally, using a network diagram that contains time estimates for each activity, the manager can determine a schedule for the start and finish dates of each activity and for the entire project. Any delays that occur along the critical path require the most attention because they delay the entire project. That is, the critical path has no slack in it; therefore, any delay along that path immediately translates into a delay in the final deadline for the completed project.

**Exhibit 4-5
Developing PERT
Charts**

Exhibit 4-6
Major Events in
Building a House

EVENT	DESCRIPTION	TIME WEEKS	PREDECESSOR ACTIVITY
A	Approve Design and Get Permits	3	None
B	Perform Excavation/Lot Clearing	1	A
C	Pour Footers	1	B
D	Erect Foundation Walls	2	C
E	Frame House	4	D
F	Instal Windows	.5	E
G	Shingle Roof	.5	E
H	Instal Brick Front and Siding	4	F, G
I	Instal Electrical, Plumbing, and Heating A/C Rough-ins	6	E
J	Instal Insulation	.25	I
K	Instal Sheetrock	2	J
L	Finish and Sand Sheetrock	7	K
M	Instal Interior Trim	2	L
N	Paint House (Interior and Exterior)	2	H, M
O	Instal All Cabinets	.5	N
P	Instal Flooring	1	N
Q	Final Touch Up and Turn Over House to Homeowner	1	O, P

Exhibit 4-7   A PERT Network for Erecting a House

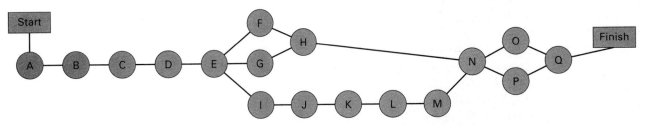

Your PERT network tells you that if everything goes as planned, it will take just over 32 weeks to complete the house. This is calculated by tracing the network's critical path: A-B-C-D-E-I-J-K-L-M-N-P-Q. Any delay in completing the events along this path will delay the completion of the entire project. For example, if it took six weeks instead of four to frame the house (event E), the entire project would be delayed by two weeks (or the time beyond that expected). Conversely, a delay of one week on installing the brick front and siding (event H) would have little effect because this event is not on the critical path. Now back to our critical path dilemma.

Notice how the critical path passes through activities N-P-Q. Looking at just these three activities, we notice from our PERT chart (Exhibit 4-6) that it takes four weeks. Wouldn't path N-O-Q be faster? In fact, the PERT network shows that it takes 3.5 weeks to complete this. So why isn't N-O-Q on the critical path? Because activity Q cannot begin until both activities O and P are completed. Although activity O takes one-half week, activity P takes one full week. Thus, the earliest we can begin Q is after one week. So what happens to the difference between the critical activity (activity P) and the noncritical activity (activity O)? The difference, in this case one-half week, becomes **slack time**. Slack time, then, is the time difference between the critical path

slack time
The difference between the critical path time and the time of all other paths.

and all other paths. And what use is there for slack? If the project manager notices a possible slippage on a critical activity, quite possibly slack time from a noncritical activity can be borrowed and temporarily assigned to the critical one.

How Is PERT Both a Planning and a Control Tool? Not only does PERT help us to estimate the times associated with scheduling a project, it also gives us clues about where our controls should be placed. Because any event on the critical path that is delayed will delay the overall project (not only making us late, but probably also overbudget), our attention needs to be focused on them at all times. For example, if in our house-building example activity H (installing the brick front and siding) is delayed by a week because supplies have not arrived, that is not a major issue. But if activity O (installing cabinets) is delayed from one-half week to one week, the entire project will be delayed by one-half week. As such, anything that has the immediate potential for delaying a project (critical activities) must be monitored very closely.

What Is Break-even Analysis?

How many units of a product must an organization sell in order to break even—that is, to have neither profit nor loss? A manager might want to know the minimum number of units that must be sold to achieve his profit objective, or whether a current product should continue to be sold or be dropped from the organization's product line. **Break-even analysis** is a widely used technique for helping managers to make profit projections.[15]

Break-even analysis is a simplistic formulation, yet it is valuable to managers because it points out the relationship among revenues, costs, and profits. To compute the break-even point (BE), the manager needs to know the unit price of the product being sold (P), the variable cost per unit (VC), and total fixed costs (TFC).

An organization breaks even when its total revenue is just enough to equal its total costs. But total cost has two parts: a fixed component and a variable component. Fixed costs are expenses that do not change, regardless of volume. Examples include insurance premiums and property taxes. Fixed costs, of course, are fixed only in the short term because, in the long run, commitments terminate and are thus subject to variation. Variable costs change in proportion to output and include raw materials, labour costs, and energy costs.

The break-even point can be computed graphically or by using the following formula:

$$BE = \frac{TFC}{P - VC}$$

This formula tells us that (1) total revenue will equal total cost when we sell enough units at a price that covers all variable unit costs, and (2) the difference between price and variable costs, when multiplied by the number of units sold, equals the fixed costs.

When Is Break-even Useful? To demonstrate, assume that Carla's Photocopying Service charges $0.10 per photocopy. If fixed costs are $27,000 a year and variable costs are $0.04 per copy, Carla can compute her break-even point as follows: $27,000 / ($0.10 –$0.04) = 450,000 copies, or when annual revenues are $45,000. This same relationship is shown graphically in Exhibit 4-8.

break-even analysis
A technique for identifying the point at which total revenue is just sufficient to cover total costs.

Exhibit 4-8
Break-Even Analysis

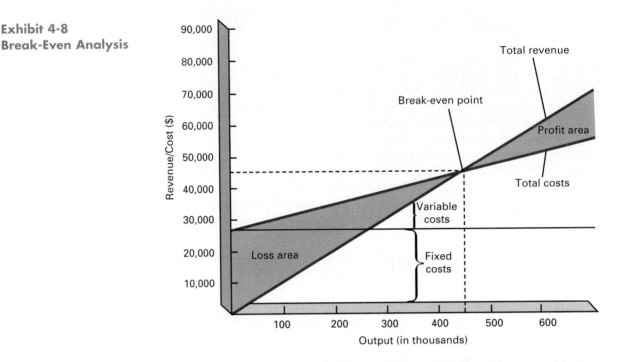

How Can Break-even Serve as a Planning Tool? As a planning tool, break-even analysis could help Carla to set her sales objective. For example, she could establish the profit she wants and then work backward to determine what sales level is needed to reach that profit. Break-even analysis could also tell Carla how much volume has to increase to break even if she's currently operating at a loss, or how much volume she can afford to lose and still break even if she's currently operating profitably. In some cases, such as the management of professional sports franchises, break-even analysis has shown the projected volume of ticket sales required to cover all costs to be so unrealistically high that the best action for management to take is to sell or close the business.

What Is Linear Programming and What Kinds of Problems Lend Themselves to It?

Paul Adams has a manufacturing plant that produces two kinds of music players: compact disc players and laser disc players. Business is good. He can sell all the music players he can produce. This is his dilemma: Given that both players go through the same production departments, how many of each type should he make to maximize his profits?

A closer look at Paul's operation tells us that he can use a mathematical technique called **linear programming** to solve his resource allocation dilemma. As we'll show, linear programming is applicable to Paul's problem, but it can't be applied to all resource allocation situations. Besides requiring limited resources and the objective of optimization, it requires that there be alternative ways of combining resources to produce a number of output mixes. There must also be a linear relationship between variables.[16] This means that a change in one variable will be accompanied by an exactly proportional change in the other. For Paul's business, this condition would be met if it took exactly twice the amount of raw materials and hours of labour to produce two of a given music player as it took to produce one.

linear programming
A mathematical technique that solves resource allocation problems.

Many different types of problems can be solved using linear programming. For instance, a few include selecting transportation routes that minimize shipping costs, allocating a limited advertising budget among various product brands, making the optimum assignment of personnel among projects, and determining how much of each product to make with a limited number of resources. To give you some idea of how linear programming is useful, let's return to Paul's problem and see how linear programming could help him to solve it. Fortunately, Paul's problem is relatively simple, so we can solve it quickly. For complex linear programming problems, computer software has been designed specifically to help develop solutions.

First, we need to establish some facts about Paul's business. Paul has computed the profit margins on the music players at $100 for the compact discs and $180 for the laser discs. He can therefore express his objective function as follows: maximum profit = $100R + $180S, where R is the number of compact discs produced and S is the number of laser discs. Paul also knows the time each compact disc must spend in each department and the monthly production capacity (1,200 hours in manufacturing and 900 hours in assembly) for the two departments (see Exhibit 4-9). The production capacity numbers act as constraints on his overall capacity. Now Paul can establish his constraint equations:

$$2R + 4S \leq 1,200$$
$$2R + 2S \leq 900$$

Of course, since neither music player can be produced in a volume less than zero, Paul can also state that $R \geq 0$ and $S \geq 0$.

Paul has graphed his solution as shown in Exhibit 4-10. The shaded area represents the options that don't exceed the capacity of either department. This area represents his feasibility region. Paul's optimal resource allocation will be defined at one of the corners within this feasibility region. Point C is the farthest from the origin and provides the maximum profits within the constraints stated. At point A, profits would be zero. At points B and D, profits would be $54,000 and $45,000, respectively. At point C, however, profits would be $57,000.

YOUNG CANADIANS

John Taggart:
Weyerhaeuser Canada

In his position as national marketing development manager for Weyerhaeuser in Canada, John Taggart is responsible for developing and implementing marketing strategies. The strong organizational culture of Weyerhaeuser (among the 30 largest foreign-owned companies operating in Canada) provides a solid foundation for his efforts.

What Is Queuing Theory and When Is It Useful?

queuing theory
A technique that balances
the cost of having a waiting line against the cost
of service to maintain
that line.

You are a supervisor for a 24-hour supermarket. One of the decisions you have to make is how many of the 18 cash registers you should keep open at any given time. **Queuing theory**, or what is frequently referred to as waiting-line theory, could assist you with this problem.

Whenever a decision involves balancing the cost of having a waiting line against the cost of service to maintain that line, it can be made more easily with queuing theory. This includes such common situations as determining how many gas pumps are needed at gas stations, tellers at bank windows, or check-in lines at airline ticket counters. In each situation, management wants to minimize cost by having as few stations open as possible, yet not so few as to test the patience of customers. Referring back to our supermarket example, during rush hours you could open all 18 registers and keep waiting time to a minimum, or you could open only one, minimize staffing costs—and risk a riot.

| | NUMBER OF HOURS REQUIRED (PER UNIT) | | |
| | COMPACT | LASER | MONTHLY PRODUCTION |
DEPARTMENT	DISCS	DISCS	CAPACITY (IN HOURS)
Manufacturing	2	4	1,200
Assembly	2	2	900
Profit per unit	$100	$180	

Exhibit 4-9   Production Data for Music Players

The mathematics underlying queuing theory is beyond the scope of this book. But you can see how the theory works in a simple example. Assume that you're a bank supervisor. One of your responsibilities (see Developing Management Skills) is assigning tellers. You have five teller windows, but you want to know whether you can get by with only one window open during an average morning. You consider 12 minutes to be the longest you would expect any customer to wait patiently in line. If it takes four minutes, on average, to serve each customer, the line should not be permitted to get longer than three deep (12 minutes @ 4 minutes per customer = 3 customers). If you know from past experience that during the morning people arrive at the average rate of two per minute, you can calculate the probability that the line will become longer than any number (n) of customers as follows:

$$P_n = \left(1 - \frac{arrival\ rate}{service\ rate}\right) \times \left(\frac{arrival\ rate}{service\ rate}\right)^n$$

where n = 3 customers, arrival rate = 2 per minute, and service rate = 4 minutes per customer. Putting these numbers into the above formula generates the following:

$$P_3 = \left(1 - \frac{2}{4}\right) \times \left(\frac{2}{4}\right)^3 = \left(\frac{1}{2}\right)\left(\frac{8}{64}\right) = \frac{8}{128} = .0625$$

What does a P_3 of .0625 mean? It tells you that the likelihood of having more than three customers in line during the morning is one chance in 16. Are you willing to live with four or more customers in line for 6 per cent of the time? If so, keeping one teller window open will be enough. If not, you'll need to add windows and assign additional personnel to staff them.

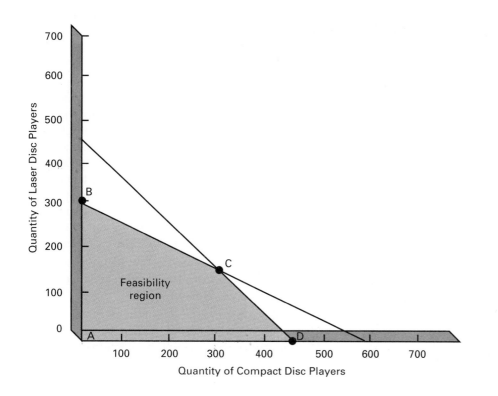

Exhibit 4-10 Graphical Solution to Paul Adams's Linear Programming Problem

DEVELOPING MANAGEMENT SKILLS

▼

FIVE STEPS TO BETTER TIME MANAGEMENT

▲

The essence of time management is to use your time effectively. This requires that you know the objectives you want to accomplish, the activities that will lead to the accomplishment of those objectives, and the importance and urgency of each activity. We've translated this into a five-step process.

▶ **1.** Make a list of your objectives. What specific objectives have you set for yourself and the unit you manage? If you're using management by objectives, these objectives are already in place.

▶ **2.** Rank the objectives according to their importance. Not all objectives are of equal importance. Given the limitations on your time, you want to make sure you give highest priority to the most important objectives.

▶ **3.** List the activities necessary to achieve your objectives. What specific actions do you need to take to achieve your objectives? Again, if you're using MBO, these action plans are already laid out.

▶ **4.** For each objective, assign priorities to the various activities required to reach the objective. This step imposes a second set of priorities. Here, you need to emphasize both importance

and urgency. If the activity is not important, you should consider delegating it to someone below you. If it's not urgent, it can usually wait. This step will identify activities that you must do, those you should do, those you'll get to when you can, and those that can be delegated to others.

▶ **5.** Schedule your activities according to the priorities you've set. The final step is to prepare a daily plan. Every morning, or at the end of the previous workday, make a list of the five or so most important things you want to do for the day. If the list grows to 10 or more activities, it becomes cumbersome and ineffective. Then set priorities for the activities on the basis of importance and urgency.

Summary

This summary is organized by the chapter Learning Objectives found on page 88.

1. Techniques for scanning the environment include reading newspapers, magazines, books, and trade journals; reading competitors' ads, promotional materials, and press releases; attending trade shows; debriefing sales personnel; and analysing competitors' products.

2. Quantitative forecasting applies a set of mathematical rules to a set of past data to predict future outcomes. Qualitative forecasting uses judgments and the opinions of knowledgeable individuals to predict future outcomes.

3. Budgets are popular planning devices because money is a universal common denominator that can be used in all types of organizations and by managers at all levels.

4. The most popular approach to budgeting is the traditional, or incremental, budget, which is based on past allocations. However, its drawbacks have led to increased interest in zero-based budgets, which make no reference to past allocations.

5. Gantt and load charts are scheduling devices. Both are bar graphs. Gantt charts monitor planned and actual activities over time; load charts focus on capacity utilization by monitoring whole departments or specific resources.

6. The five steps in developing a PERT network are (1) identifying every significant activity that must be achieved for a project to be completed; (2) determining the order in which these activities must be completed; (3) diagramming the flow of activities in a project from start to finish; (4) estimating the time needed to complete each activity; and (5) using the network diagram to determine a schedule for the start and finish dates of each activity, and for the entire project.

7. A product's break-even point is determined by the unit price of the product, its variable cost per unit, and its total fixed costs.

8. For linear programming to be applicable, a problem must have limited resources, constraints, an objective function to optimize, alternative ways of combining resources, and a linear relationship between variables.

9. Queuing theory can be used as a planning tool when the cost of having a waiting line is balanced against the costs incurred by maintaining that line.

Review and Discussion Questions

1. How is scanning the environment related to forecasting?

2. Assume that you manage a large fast-food restaurant in downtown Calgary and you want to know the amount of each type of sandwich to make and the number of cashiers to have on each shift. What type of planning tool(s) do you think will be useful to you? What type of environmental scanning, if any, would you likely do in this management job?

3. What is a scenario and how does competitor intelligence help managers to formulate one?

4. How can benchmarking improve the quality of an organization's products or processes?

5. What is a budget? Must it always be based on monetary units?

6. "Budgets are both a planning and a control tool." Explain this statement.

7. Develop a Gantt chart for writing a university term paper.

8. What is the significance of the critical path in a PERT network?

9. What is the value of break-even analysis as a planning tool?

10. How can queuing theory serve to make an operation more efficient?

Testing Your Comprehension

Circle the correct answer, then check yourself on page 471.

1. Which of the following is NOT a technique for assessing the environment?

    a) forecasting

    b) environmental scanning

    c) national weather service long-range outlook

    d) benchmarking

2. The technique by which managers identify competitors and attempt to determine what those competitors are doing is

    a) scenario analysis

    b) illegal for most organizations

    c) organizational espionage

    d) none of the above

3. A company predicts the possibility that certain legislation will be passed and considers the possible consequences to its business. This is an example of

    a) environmental scanning

    b) benchmarking

    c) building scenarios

    d) forecasting

4. The search for the best practice among other organizations is

    a) forecasting

    b) benchmarking

    c) TQM

    d) substitution effect

5. A budget that combines the revenue and expense budgets is a

    a) profit budget

    b) cash budget

    c) fixed budget

    d) variable budget

6. Which of the following is NOT true of the incremental budget?

    a) Each budget is a modified extension of past budgets.

    b) It is probably the most widely used budget today.

    c) Funds are appropriated for each division or unit; managers then use their discretion in the actual use of the unit's funds.

    d) It is essentially the same as a zero-based budget.

7. The zero-based budget
   a) requires managers to justify all proposed expenditures
   b) can provide continuity by automatically expanding budgets over the years
   c) relies heavily on an extension of the prior budget
   d) was developed by the Rockwell Corporation for the Space Shuttle program

8. When managers determine what is to be done, who is to do it, and when it is to be completed, they are exhibiting some of the components of
   a) budgeting
   b) scheduling
   c) linear programming
   d) simulation

9. If fixed costs are $8,000 and variable costs are $70 per unit, how many units must be sold at a price of $870 for the business to break even?
   a) 9.2
   b) 114.3
   c) 10
   d) 100

10. A bar graph showing time on the horizontal axis and activities to be completed on the vertical axis is a
    a) simulation chart
    b) zero-based budget
    c) Gantt chart
    d) break-even analysis

11. A load chart is a
    a) modified simulation method showing critical paths
    b) modified Gantt chart showing capacity utilization
    c) method of budgeting in an uncertain environment
    d) control devise designed to minimize extreme weight on certain bridges

12. When would a PERT network NOT provide much help?
    a) when sequencing is important
    b) for complicated jobs
    c) for independent projects
    d) for jobs with many steps involved

13. After all significant activities of a PERT network have been identified,
    a) a time estimate for each activity is prepared
    b) a diagram of all activities and events is prepared
    c) the entire schedule is determined
    d) the order of all activities is determined

14. After the manager has determined the time estimates for each activity in a PERT network,

    a) the order of events must be determined

    b) the critical path can be determined

    c) a diagram of the flow of activities can be completed

    d) a funding request is prepared

15. The difference between the duration of a critical activity and that of a noncritical activity is the

    a) break-even point

    b) critical path

    c) linear program

    d) slack time

16. The operational planning technique that attempts to minimize costs or maximize profits with limited resources and numerous options is called

    a) linear programming

    b) simulation techniques

    c) PERT network

    d) break-even analysis

17. As the "front-end" manager of an IGA your responsibilities include deciding how many checkout lines to have open during any given hour. To help you decide, you could use

    a) break-even analysis

    b) linear programming

    c) queuing theory

    d) time-management analysis

18. Which of the following is recommended as the final step in time management?

    a) prioritize objectives

    b) list goals

    c) list the activities that will accomplish your objectives

    d) prepare a daily plan

Self-Assessment Exercise

Are You an Entrepreneur?

Instructions: This quiz is designed to see if you have the traits associated with highly successful entrepreneurs. Rate yourself on each of the characteristics using a −2 to +2 scale as described at the top of the scale.

−2   I don't really have this characteristic
−1   I don't have very much of this characteristic
 0   Neutral or don't know
+1   I have this characteristic a little bit
+2   This characteristic is very strong in me

Characteristic	−2	−1	0	+1	+2
Self-confidence	___	___	___	___	___
Energy, diligence	___	___	___	___	___
Ability to take calculated risks	___	___	___	___	___
Creativity	___	___	___	___	___
Flexibility	___	___	___	___	___
Positive response to challenges	___	___	___	___	___
Dynamism, leadership					
Ability to get along with people	___	___	___	___	___
Responsiveness to suggestions	___	___	___	___	___
Responsiveness to criticism	___	___	___	___	___

Characteristic	−2	−1	0	+1	+2
Knowledge of market	___	___	___	___	___
Perseverance, determination	___	___	___	___	___
Resourcefulness	___	___	___	___	___
Need to achieve	___	___	___	___	___
Initiative	___	___	___	___	___
Independence	___	___	___	___	___
Foresight	___	___	___	___	___
Profit orientation	___	___	___	___	___
Perceptiveness	___	___	___	___	___
Optimism	___	___	___	___	___
Versatility	___	___	___	___	___
Knowledge of product and technology	___	___	___	___	___

Turn to page 464 for scoring directions and key.

Source: Robert Marx, Todd Jick, and Peter Frost, *Management Live! The Video Book* (Englewood Cliffs, N.J.: Prentice-Hall, Inc., 1991), p. 291.

Class Exercise

PERTing a Term Paper

Have you ever thought much about how you write a term paper for a course, or how long it takes? Often we just begin the project and work on it until it is finished. But that may not be the most effective way. For this exercise, you'll need to consider the following. The term paper was assigned in Week 1 of a 15-week class, and it is due by the end of Week 14. Your instructor has also included in the syllabus the following requirements. A draft of the paper must be completed by Week 10. Furthermore, it must be at least 25 pages, and contain 25 sources.

Identify the activities that need to be completed to attain your objective. Estimate times associated with each activity. Draw a PERT network of your activities and determine the critical path.

When you have completed this, answer the following:

1. How different is this process you've developed from the way in which you usually write a term paper?
2. How could you use this plan to better facilitate completing the term paper assignment? For getting a better grade on the assignment?
3. How can PERT be used as a means of managing one's time? Explain.

Case Application

Planning a Plastic Dynasty

Planning and patience most often go hand in hand, and one man who knows the virtues of patience is Vic De Zen, founder and CEO of Royal Plastics Group Ltd. of Vaughan, Ontario. Royal was started in 1970 with $58,000; the company's sales in 1994 were $453 million. That kind of growth takes foresight, planning, and a very good understanding of the external environment.

Vic De Zen came to Canada from Italy in 1962, but initially could not find work in his field—as a tool-and-die maker. He began work at Pillar Plastics in 1967. While there he helped to create dies for contracts to two companies who wanted to build houses with plastic and asbestos. This is where De Zen was first introduced to the idea that may mold Royal's future. Royal was already one of the largest extruders (forcing a substance such as a metal or a plastic through a die) of polyvinyl chloride products such as doors and windows, when it decided that there existed a huge untapped market for plastic houses. Royal designed and patented its plastic house in 1992. By the beginning of 1996 Royal had sold over 1,100 of its houses worldwide. The houses are pieced together by pre-made plastic pieces, with concrete for support—a simple construction method that seriously reduces the time it takes to put up a house. At this point Royal's primary market lies with developing countries, but De Zen believes that the market is much, much bigger, and he says it with conviction: "One day you and I will be living in plastic houses."

At the moment, Royal Plastics has two areas of concentration. Firstly, their building products such as windows, siding, and pipes are all made out of polyvinyl chloride. This is the side of the business that Royal was built on. And secondly, there is what are termed their "emerging products," which include Royal's plastic houses. This second side of the business is where Royal sees its future. Along with its houses, Royal has developed a plastic storage shed. According to Mark Badger, the company's spokesperson, "There's roughly a $1-billion market for storage sheds in North America alone."

De Zen's rapid growth is not simply due to having marketable products; a major factor in Royal's growth is the way in which the company has expanded. There are currently 50 separate Royal Plastics operations throughout Canada, the United States, and Mexico. Every factory is run by similar operating methods, but they are each incorporated separately. De Zen holds controlling interest in each of them, but they all have minority partners who manage the factories. These minority partners have worked their way up at Royal, and De Zen has rewarded them with opportunities to buy into subsidiaries. And in 1994, workers at every level in the organization were offered share-purchase options. According to De Zen, the growth of Royal's competitors in North America is inhibited by the fact that they keep 100 per cent of their companies' profit.

The plastic houses division turned a profit in 1995. Now Royal is looking at building production plants in developing countries such as Argentina, Vietnam, and China, to supply these markets more easily and cost-effectively. For De Zen, there is no limit to what he believes Royal can achieve in the marketplace. He has built up a company from $50,000 to potentially the world leader in plastic building products and housing. De Zen has perceived environmental opportunities, and acted on those opportunities, as well as following a steady growth plan. As Faris Shammas, vice-president of the Society of the Plastics Industry of Canada, states: "Royal Plastic had to develop the material, the technology, the manufacturing from zero. It takes a visionary to do that."

Questions

1. How can environmental scanning be useful to Royal Plastics in its hopes to tap housing markets throughout the world?
2. Would a PERT network be helpful to Royal Plastics in regards to building a production facility in Vietnam? If so, what would the network look like?
3. What kinds of planning tools and techniques do you think Royal Plastics could use in order to maximize its potential in the global housing market?

Source: Katrina Onstad, "The Midas Touch," *Canadian Business*, December 1995, pp. 41–51.

chapter 5

Foundations of Decision Making

Learning Objectives

What will I be able to do after I finish
this chapter?

1 • Outline the steps in the decision-making process.

2 • Define the rational decision maker.

3 • Explain the limits to rationality.

4 • Describe the perfectly rational decision-making process.

5 • Describe the bounded rational decision-making process.

6 • Identify the two types of decision problems and the two types
of decisions that are used to solve them.

7 • Identify the advantages and disadvantages of group decisions.

8 • Describe four techniques for improving group decision making.

The retail world in Canada has undergone some major shifts in the past decade. The advent of big-box stores has changed the way many people shop. Supermarkets have given way to superstores. Extremely efficient companies such as Wal-Mart have entered the marketplace and have caused the downfall of long-established retailers. Specialist chains such as Starbuck's have forced many independents out of business. The pace of changes in the way people shop seems to be accelerating, and has created a sink-or-swim environment. One industry that is undergoing significant changes, for example, is bookselling. The small independent bookstores are having a tough time struggling for market share against the new mega-bookstores. Chapters is the major player in the Canadian book world. Created from a merger of Smithbooks and Coles, Chapters has been moving away from the small bookstore outlets that were placed in practically every mall, and has been focusing on giant stores. More than 20 Chapters outlets span the nation as of the beginning of 1998, and the company has plans to open at least 75 stores by 2002. In the U.S., two chains of book superstores have completely revolutionized the bookselling industry. Barnes & Noble (which owns 13 per cent of Chapters) and Borders (half the size of its adversary) have gobbled up the U.S. market. Now the super-large store format is spreading across Canada. Bollum's Books in Vancouver (and subsequently Calgary) was the first to try the new concept in this country, back in 1995. Founder Tom Bollum offered a vast book selection, along with a coffee bar where patrons could do some reading in large, comfy chairs, authors' readings, and even puppet shows for children.[1]

In fall 1996, Winnipeg's McNally Robinson Booksellers decided to take heed of what was happening south of the border and switched from its four small stores to one 21,000-square-foot giant store. They have thereby beaten Chapters to the Winnipeg market, and hope to hold out against the chain by offering excellent service within the big-box format (the Winnipeg store also has comfy chairs, kids' play areas, and a licensed restaurant). Meanwhile, Chapters will start to feel the pressure of its first major competitor, Indigo, which plans to take its own large-format stores across Canada. And as for independent bookstores, the case in Ottawa may become a nationwide phenomenon: 35 small stores formed an alliance known as The Independents, and have begun to battle Chapters by concerting their marketing efforts, and stressing their hassle-free atmospheres and knowledgeable staffs. Yet another factor involved in the bookselling world is online sales. Amazon.com calls itself the world's biggest bookstore; it simply uses distributers and orders direct from publishing houses, thereby requiring little stock space (only enough for its 400 top sellers). Two office floors and a small staff make it easy for Amazon to offer low prices, but a massive selection (2.5 million books). Amazon's interactive Web site allows it to gain knowledge of customer tastes, and Amazon can e-mail customers to inform them of a new book in which they may be interested. Here, Canada's Internet Bookstore has opened, but so far with a much smaller selection. And finally, an American invasion may lie in the future for Canada's book industry, although currently legislation prohibits a foreign company from owning more than 49 per cent of a Canadian cultural company.

Obviously, the Canadian bookselling industry is undergoing great change, at a great pace. When faced with such major shifts, businesses must act quickly. However, there are many unknown factors. The wrong decision can be extremely costly (Bollum's

The Canadian bookselling industry has been undergoing major changes, mainly due to the advent of big-box stores.

Books filed for protection from its creditors in the spring of 1997—however, this was mainly viewed as a result of overly rapid expansion, not particularly as a result of the large-store format). So, without an existing set of guidelines, constant decisions are being made in this business. How do booksellers make decisions in this environment? In this chapter we will examine the foundations of "decision making," and you should gain an understanding of the types of situations these businesses are facing.

BARNES & NOBLE
www.barnesandnoble.com

AMAZON.COM
www.amazon.com

Planning and Decision Making

The previous two chapters discussed how companies plan—both for the long-term survival of the organization, and for the short-term day-to-day operations. Implied in those planning activities were the decisions managers make. Plans don't just come out of thin air. They are the result of careful analyses. After weighing the advantages and disadvantages of various alternatives, managers select the ones that will best serve the interests of the company. This selection process is called decision making. What kinds of planning decisions do our managers make? We've listed a few in Exhibit 5-1.

**Exhibit 5-1
Examples of Planning
Function Decisions**

1. What are the organization's long-term objectives?
2. What strategies will best achieve these objectives?
3. What should the organization's short-term objectives be?
4. What is the most efficient means of completing tasks?
5. What might the competition be considering?
6. What budgets are needed to complete department tasks?
7. How difficult should individual goals be?

The Decision-Making Process

Decision making is typically described as "choosing among alternatives." But this view is overly simplistic. Why? Because decision making is a process rather than the simple act of choosing among alternatives. Exhibit 5-2 illustrates the **decision-making process** as a set of eight steps that begins with identifying a problem, moves to selecting an alternative that can alleviate the problem, and concludes with evaluating the decision's effectiveness. This process is as applicable to your personal decision about where you're going to take your summer vacation as it is to PepsiCo's decision to introduce Crystal Pepsi. The process can also be used to describe both individual and group decisions. Let's take a closer look at the process to understand what each step encompasses.

decision-making process
A set of eight steps that include identifying a problem, selecting an alternative, and evaluating the decision's effectiveness.

What Defines a Decision Problem?

The decision-making process begins with the existence of a **problem** (step 1), or, more specifically, a discrepancy between an existing and a desired state of affairs.[2]

problem
A discrepancy between an existing and a desired state of affairs.

When it decided to market its Orbitz soft drinks, management at Clearly Canadian Beverage Corp. had to act under the assumptions of bounded rationality. Unfortunately this process does not guarantee satisfactory results—do you remember Crystal Pepsi?

Let's develop an example that illustrates this point and that we can use throughout this section. For the sake of simplicity, let's make the example something to which most of us can relate: the decision to buy a new car. Take the case of an Office Depot regional manager whose car just blew its engine. Again, for simplicity's sake, assume that it's not economical to repair the car and that public transportation is unavailable. So now we have a problem. There is a disparity between the manager's need to have a car that runs and the fact that her current one doesn't.

Unfortunately, this example doesn't tell us much about how managers identify problems. In the real world, most problems don't come with neon signs identifying them as such. While a blown engine might be a clear signal to the manager that she needs a new car, few problems are so obvious. Problem identification is subjective. Furthermore, the manager who mistakenly solves the wrong problem perfectly is likely to perform just as poorly as the manager who fails to identify the right problem and does nothing. Problem identification is neither a simple nor an unimportant part of the decision-making process.[3] How do managers become aware that they have a discrepancy? Managers have to make a comparison between their current state of affairs and some standard. What is that standard? It can be past performance, previously set goals, or the performance of some other unit within the organization or in other organizations. In our car-buying example, the standard is a previously set goal—having a car that runs.

What Is Relevant in the Decision-Making Process?

Once a manager has identified a problem that needs attention, the **decision criteria** that will be important in solving the problem must be identified (step 2).

In our car-buying example, the store manager has to assess which factors are relevant in her decision. These might include criteria such as price, model (two-door or

decision criteria
Criteria that define what is relevant in a decision.

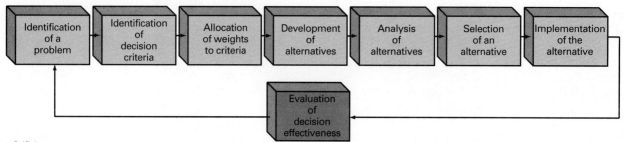

| Identification of a problem | → | Identification of decision criteria | → | Allocation of weights to criteria | → | Development of alternatives | → | Analysis of alternatives | → | Selection of an alternative | → | Implementation of the alternative |

Evaluation of decision effectiveness

**Exhibit 5-2
The Decision-Making
Process**

four-door), size (compact or intermediate), manufacturer (foreign or domestic), optional equipment (automatic transmission, air conditioning, passenger air bag, and so on), and repair records. These criteria reflect what she thinks is relevant in her decision.

Whether explicitly stated or not, every decision maker has criteria that guide her decision. Note that in this step in the decision-making process, what is not identified is as important as what is. If the store manager doesn't consider fuel economy to be a criterion, then it will not influence her final choice of car. Thus, if a decision maker does not identify a particular criterion in this second step, it's treated as irrelevant to her.

YOUNG CANADIANS

Paul Girard: Seanix Technology Inc.

Here's a story straight out of entrepreneurial fairytale land: Jonquiere, Quebec native, 22-year-old Paul Girard, leaves his job selling computers and drives to Vancouver in his van. He sells his van and borrows $12,500 from his dad to start Seanix Technology Inc. Just over a decade later, he is the sole owner of the biggest Canadian-owned manufacturer of personal computers, employing 200 people and with sales of $100 million.

SEANIX
TECHNOLOGY
www.seanix.com/
webhome.nst/public/
homepage

Why Does the Decision Maker Need to Weigh the Criteria?

The criteria listed above are not all equally important. It's necessary, therefore, to weigh the items listed in step 2 in order to give them their relative priority in the decision. We call this step allocating weights to the decision criteria (step 3).

A simple approach is merely to give the most important criterion a weight of 10 and then assign weights to the rest against this standard. Thus, in contrast to a criterion to which you assigned a five, the highest-rated factor would be twice as important. The idea is to use your personal preferences to assign a priority to the relevant criteria in your decision, as well as to indicate their degree of importance by assigning a weight to each.

Exhibit 5-3 lists the criteria and weights that our store manager developed for her car-replacement decision. Price is the most important criterion in her decision, with such factors as performance and handling having low weights. The next step requires the decision maker to list the viable alternatives that could resolve the problem (step 4). No attempt is made in this step to appraise these alternatives, only to list them. Let's assume that our manager has identified 12 cars as viable choices. They are Buick Century, Chevrolet Cavalier, Ford Escort, Geo Prism, Honda Civic, Hyundai Excel, Mazda Protégé, Nissan Sentra, Plymouth Acclaim, Pontiac Grand Am, Toyota Corolla, and Volkswagen Golf.

Once the alternatives have been identified, the decision maker must critically analyse each one (step 5). The strengths and weaknesses of each alternative become evident as they are compared with the criteria and weights established in steps 2 and 3. Each alternative is evaluated by appraising it against the criteria. Exhibit 5-4 shows the assessed values that the plant manager put on each of her 12 alternatives after she had test-driven each car. Keep in mind that the ratings given the 12 cars shown in Exhibit 5-4 are based on the assessment made by the store manager. Again, we are using a one-to-10 scale. Some assessments can be achieved in a relatively objective fashion. For instance, the purchase price represents the best price the manager can get from local dealers, and consumer magazines report data from owners on frequency of repairs. But the assessment of handling is clearly a personal judgment. The point is that most decisions contain judgments. They are reflected in the criteria chosen in step 2, the weights given to the criteria, and the evaluation of alternatives. This explains why two car buyers with the same amount of money may look at two totally distinct sets of alternatives or even look at the same alternatives and rate them differently.

Exhibit 5-4 represents only an assessment of the 12 alternatives against the decision criteria. It does not reflect the weighting done in step 3. If one choice had scored 10 on every criterion, you wouldn't need to consider the weights. Similarly, if the weights were all equal, you could evaluate each alternative merely by summing up the appropriate lines in Exhibit 5-4. For instance, the Honda Civic would have a score of 44, and the Toyota Corolla a score of 43. If you multiply each alternative assessment against its weight, you get Exhibit 5-5. To illustrate, the Nissan Sentra scored a 40 on durability, which was determined by multiplying the weight given to durability (5) by the manager's appraisal of Nissan on this criterion (8). The summation of these scores represents an evaluation of each alternative against the previously established criteria and weights. Notice that the weighting of the criteria has changed the ranking of alternatives in our example. The Honda, for example, has gone from first to third. From our analysis, both initial price and interior comfort worked against the Civic.

CRITERIA	WEIGHT
Initial price	10[a]
Interior comfort	8
Durability	5
Repair record	5
Performance	3
Handling	1

Exhibit 5-3
Criteria and Weight in Car-Buying Decision
[a] In this example, the highest rating for a criterion is 10 points.

What Determines the "Best" Choice?

The sixth step is the critical act of choosing the best alternative from among those enumerated and assessed. Since we have determined all the pertinent factors in the decision, weighted them appropriately, and identified the viable alternatives, we merely have to choose the alternative that generated the highest score in step 5. In our car example (Exhibit 5-5), the decision maker would choose the Toyota Corolla. On the basis of the criteria identified, the weights given to the criteria, and the decision maker's assessment of each car's achievement on the criteria, the Toyota scored highest (225 points) and thus became the "best" alternative.

ALTERNATIVES	CRITERIA						TOTAL
	INITIAL PRICE	INTERIOR COMFORT	DURABILITY	REPAIR RECORD	PERFORM-ANCE	HANDLING	
Buick Century	2	10	8	7	5	5	37
Chevrolet Cavalier	9	6	5	6	8	6	40
Ford Escort	8	5	6	6	4	6	35
Geo Prism	9	5	6	7	6	5	38
Honda Civic	5	6	9	10	7	7	44
Hyundai Excel	10	5	6	4	3	3	31
Mazda Protégé	4	8	7	6	8	9	42
Nissan Sentra	7	6	8	6	5	6	38
Plymouth Acclaim	9	7	4	4	4	5	33
Pontiac Grand Am	5	8	5	4	10	10	42
Toyota Corolla	6	5	10	10	6	6	43
Volkswagen Golf	8	6	6	5	7	8	40

Exhibit 5-4 Assessment of Car Alternatives

ALTERNATIVES	CRITERIA												TOTAL
	INITIAL PRICE (10)		INTERIOR COMFORT (8)		DURABILITY (5)		REPAIR RECORD (5)		PERFORM-ANCE (3)		HANDLING (1)		
Buick Century	2	20	10	80	8	40	7	35	5	15	5	5	195
Chevrolet Cavalier	9	90	6	48	5	25	6	30	8	24	6	6	223
Ford Escort	8	80	5	40	6	30	6	30	4	12	6	6	198
Geo Prism	9	90	5	40	6	30	7	35	6	18	5	5	218
Honda Civic	5	50	6	48	9	45	10	50	7	21	7	7	221
Hyundai Excel	10	100	5	40	6	30	4	20	3	9	3	3	202
Mazda Protégé	4	40	8	64	7	35	6	30	8	24	9	9	202
Nissan Sentra	7	70	6	48	8	40	6	30	5	15	6	6	209
Plymouth Acclaim	9	90	7	56	4	20	4	20	4	12	5	5	203
Pontiac Grand Am	5	50	8	64	5	25	4	20	10	30	10	10	199
Toyota Corolla	6	60	5	40	10	50	10	50	6	18	6	6	225
Volkswagen Golf	8	80	6	48	6	30	5	25	7	21	8	8	212

Exhibit 5-5 Assessment of the 12 Alternatives against the Decision Criteria

What Is Decision Implementation?

While the choice process is completed in the previous step, the decision may still fail if it is not implemented properly (step 7). Therefore, this step is concerned with putting the decision into action. **Implementation** includes conveying the decision to those affected and getting their commitment to it. As we'll demonstrate later in this chapter, groups or committees can help a manager achieve commitment. If the people who must carry out a decision participate in the process, they are more likely to endorse enthusiastically the outcome.

implementation
Conveying a decision to those affected and getting their commitment to it.

Why Evaluate Decision Effectiveness?

The last step in the decision-making process appraises the result of the decision to see whether it has corrected the problem. Did the alternative chosen in step 6 and implemented in step 7 accomplish the desired result? The evaluation of such results is detailed in chapters 15 and 16 of this book, where we look at the control function.

Rational Decision Making

Managerial decision making is assumed to be **rational**. By that we mean that managers make consistent, value-maximizing choices within specified constraints.[4] In this section, we want to take a close look at the underlying assumptions of rationality and then determine how valid these assumptions actually are.

rational
Describes choices that are consistent and value-maximizing within specified constraints.

What Is Rationality?

A decision maker who was perfectly rational would be fully objective and logical. He would define a problem carefully and would have a clear and specific goal. Moreover, the steps in the decision-making process would consistently lead toward selecting the alternative that maximizes that goal. Exhibit 5-6 summarizes the assumptions of rationality.

To What Extent Is Rationality Limited?

Managerial decision making can follow rational assumptions. If a manager is faced with a simple problem in which the goals are clear and the alternatives are few, in which the time pressures are minimal and the cost of seeking out and evaluating alternatives is low, for which the organizational culture supports innovation and risk taking, and in which the outcomes are relatively concrete and measurable, the decision process is likely to follow the assumptions of rationality.[5] But most decisions that managers face don't meet all these tests.

Hundreds of studies have sought to improve our understanding of managerial decision making.[6] Individually, these studies often challenge one or more of the assumptions of rationality. Taken together, they suggest that decision making often veers from the logical, consistent, and systematic process that rationality implies.

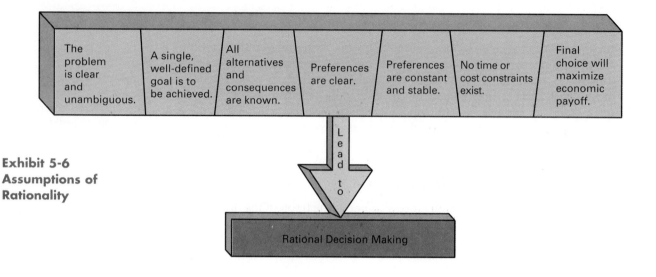

**Exhibit 5-6
Assumptions of
Rationality**

| The problem is clear and unambiguous. | A single, well-defined goal is to be achieved. | All alternatives and consequences are known. | Preferences are clear. | Preferences are constant and stable. | No time or cost constraints exist. | Final choice will maximize economic payoff. |

Lead to

Rational Decision Making

ETHICAL DILEMMAS IN MANAGEMENT

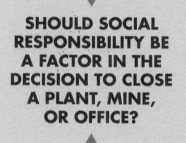

SHOULD SOCIAL RESPONSIBILITY BE A FACTOR IN THE DECISION TO CLOSE A PLANT, MINE, OR OFFICE?

MacMillan Bloedel, the Vancouver-based forestry giant, has never been known for its social responsibility. In its constant quest for profit, the company has grown to be one of the largest forest products companies in North America,

but in the process it has also cultivated perhaps the most antagonistic workforce in Canada (and of course MacBlo's public image leaves a lot to be desired as well). Laying off workers and closing down mills have major impacts on communities. Such actions can be devastating to small towns, and even to cities if the company is a major employer.

Many communities incur very high expenditures to entice and appease large employers. They build roads, schools, and hospitals for corporations and their personnel. They provide police and fire protection. Other businesses, of course, open up to ser-

vice the needs of the corporation, its workers, and their families. Management can respond by arguing that it brought more to the relationship than the community gave back—specifically, high-paying jobs that allowed the community to grow and prosper—and that, in today's global economy, hometown loyalties cannot override economic considerations. But global economies don't cut much ice in a town when a plant or mine or mill closes, and 1,000 people lose their jobs.

Should social responsibility play a part in management's decision to relocate a plant or headquarters? What do you think?

MACMILLAN BLOEDEL
www.mb-mdf.com/

If Managers Can't Be Rational, What Do They Do?

Do the limits to rationality mean that managers ignore the eight-step decision process we described at the beginning of this chapter? Not necessarily. Why? Because in spite of the limits to perfect rationality, managers are expected to appear to follow the rational process.[7] Managers know that "good" decision makers are supposed to do certain things: identify problems, consider alternatives, gather information, and act decisively but prudently (see Ethical Dilemmas in Management). Managers can thus be expected to exhibit the correct decision-making behaviours. By doing so, managers signal to their bosses, peers, and employees that they are competent and that their decisions are the result of intelligent and rational deliberation.

How many managers proceed through this process is often best explained by an alternative model—one in which a manager operates under the assumptions of **bounded rationality**.[8] In bounded rationality, managers construct simplified models that extract the essential features from the problems they face without capturing all their complexity. Then, given information-processing limitations and constraints imposed by the organization, managers attempt to behave rationally within the parameters of the simple model. The result is a satisfying decision rather than a maximizing one; that is, a decision in which the solution is "good enough."

The implications of bounded rationality on the manager's job cannot be overlooked. In situations in which the assumptions of perfect rationality do not apply (including many of the most important and far-reaching decisions that a manager makes), the details of the decision-making process are strongly influenced by the decision maker's self-interest, the organization's culture, internal politics, and power considerations (see Details on a Management Classic).

bounded rationality
Behaviour that is rational within the parameters of a simplified model that captures the essential features of a problem.

DETAILS ON A MANAGEMENT CLASSIC

Herbert Simon and Bounded Rationality

Management theory is built on the premise that individuals act rationally, and the essence of their job revolves around the rational decision-making process. However, the assumptions of rationality are rather extreme. Few people actually behave that way. Given this fact, how do managers make decisions if it's unlikely that they are perfectly rational? Herbert Simon has the answer. Simon found that within certain constraints, managers do act rationally. Since it's impossible for human beings to process and understand all the information necessary to meet the test of rationality, what they do is construct simplified models that extract the essential features from problems without capturing all their complexities.[9] Consequently, they can behave rationally (the rational decision-making model) within the limits of the simplified or bounded model.

So how do managers' actions within these boundaries differ from those within the rational model? Once a problem is identified, the search for criteria and alternatives begins. But this list of criteria is generally limited and made up of the more conspicuous choices. That is, Simon found that the decision maker will focus on easy-to-find choices—those that tend to be highly visible. In many instances, this means developing alternatives that vary only slightly from decisions that have been used in the past to deal with similar problems.

Once this limited set of alternatives is identified, the decision maker will begin reviewing them. But that review will not be exhaustive. Rather, the manager will proceed to review the alternatives only until she identifies an alternative that is sufficient, or good enough to solve the problems at hand. Thus, the first alternative to meet the "good enough" criterion ends the search, and the decision maker can then proceed to implement this acceptable course of action.▼

Decision Making: A Contingency Approach

The type of problem a manager faces in a decision-making situation often determines how that problem is treated. In this section we present a categorization scheme for problems and for types of decisions. Then we show how the type of decision making a manager uses should reflect the characteristics of the problem.

How Do Problems Differ?

well-structured problems
Straightforward, familiar, easily defined problems.

ill-structured problems
New problems in which information is ambiguous or incomplete.

Some problems are straightforward. The goal of the decision maker is clear, the problem familiar, and information about the problem easily defined and complete. Examples might include a supplier being late with an important delivery, a customer wanting to return a purchase to a retail store, a newspaper having to respond to an unexpected and fast-breaking news event, or a university's handling of a student who seeks to have a grade changed. Such situations are called **well-structured problems**. They align closely with the assumptions underlying perfect rationality.

Many situations faced by managers, however, are **ill-structured problems**. They are new or unusual. Information about such problems is ambiguous or incomplete. The selection of a new product design is one example. So, too, is the decision to invest in a new, unproven technology.

What's the Difference between Programmed and Nonprogrammed Decisions?

Just as problems can be divided into two categories, so, too, can decisions. As we will see, programmed, or routine, decision making is the most efficient way to handle well-structured problems. However, when problems are ill-structured, managers must rely on nonprogrammed decision making in order to develop unique solutions.

A waiter in a fine restaurant spills a drink on a customer's dress. What does the manager do? There is probably some standardized routine for handling the problem. For example, if it is the waiter's fault, if the damage is significant, and if the customer has asked for a remedy, the manager offers to have the dress cleaned at the restaurant's expense. This is a **programmed decision**.

programmed decision
A repetitive decision that can be handled by a routine approach.

Decisions are programmed to the extent that they are repetitive and routine and to the extent that a definite approach has been worked out for handling them. Because the problem is well-structured, the manager does not have to go to the trouble and expense of working up an involved decision process. Programmed decision making is relatively simple and tends to rely heavily on previous solutions. The "develop-the-alternatives" stage in the decision-making process is either nonexistent or is given little attention. Why? Because once the structured problem is defined, its solution is usually self-evident or at least reduced to very few alternatives that are familiar and that have proven successful in the past. In many cases, programmed decision making becomes decision making by precedent. Managers simply do what they and others have done in the same situation. The spilled drink on the customer's dress does not require the restaurant manager to identify and weigh decision criteria, nor to develop a long list of possible solutions. Rather, the manager falls back on a systematic procedure, rule, or policy.

What Are Procedures, Rules, and Policies— and Where Are They Best Used?

A **procedure** is a series of interrelated sequential steps that a manager can use to respond to a structured problem. The only real difficulty is in identifying the problem. Once the problem is clear, so is the procedure. For instance, a purchasing manager receives a request from engineering for five computer-assisted design (CAD) software packages. The purchasing manager knows that there is a definite procedure for handling this decision. Has the requisition been properly filled out and approved? If not, send the requisition back with a note explaining what is deficient. If the request is complete, the approximate costs are estimated. If the total exceeds $6,000, three bids must be obtained. If the total is $6,000 or less, only one vendor need be identified and the order placed. The decision-making process is merely the execution of a simple series of sequential steps.

A **rule** is an explicit statement that tells a manager what she ought or ought not to do. Rules are frequently used by managers when they confront a well-structured problem because they are simple to follow and they ensure consistency. In the illustration above, the $6,000 cutoff rule simplifies the purchasing manager's decision about when to use multiple bids.

A third guide for making programmed decisions is a **policy**. It provides guidelines to channel a manager's thinking in a specific direction. In contrast to a rule, a policy establishes parameters for the decision maker rather than specifically stating what should or should not be done. As an analogy, think of the Ten Commandments as rules and the Canadian Constitution as policy. The latter requires judgment and interpretation, the former do not.

procedure
A series of interrelated sequential steps that can be used to respond to a structured problem.

rule
An explicit statement that tells managers what they ought or ought not to do.

policy
A guide that establishes parameters for making decisions.

What Do Nonprogrammed Decisions Look Like?

Deciding whether to merge with another organization, how to restructure an organization to improve efficiency, or whether to close an unprofitable division are examples of **nonprogrammed decisions**. Such decisions are unique and nonrecurring. When a manager confronts an ill-structured problem or one that is novel, there is no cut-and-dried solution. It requires a custom-made response.

The creation of a marketing strategy for a new product represents an example of a nonprogrammed decision. It will be different from previous marketing decisions because the product is new, a different set of competitors exists, and other conditions that may have existed when previous products were introduced years earlier have changed.

Bombardier's decision to produce its Global Express business jet is an example of nonprogrammed decision making. While Bombardier's aerospace expertise cannot be argued, the company had never produced and marketed a high-end business jet. Bombardier decided to go head-to-head with Gulfstream, which dominates the U.S. market, and bring out a business jet that would fly 6,700 miles without refuelling. Gulfstream responded to this new competitive threat by hurrying a long-range jet of their own to market—the GV. The GV beat the Global Express to market, as the latter was not ready until 1998. However, while Gulfstream's jet is based on a 1960s' jet design, Bombardier's has been built entirely from scratch. Forecasts for the Global Express look favourable, but the process has required Bombardier's management to face a completely new set of variables in their decision making.

nonprogrammed decisions
Unique decisions that require a custom-made solution.

GULFSTREAM
www.gulfstreamaircraft.
com/

MANAGERS WHO MADE A DIFFERENCE

Stephen Bachand: Canadian Tire

When Stephen Bachand agreed to take over as CEO of Canadian Tire, the 71-year-old institution was facing some hard times, and its prospects looked grim. Many of the smaller stores in the chain were losing money, service was often poor, and inventory was not always being kept up. The result: customers were going to stores only to find their desired product out of stock. Moreover, the marketplace was on the verge of being invaded on a large scale by major American chains such as Home Depot and Wal-Mart.[10]

However, Canadian Tire was still a powerful force in Canadian retailing, accounting for roughly a third of the nation's retail sales in both sporting goods and hardware, and nearly half of all auto parts. The challenge was to hold on to market share in the face of new competition, while bringing Canadian Tire stores into the customer-oriented '90s. To achieve these goals, Bachand had to have the cooperation of the individual store owners. These owners collectively hold a significant number of shares in the corporation itself. This is a fairly uncommon relationship between a head office and its store owners, and Bachand was forced to gain the approval of these dealers before he could institute any changes. This he did, and together they developed a strategy to bring Canadian Tire back up to previous levels of profitability.

The company instituted a $1-billion renovation program, making stores more shopper-friendly—with space, more competitive prices, wider selection, and more stock. By 1997, 100 new stores had replaced the old, out-of-date versions. And the

company plans to overhaul another 140 within the next three years. The objective is to meet the new competition head-on, and so far it has been working successfully. In every year since Bachand's appointment as CEO, Canadian Tire has reported increased revenue. Revenues for 1996 set a company record, at $3.91 billion. Profits are steadily climbing as a result of increased sales coupled with cost-cutting measures in shipping, distribution, and marketing.

When Canadian Tire turned three-quarters of a century old in 1997, all signs were pointing to increasing success in the Canadian retail market. With Stephen Bachand at the helm, Canadian Tire looks well on its way to completing the last quarter of its first century very profitably.▼

An example of the dangers inherent in nonprogrammed decisions is that of the Internet cafes that have sprung up—and then often shut down—in Canada. The combination of Internet access and a coffee-shop atmosphere seemed a few years ago to be a brilliant coupling. But this type of venture requires a vast array of nonprogrammed decisions. Owners were going into the business virtually blind, and they often did not take into account many factors. For one thing, it takes a fair amount of coffee to pay off the high-tech virtual reality games that many of these cafes decided they needed. This market was ruled by public tastes, which had not been gauged. What seemed like a great new idea often proved to be a hectic, and doomed, struggle for survival.

How Can You Integrate Problems, Types of Decisions, and Level in the Organization?

Exhibit 5-7 describes the relationship between the types of problems, the types of decisions, and level in the organization. Well-structured problems are responded to with programmed decision making. Ill-structured problems require nonprogrammed decision making. Lower-level managers essentially confront familiar and repetitive problems; therefore, they most typically rely on programmed decisions such as standard operating procedures. However, the problems confronting managers are more likely to become ill-structured as the managers

Neptec Design Group of Kanata, Ontario, faced many nonprogrammed decisions during the development of a vision system for guiding robotic arms in space, which has led to a $20-million contract with NASA.

move up the organizational hierarchy. Why? Because lower-level managers handle the routine decisions themselves and pass upward only decisions that they find unique or difficult. Similarly, managers pass down routine decisions to their employees in order to spend their time on more problematic issues.

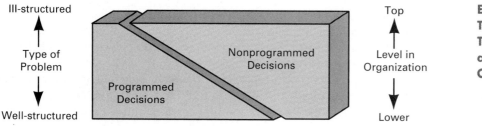

Exhibit 5-7
Types of Problems, Types of Decisions, and Level in the Organization

Few managerial decisions in the real world are either fully programmed or nonprogrammed. These are extremes, and most decisions fall somewhere in between. Few programmed decisions are designed to eliminate individual judgment completely. At the other extreme, even the most unique situation requiring a nonprogrammed decision can be helped by programmed routines.

A last point on this topic is that organizational efficiency is facilitated by the use of programmed decision making, which may explain its wide popularity. Wherever possible, management decisions are likely to be programmed. Obviously, this is not too realistic at the top of the organization, since most of the problems that top management confronts are of a nonrecurring nature. But there are strong economic incentives for top management to create policies, standard operating procedures (SOPs), and rules to guide other managers.

Programmed decisions minimize the need for managers to exercise discretion. This is relevant because discretion costs money. The more nonprogrammed decision making a manager is required to do, the greater the judgment needed. Since sound judgment is an uncommon quality, it costs more to acquire the services of managers who possess this ability.

YOUNG CANADIANS

David Weiser:
Megatoon Entertainment Group

David Weiser of Quebec City definitely has the entrepreneurial spirit. He cofounded Megatoon Entertainment Group, an animation studio. After major success, Megatoon was sold and Weiser went on to start the largest Internet provider in the Quebec City area. Selling that for millions, Weiser then founded CH!WAWA Communications, an entertainment development company. And all of this was done by age 25.

**MEGATOON
ENTERTAINMENT
GROUP**
www.megatoon.com

Group Decision Making

Many decisions in organizations, especially important decisions that have a far-reaching impact on organizational activities and personnel, are made in groups. It's a rare organization that doesn't at some time use committees, task forces, review panels, study teams, or similar groups as vehicles for making decisions. Studies tell us that managers spend up to 40 per cent or more of their time in meetings.[11] Undoubtedly, a large portion of that time is involved with defining problems, arriving at solutions to those problems, and determining the means for implementing the solutions. It's possible, in fact, for groups to be assigned any of the eight steps in the decision-making process.

What Are the Advantages to Group Decision Making?

Individual and group decisions each have their own set of strengths. Neither is ideal for all situations. Let's begin by reviewing the advantages that group decisions have over individual decisions. Group decisions provide more complete information. There is often truth to the axiom that two heads are better than one. A group will bring a diversity of experience and perspectives to the decision process that an individual, acting alone, cannot. Groups also generate more alternatives. Because groups have a greater quantity and diversity of information, they can identify more alternatives than can an individual. This is most evident when group members represent different specialties.

Furthermore, group decision making increases acceptance of a solution. Many decisions fail after the final choice has been made because people do not accept the solution. However, if the people who will be affected by a certain solution and who will help implement it get to participate in the decision making itself, they will be more likely to accept the decision and to encourage others to accept it. And last, this process increases legitimacy. The group decision-making process is consistent with democratic ideals; therefore, decisions made by groups may be perceived as more legitimate than decisions made by a single person. The fact that the individual decision maker has complete power and has not consulted others can create a perception that a decision was made autocratically and arbitrarily.

What Are the Disadvantages to Group Decision Making?

If groups are so good, how did the phrase "a camel is a racehorse put together by a committee" become so popular? The answer, of course, is that group decisions are not without their drawbacks. There are several major disadvantages of group decision making. First, it is time-consuming. It takes time to assemble a group. Second, the interaction that takes place once the group is in place is frequently inefficient. The result is that groups almost always take more time to reach a solution than it would take an individual making the decision alone. There may also be a situation where there is minority domination. Members of a group are never perfectly equal. They may differ in rank in the organization, experience, knowledge about the problem, influence with other members, verbal skills, assertiveness, and the like. This creates the opportunity for one or more members to use their advantages to dominate others in the group. A minority that dominates a group frequently has an undue influence on the final decision.

Another problem focuses on the pressures to conform. There are social pressures to conform in groups that can lead to what has been called **groupthink**.[12] This is a form of conformity in which group members withhold deviant, minority, or unpopular views to give the appearance of agreement. Groupthink undermines critical thinking in the group and eventually harms the quality of the final decision (see Details on a Management Classic). And finally, there is ambiguous responsibility. Group members share responsibility, but who is actually responsible for the outcome? In an individual decision, it is clear who is responsible. In a group decision, the responsibility of any single member is watered down.

groupthink
The withholding by group members of different views in order to appear in agreement.

When Are Groups Most Effective?

Whether groups are more effective than individuals depends on the criteria you use for defining effectiveness. Group decisions tend to be more accurate. The evidence indicates that, on the average, groups make better decisions than do individuals.[13] This doesn't mean, of course, that all groups outperform every individual. Rather, group decisions have been found to be better than those that would have been reached by the average individual in the group. However, they are seldom better than the performance of the best individual.

If decision effectiveness is defined in terms of speed, individuals are superior. Group decisions are characterized by give and take, which consumes time.

Effectiveness may mean the degree to which a solution demonstrates creativity. If creativity is important, groups tend to be more effective than individuals.[14] This requires, however, that the forces that foster groupthink be constrained.

DETAILS ON A MANAGEMENT CLASSIC

Irving L. Janis and Groupthink

Have you ever been in a situation where a number of people were sitting around discussing a particular item—and you had something to say that ran contrary to the majority views that dominated the group. What did you do? Remain silent? Would you be surprised if you later learned that others shared your views and also had remained silent? What you experienced is what Irving Janis termed groupthink.[15]

Groupthink relates to a situation in which a group's ability to appraise alternatives objectively and arrive at a quality decision is jeopardized. Because of pressures applied for conformity, groups often deter individuals from critically appraising unusual, minority, or unpopular views. Consequently, there is a deterioration of an individual's mental efficiency, reality testing, and moral judgment as a result of the group's pressure.

How does groupthink occur? The following are examples where groupthink is evident:

▶ **1.** Group members rationalize any resistance to the assumptions they have made.
▶ **2.** Members apply direct pressure on those who momentarily express doubts about any of the group's shared views, or who question the validity of arguments favoured by the majority.
▶ **3.** Members who have doubts or hold differing points of view seek to avoid deviating from what appears to be group consensus.
▶ **4.** There appears to be an illusion of unanimity. If someone does not speak, it is assumed that he is in full accord.

Although we can recognize that the above may affect groups' decisions, just how much of a problem is it? Several research studies have found that groupthink symptoms were associated with poorer quality decision outcomes. None was more noteworthy than the decision of Lyndon Johnson's administration to escalate the Vietnam War by increasing the tonnage of bombs dropped on North Vietnam—despite continual information that bombing them was not bringing the war any closer to conclusion. Conversely, where groupthink symptoms were not found, such as in the case of President Kennedy and his staff's handling of the Cuban Missile Crisis in 1961, these decisions were viewed as being successful.

Research has found that groupthink can be minimized if the following conditions exist in group decision making: The group is cohesive, fosters open discussion, and is led by an impartial leader who seeks input from all members; furthermore, individuals external to the group become aware of who the group is and what decision it is making.▼

Another criterion for effectiveness is the degree of acceptance that the final decision achieves. As was previously noted, because group decisions have input from more people, they are likely to result in solutions that will be more widely accepted.

The effectiveness of group decision making is also influenced by the size of the group. The larger the group, the greater the opportunity for heterogeneous representation.

DEVELOPING MANAGEMENT SKILLS

▼ CONDUCTING A GROUP MEETING ▲

▶ **1. Prepare and distribute an agenda well in advance of the meeting.** An agenda defines the meeting's purpose for participants and plans boundaries between relevant and irrelevant discussion topics. Also, the agenda can serve as an important vehicle for pre-meeting discussions with participants.

▶ **2. Consult with participants before the meeting to ensure proper participation.** Let participants know that their input is valuable and that you welcome them speaking up at the meeting when they have something to offer.

▶ **3. Establish specific time parameters for the meeting—when it will start and end.** This helps to keep the meeting on time and focused on the important matters.

▶ **4. Maintain focused discussion during the meeting.** Items not on the agenda should not be given substantial time during the meeting. If an issue is important, maybe another meeting, with its own agenda, should be held to address that issue.

▶ **5. Encourage and support participation by all members.** If you have done a good job in the second step, participants should come prepared to talk but still may need some encouragement at the meeting. Sometimes direct questions about what they think will get them to talk.

▶ **6. Encourage the clash of ideas.** Remember, you want as much information about a topic to surface as possible. Disagreements are fine. That indicates that different voices are being heard. Better to work the differences out now than to have them surface later.

▶ **7. Discourage the clash of personalities.** Disagreements can enhance the process, but they should be substantive disputes. Differences due to personal dislikes are a disaster in a meeting.

▶ **8. Bring closure by summarizing accomplishments and allocating follow-up assignments.** This lets participants understand what occurred in the meeting and what they may have to do before the next meeting. This is, in essence, planning.

On the other hand, a larger group requires more coordination and more time to allow all members to contribute. What this means is that groups probably should not be too large: a minimum of five to a maximum of about 15. Evidence indicates, in fact, that groups of five and, to a lesser extent, seven are the most effective.[16] Because five and seven are odd numbers, strict deadlocks are avoided. Effectiveness should not be considered without also assessing efficiency. Groups almost always stack up a poor second in efficiency to the individual decision maker. With few exceptions, group decision making consumes more work hours than does individual decision making. In deciding whether to use groups, then, primary consideration must be given to assessing whether increases in effectiveness are more than enough to offset the losses in efficiency.

How Can You Improve Group Decision Making?

When members of a group meet face to face and interact with one another, they create the potential for groupthink. They can censor themselves and pressure other group members into agreement. Four ways of making group decision making more creative have been suggested: brainstorming, the nominal group and Delphi techniques, and electronic meetings. We've also provided some thoughts regarding how to conduct a meeting (see Developing Management Skills).

brainstorming
An idea-generating process that encourages alternatives while withholding criticism.

What Is Brainstorming? Brainstorming is a relatively simple technique for overcoming pressures for conformity that retard the development of creative alternatives.[17] It does this by using an idea-generating process that specifically encourages any and all alternatives while withholding any criticism of those alternatives. In a typical brainstorming session, a half-dozen to a dozen people sit around a table. The group leader states the problem in a clear manner that is understood by all participants. Members then "freewheel" as many alternatives as they can in a given time. No criticism is allowed, and all the alternatives are recorded for later discussion and analysis. Brainstorming, however, is merely a process for generating ideas. The next two techniques go further by offering ways to arrive at a preferred solution.[18]

How Do the Nominal Group Technique and the Delphi Technique Function? The **nominal group technique** restricts discussion during the decision-making process; hence the term. Group members must be present, as in a traditional committee meeting, but they are required to operate independently. The chief advantage of this technique is that it permits the group to meet formally but does not restrict independent thinking, as so often happens in the traditional interacting group.

nominal group technique
A decision-making technique in which group members are physically present but operate independently.

Delphi technique
A group decision-making technique in which members never meet face to face.

A more complex and time-consuming alternative is the **Delphi technique**, which is similar to the nominal group technique except that it does not require the physical presence of the group members. This is because the Delphi technique never allows the group members to meet face to face. Like the nominal group technique, the Delphi technique shields group members from the undue influence of others. It also does not require the physical presence of the participants. So, for instance, Minolta could use the technique to query its sales managers in Tokyo, Hong Kong, Paris, London, New York, Toronto, Mexico City, and Melbourne as to the best worldwide price for one of the company's new cameras. The cost of bringing the executives together at a central location is avoided, yet input from Minolta's major markets is obtained. Of course, the Delphi technique has its drawbacks. The method is extremely time-consuming. It is frequently not applicable when a speedy decision is necessary. Further, the method might not develop the rich array of alternatives that the interacting or nominal groups do. The ideas that might surface from the heat of face-to-face interaction might never arise. Specific steps for conducting either the nominal group or the Delphi techniques are presented in Exhibit 5-8.

electronic meetings
Decision-making groups that interact by way of linked computers.

Companies such as Minolta and IBM use electronic meetings to bring people from all parts of the world together.

How Can Electronic Meetings Enhance Group Decision Making? The most recent approach to group decision making blends the nominal group technique with sophisticated computer technology.[19] It's called the **electronic meeting**.

Once the technology for the meeting is in place, the concept is simple. Up to 50 people sit around a horseshoe-shaped table that is empty except for a series of computer terminals. Issues are presented to participants, who type their responses onto their computer screens. Individual comments, as well as aggregate votes, are displayed on a projection screen in the room.

The major advantages to electronic meetings are anonymity, honesty, and speed. Participants can anonymously type any message they want, and it will flash on the screen for all to see at the push of a board key. It also allows people to be brutally honest with no penalty. And it's fast—chitchat is eliminated, discussions don't digress, and many participants can "talk" at once without stepping on others' toes.

The Nominal Group Technique:

▶ **1.** Members meet as a group; but before any discussion takes place, each member independently writes down his or her ideas on the problem.

▶ **2.** This silent period is followed by each member presenting one idea to the group. Each member takes his or her turn, going around the table, presenting one idea at a time until all ideas have been presented and recorded (typically on a flip chart or chalkboard). No discussion takes place until all ideas have been recorded.

▶ **3.** The group now discusses the ideas for clarity and evaluates them.

▶ **4.** Each group member silently and independently assigns a rank to the ideas. The final decision is determined by the idea with the highest aggregate ranking.

The Delphi Technique:

▶ **1.** The problem is identified, and members are asked to provide potential solutions through a series of carefully designed questionnaires.

▶ **2.** Each member anonymously and independently completes the first questionnaire.

▶ **3.** Results of the first questionnaire are compiled at a central location, transcribed, and reproduced.

▶ **4.** Each member receives a copy of the results.

▶ **5.** After viewing the results, members are again asked for their solutions. The results typically trigger new solutions or cause changes in the original position.

▶ **6.** Steps 4 and 5 are repeated as often as necessary until consensus is reached.

Exhibit 5-8
Steps in the Nominal Group Technique and the Delphi Technique

Experts claim that electronic meetings are as much as 55 per cent faster than traditional face-to-face meetings.[20] Phelps Dodge Mining, for instance, used the approach to cut its annual planning meeting from several days down to 12 hours. However, there are drawbacks. Those who can type quickly can outshine those who may be verbally eloquent but are lousy typists; those with the best ideas don't get credit for them; and the process lacks the informational richness of face-to-face oral communication. But because this technology is only in its infancy, the future of group decision making is very likely to include extensive use of electronic meetings.

The Effect of National Culture on Decision-Making Styles

The way decisions are made—whether by group, participatively, or autocratically by an individual manager—and the degree of risk a decision maker is willing to take are just two examples of decision variables that reflect a country's cultural environment. Decision making in Japan, for instance, is much more group-oriented than in Canada, and characteristics of the Japanese national culture can explain why.[21]

The Japanese value conformity and cooperation. One can see this in their schools as well as in their business organizations. Before making decisions, Japanese

CEOs collect a large amount of information, which is then used in consensus-forming group decisions. Since employees in Japanese organizations have high job security, managerial decisions take a long-term perspective rather than focusing on short-term profits, as is often the practice in Canada.

Senior managers in other nations—including France, Germany, and Sweden—also adapt their decision styles to their country's culture. In France, for instance, autocratic decision making is widely practised, and managers avoid risks. Managerial styles in Germany reflect the German culture's concern for structure and order. There are extensive rules and regulations in German organizations. Managers have well-defined responsibilities and accept that decisions must go through channels. Decision styles of Swedish managers differ considerably from those of their French and German counterparts. Managers in Sweden are more aggressive; they take the initiative with problems and are not afraid to take risks. Senior managers in Sweden also push decisions down in the ranks. They encourage lower-level managers and employees to take part in decisions that affect them.

These examples are meant to remind you that managers need to modify their decision styles to reflect the national culture of the country in which they live, as well as to reflect the organizational culture of the firm in which they work.

Summary

This summary is organized by the chapter Learning Objectives found on page 114.

1. Decision making is an eight-step process: (1) formulation of a problem, (2) identification of decision criteria, (3) allocation of weights to the criteria, (4) development of alternatives, (5) analysis of alternatives, (6) selection of an alternative, (7) implementation of the alternative, and (8) evaluation of decision effectiveness.

2. The rational decision maker is assumed to have a clear problem, have no goal conflict, know all options, have a clear preference ordering, keep all preferences constant, have no time or cost constraints, and select a final choice that maximizes her economic payoff.

3. Rationality assumptions don't apply in many situations because problems aren't simple, goals are not clear, alternatives are many, and there are time and cost constraints; decision makers sometimes increase commitment to a previous choice to confirm its original correctness; prior decision precedents constrain current choices; there is rarely agreement on a single goal; decision makers must face time and cost constraints; and most organizational cultures discourage taking risks and searching for innovative alternatives.

4. In the perfectly rational decision-making process: (1) the problem identified is important and relevant; (2) all criteria are identified; (3) all criteria are evaluated; (4) a comprehensive list of alternatives is generated; (5) all alternatives are assessed against the decision criteria and weights; (6) the decision with the highest economic outcome is chosen; (7) all organizational members embrace the solution chosen; and (8) the decision's outcome is objectively evaluated against the original problem.

5. In the bounded rational decision-making process managers construct simplified models that extract essential features from the problems they face without capturing all their complexity. They then attempt to act rationally within this simplified model.

6. Managers face well- and ill-structured problems. Well-structured problems are straightforward, familiar, easily defined, and solved using programmed decisions. Ill-structured problems are new or unusual, involve ambiguous or incomplete information, and are solved using nonprogrammed decisions.

7. Groups offer certain advantages: more complete information, more alternatives, increased acceptance of a solution, and greater legitimacy. On the other hand, groups are time-consuming, can be dominated by a minority, create pressures to conform, and cloud responsibility.

8. Four ways of improving group decision making are brainstorming, the nominal group technique, the Delphi technique, and electronic meetings.

Review and Discussion Questions

1. Explain how decision making is related to the planning process.

2. Describe a decision you have made that closely aligns with the assumptions of perfect rationality. Compare this with the process you used to select your university. Is there a deviation? Explain.

3. What are the steps of the rational decision-making model?

4. How is implementation important to the decision-making process?

5. What is a satisficing decision?

6. Why might a manager use a simplified decision model?

7. What's the difference between a rule and a policy?

8. Is the order in which alternatives are considered more critical under assumptions of perfect rationality or bounded rationality? Why?

9. What is groupthink? What are its implications for decision making?

10. Why do you think organizations have increased the use of groups for making decisions during the past 20 years? When would you recommend using groups to make decisions?

Testing Your Comprehension

Circle the correct answer, then check yourself on page 471.

1. Which of the following sequences is correct for the decision-making process?
   a) identify decision criteria, analyse alternatives, allocate weights to criteria
   b) analyse alternatives, select an alternative, implement the alternative
   c) select an alternative, evaluate decision effectiveness, weight the criteria
   d) analyse alternatives, develop alternatives, allocate weights to criteria

2. Which of the following is NOT a prerequisite for identifying a problem?
   a) managers must be rational
   b) managers must be aware of some discrepancy
   c) managers must be under pressure to take action
   d) managers must have the resources to be able to act

3. When British Airway's U.S. manager observed that her market share had slipped in relation to Avianca Air, she was
   a) recognizing a discrepancy by comparison with another unit in the organization
   b) analysing alternatives
   c) recognizing a discrepancy by comparison with past performance
   d) identifying decision criteria

4. Once a problem is formulated, the next step is to
   a) select an alternative
   b) list all possible solutions
   c) observe a discrepancy
   d) decide what is critical in the decision

5. The decision criteria are
   a) factors that determine what is important
   b) used to implement a decision
   c) what we use to spot a discrepancy
   d) guidelines for deciding who can make a decision

6. When a manager prioritizes all the features a new purchase should have, he is practising
   a) selecting criteria
   b) formulating a problem
   c) weighting criteria
   d) analysing alternatives

7. After implementation has been accomplished
   a) the decision-making process is complete
   b) the control function of management becomes important
   c) the alternatives are ranked
   d) the manager must complete written evaluation forms

8. Bounded rationality refers to the idea that
   a) managers are bound by ethical considerations to be rational
   b) managers will promote rationalization as an aid to decision making
   c) managers employ model construction to simplify decision making
   d) managers are to behave according to rational guidelines within the bounds of their authority in the workplace

9. The tendency for decision makers to base their judgments on information that is readily accessible to them is best referred to as
   a) escalation of commitment
   b) representative heuristic
   c) bounded rationality
   d) none of the above

10. Well-structured problems are
    a) new
    b) closely aligned with the assumptions of perfect rationality
    c) ambiguous
    d) characterized by limited information

11. When a decision maker relies on a programmed decision, she
    a) may fall back on rules, procedures, or policies
    b) will develop many alternatives from which to select a solution
    c) will spend considerable time on the decision
    d) must be dealing with a unique or unusual problem

12. A procedure can be defined as a
    a) method to guide a manager's thinking in one general direction
    b) hierarchy of authority relationships in an organization
    c) series of interrelated sequential steps for problem solving
    d) collection of explicit statements about what a manager can or cannot do

13. A rule is BEST described by which of the following?
    a) a general guideline designed to direct a manager's focus
    b) a series of interrelated sequential steps
    c) a prohibition against desired activity
    d) an explicit and specific statement of correct behaviour

14. A policy typically contains
    a) parameters to constrain behaviour, not specific rules
    b) nothing but explicit, unambiguous terminology
    c) a sequence of steps to follow for approved decision making
    d) specific rules

15. Group decisions will usually be superior to individual decisions when
    a) speed is a concern
    b) accuracy is critical
    c) minimizing the tendency of groupthink is important
    d) flexibility is needed

16. Which of the following is NOT an example of a situation in which groupthink occurs?
    a) Group members rationalize any resistance to the assumptions they have made.
    b) Group members apply direct pressure on those who express doubts.
    c) Group members avoid openly showing lack of consensus.
    d) Group members question those who are silent and try to sway them.

17. Which of the following statements is correct regarding national culture and decision making?
    a) In Sweden, employees are empowered to make decisions on matters that directly affect them.
    b) In Japan, *ringisei* reflects an efficient way for managers to make individual decisions regarding strategic directions.
    c) In Egypt, time pressure in making decisions promotes individual rather than group decision making.
    d) In France, risk avoidance is best achieved through participative decision making.

Self-Assessment Exercise

What's Your Intuitive Ability?

For each of the following questions, select the response that first appeals to you by circling the letter of that response. Be honest with yourself.

1. When working on a project, do you prefer to:
   a. be told what the problem is, but left free to decide how to solve it?
   b. get very clear instructions about how to go about solving the problem before you start?

2. When working on a project, do you prefer to work with colleagues who are:
   a. realistic?
   b. imaginative?

3. Do you admire people most who are:
   a. creative?
   b. careful?

4. Do the friends you choose tend to be:
   a. serious and hard working?
   b. exciting and often emotional?

5. When you ask a colleague for advice on a problem you have, do you:
   a. seldom or never get upset if she questions your basic assumptions?
   b. often get upset if he questions your basic assumptions?

6. When you start your day, do you usually:
   a. seldom make or follow a specific plan?
   b. make a plan first?

7. When working with numbers, do you find that you:
   a. seldom or never make factual errors?
   b. often make factual errors?

8. Do you find that you:
   a. seldom daydream during the day and really don't enjoy doing so?
   b. frequently daydream during the day and enjoy doing so?

9. When working on a problem do you:
   a. prefer to follow the instructions or rules when they are given to you?
   b. often enjoy circumventing the instructions or rules when they are given to you?

10. When you are trying to put something together, do you prefer to have:
    a. step-by-step written instructions on how to assemble the item?
    b. a picture of how the item is supposed to look once assembled?

11. Do you find that the person who irritates you the most is the one who appears to be:
    a. disorganized?
    b. organized?

12. When an unexpected crisis comes up that you have to deal with, do you:
    a. feel anxious about the situation?
    b. feel excited by the challenge of the situation?

Turn to page 464 for scoring directions and key.

Source: Weston H. Agor, _AIM Survey_ (El Paso, Tex.: ENP Enterprises, 1989), Part I. With permission.

Class Exercise

Contrasting Individual and Group Decision Making

Objective: To contrast individual and group decision making.

Time: Fifteen minutes.

Procedure: **A.** You have five minutes to read the following story* and respond to each of the 11 questions as either *true, false,* or *unknown* (indicated by a question mark). Begin.

The Story: A sales clerk had just turned off the lights in the store when a man appeared and demanded money. The owner opened a cash register. The contents of the cash register were scooped up, and the man sped away. A member of the police force was notified promptly.

Statements about the Story:

1. A man appeared after the owner had turned off his store lights.	T	F	?
2. The robber was a *man.*	T	F	?
3. The man did not demand money.	T	F	?
4. The man who opened the cash register was the owner.	T	F	?
5. The store owner scooped up the contents of the cash register and ran away.	T	F	?
6. Someone opened a cash register.	T	F	?
7. After the man who demanded the money scooped up the contents of the cash register, he ran away.	T	F	?
8. While the cash register contained money, the story does *not* state *how much.*	T	F	?
9. The robber demanded money of the owner.	T	F	?
10. The story concerns a series of events in which only three persons are referred to: the owner of the store, a man who demanded money, and a member of the police force.	T	F	?
11. The following events in the story are true: Someone demanded money, a cash register was opened, its contents were scooped up, and a man dashed out of the store.	T	F	?

B. When your five minutes are up, form groups of four to five members each. Group members have 10 minutes to discuss their answers and agree on the correct answers to each of the 11 statements.

C. Your instructor will give you the correct answers. How many correct answers did you get at the conclusion of Step A? How many did your group achieve at the conclusion of Step B? Did the group outperform the average individual? The best individual? Discuss the implications of these results.

---

* Adapted from W.V. Haney, *Communication and Interpersonal Relations,* 6th ed. (Homewood, Ill.: Richard D. Irwin, Inc., 1992), pp. 232–233. Reprinted by special permission.

Case Application

Nike's Fight for Top Spot

During the physical fitness boom of the 1970s, millions of previously unathletic people became interested in exercise. During that time, the fastest-growing segment of the physical fitness market was joggers. In fact, it was estimated that by the late 1970s, almost 30 million people were jogging, and another 10 million wore running shoes for leisure. For most of those 40 million people, there was only one real choice in athletic shoes: Nike.[22]

Nike was founded by Philip Knight, a track star from the University of Oregon. While importing shoes to the U.S., Nike's big breakthrough came in 1975 with the development of the "waffle" sole—a sole with tiny rubber studs that made it spongier than any other on the market. From that point on, Nike's sales skyrocketed. Today, Nike has sales of more than $3.8 billion (U.S.), with nearly 25 per cent of the world market.

Nike's success can be traced to several of Knight's core values. First, the company emphasizes research and development. Second, the company provides a variety of styles and models to satisfy everyone's tastes. Third, Knight wants his company to be on the "hearts, minds, and feet" of every individual. To achieve this last goal, Nike has relied heavily on a phenomenal marketing campaign.

Being an athlete, Knight recognized that professional sports heroes could influence a lot of people. He believed that if he could get high-profile athletes to become part of the Nike team, the company could "build new product lines and marketing campaigns around them." The athletes' dominating presence and the consumers' passion for imitating their idols would enable Knight to achieve his goal of running the number one athletic shoe and apparel company in the world. That formula seems to have worked! But success is not something that Knight can take for granted. When you are number one, everyone else is at your heels trying to overtake you.

Reebok is currently number two. With revenues of more than $3 billion (U.S.), Reebok is in a good position to attempt to overtake Nike. Its president, Paul Fireman, has been successful in filling in niches that Nike has overlooked. For instance, when Nike was producing jogging and other athletic shoes primarily for men, Reebok recognized that a large segment of the population was being ignored. Accordingly, Reebok developed its white leather shoes for women who needed good athletic shoes—and the market exploded. In fact, by the late 1980s, Reebok had a greater market share than did Nike. That lasted until Nike regained top spot with its Air Jordan line of shoes.

Fireman has answered with professional athlete sponsors for Reebok, including Michael Chang, Emmett Smith, and Shaquille O'Neal. The war is on.

Questions

1. What decisions did Nike's management make that helped lead to its success?

2. By the late 1980s, Nike had missed a large part of the market and had given Reebok the opportunity to overtake it. How did poor decision making lead to Nike's reduced market share? Do you think that uncertainty played a role in Nike's decisions?

3. Now that Nike has regained preeminence in the athletic shoe and apparel market, what do you think Reebok could do to surpass Nike?

NIKE
www.nike.com

Transat AT Inc.

Transat has always followed a growth strategy of acquiring poorly managed companies, bringing them into the fold, and turning them around. According to Transat's CEO Jean-Marc Eustache, "Internal growth takes too long, and buying a company that is doing very well is too expensive. All our acquisitions have been opportunities—cheap, but not doing well." This strategy has thus far worked wonders for the Montreal-based tour operator, which has become Canada's leading tour operator (but only slightly ahead of the other two major players in the Canadian market—Sunquest Vacations and First Choice Holidays—both Toronto-based but now British-owned).

Consolidation of the global industry, as mentioned in the video, is occurring at a rapid pace. When Eustache mentioned in the *Venture* program that he would like to be one of the five or six biggest operators worldwide in the next couple of years, he was speaking about an imperative situation for Transat. Industry experts believe that by the year 2001 there will only be six companies dominating the global industry. This means that Transat will have to doggedly pursue its acquisition strategy and international expansion in order to compete. At its present level, Transat will not remain large enough to fend off competition, will be squeezed out of market share, and will eventually be bought out. The bigger operators can command the best deals from hotels and resorts, and take precedence over smaller operations that often find they cannot book rooms.

Transat's operations to date have been very profitable, mainly due to the fact that the company originally modelled itself after European companies that combine many facets of the travel industry into one organization. Transat controls seven major tour operators and 321 travel agencies, along with a fleet of 17 planes. Since Transat does not have to operate regular flight schedules like, for example, Air Canada, the company does not have to deal with flying when underbooked. The vacation packages guarantee that seats will be filled, and Transat has the ability to determine how many, and which, of its aircraft it will use. (This is important because with a mix of new and old planes, Transat can keep its new ones constantly operational to make them profitable. The debt load of a Boeing 757 sitting in a hanger can bleed cash quickly—just ask Canadian Airlines.) Air Transat, the company's airline, boasts an average seat occupancy of more than 90 per cent throughout the year, far above any of the other Canadian airlines.

But Transat's acquisition of Look Voyages SA in France has been Transat's first major stumbling block. The takeover looked like a brilliant opportunity to further the company's aims of having its business equally divided among Canada, France, and the U.K. (currently the numbers are 68 per cent/27 per cent/5 per cent). But Look turned out to be in much worse financial shape than Transat originally believed. The turn-around of this company could take a while, and Transat's expansion strategy cannot afford to lose time. As for the move into the U.K., Transat still has not found a suitable acquisition. An alternative way to gain a hold on this market may have to be a strategic alliance. It will be interesting to see what happens with Transat's operations in the coming years.

Questions

1. Using bounded rationality, how do you think Transat should deal with its current situation?

2. What are the programmed decisions in this industry? What are the nonprogrammed ones?

3. How might decision making at Transat differ from decision making at, say, a tour operator in France?

Video Resource: "Transat Air," _Venture_ 634 (March 16, 1997).

Additional Sources: Luis Millan, "If It Ain't Broke, Don't Buy It," _Canadian Business_, October 10, 1997, pp. 6-41; Julie Balow, "Spreading Its Wings," _Report on Business Magazine_, February 1997, pp. 8-52.

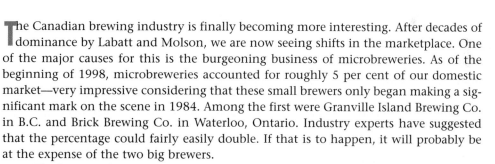

Canadian Microbreweries

The Canadian brewing industry is finally becoming more interesting. After decades of dominance by Labatt and Molson, we are now seeing shifts in the marketplace. One of the major causes for this is the burgeoning business of microbreweries. As of the beginning of 1998, microbreweries accounted for roughly 5 per cent of our domestic market—very impressive considering that these small brewers only began making a significant mark on the scene in 1984. Among the first were Granville Island Brewing Co. in B.C. and Brick Brewing Co. in Waterloo, Ontario. Industry experts have suggested that the percentage could fairly easily double. If that is to happen, it will probably be at the expense of the two big brewers.

The beer market in Canada is experiencing new competition from three distinct areas. First, there is the growth of the microbreweries. Second, free trade with the U.S. has allowed American imports, such as Stroh, which have made significant inroads into Ontario and Quebec, offering a cheaper alternative than domestic brands. Third, the brew-it-yourself industry is growing at a rapid pace. In B.C., for example, the Western Brewers Association estimates that u-brews account for 10 per cent of the provincial market. (This may well be an exaggeration, since B.C. breweries are trying to have controls placed on this industry, which it deems to have an unfair advantage.) John Sleeman has said that if the rules governing u-brews are not tightened (currently, u-brews are charged lower taxes), he will look into getting into the business himself.

The industry changes can be seen in the new ways Molson and Labatt are fighting for market share. "Generally, there was an unwritten code among brewers not to do anything to disparage each other in terms of their products," says Rick Knudson, now managing director at Okanagan Spring Brewery in B.C. This "agreement" seems, in the new industry climate, to have been thrown out the window by the Big Two. Molson attacked Labatt's Kokanee brand in full-page newspaper ads, declaring that Labatt's attempts to market Kokanee as a B.C. brew were misleading (it is made in Ontario—prompting Molson's slogan, B.C. or B.S.?). This sort of behaviour hints at some nervous desperation between the Big Two (who still control 90 per cent of the domestic market). Such marketing attacks have not occurred among the microbreweries, who perhaps do not wish to tempt the wrath of Molson and Labatt. For now these small independents are content in the knowledge that taste is on their side.

The question is, How far can the micros go in their fight for domestic market share? Sleeman's believes that it can carve out a significant amount of the market for itself, but many Canadian micros believe that the most profitable course of action is to take their product south. Unibroue Inc. of Chambly, Que., Big Rock of Calgary, Moosehead in N.S., and Upper Canada Brewing and Niagara Falls Brewing, both of Ontario, are all putting heavy focus on the U.S. market. While *Venture* mentioned the daunting figure of 400 microbreweries in the U.S. (there are about 75 in Canada), it didn't take into consideration the fact that there are only two-thirds as many *per capita* in the U.S., thus seemingly leaving a large market untapped.

Questions

1. What advantages would a microbrewery have in terms of differences between mechanic and organic organizations?

2. How would environment affect structure for a microbrewer such as McAuslan in Montreal, makers of St. Ambroise and other brands?

3. What problems might Sleeman's Brewery of Guelph, Ont., have regarding span of control, considering the fact that they have recently purchased Okanagan Spring Brewery in B.C., and are considering opening a production facility in Quebec? Also take into consideration the company's national expansion aims.

Video Resource: "Micro Brew," *Venture* 595 (June 16, 1996).

Additional Sources: Peter Morton, "More Trouble Brewing: Beer Wars Continue," *The Financial Post*, October 4, 1997, p. 16; Peter Boisseau, "The Suds Stud," *Canadian Business*, July 1997, pp. 36-43; Stephen Beaumont, "A Little Beer Goes a Long Way," *Canadian Business*, July 1996, pp. 54-57; John Schofield, "Stirring Up a Batch of Trouble," *Maclean's*, February 17, 1997, p. 54.

chapter 6

Foundations of Organizing

Learning Objectives

What will I be able to do after I finish this chapter?

1 • Define organization structure.

2 • Identify the advantages and disadvantages of division of labour.

3 • Contrast power with authority.

4 • Explain why wider spans of control are related to increased efficiency.

5 • Identify the five different ways by which management can departmentalize.

6 • Contrast mechanistic and organic organizations.

7 • Explain the strategy-determines-structure thesis.

8 • Summarize the effect of size on structure.

9 • Explain the effect of technology on structure.

10 • Describe how environmental uncertainty affects structure.

f you look in *Report on Business Magazine*'s list of top private companies in Canada, you will invariably find Asea Brown Boveri. R.O.B.'s 1997 report had ABB's annual revenue listed at $592 million. Nothing to scoff at, certainly, but ABB's Canadian operations are just a small part of this $30-billion international company whose worldwide operations span 140 countries. Headquartered in Zurich, Switzerland, Percy Barnevik is in charge of running this world leader in high-speed trains, robotics, and environmental control.[1]

ABB was formed in 1988 through a merger of Asea, a Swedish engineering group, with Brown Boveri, a Swiss competitor. As CEO of the newly created organization, Percy has inherited a company that had nearly 210,000 employees—some 2,000 being part of the headquarters staff. One of Barnevik's first challenges was to organize this giant to meet its strategic goal of becoming a world-class operation. Here's what he did.

First, Barnevik cut the headquarters staff from 2,000 to 176 people. In doing so he decentralized decision making down to the operating levels. He then divided the organization into 1,300 separate companies, each focusing on a particular customer and market. And he continues to refine these units; he has sold or consolidated 300 of the less profitable ones. But probably his most innovative idea was to introduce a dual chain of command. Barnevik recognizes that "globalization requires a global organization." ABB has approximately 100 managers who run their operations with a local board of directors. Most of these managers are citizens of the country in which they work. In addition, there are about 60 global managers who are organized into eight segments, in such areas as financial services; trans-

portation; process automation and engineering; electrical equipment; and three electric power businesses of power generation, transportation, and distribution. This structure makes it easier for "local" managers to capitalize on information and other technologies from different countries, and transport these "best practices" to various parts of the organization.

Have Percy Barnevik's actions been successful? By most accounts, the answer is yes. Through reorganization, ABB has improved customer service measures by 50 per cent and has reduced cycle times for producing products. ABB has also been recognized by *The Financial Times* as the most admired company in Europe. But Barnevik isn't done. What has occurred to date reflects the dynamic environment of ABB. Tomorrow, however, may require more changes and different directions. As technology improves, it will directly affect ABB's business. Therefore, Percy Barnevik is keeping the organization fluid in an effort to remain competitive.

Percy Barnevik understands the challenges organizations face today in their efforts to become and remain competitive.

ASEA BROWN
BOVERI
www.abb.com/

What Is Organization Structure?

Organization structure describes the organization's framework. Just as human beings have skeletons that define their shapes, organizations have structures that define theirs. An organization's structure can be dissected into three parts: complexity, formalization, and centralization.[2] We have briefly described each in Exhibit 6-1.

When managers construct or change an organization's structure, they are engaged in organization design. When we discuss managers making structural decisions—for example, determining the level at which decisions should be made or the number of standardized rules for employees to follow—we are referring to organization design. In the next chapter, we'll show how the three components of an organization—its complexity, formalization, and centralization—can be mixed and matched to create various organization designs.

organization structure
An organization's framework as expressed by its degree of complexity, formalization, and centralization.

Basic Organization Design Concepts

The classical concepts of organization design were formulated by management writers in the early years of this century (see Details on a Management Classic). These classical theorists offered a set of principles for managers to follow in organization design. More than six decades have passed since most of these principles were originally proposed. Given the passing of that much time and all the changes that have taken place in our society, you might think that these principles would be fairly worthless today. Surprisingly, they're not—although they may not be in place as strongly as they were in the 1930s. Nonetheless, for the most part, they still provide valuable insights into designing effective and efficient organizations. Of course, we have also gained a great deal of knowledge over the years as to the limitations of these principles.

We'll discuss the five basic classical principles that have guided organization design decisions over the years. We'll also present an updated analysis of how each has had to be modified to reflect the increasing sophistication and changing nature of organizational activities.

**Exhibit 6-1
Characteristics of
Organizational
Structure**

Complexity:	The amount of horizontal, vertical, and spatial differentiation that exists in an organization. The degree of complexity is a function of the extent to which activities are divided horizontally into separate departments (like accounting and marketing), the number of vertical layers in an organization (such as president, senior vice-president, vice-president, director, department manager, unit manager, supervisor), or the geographic dispersement of organizational activities (such as one located in Moncton, New Brunswick, and Saskatoon, Saskatchewan).
Formalization:	Formalization refers to the degree to which an organization relies on rules and procedures to direct the behaviour of employees.
Centralization:	Refers to the location where decisions are made. Centralized decisions are made by top management. Decentralized decisions are made by the level of individual closest to the problem.

DETAILS ON A MANAGEMENT CLASSIC

Max Weber and the Ideal Structure: Bureaucracy

The central theme in Weber's bureaucratic model is standardization.[3] The behaviour of people in bureaucracies is predetermined by the standardized structure and processes. The model itself can be dissected into three groups of characteristics—those that relate to the structure and function of the organization, those that deal with means of rewarding effort, and those that deal with protection for individual members.

Weber's model stipulates a hierarchy of offices, with each office under the direction of a higher one. Each of these offices is differentiated horizontally by division of labour. This division of labour creates units of expertise, defines areas of action consistent with competence of unit members, assigns responsibilities for carrying out these actions, and allocates commensurate authority to fulfil these responsibilities. All the while, written rules govern the performance of members' duties. This imposition of structure and functions provides a high level of specialized expertise, coordination of roles, and control of group members through standardization.

The second group of characteristics in Weber's model relates to rewards. Members receive salaries in relation to their rank in the organization. Promotions are based on objective criteria such as seniority or achievement. Since members are not owners, it is important that there be a clear separation of their private affairs and property from the organization's property and affairs. It is further expected that commitment to the organization is paramount, the position in the organization being the employee's sole occupation.

Finally, Weber's model seeks to protect the rights of individuals. In return for a career commitment, members receive protection from arbitrary actions by employers, clear knowledge of their responsibilities and the amount of authority their boss holds, and the ability to appeal decisions that they see as unfair or outside the parameters of their boss's authority.

Weber believed that organizations that were structured around these three sets of characteristics would be more rational and efficient. Career advancement would be based on individual qualifications as opposed to favouritism. Employee commitment would be maximized and conflicts of interest would be eliminated by providing lifetime employment and separating employees' off-the-job roles from those required to fulfil organizational goals.▼

What Is Division of Labour?

division of labour
The breakdown of jobs into narrow, repetitive tasks.

As envisioned by classical management writers, **division of labour** means that rather than an entire job being done by one individual, it is broken down into a number of steps—each step being completed by a separate individual. In essence, individuals specialize in doing part of an activity rather than the entire activity. Assembly line production, in which each worker does the same standardized task over and over again, is an example of division of labour.

Division of labour makes efficient use of the diversity of skills that workers hold. In most organizations, some tasks require highly developed skills; others can be performed by the untrained. If all workers were engaged in each step of, say, an organization's manufacturing process, all would have to have the skills necessary to perform both the most demanding and the least demanding jobs. The result would be that except when performing the most highly skilled or highly sophisticated tasks, employees would be working below their skill level. Because skilled workers are paid more than are unskilled workers and their wages tend to reflect their highest level of skill, it represents an inefficient use of resources to have highly skilled workers do easy tasks.

The classical writers viewed division of labour as an unending source of increased productivity. At the turn of the twentieth century and earlier, this generalization was undoubtedly accurate. Because specialization was not widely practised, its introduction almost always generated higher productivity. But a good thing can be carried too far. There is a point at which the human diseconomies from division of labour—which surface as boredom, fatigue, stress, low productivity, poor quality work, increased absenteeism, and high turnover—exceed the economic advantages (see Exhibit 6-2).

We see the results of division of labour in operating rooms. In this environment, doctors, nurses, and other medical professionals each perform a precise and repetitive set of tasks.

By the 1960s, that point had been reached in a number of jobs. In such cases, productivity could be increased by enlarging, rather than narrowing, the scope of job activities.[4] For instance, in the next chapter, we'll discuss successful efforts to increase productivity by giving employees a variety of activities to do, allowing them to do a whole and complete piece of work, and putting them together into teams. Each of these ideas, of course, runs counter to the division of labour concept. Yet, overall, the division of labour concept is alive and well in most orga-

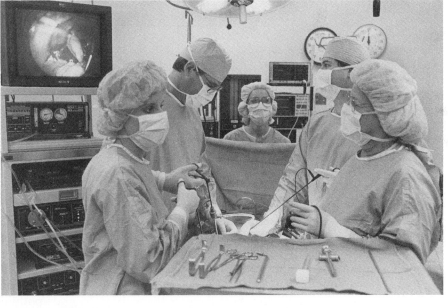

nizations today. We have to recognize the economies it provides in certain types of jobs, but we also have to recognize its limitations.

What Is the Unity of Command?

The classical writers professing the **unity of command** principle argued that a subordinate should have one and only one superior to whom she is directly responsible. No person should report to two or more bosses. Otherwise, an employee might have to cope with conflicting demands or priorities from several superiors. In those rare instances when the unity of command principle had to be violated, the classical viewpoint always explicitly designated that there be a clear separation of activities and a supervisor responsible for each.

unity of command
The principle that a subordinate should have one and only one superior to whom she is directly responsible.

**Exhibit 6-2
Economies and
Diseconomies of
Division of Labour**

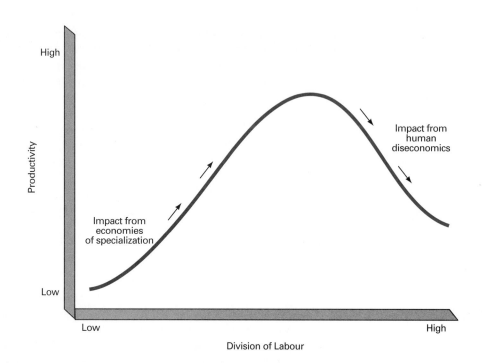

High

Productivity

Impact from
human
diseconomics

Impact from
economies
of specialization

Low

Low

High

Division of Labour

authority
The rights, inherent in a
managerial position, to
give orders and expect
them to be obeyed.

**Army drill instructors
exemplify individuals
who give orders and
expect the orders to
be obeyed. This drill
sergeant's emphasis
is on accomplishing
tasks. The recruits'
emphasis is on
accepting authority
figures.**

   The unity of command concept was logical when organizations were comparatively simple. Under most circumstances it is still sound advice, and most contemporary organizations closely adhere to this principle. Yet there are instances, which we'll introduce in the next chapter, when strict adherence to the unity of command creates a degree of inflexibility that hinders an organization's performance.[5]

What Is Authority and Responsibility?

Authority refers to the rights, inherent in a managerial position, to give orders and expect the orders to be obeyed. Authority was a major tenet of the classical writers; it was viewed as the glue that held the organization together. It was to be delegated downward to subordinate managers, giving them certain rights while providing certain prescribed limits within which to operate (see Details on a Management Classic). Each management position has specific inherent rights that incumbents acquire from the position's rank or title. Authority, therefore, relates to one's position within an organization and ignores the personal characteristics of the individual manager. It has nothing directly to do with the individual. The expression, "The king is dead; long live the king," illustrates the concept. Whoever is king acquires the rights inherent in the king's position. When a position of authority is vacated, the person who has left the position no longer has any authority. The authority remains with the position and its incumbent.

DETAILS ON A MANAGEMENT CLASSIC

Stanley Milgram and Following Orders

Stanley Milgram, a social psychologist at Yale University, wondered how far individuals would go in following orders.[6] If subjects were placed in the role of a teacher in a learning experiment and told by the experimenter to administer a shock to a learner each time that learner made a mistake, would the subjects follow the commands of the experimenter? Would their willingness to comply decrease as the intensity of the shock was increased?

To test these hypotheses, Milgram hired a set of subjects. Each was led to believe that the experiment was to investigate the effect of punishment on memory. Their job was to act as teachers and administer punishment whenever the learner made a mistake on a learning test. Punishment in this case was administered by electric shock. The subject sat in front of a shock generator with 30 levels of shock; beginning at zero and progressing in 15-volt increments to a high of 450 volts. The demarcations of these positions ranged from "slight shock" at 15 volts to "danger: severe shock" at 450 volts. And to add realism to the experiment, the subjects received a sample shock of 45 volts and saw the learner strapped in an electric chair in an adjacent room. Of course, the learner was an actor, and the electric shocks were phoney—but the subjects didn't know this.

The subjects were instructed to shock the learner each time he made a mistake. And subsequent mistakes would result in an increase in shock intensity. Throughout the experiment, the subject got verbal feedback from the learner. At 75 volts, the learner began to grunt and moan; at 150 volts, he demanded to be released from the experiment; at 180 volts he cried out that he could no longer stand the pain; and at 300 volts, he insisted he be let out because of a heart condition. After 300 volts, the learner did not respond to further questions.

Most subjects protested and, fearful they might kill the learner if the increased shocks were to bring on a heart attack, insisted they could not go on. But the experimenter responded by saying that they had to, that was their job. The majority of the subjects dissented. But dissension isn't synonymous with disobedience. Sixty-two per cent of the subjects increased the shock level to the maximum of 450 volts. The average level of shock administered by the remaining 38 per cent was nearly 370 volts—more than enough to kill even the strongest human.

What can we conclude from Milgram's results? Well, one obvious conclusion is that authority is a potent source of getting people to do things. Subjects in Milgram's experiment administered levels of shock far above that which they wanted to—but they did it because they were told they had to do so. And that's in spite of the fact that they could have voluntarily walked out of the room at any time.▼

When we delegate authority, we must allocate commensurate **responsibility**. That is, when one is given "rights," one also assumes a corresponding "obligation" to perform. Allocating authority without responsibility creates opportunities for abuse, and no one should be held responsible for something over which he has no authority.

responsibility
An obligation to perform assigned activities.

line authority
The authority that entitles a manager to direct the work of an employee.

chain of command
The flow of authority from the top to the bottom of an organization.

staff authority
Authority that supports, assists, and advises holders of line authority.

Are There Different Types of Authority Relationships? The classical writers distinguished between two forms of authority relations: line authority and staff authority. **Line authority** is the authority that entitles a manager to direct the work of an employee. It is the employer-employee authority relationship that extends from the top of the organization to the lowest echelon, following what is called the **chain of command**. This is shown in Exhibit 6-3. As a link in the chain of command, a manager with line authority has the right to direct the work of employees and to make certain decisions without consulting others. Of course, in the chain of command, every manager is also subject to the direction of her supervisor.

Sometimes the term line is used to differentiate line managers from staff managers. In this context, line emphasizes managers whose organizational function contributes directly to the achievement of organizational objectives. In a manufacturing firm, line managers are typically in the production and sales functions, whereas managers in human resources management and accounting are considered staff managers. But whether a manager's function is classified as line or staff depends on the organization's objectives. For example, at Drake Personnel Services, a supplier of temporary employees, interviewers have a line function. Similarly, at the accounting firm of Price Waterhouse, accounting is a line function.

As organizations get larger and more complex, line managers find that they do not have the time, expertise, or resources to get their jobs done effectively. In response, they create **staff authority** functions to support, assist, advise, and generally reduce some of the informational burdens they have. The hospital administrator can't effectively handle all the purchasing of supplies that the hospital needs, so she creates a

Exhibit 6-3
The Chain of Command

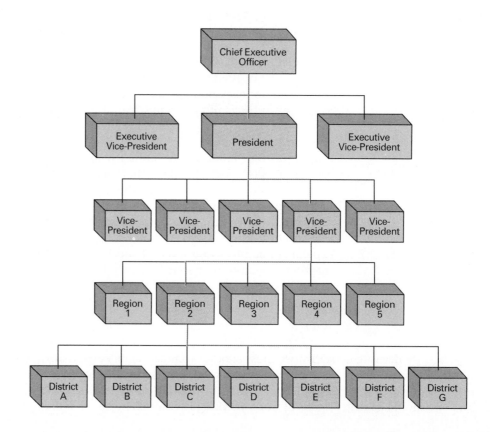

purchasing department. The purchasing department is a staff department. Of course, the head of the purchasing department has line authority over her subordinate purchasing agents. The hospital administrator might also find that she is overburdened and needs an assistant. In creating the position of assistant to the hospital administrator, she has created a staff position. Exhibit 6-4 illustrates line and staff authority.

How Is the Contemporary View of Authority and Responsibility Different from the Classical View? The classical writers were enamoured with authority. They actively assumed that the rights inherent in one's formal position in an organization were the sole source of influence. They believed that managers were all-powerful. This might have been true 60 or more years ago. Organizations were simpler. Staff was less important. Managers were only minimally dependent on technical specialists. Under such conditions, influence is the same as authority; and the higher a manager's position in the organization, the more influence he had. However, those conditions no longer hold. Researchers and practitioners of management now recognize that you don't have to be a manager to have power, nor is power perfectly correlated to one's level in the organization. Authority is an important concept in organizations, but an exclusive focus on authority produces a narrow, unrealistic view of its influence. Today, we recognize that authority is but one element in the larger concept of power.[7]

How Do Authority and Power Differ? The terms authority and power are frequently confused. Authority is a right, the legitimacy of which is based on the authority figure's position in the organization. Authority goes with the job. **Power**, on the other hand, refers to an individual's capacity to influence decisions. Authority is part of the larger concept of power. That is, the formal rights that come with an individual's position in the organization are just one means by which an individual can affect the decision process.

power
The capacity to influence decisions.

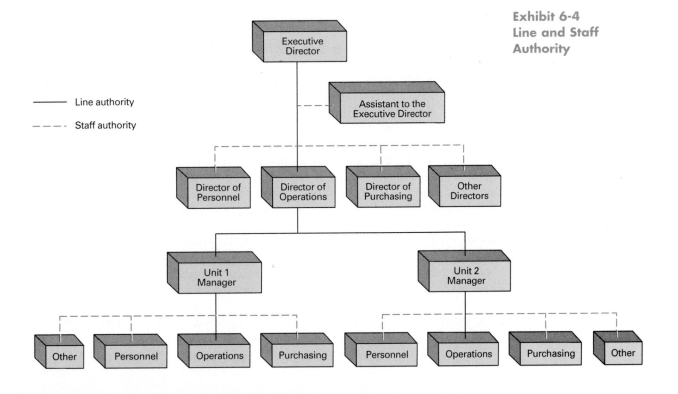

**Exhibit 6-4
Line and Staff
Authority**

ETHICAL DILEMMAS IN MANAGEMENT

▼

SHOULD YOU FOLLOW ORDERS WITH WHICH YOU DON'T AGREE?

▲

A few years back, a study of business executives revealed that most had obeyed orders that they had found personally objectionable or unethical.[8] Far more thought-provoking was a survey taken among the public in the U.S. near the end of the Vietnam War. In spite of public dismay over the actions of some military personnel during that war, about half the respondents said that they would have shot civilian men, women, and children in cold blood if they had been ordered to do so by their commanding officer.[9]

If you were asked to follow orders that you believed were unconscionable, would you comply? For example, what if your boss asked you to destroy evidence that he had been stealing a great deal of money from the organization?

What if you merely disagreed with the orders? For instance, what if your boss asked you to bring her coffee each morning even though no such task is included in your job description? What would you do?

Exhibit 6-5 visually depicts the difference between authority and power. The two-dimensional arrangement of boxes in Part A portrays authority. The area in which the authority applies is defined by the horizontal dimension. Each horizontal grouping represents a functional area. The influence one holds in the organization is defined by the vertical dimension in the structure. The higher one is in the organization, the greater one's authority.

Power, on the other hand, is a three-dimensional concept (see the cone in Part B of Exhibit 6-5). It includes not only the functional and hierarchical dimensions, but also a third dimension called centrality. While authority is defined by one's vertical position in the hierarchy, power is made up of both one's vertical position and one's distance from the organization's power core, or centre.

Think of the cone in Exhibit 6-5 as being an organization. The centre of the cone is the power core. The closer you are to the power core, the more influence you have on decisions. The existence of a power core is, in fact, the only difference between A and B in Exhibit 6-5. The vertical hierarchy dimension in A is merely one's level on the outer edge of the cone. The top of the cone corresponds to the top of the hierarchy, the middle of the cone to the middle of the hierarchy, and so on. Similarly, the functional groups in A become wedges in the cone. Each wedge represents a functional area.

The cone analogy explicitly acknowledges two facts: (1) the higher one moves in an organization (an increase in authority), the closer one moves to the power core; and (2) it is not necessary to have authority in order to wield power, because one can move horizontally inward toward the power core without moving up.

Have you ever noticed that company secretaries usually have a great deal of power, even though they have little authority? As gatekeepers for their bosses, secretaries have considerable say over whom their bosses see, and when. Furthermore, because they are regularly relied upon to pass information on to their bosses, they have some control over what their bosses hear. It's not unusual for $75,000-a-year middle managers to tread very carefully in order not to upset their boss's $25,000-a-year secretary. Why? Because the secretary has power! The secretary may be low in the authority hierarchy but close to the power core. Low-ranking employees who have relatives, friends, or associates in high places might also be close to the power core. So,

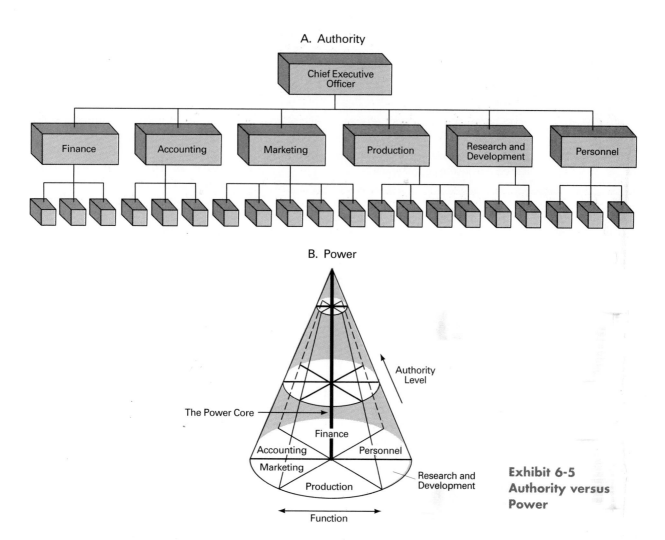

**Exhibit 6-5
Authority versus
Power**

too, are employees with scarce and important skills. The lowly production engineer with 20 years of experience in a company might be the only one in the firm who knows the inner workings of all the old production machinery. When pieces of this old equipment break down, no one but this engineer understands how to fix them. Suddenly, the engineer's influence is much greater than it would appear from his level in the vertical hierarchy. So what does this tell us about power? It states that power can come from different areas (see Developing Management Skills). John French and Bertram Raven have identified five sources or bases of power: coercive, reward, legitimate, expert, and referent.[10] We have summarized them in Exhibit 6-6.

What Is the Span of Control?

How many employees can a manager efficiently and effectively direct? This question of **span of control** received a great deal of attention from early writers. While there was no consensus on a specific number, the classical writers favoured small spans—typically no more than six—in order to maintain close control.[11] However, several writers did acknowledge level in the organization as a contingency variable. They

span of control
The number of subordinates a manager can direct efficiently and effectively.

Coercive Power:	Power that is dependent on fear.
Reward Power:	Power based on the ability to distribute anything that others may value.
Legitimate Power:	Power based on one's position in the formal hierarchy.
Expert Power:	Power based on one's expertise, special skill, or knowledge.
Referent Power:	Power based on identification with a person who has desirable resources or personal traits.

Exhibit 6-6
Types of Power

argued that as a manager rises in an organization, she has to deal with a greater number of ill-structured problems, so top managers need a smaller span than do middle managers, and middle managers require a smaller span than do supervisors.

Why Is the Span of Control Concept Important? The span of control concept is important because, to a large degree, it determines the number of levels and managers an organization has. All things being equal, the wider or larger the span, the more efficient the organization design.

How Does the Contemporary View of Span of Control Differ from the Classical View? In 1992, Wal-Mart surpassed Sears as the number-one retailer in the United States. Management writer Tom Peters predicted this result a few years earlier: "Sears doesn't have a chance," he said. "A twelve-layer company can't compete with a three-layer company."[12] Peters might have exaggerated the point a bit, but it clearly reflects the fact that in recent years the pendulum has swung toward designing flat structures with wide spans of control. The Canadian telephone companies are experiencing really strong competitive pressure and many are having trouble adjusting rapidly because of the inflexibility of their multilevel structures.

More organizations are increasing their spans of control. The span for managers at such companies as General Electric and Reynolds Metals has expanded to 10 or 12 subordinates—twice the number of 15 years ago.[13] The span of control is increasingly being determined by looking at contingency variables. It's obvious that the more

DEVELOPING MANAGEMENT SKILLS

▼ BUILDING A POWER BASE ▲

▶ **1. Gain control over organizational resources that are scarce and important.** In doing so, you generate expert and referent power.

▶ **2. Make yourself appear indispensable.** It's difficult to remove someone who is seen as critical to an operation's success.

▶ **3. Be visible.** By maintaining a high profile and being available, you aid in developing an appearance of being indispensable.

▶ **4. Develop powerful allies.** Powerful allies in the organization can provide you with important information and also help protect you from attacks by others.

▶ **5. Avoid tainted members.** Carefully keep your distance from organizational members whose status is questionable.

Don't be judged by the company you keep. Given the reality that effectiveness has a large subjective component, your own effectiveness might be called into question if you are perceived as being too closely associated with tainted people.

▶ **6. Support your boss.** Your immediate future is in the hands of your current boss. Since he evaluates your performance, you will typically want to do whatever is necessary to have your boss on your side. Make every effort to help your boss succeed.

training and experience employees have, the less direct supervision they need. Managers who have well-trained and experienced employees can function with a wider span. Other contingency variables that will determine the appropriate span include similarity of subordinate tasks, the complexity of those tasks, the physical proximity of subordinates, the degree to which standardized procedures are in place, the sophistication of the organization's management information system, the strength of the organization's culture, and the preferred style of the manager.[14]

YOUNG CANADIANS

Phil and Richard Smart

Phil and Richard Smart sold their Burlington, Ontario-based software company for millions before either of the brothers had reached 30. By selling to a large company, the Smarts' products will reach new markets worldwide, and the administrative growing pains will be taken care of—leaving the pair to focus on product development. The company that purchased the Smarts' company is Symix Systems Inc. of Columbus, Ohio. The Smart brothers' company had been called Visual Applications Software Inc.

Can You Identify the Five Ways to Departmentalize?

The classical writers argued that activities in the organization should be specialized and grouped into departments. Division of labour creates specialists who need coordination. This coordination is facilitated by putting specialists together in departments under the direction of a manager. Creation of these departments is typically based on the work functions being performed, the product or service being offered, the target customer or client, the geographic territory being covered, or the process being used to turn inputs into outputs. No single method of departmentalization was advocated by the classical writers. The method or methods used should reflect the grouping that would best contribute to the attainment of the organization's objectives and the goals of individual units.

What Do the Five Departmentalizations Look Like? One of the most popular ways to group activities is by functions performed, or **functional departmentalization**. A manufacturing manager might organize her plant by separating engineering, accounting, manufacturing, personnel, and purchasing specialists into common departments (see Exhibit 6-7). Functional departmentalization can be used in all types of organizations. Only the functions change to reflect the organization's objectives and activities. A hospital might have departments devoted to research, patient care, accounting, and so forth. A professional baseball franchise might have departments labelled player personnel, ticket sales, and travel and accommodations.

functional departmentalization Grouping activities by functions performed.

Exhibit 6-7
Functional
Departmentalization

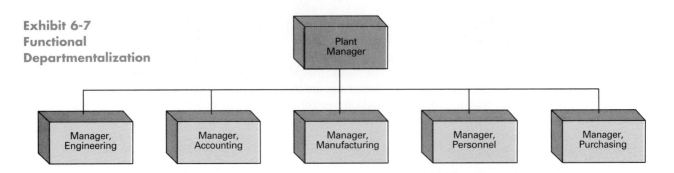

product departmentalization
Grouping activities by product line.

Exhibit 6-8 illustrates the **product departmentalization** method used at Sun Petroleum Products. Each major product area in the corporation is placed under the authority of a vice-president who is a specialist in, and is responsible for, everything having to do with his product line. Notice, for example, in contrast to functional departmentalization, that manufacturing and other major activities have been divided up to give the product managers (vice-presidents, in this case) considerable autonomy and control. If an organization's activities are service-related rather than product-related, each service would be autonomously grouped. For instance, an accounting firm would have departments for tax, management consulting, auditing, and the like. Each offers a common array of services under the direction of a product or service manager.

Exhibit 6-8   Product Departmentalization

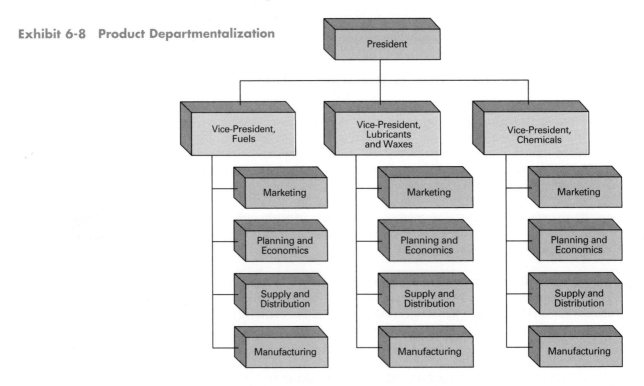

The particular type of customer the organization seeks to reach can also be used to group employees. The sales activities in an office-supply firm, for instance, can be broken down into three departments to serve retail, wholesale, and government customers (see Exhibit 6-9). A large law office can segment its staff on the basis of whether it serves corporate or individual clients. The assumption underlying **customer departmentalization** is that customers in each department have a common set of problems and needs that can best be met by having specialists for each.

Another way to departmentalize is on the basis of geography or territory—**geographic departmentalization**. The sales function might have western, southern, midwestern, and eastern regions (see Exhibit 6-10). A large school district might have six high schools to provide for each of the major geographic territories within the district. If an organization's customers are scattered over a large geographic area, this form of departmentalization can be valuable.

customer departmentalization
Grouping activities on the basis of common customers.

geographic departmentalization
Grouping activities on the basis of territory.

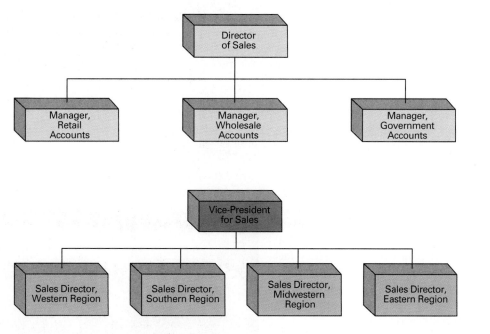

Exhibit 6-9
Customer
Departmentalization

Exhibit 6-10
Geographic
Departmentalization

Exhibit 6-11
Process
Departmentalization

Exhibit 6-11 represents an example of **process departmentalization** by depicting the various departments in a motor vehicle department. If you have ever been to a motor vehicle office to get a driver's licence, you probably went through several departments before receiving your licence. In some areas, applicants must go through three steps, each handled by a separate department: (1) validation, by the motor vehicles division; (2) processing, by the licensing department; and (3) payment collection, by the treasury department.

How Does the Contemporary View of Departmentalization Differ from the Classical View? Most large organizations continue to use most or all of the departmental groups suggested by the classical writers. Black & Decker, for instance, organizes each of its divisions along functional lines, organizes its manufacturing units around processes, departmentalizes sales around geographic regions, and divides

process departmentalization
Grouping activities on the basis of product or customer flow.

each sales region into customer groupings. But a recent trend needs to be mentioned. That is, rigid departmentalization is being complemented by the use of teams that cross over traditional departmental lines.

Today's competitive environment has refocused the attention of management on its customers. To better monitor the needs of customers and to be able to respond to changes in those needs, many organizations have given greater emphasis to customer departmentalization. Xerox, for example, has eliminated its corporate marketing staff and placed marketing specialists out in the field.[15] This allows the company to better identify its customers and to respond faster to their requirements.

We are also seeing a great deal more use of teams today as a device for accomplishing organizational objectives. Some of the organizations using cross-departmental teams include Ford, Imperial Oil, Rubbermaid, most large Canadian hospitals, and a number of government departments. As tasks have become more complex and as more diverse skills are needed to accomplish these tasks, management has increasingly introduced the use of teams and task forces.

The Contingency Approach to Organization Design

If we combine the classical principles, we arrive at what most of the early writers believed to be the ideal structural design: the mechanistic or bureaucratic organization. Today

we recognize that there is no single "ideal" organization design for all situations. Rather, the ideal organization design depends on contingency factors. In this section, we'll look at two generic models of organization design and then look at the contingency factors that favour each.

How Is a Mechanistic Organization Different from an Organic Organization?

mechanistic organization
A structure that is high in complexity, formalization, and centralization (bureaucracy).

bureaucracy
A form of organization marked by division of labour, hierarchy, rules and regulations, and impersonal relationships (mechanistic).

Exhibit 6-12 describes two diverse organizational forms.[16] The **mechanistic organization** (or **bureaucracy**) was the natural result of combining the classical principles. Adherence to the unity of command principle ensured the existence of a formal hierarchy of authority, with each person controlled and supervised by one superior. Keeping the span of control small at increasingly higher levels in the organization cre-

What can happen to a company that offers early retirement to reduce the number of employees, and twice as many people as expected opt to retire? Texas Instruments created work teams among the remaining employees. These teams have helped the company increase sales per employee from $88,300 in 1989 to $122,820 in 1992.

ated tall, impersonal structures. As the distance between the top and the bottom of the organization expanded, top management would increasingly impose rules and regulations. Because top managers couldn't control lower-level activities through direct observation and ensure the use of standard practices, they substituted rules and regulations. The classical writers' belief in a high degree of division of labour created jobs that were simple, routine, and standardized. Further specialization through the use of departmentalization increased impersonality and the need for multiple layers of management to coordinate the specialized departments.

The **organic organization** (also referred to as an **adhocracy**) is a direct contrast to the mechanistic form. It is low in complexity, low in formalization, and decentralized. The organic organization is a highly adaptive form that is as loose and flexible as the mechanistic organization is rigid and stable. Rather than having standardized jobs and regulations, the adhocracy's loose structure allows it to change rapidly as needs require. Adhocracies have division of labour, but the jobs people do are not standardized. Employees tend to be professionals who are technically proficient and trained to handle diverse problems. They need very few formal rules and little direct supervision because their training has instilled in them standards of professional conduct. For instance, a computer engineer who is given an assignment doesn't need to be given procedures on how to do it. The engineer can solve most problems alone or after conferring with colleagues. Professional standards guide her behaviour. The organic organization is low in centralization in order for the professional to respond quickly to problems and because top management cannot be expected to possess the expertise to make the necessary decisions.

organic organization
A structure that is low in complexity, formalization, and centralization (adhocracy).

adhocracy
A structure that is low in complexity, formalization, and centralization (organic).

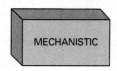

MECHANISTIC

ORGANIC

**Exhibit 6-12
Mechanistic
versus Organic
Organizations**

☐ Rigid hierarchical relationships

☐ Fixed duties

☐ High formalization

☐ Formalized communication channels

☐ Centralized decision authority

☐ Collaboration (both vertical and horizontal)

☐ Adaptable duties

☐ Low formalization

☐ Informal communication

☐ Decentralized decision authority

What Contingency Variables Affect Organization Design Options?

Several variables have been found to affect an organization's structure. The more popular of these are strategy, size, technology, and environment. Let's briefly look at each of these.

How Does Strategy Affect Structure? An organization's structure is a means to help management achieve its objectives. Since objectives are derived from the organization's overall strategy, it is only logical that strategy and structure should be closely linked. More specifically, structure should follow strategy. If management makes a significant change in its organization's strategy, it will need to modify structure to accommodate and support this change.

The first important research on the strategy-structure relationship was a study of close to 100 large U.S. companies conducted by Alfred Chandler.[17] After tracing the development of these organizations over a 50-year period, and compiling extensive case histories of companies such as du Pont, General Motors, Standard Oil of New Jersey, and Sears, Chandler concluded that changes in corporate strategy precede and lead to changes in an organization's structure. Specifically, he found that organizations usually begin with a single product or line. The simplicity of the strategy requires only a simple or loose form of structure to execute it. Decisions can be centralized in the hands of a single senior manager, while complexity and formalization will be low. As organizations grow, their strategies become more ambitious and elaborate.

From the single product line, companies often expand their activities within their industry by acquiring suppliers or selling their products directly to customers. Bombardier is a prime example of a Canadian company that has developed an organizational structure that meets the needs of its diverse production. This vertical integration strategy leads to increased interdependence between organizational units, and creates the need for a more complex coordination device. This is achieved by redesigning the structure to form specialized units based on functions performed. Finally, if growth proceeds further into product diversification, structure needs to be adjusted again to gain efficiency. A product diversification strategy demands a structural form that allows for the efficient allocation of resources, accountability for performance, and coordination between units. This can be achieved best by creating many independent divisions, each responsible for a specified product line.

Recent research has generally confirmed the strategy-structure relationship but has used the strategy terminology presented in Chapter 3.[18] For instance, organizations pursuing a differentiation strategy must innovate to survive. Unless they can maintain their uniqueness, they may lose their competitive advantage. An organic organization matches best with this strategy because it is flexible and maximizes adaptability. In contrast, a cost-leadership strategy seeks stability and efficiency. Stability and efficiency help to produce low-cost goods and services. This, then, can best be achieved with a mechanistic organization.

Bombardier's beginnings lay in the manufacturing of snowmobiles. Then in the early 1970s they began to produce subway and railway cars, and in the mid-1980s moved into the aerospace industry. Today all three sectors enjoy excellent profit.

YOUNG CANADIANS

Carolyn Farha:
Linda Lingerie Inc.

Carolyn Farha, president of Montreal's Linda Lingerie Inc., realized that her company was too dependent on one customer, and moved into new markets to lessen risk. This strategy proved to be timely: Eaton's filed for bankruptcy protection, leaving many suppliers with unpaid orders and uncertain futures.

How Does Organizational Size Affect Structure? There is considerable historical evidence that an organization's size significantly affects its structure.[19] For instance, large organizations—those typically employing 2,000 or more employees—tend to have more division of labour, horizontal and vertical differentiation, and rules and regulations than do small organizations. However, the relationship isn't linear. Rather, size affects structure at a decreasing rate. The impact of size becomes less important as an organization expands. Why is this? Essentially, once an organization has around 2,000 employees, it is already fairly mechanistic. An additional 500 employees will not have much impact. On the other hand, adding 500 employees to an organization that has only 300 members is likely to result in a shift toward a more mechanistic structure.

How Does Technology Affect Structure? Every organization uses some form of technology to convert its inputs into outputs. To attain its objectives, the organization uses equipment, materials, knowledge, and experienced individuals, and puts them together into certain types and patterns of activities. For instance, university instructors teach students by a variety of methods: formal lectures, group discussions, case analyses, programmed learning, and so forth. Each of these methods is a type of technology. Over the years, several studies regarding the effect of technology have been conducted.[20] For instance, in one study Joan Woodward found that distinct relationships exist between size of production runs and the structure of the firm. Additionally, she found that the effectiveness of the organizations was related to "fit" between technology and structure.[21] Most of these studies, like Woodward's, have focused on the processes or methods that transform inputs into outputs and how they differ by their degree of routineness. For example, mass production of steel and automobiles or refining petroleum is characteristic of routine technology. As such, with a more routine technology, the more standardized the structure can be. Conversely, Spar Aerospace's development of the Canadarm—the extending arm used by the

The Canadarm has been Canada's major contribution to the NASA space program. It is an extending arm that allows astronauts to manipulate objects outside the shuttle.

NASA space shuttles—would be indicative of a nonroutine technology. Since the technology is more nonroutine, the structure is more organic.[22]

How Does Environment Affect Structure? In Chapter 2, we introduced the organization's environment as a constraint on managerial discretion. Research has demonstrated that environment is also a major influence on structure.[23] Essentially, mechanistic organizations are most effective in stable environments. Organic organizations are best matched with dynamic and uncertain environments.

The evidence on the environment-structure relationship helps to explain why so many managers have restructured their organizations to be lean, fast, and flexible. Global competition, accelerated product innovation by all competitors, and increased demands from customers for higher quality and faster deliveries are examples of dynamic environmental forces. Mechanistic organizations tend to be ill-equipped to respond to rapid environmental change. As a result, we're seeing managers redesigning their organizations to make them more organic.

Organizational Structures Reflect Cultural Values

An organization's structure must adapt to its environment. Included in that environment is the national culture of the country in which the organization is located. Research confirms that organizations mirror, to a considerable degree, the cultural values of their host country.[25]

In a country with a high power distance rating, people prefer that decisions be centralized. Similarly, uncertainty avoidance relates to formalization. High uncertainty avoidance relates to high formalization. Based on these relationships, we find certain patterns. French and Italian managers tend to create rigid bureaucracies that are high in both centralization and formalization. Managers in India prefer centralization and low formalization. Germans prefer formalization with decentralization.

The extensive use of work teams in a country like Japan can also be explained in terms of national culture. Japan scores high on collectivism. In such a culture, employees prefer more organic organizations built around work teams. In contrast, employees in India—where power distance values are high—are likely to perform poorly in teams. They feel more comfortable working in mechanistic, authority-dominated structures.

A recent study of managers' perceptions of the "ideal" organization in the People's Republic of China (PRC) found preferences for structures that fit with their culture.[26] Executives in the PRC favoured high participation in their organizations. The researchers noted that this reflected the cultural value placed on allowing workers formal participation in the planning process as well as retaining some worker authority over the appointment and retention of managers. Managers in the PRC also have an aversion to conflict and a need to "save face," which fosters a mechanistic structure with clear lines of authority and unambiguous standard operating procedures. In addition, managers in the PRC were found to shun internal competition and individual risk-taking initiatives. This is consistent with traditional Chinese values of collective responsibility.

MANAGERS WHO MADE A DIFFERENCE

Terry McBride: Nettwerk Records

NETTWERK
RECORDS
www.nettwerk.com

Managing an independent record label has never been an easy occupation. Without the muscle of the large labels, independents have always had to gamble on acts the big companies wouldn't touch. It is a lot of work with little monetary reward—unless the dream materializes, and one of the label's acts starts selling records. I.R.S. eventually got a taste of success with R.E.M., but had to be satisfied with proceeds from record sales up to the album *Document*. With the band's breakthrough album *Green*, R.E.M. decided to go with Warner Brothers, a major label that could supply world-class marketing and distribution. This was another plight of the independent—not having the resources to keep artists when they reached a certain level of popularity.[24]

Today, many independent labels have distribution deals with the large record companies, thereby solving many problems associated with getting CDs and tapes into stores. But there is a lot more competition in the business. After the success of SubPop in Seattle, independent labels have been springing up everywhere, hoping to find the next big scene.

Enter Nettwerk Records of Vancouver. Formed in 1985 by Terry McBride with two partners, Ric Arboite and Mark Jowett, Nettwerk has become one of Canada's leading independent labels, managing such Canadian artists as Sarah McLachlan and Moist. Nettwerk has grown through a truely hands-on, all-encompassing approach to promoting its artists. As the label signed artists, it found that these unknowns were represented by no management. So McBride took it upon himself to perform this role. As it turned out, this strategy led to a company philosophy that has paid off greatly for Nettwerk. The do-it-yourself ethic has given the label a high level of control over its business. Different arms have developed, such as a publishing entity, a multimedia division, and a merchandising department to sell T-shirts and other such products.

This structure has allowed McBride to develop a familial relationship with Nettwerk's artists, such as their biggest success, Sarah McLachlan. McBride and Nettwerk's involvement in all areas of their artists' careers includes such aspects as being a partner in McLachlan's "Lilith Fair" tour— an unprecedented female-oriented show that many in the industry believed could never succeed. Moreover, Nettwerk is a very organic organization with a specific plan in place to keep things this way as the company grows. Terry McBride sums it up in this manner: "Whenever we do something new, we bring the other key people in the company into the ownership of that new entity. Because a lot of growing a young company and keeping it dynamic is keeping the key people there. If in essence they're working for themselves, in the end there's probably a better chance that we're still gonna be around here in 10 or 15 years."▼

Summary

This summary is organized by the chapter Learning Objectives found on page 145.

1. An organization's structure is a measure of its degree of complexity, formalization, and centralization.

2. The advantages of division of labour relate to economic efficiencies. It makes efficient use of the diversity of skills that workers hold. Skills are developed through repetition. Less time is wasted. Training is also easier and less costly. The disadvantage of division of labour is that it can result in human diseconomies. Excessive division of labour can cause boredom, fatigue, stress, low productivity, poor quality work, increased absenteeism, and high turnover.

3. Authority relates to rights inherent in a position. Power describes all means by which an individual can influence decisions, including formal authority. Authority is synonymous with legitimate power. However, a person can have coercive, reward, expert, or referent power without holding a position of authority. Thus, authority is actually a subset of power.

4. Wider spans of control mean that a manager has more subordinates reporting to her. The more subordinates that a manager can effectively supervise, the lower the cost of administrative overhead, and the more efficient the manager becomes.

5. Managers can departmentalize on the basis of function, product, customer, geography, or process. In practice, most large organizations use all five.

6. The mechanistic organization or bureaucracy rates high in complexity, formalization, and centralization. The organic organization or adhocracy scores low on these same three structural dimensions.

7. The strategy-determines-structure thesis argues that structure should follow strategy. As strategies move from single product to vertical integration to product diversification, structure must move from organic to mechanistic.

8. Size affects structure at a decreasing rate. As size increases, so, too, do specialization, formalization, vertical differentiation, and decentralization. But size has less of an impact on large organizations than on small ones because once an organization has about 2,000 employees, it tends to be fairly mechanistic.

9. All other things being equal, the more routine the technology, the more mechanistic the organization should be. The more nonroutine the technology, the more organic the structure should be.

10. All other things being equal, stable environments are better matched with mechanistic organizations, while dynamic environments fit better with organic organizations.

Review and Discussion Questions

1. Reconcile the following two statements: (a) An organization should have as few levels as possible to foster coordination; and (b) An organization should have narrow spans of control to facilitate control.

2. Which is more efficient—a wide or a narrow span of control? Why?

3. Why did the classical writers argue that authority should equal responsibility?

4. Can the manager of a staff department have line authority? Explain.

5. How are authority and organization structure related?

6. What are the five sources of power?

7. Why is an understanding of power important?

8. In what ways can management departmentalize?

9. Is your university organized as a mechanistic or an organic organization? Is this the type of structure you would ideally choose for it? Explain.

10. Under what conditions is the mechanistic organization most effective? When is the organic organization most effective?

Testing Your Comprehension

Circle the correct answer, then check yourself on page 471.

1. Determining where decisions are made in the organization's hierarchy
   a) defines spatial differentiation
   b) refers to work specialization
   c) defines the degree of centralization
   d) refers to the process of organization design

2. The early management writers proposed
   a) one set of organizational principles for all organizations
   b) the separation of authority and responsibility
   c) an organic structure
   d) a simple structure as the basis for all organizations

3. The idea that jobs should be broken down into the simplest of steps, with one step generally assigned to each individual, refers to
   a) span of control
   b) division of labour
   c) chain of command
   d) line authority

4. The classical writers professing the unity of command principle argued that if the principle was not adhered to
   a) supervisors could not keep abreast of what their subordinates were doing
   b) decision making would be slow
   c) employees would have potential trouble coping with conflicting priorities and demands
   d) there would not be enough flexibility

5. A manager's entitlement to direct the work of an employee is the result of
   a) line authority
   b) chain of command
   c) staff authority
   d) autocratic control

6. Which of the following statements is LEAST accurate regarding power?
   a) Functional departments are wedges in the core.
   b) The closer one is to the outer edge of the core, the more power one has.
   c) The organization's hierarchy is directly represented at the edge of the core.
   d) The closer one is to the power core, the more influence one has on decisions.

7. The rights inherent in one's job constitute _____, while the capacity to influence decisions is _____.
   a) power; authority
   b) power; responsibility
   c) authority; responsibility
   d) authority; power

8. Concerning the span of control, early management writers believed that
   a) stronger managers should have a larger span of control
   b) top managers should have a larger span of control
   c) lower-level managers should have a larger span of control
   d) newer managers should have a larger span of control

9. When the manager of an insurance claims department groups together all construction claims personnel under one manager, _____ is being demonstrated.
   a) functional departmentalization
   b) geographic departmentalization
   c) process departmentalization
   d) product departmentalization

10. Which of the following statements is INCONSISTENT with the relationship between strategy and structure?
    a) A change in strategy is followed by a change in structure.
    b) Strategy is a major influence on structure.
    c) A change in structure will result in a change in strategy.
    d) None of the above are inconsistent with the relationship between strategy and structure.

11. All of the following are features of the organic organization EXCEPT:
    a) low formalization
    b) informal communication
    c) fixed duties
    d) decentralized decision authority

12. If an organization's production necessitates nonroutine technology, the organization's structure would be most effective if it were
    a) standardized
    b) bureaucratic
    c) organic
    d) mechanistic

13. In India, employees are likely to perform poorly in teams because
    a) India scores high on collectivism
    b) power distance values are high
    c) employees prefer more organic organizations
    d) formalization is preferred in organizations

Self-Assessment Exercise

How Power Oriented Are You?

Answer the following 10 questions based on a scale of 1 (disagree a lot); 2 (disagree a little); 3 (neutral); 4 (agree a little); or 5 (agree a lot).

	Disagree				Agree
Statement	*A Lot*	*A Little*	*Neutral*	*A Little*	*A Lot*
1. The best way to handle people is to tell them what they want to hear.	1	2	3	4	5
2. When you ask someone to do something for you, it is best to give the real reason for wanting it rather than giving reasons that might carry more weight.	1	2	3	4	5
3. Anyone who completely trusts anyone else is asking for trouble.	1	2	3	4	5
4. It is hard to get ahead without cutting corners here and there.	1	2	3	4	5
5. It is safest to assume that all people have a vicious streak, and it will come out when they are given a chance.	1	2	3	4	5
6. One should take action only when it is morally right.	1	2	3	4	5
7. Most people are basically good and kind.	1	2	3	4	5
8. There is no excuse for lying to someone else.	1	2	3	4	5
9. Most people forget the death of their father more easily than the loss of their property.	1	2	3	4	5
10. Generally speaking, people won't work hard unless they're forced to do so.	1	2	3	4	5

Turn to page 465 for scoring directions and key.

Source: R. Christie and F.L. Geis, *Studies in Machiavellianism* (London, England: Academic Press, 1970). Reprinted by permission.

Class Exercise

How Is Your School Organized?

Every university or college displays a specific type of organizational structure. That is, if you are a Business major, your classes are often "housed" in a department, school, or college of business. But have you ever asked why? Or is it something you just take for granted?

In Chapter 3 you had an opportunity to assess your university's strengths, weaknesses, and comparative advantage and see how this fits into its strategy. Now in this chapter, we have built a case that structure follows strategy. Given your analysis in Chapter 3 (if you have not done so, you may want to turn to page 76 for the strategy part of this exercise), analyse your university's overall structure in terms of formalization, centralization, and complexity. Furthermore, look at the departmentalization that exists. Is your university more organic or mechanistic? Now analyse how well its structure fits with its strategy. Do the same thing for your university size, technology, and environment. That is, assess its size, degree of technological routineness, and environmental uncertainty. Based on these assessments, what kind of structure would you predict your university to have? Does it have this structure now? Compare your findings with those of other classmates. Are there similarities in how each viewed the organization? Differences? What do you believe has attributed to these findings?

Case Application

Greyhound Canada Rolls Over

Greyhound Canada Transportation Corp. had a very bad year in 1997. In fact, it was the culmination of many bad years, but this year saw the demise of the company's Greyhound Air, and then the takeover bid by Laidlaw Inc. for Greyhound Canada's bus and courier business. Greyhound began to feel the effects of the changing industry in the early 1990s. Travel by bus was becoming less and less popular (and indeed, the railway lines in Canada have been struggling for a long time) due to the emergence of cheap airline flights. Charter airlines have been putting pressure on the travel industry, with major airlines attempting to remain competitive in price, and bus and train companies trying to redefine themselves in the marketplace.[27]

The shifts in the transportation industry led Greyhound Canada into a disastrous foray. Critics viewed it as the act of a desperate organization: Greyhound was going to move into the airline business. You may remember the television advertisements, with a greyhound sauntering up to the wheels of a 727, lifting its hind leg, and "marking its territory." Clever ad—but over the next year and a half, the marketplace was "lifting its hind leg" with a different intent. Greyhound Air was down the toilet.

From the beginning it didn't look like Greyhound Air really knew what it was doing. The airline didn't have an operating licence obtained for its first day of operation. Greyhound was entering a market it didn't know well, and one which has seen the demise of many companies. For Greyhound Air, it was one long money-losing slide. Meanwhile, Greyhound Canada was not succeeding in turning its fortunes around, and Greyhound Air was just another weight to carry. Before the company could shed itself of Greyhound Air, Laidlaw came in with a takeover bid.

Questions

1. Do you think Greyhound Air was mechanistic or organic? Which type of organization would be most suited to the industry Greyhound Air was operating in, and why?

2. How could Greyhound Canada Transportation Corp. (not Greyhound Air) have made changes to its organization to better deal with changes in the transportation industry?

GREYHOUND CANADA
www.greyhound.ca/

LAIDLAW INC.
www.laidlaw.com/

chapter

7

Organization Design for the Twenty-first Century

Learning Objectives

What will I be able to do after I finish this chapter?

1 • Define the simple structure.

2 • Describe the strengths of the functional structure.

3 • Contrast the divisional and functional structures.

4 • Explain the strengths of the matrix structure.

5 • Describe the recent popularity of the network structure.

6 • Define a strategic alliance.

7 • Identify the advantages of using organic appendages.

8 • Explain what is meant by the term horizontal organization.

9 • Explain the preferred structural design for TQM programs.

10 • Describe what is meant by the term organization culture.

11 • Contrast job specialization, job enlargement, and job enrichment.

As the world of business becomes more and more complex, innovative ideas on how to structure organizations are beginning to spring up. Two small businesses in Toronto have taken the idea of divisional structure, combined it with entrepreneurial ownership and drive, added the element of partnership and collaboration, and come up with something that makes a lot of sense—and works. The two companies are Nuroc Plumbing and Heating Supplies Ltd., and Independent Electric Supply Inc.[1]

The alliance is the brainchild of Paul Mashinter, a partner at Ernst & Young. He put the two firms together because Bob Branscombe at Independent Electric was looking for an investor to buy out his partner, and Gary Tester, Paul Rocamora, and John Hudson of Nuroc were looking for ways to expand their business. By putting the two firms together, Branscombe could arrange the buyout of his partner, and Nuroc could expand its customer base without opening another outlet or acquiring another company. The two companies now share information, customers, and support infrastructure. For instance, they jointly invested in a new IBM computer, saving them $30,000. The computer is set up at Nuroc, uses Independent's software, and has a direct access linking the two companies located on opposite sides of Toronto. They are exploring collaborating on inventory systems and trying to develop a common invoice for customers. As a result of the partnership, Independent's customer base doubled in the first year, and sales increased 17 per cent. It also gave Independent a larger line of credit at the bank. The owners still run their companies, but they consult with one another weekly. Nuroc's financial controller visits Independent once or twice a week. When Bob Branscombe wanted to buy a new truck, he and Gary Tester researched the purchase together. Branscombe says, "I use Nuroc as a sounding board on a regular basis."

Given that small businesses are driving the growth in the Canadian economy, the model that Nuroc and Independent have created may turn out not only to answer the needs of entrepreneurs to maintain control over their own businesses, but also to enable businesses to grow without having to raise large amounts of capital and become burdened by heavy debt and overhead costs.

Bob Branscombe (left), Gary Tester (right), and Paul Rocamora (middle), have created a new form of small business venture that may become a model for the next decade.

INDEPENDENT ELECTRIC SUPPLY INC.
www.independent electric.com/

In this chapter, we'll show that there are a number of structural options at management's disposal. There are traditional structures, such as the functional bureaucracy, which have been dominant organizational structures since the 1930s. Although these structures worked well in the past, today's managers are looking at new and unique ways of reorganizing. Accordingly, we'll explore some of the new organization design options, taking a look at matrix, network, and horizontal structures.

Keep in mind that organizational design decisions are typically made by senior executives, possibly with input from mid-level managers. This realization, however, should not diminish our desire to understand how these structures work. Why? Because each of us works in some type of structure, and we need to know why we are "arranged" the way we are. Also, given the changing environment and the needs for organizations to rapidly adapt, we should understand what the organizations for which we'll be working "tomorrow" are going to look like.

Even though structures may dictate specific work activities, every organization has a personality that influences how its members behave. This personality is the organization's culture. We'll explore the concept of organizational culture in this chapter and discuss what goes into its development.

Finally, we'll close this chapter with a discussion of how jobs can be designed to better facilitate employee productivity. We'll show that understanding job design is important for managers at all levels.

Traditional Organization Designs

Traditional organization designs typically come in one of three varieties—the simple structure, the functional structure, and the divisional structure. Most organizations in North America are small. In Canada, the vast majority of new jobs in the economy for the last 15 years have been created by small business—more than 85 per cent of new jobs created from 1980 to 1990 were from small business, with roughly half of these being created by firms with fewer than five employees, and about a quarter by firms with between five and 20 employees. The same scenario exists in the United States. Between 1980 and 1990, Fortune 500 companies *cut* 3.4 million jobs,[2] but companies with fewer than 500 employees *created* more than 13 million jobs.[3] Small organizations don't require a highly complex, formal structural design. What they need is a simple structure—one that minimizes structural complexity.

When contingencies such as strategy, size, or technology favour a highly complex, formalized, and centralized (mechanistic) organization design, one of two options is traditionally considered—a functional or divisional structure. The functional structure's primary focus is on achieving the efficiencies of division of labour by grouping like specialists together. The divisional structure creates self-contained, autonomous units that are usually organized along mechanistic lines. Let's explore these three—simple, functional, and divisional—traditional structures.

What Is the Simple Structure?

If bureaucracy is the term that best describes most large organizations, simple structure is the one that best characterizes most small ones. A **simple structure** is defined more by what it is not than by what it is. It is not an elaborate structure.[4] If you see an organization that appears to have almost no structure, it is probably of the simple variety. By that we mean that it is low in complexity, has little formalization, and has its authority centralized in a single person. The simple structure is a "flat" organization; it usually has only two or three vertical levels, a loose body of empowered employees (see Developing Management Skills), and one individual in whom the decision-making authority is centralized.

simple structure
An organization that is low in complexity and formalization but high in centralization.

**Exhibit 7-1
Organization Chart for a Simple Structure (Gino Ceccardi's Men's Store)**

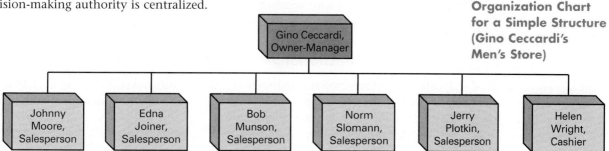

DEVELOPING MANAGEMENT SKILLS

▼ EMPOWERING EMPLOYEES ▲

▶ **1. Be sure employees have the abilities and motivation to perform empowered tasks.** Unless employees have the ability and desire to perform the empowered tasks, no amount of "empowerment" will work. Thus, when filling empowered jobs, employees should be screened for their ability to perform in an empowered setting or be appropriately trained to do so.

▶ **2. Clarify the assignment and decisions to be empowered.** Empowerment may mean many things to different employees—especially if left up to them to decide. Be specific about what employees can and cannot do.

▶ **3. Specify employees' range of discretion.** Similar to step two, you must let employees know how much freedom they can exercise. By knowing, they can then act freely within that range. Outside of the range, they should consult you.

▶ **4. Inform others that empowerment has occurred.** Why? Because others in the organization may think your employees are acting on their own or without your "approval." Letting others know what you've "given" your employees will help all parties involved to be effective in their jobs.

▶ **5. Establish feedback controls.** Remember, empowerment does not mean abdication. You still have ultimate responsibility for whatever you have pushed downward. As such, getting feedback on what is happening in your unit is necessary.

The simple structure is most widely practised in small businesses in which the manager and the owner are one and the same. This, for example, is illustrated in Exhibit 7-1—an organization chart for a men's retail store. Gino Ceccardi owns and manages this store. Although Gino employs five full-time salespeople, a cashier, and extra personnel for weekends and holidays, he "runs the show."

The strengths of the simple structure should be obvious. It is fast, flexible, and inexpensive to maintain, and accountability is clear. One major weakness is that it is effective only in small organizations. It becomes increasingly inadequate as an organization grows because its low formalization and high centralization result in information overload at the top. As size increases, decision making becomes slower and can eventually come to a standstill as the single executive tries to continue making all the decisions. This proves to be the undoing of many small businesses. When a company's sales begin to exceed about $5 million a year, it's very difficult for the owner-manager to make all the choices. If the structure isn't changed and made more elaborate, the firm is likely to lose momentum, and eventually to fail. The simple structure's other weakness is that it is risky: everything depends on one person. One heart attack or a fatal auto accident on the way to work can literally destroy the organization's information and decision-making centre.

What Is the Functional Structure?

functional structure
A design that groups similar or related occupational specialties together.

We introduced functional departmentalization in the previous chapter, so the idea of organizing around functions is already familiar to you. The **functional structure** merely expands the functional orientation to make it the dominant form for the entire organization. As depicted in Exhibit 7-2, management can choose to organize

Exhibit 7-2   Functional Structure in a Manufacturing Organization

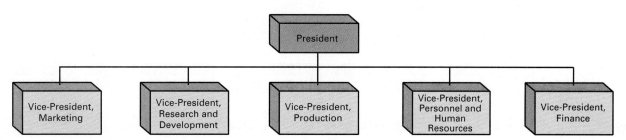

its structure by grouping similar and related occupational specialties together. When it does this, management has chosen a functional structure.

Can You Identify the Major Strength of the Functional Structure? The strength of the functional structure lies in the advantages that accrue from specialization. Putting like specialties together results in economies of scale, minimizes duplication of personnel and equipment, and makes employees comfortable and satisfied because it gives them the opportunity to "talk the same language" as their peers.

What Are the Weaknesses of the Functional Structure? The most obvious weakness of the functional structure is that the organization frequently loses sight of its best interests in the pursuit of functional goals. No one function is totally responsible for end results, so members within individual functions become insulated and have little understanding of what people in other functions are doing. Because only top management can see the whole picture, it must assume the coordination role. The diversity of interests and perspectives that exists between functions can result in continual conflict between functions as each tries to assert its importance. An additional weakness of the functional structure is that it provides little or no training for future senior managers. Functional managers only see one narrow segment of the organization—the one dealing with their function. Exposure to other functions is limited. As a result, the structure does not give these managers a broad perspective on the organization's activities.

What Is the Divisional Structure?

The CBC, General Motors, and Bombardier are examples of organizations that have adopted the divisional structure. An illustration of what this structural form looks like at Hershey Foods Corporation can be seen from the organization chart in Exhibit 7-3.

The **divisional structure**, which was pioneered in the 1920s by General Motors and du Pont, is designed to foster self-contained units. Each unit or division is generally autonomous, with a division manager responsible for performance and holding complete strategic and operational decision-making authority. At Hershey Foods, each of the groups is a separate division headed by a group president who is totally responsible for results. As in most divisional structures, a central headquarters provides support services to the divisions. This typically includes financial and legal services. Of course, the headquarters also acts as an external overseer to coordinate and control the various divisions. Divisions are, therefore, autonomous within given parameters. Division managers are usually free to direct their division as they see fit, as long as it is within the overall guidelines set down by headquarters.

divisional structure
An organization structure made up of autonomous, self-contained units.

Exhibit 7-3 Divisional Structure at Hershey Foods Corp.

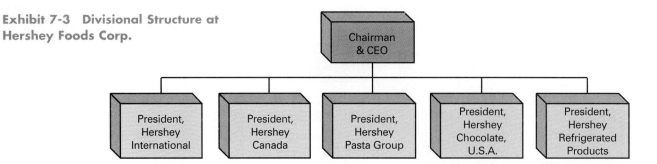

Chairman & CEO

President, Hershey International

President, Hershey Canada

President, Hershey Pasta Group

President, Hershey Chocolate, U.S.A.

President, Hershey Refrigerated Products

A closer look at divisional structures reveals that their "innards" contain functional structures. The divisional framework creates a set of autonomous "little companies." Within each of these companies lies another organizational form, and it is almost always of the functional variety.

Some large companies, like General Motors, structure themselves around self-contained units— like that of GM's Buick Division.

Can You Identify the Strengths of the Divisional Structure? What advantages does the divisional structure offer? It focuses on results. Division managers have full responsibility for a product or service. The divisional structure also frees the headquarters staff from being concerned with day-to-day operating details so that they can pay attention to long-term and strategic planning.

In contrast to functional structures, the divisional form is also an excellent vehicle for developing senior executives. Division managers gain a broad range of experience in running their autonomous units. The individual responsibility and independence give them an opportunity to run an entire company, with all its frustrations and satisfactions. So a large organization with 15 divisions has 15 division managers who are developing the kind of generalist perspective that is needed in the organization's top spots.

What Is the Primary Weakness of the Divisional Structure? The major disadvantage of the divisional structure is duplication of activities and resources. Each division, for instance, may have a marketing research department. In the absence of autonomous divisions, all of the organization's marketing research might be centralized and done for a fraction of the cost that divisionalization requires. Thus, the divisional form's duplication of functions increases the organization's costs and reduces efficiency.

Designs for a Changing World

In this section, we present a selection of more organic design options. These include the matrix, network, task force, and committee structures (see Managers Who Made a Difference). We'll also introduce you to an increasingly popular design that is moving us toward the boundary-free organization—the horizontal structure.

MANAGERS WHO MADE A DIFFERENCE

Jean Monty and John Roth: Northern Telecom

Northern Telecom is a manufacturer of telecommunications equipment (in fact, the sixth-largest in the world) based in Brampton, Ontario. In the early 1990s, Nortel was experiencing a very bad run. Research and development funds were being cut back, leading to increasingly inferior products, which in time led to dissatisfied customers, poor employee morale, and, finally, a disastrous bottom line. In 1993 all of this culminated in the company experiencing losses of $884 million (U.S.).[5]

This is when Jean Monty stepped in to take control of the sinking ship. Monty was chairman of Bell Canada, another subsidiary of BCE, the parent company of Nortel. His first order of business at Nortel was to boost research and development spending, recognizing that R&D was the lifeblood of a company like Nortel. In an industry of constant technological innovation, a company either stays ahead of the technological trends, or it suffers heavily by allowing itself to fall behind. While Monty's predecessor had been consumed by the idea of cost-cutting—a common preoccupation of large organizations at the time—Monty had a different strategy. In his own words: "We invested massively, particularly in R&D, and we didn't try to shrink ourselves to greatness."

Understanding the nature of a company's industry is essential. Whereas Monty's predecessor perhaps had a difficulty with "being able to see the forest for the trees," Monty was able to look beyond the smaller matters and focus on what was important for the organization as a whole. In 1997 *Report on Business Magazine*'s list of top R&D companies, Nortel ranked number one (the same as the previous year), with R&D spending at $2.6 million. Moreover, in the profit rankings Nortel came in at number seven in Canada, with more than $600 million in profit on close to $13 billion in revenue. Quite an impressive turnaround.

Jean Monty also recognized the abilities of John Roth, a manager in the company with an engineering background. Roth quickly moved to chief operating officer while Monty was chief executive officer. With Monty's work done at Nortel, he has returned to BCE, and has handed the reigns of power at Nortel over to Roth. The appointment of Roth should ensure Nortel's position as an industry-leading innovator. He possesses a great technical knowledge of the company's products, and is primarily interested in furthering this focus on innovation while moving into new markets the world over. And the timing of Nortel's turnaround couldn't be better, as global deregulation of the telecommunications industry leads to new telephone companies springing up constantly; the market for telecom equipment is growing to service these companies. This market is expected to reach $300 billion by 2000. John Roth is undoubtedly relishing the prospects for his company.▼

John Roth, CEO of Northern Telecom, should ensure the company's position as an industry-leading innovator.

matrix structure
A structural design that assigns specialists from functional departments to work on one or more projects that are led by a project manager.

What Is the Matrix Structure?

The functional structure offers the advantages that accrue from specialization. The divisional structure has a greater focus on results but suffers from duplication of activities and resources. Does any structure combine the advantages of functional specialization with the focus and accountability that product departmentalization provides? The answer is yes, and it's called the **matrix structure**.[5]

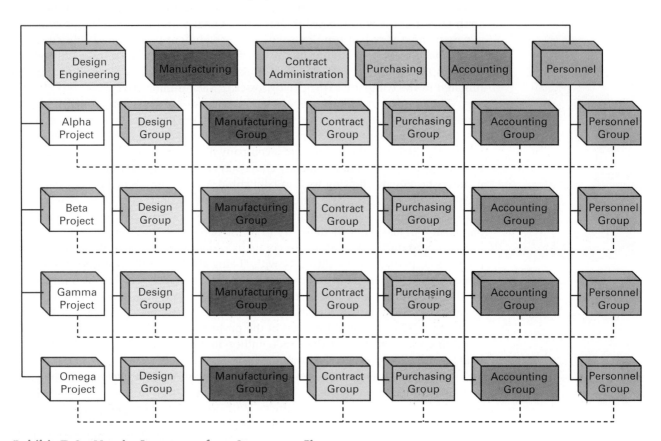

Exhibit 7-4 Matrix Structure of an Aerospace Firm

Remember earlier we stated that functional departmentalization is used to gain the economies from specialization. The matrix overlaps the functional departments with a set of managers who are responsible for specific products, projects, or programs within the organization. (We will use these terms—products, projects, programs—interchangeably, since matrix structures can use any of the three.) Exhibit 7-4 illustrates the matrix structure of an aerospace firm. Notice that along the top of the figure are the familiar functions of engineering, accounting, human resources management, and so forth. Along the vertical dimension, however, the various projects that the aerospace firm is currently working on have been added. Each project is directed by a manager who staffs his project with people from the functional departments. The addition of this vertical dimension to the traditional horizontal functional departments, in effect, weaves together elements of functional and product departmentalization—hence the term matrix.

What Is Unique About the Matrix? In Chapter 4, we introduced the concept of PERT and project management. In part, much of that discussion related directly to a matrix structure. How? Project management looks at employing specific resources (functional) on specific work activities (projects). Accordingly, when you work in a project management setting, you are actually working in a form of a matrix.

The most unique characteristic of the matrix is that employees in this structure have at least two bosses: their functional departmental manager and their product or project managers—just like those working for ABB, a global equipment corporation. The project managers have authority over the functional members who are part of that manager's project team. The purchasing specialists, for instance, who are responsible for procurement activities on the Gamma project, are responsible to both the manager of purchasing and the Gamma project manager. Authority is shared between the two managers. Typically, this is done by giving the project manager authority over project employees relative to the project's goals. However, decisions such as promotions, salary recommendations, and annual reviews remain the functional manager's responsibility. To work effectively, project and functional managers must communicate regularly and coordinate the demands upon their common employees.

Companies like the Jet Propulsion Lab in Pasadena, California, use a matrix structure to facilitate coordination of multiple complex projects.

network structure
A small centralized organization that relies on other organizations to perform its basic business functions on a contract basis.

What Are the Strengths and Weaknesses of a Matrix Structure? The primary strength of the matrix is that it can facilitate coordination of a multiple set of complex and interdependent projects while still retaining the economies that result from keeping functional specialists grouped together. The major disadvantages of the matrix lie in the confusion it creates and its propensity to foster power struggles. When you dispense with the unity of command principle, you significantly increase ambiguity. Confusion can exist over who reports to whom. This confusion and ambiguity, in turn, plant the seeds for power struggles. Because the relationships between functional and project managers typically are not specified by rules and procedures, they need to be negotiated, and this gives rise to power struggles. Deciding whether to implement the matrix requires managers to weigh these disadvantages against the advantages.

How Does the Network Structure Work?

A new form of organization design is currently gaining popularity. It allows management great flexibility in responding to new technology, fashion, or low-cost foreign competition. It is the **network structure**—a small central organization that relies on other organizations to perform manufacturing, distribution, marketing, or other crucial business functions on a contract basis.[7]

Nike uses the network structure to create great flexibility in responding to new athletic shoes.

The network structure is a viable option for the small organization. Behavioural Science Systems Ltd., a management consultancy that operates in Canada, Britain, and Southeast Asia, links its consultants on a computer network. It maintains a head office in London, England—which none of the consultants ever visits! Their business is done at the client's place of business, and the office is only used to provide the supporting infrastructure of financial controls, coordination of materials production, etc. James Naisbitt, the futurist and author of *Megatrends*, likewise has an office in Washington, DC, that he never visits; he lives and works out of a small town in Colorado, with faxes, phones, computers, and Federal Express to link him with his clients.

The network structure is also applicable to large organizations such as Nike, Esprit, and Liz Claiborne, which have found that they can sell hundreds of millions of dollars' worth of products every year and earn a very competitive return with few or no manufacturing facilities of their own and only a few hundred employees. What these firms have done is to create an organization of relationships. They contract with independent designers, manufacturers, commissioned sales representatives, or the like, to perform the functions they need for a set fee.

Other large companies have developed variants of the network structure by farming out just a limited set of functions. Hudson Bay creates the design specifications for its clothing requirements and contracts out its manufacture largely to Asian suppliers. Nova Scotia's Maritime Telegraph & Telephone contracts out its computer and information systems operations. And most book publishing companies—the large ones as well as the small ones—rely on outside contractors for editing, designing, printing, and binding.

The network stands in sharp contrast to divisional structures that have many vertical levels of management or which seek to control their destiny through ownership. In such organizations, research and development are done in-house, production occurs in company-owned manufacturing plants, and sales and marketing are performed by their own employees. To support all this, management has to employ extra personnel, including accountants, human resource specialists, and lawyers. In the network structure, most of these functions are bought outside the organization. This gives management a high degree of flexibility and allows the organization to concentrate on what it does best. For most Canadian firms, that means focusing on design or marketing.

Exhibit 7-5 shows a network structure in which management contracts out all of the primary functions of the business. The core of the network organization is a small group of managers. Their job is to oversee directly any activities that are done in-house and to coordinate relationships with the other organizations that manufacture, distribute, and perform other crucial functions for the network organization. The dotted lines in Exhibit 7-5 represent those contractual relationships. In essence, managers in network structures spend most of their time coordinating and controlling external relations.

Exhibit 7-5 Network Structure

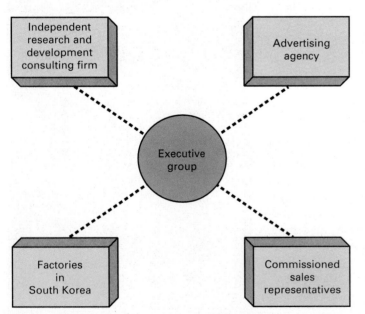

Where Would a Network Structure Best Fit? The network organization is not appropriate for all endeavours. It fits industrial companies such as toy and apparel firms, which require very high flexibility to respond quickly to market changes. It also fits firms whose manufacturing operations require low-cost labour and can best be utilized by contracting with foreign suppliers. On the negative side, management in network structures lacks the close control of manufacturing operations that exists in more traditional organizations. Reliability of supply is also less predictable. Finally, any innovation in design that a network organization acquires is susceptible to being "ripped off." It is very difficult, if not impossible, to closely guard innovations that are under the direction of management in another organization. Yet with computers in one organization now interfacing and communicating directly with computers in other organizations, the network structure is becoming an increasingly viable alternative.

What Is a Strategic Alliance? Before we leave networks, we'd like to introduce another element that is gaining momentum in a number of large companies like Canadian Pacific Railway (which has teamed up with Norfolk Southern Railway in the U.S., to gain access to the U.S. market), and small ones like the two mentioned at the start of the chapter—Nuroc Plumbing and Heating and Independent Electric Supply. This new "structure" revolves around building a **strategic alliance**.[8] Just as there were dotted-line relationships with a headquarters staff and its suppliers in a network, a strategic alliance allows organizations to cooperate with one another, sharing resources, and spreading development costs and risks.

strategic alliance
Joint partnerships between two or more firms that are created to gain a competitive advantage in a market.

A strategic alliance, then, exists when two separate companies come together to develop a joint product or share marketing capabilities. This usually happens when one company needs specific resources or skills that another company has. A recent example of such an alliance is Calgary's Applied Terravision Systems, Inc., teaming up with U.S.-based Oracle Corp., the second-largest software company in the world.[9] The alliance will greatly help to further the development of Applied Terravision's software packages for the oil and gas industry, with financing and expertise from Oracle. And Oracle's worldwide distribution network will give the small Canadian company access to markets it could not otherwise easily reach.

Can Mechanistic and Organic Structures Be Combined?

The design options previously described are intended for organization-wide application. Sometimes, however, management might want to maintain an overall mechanistic structure but gain the flexibility of an organic structure. An alternative is to append an organic structural unit to a mechanistic organization. Two examples of such appendages are the task force and the committee structure.

What Is a Task Force? The **task force structure** is a temporary structure created to accomplish a specific, well-defined, and complex task that requires the involvement of personnel from a number of organizational subunits. It can be thought of as a scaled-down version of the temporary matrix. Members serve on the task force until its goal is achieved. Then the task force is disbanded, and its members move on to a new task force, return to their permanent functional department, or leave the organization.[10]

task force structure
A temporary structure created to accomplish a specific, well-defined, complex task that requires the involvement of personnel from a number of organizational subunits.

The task force is a common tool of consumer product firms. For instance, when the Kellogg Company decides to create a new breakfast cereal, it brings together people with expertise in product design, food research, marketing, manufacturing,

KELLOGG
COMPANY
www.kelloggs.com/

committee structure
A structure that brings together a range of individuals from across functional lines to deal with problems.

finance, and other relevant functions to formulate the product, design its package, determine its market, compute its manufacturing costs, and project its profits. Once the problems have been worked out and the product is ready to be mass produced, the task force disbands, and the cereal is integrated into the permanent structure. At Kellogg, the new cereal is then assigned its own product manager and becomes a part of Kellogg's matrix structure.

What Is a Committee Structure? Another option that combines a range of individual experiences and backgrounds for dealing with problems and cuts across functional lines is the **committee structure**. Committees may be temporary or permanent in nature. A temporary committee is typically the same as a task force. Permanent committees facilitate the unity of diverse inputs as does the task force, but they offer the stability and consistency of the matrix. However, committees are appendages. Members of the committee are permanently attached to a functional department. They can meet at regular or irregular intervals to analyse problems, make recommendations or final decisions, coordinate activities, or oversee projects. As a result, they are mechanisms for bringing together the input of diverse departments. Universities frequently use permanent committees for everything from student admissions to faculty promotions and alumni relations. Large business firms use committees as coordinating and control mechanisms. For instance, many firms have a compensation committee to review salary and bonuses provided to management personnel, and an audit committee to objectively evaluate the organization's operations. A few firms even use the committee as the central coordinating device in their structure. Many companies have a management committee that consists of the firm's top managers. They debate and pass on decisions to such disparate areas as strategic planning, public affairs, personnel, and merchandising. Permanent subcommittees are used to focus on key parts of the business, while temporary committees are formed for specific issues.

Why Is There Movement Toward a Boundary-free Organization?

Recall our discussion in Chapter 2 regarding the challenges that managers face. Two of these—downsizing and reengineering—are particularly relevant to today's organization structural changes.[11] How? To answer, let's briefly review some facts regarding traditional structures. These bureaucratic designs were highly complex and formalized, and decisions were made in a centralized fashion—resulting in rigid, often massive, vertical structures. Although they were designed to promote efficiency, they did not lend themselves well to helping management adapt quickly to a changing environment.[12]

Network organizations and strategic alliances are structural responses to a rapidly changing environment. Both blur the historic boundaries surrounding an organization by increasing the interdependence with which it interacts. In terms of quantum change, managers are increasingly turning to still another structural option that downplays rigid boundaries. This can involve horizontal changes in the organization (like using task forces), vertical integration (multilevel teams), or interorganizational blends (for example, strategic alliances) (see Exhibit 7-6). Only this time the focus is on the inside of the organization (intraorganizational) rather than between organizations (interorganizational). We're talking about the horizontal structure.

Horizontal:	Crossfunctional teams and task forces can be used to break down the traditional horizontal differentiation derived from division of labour.
Vertical:	Multilevel teams, empowerment, and 360-degree performance evaluations can be used to break down vertical barriers derived from authoritative hierarchies.
Interorganizational:	Strategic alliances, interorganizational computer networks, and using customers' input in the evaluation of employees can be used to break down the barriers derived from the classical organization design principles of bureaucracies.

Exhibit 7-6 Methods Used in the Boundary-free Organization to Break Down Horizontal, Vertical, and Interorganizational Barriers

What Is a Horizontal Structure? A horizontal structure is really nothing new. **Horizontal structures** are organization design options that reflect very flat structures. If you're making the connection to a few pages back when we discussed simple structures, you're on the right track. What's new about these structures, however, is that they are being used not only in small businesses but in giant companies such as du Pont, General Electric, and Motorola.[13]

Horizontal organizations, as the term implies, cut across all aspects of the organization. Rather than having functional specialties located in departments working on distinctive tasks, these internally boundary-free organizations group employees to accomplish some core processes.[14] A **core process** is a basic focus of the business, like Bell Northern Research's product development. Core processes, then, encompass the entire work to be accomplished, from beginning to end, rather than focus on individualized job tasks. Let's look at an example to help clarify what we mean by core processes.

Ryder Systems, the company that rents and leases trucks, recently reorganized to focus on its mainstay business.[15] Previously, it took almost an entire year from the time managers decided to purchase a vehicle until the truck was ready for customer use. There were upwards of 17 functional departments that were required to get involved, even if it was only to sign some papers. Ryder managers knew they couldn't remain competitive in this self-moving market unless they made drastic changes. Competition from companies such as U-Haul mandated that something be done.

Ryder's management wanted to eliminate the unnecessary activities involved in this drawn-out process. They realized they had a single core process—purchase a vehicle and prepare it for customer rental.[16] Ryder was able to eliminate the involvement of 15 functional areas by creating a single "team" that did all the activities from start to finish. The result? Ryder reduced its cycle time to four months.

horizontal structure
An organization design option characterized by very flat structures.

core process
A basic focus of the business.

RYDER MOVING SERVICES
www.yellowtruck.com/ cgi-bin/pf/main.htm

Ryder eliminated 15 functional departments, flattened the organization by creating teams, and reduced its cycle time by 66 per cent in delivering new trucks to customers.

Horizontal organizations are not just "flatter" organizations. To achieve what Ryder did required an internal revolution.[17] This means that managers must break down the traditional hierarchies that have existed for many decades. In doing so, horizontal organizations will require work teams—groups of employees who come from all specialties working together for a common objective. These multidisciplinary teams will be given the authority to make the necessary decisions to do the work and will be held accountable for measurable outcomes.[18]

As these changes are made, employees in horizontal organizations will also see new ways of being evaluated. Rather than being measured on individual performance, employees will be rewarded based on how the team performs. Also, team members will be rewarded for mastering multiple skills, rather than just a select few. But probably the biggest difference will be who evaluates employees. In traditional structures, one's supervisor conducts the performance evaluation. In a horizontal organization, supervisory evaluations will no longer be the only ones. For instance, at General Electric, CEO Jack Welch has implemented what he calls a 360-degree appraisal process.[19] At GE, team members are evaluated by team leaders, peer members, and other employees with whom they work.[20]

Is There a Typical Form of Horizontal Organization? Horizontal organizations can almost be described in much the same way that we described simple structures. They are more representative of what they don't have than what they do have. However, all horizontal organizations share one common element. That is, they're flat. Beyond that, each is specifically tailored to the organization's core process. Although designs will vary, there is some indication that horizontal organizations may share the following characteristics.[21] They will have few senior executives. Those that are present will more than likely be from two critical areas that permeate all core processes: finance and human resources. Beyond these, the remaining employees will form multidisciplinary teams. Although there will be team or process leaders, it is estimated that horizontal organizations will have no more than three or four layers of management. That means from CEO to employee, there will be two management groups. So what might this structure look like?

The network structure probably gives us the foundation for a horizontal framework. Unlike the network, however, the outlying areas will represent organizational teams, not contractual relationships. One design that typifies horizontal organizations is that of Eastman Chemical Company.[22] Eastman's organization chart can best be conceptualized as a pepperoni pizza. At the centre of the pizza is the small staff of executives who set the strategic direction. Around the circle are many pepperoni, each representing a multidisciplinary team "responsible for managing a business, a geographic area, or a core competency."[23] And what does the cheese that covers the pizza signify? In a true horizontal fashion, even teams must cross over to assist one another. The cheese, then, on Eastman's pizza shows how all team members are strung together.

Organizational charts, such as Eastman's, tell employees that they are all important to the organization's success. Being part of a pie, or whatever analogy is used, indicates that all employees are "equal" and are working toward a common goal. In fact, this addresses one of the problem areas that is inherent in traditional structures. On typical organizational charts, employees are often shown at the very bottom of a pyramid—reinforcing to organizational members who is in power and who has authority over them. Employees do not need to be told that they are perceived as the lowest cog in the organization. In fact, Pepsico has inverted its organization chart to

EASTMAN
CHEMICAL CO.
www.eastman.com/

show that its field representatives are the number one reason for company success. Having management at the bottom of the pyramid shows Pepsi employees what management is supposed to be—a team that exists to support worker efforts.[24]

Whether or not a specific "picture" is used to represent horizontal organizations, these structures will follow a common format. That is, no matter what they look like, horizontal organizations will focus and organize around core processes that meet strategic goals and will have empowered multidisciplinary teams working to achieve these objectives. But keep one thing in mind. Horizontal organizations must be used where appropriate. In some industries where efficiency of mass production is warranted, a traditional structure may better serve the organization. The question raised then is, When do the different structures work best? The answer will depend on the environment in which a company operates.

So What's the Key to Organization Design?

The right organization design, like many activities in management, is dependent on the situation. As such, conditions making one organization design preferable eliminate others. In Exhibit 7-7, we have summarized the options we have discussed and note the conditions that favour the use of each.

STRUCTURE	ADVANTAGES	BEST USED
Simple	Speed, flexibility, economy	In small organizations; during formative years of development; in simple and dynamic environments
Functional	Economies through specialization	In single-product or single-service organizations
Divisional	High accountability for results	In large organizations, in multiple-product or multiple-market organizations
Matrix	Economies through specialization and accountability for product results	In organizations with multiple products or programs that rely on functional expertise
Network	Speed, flexibility, economy	In industrial firms; during formative years of development; when many reliable suppliers are available; when low-cost foreign labour is available
Task Force	Flexibility	In organizations with important tasks that are unique and unfamiliar, that require expertise that crosses functional lines
Committee	Flexibility	In organizations with tasks that require expertise that crosses functional lines
Horizontal	Speed, flexibility, customer focus	In large organizations facing complex and dynamic environments; when tasks require expertise that crosses functional lines; when ability to deal with rapid change is paramount

Exhibit 7-7   Organization Design Options

TQM and Structural Design

Several concepts introduced in this and the prior chapter have direct relevance to the Total Quality Management movement. These include vertical differentiation, division of labour, and centralization.

One common characteristic of TQM programs is an effort to reduce vertical differentiation. By widening spans of control and flattening organizations, management cuts overhead and improves vertical communication. A second common TQM characteristic is reduced division of labour. High division of labour emphasizes specialization, promotes an "us versus them" mentality, and retards collaboration and horizontal communication. In contrast, TQM encourages the use of teams that cut across functional specializations (see Ethical Dilemmas in Management).

Finally, TQM emphasizes decentralized decision making. Authority and responsibility are pushed as far down, and as close to the customer, as possible. The reason, of course, is that TQM's success depends on quickly and continually responding to the changing needs of customers.

Amoco Production Company illustrates the effectiveness of these structural changes.[25] The company realized that its matrix structure—six tiers of management cross-laden with a multitude of functional units—had become too cumbersome. Geologists, for instance, were spending nearly 40 per cent of their time in committee meetings trying to get approvals to search for oil when they actually could have been searching for oil. So Amoco's management reorganized. They eliminated three layers of management and dismantled the functional hierarchies. Workers were grouped into units of approximately 500, organized around multidisciplinary teams, and given considerable authority to make decisions. Noted one unit leader, "We're finding more oil and getting better financial results with the same number of professionals and fewer managers."[26]

YOUNG CANADIANS

Mark Knodell: Continental Connections Trading

Mark Knodell knows the value of customer satisfaction. His company, Continental Connections Trading, is a Bedford, N.S.-based brokerage between Atlantic Canadian fish suppliers and international markets. Knodell found it difficult to get business until finally being given the opportunity to ship $300 worth of fish to Greece. He lost money on the deal, but made sure the job was done well. Now that client gives CCT $300,000 orders and is just part of an international roster of clients Knodell has personally brought on board due to his commitment to quality.

Organization Culture and Structural Design

We know that every individual has something that psychologists have termed "personality." An individual's personality is made up of a set of relatively permanent and stable traits. When we describe someone as warm, innovative, relaxed, or conservative, we are describing personality traits. An organization, too, has a personality, which we call the organization's culture.

What Is Organization Culture?

What do we specifically mean by the term **organization culture**? We use the term to refer to a system of shared meaning. Just as tribal cultures have totems and taboos that dictate how each member will act toward fellow members and outsiders, organizations have cultures that govern how their members should behave. In every organization, there are systems or patterns of values, symbols, rituals, myths, and practices that have evolved over time.[27] These shared values determine, to a large degree, what employees see and how they respond to their world.[28]

organization culture
A system of shared meaning within an organization that determines, to a large degree, how employees act.

How Can Cultures Be Assessed?

Though we currently have no definitive method for measuring an organization's culture, preliminary research suggests that cultures can be analysed by assessing how an organization rates on 10 characteristics.[29] We have listed these characteristics in Exhibit 7-8.

    These 10 characteristics are relatively stable and permanent over time. Just as an individual's personality is stable and permanent—if you were outgoing last month, you're likely to be outgoing next month—so, too, is an organization's culture.

    General Motors has been almost universally described as a cold, formal, risk-aversive firm. It was that way in the 1930s, and it is basically the same today. In contrast, Hewlett-Packard is an informal, loosely structured, highly humanistic organization. Both General Motors and Hewlett-Packard have been essentially successful over the decades despite having completely different cultures.

GENERAL MOTORS
www.gm.com/

► **1.** Member identity: the degree to which employees identify with the organization as a whole rather than with their type of job or field of professional expertise.

► **2.** Group emphasis: the degree to which work activities are organized around groups rather than individuals.

► **3.** People focus: the degree to which management decisions take into consideration the effect of outcomes on people within the organization.

► **4.** Unit integration: the degree to which units within the organization are encouraged to operate in a coordinated or interdependent manner.

► **5.** Control: the degree to which rules, regulations, and direct supervision are used to oversee and control employee behaviour.

► **6.** Risk tolerance: the degree to which employees are encouraged to be aggressive, innovative, and risk-seeking.

► **7.** Reward criteria: the degree to which rewards such as salary increases and promotions are allocated on employee performance criteria in contrast to seniority, favouritism, or other nonperformance factors.

► **8.** Conflict tolerance: the degree to which employees are encouraged to air conflicts and criticisms openly.

► **9.** Means-end orientation: the degree to which management focuses on results or outcomes rather than the techniques and processes used to achieve those outcomes.

►**10.** Open-systems focus: the degree to which the organization monitors and responds to changes in the external environment.

**Exhibit 7-8
Cultural
Characteristics**

Robert Schad, CEO of Husky Injection Molding Systems in Bolton, Ontario, has established a strong culture wherein workers are encouraged to set goals for themselves and are offered incentives; and personal fitness is strongly supported, with state-of-the-art fitness facilities and subsidized health-conscious cafeterias.

strong culture
Organizations in which the key values are accepted, intensely held, and widely shared.

Where Does an Organization's Culture Come From?

An organization's culture usually reflects the vision or mission of the organization's founders. Because the founders have the original idea, they also have biases on how to carry out the idea. They are unconstrained by previous customs or ideologies. The founders establish the early culture by projecting an image of what the organization should be. The small size of most new organizations also helps the founders impose their vision on all organizational members. An organization's culture, then, results from the interaction between (1) the founders' biases and assumptions, and (2) what the first employees learn subsequently from their own experiences.[30]

Thomas Watson at IBM and Frank Stronach at Magna are just two examples of individuals who have had an immeasurable influence on shaping their organizations' cultures. For instance, Watson's views on research and development, product quality, employee attire, and compensation policies are still evident at IBM, although he died in 1956. Frank Stronach's belief that business units must remain small to be effective, and that Magna's design and development functions must be a part of their customers' design and development functions are two of the major differentiating factors that make Magna stand out in the automobile industry.

Does Culture Influence Structure?

An organization's culture may have an effect on an organization's structure depending on how strong, or weak, the culture may be. For instance, in organizations where there is a **strong culture**—one in which the dominant values of organizational members are accepted, intensely held, and widely shared—behavioural consistency of employees increases. In a sense, culture can act as a substitute for formalization.

In our last chapter, we discussed how formalization's rules and regulations act to regulate employee behaviour. High degrees of formalization in an organization create predictability, orderliness, and consistency. Strong cultures achieve the same end without the need for written documentation. Therefore, we can view formalization and culture as two different roads to a common destination. The stronger an organization's culture, the less managers need to be concerned with developing formal rules and regulations to guide employee behaviour. Instead, those guides will be internalized in employees when they accept the organization's culture. If an organization's culture is weak— where there are no dominant shared values—its effect on structure is less clear.

Operations Technology

High-tech manufacturing is quickly becoming a global phenomenon. By using technology developed elsewhere (called technology transfer), developing countries can bypass stages of development. This makes for a much greater level of competition in all industries, and therefore a greater need for organizations to stay on top of progress in operations technology. For instance, New Brunswick has traditionally lagged far behind other Canadian provinces in economic terms. But the development of a state-of-the-art fibre optics telephone system has allowed N.B. to lure many call centres of the major Canadian corporations away from economic hubs such as Toronto.

In this section we look at key issues related to operations technology: design, production, customer service, distribution, continuous improvement processes, and reengineering work processes.

How Can Products Be Designed More Efficiently?

Technology is redefining how the design of products is accomplished. For instance, computer-aided design is generating substantial improvements in design productivity. And sophisticated computer networks are allowing designers to collaborate as never before.

Computer-aided design (CAD) has essentially made manual drafting obsolete. Computational and graphics software allow the geometry of a product or component to be graphically displayed and manipulated on video monitors. Alternative designs can be created and evaluated quickly, and the cost in time and materials of developing mock-ups and prototypes is often eliminated. The best CAD software lets engineers plan products, test them on-screen, and even design tools to make them.

computer-aided design (CAD)
The use of computational and graphics software that allows the geometry of a product or component to be graphically displayed and manipulated on video monitors.

In What Ways Can Production Processes Be Enhanced?

Technological advances over the past 20 years have completely revolutionized the way products are manufactured. First there were robotics and just-in-time inventory systems. Today we have entered the stage of mass customization called flexible manufacturing systems.

What Is Robotics? Robots, of course, are machines that act like human beings. By the late 1970s, manufacturing firms began adding robots to assembly lines. From those initial basic robots came industrial **robotics**—computer-controlled machines that manipulate materials and perform complex functions. The leaders of this move to industrial robotics were the Japanese. By 1990, they already had more than two million manufacturing robots in use.[31]

But robots were not without their problems. They were useful in handling simple jobs, but they often failed when tasks became more complicated. Today, robots are playing more of a support role in larger computer-based manufacturing systems.

robotics
Computer-controlled machines that manipulate materials and perform complex functions.

How Do Just-in-time Inventory Systems Operate? Large companies, such as Bombardier, Ford, and General Electric, can have up to billions of dollars tied up in inventories. It is not unusual for even small firms to have millions in inventory. So anything management can do to significantly reduce the size of its inventory will improve its organization's productivity.

Just-in-time (JIT) inventory systems change the technology around which inventories are managed. Inventory items arrive when they are needed in the production process instead of being stored in stock. Companies such as Xerox Canada are becoming increasingly committed to this idea of "keeping their warehouses on the road."

just-in-time (JIT) inventory
A system in which inventory items arrive when they are needed in the production process instead of being stored in stock.

kanban
The Japanese word for "card" or "sign"; the basis of JIT inventory systems.

In Japan, JIT systems are called *kanban*, a word whose definition gets to the essence of the JIT concept. **Kanban** is Japanese for "card" or "sign." Japanese suppliers ship parts in containers, with each container having a card, or *kanban*, slipped into a side pocket. When a production worker at the manufacturing plant opens a container, she takes out the card and sends it back to the supplier. Receipt of the card initiates the shipping of a second container of parts that, ideally, reaches the production worker just as the last part in the first container is being used up. The ultimate goal of a JIT inventory system is to eliminate raw material inventories by precisely coordinating production and supply deliveries. When the system works as designed, it results in a number of positive benefits for a manufacturer: reduced inventories, reduced set-up times, better work flow, shorter manufacturing time, less space consumption, and even higher quality goods. Of course, suppliers who can be depended on to deliver quality materials on time must be found. Because there are no inventories, there is no slack in the system to compensate for defective materials or delays in shipments.

What Are Flexible Manufacturing Systems? Flexible manufacturing systems look like something out of a science-fiction movie in which remote-controlled carts deliver basic casting to a computerized machining centre. With robots positioning and repositioning the casting, the machining centre calls upon its hundreds of tools to perform varying operations that turn the casting into a finished part. Completed parts, each a bit different from the others, can be finished at a rate of one every 90 seconds. Neither skilled machinists nor conventional machine tools are used. Nor are there any costly delays for changing dies or tools in this factory. A single machine can make dozens or even hundreds of different parts in any order management wants. This is the world of **flexible manufacturing systems**.

At Fred Deeley Imports, the Canadian distributor for Harley Davidson, a JIT process called crossdocking is used wherein inventory comes in one end of the warehouse and is rearranged without shelving to be sent out to retailers, keeping product always on the move.

flexible manufacturing systems
Systems that, by integrating computer-aided design, engineering, and manufacturing, can produce low-volume, customized products at a cost comparable to that of high-volume, standardized products.

In a global economy, manufacturing organizations that can respond rapidly to change have a competitive advantage. They can, for instance, better meet the diverse needs of customers and deliver products faster than their competitors. When customers were willing to accept standardized products, fixed assembly lines made sense. But nowadays flexible technologies are increasingly necessary to compete effectively.

The unique characteristic of flexible manufacturing systems is that by integrating computer-aided design, engineering, and manufacturing, they can produce low-volume products for customers at a cost comparable to what had previously been possible only through mass production. Flexible manufacturing systems are, in effect, repealing the laws of economies of scale. Management no longer has to mass produce

At Celestica Inc.'s Toronto factory, the production line can be, and often is, changed in less than 48 hours to produce a different product. The introduction of a flexible manufacturing system has made this company vastly more profitable than before.

thousands of identical products to achieve low per-unit production costs. With flexible manufacturing, when management wants to produce a new part, it does not change machines—it simply changes the computer program. In this way management is able to respond to each customer's unique taste, specification, and budget.

In What Ways Can Service Be Improved?

Consistent with the quality movement, technology can be used to revitalize customer service. It can provide the ability to identify and track individual customers, to monitor service levels by customer representatives, and to assist customers in specifying, acquiring, fixing, or returning products.

Managers are using technology to improve their customer service strategies in three ways. First, technology can *personalize* service that was previously standardized. It can allow managers to individualize service for each customer's unique needs. This sort of service has traditionally been the domain of small local businesses. For instance if you were to walk into The Odd Book bookstore in Wolfville, Nova Scotia, being a resident and frequent customer, Jim Tillotson would be able to refer you to a number of books to suit your taste. A large bookstore such as Chapters would not. However, by keeping computer records of individual purchases (using a system such as a frequent-shopper discount card), a large bookstore could offer a similar service. Many Canadian companies, such as Mountain Equipment Co-Op, use customer information to offer more personalized service.

Second, technology can *augment* service by providing the customer with additional support related to the acquisition or use of the product. Hertz used this strategy when it created its Gold Card service. Its computer system has your credit card number for billing, your car style and size preference, insurance data, and drivers' licence information. One short phone call makes your reservation. Then, when you arrive at your destination, an electronic sign with your name on it indicates where your car is located. The paperwork is already done and your contract is sitting in your waiting car. When your trip is complete and you drop the car off, you bypass the line at the checkout counter. All you have to do is hand the keys and contract to the lot attendant, who records the time, date, and mileage in his hand-held computer.

Third, technology can *transform* your business. That is, it can allow an organization to develop fundamentally new business practices, and to reinvent itself. By using technology, a business can offer superior service to customers, through flexible manufacturing systems, for example, or less complicated improvements to operations.

How Does Technology Enhance Product Distribution?

MONTY PYTHON
www.pythononline.com

Traditional distribution technology relied heavily on sales agents or brokers, wholesalers, and retailers. It was not unusual for a product to go through two or three intermediaries before reaching the consumer. New technologies are increasingly cutting out these intermediaries. Management has been investing heavily in multiple-distribution technologies to get closer to the customer, while also cutting costs, providing quicker deliveries and better service, and better meeting the needs of a diverse customer base. The two most recent breakthroughs in distribution technology are home shopping through television and electromic shopping via the Internet. Both allow manufacturers to directly reach customers.

While home shopping through television stations specifically devoted to this method of sales is a growing phenomenon, the latest and potentially most exciting distribution channel made possible by computer technology is marketing products directly to customers on the Internet. Just about every major business firm (and many of the small ones), educational institution, and not-for-profit organization in Canada is setting up a site on the World Wide Web, and creating a home page. This represents a relatively cheap way for organizations to reach more than 20 million customers. Visiting the Monty Python Web site, for instance, you can listen to songs, look at cartoons, play games, and, of course, purchase an array of Python merchandise. Toronto Dominion Bank has turned its Web site into a one-stop financial shopping centre, containing 300 "pages" of general financial information about savings plans, mortgages, and other financial products and services.[32]

The Shopping Channel Ltd., controlled by media magnate Ted Rogers, allows manufacturers to sell directly to customers. In the U.S., per capita each household spends $30 a year through home shopping, while here the figure is $5, but Canada's home shopping industry is growing quickly.

Is 99.9 Per Cent Good Enough?

We have already discussed the philosophy of management known as total quality management (TQM), which is driven by the constant attainment of customer satisfaction through the continuous improvement of all organizational processes. Managers in many organizations, especially in North America, have been criticized for accepting a level of performance that is below perfection. TQM, however, argues that good isn't good enough. Is it acceptable for Canada Post to lose every thousandth letter, or for University Hospital in London, Ontario, to lose every thousandth patient who comes in for a routine operation?

TQM programs seek to achieve continuous process improvements so that variability is constantly reduced. When variations are eliminated, the uniformity of the product or service is increased. Uniformity, in turn, results in lower costs and higher quality.

Continuous improvement runs counter to the more typical North American management approach of seeing work projects as being linear—with a specific beginning and end. For example, Canadian managers traditionally looked at cost-cutting as a short-term project. They set a goal of, say, cutting costs by 20 per cent, achieved it, and then said, "All right, good job, our cost-cutting is finished." The Japanese, on the other hand, have regarded cost control as something that never ends. The search for continuous improvement creates a race without a finish line, never providing one the opportunity to stop, rest after a victory, and become slow and lazy again.

The search for never-ending improvement requires a circular approach rather than a linear one. Management plans a change, does it, checks the results, and, depending on the outcome, acts to standardize the change or begin the cycle of improvement again with new information, then repeats the process. The cycle treats all organizational processes as being in a constant state of improvement.

Standard Aero in Winnipeg is an aircraft engine repair company whose TQM efforts cost millions but result in continual improvements in productivity, bringing it more contracts.

Will Reengineering Enhance Work Processes?

We have already described reengineering as considering how things would be done if you could start all over from scratch.

The term reengineering comes from the historical process of taking apart an electronics product and designing a better version. Michael Hammer coined the term for organizations. When he found companies using computers simply to automate outdated processes rather than finding fundamentally better ways of doing things, he realized that the principles of reengineering electronics products could be applied to business. So, as applied to organizations, reengineering means starting with a clean sheet of paper, rethinking and redesigning the processes by which the organization creates value and does work, and eliminating operations that have become antiquated in the computer age.

What Are the Key Elements of Reengineering? Three key elements of reengineering are identifying an organization's distinctive competencies; assessing core processes; and reorganizing horizontally by process.

An organization's distinctive competencies are the unique skills and resources that determine its competitive weapons. Distinctive competencies define what it is that the organization can do better than its competition can. It might have superior store locations, more knowledgeable sales personnel, or superior technical support. Why is identifying distinctive competencies so important? Because it guides decisions regarding what activities are crucial to the organization's success.

Management also needs to assess the core processes that clearly add value to the organization's distinctive competencies. These are the processes that transform materials, capital, information, and labour into products and services that the customer values. When the organization is viewed as a series of processes—ranging from strategic planning to after-sales customer support—management can determine to what degree each adds value. Not surprisingly, this **process value analysis** typically uncovers many activities that add little or nothing of value and whose only justification is "we've always done it this way."

Reengineering requires management to reorganize around horizontal processes. This orientation means using cross-functional and self-managed teams. It means focusing on processes rather than on functions. It also means cutting out levels of middle management. As Hammer has pointed out, "Managers are not value-added. A customer never buys a product because of the caliber of management. Management is, by definition, indirect. So, if possible, less is better. One of the goals of reengineering is to minimize the necessary amount of management."[33]

Why Reengineering Now? Isn't reengineering something management should have been doing all along? Why has it become such a hot topic over the past five to 10 years? The answers, according to Mike Hammer, are a changing global environment and organizational structures that have become top-heavy.

Traditional bureaucratic organizations worked well in times of stable growth. Activities could be fragmented and specialized to gain economic efficiencies. That description fits the environment faced by most North American organizations in the 1950s, 1960s and much of the 1970s. But most organizations today operate in a much different environment. Customers are far more informed and sophisticated than they were 30 years ago. Moreover, markets, production, and capital can be moved all over the world. Investors in Australia, for example, can put their money into opportunities

process value analysis
Analysing core processes that by transforming materials, capital, information, and labour into products and services that customers value, add value to an organization's distinctive competencies.

in Canada, Japan, the U.S., or anywhere else in the world—if they see better returns than they can get at home. Customers worldwide now demand quality, service, and low cost. If one organization can't provide it, they will get it from somewhere else.

Work specialization, bureaucratic departments, managers supervising few employees, and other such factors drove down direct labour costs, but the bureaucracies they created had massive overhead costs. To coordinate all the fragmentation and specialization, the organization needed numerous levels of middle management. So, although bureaucracies drove down costs at the operating level, they required increasingly expensive coordinating systems. Organizations challenged the traditional way of doing things when they introduced teams, moved decision making down to the people closest to the problems, made managers supervise more employees, and eliminated layers of management.

Information Technology

Information technology (IT) is one of the fastest-growing industries in Canada. The industry in this country was worth an estimated $64 billion in 1997, and has since been growing steadily. A broad definition of the IT industry is as follows: "A combination of computer applications and communications. Computer applications include software, hardware, and related services such as multimedia. Communications involve the transmission of information, through such venues as cable or telephone wires, as well as wireless communications such as satellite or radio."[34]

Information technology is revolutionizing the ways organizations operate. In this section we will highlight how this technology is reshaping office work flows, changing the way internal communications are handled, and providing high-tech support for organizational decision making.

What Is Workflow Automation?

In the typical office, information spends most of its time moving from desk to desk. For instance, consider the creation of a marketing plan. The marketing director approves the creation of the plan. A product manager is given responsibility for overseeing the plan's development. Staff marketing researchers gather the necessary data. A senior researcher than writes the first draft and sends it on to the product manager. This whole process requires documents to be passed along from one desk to another as the plan is developed, reviewed, edited, and rewritten, until eventually a final document is agreed upon and approved. This process can take weeks or even months because the document can sit on someone's desk for days before he even looks at it. In fact, it is estimated that gathering and transferring paper documents can take up as much as 90 per cent of the time needed to finish typical office tasks.

Workflow automation can solve much of this delay. It greatly improves the process of creating and transferring documents by automating the flow of information. Workflow automation begins by examining how documents, business forms, and other information wend their way through an organization. It looks for bottlenecks and outdated procedures that slow things down and add to costs. Once new routines are laid out, workflow software is installed on computer networks to

workflow automation
Use of computer software to automatically process and route documents and information through an organization.

instantly convey all information to the right desk—whether it's a digital image of an invoice, an e-mail question from a customer, or any other type of information. This software makes the movement of documents automatic, eliminating the need for a person to figure out who should get the information next and then get it to them. It also collapses the travel times and avoids misrouting. The system can also be programmed to send documents along different paths depending on content.

How Does Technology Enhance Internal Communications?

Information technology is reshaping communications within organizations in many ways. For example, it is significantly improving management's ability to monitor organizational performance and is allowing employees to have more complete information to make faster decisions. But if we had to identify the two most important developments in information technology, in terms of their impact on internal organizational communications, they would probably be digitalization and the wireless phenomenon.

Organizations are converting internal information from analog language to digital. Telephones, for instance, have traditionally used an analog signal—an electric wave-form representation of sound. Computers, on the other hand, use a digital language—combinations of zeros and ones—to communicate. Organizations are aggressively changing all of their internal communication systems to the digital format. Why? Analog is slower, less accurate, and prone to interruptions and distortions. Moreover, any information—numbers, words, voices, or pictures—can be digitized. So, by converting to a completely digital format, organizations will have put in place a system that can permit managers and employees to communicate in any form. Any information can be delivered to any instrument capable of displaying it. A television, for instance, can receive and display computer text, or a radio can receive a phone call.

Combine digitalization and wireless networks and you have revolutionized internal communications. Wireless products—such as personal pagers, cellular telephones, and computers with modems—are making it possible for people in organizations to be fully accessible to each other at any time, from any place. Employees won't have to be at their desks with their computers plugged in to communicate with others in the organization. "I think wireless communications is probably the last communications breakthrough of our lifetimes," says Kenneth Forbes III, CEO of Mobile Digital Corp.[35] Or, as another senior manager put it, "The last 100 years have been the wireline century. We have just embarked on the wireless century."[36]

In What Ways Does Technology Assist Decision Making?

Information technology is providing managers with a wealth of decision-making support. Examples include expert systems, neural networks, groupware, and specific problem-solving software.

expert systems
Software programs that use the encoded relevant experience of a human expert to analyse and solve ill-structured problems.

Expert systems use software programs to encode the relevant experience of a human expert and allow a system to act like that expert in analysing and solving ill-structured problems. The essence of expert systems is that (1) they use specialized knowledge about a particular problem area rather than general knowledge that would apply to all problems; (2) They use qualitative reasoning rather than numeric calculations; and (3) they perform at a level of competence that is higher than that of non-expert humans.[37] They guide users through problems by asking them a set of sequential questions about the situation, and drawing conclusions based on the answers. The conclusions are based on programmed rules that have been modeled on the actual reasoning processes of experts who have previously confronted similar problems. Once in place, these systems are allowing employees and lower-level managers to make high-quality decisions that previously could only have been made by senior managers. Expert systems are being used in such diverse areas as medical diagnosis, mineral and oil exploration, equipment fault-locating, credit approval, and financial planning. For instance, IDS Financial Services has encoded the expertise of its best financial-planning account managers in an expert system program. "Now even the worst of our 6,500 planners is better than our average planner used to be," IDS's chairman has said.[38]

Neural networks are the next step beyond expert systems. They use computer software to imitate the structure of, and connections among, brain cells. Neural networks have the ability to distinguish patterns and trends too subtle or complex for human beings to distinguish. For instance, people can't easily assimilate more than two or three variables at once, but neural networks can perceive correlations among hundreds of variables. As a result, they can perform many operations simultaneously, recognizing patterns, making associations, generalizing about problems they haven't been exposed to before, and learning through experience.

neural networks
Computer software that by imitating the structure of and connections between brain cells, distinguish patterns and trends too subtle or complex for human beings.

We have already mentioned the concept of electronic meetings as one means of improving group decision making. Although electronic meetings have assisted in the decision-making process, groups today are interacting electronically for a number of reasons. **Groupware** is a term used to describe the multitude of software programs that have developed to facilitate group interaction and decision making. Other examples of groupware applications are videoconferencing group meetings, disseminating presentations, augmenting face-to-face customer visits, and even conducting preliminary interviews for job candidates.[39]

groupware
Software programs that facilitate group interaction and decision making by people at different locations.

Job Design Options

If you put an organization under a microscope, you would find that it is composed of thousands, maybe even millions, of tasks. These tasks, in turn, are aggregated into jobs.[40] The jobs that people do in any organization should not evolve by chance. Managers should design jobs thoughtfully to reflect the organization's technology, as well as the skills, abilities, and preferences of its employees. When this is done, employees can reach their full productive capabilities.

We use the term **job design** to refer to the way tasks are combined to form complete jobs. Some jobs are routine because the tasks are standardized and repetitive; others are nonroutine. Some require a large number of varied and diverse skills; others are narrow in scope. Some jobs constrain employees by requiring them to follow very precise procedures; others allow employees substantial freedom in how they do their work. Some jobs are most effectively accomplished by groups of employees working as a team, whereas other jobs are best done by individuals acting independently. Our point is that jobs differ in the way their tasks are combined, and these different combinations create a variety of job designs. Exhibit 7-9 describes some popular job design options.

job design
The way in which tasks are combined to form complete jobs.

job characteristics model (JCM)
A framework for analysing and designing jobs; identifies five primary job characteristics, their interrelationships, and their impact on outcome variables.

skill variety
The degree to which a job includes a variety of activities that call for a number of different skills and talents.

task identity
The degree to which a job requires completion of a whole and identifiable piece of work.

task significance
The degree to which a job has a substantial impact on the lives or work of other people.

autonomy
The degree to which a job provides substantial freedom, independence, and discretion to an individual in scheduling and carrying out his work.

What Is the Job Characteristics Model?

None of the approaches listed in Exhibit 7-9 provides a conceptual framework for analysing jobs or for guiding managers in designing jobs. The **job characteristics model (JCM)**, however, offers such a framework.[41] It identifies five primary job characteristics, their interrelationships, and their impact on employee productivity, motivation, and satisfaction.

According to the JCM, any job can be described in terms of five core dimensions, defined as follows: **skill variety**, the degree to which a job requires a variety of activities so that an employee can use a number of different skills and talents; **task identity**, the degree to which a job requires completion of a whole and identifiable piece of work; **task significance**, the degree to which a job has a substantial impact on the lives or work of other people; **autonomy**, the degree to which a job provides substantial freedom, independence, and discretion to the individual in scheduling the

Job Specialization:	Under job specialization, jobs are divided into minute, specialized tasks. Job specialization is synonymous with the early management writers.
Job Rotation:	Job rotation is designed to allow workers to diversify their activities and avoid boredom. There are actually two types of rotation: vertical and horizontal. Vertical rotation refers to promotions and demotions. However, traditional job rotation involves lateral transfers of workers among jobs involving different tasks.
Job Enlargement:	Job enlargement increases the number of different tasks required in a job and decreases the frequency with which the job cycle is repeated. By increasing the number of tasks an individual performs, job enlargement increases job diversity.
Job Enrichment:	Job enrichment increases job depth. This option allows employees greater control over their work. They're allowed to assume some of the tasks typically done by their supervisors—particularly planning and evaluating their own work.
Integrated Work Teams:	In integrated work teams, a large number of tasks are assigned to a group. The group then decides the specific assignments of members and is responsible for rotating jobs among the members as the tasks require. The team still has a supervisor who oversees the group's activities.
Self-Managed Work Teams:	Self-managed work teams are more vertically integrated and have a wider range of discretion than their integrated counterparts. The self-managed work team is given a goal to achieve and then is free to determine work assignments, rest breaks, inspection procedures, and so forth. These teams often even select their own members and have the members evaluate one another's performances. As a result, supervisory positions become less important and may sometimes be eliminated.

Exhibit 7-9   Some Examples of Job Design Options

work and determining the procedures to be used in carrying it out; and **feedback**, the degree to which carrying out the work activities required by a job results in the individual's obtaining direct and clear information about the effectiveness of her performance (see Details on a Management Classic).

What Guidance Can the JCM Offer Managers in Designing Jobs?

The JCM provides specific guidance to managers in designing jobs. The following suggestions, which derive from the JCM, specify the types of changes in jobs that are most likely to lead to improvements in each of the five core dimensions:

► **1. Combine tasks.** Managers should put existing fractionalized tasks back together to form a new, larger module of work. This increases employees' skills and allows them to complete the whole job.

► **2. Create natural work units.** Managers should design tasks that form an identifiable and meaningful whole. This increases employee "ownership" of the work and encourages employees to view their work as meaningful and important rather than as irrelevant and boring.

► **3. Establish client relationships.** The client is the user of the product or service that the employee works on. Wherever possible, managers should establish direct relationships between workers and their clients. This increases employees' skills and provides them with feedback.

► **4. Expand jobs vertically.** Vertical expansion gives employees responsibilities and controls that were formerly reserved for management. It partially closes the gap between the "doing" and "controlling" aspects of the job, and it increases employee autonomy.

► **5. Open feedback channels.** By increasing feedback, employees learn not only how well they are performing their jobs but also whether their performances are improving, deteriorating, or remaining at a constant level. Ideally, employees should receive performance feedback directly, as they do their jobs, rather than from management on an occasional basis.[42]

feedback
The degree to which carrying out the work activities required by a job results in an individual's obtaining direct and clear information about the effectiveness of her performance.

DETAILS ON A MANAGEMENT CLASSIC

J. Richard Hackman and Greg R. Oldham: The Job Characteristics Model

The dominant framework today for defining task characteristics and understanding their relationships to employee motivation is Hackman and Oldham's job characteristics model (JCM).[43] Research on the JCM has found that the first three dimensions— skill variety, task identity, and task significance—combine to create meaningful work. That is, if these three characteristics exist in a job, we can predict that the person will view his job as being important, valuable, and worthwhile. Jobs that allow autonomy give the job incumbent a feeling of personal responsibility for the results, and jobs that provide feedback let the employee know how effectively she is performing.

From a motivational standpoint, the JCM says that internal rewards are obtained when one *learns* (knowledge of results) that one *personally* (experienced responsibility) has performed well on a task that one *cares about* (experienced meaningfulness).[44] The more these three conditions are present, the greater will be the employee's motivation, performance, and satisfaction.[45]

The core dimensions can be combined into a single index called the Motivating Potential Score (MPS). The MPS is calculated as follows:

$$\begin{array}{c} \text{Motivating} \\ \text{Potential} \\ \text{Score (MPS)} \end{array} = \left[\frac{\begin{array}{ccc} \text{Skill} & \text{Task} & \text{Task} \\ \text{Variety} + \text{Identity} + \text{Significance} \end{array}}{3} \right] \times \text{Autonomy} \times \text{Feedback}$$

What does the JCM tell us? To score high on motivating potential, managers must design jobs so that they are high on at least one of the three factors that lead to experiencing meaningfulness (skill variety, task identity, or task significance). Furthermore, jobs must also be high on both autonomy and feedback. Creating jobs that meet these requirements will result in a high motivating potential score. In doing so, motivation, performance, and satisfaction will be positively affected, while the likelihood of absenteeism and turnover will be lessened.[46]▼

Summary

This summary is organized by the chapter Learning Objectives found on page 171.

1. The simple structure is low in complexity, has little formalization, and has authority centralized in a single person. It is widely used in small businesses.

2. The functional structure groups similar or related occupational specialties together. It takes advantage of specialization and provides economies of

scale by allowing people with common skills to work together.

3. The divisional structure is composed of autonomous units, with managers having full responsibility for a product or service. However, these units are frequently organized as functional

structures inside their divisional framework. So divisional structures typically contain functional structures within them.

4. By assigning specialists from functional departments to work on one or more projects led by project managers, the matrix structure combines functional and product departmentalization. Thus, it has the advantage of both specialization and high accountability.

5. The recent popularity of the network structure is due to its high flexibility. It allows management to perform manufacturing, distribution, marketing, or other crucial business functions with a minimal commitment of resources.

6. A strategic alliance allows for different organizations to combine resources, skills, and share costs and risks in an effort to produce a joint product.

7. Organic appendages allow organizations to be responsive and flexible while, at the same time, maintaining an overall mechanistic structure.

8. The term horizontal organization refers to a structural design characterized by multidisciplinary teams who perform core processes.

9. TQM encourages low vertical differentiation, minimal division of labour, and decentralized decision making.

10. Organization culture is a system of shared meaning within an organization that determines, to a large degree, how employees act.

11. Job specialization is concerned with breaking down jobs into ever-smaller tasks. Job enlargement is the reverse. It expands jobs horizontally by increasing their scope. Like enlargement, job enrichment expands jobs, but it does so vertically rather than horizontally. Enriched jobs increase depth by allowing employees greater control over their work.

Review and Discussion Questions

1. Show how both the functional and matrix structures might create conflict within an organization.

2. What are the strengths and weaknesses of
   a. the functional structure
   b. the divisional structure

3. Why is the simple structure inadequate in large organizations?

4. Can an organization have no structure?

5. When should management use
   a. the matrix structure
   b. the network structure
   c. a committee

6. Of the following structural designs—functional, divisional, simple, network, or matrix—which one would you most prefer to work in? Least prefer? Why?

7. "What a manager does in terms of the organizing function depends on what level she occupies in the organizational hierarchy." Discuss.

8. Describe the characteristics of a horizontal organizational structure. How do you think "tomorrow's" employees will accept these characteristics?

9. Contrast job enlargement and job enrichment in terms of the job characteristics model.

10. Define organizational culture.

11. Contrast organizational culture with formalization.

12. Classrooms have cultures. Describe your class culture. How does it affect your instructor?

Testing Your Comprehension

Circle the correct answer, then check yourself on page 471.

1. Which of the following is LEAST likely to be a disadvantage of the functional structure?

   a) little cross-training among managers

   b) optimization of goals at the department level rather than at the organizational level

   c) insulation among various departments that often results in suboptimization of organizational goals

   d) duplication of facilities, people, and information

2. A major advantage of the simple structure is

   a) clear responsibility and accountability

   b) low risk

   c) appropriateness for almost any business

   d) ability to build managers through participative decision making

3. Which of the following statements is INCORRECT regarding divisional structures?

   a) A divisional structure's roots are based in product departmentalization.

   b) A major disadvantage of the divisional structure is its duplication of resources.

   c) A divisional structure manager is required to seek corporate approval for implementing tactical plans.

   d) An advantage of the divisional structure is that it focuses on results.

4. Which of the following is NOT a strength of the matrix structure?

   a) the accountability of the divisional structure

   b) the efficiency from specialization attributable to the functional structure

   c) elimination of the duplication of resources and facilities

   d) minimization of ambiguity in reporting relationships

5. A centralized organization that relies on other organizations for many of its functions is an example of

   a) a neural network

   b) a network structure

   c) an expert system

   d) horizontal structure

6. A temporary structure designed to accomplish a specific goal, using personnel from different areas in an organization is

   a) a task force

   b) a strategic alliance

   c) a committee structure

   d) a core process

7. Which of the following statements describes a benefit of computer-aided design?

   a) Computer-aided design has made manual drafting obsolete.

   b) Computer-aided design enhances customization in manufacturing.

   c) Computer-aided design involves computer-controlled machines and materials manipulation.

   d) All of the above are benefits of computer-aided design.

8. The Japanese word *kanban* is best associated with which of the following operations technology concepts?

   a) robotics

   b) computer-aided design

   c) flexible manufacturing systems

   d) just-in-time inventory systems

9. Which of the following statements is correct regarding flexible manufacturing systems?

   a) Flexible manufacturing systems ensure that inventory items arrive when they are needed in the production process rather than being stored in stock.

   b) Flexible manufacturing systems permit organizations to rapidly change their production setups to more fully meet customers' needs.

   c) Flexible manufacturing systems permit an organization to more effectively meet customer needs, but to do so at an increased cost per unit produced.

   d) Flexible manufacturing systems can be used to enhance information technology.

10. What is the point of the question "Is 99.9 per cent good enough?"

    a) Sometimes "good" isn't good enough.

    b) Continuous process improvement will never reach perfection.

    c) TQM efforts have lost their luster in manufacturing corporations.

    d) TQM without reengineering will not achieve corporate goals of 100-per-cent effectiveness.

11. The process by which an organization improves how it creates documents and transfers the flow of information is best defined as

    a) information technology

    b) neural networks

    c) workflow automation

    d) computer-assisted information design

12. Expert systems

    a) use software programs to model how someone analyses and solves an ill-structured problem

    b) use software programs to imitate the structure of the brain cells and the connections among them

    c) is a term used to describe software programs that help to facilitate group decision making

    d) enable managers with minimal statistical background to solve organizational problems that require quantitative techniques

13. You are a senior manager of a global manufacturing company. You would like to obtain input from several of your plant managers regarding the advantages and disadvantages of installing the newest robotic technology. Several thousand miles separate you and your plant managers, who are working on four continents. Given this background information, and your desire to involve them in making a decision, which of the following information technology support systems would you use to most efficiently get your managers' input?

    a) an expert system
    b) a neural network
    c) electronic mail
    d) groupware

14. The degree to which the job requires an assortment of different activities so the worker can use a number of different skills and talents is best defined as

    a) autonomy
    b) task identity
    c) task significance
    d) none of the above

15. Which of the following was NOT identified in the job characteristics model as a core job dimension?

    a) skill ability
    b) task identity
    c) autonomy
    d) feedback

16. An inspector working at a nuclear plant recognizes that her job is important to members of the surrounding community. Given this perception, which of the five core job dimensions of the job characteristics model is being affected?

    a) autonomy
    b) task identity
    c) task significance
    d) feedback

17. The social information processing model argues that

    a) information technology contributes extensively to worker obsolescence
    b) employees adopt attitudes and behaviours in response to cues provided by others around them
    c) employees process information about the job's actual requirements and form their likes and dislikes about the job on the basis of factual data
    d) employee motivation and satisfaction are not affected by challenging or autonomous work

18. Requiring full-time employees to be in the office between 9:00 a.m. and 2:00 p.m. each day but permitting them to schedule the remaining work hours to match their individual needs represents which type of work schedule option?

   a) worker autonomy

   b) core work hours

   c) job sharing

   d) flextime

Self-Assessment Exercise

Is an Enriched Job for You?

Instructions: People differ in what they like and dislike in their jobs. Listed below are 12 pairs of jobs. For each pair, indicate which job you would prefer. Assume that everything else about the jobs is the same—pay attention only to the characteristics actually listed for each pair of jobs. If you would prefer the job in the left-hand column (Column A), indicate how much you prefer it by putting a check mark in a blank to the left of the Neutral point. If you prefer the job in the right-hand column (Column B), check one of the blanks to the right of Neutral. Check the Neutral blank only if you find the two jobs equally attractive or unattractive. Try to use the Neutral blank rarely.

COLUMN A		COLUMN B
1. A job that offers little or no challenge.	Strongly prefer A — Neutral — Strongly prefer B	A job that requires you to be completely isolated from co-workers.
2. A job that pays very well.	Strongly prefer A — Neutral — Strongly prefer B	A job that allows considerable opportunity to be creative and innovative.
3. A job that often requires you to make important decisions.	Strongly prefer A — Neutral — Strongly prefer B	A job in which there are many pleasant people to work with.
4. A job with little security in a somewhat unstable organization.	Strongly prefer A — Neutral — Strongly prefer B	A job in which you have little or no opportunity to participate in decisions that affect your work.
5. A job in which greater responsibility is given to those who do the best work.	Strongly prefer A — Neutral — Strongly prefer B	A job in which greater responsibility is given to loyal employees who have the most seniority.
6. A job with a supervisor who sometimes is highly critical.	Strongly prefer A — Neutral — Strongly prefer B	A job that does not require you to use much of your talent.
7. A very routine job.	Strongly prefer A — Neutral — Strongly prefer B	A job in which your co-workers are not very friendly.
8. A job with a supervisor who respects you and treats you fairly.	Strongly prefer A — Neutral — Strongly prefer B	A job that provides constant opportunities for you to learn new and interesting things.
9. A job that gives you a real chance to develop yourself personally.	Strongly prefer A — Neutral — Strongly prefer B	A job with excellent vacations and fringe benefits.
10. A job in which there is a real chance you could be laid off.	Strongly prefer A — Neutral — Strongly prefer B	A job with very little chance to do challenging work.

COLUMN A		COLUMN B
11. A job with little freedom and independence to do your work in the way you think best.	Strongly prefer A Neutral Strongly prefer B	A job with poor working conditions.
12. A job with very satisfying team-work.	Strongly prefer A Neutral Strongly prefer B	A job that allows you to use your skills and abilities to the fullest extent.

Turn to page 465 for scoring directions and key.

Source: J.R. Hackman and G.R. Oldham, *The Job Diagnostic Survey: An Instrument for the Diagnosis of Jobs and the Evaluation of Job Redesign Projects*, Technical Report No. 4 (New Haven, Conn.: Yale University, Department of Administrative Sciences, 1974). With permission.

Class Exercise

What Kind of Organization Design Do You Want to Work For?

Do you have an idea of what type of organization you'd like to work for? Most likely you have given it some thought, but that focus has probably been on the type of job, or maybe its location. What about the personality of the organization? How much consideration have you given to the culture you'd work best in?

For this exercise, first complete the questions below and score them. Then, in your group, compare responses. Are there group members who prefer to work in more bureaucratic organizations? Others who prefer to work in smaller companies? Discuss with your group members why you feel that type of organization will best suit you. Also, imagine that you work in an organization whose culture is the opposite of your preference. How might that affect your work? Discuss with your class members.

For each of the following statements, circle the level of agreement or disagreement that you personally feel:

SA = Strongly Agree
A = Agree
U = Uncertain
D = Disagree
SD = Strongly Disagree

1. I like being part of a team and having my performance assessed in terms of my contribution to the team.   SA A U D SD

2. No person's needs should be compromised in order for a department to achieve its goals.   SA A U D SD

3. I prefer a job where my boss leaves me alone.   SA A U D SD

4. I like the thrill and excitement of taking risks.   SA A U D SD

5. People shouldn't break rules.   SA A U D SD

6. Seniority in an organization should be highly rewarded.   SA A U D SD

7. I respect authority.   SA A U D SD

8. If a person's job performance is inadequate, it's irrelevant how much effort he made.   SA A U D SD

9. I like things to be predictable.   SA A U D SD

10. I'd prefer my identity and status to come from my professional expertise rather than from the organization that employs me.   SA A U D SD

For items 5, 6, 7, and 9, give yourself +2 for each strongly agree, +1 for agree, 0 for uncertain, −1 for disagree, and −2 for strongly disagree. For items 1, 2, 3, 4, 8, and 10, reverse the scoring (strongly agree = −2, and so forth). Add up your total. Your score will fall somewhere between +20 and −20. The higher your score (positive), the more comfortable you'll be in a stable, rule-oriented culture. This is synonymous with large companies and government agencies. Negative scores indicate a preference for small, innovative, flexible, team-oriented cultures that are more likely to be found in research units or small businesses.

Case Application

Flattening the Structure at Imedia Inc.

If we look at companies that are growing fastest and are most successful today, we see some common characteristics. Many of these firms have no senior manager of marketing or human resources. Many have no chief financial officer. And many do not rely on an information systems department for their communication needs. Rather, those specialized activities have been pushed down and assumed by individuals lower in the organization. In management terms, we say that what is occurring is empowering.[47]

Jo-Anne Dressendofer is the president of Imedia Inc., a marketing firm. Dressendofer always believed in keeping the company simple. When she started Imedia, she set herself up as the only manager and had all 30 of her employees report directly to her. This structure, to Dressendofer, was consistent with the lean-and-mean trend. Her employees, however, didn't see it that way. It was not that any of them disliked reporting directly to the president—they simply became fed up with Dressendofer making all of the decisions. The Imedia staff had to seek her permission to do, in their view, even the most mundane of tasks. This frustration went on for more than three years, until several of her staff marched into her office to confront her. Their demand: either she let go of the tight reins immediately, or they would quit.

Recognizing that she couldn't afford to lose these critical employees without losing a substantial part of her business, Dressendofer agreed. She immediately implemented a team management structure, giving employee groups responsibility for many activities and decisions. During the first year following the reorganization, she witnessed some startling changes. Although some employees initially had difficulty in accepting a major role in company decisions, the firm's sales increased by more than $1 million. That was almost a 50-per-cent increase in revenues—in only one year. Now, employees are more creative, more productive, and happier at work. And of course, Jo-Anne Dressendofer is much happier as well.

Questions

1. How would you characterize the "old" structure of Imedia—mechanic or organic? The new one? Give examples to support your choice.

2. Top management is usually involved in making organization design changes. Employees frequently do not have input. Do you believe that Jo-Anne Dressendofer made the design changes because they were appropriate, or because of pressure from her employees? Discuss your position.

3. What effect do you believe the organization's culture had on the structure changes? Explain.

chapter 8

Human Resource Management

Learning Objectives

What will I be able to do after I finish this chapter?

1 • Describe the strategic human resource management process.

2 • Discuss the influence of government regulations on human resource decisions.

3 • Differentiate between job descriptions and job specifications.

4 • Contrast recruitment and decruitment options.

5 • Explain the importance of validity and reliability in selection.

6 • Describe the selection devices that work best with various kinds of jobs.

7 • Identify various training methods.

8 • Outline the five stages in a career.

9 • Explain the collective bargaining process.

10 • Describe how HRM practices can facilitate workforce diversity.

Husky Injection Molding Systems is a manufacturer of injection molding machines, located in Bolton, Ontario. The machines Husky produces are used to manufacture plastics products such as car parts, children's toys, and food containers. The company is the third largest of its kind worldwide, with revenues of more than $600 million. But these figures are not the most remarkable aspects of the company. What truely makes Husky unique is the incredible dedication the company has to its human resources. Founder Robert Schad has created an environment geared towards hiring the right people, getting the most out of them, and keeping them happy. According to Schad, "You build something to last if you treat workers well."[1]

To that end, Schad instituted a rotating employee council, consisting of employees from all levels, which meets with him every month. Representatives poll fellow workers to determine what should be discussed, and transcripts of the meetings' minutes accompany everyone's paycheques. Every employee is included in a profit-sharing plan, and people holding specialized jobs are allowed to purchase shares of the company (Schad and his family own 65 per cent). Salaries are above the industry average, and the employees are kept informed of the company's performance through annual reports and monthly newsletters.

Physical health is a primary concern at Husky. Employees have a state-of-the-art fitness centre at their disposal, as well as a medical doctor, nurse, naturopath, chiropractor, and massage therapist. What's more, employees get a $500 credit every year for vitamins. These investments in Husky's workforce pay off on the bottom line. The company spends only a third of the industry average in drug costs for employees, and absenteeism is roughly a quarter of that in other manufacturing companies.

Employees seem content at Husky, and why wouldn't they be—with facilities such as Husky's $5-million child-care centre, and company perks such as tuition and books being fully paid for by the company for any employee wishing to go to university or college?

Obviously Robert Schad believes that keeping his workers happy is good for business, and it would be hard to argue the point in the face of Husky's performance; the company is heading into the new millenium with astounding revenue growth.

Employees are treated as the organization's most important resource at Husky Injection Molding Systems.

HUSKY INJECTION MOLDING SYSTEMS www.husky.on.ca/ home.htm

As Husky illustrates, the quality of an organization is, to a large degree, merely the summation of the quality of its people. Getting, training, and keeping competent employees is critical to the success of every organization, whether the organization is just starting or well established. Therefore, part of every manager's job in the organizing function is putting the right person into the right job.

Managers and Human Resource Management

Some readers may be thinking, "Sure, personnel decisions are important, but aren't they made by people in human resource departments? These aren't decisions that all managers are involved in."

It's true that in large organizations, a number of the activities grouped under the label **human resource management (HRM)** often are done by specialists in human resources. However, not all managers work in organizations that have formal HRM functions; and even those who do still have to be engaged in some human resource activities. Small business managers are an obvious example of individuals who frequently must do their hiring without the assistance of HRM. But even managers in billion-dollar corporations are involved in recruiting candidates, reviewing application forms, interviewing applicants, inducting new employees, making decisions about employee training, and providing career advice to employees. Whether or not an organization has an HRM department, every manager is involved with human resource decisions in her unit.

human resource management (HRM)
Function in management concerned with getting, training, motivating, and keeping employees.

The Human Resource Management Process

Exhibit 8-1 introduces the key components of an organization's human resource management process. It represents nine activities, or steps, that, if properly executed, will staff an organization with competent, high-performing employees who are capable of sustaining their performance level over the long term.

The first four steps represent strategic human resource planning, the adding of staff through recruitment, the reduction in staff through decruitment, and selection, resulting in the identification and selection of competent employees. Once you've got competent people, you need to help them adapt to the organization and ensure that their job skills and knowledge are kept current. You do this through orientation and training. The last steps in the HRM process are designed to identify performance problems, correct them, and help employees to sustain a high level of performance over their entire career. The activities involved here include performance appraisal, career development, and, where employees are unionized, labour-management relations. Because performance appraisals focus on behavioural control, we'll delay this discussion until Chapter 16.

Notice in Exhibit 8-1 that the entire HRM process is influenced by the external environment. In Chapter 2 we introduced constraints that the environment (both specific and general) places on management. Those constraints are probably most severe in the management of human resources. Before we review the nine steps in the process, therefore, we will briefly examine how environmental forces influence the process.

Important Environmental Factors Affecting HRM

Numerous environmental forces impinge on human resource management activities. In unionized organizations, many key personnel decisions are regulated by the terms of collective bargaining agreements. These agreements usually define such things as wages, work hours, criteria for promotions, and layoffs; training eligibility; and disci-

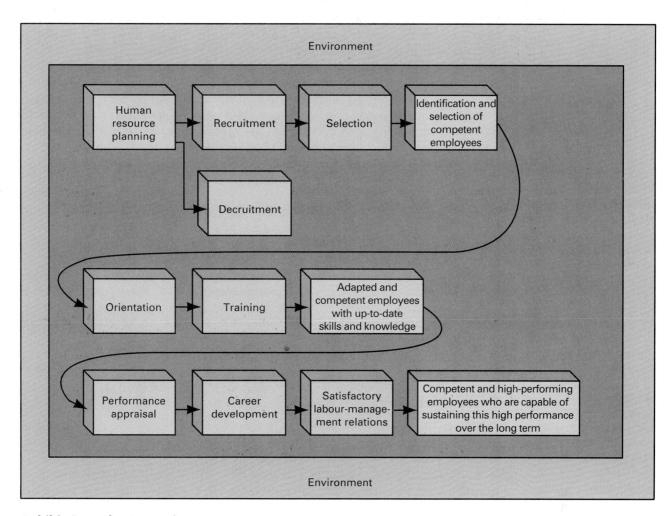

Exhibit 8-1   The Strategic Human Resources Management Process

plinary practices. But no environmental constraint can match the influence of government laws and regulations.

Since the mid-1960s, the federal government has greatly expanded its influence over HRM decisions by enacting a wealth of laws and regulations (see Exhibit 8-2 for examples). As a result of this legislation, employers today must ensure that equal employment opportunities exist for job applicants and current employees. Decisions regarding who will be hired, for example, or which employees will be chosen for a management training program must be made without regard to race, sex, religion, age, colour, national origin, or disability. Exceptions can occur only for requirements that are **bona fide occupational qualifications (BFOQ)**. This explains why, for instance, airlines today have flight attendants of both sexes and of varying ages. In the early 1960s, airlines hired almost exclusively flight attendants who were young, attractive females. But age, beauty, and gender are not BFOQs for this job; and so such criteria had to be dropped.

The picture of companies being controlled by the 'old boys club' has largely disappeared, but the days of male dominance in the boardroom are not as far behind us as we may like to think. Management has certainly vastly changed—today 61 per cent

bona fide occupational qualifications (BFOQ)
A criterion such as sex, age, or national origin may be used as a basis for hiring if it can be clearly demonstrated to be job related.

of major Canadian companies have at least one female director; however, there is still much growth to be achieved—in the U.S. this figure is 98 per cent. While women make up 45 per cent of the labour force and 57 per cent of graduate degree holders, only 2 per cent of CEOs among Canada's top 500 companies are female.[2] Still, it no longer comes as a surprise when a woman is chosen to head up a major Canadian company. Some of our top producers are run by women, including both Ford Canada (Bobbie Gaunt) and General Motors Canada (Maureen Kempston Darkes). In England, on the other hand, the appointment of Marjorie Scardino as CEO of the media company Pearson in 1997 was the first such appointment of a woman in a top 100 firm, and this novel situation was met by an intrigued, dumbfounded, and fawning media.

affirmative action programs
Programs that enhance the organizational status of members of protected groups.

Many organizations have **affirmative action programs** to ensure that decisions and practices enhance the employment, upgrading, and retention of members of protected groups, such as minorities and females. That is, not only will the organization refrain from discrimination, but it will also actively seek to enhance the status of members from protected groups. Our conclusion is that managers are not completely free to choose whom they hire, promote, or fire. While these regulations have significantly helped to reduce discrimination and unfair employment practices in organizations, they have, at the same time, also reduced management's discretion over human resource decisions.

strategic human resource planning (SHRP)
The process by which management ensures that it has the right personnel, who are capable of completing tasks that help the organization reach its objectives.

Strategic Human Resource Planning

Strategic human resource planning (SHRP) is the process by which management ensures that it has the right number and kinds of people in the right places and at the right times, who are capable of effectively and efficiently completing tasks that will help the organization achieve its overall objectives. Strategic human resource planning, then, translates the organization's objectives (assuming, of course, that they have been established) in terms of the workers needed to meet those objectives.[3]

SHRP can be condensed into two steps: (1) assessing current human resources, and (2) assessing future human resource needs and developing a program to meet future human resource needs.

human resource inventory
A database containing information on employees' skills and competencies.

job analysis
An assessment that defines jobs and the behaviours necessary to perform them.

LAW OR REGULATION

Canadian Human Rights Act
Canada Labour Code
Official Languages Act
Privacy Act
Access to Information Act

**Exhibit 8-2
Major Canadian Federal Laws and Regulations Related to HRM**

How Does an Organization Conduct an Employee Assessment?

Management begins by reviewing its current human resource status. This is typically done by generating a **human resource inventory**. In an era of sophisticated computer systems, it is not too difficult for most organizations to generate a human resource inventory report. The input for this report is derived from forms completed by employees. Such reports might list the name, education, training, prior employment, languages spoken, capabilities, and specialized skills of each employee in the organization. This inventory allows management to assess which talents and skills are available.

Another part of the current assessment is the **job analysis**. While the human resource inventory is concerned with telling management what individual employees can do, job analysis is more fundamental. It defines the jobs within the organization and the behaviours that are necessary to perform those jobs. For instance, what are the duties of a purchasing specialist, grade 3, who works for Ford of Canada? What minimal knowledge, skills, and abilities are necessary for the adequate performance of this particular job? How do the requirements for a purchasing specialist, grade 3, compare with those for a purchasing specialist, grade 2, or for a purchasing analyst? These are questions that job analysis can answer. It seeks to determine the kind of people needed to fill each job and culminates in job descriptions and job specifications.

There are several methods for analysing jobs. There is the observation method, in which employees are either watched directly or filmed on the job. Employees can also be interviewed individually or in a group. A third method is the use of structured questionnaires on which employees check or rate the items they perform in their jobs from a long list of possible task items. A fourth method is the use of a technical conference, at which "experts"—usually supervisors with extensive knowledge of a job—identify its specific characteristics. A fifth method is to have employees record their daily activities in a diary or notebook, which can then be reviewed and structured into job activities. In practice, usually some combination of the above is used.[4]

Information gathered by using one or more of these methods allows management to draw up a **job description** and **job specification**. The former is a written statement of what a jobholder does, how it is done, and why it is done. It typically portrays job content, environment, and conditions of employment. The job specification states the minimum acceptable qualifications that an incumbent must possess to perform a given job successfully. It identifies the knowledge, skills, and abilities needed to do the job effectively.

The job description and specification are important documents when managers begin recruiting and selecting. The job description can be used to describe the job to potential candidates. The job specification keeps the manager's attention on the list of qualifications necessary for an incumbent to perform a job and assists in determining whether candidates are qualified. Consequently, hiring individuals based on the information contained in these two documents helps to ensure that the hiring process is not discriminatory.

job description
A written statement of what a jobholder does, how it is done, and why it is done.

job specification
A statement of the minimum acceptable qualifications that an incumbent must possess to perform a given job successfully.

How Are Future Employee Needs Determined?

Future human resource needs are determined by the organization's objectives and strategies. Demand for human resources is a result of demand for the organization's products or services. On the basis of its estimate of total revenue, management can attempt to establish the number and mix of human resources needed to reach these revenues. In some cases, the situation may be reversed. Where particular skills are necessary and in scarce supply, the availability of satisfactory human resources determines revenues. This might be the case, for example, in a tax-consulting firm that finds it has more business opportunities than it can handle. Its only limiting factor in building revenues might be its ability to locate and hire staff with the qualifications necessary to satisfy the consulting firm's clients. In most cases, however, the overall organizational goals and the resulting revenue forecast provide the major input determining the organization's human resource demand requirements.

After it has assessed both current capabilities and future needs, management is able to estimate shortages—both in number and in kind—and to highlight areas in which the organization is overstaffed. A program can then be developed that matches these estimates with forecasts of future labour supply. So strategic human resource planning provides not only information to guide current staffing needs but also projections of future employee needs and availability.

YOUNG CANADIANS

Vito Monopoli and Albert Divalerio: Mondiv Food Products

Vito Monopoli and Albert Divalerio began Mondiv Food Products, a Boisbriand, Quebec-based producer of premium pasta sauces, at the ages of 26 and 25 respectively. Five years later the company has sales of $5 million, and is up to 35 employees from the original two. Mondiv set itself apart from its competition by offering excellent quality (a result of ingredients used) for a low cost.

Recruitment and Selection

recruitment
The process of locating, identifying, and attracting capable applicants.

decruitment
Techniques for reducing the labour supply within an organization.

Once managers know their current SHRP status (whether they are understaffed or overstaffed), they can begin to do something about it. If one or more vacancies exist, they can use the information gathered through job analysis to guide them in **recruitment**—that is, the process of locating, identifying, and attracting capable applicants.[5] On the other hand, if strategic human resource planning indicates a surplus, management will want to reduce the labour supply within the organization. This activity is called **decruitment**.[6]

Where Does a Manager Look to Recruit Potential Candidates? Candidates can be found by using several sources. Exhibit 8-3 offers some guidance. The source that is used should reflect the local labour market, the type or level of position, and the size of the organization.

Are Certain Recruiting Sources Superior to Others? Do certain recruiting sources produce superior candidates? The answer is yes. The majority of studies find that employee referrals prove to be superior.[7] The explanation for this finding is intuitively logical. First, applicants referred by current employees are prescreened by these employees. Because the recommenders know both the job and the person being recommended, they tend to refer applicants who are better qualified for the job. Second, because current employees often feel their reputation in the organization is at stake with a referral, they tend to refer others only when they are reasonably confident that the referral won't make them look bad.

How Does a Manager Handle Decruitment? In the past decade, most large Canadian corporations, as well as many government agencies, small businesses, and

SOURCE	ADVANTAGES	DISADVANTAGES
Internal Searches	Low cost; build employee morale; candidates are familiar with organization	Limited supply; may not increase proportion of protected group employees
Advertisements	Wide distribution can be targeted to specific groups	Generate many unqualified candidates
Employee Referrals	Knowledge about the organization provided by current employees; can generate strong candidates because a good referral reflects on the recommender	May not increase the diversity and mix of employees
Public Employment Agencies	Free or nominal cost	Candidates tend to be lower skilled, although some skilled employees available
Private Employment Agencies	Wide contacts; careful screening; short-term guarantees often given	High cost
School Placement	Large, centralized body of candidates	Limited to entry-level positions
Temporary Help Services	Fill temporary needs	Expensive
Employee Leasing and Independent Contractors	Fill temporary needs, but usually for more specific, longer-term projects	Little commitment to organization other than current project

foreign companies, have been forced to engage in some decruitment activities.[8] The decline in many manufacturing industries, market changes, foreign competition, and mergers have been the primary causes of personnel cutbacks. Decruitment is not a pleasant task for any manager to perform. But as many organizations are forced to shrink the size of their workforce or restructure their skill composition, decruitment is becoming an increasingly relevant activity in human resource management (see Managers Who Made a Difference).

What are a manager's decruitment options? Obviously, people can be fired. But other choices may be more beneficial to the organization and the employee.[9] Exhibit 8-4 summarizes a manager's major options.

Exhibit 8-3
Major Sources of
Potential Job

Is There a Basic Premise to Selecting Job Candidates?

The **selection process** is a prediction exercise. It seeks to predict which applicants will be successful if hired. "Successful" in this case means performing well on the criteria the organization uses to evaluate its employees. In filling a sales position, for example, the selection process should be able to predict which applicants will generate a high volume of sales; for a position as a high school teacher, it should predict which applicants will be effective educators. Consider, for a moment, that any selection decision can result in four possible outcomes. As shown in Exhibit 8-5, two of these outcomes would indicate correct decisions, but two would indicate errors.

A decision is correct when the applicant was predicted to be successful and later proved to be successful on the job; or when the applicant was predicted to be unsuccessful and later performed accordingly. In the former case, we have successfully accepted; in the latter case, we have successfully rejected.

selection process
The process of screening job applicants to ensure that the most appropriate candidates are hired.

Exhibit 8-4   Decruitment Options

OPTION	DESCRIPTION
Firing	Permanent involuntary termination
Layoffs	Temporary involuntary termination; may last only a few days or extend to years
Attrition	Not filling openings created by voluntary resignations or normal retirements
Transfers	Moving employees either laterally or downward; usually does not reduce costs but can reduce intraorganizational supply-demand imbalances
Reduced Workweeks	Having employees work fewer hours per week, share jobs, or perform their jobs on a part-time basis
Early Retirements	Providing incentives to older and more senior employees for retiring before their normal retirement date
Job Sharing	Having employees, typically two part-timers, share one full-time position

**Exhibit 8-5
Selection Decision
Outcomes**

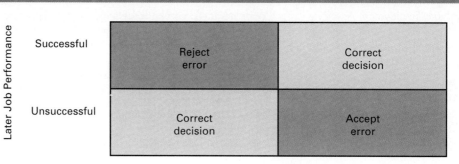

Problems occur when we make errors by rejecting candidates who would later perform successfully on the job (reject errors) or accepting those who subsequently perform poorly (accept errors). These problems are, unfortunately, far from insignificant. A generation ago, reject errors meant only that the costs of selection would be increased because more candidates would have to be screened. Today, selection techniques that result in reject errors can open the organization to charges of employment discrimination, especially if applicants from protected groups are disproportionately rejected. Accept errors, on the other hand, have very obvious costs to the organization, including the cost of training the employee, the costs generated or profits foregone because of the employee's incompetence, and the cost of severance and the subsequent costs of further recruiting and selection screening. The major thrust of any selection activity is therefore to reduce the probability of making reject errors or accept errors, while increasing the probability of making correct decisions. We do this by using selection activities that are both reliable and valid.

reliability
The ability of a selection device to measure the same thing consistently.

What Is Reliability? Reliability addresses whether a selection device measures the same thing consistently. For example, if a test is reliable, any single individual's score should remain fairly stable over time, assuming that the characteristics it is measuring are also stable.

The importance of reliability should be evident. No selection device can be effective if it is low in reliability. That is equivalent to weighing yourself every day on an erratic scale. If the scale is unreliable—randomly fluctuating, say, 10 to 15 pounds every time you step on it—the results will not mean much. To be effective predictors, selection devices must possess an acceptable level of consistency.

MANAGERS WHO MADE A DIFFERENCE

Daniel Branda: Hewlett-Packard Canada

HEWLETT-PACKARD CANADA

hpclweb.external.hp.com/

Daniel Branda has a very good reason to appreciate Hewlett-Packard's approach to resorting to layoffs only as a last-case scenario. Branda's job became redundant in the early 1990s, and, whereas many organizations might have laid off an employee in his position, H.P. offered him the choice of a new position, albeit at a lower salary. Branda decided to stay with Hewlett-Packard during the uncertain years of the recession, and the decision paid off. Within two years Branda had proved himself through his work and had managed a succession of promotions that led him to the position of chief executive of Hewlett-Packard Canada. The appointment marked an amazingly fast rebound from being demoted during cutbacks. Branda has not forgotten the opportunity his company gave him during those years when massive layoffs became commonplace among large organizations. Today, Branda would take virtually any measure necessary to avoid cutting jobs.[10]

Hewlett-Packard's attitude toward its workforce has proven to be a boon to the company's welfare. H.P. has made only negligible cutbacks in its employee base (it did offer a voluntary retirement option during the last recession) and has continually rebounded from economic downturns with a growth in its workforce.

It is, in many ways, a matter of being able to see the forest by looking beyond the trees. To find the best possible direction to take, a manager must look beyond simple solutions and view the situation in its entirety. If, for instance, a company such as H.P. Canada is faced with a decrease in growth in the educational market, is the best solution to cut jobs and become more efficient in a smaller market? Or should the company move its focus to an emerging-growth market such as the consumer and financial institution market, where the skills of its employees can be steered in a new direction, and the company can continue to grow? For Hewlett-Packard, the choice is obvious.

As Daniel Branda has said, "Chopping 10 per cent of your workforce might improve your numbers for three to six months, but then what? If revenues and profits are falling, it's probably not because you have too many people. It's because you have a structural problem that needs fixing. Downsizing doesn't get to the cause of the problem." ▼

validity
The proven relationship that exists between a selection device and some relevant criterion.

What Is Validity? Any selection device that a manager uses—such as an application form, test, interview, or physical examination—must also demonstrate **validity**. That is, there must be a proven relationship between the selection device and some relevant criterion. For example, the law prohibits management from using a test score as a selection device unless there is clear evidence that, once on the job, individuals with high scores on this test outperform individuals with low test scores.

The burden is on management to prove that any selection device it uses to differentiate applicants is related to job performance. While management can give applicants an intelligence test and use the results to help make selection decisions, it must be prepared to demonstrate, if challenged, that this intelligence test is a valid measure—that is, that scores on the test are positively related to later job performance.

Are There Selection Devices That Every Manager Should Use?

Managers can use a number of selection devices to reduce accept and reject errors. The best-known devices include an analysis of the prospect's completed application form, written and performance-simulation tests, interviews, background investigations, and, in some cases, a physical examination. Let's briefly review each of these devices, giving particular attention to the validity of each in predicting job performance. After we review the devices, we will discuss when each should be used.

What Is the Application Form? Almost all organizations require candidates to complete an application. It may be only a form on which a prospect gives his name, address, and telephone number. At the other extreme, it might be a comprehensive personal history profile, detailing the applicant's activities, skills, and accomplishments (see Ethical Dilemmas in Management).

Hard and relevant biographical data that can be verified—for example, rank in high school graduating class—have shown to be valid measures of performance for some jobs.[11] Also, when application form items have been appropriately weighted to reflect job relatedness, the device has proven a valid predictor for such diverse groups as salesclerks, engineers, factory workers, district managers, clerical employees, and technicians.[12] But, typically, only a couple of items on the application prove to be valid predictors, and then only for a specific job. Use of weighted applications for selection purposes is difficult and expensive because the weights have to be validated for each specific job and must be continually reviewed and updated to reflect changes in weights over time.

Do Written Tests Serve a Useful Purpose? Typical written tests include tests of intelligence, aptitude, ability, and interest. Such tests have long been used as selection devices, although their popularity has run in cycles. Written tests were widely used for 20 years following World War II. Beginning in the late 1960s, however, they fell into disfavour. Written tests were frequently characterized as discriminatory, and many organizations couldn't validate that their written tests were job-related.[13] But since the late 1980s, written tests have made a comeback.[14] Managers have become increasingly aware that poor hiring decisions are costly and that properly designed tests could reduce the likelihood of these decisions occurring. In addition, the cost of developing and validating a set of written tests for a specific job has come down markedly. "Ten years ago," says an executive at Personnel Decisions Inc., "if an employer called us and wanted to put together a test battery for salespeople or copywriters, we told him [or her] it would take $100,000 and six months. Now we're talking about $6,000 and a couple of weeks."[15]

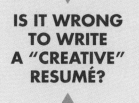

ETHICAL DILEMMAS IN MANAGEMENT

IS IT WRONG TO WRITE A "CREATIVE" RESUMÉ?

Almost all of us have written, or will write, a resumé to give to prospective employers. It summarizes our background, experiences, and accomplishments. Should it be 100-per-cent truthful? Let's take a few examples.

Person A leaves a job where his title was "credit clerk." When looking for a new job, he describes his previous title as "credit analyst." He thinks it sounds more impressive. Is this retitling of a former job wrong?

Person B made $2,700 a month when she left her previous job. On her resumé, she says that she was making $2,900. Is that wrong?

Person C, about eight years ago, took nine months off between jobs to travel overseas. Afraid that people might consider her unstable or lacking in career motivation, on her resumé she states that she was engaged in "independent consulting activities" during the period. Was she wrong?

Person D is 50 years old with an impressive career record. He spent five years in university 30 years ago, but he never got a degree. He is being considered for a $150,000-a-year vice-presidency at another firm. He knows that he has the ability and track record to do the job, but he won't get the interview if he admits to not having a university degree. He knows that the probability that anyone would check his school records is very low. Should he put on his resumé that he completed his degree?

Falsehoods on resumés are widespread. A recent survey of 200 applicants found that 30 per cent reported incorrect dates of employment. Eleven per cent misrepresented reasons for leaving a previous job to cover up the fact that they were fired. Some falsely claimed degrees or totally fabricated work histories. In a larger study of 11,000 applicants, 488 failed to disclose criminal records; most of these were drug or alcohol offences, but some were as serious as rape or attempted murder.[16]

Is it wrong to write a "creative" resumé? What deviations from the truth, if any, would you make?

A review of the evidence finds that tests of intellectual ability, spatial and mechanical ability, perceptual accuracy, and motor ability are moderately valid predictors for many semiskilled and unskilled operative jobs in industrial organizations.[17] And intelligence tests are reasonably good predictors for supervisory positions.[18] However, an enduring criticism of written tests is that intelligence, and other tested characteristics, can be somewhat removed from the actual performance of the job itself. For example, a high score on an intelligence test is not necessarily a good indicator that the applicant will perform well as a computer programmer. This criticism has led to an increased use of performance-simulation tests.

What Are Performance-simulation Tests? What better way to find out whether an applicant for a technical writing position at Spar Aerospace can write technical manuals than by having her do it? The logic of this question has led to the expanding interest in performance-simulation tests. Undoubtedly, the enthusiasm for these tests lies in the fact that they are based on job analysis data and therefore should more easily meet the requirement of job relatedness than do written tests. Performance-simulation tests are made up of actual job behaviours rather than of surrogates. The best-known performance-simulation tests are **work sampling** (a miniature replica of the job) and **assessment centres** (simulating real problems that one may face on the job). The former is suited to routine jobs, the latter to selecting managerial personnel. We've identified characteristics of these two in Exhibit 8-6.

work sampling
A personnel selection device in which job applicants are presented with a miniature replica of a job and are asked to perform tasks central to that job.

assessment centres
Places in which job candidates undergo performance-simulation tests that evaluate managerial potential.

**Exhibit 8-6
Characteristics of
Work Sampling and
Assessment Centres**

METHOD	ACTIVITIES	BEST USED FOR
Work Sampling	Presents applicants with a miniature replica of the job	Matching the knowledge, skills, and abilities needed for successful performance on each job and an applicant's ability to demonstrate proficiency on these elements
Assessment Centres	An elaborate set of performance-simulation tests that simulate real problems individuals may confront on the job. Usually includes interviews, in-basket problem-solving exercises, group discussions, and business decision games	Evaluating a candidate's managerial potential

Is the Interview Effective? The interview, along with the application form, is an almost universal selection device.[19] Few of us have ever gotten a job without one or more interviews. The irony of this is that the value of the interview as a selection device has been the subject of considerable debate.[20]

Interviews can be reliable and valid selection tools, but too often they're not. When interviews are structured and well organized, and when interviewers are held to common questioning, interviews are effective predictors.[21] But those conditions don't characterize most interviews. The typical interview—in which applicants are asked a varying set of essentially random questions in an informal setting—usually provides little in the way of valuable information.

There are all kinds of potential biases that can creep into interviews if they are not well structured and standardized. To illustrate, a review of the research leads us to the following conclusions:

▶ **1.** Prior knowledge about the applicant will bias the interviewer's evaluation.

▶ **2.** The interviewer tends to hold a stereotype of what represents a "good" applicant.

▶ **3.** The interviewer tends to favour applicants who share her own attitudes.

▶ **4.** The order in which applicants are interviewed will influence evaluations.

▶ **5.** The order in which information is elicited during the interview will influence evaluations.

▶ **6.** Negative information is given unduly high weight.

▶ **7.** The interviewer may make a decision concerning the applicant's suitability within the first four or five minutes of the interview.

▶ **8.** The interviewer may forget much of the interview's content within minutes of its conclusion.

▶ **9.** The interview is most valid in determining an applicant's intelligence, level of motivation, and interpersonal skills.[22]

What can managers do to make interviews more valid and reliable? Specifically, we suggest (1) structuring a fixed set of questions for all applicants; (2) having detailed information about the job for which applicants are interviewing; (3) minimizing any foreknowledge of applicants' background, experience, interests, test scores, or other characteristics; (4) asking behavioural questions that require applicants to give detailed accounts of actual job behaviours (for example, Give me a specific example of a time you had to reprimand an employee, tell me what action you took, and describe the result); (5) using a standardized evaluation form; (6) taking notes during the interview; and (7) avoiding short interviews that encourage premature decision making (see Developing Management Skills.)[23]

What Is a Background Investigation? Background investigations are of two types: verifications of application data and reference checks. The first type has proven to be a valuable source of selection information, whereas the latter is essentially worthless. Let's briefly review each.

Several studies indicate that verifying "facts" given on the application form pays dividends. A significant percentage of job applicants—upward of 15 per cent—exaggerate or misrepresent dates of employment, job titles, past salaries, or reasons for leaving a prior position.[24] Confirmation of hard data on the application with prior employers is therefore a worthwhile endeavour.

The reference check is used by many organizations, but is extremely difficult to justify. Whether they are work related or personal, references provide little valid information for the selection decision.[25] Why? Employers are frequently reluctant to give candid evaluations of a former employee's job performance for fear of legal repercussions. In fact, a survey found that only 55 per cent of human resource executives would "always" provide accurate references to a prospective employer. Moreover, 7 per cent said they would never give an accurate reference.[26] Personal likes and dislikes also heavily influence the type of recommendation given. Personal references are likely to provide biased information. Who among us doesn't have three or four friends who will speak in glowing terms about our integrity, work habits, positive attitudes, knowledge, and skills?

All applicants will eventually go through some type of interview. But do the interviewers give all candidates a fair shake? Research has shown that they may not. However, following some basic steps, like structuring the interview, can help immensely.

Is a Physical Examination Necessary? For jobs with certain physical requirements, the physical examination has some validity. Today, however, this includes a very small number of jobs. In many cases, the physical examination is done primarily for insurance purposes—especially if a company has an insurance policy that does not provide medical coverage for preexisting conditions.

Great care must be taken to ensure that physical requirements are job-related and do not discriminate. Some physical requirements may exclude certain disabled persons, when, in fact, such requirements do not affect job performance.

DEVELOPING MANAGEMENT SKILLS

▼ INTERVIEWING SKILLS ▲

▶ **1. Review job description and job specification.** Reviewing pertinent information about the job provides valuable information about what you'll assess the candidate on. Furthermore, relevant job requirements help to eliminate bias.

▶ **2. Prepare a structured set of questions you want to ask all applicants for the job.** By having a set of prepared questions, you ensure that the information you wish to elicit is attainable. Furthermore, by asking similar questions, you are able to better compare all candidates' answers.

▶ **3. Prior to meeting a candidate, review his application form and resumé.** Doing so helps you to create a complete picture of the candidate in terms of what is represented on the resumé/

application, and what the job requires. You will also begin to identify areas to explore in the interview. That is, areas not clearly defined on the resumé/application that are essential for your job become a focal point in your discussion with the candidate.

▶ **4. Open the interview by putting the applicant at ease and by providing a brief preview of the topics to be discussed.** Interviews are stressful for job candidates. By opening with small talk—e.g., the weather, etc.—you give the candidate time to adjust to the interview setting. By providing a preview of topics to come, you are giving the candidate an "agenda." This helps the candidate to begin framing what she will say in response to your questions.

▶ **5. Ask your questions and listen carefully to the applicant's answers.** Select follow-up questions that naturally flow from the answers given. Focus on the responses as they relate to information you need to ensure that the

candidate meets your job requirements. Any uncertainty you may still have requires a follow-up question to further probe for the information.

▶ **6. Close the interview by telling the applicant what's going to happen next.** Applicants are anxious about the status of your hiring decision. Be up front with the candidate regarding others who will be interviewed and the remaining steps in the hiring process. If you plan to make a decision in two weeks or so, let the candidate know what you intend to do. And, tell the applicant how you will respond to her about your decision.

▶ **7. Write your evaluation of the applicant while the interview is still fresh in your mind.** Don't wait until the end of your day, after interviewing several candidates, to write your analysis of a candidate. Memory can fail you! The sooner you complete your write-up after an interview, the better chance you have of accurately recording what occurred in the interview.

What Selection Device Works Best and When? Many selection devices are of limited value to managers in making selection decisions. An understanding of strengths and weaknesses of each will help you to determine when one or the other should be used. We offer the following advice to guide your choices.

Since the validity of selection devices varies for different types of jobs, you should use only devices that predict for a given job (see Exhibit 8-7). The application form offers limited information. Traditional written tests are reasonably effective devices for routine jobs. Work samples, however, are clearly preferable to written tests. For supervisory and managerial selection, the assessment centre is strongly recommended. If the interview has a place in the selection decision, it is probably among less-routine jobs, particularly managerial positions. The interview is a reasonably good device for discerning intelligence and interpersonal skills.[27] These are more likely to be related to job performance in nonroutine activities. Verification of application data

SELECTION DEVICE	POSITION[a]			
	SENIOR MANAGEMENT	MIDDLE AND LOWER MANAGEMENT	COMPLEX NONMAN-AGERIAL	ROUTINE OPERATIVE
Application form	2	2	2	2
Written tests	1	1	2	3
Work samples	—	—	4	4
Assessment centre	5	5	—	—
Interviews	4	3	2	2
Verification of application data	3	3	3	3
Reference checks	1	1	1	1
Physical exam	1	1	1	2
[a] Validity is measured on a scale from 5 (highest) to 1 (lowest).				

**Exhibit 8-7
Quality of
Selection Devices
as Predictors**

is valuable for all jobs. Finally, physical examinations only provide valid selection information in rare instances.

What Should One Look for in Selecting Managers for Global Assignments?
Transferring managers into new and different national cultures, without careful thought and proper selection, sets those managers up to fail. Most research on the transfer of managers between diverse countries—particularly the moving of Canadian executives overseas—indicates a fairly high failure rate.

Why don't more managers succeed when they are placed in foreign countries? One possible reason is that most organizations still select transfer candidates on the basis of technical competence alone, ignoring other predictors of success, such as language skills, flexibility, and family adaptability.[28]

Orientation and Training

If we have done our recruiting and selecting properly, we should have hired competent individuals who can perform successfully. But successful performance requires more than possession of certain skills. New hires must be acclimated to the organization's culture and be trained to do the job in a manner consistent with the organization's objectives. To achieve these ends, HRM embarks on two processes: orientation and training.

How Do We Introduce New Hires to the Organization?

Once a job candidate has been selected, he needs to be introduced to the job and organization. This introduction is called **orientation**. The major objectives of orientation are to reduce the initial anxiety all new employees feel as they begin a new job; to familiarize new employees with the job, the work unit, and the organization as a whole; and to facilitate the outsider-insider transition. Job orientation expands on the

orientation
The introduction of a new employee to his job and the organization.

information the employee obtained during the recruitment and selection stages. The new employee's specific duties and responsibilities are clarified, as well as how her performance will be evaluated. This is also the time to rectify any unrealistic expectations new employees might hold about the job. Work-unit orientation familiarizes the employee with the goals of the work unit, makes clear how his job contributes to the unit's goals, and includes introduction to his coworkers. Organization orientation informs the new employee about the organization's objectives, history, philosophy, procedures, and rules. This should include relevant personnel policies regarding work hours, pay procedures, overtime requirements, and benefits. A tour of the organization's physical facilities is often part of the organization orientation.

YOUNG CANADIANS

Andrew Badia: Iris Hosiery Inc.

Quebec's Entrepreneur of the Year for 1997, according to *Canadian Business* magazine, Andrew Badia has a sock manufacturing company, Iris Hosiery Inc. in Montreal (he is both founder and president), that owes much of its success to Badia's commitment to his workforce. "My employees are very important to me. They get full benefits, medical coverage, . . . and subsidized lunches in the cafeteria," says Badia.

Management has an obligation to make the integration of the new employee into the organization as smooth and as free of anxiety as possible. Successful orientation, whether formal or informal, results in an outsider-insider transition that makes the new member feel comfortable and fairly well adjusted, lowers the likelihood of poor work performance, and reduces the probability of a surprise resignation by the new employee only a week or two into the job.

What Is Employee Training?

On the whole, planes don't cause airline accidents, people do. Most collisions, crashes, and other mishaps—about 74 per cent to be exact—result from errors by the pilot or air traffic controller, or inadequate maintenance. Weather and structural failures cause only 15

Honeywell Ltd., of Scarborough, Ontario, provides training for its workforce in such areas as TQM, JIT techniques, and team skills, as well as an education program called Learning for Life that offers courses in subjects such as English, math, computer science, and communications.

per cent of accidents.[29] We cite these statistics to illustrate the importance of training in the airline industry. These maintenance and human errors could be prevented or significantly reduced by better employee training.

As job demands change, employee skills have to be altered and updated. It has been estimated that North American firms spend more than $50 billion annually on formal courses and training programs to build workers' skills.[30] Management, of course, is responsible for deciding when subordinates are in need of training and what form that training should take.

career
The sequence of positions occupied by a person during a lifetime.

How Are Employees Trained? Most training takes place on the job. This can be attributed to the simplicity of such methods and their usually lower cost. However, on-the-job training can disrupt the workplace and result in an increase in errors while learning takes place. Also, some skill training is too complex to learn on the job. In such cases, it should take place outside the work setting.

What Are Some of the Typical Methods Used? There are many different types of training methods that are available for organizations to use. For the most part, however, we can classify them in two ways. That is, training methods can be viewed as on-the-job or off-the-job. We have summarized the more popular of these training methods in Exhibit 8-8.

Career Development

The term career has a number of meanings. In popular usage, it can mean advancement ("his career is progressing nicely"), a profession ("she has chosen a career in medicine"), or a lifelong sequence of jobs ("his career has included 15 jobs in six different organizations"). For our purposes, we define a **career** as the sequence of positions occupied by a person during a lifetime.[31] By this definition, it is apparent that we all have, or will have, careers. Moreover, the concept is as relevant to transient, unskilled labourers as to engineers or physicians.

Why should an organization be concerned with careers? More specifically, why should management spend time on career development? Focusing on careers forces management to adopt a long-term perspective on its human resources. An effective career-development program ensures that needed talent will be available and that women and minorities will get opportunities for growth and development. It also improves the organization's ability to attract and retain highly talented personnel.

An example of a company that understands the value of its human resources is Brunswick Mining and Smelting of Fredericton, New Brunswick.[32] The company began a literacy campaign in conjunction with its union, in order to improve the reading, writing, and numeracy skills of workers. The company sponsored employees to finish high school equivalency courses, and provided after-hours tutoring in both official languages. As the company's manager of corporate affairs, Roger Clinch, puts it: "We believe that the most experienced workers have the most to offer, but this is a technologically changing world and if we can take that experience and add the ability to adapt to the new technology, we believe it's a benefit to the company."

Individuals being trained as pilots are often trained on flight simulators. Why? In a simulator all aspects of flying a plane can be experienced. And if trainees react improperly, the simulator can be reset, and the individuals can try again. A mistake while actually flying could be tragic and costly.

BRUNSWICK MINING AND SMELTING
www.abc-canada.org/data/dataatlantic2.html

Exhibit 8-8
Typical Training
Methods

Sample On-the-Job Training Methods	
Job Rotation:	Lateral transfers allowing employees to work at different jobs. Provides good exposure to a variety of tasks.
Understudy Assignments:	Working with a seasoned veteran, coach, or mentor. Provides support and encouragement from an experienced worker. In the trades industry, this may also be an apprenticeship.
Sample Off-the-Job Training Methods	
Classroom Lectures:	Lectures designed to convey specific technical, interpersonal, or problem-solving skills.
Films and Videos:	Using the media to explicitly demonstrate technical skills that are not easily presented by other training methods.
Simulation Exercises:	Learning a job by actually performing the work (or its simulation). May include case analyses, experiential exercises, role playing, and group interaction.
Vestibule Training:	Learning tasks on the same equipment that one actually will use on the job, but in a simulated work environment.

exploration career stage
A career stage that usually ends in one's mid-20s as one makes the transition from school to work.

establishment career stage
A period in which one begins to search for work. It includes getting one's first job.

mid-career stage
A period marked by continuous improvement in performance, levelling off in performance, or deterioration in performance.

late-career stage
A period in which one is no longer learning about one's job, and is not expected to be trying to outdo one's levels of performance from previous years.

decline career stage
The final phase in one's career, usually marked by retirement.

realistic job preview (RJP)
Exposing job candidates to both negative and positive information about a job and an organization.

Do All Employees Progress Through Career Stages?

The most popular way of analysing and discussing careers is to view them as a series of stages.[33] We'll look at a five-stage model that applies to most people during their adult years, regardless of the type of work they do.

Most individuals begin to form ideas about their careers during their elementary and secondary school years. Their careers begin to wind down as they reach retirement age. We can identify five career stages that most people will go through during these years: **exploration**, **establishment**, **mid-career**, **late career**, and **decline**. These stages and the challenges for individuals are depicted in Exhibit 8-9.

How Can You Apply the Career Stage Model?

The concept of career stages can be of great benefit to managers. The following are some possible insights. New employees often hold unrealistic expectations about their work. A **realistic job preview (RJP)**—in which job candidates are exposed to negative as well as positive information about the job and organization—can reduce the number of surprise resignations[34] (see Details on a Management Classic). Employees in the establishment stage need training and mentoring to ensure that they have the abilities to perform their jobs well and to provide them with guidance and encouragement.

Managers should keep an eye out for employees who, in mid-career, fail to understand that they are no longer apprentices and that mistakes now carry penalties. Disciplinary action is more likely to be necessary at this stage, when employees first start to show signs of insecurity. Younger employees may be threats. Mid-career failures will occur, but so too will frustration, boredom, and burnout. Managers should be prepared to help employees with their insecurities and consider ways of making jobs more interesting or varied.

Individuals in their late careers make excellent mentors. Managers should exploit this resource. Managers also need to recognize that people in the late-career stage frequently undergo significant changes in personal priorities. They may become less interested in work, or prefer more free time or a less stressful position instead of

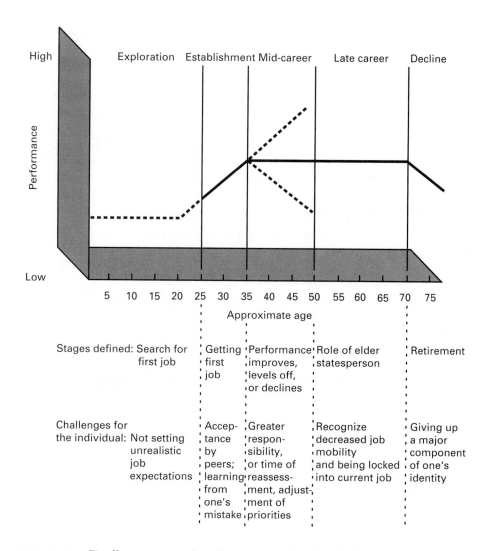

**Exhibit 8-9
Stages in Career
Development**

Source: D.T. Hall, *Careers in Organizations* (Glenview, IL: Scott Foresman and Company, 1976), p. 57. Reprinted with permission of the author.

more money. Finally, managers should recognize that the decline stage is difficult for every employee to confront. Periods of depression are not uncommon. Employees may also become more hostile and aggressive.

Labour-Management Relations

Why Are Good Labour-Management Relations Important?

For many managers in unionized organizations, the management of human resources is largely composed of procedures and policies laid out in the labour contract. Decisions about wages, hours, and terms and conditions of employment are no longer unilateral prerogatives of management for jobs within the union's province. Such decisions are substantially made at the time the labour contract is negotiated. However, the development of good **labour-management relations**, the formal interaction between **labour unions** and an organization's management, can produce a number of positive outcomes for management during these negotiations: for instance, work

labour-management relations
The formal interactions between unions and an organization's management.

labour union
An organization that represents workers and seeks to protect their interests through collective bargaining.

**CHRYSLER
CANADA**
chryslercanada.ca/

rules that don't place unreasonable constraints on managerial decision options, employment stability, and reduced threats of costly strikes and work stoppages.[35]

Chrysler Canada is a good example of how management and unions can cooperate to make an organization stronger and better. The recession and the threat of the Japanese car makers have brought the goal of both groups together—to make a better and more competitive car. Workers at Chrysler were given a say both in designing the new plant layout in Bramalea, Ontario, and in the design of the cars. They also have much greater authority than before; a worker can shut down the assembly line if she notices a problem. The absenteeism rate at the Bramalea plant is 1.9 per cent, the lowest of any Chrysler assembly plant, the average rate being between 4.5 and 5 per cent.

What Is the Collective Bargaining Process?

collective bargaining
A process for negotiating a union contract and for administrating the contract after it has been negotiated.

When we talk about the **collective bargaining** process, we are referring to the negotiation, administration, and interpretation of a labour contract. The following discussion summarizes how the process typically flows. See also Exhibit 8-10.

Efforts to organize a group of employees may begin when employee representatives ask union officials to visit the employees' organization and solicit members, or when the union itself initiates a membership drive. Federal legislation requires a union to secure signed authorization cards from 50 per cent of the employees, after which the union is automatically certified. Provincial legislation varies, but generally if 50 to 55 per cent of employees sign authorization cards, a vote on unionization is ordered. Occasionally, employees become dissatisfied with a certified union. In such instances, employees may request a decertification election. If a majority of the members vote for decertification, the union is out.

Once a union has been certified, management will begin preparing for negotiations. It will gather information on the economy, copies of recently negotiated contracts between other unions and employers, cost-of-living data, labour market statistics, and similar environmental concerns. It will also gather internal information on grievance and accident records, employee performance reports, and overtime figures.

This information will tell management the organization's current labour-performance status, what similar organizations are doing, and what it can anticipate from the economy in the near future. Management then uses these data to determine what it can expect to achieve in the negotiation. What can it expect the union to ask for? What is management prepared to acquiesce on?

Negotiation customarily begins when the union delivers a list of demands to management. These are typically ambitious in order to create room for trading in the later stages of negotiation. Not surprisingly, management's initial response is typically to counter by offering little more than the terms of the previous contract. In recent years, some managements have even begun by proposing a reduction in wages and benefits and demanding that the union take a lesser role in the organization's decision-making process. These introductory proposals usually initiate a period of long and intense bargaining. Compromises are made, and after an oral agreement is achieved, it is converted into a written contract. Finally, negotiation concludes with the union's representatives submitting the contract to its members for ratification.

Once a contract is agreed upon and ratified, it must be administered. The way in which it will be administered is set out in the contract itself. Probably the most important element of contract administration has to do with the spelling out of a procedure for handling contractual disputes. Almost all collective bargaining agreements contain formal procedures for resolving grievances over the interpretation and application of the contract.

DETAILS ON A MANAGEMENT CLASSIC

John P. Wanous and the Realistic Job Preview

Managers who treat the recruiting and hiring of employees as if the applicants must be sold on the job and exposed only to an organization's positive characteristics set themselves up to have a workforce that is dissatisfied and prone to high turnover. That is the conclusion of John P. Wanous.[36]

Every job applicant acquires, during the hiring process, a set of expectations about the company and about the job for which he is interviewing. When the information an applicant receives is excessively inflated, a number of things happen that have potentially negative effects on the company. First, Wanous found that mismatched applicants who would probably become dissatisfied with the job and quit soon would be less likely to withdraw from the search process. Second, he found the absence of accurate information builds unrealistic expectations. Consequently, if hired, the new employees are likely to become quickly dissatisfied—leading to premature resignations. Third, new hires are prone to become disillusioned and less committed to the organization when they face the "harsh" realities of the job. In many cases, Wanous revealed, these individuals feel that they were duped or misled during the hiring process and, therefore, may become problem employees.

To increase job satisfaction among employees and to reduce turnover, Wanous advocated providing applicants with a realistic job preview (RJP). An RJP includes both the positive and negative information about the job and the company. For example, in addition to the positive comments typically expressed in the interview, the candidate would be told of the downside of joining the company. For instance, she might be told that there are limited opportunities to talk to coworkers during work hours, that promotional advancement is slim, or that work hours fluctuate so erratically that employees may be required to work during typically off-hours (nights and weekends). Wanous's research, supported by others, indicates that applicants who have been given a more realistic job preview hold lower and more realistic job expectations for the jobs they'll be performing and are better able to cope with the job and its frustrating elements. The result is fewer unexpected resignations by new employees.

For managers, realistic job previews offer a major insight into the HRM process. That is, retaining good people is as important as hiring them in the first place. Presenting only the positive aspects of a job to a job applicant may initially entice him to join the organization, but it may be an affiliation that both parties quickly regret.▼

HRM and Workforce Diversity

We've previously discussed the changing makeup of the workforce in several places in this book. Let's now consider how workforce diversity will affect such basic HRM concerns as recruitment and selection.

Improving workforce diversity requires managers to widen their recruiting net. For example, the popular practice of relying on current employee referrals as a source

Exhibit 8-10 Stages of the Collective
Bargaining Process

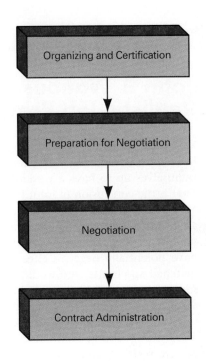

of new job applicants tends to result in candidates who have similar characteristics to current employees. So managers have to look for applicants in places where they haven't typically looked before. To increase diversity, managers are increasingly turning to nontraditional recruitment sources, including women's job networks, over-50 clubs, urban job banks, disabled people's training centres, ethnic newspapers, and gay-rights organizations.

Once a diverse set of applicants exists, efforts must be made to ensure that the selection process doesn't discriminate. Moreover, applicants need to be made comfortable with the organization's culture and be made aware of management's desire to accommodate their needs.

The insider-outsider transition (orientation) is often more difficult for women and minorities. Many organizations today provide special workshops to raise diversity consciousness among current employees, as well as programs for new employees that focus on diversity issues. The thrust of these efforts is to increase individual understanding of the differences that each of us brings to the workplace.

**SYNCRUDE
CANADA LTD.**
www.syncrude.com/
0_00.htm

Syncrude Canada Ltd. is Canada's largest mine—an oil mine. It sits on the Alberta oil sands, which contain more energy than all the crude oil reserves of the Middle East. It has changed Fort McMurray from a small river town into a bustling centre of 30,000 people. Capital investment in the project is about $4.3 billion. A 1997 survey listed Syncrude's R&D spending at $30 million, while annual revenues were more than $2 billion.[37] But all this notwithstanding, it is also a sparkling example of effective human resource management.

Gender equality is an area in which it excels: about 700 of Syncrude's employees are women, of whom 450 are in "nontraditional" jobs, a result of the company's Bridges program that helps women move away from clerical tasks and other traditional jobs. For instance, one-quarter of the heavy-equipment operators are women. Syncrude is also Canada's largest industrial employer of First Nations people, with about 300 on the payroll. In addition, it operates programs for natives among its suppliers that encourage and support entrepreneurship and job opportunities. Everyone with supervisory responsibilities (about 1,000 people) undergoes training that facilitates teamwork and the ability to manage diversity. The training centres on leadership, communications, and cultural sensitivity. The company spends between 5 and 7 per cent of annual payroll costs on training. Employees work within teams that allow them to participate in decisions and even customize their job descriptions.

Diversity of the workforce is something that all employees must understand and accept. At this training seminar, these employees are learning to better appreciate one another.

Summary

This summary is organized by the chapter Learning Objectives found on page 208.

1. The human resource management process seeks to staff the organization and sustain high employee performance through human resource planning, recruitment or decruitment, selection, orientation, training, performance appraisal, career development, and labour-management relations.

2. Since the mid-1960s, the U.S. government has greatly expanded its influence over HRM decisions by enacting new laws and regulations. Because of the government's effort to provide equal employment opportunities, management must ensure that key HRM decisions—such as recruitment, selection, training, promotions, and terminations—are made without regard to race, sex, religion, age, colour, or national origin. Extensive financial penalties can be imposed on organizations that fail to follow these laws and regulations.

3. A job description is a written statement of what a jobholder does, how it's done, and why it's done. A job specification states the minimum acceptable qualifications that an incumbent must possess to perform a given job successfully.

4. Recruitment seeks to develop a pool of potential job candidates. Typical sources include an internal search, advertisements, employee referrals, employment agencies, school placement centres, and temporary help services. Decruitment reduces the labour supply within an organization through options such as firing, layoffs, attrition, transfers, reduced workweeks, early retirements, and job sharing.

5. The quality of a selection device is determined by its validity and reliability. If a device is not valid, then no proven relationship exists between it and relevant job criteria. If a selection device isn't reliable, then it cannot be assumed to be a consistent measure.

6. Selection devices must match the job in question. Work sampling works best with low-level jobs. Assessment centres work best for managerial positions. The validity of the interview as a selection device increases at progressively higher levels of management.

7. Employee training can be on-the-job or off-the-job. Popular on-the-job methods include job rotation, understudying, and apprenticeships. The more popular off-the-job methods are classroom lectures, films, and simulation exercises.

8. The five career stages are exploration, establishment, mid-career, late-career, and decline.

9. The collective bargaining process begins with a union-organizing effort and attainment of certification. Once a union has been certified, management begins preparation for negotiations by reviewing internal documents and environmen-

tal data. Negotiations then proceed, which often involve long and intense bargaining, leading to a written contract. Once a contract is agreed upon and ratified, it must be administered, and a procedure must be spelled out for handling contract disputes.

10. HRM practices can facilitate workforce diversity by widening the recruitment net, eliminating any discriminatory practices in the selection process, making applicants aware of the organization's willingness to accommodate their needs, and providing programs that focus on diversity issues.

Review and Discussion Questions

1. How does HRM affect all managers?
2. What are the possible sources for finding new employees?
3. Contrast reject errors and accept errors. Which one is most likely to open an employer to charges of discrimination? Why?
4. Why is decruitment now a major concern for managers?
5. What are the major problems of the interview as a selection device?
6. What is the relationship between selection, recruitment, and job analysis?
7. Do you think there are moral limits on how far a prospective employer should delve into an applicant's life by means of interviews and tests? Explain your position.
8. Identify three skill categories for which organizations do employee training.
9. What is the goal of orientation?
10. Do you believe that the government should be able to influence the HRM process of organizations through legislation and regulations? Support your position.
11. Assuming that management is already responsive to employee needs, do you think that labour unions benefit employees? Support your position.

Testing Your Comprehension

Circle the correct answer, then check yourself on page 471.

1. Which of the following is LEAST likely to be a reason to adopt an affirmative action program?
   a) the potential cost of defending discrimination lawsuits
   b) because discrimination does still exist, there are many above-average minority persons as potential employees
   c) organizational social responsibility
   d) to comply with federal legislation mandating affirmative action

2. As a result of federal legislation since the mid-1960s, employers must ensure that equal employment opportunities exist for
   a) every employee of their organization and all those organizations with which they do interstate business
   b) current employees
   c) current employees and job applicants
   d) job applicants

3. Strategic human resource planning is the process by which management
   a) plans for future business needs in terms of land, labour, and capital
   b) develops its restructuring plan
   c) ensures that the organization has the right personnel
   d) allocates resources to product line-managers

4. The document describing how a job fits into the organization's strategic direction is called
   a) a job description
   b) a job evaluation
   c) a job specification
   d) a job analysis

5. A human resource inventory is
   a) a statement of what a current jobholder does, how it is to be done, and the accountabilities of the job
   b) a statement indicating employees' education, capabilities, and specialized skills
   c) a statement of the minimum qualifications required for job candidates to be successful on the job
   d) none of the above

6. Where there exists a proven relationship between a selection device and job performance, there is
   a) no discrimination
   b) reliability
   c) validity
   d) selectivity

7. Which of the following is NOT a benefit attained from an internal recruiting search?

    a) building employee morale

    b) reducing recruiting costs

    c) reducing orientation time

    d) facilitating affirmative action goals

8. Which of the following is MOST CORRECT concerning the interview as a selection method for hiring a job candidate?

    a) interviews should be structured before any interview is conducted.

    b) Interviewers should check an applicant's background data before conducting an interview.

    c) Negative information about a job candidate is often discounted or overlooked.

    d) Most interviewers wait until a candidate is leaving the interview before making a decision.

9. All of the following should be primary concerns of job orientation, EXCEPT

    a) to familiarize new employees with their job activities

    b) to ease the initial anxiety of beginning a new job

    c) to allow employers to discern where, how, and if the employee will fit into the organization's culture

    d) to facilitate the outsider-insider transition

10. Which of the following statements BEST reflects the difference between employee training and employee development?

    a) Employee training focuses on job skills needed for future positions. Employee development focuses on skills needed for current jobs.

    b) Employee development primarily involves off-the-job training methods. Employee training primarily involves on-the-job training methods.

    c) Employee training focuses on skills needed for current jobs. Employee development focuses on skills needed for future positions.

    d) Employee development focuses on current employees. Employee training focuses on potential job applicants.

11. With regard to John P. Wanous's outlines for providing employees with a realistic job preview, all of the following may occur if this is NOT done, EXCEPT

    a) newly hired workers may become problem employees

    b) premature resignations may occur

    c) unrealistic job expectations may be built up by employees

    d) employees would be informed of the downsides of joining the company

12. All of the following should help to boost workforce diversity EXCEPT

    a) impressing upon employees the idea that management wants to accommodate their needs

    b) using current employee referrals as a source of new job applicants

    c) providing workshops to raise diversity consciousness

    d) making efforts to ensure that discrimination is excluded from the selection process for new job applicants

Self-Assessment Exercise

How Do You Define Life Success?

People have different ideas about what it means to be successful. Rate each of the following ideas on life success by circling the number that best represents its importance to you.

	ALWAYS IMPORTANT	VERY OFTEN IMPORTANT	FAIRLY OFTEN IMPORTANT	OCCASIONALLY IMPORTANT	NEVER IMPORTANT
1. Getting others to do what I want	5	4	3	2	1
2. Having inner peace and contentment	5	4	3	2	1
3. Having a happy marriage	5	4	3	2	1
4. Having economic security	5	4	3	2	1
5. Being committed to my organization	5	4	3	2	1
6. Being able to give help, assistance, advice, and support to others	5	4	3	2	1
7. Having a job that pays more than peers earn	5	4	3	2	1
8. Being a good parent	5	4	3	2	1
9. Having good job benefits	5	4	3	2	1
10. Having a rewarding family life	5	4	3	2	1
11. Raising children to be independent adults	5	4	3	2	1
12. Having people work for me	5	4	3	2	1
13. Being accepted at work	5	4	3	2	1
14. Enjoying my non-work activities	5	4	3	2	1
15. Making or doing things that are useful to society	5	4	3	2	1
16. Having high income and the resulting benefits	5	4	3	2	1
17. Having a sense of personal worth	5	4	3	2	1
18. Contributing to society	5	4	3	2	1
19. Having long-term job security	5	4	3	2	1
20. Having children	5	4	3	2	1
21. Getting good performance evaluations	5	4	3	2	1
22. Having opportunities for personal creativity	5	4	3	2	1
23. Being competent	5	4	3	2	1
24. Having public recognition	5	4	3	2	1
25. Having children who are successful emotionally and professionally	5	4	3	2	1

	ALWAYS IMPORTANT	VERY OFTEN IMPORTANT	FAIRLY OFTEN IMPORTANT	OCCASIONALLY IMPORTANT	NEVER IMPORTANT
26. Having influence over others	5	4	3	2	1
27. Being happy with my private life	5	4	3	2	1
28. Earning regular salary increases	5	4	3	2	1
29. Having personal satisfaction	5	4	3	2	1
30. Improving the well-being of the workforce	5	4	3	2	1
31. Having a stable marriage	5	4	3	2	1
32. Having the confidence of my bosses	5	4	3	2	1
33. Having the resources to help others	5	4	3	2	1
34. Being in a high-status occupation	5	4	3	2	1
35. Being able to make a difference in something	5	4	3	2	1
36. Having money to buy or do anything	5	4	3	2	1
37. Being satisfied with my job	5	4	3	2	1
38. Having self-respect	5	4	3	2	1
39. Helping others to achieve	5	4	3	2	1
40. Having personal happiness	5	4	3	2	1
41. Being able to provide quality education for my children	5	4	3	2	1
42. Making a contribution to society	5	4	3	2	1

Turn to page 466 for scoring directions and key.

Source: Barbara Parker and Leonard H. Chusmir, *Development and Validation of the Life Success Measures Scale.* (Miami, Fla.: Florida International University, 1991). Used with permission.

Class Exercise

Decruitment

Every manager, at some point in her career, will be faced with one of the more difficult tasks of managing—laying off employees. No matter how unpleasant this may be to some, when it is necessary, it must be done. Assume you are the manager in the information-processing department of a large corporation, and you have been notified that you must permanently reduce your staff by two individuals.[35] Below are some data about your employees.

Cara Burns. Inuit female, age 34. Cara has been employed with your company for five years, all in your department. Her evaluations over the past three years have been above average, and outstanding. Cara has a Master degree in computer science. She has been on short-term disability the past few weeks due to the birth of her second child and is expected to return to work in 20 weeks.

Bill Volkme. White male, age 30. Bill has been with you for four months and has 11 years of experience in the company in computer operations. He has an associate's degree in data processing and Bachelor and Master degrees in business. Last month Bill got married, and he and his new wife just bought an expensive home. Bill's evaluations over the past three years have been average, but he did save the company $550,000 on a suggestion he made regarding computer software vendors.

Louis-Claude Vachon. French-Canadian male, age 59. Louis-Claude has been with the company almost 40 years. He started as a janitor and worked up to data processor by attending technical school at night. Louis-Claude's evaluations over the past three years in your department have been outstanding. He is committed to getting the job done and devoting whatever it takes. He has three grown children, all college educated. Furthermore, when you took over the job as manager in this department, he made every effort to help you succeed by providing all the historical information you needed.

Leslie Anderson. White female, age 35. Leslie has been with your company 14 months. Five years ago, Leslie was in an automobile accident that left her wheelchair bound. Rumours have it that she is about to receive several million dollars from the insurance company of the driver that hit her. Her performance last year was above average. She has a Bachelor degree in computer programming.

Robert Oboke. Nigerian-born male, age 41. Bob just completed his Master degree in computer science. Bob has been with your department the past three years. His evaluations have been good to above-average. Five years ago, Bob won a lawsuit against your company for discriminating against him in a promotion to a supervisory position. Rumours have it that now, with his new degree, Bob is actively pursuing another job outside the company.

Given these five brief descriptions, make a decision on which two employees will be laid off. Then, in your group, seek consensus on which two the group would let go. In both cases, be prepared to defend your action, especially assuming that it may be challenged in court.

Case Application

A World Away—Only a Four-hour Flight from Toronto

Human resource management is not a simple aspect of business even in the best of circumstances, but it can become very difficult when a foreign environment is added to the mix. Delta Hotels and Resorts of Toronto is dealing with the human resource challenges that come with being the biggest hotelier in a foreign country that also happens to be one of the last remaining bastions of communism in the world: Cuba. Operating in Cuba provides Delta with great opportunity for profit, as it is a virtually untapped market and the Canadian company can do business there free of any competition from the large American firms. However, there are also some drawbacks to doing business in Cuba. Apart from the uncertain political future of the small island nation (Fidel Castro turned 71 in 1998, and has not set the country up with a successor), foreign investors must play by certain rules.

A state-controlled organization owns the properties on which Delta's resorts stand, and also controls the labour supply. Delta can only employ a handful of non-Cubans in its hotels. While Cubans generally have a high level of education, cultural differences present obstacles in small matters that would be taken for granted in Canada. Here is a list of some of the everyday problems Delta managers faced in Cuba: waiters would be wary of looking guests in the eyes, and be reluctant to offer refills of coffee or tea; janitorial personnel would refuse to stock the washrooms in the lobbies with toilet paper, for fear it would be stolen; maids would seek out a manager to ask permission before allowing the guests to have extra towels. It is essential for Delta to provide its guests with service on a par with what they would get at any of their other hotels or resorts. If Delta fails to provide this service, it will surely lose its customers. Therefore, little details such as these must be worked out with the staff.

Cuban employees are paid by the state and receive the equivalent of about US$12.50 a month (250–400 pesos). These low wages force Delta to contribute to its staff's welfare in other ways, such as offering free meals in cafeterias, and free monthly supplies of tooth-brushes, soap, detergent, shampoo, etc. Employees, of course, also receive tips, most often in Canadian or other foreign funds—very lucrative on the black market. These benefits keep employees happy and motivated. For Delta, there are benefits to the Cuban system. Strikes are nonexistent, and vacant positions are never a problem to fill. Still, managers must constantly stay on top of operations at the Cuban resorts, and human resources management is one of the main challenges of doing business in Cuba.

DELTA HOTELS AND RESORTS
www.deltahotels.com/

Questions

1. Since Delta cannot control recruitment for its workforce in Cuba, what methods could you suggest to help Delta create a skilled, efficient workforce?

2. If Cuba were eventually to change to a free-market economy, what effects would you foresee this having on Delta's human resource management in Cuba?

3. If the United States were to remove its embargo on Cuba, what human resource advantages do you think Delta would have over any new American competitors?

Source: Tamsen Tillson, "Rooms at the Revolution," *Canadian Business*, February 1996, pp. 75–76.

chapter **9**

Managing Change and Innovation

Learning Objectives

What will I be able to do after I finish this chapter?

1 • Describe what managers can change in organizations.

2 • Identify the external and internal forces for change.

3 • Explain how managers can serve as change agents.

4 • Contrast the "calm waters" and "white water rapids" metaphors of change.

5 • Explain why people are likely to resist change.

6 • Explain how TQM is a change effort.

7 • Differentiate between creativity and innovation.

8 • Explain how organizations can stimulate innovation.

Michael Cowpland, as CEO of Corel, is an expert at managing change and innovation.

COREL CORP
www.corel.com/

MICROSOFT CORP.
www.microsoft.com/
microsoft.htm

change
An alteration in structure, technology, or people.

Change is a fact of life in the business world, but some industries feel the effects of this force more than others. Software production is a field wherein change is practically the only constant. No one knows this better than Michael Cowpland, CEO and founder of Ottawa-based Corel Corp. Corel came into being in 1985 with 30 employees. Today it has more than 1,500 employees worldwide, with revenues of more than $400 million, and is, in fact, second only (but a far, far second) to Microsoft in the software market.[1]

During its short existence Corel has flirted with disaster many times, but has continually strived to change with the marketplace and to stay in pace with technology. The company made its fortune with its Corel Draw graphic design program, which captured more than 80 per cent of the market. But Cowpland realized that to sit on his heels and allow Corel to become complacent with its success could be disastrous. One of the company's great strengths is the ability to minimize the mistakes that are inevitable in such a volatile business. Corel has been willing to bow out gracefully from certain projects that have not lived up to expectations; such as abandoning development of a hand-held computer in December 1996, and selling its CD-ROM division in April 1997. Meanwhile, Corel has made major moves such as purchasing WordPerfect for $185 million (U.S.). This acquisition put Corel in direct competition with industry giant Microsoft over the office-suite software market. In early 1997 Corel declared that Java-based software, with its universal programming technology (removing the barriers between Macintosh and PC) would be Corel's plan of attack versus Microsoft, along with increased focus on expanding Internet markets. However, the Java strategy had to be abandoned later in the year because demand for Java programs in the marketplace was not yet sufficient to sustain a massive investment by Corel. In this case Corel's pursuit of leading-edge technology got ahead of the realities of its industry—profitability of innovation is never independent of the marketplace.

Still, Corel tries not only to keep up with technology, but to anticipate it. By constantly evolving, the company does not allow itself to be left behind. Corel's agility has brought it great success in an ever-changing industry, and Michael Cowpland's ability to adjust to change and to use it to his advantage is his strongest asset.

What Is Change?

If it weren't for **change**, the manager's job would be relatively easy. Planning would be without problems because tomorrow would be no different from today. The issue of organization design would be solved. Since the environment would be free from uncertainty, there would be no need to adapt. All organizations would be tightly structured. Similarly, decision making would be dramatically simplified because the outcome of each alternative could be predicted with almost certain accuracy. It would, indeed, simplify the manager's job if, for example, competitors didn't introduce new products or services, if customers didn't make new demands, if government regulations were never modified, or if employees' needs didn't change.

However, change is an organizational reality. Handling change is an integral part of every manager's job. But what can a manager change? The manager's options essentially fall into one of three categories: altering structure, technology, or people (see Exhibit 9-1). Changing structure includes any alteration in authority relations, coordination mechanisms, degree of centralization, job redesign, or similar structural variables. Changing technology encompasses modifications in the way work is processed, or methods and equipment are used. Changing people refers to changes in employee attitudes, expectations, perceptions, or behaviour. In this chapter, we'll look at the key managerial issues related to managing change.

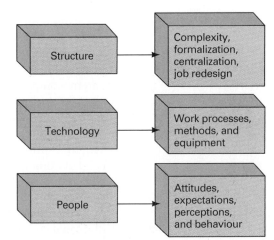

Exhibit 9-1
Three Categories of Change

Forces for Change

In Chapter 2, we pointed out that there are both external and internal forces that constrain managers. These same forces also bring about the need for change. Let's briefly look at the factors that can create the need for change.

What Are the External Forces Creating a Need for Change?

The external forces that create the need for change come from various sources. One such force can be the introduction of new competition in a marketplace. The arrival of Second Cup coffee stores in Montreal has forced A.L. Van Houte (which has historically dominated the specialty coffee business in Quebec) to re-fashion its image with store renovations and a change in focus, to compete for the growing market of customers under age 25.[2] Another example would be the older telephone companies, which must adapt to competition from Sprint and other long-distance carriers.

Government laws and regulations are a frequent impetus for change. The northern cod have been severely depleted on the Grand Banks and Newfoundland's economy has been severely damaged, causing heavy unemployment. Fishery Products International, the giant Newfoundland-based fish processor, has been forced to

SECOND CUP
COFFEE CO.
www.northernlife.com/
second/

Louis Deveau and son Jean-Paul of Acadian Seaplants Ltd., a seaweed supplier in Dartmouth, Nova Scotia, were working on ways to cultivate new seaweed products when they lost their sole customer. Acadian pushed ahead with product research, coupled with market research, and found a potentially huge market in Asia for a type of seaweed that they have developed the technology to cultivate.

change its business focus away from harvesting, to the processing of fish that it acquires from around the world. The furore over the federal anti-tobacco law, Bill C-71, began in earnest in early 1997. The planned restrictions on tobacco sponsorships threatened to affect far more than just the cigarette industry. Even though the ban on cigarette company sponsorship would not take effect until October 1998, organizers of such major cultural events as the Montreal International Jazz Festival, the Player's Grand Prix of Canada, the du Maurier Open Tennis Championship, and the Benson & Hedges International Fireworks Competition immediately had to begin considering alternative forms of funding to ensure a future.

**TELEGLOBE
CANADA**
www.teleglobe.ca/en/
canada/index.html

Pollution laws have changed the way companies in industries such as pulp and paper and mining run their operations. Changes in allowable emissions have forced the automobile industry to redesign its vehicles.

When the federal government told them that their monopoly on transatlantic calls would end in October 1998, Teleglobe Canada of Montreal decided to realign its business focus. Teleglobe moved into the U.S. to compete there in the growing market for international long-distance calling.[3]

NAFTA, the North American Free Trade Agreement, has opened up a number of markets for Canadian companies—but has also opened up Canadian markets to competitors from the United States and Mexico. Chains such as The Bay and Sears must adapt to competition from market entrants such as Price-Costco and Wal-Mart.

Technology also creates the need for change. Recent developments in sophisticated and extremely expensive diagnostic equipment have created significant economies of scale for hospitals and medical centres. The assembly line in many industries is undergoing dramatic changes as employers replace human labour with technologically advanced mechanical robots. The fluctuation in labour markets also forces managers to initiate change. For instance, the shortage of medical practitioners forces hospitals to redesign jobs and alter their reward and benefit packages.

Economic changes, of course, affect almost all organizations. For instance, a global firm's profits can vary dramatically depending on the strength of its home currency and the currencies of the countries in which it operates. When the Mexican peso was being steadily and drastically devalued early in 1995, the Bank of Nova Scotia suffered huge losses. By February, the value of the bank's $102-million investment in a Mexican bank had shrunk to as little as $35 million.[4] Similarly, Labatt's investments in a Mexican brewery made the Canadian brewery susceptible to the peso's plunge.

What Are the Internal Forces Creating a Need for Change?

In addition to the external forces noted above, internal forces can also stimulate the need for change. These internal forces tend to originate primarily from the internal operations of the organization or from the impact of external changes.

When management redefines or modifies its strategy, it often introduces a host of changes. As noted at the beginning of this chapter, Corel Corp.'s need to be competitive has required a major reorganization in how the business operates. The introduction of new equipment represents another internal force for change. Employees may have their jobs redesigned, need to undergo training to operate the new equipment, or be required to establish new interaction patterns within their formal group. An organization's workforce is rarely static. Its composition changes in terms of age, education, sex, nationality, and so forth. In a stable organization where managers have been in their positions for years, there might be a need to restructure jobs to retain the more ambitious employees, affording them some upward mobility. The compensation and benefits systems might also need to be reworked to reflect the needs of a diverse workforce. Employee attitudes, such as increased job dissatisfaction, may lead to increased absenteeism, more voluntary resignations, and even strikes. Such events will, in turn, often lead to changes in management policies and practices.

For Rockwell International of Canada, it is essential to keep management and labour relations at a strong level. The reasons for this are several, but principally, being a just-in-time supplier of parts to Chrysler has increased pressure to avoid a strike. It's normal for manufacturers working on a just-in-time system to finish making a batch of parts only 60 to 90 minutes before they are needed at the customer's plant. Inventory levels are kept at a minimum so that when problems arise there are tremendous pressures on everybody to find a solution—a big change from the days when strikes and walkouts were common. As Guido Tonin, chairman of the Canadian Auto Workers plant committee at Rockwell's plant in Milton, Ontario, says, "We're the only supplier for Chrysler and we don't want to lose that customer. If we lose Chrysler, we've lost our jobs."[5]

How Can a Manager Serve as a Change Agent?

Changes within an organization need a catalyst. People who act as catalysts and assume the responsibility for managing the change process are called **change agents**.

Any manager can be a change agent. As we review the topic of change, we assume that it is initiated and carried out by a manager within the organization. However, the change agent can be a nonmanager—for example, an internal staff specialist or outside consultant whose expertise is in change implementation. For major systemwide changes, internal management will often hire outside consultants to provide advice and assistance. Because they are from the outside, they often can offer an objective perspective usually lacking in insiders. However, outside consultants may be at a disadvantage because they have an inadequate understanding of the organization's history, culture, operating procedures, and personnel. Outside consultants are also prone to initiate more drastic changes than are insiders, which can be either a benefit or a disadvantage—because they do not have to live with the repercussions after the change is implemented. In contrast, internal managers who act as change agents may be more thoughtful (and possibly more cautious) because they must live with the consequences of their actions.

ROCKWELL
INTERNATIONAL
www.rockwell.com/

change agents
People who act as catalysts and manage the change process.

Two Different Views on the Change Process

We often use two very different metaphors to clarify the change process.[6] One envisions the organization as a large ship crossing a calm sea. The ship's captain and crew know exactly where they're going because they've made the trip many times before. Change surfaces as the occasional storm, a brief distraction in an otherwise calm and predictable trip. In the other metaphor, the organization is seen as a small raft navigating a raging river with uninterrupted white water rapids. Aboard the raft are half-a-dozen people who've never worked together before, who are totally unfamiliar with the river, who are unsure of their eventual destination, and, as if things weren't bad

YOUNG CANADIANS

Carol Borghesi: BC Tel

Carol Borghesi's fast rise through the management ranks at BC Tel has been the result of exceptional skill and foresight. One of her greatest feats was to understand the possible consequences of deregulation in the long-distance phone market, and to take immediate action to defend against the changing environment and its new competition. Borghesi convinced senior management to let her create a Corporate Call Centre dedicated to preserving customer loyalty.

BC TEL
www.bctel.net/

enough, who are travelling in the pitch-dark of night. In the white water rapids metaphor, change is a natural state, and managing change is a continual process.

These two metaphors present very different approaches to understanding and responding to change. Let's take a closer look at each one.

What Is the "Calm Waters" Metaphor?

Until recently, the "calm waters" metaphor dominated the thinking of practising managers and academics. It is best illustrated in Kurt Lewin's three-step description of the change process[7] (see Exhibit 9-2).

According to Lewin, successful change requires unfreezing the status quo, changing to a new state, and refreezing the new change to make it permanent. The status quo can be considered an equilibrium state. To move from this equilibrium, unfreezing is necessary. It can be achieved in one of three ways:

► **1.** The driving forces, which direct behaviour away from the status quo, can be increased.
► **2.** The restraining forces, which hinder movement from the existing equilibrium, can be decreased.
► **3.** The two approaches can be combined.

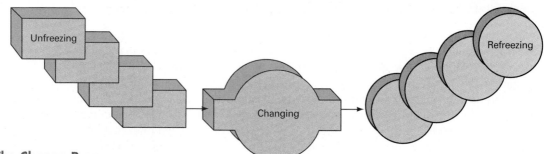

Exhibit 9-2 The Change Process

Once unfreezing has been accomplished, the change itself can be implemented. However, the mere introduction of change does not ensure that it will take hold. The new situation, therefore, needs to be refrozen so that it can be sustained over time. Unless this last step is attended to, there is a strong chance that the change will be short-lived and employees will revert to the previous equilibrium state. The objective of refreezing, then, is to stabilize the new situation by balancing the driving and restraining forces.

Note how Lewin's three-step process treats change as a break in the organization's equilibrium state. The status quo has been disturbed, and change is necessary to establish a new equilibrium state. This view might have been appropriate to the relatively calm environment that most organizations faced in the 1950s, 1960s, and early 1970s. But the "calm waters" metaphor is increasingly obsolete as a way to describe the kind of seas that current managers have to navigate.

What Is the "White Water Rapids" Metaphor?

The "white water rapids" metaphor takes into consideration the fact that environments are both uncertain and dynamic. To get a feeling for what managing change might be like when you have to continually maneuver in uninterrupted rapids, consider attending a university that had the following characteristics: Courses vary in length. Unfortunately, when you sign up, you don't know how long a course will last. It might go for two weeks or 30 weeks. Furthermore, the instructor can end a course any time he wants, with no prior warning. If that isn't bad enough, the length of the class changes each time it meets—sometimes it lasts 20 minutes, while other times it runs for three hours—and determination of the time of the next class meeting is set by the instructor during the previous class. Oh yes, there's one more thing. The exams are all unannounced, so you have to be ready for a test at any time. To succeed there, you would have to be incredibly flexible and be able to respond quickly to every changing condition. Students who were too structured or slow on their feet wouldn't survive.

**STENTOR
ALLIANCE**
www.stentor.ca/

YOUNG CANADIANS

Daniele Bertrand: Stentor Alliance

Daniele Bertrand joined the Stentor Alliance (members are Canadian regional telecommunications companies) as the industry adjusted to long distance competition. As deregulation continued, it became increasingly important to outline the companies' shared vision to such stakeholders as the federal government. Bertrand was instrumental in convincing the companies to develop a unified vision and to create the Stentor Innovation Centre. As president of the centre, Bertrand looks for new growth opportunities for the industry.

A growing number of managers are coming to accept that their job is much like what a student would face in such a university. The stability and predictability of the "calm waters" metaphor don't exist. Disruptions in the status quo are not occasional and temporary, followed by a return to calm waters. Many of today's managers never get out of the rapids. They face constant change, bordering on chaos. These managers are being forced to play a game they've never played before, which is governed by rules that are created as the game progresses.[8]

"White water rapids" may seem to be an overly drastic metaphor, but we assure you it is not. On a large scale, the airline industry has gone through rapid, white water changes. A number of very big carriers have gone bankrupt—Pan Am, Eastern, People's. Almost every major player has merged or formed associations with other airlines—Canadian with American Air Lines, and Air Canada with Continental, British Airways with Quantas. Commuter airlines have sprung out of nowhere; hub-and-spoke, in which airlines fly their routes in and out of "hub" airports, has changed routings; there have been widespread price wars; and virtually every airline has a frequent-flyer program. Anyone who doubts the "white water" nature of this business need only look at the continual struggles of Canadian Airlines to stay aloft. The company has been battling for its life for years, and has constantly made changes to try to survive; for example, in 1997 it reduced dependence on domestic flights where it was losing money drastically, and moved to increase transborder routes where chances for profit seemed brighter.[9]

Do you remember when you ordered something, having to wait days or weeks for delivery? Not anymore. The big wholesale distributors for things like computers and software fight over what they call "differentials"—how quickly and well they service their retail customers.[10] Ingram, a Toronto-based distributor, offers same-day delivery for orders placed before 11:30 a.m. Merisel, another distributor, instantly flashes order data on a salesperson's computer screen when the customer calls—for a 20-second-per-call saving! A similar change has happened to home-delivery pizza. Now in a number of markets, delivery is guaranteed within 15 minutes—because the pizza is made in the delivery van.

Book publishing was once thought of as an industry that experienced little change. Now, faced with high-tech publishing systems, mega-mergers, and takeovers among publishing companies, even this industry is facing white water rapids.

DETAILS ON A MANAGEMENT CLASSIC

Coch and French: Resistance to Change

One of the most famous studies on organizational change took place in the late 1940s at a plant of the Harwood Manufacturing Company where pajamas were made.[11] The plant employed about 500 people and had a long history of disruptions every time changes were made in the way work progressed. Although the changes were typically minor—for example, pajama folders who formerly folded tops with prefolded bottoms would be required to fold the bottoms as well—the employees resisted. They would complain bitterly and would openly refuse to make the changes. Production decreased; grievances, absenteeism, and job turnover increased.

The usual way that Harwood's management made these changes was autocratically. Management made the decision, then would call a group meeting where they would announce the changes to employees. The changes would be implemented immediately. Then, as mentioned, the employees rebelled. So Harwood's executives brought in a consultant as a change agent to help with their problem. As an experiment, the consultant arranged for the next change to be conducted in three groups, using three different methods. In the first group, the change was initiated in the usual manner—autocratically. This was the control group. The second group involved employee participation through selective representatives. These representatives, with management, worked out the details of the change, then tried the new methods and trained others in the new procedures. In the third group, there was full participation. All employees shared in designing the new methods with management.

The change agent gathered data over a 40-day period and what he found strongly supported the value of participation. In the control group, resistance occurred as before. Seventeen per cent of the employees quit their jobs during the 40-day period and grievances and absenteeism increased. However, in the representative and full participation groups, there were no resignations, only one grievance, and no absenteeism. Moreover, participation was positively related to productivity. In the control group, output actually dropped from an average of 60 units per hour to 48 during the experimental period. The participation group generated 68 units per hour, and the total participation group averaged 73 units per hour.

The conclusion of the Coch and French study holds a major key for today's organizational change. That is, for permanent change to occur without extensive resistance, employees must be involved. Without employee involvement in things that directly affect their work, companies run the risk of negating any possible gain a change can bring about or, worse, making the situation more serious than it was originally.▼

Does Every Manager Face a World of Constant and Chaotic Change?

Not every manager faces a world of constant and chaotic change. However, the set of managers who don't is dwindling rapidly.

Managers in such businesses as high-fashion apparel and computer software have long confronted a world of white water rapids. These managers used to look with envy at their counterparts in industries such as auto manufacturing, oil exploration, banking, publishing, telecommunications, and air transportation, who historically faced a stable and predictable environment. That might have been true in the 1960s, but it's not true in the 1990s!

Few organizations today can treat change as the occasional disturbance in an otherwise peaceful world. Even these few do so at great risk. Too much is changing too fast for any organization or its managers to be complacent.[12] Most competitive advantages last less than 18 months. A firm such as People Express—a no-frills, no-reservations airline—was described in business periodicals as the model "new look" firm, then went bankrupt a short time later. As management writer Tom Peters has aptly noted, the old saying "If it ain't broke, don't fix it" no longer applies. In its place, he suggests "If it ain't broke, you just haven't looked hard enough. Fix it anyway."[13] Of course, what Peters is saying is consistent with current reengineering trends. Recall from our discussion of reengineering in Chapter 2 that management needs to rethink all of the activities and processes in its organization. The quantum change required to remain competitive in today's global marketplace cannot be overstated.

Organizational Change

Individuals who spent 20 years as mail sorters for the post office were likely to resist automatic letter sorters more actively than were recent hires. The latter had less personal investment in the old system and were less threatened by automation.

As change agents, managers should be motivated to initiate change because they're concerned with improving their organization's effectiveness. However, change can be a threat to managers. It can also be a threat to nonmanagerial personnel. Organizations, and people within them, can build up inertia that propels them to resist any change, even if that change might be beneficial (see Details on a Management Classic). In this section, we want to review why people in organizations resist change and what can be done to lessen this resistance.

Why Do People Resist Change?

It has been said that most people hate any change that doesn't jingle in their pockets. This awareness of resistance to change is well documented.[14] But why do people resist change? An individual is likely to resist change for three reasons: uncertainty, concern over personal loss, and the belief that the change is not in the organization's best interest[15] (see Exhibit 9-3).

Changes substitute ambiguity and uncertainty for the known. Regardless of how much you may dislike some of the work associated with attending university, at least you know the ropes. You understand what is expected of you. When you leave and venture out into the world of full-time employment, regardless of how anxious you are to get out of school, you will have to trade the known for the unknown. Employees in organizations hold the same dislike for uncertainty. For example, the introduction in manufacturing plants of quality control methods based on sophisticated statistical models means that many quality control inspectors will have to learn these new methods. Some inspectors may fear that they will

Exhibit 9-3
Reasons for Resistance to Change

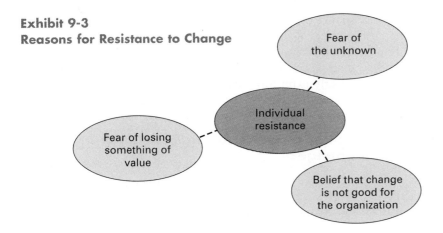

be unable to do so. They may, therefore, develop a negative attitude toward statistical control techniques, or behave dysfunctionally if required to use them.

The second cause of resistance is the fear of losing something already possessed. Change threatens the investment one has already made in the status quo. The more that people have invested in the current system, the more they resist change. Why? They fear the loss of status, money, authority, friendships, personal convenience, or other benefits that they value. This explains why senior employees resist change more than do relatively new employees to an organization. Senior employees have generally invested more in the current system and, therefore, have more to lose by adapting to a change.

TECHNIQUE	WHEN USED	ADVANTAGE	DISADVANTAGE
Education and communication	When resistance is due to misinformation	Clear up misunderstandings	May not work where mutual trust and credibility are lacking
Participation	When resisters have the expertise to make a contribution	Increases involvement and acceptance	Time-consuming; has potential for a poor solution
Facilitation and support	When resisters are fearful and anxiety-ridden	Can facilitate needed adjustments	Expensive; no guarantee of success
Negotiation	Necessary when resistance comes from a powerful group	Can "buy" commitment	Potentially high cost; opens door for others to apply pressure, too
Manipulation and co-optation	When a powerful group's endorsement is needed	Inexpensive easy way to gain support	Can backfire, causing change agent to lose credibility
Coercion	When a powerful group's endorsement is needed	Inexpensive, easy way to gain support	May be illegal; may undermine change agent's credibility

Exhibit 9-4   Techniques for Reducing Resistance to Change

A final cause of resistance is a person's belief that the change is incompatible with the goals and best interests of the organization. If an employee believes that a new job procedure proposed by a change agent will reduce productivity or product quality, that employee can be expected to resist the change. If the employee expresses her resistance positively (clearly expressing it to the change agent, along with substantiation), this form of resistance can be beneficial to the organization.

What Are Some Techniques for Reducing Resistance to Organizational Change?

When management sees resistance to change as dysfunctional, what actions can it take? Several tactics have been suggested for use by managers or other change agents in dealing with resistance to change[16] (see Developing Management Skills).

Change and TQM

Total Quality Management is essentially a continuous, incremental change program. It is compatible with the white water rapids metaphor of change that we discussed earlier. In this section, we want to draw on our knowledge of change processes to consider how managers can effectively implement TQM.

First, let's briefly review the key components of TQM. You'll remember that it focuses on customer needs, emphasizes participation and teamwork, and seeks to create a culture in which all employees strive to improve continuously not only the quality of the organization's products or services, but also such factors as work processes and customer response time. It might be helpful if we look at TQM in terms of the three areas toward which management can direct its change efforts: structure, technology, and people (see Exhibit 9-5).

As first discussed in Chapter 7, the structure of an organization that expects to implement TQM effectively will be decentralized; will have reduced vertical differentiation, wider spans of control, and reduced division of labour; and will support cross-functional teams. These structural components give employees the authority and means to implement process improvements. For instance, the creation of work teams that cut across departmental lines allows people who understand a problem best to solve that problem. And cross-functional teams encourage cooperative problem solving rather than "us versus them" blame placing.

TECHNOLOGY	STRUCTURE	PEOPLE	CHANGE AGENT

Flexible process
Education and training
  of workers
	Decentralization
	Reduced vertical
	  differentiation
	Reduced division
	  of labour
	Wider spans of control
	Cross-functional teams
		Education and training
		Supportive performance
		  evaluation and reward
		  system
			Active leadership from
			  the top

Exhibit 9-5   Factors that Facilitate Continuous Incremental Improvement

The primary focus on technological change in TQM is directed at developing flexible processes to support continuous improvement. Employees committed to TQM are constantly looking for things to fix. Thus, work processes must be adaptable to continual change and fine-tuning. To achieve this, TQM requires an extensive commitment to educating and training workers. The organization must provide employees with skills training in problem solving, decision making, negotiation, statistical analysis, and team building.[17] For example, employees need to be able to analyse and act on data. An organization with a TQM program should provide work teams with quality data such as failure rates, reject rates, and scrap rates. It should provide feedback data on customer satisfaction. It should give the teams the necessary information to create and monitor process control charts. And, of course, the structure should allow the work teams to make continual improvements in the operations based on process control data.

The people dimension of TQM requires a workforce committed to the organization's objectives of quality and continual improvement. Again, this necessitates proper education and training. It also demands a performance evaluation and reward system that supports and encourages TQM objectives. For example, successful programs put quality objectives into bonus plans for executives, and incentives for operating employees.[18]

The discussion above is critical for change to be promoted and implemented. But remember, too, that needed change may require more than incremental movements. In these cases, radical or massive changes are in order. When that occurs—a process we described in Chapter 2 when we discussed reengineering—the same principles may hold but on a much larger scale. That is, to be competitive, organizations may need to reengineer or initiate quantum change. Then to remain competitive, managers must seek continuous improvements. For example, consider our wave analogy. Reengineering can be likened to a big, sweeping tidal wave. As it hits, everything in its path is scattered. But the energies behind tidal waves cannot continue forever. Instead, what it began to set adrift is now propelled to its new destination by a number of smaller waves (continuous improvement).

Stimulating Innovation

"Innovate or die!" That has increasingly become the rallying cry of today's contemporary managers. In the dynamic world of global competition, organizations must create new products and services and adopt state-of-the-art technology if they are to compete successfully. The standard of innovation to which many organizations strive is that achieved by the 3M Company.[19] 3M has developed a reputation for being able to stimulate innovation over a long period of time. One of its stated objectives is that 25 per cent of each division's profits are to come from products less than five years old. Toward that end, 3M typically launches more than 200 new products each year. During a recent five-year period, 3M generated better than 30 per cent of its $13 billion in revenues from products introduced during the previous five years.

3M COMPANY
www.mmm.com/

What's the secret to 3M's success? What, if anything, can other managers do to make their organizations more innovative? In the following pages, we'll try to answer these questions as we discuss the factors behind innovation.

How Do Creativity and Innovation Differ?

creativity
The ability to combine ideas in a unique way or to make unusual associations between ideas.

innovation
The process of taking a creative idea and turning it into a useful product, service, or method of operation.

In general usage, **creativity** means the ability to combine ideas in a unique way or to make unusual associations between ideas.[20] An organization that stimulates creativity is one that develops novel approaches to things or unique solutions to problems. **Innovation** is the process of taking a creative idea and turning it into a useful product, service, or method of operation. Thus, the innovative organization is characterized by the ability to channel its creative juices into useful outcomes. When managers talk about changing an organization to make it more creative, they usually mean that they want to stimulate innovation.

Telecommunications companies operate in an industry that demands constant innovation—Canada's two largest telecommunications firms, Northern Telecom and BCE Inc., each spend more than $2 billion annually on research and development. A company such as Ottawa-based Corel Corp. must also strive constantly to stay ahead of competition from U.S. powerhouses Microsoft and Oracle. Corel spends roughly 14 per cent of its revenue on new research and development. Staying at the forefront of its industry's technology keeps Corel on pace in its dogged pursuit of Microsoft.[21]

Vancouver-based Ballard Power Systems received $450 million in investment from German automaker Daimler-Benz in 1997, enough to keep the company's development of its fuel-cell engine going until it is ready for the market. The engine, which converts hydrogen to electricity without combustion, is on the leading edge of innovation.

MANAGERS WHO MADE A DIFFERENCE

Colin Patey at the Waterford Hospital

Hospitals haven't traditionally been held up as examples of change. In fact, until the 1990s "change" was a word to be avoided in the health care system in Canada. But two factors have altered that: first, severe pressure on funding, and second, consumer demand for better service. Big hospitals are big business; they have budgets in the hundreds of millions of dollars and are managed professionally. But being staffed largely by professionals—doctors, nurses, pharmacists, and other specialists—they tend to have reasonably well-defined "territories" that are well guarded. Cooperation is often difficult to attain. Things have changed, however, and the health care system in Newfoundland has led the way in many areas.

An outstanding leader of change in the health care system is Colin Patey, executive director of the Waterford Hospital in St. John's, Newfoundland. Whether or not Patey watched *Star Trek* when he was a boy, he can perhaps best be described as something of a Captain Kirk—daring to boldly go where no one has gone before. In 1990, when he joined the Waterford Hospital as executive director, it was an institution in gridlock. As Peter Dawe, the director of the hospital's foundation, describes it, "This was the epitome of a bureaucratic institution; nothing happened, nothing

changed. There were a lot of problems identified—I mean, everybody knew the problems, but nobody did anything about them." Because he came to the Waterford with a reputation for change, as he took on his new post Patey was greeted with a strike. And, for good measure, after he had successfully dealt with that and begun to gain the trust of the staff, he was told by the government to take $2 million out of his budget.

Large budget cuts most often translate into staff cuts. But Patey knew that if he was ever to get the staff motivated, committed to change, and proud of themselves and their hospital, he would have to avoid the "easy" route of simply cutting jobs. He had to involve staff at all levels in the process of operating the hospital more efficiently and effectively. So, rather than go to his executive team for suggestions as to how they would effect the cuts, he went to the entire hospital! Working on the belief that it is the people working on a job who know most about it, he put the problem to them: how to operate with $2 million less, provide the same level of patient care, and not lose any jobs. Within a short period, all the solutions were provided and the budget cut was absorbed without loss of jobs.

It is virtually impossible to gain commitment to change in a climate of low trust. But once Patey had earned the trust of the staff, he set about creating a vision for the hospital to which everyone could subscribe and that would instil pride in individuals and their institution. Change implies risks, and it also requires a high degree of openness. As part of his change plan, Patey did things such as inviting the CBC into the hospital to produce a documentary; involving all the stakeholders in the hospital—doctors, nurses, staff, patients, the board, and the community—to express their views on its mission; changing the focus of his executive team from "the problems are too large to handle" to "one problem at a time, and one step at a time." And an element of successful change which is often overlooked, communication—of the changes, of the problems, and most importantly of the successes—was tackled head-on by a communications professional.

In 1995, the Waterford hospital came under one board that amalgamated all the hospitals in St. John's. But it wasn't the same hospital that Colin Patey had joined in 1990. Hundreds of patients had been reintroduced into the community with careful and comprehensive support; the new openness of the hospital was clearly symbolized by physical changes to the facilities; locked wards had been unlocked; outpatient services had flourished; the hospital had benchmarked what it considered to be the best providers of psychiatric care in Canada and focused on bringing the Waterford's services to those levels; ownership of the change had been embedded at all levels; and there was real pride of ownership by the staff. Managers of successful change make a very big difference, and Colin Patey is one of them.▼

How Can a Manager Foster Innovation?

There are three sets of variables that have been found to stimulate innovation. They pertain to the organization's structure, culture, and human resource practices.

How Do Structural Variables Affect Innovation? Based on extensive research, we can make three statements regarding the effect of structural variables on innovation.[22] First, organic structures positively influence innovation. Because they're lower in vertical differentiation, formalization, and centralization, organic structures facilitate the flexibility, adaptation, and cross-fertilization that make the adoption of innovations easier. Second, the easy availability of plentiful resources provides a key building block for innovation. An abundance of resources allows management to afford to purchase innovations, bear the cost of instituting innovations, and absorb failures. Finally, frequent interunit communication helps to break down possible barriers to innovation.[23] Committees, task forces, and other such mechanisms facilitate interaction across departmental lines and are widely used in successfully innovative organizations. 3M, for instance, is highly decentralized and takes on many of the characteristics of small, organic organizations. The company also has the "deep pockets" needed to support its policy of allowing scientists and engineers to use up to 15 per cent of their time on projects of their own choosing.

How Does an Organization's Culture Affect Innovation? Innovative organizations tend to have similar cultures.[24] They encourage experimentation. They reward both successes and failures. They celebrate mistakes. An innovative culture is likely to have the following seven characteristics:

▶ 1. **Acceptance of ambiguity.** Too much emphasis on objectivity and specificity constrains creativity.
▶ 2. **Tolerance of the impractical.** Individuals who offer impractical, even foolish, answers to "what if" questions are not stifled. What seems impractical at first might lead to innovative solutions.
▶ 3. **Low external controls.** Rules, regulations, policies, and similar controls are kept to a minimum.
▶ 4. **Tolerance of risk.** Employees are encouraged to experiment without fear of consequences should they fail. Mistakes are treated as learning opportunities.
▶ 5. **Tolerance of conflict.** Diversity of opinions is encouraged. Harmony and agreement between individuals and/or units are not assumed to be evidence of high performance.
▶ 6. **Focus on ends rather than means.** Goals are made clear, and individuals are encouraged to consider alternative routes toward their attainment. Focusing on ends suggests that there might be several right answers to any given problem.
▶ 7. **Open systems focus.** The organization closely monitors the environment and responds rapidly to changes as they occur.

ETHICAL DILEMMAS IN MANAGEMENT

WHAT WOULD YOU DO IF YOU HAD DETAILS ON A COMPETITOR'S TRADE SECRET?

A disgruntled employee who works for one of your key competitors mails you samples of a top-secret new product that your competitor is working on. He even offers, for a small fee, to help you unravel its groundbreaking technology. You realize that this new technology will make your competition's new products unbeatable. Should you send the samples back to the employee and turn him in to his employer? Or should you turn the samples over to your research and development team for analysis, and encourage them to break the code? Sound far-fetched? Not really. This dilemma was actually faced by managers at Johnson & Johnson.[25]

Philip A. Stegora, a disgruntled employee at 3M Company, got hold of some samples of a new casting tape that 3M developed for doctors to use to set broken bones. He mailed the tape to Johnson & Johnson and offered to help them unravel 3M's technology for a fee of only $20,000. As the manager at J&J who received the package, you'd love to understand the technology that 3M has developed. The new products that might evolve from this technology could be unbeatable in the $200-million market for casting tapes. What would you do?

What Human Resource Variables Affect Innovation? Within the human resources category, we find that innovative organizations actively promote the training and development of their members so that their knowledge remains current, offer their employees high job security to reduce the fear of getting fired for making mistakes, and encourage individuals to become champions of change. Once a new idea is developed, champions of change actively and enthusiastically promote the idea, build support, overcome resistance, and ensure that the innovation is implemented. Recent research finds that champions have common personality characteristics: extremely high self-confidence, persistence, energy, and a tendency to take risks. Champions also display characteristics associated with dynamic leadership. They inspire and energize others with their vision of the potential of an innovation and through their strong personal conviction in their mission. They are also good at gaining the commitment of others to support their mission. And champions have jobs that provide considerable decision-making discretion (see Ethical Dilemmas in Management). This autonomy helps them introduce and implement innovations in organizations.[26]

Summary

This summary is organized by the chapter Learning Objectives found on page 239.

1. Managers can change the organization's structure by altering complexity, formalization, or centralization variables or by redesigning jobs; changing the organization's technology by altering work processes, methods, and equipment; or changing people by altering attitudes, expectations, perceptions, or behaviour.

2. External forces for change include the marketplace, government laws and regulations, technology, labour markets, and economics. Internal forces of change include organizational strategy, equipment, the workforce, and employee attitudes.

3. Managers can serve as change agents by becoming the catalyst for change in their units and by managing the change process.

4. The "calm waters" metaphor views change as a break in the organization's equilibrium state. Organizations are seen as stable and predictable, disturbed by an occasional crisis. The "white water rapids" metaphor views change as continual and unpredictable. Managers must deal with ongoing and almost chaotic change.

5. Change is often resisted because of the uncertainty it creates, concern for personal loss, and a belief that it might not be in the organization's best interest.

6. TQM is essentially a change effort, as it focuses on continuous, incremental change in aspects of the organization's operations.

7. Creativity is the ability to combine ideas in a unique way or to make unusual associations between ideas. Innovation is the process of taking creative ideas and turning them into a useful product, service, or method of operation.

8. Organizations that stimulate innovation will have structures that are flexible, easy access to resources, and fluid communication; a culture that is relaxed, supportive of new ideas, and encourages monitoring of the environment; and creative people who are well trained, current in their fields, and secure in their jobs.

Review and Discussion Questions

1. Why is handling change an integral part of every manager's job?
2. What internal and external forces create the need for organizations to change?
3. Who are change agents?
4. Do you think that a low-level employee could act as a change catalyst? Explain.
5. Describe Lewin's three-step change process.
6. Is TQM consistent with the goal of introducing revolutionary change into an organization? Discuss.
7. How do creativity and innovation differ? Give an example of each.
8. How can an innovative culture make an organization more effective? Could such an innovative culture make an organization less effective? Explain.
9. How can management foster innovation?
10. Can changes occur in an organization without a champion to foster innovation? Explain.

Testing Your Comprehension

Circle the correct answer, then check yourself on page 472.

1. Some of your employees who ride the subway show up for work one hour late every day. Leaving their homes earlier does not work because of construction delays on the subway. You decide to allow these people, and other employees, to start work one hour later. Of course, they work an hour later in the afternoon. What type of change did you make?
   a) people-oriented
   b) technological
   c) structural
   d) environmental

2. A participative approach to overcoming resistance to change works best when
   a) there is close alignment of the goals of all concerned
   b) the source of resistance is misinformation or poor communication
   c) obsolescent skills are a concern of the individuals resisting the change
   d) coercion, manipulation, and cooptation have failed

3. Which of the following is the correct order of change in the "calm waters" metaphor?
   a) unfreezing—changing—refreezing
   b) unfreezing—refreezing—changing
   c) freezing—refreezing—changing
   d) freezing—changing—unfreezing

4. The MOST relevant disadvantage of using outside consultants as change agents is
   a) the cost
   b) internal members do not accept external recommendations
   c) they do not have to live with the repercussions after the change
   d) they cannot offer an objective perspective

5. If resistance to change is caused by misinformation, which of the following tactics would BEST reduce change resistance?
   a) participation
   b) facilitation and support
   c) negotiation
   d) education and communication

6. Innovation refers to
   a) a decision-making technique
   b) the implementation of a creative idea
   c) a type of process consultation
   d) a type of automation

7. A culture conducive to creativity and innovation would probably have a high _____ and a low _____.

   a) tolerance of risk; division of labour

   b) external control; tolerance of risk

   c) tolerance of conflict; acceptance of ambiguity

   d) tolerance of risk; tolerance of the impractical

8. The Coch and French study would suggest that the best way for an organization to overcome resistance to change would be to

   a) have management inform workers of the need for change by giving specific examples and reasons

   b) have management make decisions and implement them

   c) allow for employee participation in the design of change measures

   d) bring in an outside consultant to act as a change agent

9. An employee is likely to resist change in an organization for all of the following reasons EXCEPT

   a) concern over possible personal loss

   b) belief that change is not good for the organization

   c) change can only improve an organization's effectiveness at the management level

   d) fear of the unknown

10. All of the following can justifiably be said of TQM EXCEPT

    a) TQM as a program involves continuous change.

    b) High division of labour is usually necessary for effective TQM implementation.

    c) TQM focuses on customer needs.

    d) TQM emphasizes teamwork and participation.

11. A company such as 3M could best be described as:

    a) creative

    b) resistant to change

    c) innovative

    d) centralized

12. All of the following statements regarding the effect of structural variables on innovation are true EXCEPT

    a) Formalization and centralization facilitate the adoption of innovation.

    b) Communication among units reduces barriers to innovation.

    c) The availability of resources has an effect on an organization's innovative capacity.

    d) Organic structures can adversely effect innovation.

Self-Assessment Exercise

How Ready Are You for Managing in a Turbulent World?

Instructions: Listed below are some statements that a 37-year-old manager made about his job at a large, successful corporation. If your job had these characteristics, how would you react to them? After each statement are five letters, A to E. Circle the letter that best describes how you think you would react according to the following scale:

A I would enjoy this very much; it's completely acceptable.

B This would be enjoyable and acceptable most of the time.

C I'd have no reaction to this feature one way or another, or it would be about equally enjoyable and unpleasant.

D This feature would be somewhat unpleasant for me.

E This feature would be very unpleasant for me.

1. I regularly spend 30 to 40 per cent of my time in meetings. A B C D E

2. A year and a half ago, my job did not exist, and I have been essentially inventing it as I go along. A B C D E

3. The responsibilities I either assume or am assigned consistently exceed the authority I have for discharging them. A B C D E

4. At any given moment in my job, I have on the average about a dozen phone calls to be returned. A B C D E

5. There seems to be very little connection in my job between the quality of my performance and my actual pay and fringe benefits. A B C D E

6. About two weeks a year of formal management training is needed in my job just to stay current. A B C D E

7. Because we have very effective equal employment opportunity (EEO) in my company and because it is thoroughly multinational, my job consistently brings me into close working contact at a professional level with people of many races, ethnic groups, and nationalities, and of both sexes. A B C D E

8. There is no objective way to measure my effectiveness. A B C D E

9. I report to three different bosses for different aspects of my job, and each has an equal say in my performance appraisal. A B C D E

10. On average, about a third of my time is spent dealing with unexpected emergencies that force all scheduled work to be postponed. A B C D E

11. When I have to meet with the people who report to me, it takes my secretary most of a day to find a time when we are all available, and even then, I have yet to have everyone present for the entire meeting. A B C D E

12. The university degree I earned in preparation for this type of work is now obsolete, and I probably should go back for another degree. A B C D E

13. My job requires that I absorb 100–200 pages per week of technical materials. A B C D E

14. I am out of town overnight at least one night per week. A B C D E

15. My department is so interdependent with several other departments in the company that all distinctions about which ones are responsible for which tasks are quite arbitrary. A B C D E

16. I will probably get a promotion in about a year to a job in another division that has most of these same characteristics. A B C D E

17. During the period of my employment here, either the entire company or the division I worked in has been reorganized every year or so. A B C D E

18. While there are several possible promotions I can see ahead of me, I have no real career path in an objective sense. A B C D E

19. While there are several possible promotions I can see ahead of me, I think I have no realistic chance of getting to the top levels of the company. A B C D E

20. While I have many ideas about how to make things work better, I have no direct influence on either the business policies or the personnel policies that govern my division. A B C D E

21. My company has recently put in an "assessment centre" where all other managers and I will be required to go through an extensive battery of psychological tests to assess our potential.

                                      A B C D E

22. My company is a defendant in an antitrust suit, and if the case comes to trial, I will probably have to testify about some decisions that were made a few years ago.   A B C D E

23. Advanced computer and other electronic office technology is continually being introduced into my division, necessitating constant learning on my part.   A B C D E

24. The computer terminal and screen I have in my office can be monitored in my bosses' offices without my knowledge.   A B C D E

Turn to page 467 for scoring directions and key.

Source: From Peter B. Vaill, *Managing as a Performing Art: New Ideas for a World of Chaotic Change* (San Francisco: Jossey-Bass, 1989), pp. 8–9. With permission.

Class Exercise

The Celestial Aerospace Company

Objectives:

1. To illustrate how forces for change and stability must be managed in organizations.
2. To illustrate the effects of alternative change techniques on the relative strength of forces for change and forces for stability.

The Situation:

The marketing division of the Celestial Aerospace Company (CAP) has gone through two major reorganizations in the past three years. Initially, its structure changed from a functional to a matrix form. But the matrix form did not satisfy some functional managers. They complained that the structure confused the authority and responsibility relationships. In reaction to these complaints, the marketing department revised the structure back to the functional form. This new structure maintained market and project teams, which were managed by project managers with a few general staff personnel. But no functional specialists were assigned to these groups. After the change, some problems began to surface. Project managers complained that they could not obtain necessary assistance from functional staffs. It not only took more time to obtain necessary assistance but also created problems in estab-lishing stable relationships with functional staff members. Since these problems affected their services to customers, project managers demanded a change in the organizational structure—probably again toward a matrix structure. Faced with these complaints and demands from project managers, the vice-president is pondering another reorganization. He has requested an outside consultant (you) to help him form a reorganization plan.

1. Divide yourselves into groups of five to seven and take the role of consultants.
2. Each group should identify the forces necessitating the change and the resistance to that change found in the company.
3. Each group should develop a set of strategies for dealing with the resistance to change and explain how it would implement these strategies.
4. Reassemble the class and hear each group's recommendations and explanations.

Source: Adapted from K.H. Chung and L.C. Megginson, *Organizational Behavior* (New York: Harper & Row, 1981), pp. 498–99. With permission.

Case Application

Hot Off the Press: Thomson Corp.

Managing change is something that Michael Brown knows well. As the executive in charge of Thomson Corp.'s strategic management, Brown sees innovation as the Canadian media giant's future. Thomson has built itself into the major force in the Canadian print news media, with a chain of newspapers across the country. Now Thomson is in the midst of a major change. Recently the company has sold 46 of its newspapers in North America. In 1995 Thomson brought in an estimated US$1 billion from the sale of newspaper groups in the U.K., Canada, and the U.S. Now Thomson is changing its focus, and is moving into information products for businesses and professionals. Thomson now provides information services in five professional fields: tax, law, accounting, and human resources; science and engineering; financial services; health and medical; and education and libraries. In 1994 the company purchased 40 businesses to further its ambitions in these fields, paying US$904 million.

The decision to move into this new area of operations, while being a major manoeuvre, was a strategic move based on solid figures. From 1987 to 1993, Thomson's newspaper holdings dropped in profit by 37.9 per cent, while the company's specialized information business profit increased by more than 200 per cent. This pattern has continued, and while the newspaper industry appears to be recovering from the recession, Thomson believes that its best interests lie in this new field. Now major changes are afoot at Thomson. The company must redefine its corporate mission to adjust to its new market, and the structure of the corporation will probably undergo major changes.

After being the sleeping giant of the Canadian publishing world for so long, it seems as if Thomson has decided to come out of hibernation and face a new and exciting challenge. The new shape of Thomson's operations will be subject to more rapid transformation than the corporation has ever known. In time, electronic publishing ventures may well represent the core of the organization's business. Thomson may be set for great things in the future. Of Thomson's new direction, Brown has this to say: "There's more change and more opportunity than ever before. Through commitment to innovation, technology and excellence, I believe we will become the largest information company in the world."

Questions

1. What kinds of difficulties can you foresee Thomson having in changing from a calm-waters environment to a white-water rapids environment?

2. What types of internal resistance to change might Thomson face?

3. How can Thomson overcome resistance to change within its organization?

Source: Harvey Schachter, "Information Overload," *Canadian Business*, November 1995, pp. 34–47.

Eaton's: Slow, Sluggish, Complacent, Crippled

CBC ✺

"The Empire Strikes Out." "Vultures Closing In." "Safe and Dull—and in Danger." The media in the year 1997 was peppered with such headlines, referring to the filing for bankruptcy protection of T. Eaton Co. Ltd., the 127-year-old department store chain based in Toronto. Many of the stores had been losing money for years while management seemingly carried on as if it were business as usual. For the fiscal year before filing for court protection, Eaton's posted losses of $120 million.

Business analysts had been talking about Eaton's woes for years, but when the bottom finally fell out, there was still great shock that such a venerable institution could sink to such depths. But it was both a lesson and a warning: even giant corporations cannot afford to be complacent. Companies that are slow to change with the times quickly lose any competitive advantage in today's business climate.

Department stores began to feel the effects of new competition when big-box stores started to emerge over the past two decades. These "category killers," as they are often called due to their total domination of a specific segment of retailing, operate in their chosen domains much more efficiently than department stores that seek to offer everything under one roof. Moreover, the fast rise of discount chains such as Wal-Mart—which stormed into Canada in the mid-1990s—offered excellent customer service and low prices without the overhead of grand-looking stores. Some Canadian institutions changed to better compete in this new environment (such as Canadian Tire—see Managers Who Made a Difference, Chapter 5). Eaton's itself unveiled a new strategy, coined "Eaton 2000, a Vision of Our Future," but it seemed as if the Eaton family was simply paying lip service to new business trends. The changes implemented did not get to the root problems plaguing the company.

Questions

1. What sort of problems would a company like Eaton's, with an ingrained corporate culture, face if reengineered to cope with the changing industry climate?

2. Do you think it would be easier for a smaller company such as Sport Chek to apply the concepts of TQM than it would be for a company such as Eaton's? How could TQM efforts have benefitted Eaton's?

3. If you had been CEO at Eaton's during the 1990s, what would you have done to try to prevent such a decline?

Video Resource: "Eaton's Troubles," *Venture* 635 (March 23, 1997).

Additional Sources: Tom Fennell, "Show Him the Money," *Maclean's*, September 1, 1997, p. 46; Jennifer Wells, "The Empire Strikes Out," *Maclean's*, March 10, 1997, pp. 32–35; Tom Fennell, "Eaton's Chooses a 'Brand-new' Chief," *Maclean's*, June 16, 1997, p. 49; Elizabeth Church, "If I Ran Eaton's. . .," *The Globe and Mail*, March 6, 1997, p. B6; Ian MacLeod, "'Safe and Dull'— and in Danger," *The Montreal Gazette*, February 28, 1997, p. D1; Francois Shalom, "Eaton's on Chopping Block," *The Montreal Gazette*, February 28, 1997, p. A1.

Macmillan Bloedel's Misfortunes

CBC 🔴

As the *Venture* program showed, Macmillan Bloedel has been facing a steady decline in its profits during the 1990s. The downturn in the forest products industry has struck a heavy blow to the Vancouver-based giant. But to say that the falling market prices for forest products have been solely responsible for MacBlo's woes would be to excuse the company from any fault in its management. And in the end, it is with management that the fault must always lie.

MacBlo's inability to deal with shifts in the marketplace has left it a sitting duck in the face of global competition. For years MacBlo's only major forms of cost control were shutting down mills and laying off workers. These are obviously short-term solutions to a deep-seated problem. MacBlo has seemed to lack any focus in direction. As major mergers such as that of Abitibi-Stone reconfigure the Canadian industry, and as companies devote themselves to the efficient production of a single product with heavy investments in state-of-the-art technology, Macmillan Bloedel has apparently believed it could continue to dominate by maintaining its status quo. This could be a fatal mistake.

When Thomas Stephens took over as CEO in September 1997, it was seen as a ray of hope for the ailing forestry company. His predecessor Robert Findlay had been with the company for decades and was perhaps too much a part of MacBlo's corporate culture to deal with the major changes necessary. A restructuring plan begun in 1994 was largely ineffectual, for the most part comprising superficial changes to the operations. Stephens may benefit from the fact that he is an outsider to the company (and one with major turnaround experience), but this is a task that probably requires major upheaval in the company. MacBlo has been going into new product development apparently out of desperation for new markets, but it does not have the expertise or technology to compete successfully with these products. As Adam Zimmerman stated on the video, "They're everything and yet they're nothing." MacBlo's lack of focus has cost it its high standing in the world industry. And when Zimmerman states that, "it's unlikely that any swashbuckler can come in there and turn [MacBlo] around," it's clear that the company's misfortunes stem from deep-rooted problems. But surely major change is necessary if MacBlo is to survive.

Questions

1. What factors might make MacBlo resistant to change?

2. Given that the logging industry is in a state of uncertainty (with provinces cutting the amount of trees allowed to be harvested, protestors calling for an end to logging, and the success of regeneration through replanting as yet mostly unproven), what sorts of changes should MacBlo be prepared to face in the coming decades?

3. How could TQM methods benefit Macmillan Bloedel?

Video Resource: "MacBlo in Trouble," *Venture* 639 (April 20, 1997).

Additional Sources: Paul Waldie, "MacBlo Appoints New CEO," *The Globe and Mail*, September 17, 1997, p. B1; Mark Stephenson, "Be Nice For A Change," *Canadian Business*, November, 1993, pp. 81–85.

chapter 10

Foundations of Behaviour

Learning Objectives

What will I be able to do after I finish this chapter?

1 • Define the focus and goals of organizational behaviour.

2 • Identify and describe the three components of attitudes.

3 • Explain the role consistency plays in attitudes.

4 • Define cognitive dissonance.

5 • Explain why companies use attitude surveys.

6 • Identify the six personality traits linked to organizational behaviour.

7 • Describe Holland's personality–job fit theory.

8 • Define perception and describe the factors that can shape or distort perception.

9 • Describe attribution theory.

10 • Explain how managers can shape employee behaviour.

In a general and traditional view of how organizations operate, management and labour have usually been seen as being set against each other, with each trying to promote its own aims. This unfortunate situation is now understood by most organizations to be counter-productive. But the idea of two separate camps, pitted against each other yet having to work together, has certainly not disappeared from the Canadian business world. Moves toward flat structures with wider spans of control and more organic organizations have helped to rectify some problems in the workplace, but many companies are far from boasting a harmonious working environment. In 1997, Safeway in Alberta discovered the hard way just what the price can be of not understanding its workforce.[1]

Management at Safeway showed how little they understood the behavioural aspects of their organization. Some 10,000 Safeway employees went on a strike that lasted 75 days, and may well have caused irreparable damage to 74 stores. The reason for the strike stemmed from an earlier situation. Four years earlier, Safeway opened its books to employees to show how new superstore competition had eroded earnings to the point that Safeway was losing money, and its market share had fallen from 70 per cent to only 30 per cent. Management asked its workforce to make wage concessions and the workers agreed to a $2.85-per-hour rollback. The future of the company seemed to depend on it. However, management promised that when profits returned, employees would get wage increases. Profits did indeed return, but the public promise of compensation to employees did not materialize.

Management seemed to believe that they could take the labour force for granted. This proved to be a serious mistake. The strike was a costly one. Customers sympathized with the plight of the workers who were deemed to have been cheated by a lying management. In communities where most people know someone who works at Safeway, neighbours, friends, and aquaintances were not about to cross a picket line. In the grocery business, customer loyalty is seen as essential—once a customer decides to shop somewhere else, it is extremely difficult to win him back. The strike cost Safeway about $24 million in profit, but more importantly it cost it many customers who may never return.

In the end Safeway made concessions to the union, but both sides were ultimately losers in the dispute. Apart from costing the union $10 million, the strike caused rifts between striking workers and those who crossed the picket line—and both groups eventually had to return to work together. Tensions between labour and management have certainly not lessened to any great degree. And Safeway found itself having to contend with a diminished market share. An incident such as this is very damaging to an organization—and anything that affects the bottom line inevitably affects both the workforce and management. This situation was a prime example of the dangers involved in management not having a basis of understanding with its employees.

Managers at Safeway stores in Alberta discovered the hard way just what the price of not understanding their organization's behavioural aspects could be.

Safeway's situation illustrates the need for managers to better understand their employees. This chapter looks at a number of factors that influence employee behaviour and the implications of those factors for management practice.

Toward Explaining and Predicting Behaviour

behaviour
The actions of people.

**organizational
behaviour**
The study of the actions
of people at work.

The material in this and the following four chapters draws heavily on the field of study that has come to be known as organizational behaviour (OB). While it is concerned with the subject of **behaviour**—that is, the actions of people—**organizational behaviour** is concerned more specifically with the actions of people at work.

One of the challenges to understanding organizational behaviour is that it addresses a number of issues that are not obvious. Like an iceberg, a lot of organizational behaviour is not visible to the naked eye (see Exhibit 10-1). What we tend to see when we look at organizations are their formal aspects—strategies, objectives, policies and procedures, structure, technology, formal authority, and chains of command. But just under the surface lie a number of informal elements that managers need to understand. As we'll show, OB provides managers with considerable insight into these important, but hidden, aspects of the organization.

**Exhibit 10-1
The "Organization as
an Iceberg" Metaphor**

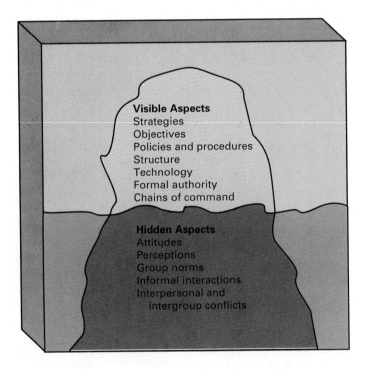

Visible Aspects
Strategies
Objectives
Policies and procedures
Structure
Technology
Formal authority
Chains of command

Hidden Aspects
Attitudes
Perceptions
Group norms
Informal interactions
Interpersonal and
    intergroup conflicts

What Is the Focus of Organizational Behaviour?

Organizational behaviour focuses primarily on two major areas. First, OB looks at individual behaviour. Based predominantly on contributions from psychologists, this area includes such topics as attitudes, personality, perception, learning, and motivation. Second, OB is concerned with group behaviour, which includes norms, roles, team building, and conflict. Our knowledge about groups comes basically from the work of sociologists and social psychologists. Unfortunately, the behaviour of a group of employees cannot be understood by merely summing up the actions of each individual, because individuals in groups behave differently from individuals acting alone. You see this characteristic when a street gang in a large city harasses innocent citizens. The gang members, acting individually, might never engage in such behaviour. Put them together, and they act differently. Therefore, because employees in an organization are both individuals and members of groups, we need to study them at two levels. In this chapter, we'll provide the foundation for understanding individual behaviour. In the next chapter, we'll introduce basic concepts related to understanding group behaviour.

What Are the Goals of Organizational Behaviour?

The goals of OB are to explain and to predict behaviour. Why do managers need this skill? Simply, in order to manage their employees' behaviour. We know that a manager's success depends on getting things done through other people. Toward this goal, the manager needs to be able to explain why employees engage in some behaviours rather than others and to predict how employees will respond to various actions the manager might take.

What employee behaviours are we specifically concerned about explaining and predicting? The emphasis will be on employee productivity, absenteeism, and turnover. In addition, we'll also look at job satisfaction. While job satisfaction is an attitude rather than a behaviour, it is an outcome about which many managers are concerned.

In the following pages, we'll address how an understanding of employee attitudes, personality, perception, and learning can help us to predict and explain employee productivity, absence and turnover rates, and job satisfaction.

Attitudes

Attitudes are evaluative statements—either favourable or unfavourable—concerning objects, people, or events. They reflect how an individual feels about something. When a person says, "I like my job," he is expressing an attitude about work.

To better understand the concept of attitudes, we should look at an attitude as being made up of three components: cognition, affect, and behaviour.[2] The **cognitive component of an attitude** makes up the beliefs, opinions, knowledge, or information held by a person. The belief that "discrimination is wrong" illustrates a cognition. The **affective component of an attitude** is the emotional or feeling segment of an attitude. Using our example, this component would be reflected in the statement, "I don't like Jon because he discriminates against minorities." Finally, affect can lead to behavioural outcomes. The **behavioural component of an attitude** refers to an intention to behave in a certain way toward someone or something. So, to continue our example, I might choose to avoid Jon because of my feelings about him. Looking at attitudes as being made up of three components—cognition, affect, and behaviour—helps to show the complexity. But for the sake of clarity, keep in mind that the term attitude usually refers only to the affective component.

Naturally, managers aren't interested in every attitude an employee might hold. They're specifically interested in job-related attitudes. The three most popular of these are job satisfaction, job involvement, and organizational commitment.[3] **Job satisfaction** is an employee's general attitude toward her job. When people speak of employee attitudes, more often than not they mean job satisfaction. **Job involvement** is the degree to which an employee identifies with her job, actively participates in it, and considers her job performance important to her self-worth. Finally, **organizational commitment** represents an employee's orientation toward the organization in terms of her loyalty to, identification with, and involvement in the organization.

attitudes
Evaluative statements concerning objects, people, or events.

cognitive component of an attitude
The beliefs, opinions, knowledge, or information held by a person.

affective component of an attitude
The emotional or feeling segment of an attitude.

behavioural component of an attitude
An intention to behave in a certain way toward someone or something.

job satisfaction
A person's general attitude toward her job.

job involvement
The degree to which an employee identifies with her job, actively participates in it, and considers her job performance important to her self-worth.

organizational commitment
An employee's orientation toward the organization in terms of his loyalty to, identification with, and involvement in the organization.

Do an Individual's Attitude and Behaviour Need to Be Consistent?

Did you ever notice how people change what they say so it doesn't contradict what they do? Perhaps a friend of yours has consistently argued that American cars were poorly built and that he'd never own anything but a foreign import. But his dad gives him a late-model American-made car, and suddenly they're not so bad. Or, when going through sorority rush, a new freshman believes that sororities are good and that pledging a sorority is important. If she fails to make a sorority, however, she may say, "I recognized that sorority life isn't all it's cracked up to be, anyway!"

Research has generally concluded that people seek consistency among their attitudes and between their attitudes and their behaviour.[4] This means that individuals try to reconcile differing attitudes and align their attitudes and behaviour so they appear rational and consistent. When there is an inconsistency, individuals will take steps to correct it. This can be done by altering either the attitudes or the behaviour, or by developing a rationalization for the discrepancy.

For example, a recruiter for Ontario Electronics Ltd. (OEL), whose job it is to visit university campuses, identify qualified job candidates, and sell them on the advantages of OEL as a place to work, would be in conflict if he personally believed OEL had poor working conditions and few opportunities for new graduates. This recruiter could, over time, find his attitudes toward OEL becoming more positive. He may, in effect, convince himself by continually articulating the merits of working for OEL. Another alternative would be for the recruiter to remain negative about OEL and the opportunities within the firm for prospective candidates. However, the recruiter might acknowledge that although OEL is an undesirable place to work, his obligation as a professional recruiter is to present the positive side of working for the company. He might, therefore, rationalize that no workplace is perfect and that his job is not to present both sides of the issue but rather to present a rosy picture of the company.

What Is Cognitive Dissonance Theory?

Can we additionally assume from this consistency principle that an individual's behaviour can always be predicted if we know his attitude on a subject? The answer to this question is, unfortunately, more complex than merely a yes or a no.

cognitive dissonance
Any incompatibility between two or more attitudes or between behaviour and attitudes.

Leon Festinger, in the late 1950s, proposed the theory of **cognitive dissonance**.[5] This theory sought to explain the relationship between attitudes and behaviour. Dissonance in this case means inconsistency. Cognitive dissonance refers to any incompatibility that an individual might perceive between two or more of his attitudes, or between his behaviour and attitudes. Festinger argued that any form of inconsistency is uncomfortable and that individuals will attempt to reduce the dissonance and, hence, the discomfort. Therefore, individuals will seek a stable state where there is a minimum of dissonance.

Of course, no individual can completely avoid dissonance. You know that cheating on your income tax is wrong, but you may "fudge" the numbers a bit every year, and hope you're not audited. Or you tell your children to brush after every meal, but you might not. So how do people cope? Festinger proposed that the desire to reduce dissonance is determined by the importance of the elements creating the dissonance, the degree of influence the individual believes he has over the elements, and the rewards that may be involved in dissonance (see Details on a Management Classic).

Leon Festinger and Cognitive Dissonance Theory

Cognitive dissonance theory argues that individuals' motivation to change their attitudes is based on their desire to appear consistent. In other words, individuals strive to appear rational. According to Leon Festinger, how this level of rationality is achieved is contingent on individuals' perception of the importance of and control over what is affecting them, as well as on the reward structures that are in place to make the inconsistencies more palatable.[6]

If the elements creating the dissonance are relatively unimportant, the pressure to correct this imbalance will be low. For example, a required class that you must take next semester is offered only at 11:00 a.m., at the same time that you wanted to take an elective class from a popular professor. You know, however, that this professor offers the class frequently, and it can easily be taken another time. But consider a case where the issues are important. For example, a manager—Mrs. Ryan—believes strongly that no company should lay off employees. Unfortunately, Mrs. Ryan, because of the requirements of her job, is placed in the position of having to make decisions that would trade off her company's strategic direction against her attitudes on layoffs. She knows that restructuring in the company may result in some jobs no longer being needed; and this is in the best economic interest of her firm. What will she do? Undoubtedly, Mrs. Ryan is experiencing a high degree of cognitive dissonance. Because of the importance of the elements in this example, we cannot expect Mrs. Ryan to ignore the inconsistency. As such, there are several paths that she can follow to deal with her dilemma. She can change her behaviour (lay off employees). Or she can reduce dissonance by concluding that the dissonant behaviour is not so important after all ("I've got to make a living, and in my role as a decision maker, I often have to place the good of my company above that of individual organizational members."). A third alternative would be for Mrs. Ryan to change her attitude ("There is nothing wrong in laying off employees."). Still another choice would be to seek out more consonant elements to outweigh the dissonant ones ("The long-term benefits to the surviving employees from our restructuring more than offset the cost associated with the retrenchment effort.").

The degree of influence that individuals believe they have over the elements also will have an impact on how they will react to the dissonance. If they perceive the dissonance to be an uncontrollable result—something over which they have no choice—they are less likely to be receptive to attitude change. If, for example, the dissonance-producing behaviour was required as a result of the boss's directive, the pressure to reduce dissonance would be less than if the behaviour were performed voluntarily. While dissonance exists, it can be rationalized and justified.

Finally, rewards influence the degree to which individuals are motivated to reduce dissonance. High dissonance, when accompanied by high rewards, tends to reduce the tension inherent in the dissonance. The reward acts to reduce dissonance by increasing the consistency side of the individual's balance sheet.

These moderating factors suggest that the fact that individuals experience dissonance does not necessarily mean they will move directly toward consistency, that is, toward reduction of this dissonance. If the issues underlying the dissonance are of minimal importance, if an individual perceives that the dissonance is externally imposed and is substantially uncontrollable by him or her, or if rewards are significant enough to offset the dissonance, the individual will not be under great tension to reduce the dissonance.▼

What conclusions about organizational behaviour can we draw from Festinger's work? Cognitive dissonance can help us to predict the willingness of employees to engage in attitude or behavioural change. If employees are required, for example, by the demands of their job to say or do things that contradict their personal opinions, they will tend to modify their beliefs to make them more compatible with what they have said or done. Additionally, the greater the inconsistency, the more likely one is to reduce it.

How Can Managers Be Kept Informed About Employee Attitudes?

To keep informed of their workers' attitudes, an increasing number of organizations are regularly surveying their employees. Exhibit 10-2 illustrates what an attitude survey might look like. Typically, **attitude surveys** present the employee with a set of statements or questions. Ideally, the items will be tailor-made to obtain the specific information that management desires. An attitude score is achieved by summing up responses to individual questionnaire items. These scores can then be averaged for job groups, departments, divisions, or the organization as a whole. General Electric, for example, in surveying more than 20,000 of its employees, found that more than half of the respondents were dissatisfied with the information and the recognition they received from the company and with their opportunities for advancement.[7] As a result, management instituted regular monthly information meetings, brought in experts to answer questions, and began printing a newsletter. One year later, a follow-up survey found that the number of employees dissatisfied with the information they received had dropped to zero, while the number dissatisfied with promotional opportunities fell from 50 to 20 per cent.

How Can an Understanding of Attitudes Help Managers Be More Effective?

We know that employees can be expected to try to reduce dissonance. Therefore, not surprisingly, there is relatively strong evidence that committed and satisfied employees have lower rates of turnover and absenteeism.[8] Because most managers want to minimize the number of resignations and absences—especially among their more productive employees—they should do things that will generate positive job attitudes. Dissonance, however, can be managed. If employees are required to engage in activities that appear inconsistent to them or that are at odds with their attitudes, managers should remember that pressure to reduce the dissonance is lessened when the employee perceives that the dissonance is externally imposed and uncontrollable. The pressure is also lessened if rewards are significant enough to offset the dissonance.

But let's not confuse satisfied workers with happy workers. We need to be aware of a debate that has lasted for more than five decades. That is, are happy workers more pro-

attitude surveys
Eliciting responses from employees through questionnaires about how they feel about their jobs, work groups, supervisors, and the organization.

GENERAL
ELECTRIC
www.ge.com/

Exhibit 10-2
Sample Attitude
Survey

Please answer each of the following statements using the following rating scale:

5 = Strongly agree
4 = Agree
3 = Undecided
2 = Disagree
1 = Strongly disagree

Statement	Rating
1. This company is a pretty good place to work.	_____
2. I can get ahead in this company if I make the effort.	_____
3. This company's wage rates are competitive with those of other companies.	_____
4. Employee promotion decisions are handled fairly.	_____
5. I understand the various fringe benefits the company offers	_____
6. My job makes the best use of my abilities.	_____
7. My workload is challenging but not burdensome.	_____
8. I have trust and confidence in my boss.	_____
9. I feel free to tell my boss what I think.	_____
10. I know what my boss expects of me.	_____

ductive? The results of several research studies in the past have provided important implications for managers.[9] They suggest that the goal of making employees happy on the assumption that this will lead to high productivity is probably misdirected. Managers who follow this strategy could end up with a very happy but poorly performing group of employees. Managers would get better results by directing their attention primarily to what will help employees become more productive. Successful job performance should then lead to feelings of accomplishment, increased pay, promotions, and other rewards—all desirable outcomes—which, in then, lead to satisfaction with the job.

Personality

Some people are quiet and passive while others are loud and aggressive. When we describe people using terms such as quiet, passive, loud, aggressive, ambitious, extroverted, loyal, tense, or sociable, we are categorizing them in terms of personality traits. An individual's **personality** is the combination of the psychological traits we use to classify that person.

personality
A combination of psychological traits that classifies a person.

Can Behaviour Be Predicted from Personality Traits?

There are literally dozens of personality traits. However, six have received the bulk of attention in the search to link personality traits to behaviour in organizations. They include locus of control, authoritarianism, Machiavellianism, self-esteem, self-monitoring, and risk propensity.

YOUNG CANADIANS

Jen Holland:
Sunnybrook Health Science Centre

Jen Holland at Sunnybrook Health Science Centre in Toronto does not fit most people's idea of a manager (suit-and-tied and sitting behind a desk). But Jen has to use managerial skills to head up research projects such as one to develop an early detection system for the infection of pathogenic bacteria. A simple system for this could save hospitals thousands of work hours. In order to successfully complete a project such as this, Jen needs to use organizational skills for such tasks as planning, developing work processes, and functioning with other departments.

locus of control
A personality attribute that measures the degree to which people believe they are masters of their own fate.

authoritarianism
A measure of a person's belief that there should be status and power differences among people in organizations.

Machiavellianism
A measure of the degree to which people are pragmatic, maintain emotional distance, and believe that ends can justify means.

MACHIAVELLI ONLINE
www.sas.upenn.edu/ ~pgrose/mach/

Who has control over people's behaviour? Some people believe that they control their own fate. Others see themselves as pawns of fate, believing that what happens to them in their lives is due to luck or chance. The **locus of control** in the first case is internal; these people believe that they control their destiny (see Managers Who Made a Difference). In the second case it is external; these people believe that their lives are controlled by outside forces.[10] The evidence indicates that employees who rate high in externality are less satisfied with their jobs, more alienated from the work setting, and less involved in their jobs than are those who rate high in internality.[11] A manager might also expect to find that externals blame a poor performance evaluation on their boss's prejudice, their coworkers, or other events outside their control, whereas internals explain the same evaluation in terms of their own actions.

Authoritarianism refers to a belief that there should be status and power differences among people in organizations.[12] The extremely high authoritarian personality is intellectually rigid, judgmental of others, deferential to those above, exploitative of those below, distrustful, and resistant to change. Because few people are extreme authoritarians, our conclusions must be guarded. It seems reasonable to postulate, however, that possessing a high authoritarian personality would be negatively related to the performance of a job that demands sensitivity to the feelings of others, tact, and the ability to adapt to complex and changing situations.[13] On the other hand, in a job that is highly structured and in which success depends on close conformance to rules and regulations, the highly authoritarian employee should perform quite well.

Closely related to authoritarianism is the characteristic of **Machiavellianism** ("Mach"), named after Niccolo Machiavelli, who wrote in the sixteenth century on how to gain and manipulate power. An individual who is high in Machiavellianism—in contrast to someone who is low—is pragmatic, maintains emotional distance, and believes that ends can justify means.[14] "If it works, use it" is consistent with a high Mach perspective. Do high Machs make good employees? That answer depends on the type of job and whether you consider ethical implications in evaluating performance. In jobs that require bargaining skills (such as labour negotiator) or that have substantial rewards for winning (such as commissioned salesperson), high Machs are productive. In jobs in which ends do not justify the means or that lack absolute standards of performance, it is difficult to predict the performance of high Machs.

People differ in the degree to which they like or dislike themselves. This trait is called **self-esteem**.[15] The research on self-esteem (SE) offers some interesting insights into organizational behaviour. For example, self-esteem is directly related to expectations for success. High SEs believe that they possess more of the ability they need in order to succeed at work. Individuals with high SE will take more risks in job selection and are more likely to choose unconventional jobs than are people with low SE.

The most common finding on self-esteem is that low SEs are more susceptible to external influence than are high SEs. Low SEs depend on the receipt of positive evaluations from others. As a result, they are more likely to seek approval from others and more prone to conform to the beliefs and behaviours of those they respect than are high SEs. In managerial positions, low SEs will tend to be concerned with pleasing others and are, therefore, less likely to take unpopular stands than are high SEs.

Not surprisingly, self-esteem has also been found to be related to job satisfaction. A number of studies confirm that high SEs are more satisfied with their jobs than are low SEs.

Another personality trait that has recently received increased attention is **self-monitoring**.[16] It refers to an individual's ability to adjust her behaviour to external, situational factors. Individuals high in self-monitoring can show considerable adaptability in adjusting their behaviour to external, situational factors. They are highly sensitive to external cues and can behave differently in different situations. High self-monitors are capable of presenting striking contradictions between their public persona and their private selves. Low self-monitors can't alter their behaviour. They tend to display their true dispositions and attitudes in every situation; hence, there is high behavioural consistency between who they are and what they do.

The research on self-monitoring is in its infancy; thus, predictions are hard to make. However, preliminary evidence suggests that high self-monitors tend to pay closer attention to the behaviour of others and are more capable of conforming than are low self-monitors.[17] We might also hypothesize that high self-monitors will be more successful in managerial positions where individuals are required to play multiple, and even contradicting, roles. The high self-monitor is capable of putting on different "faces" for different audiences.

People differ in their willingness to take chances—their propensity for **risk taking**. This preference to assume or avoid risk has been shown to have an impact on how long it takes individuals to make a decision and how much information they require before making their choice. For instance, in a recent study, a group of individuals worked on simulated HRM exercises that required them to make hiring decisions.[18] High-risk-taking individuals made more rapid decisions and used less information in making their choices than did the low-risk-taking individuals. Interestingly, the decision accuracy was the same for both groups.

While it is generally correct to conclude that managers in organizations are risk aversive,[19] there are still individual differences on this dimension.[20] As a result, it makes sense to recognize these differences and even to consider aligning risk-taking propensity with specific job demands. For instance, a high-risk-taking propensity may lead to effective performance for a stock trader in a brokerage firm. This type of job demands rapid decision making. On the other hand, this personality characteristic might prove a major obstacle to accountants performing auditing activities, a job better filled by someone with a low-risk-taking propensity.

self-esteem
An individual's degree of like or dislike for herself.

self-monitoring
A personality trait that measures an individual's ability to adjust her behaviour to external, situational factors.

risk taking
The willingness to take chances.

MANAGERS WHO MADE A DIFFERENCE

David Peacock and Ian Chamandy, Founders of YOUtv

Ian Chamandy and David Peacock of Toronto had a great idea for a business. Produce and supply video booths for informal guest comments at weddings. But in development, the project took a major shift as the two men realized there was an even greater market to be tapped with this technology. Private video booths could be used by organizations to garner valuable information from customers, potential customers, and employees. After raising the seed money for the project, the pair convinced three retail outlets to put booths in their stores. They did this without charge, hoping that the results would convince the stores' head offices that this was a valuable tool. It worked. Having customers make informal comments directed at the manager or CEO, without having to actually do it face-to-face, afforded people the honesty that comes with anonymity.[21]

The feedback received from these videos was excellent: opinions on better sales techniques, problems with products or display, ideas for new products, and more. Once again the partners realized a better avenue of business than that which they had originally targeted. Instead of selling these video booths, they would focus on collecting and analysing the information taken from them. The two understood that the information could be of great value to a variety of businesses, and that selling this information would be far more lucrative than simply selling the machines. Clients to date have included such heavy-hitters as Bell Canada, Loblaws, Apple Computer, Cadbury's, and Famous Players cinemas. The company plans to expand across North America. YOUtv wants to place its Listening Posts not only in stores, but in various businesses and factories. A tool such as this could provide organizations with invaluable information concerning employees' attitudes, and provide managers with a better grasp of the behavioural aspects of their organization's workforce.▼

YOUTV
www.youtv.com/

LOBLAW COMPANIES LTD.
www.loblaw.com/

APPLE COMPUTER
www.apple.com

CADBURY'S
www.cadbury.co.uk/

How Do We Match Personalities and Jobs?

Obviously, individual personalities differ. So, too, do jobs. Following this logic, efforts have been made to match the proper personalities with the proper jobs. The best documented personality–job fit theory has been developed by psychologist John Holland.[22] His theory states that an employee's satisfaction with his job, as well as his propensity to leave that job, depends on the degree to which the individual's personality matches his occupational environment. Holland has identified six basic personality types that an organization's employees might possess. Exhibit 10-3 describes each of the six types, their personality characteristics, and examples of congruent occupations.

TYPE	PERSONALITY CHARACTERISTICS	SAMPLE OCCUPATIONS
Realistic — Prefers physical activities that require skill, strength, and coordination	Shy, genuine, persistent, stable, conforming, practical	Mechanic, drill press operator, assembly line worker, farmer
Investigative — Prefers activities involving thinking, organizing, and understanding	Analytical, original, curious, independent	Biologist, economist, mathematician, news reporter
Social — Prefers activities that involve helping and developing others	Sociable, friendly, cooperative, understanding	Social worker, teacher, counsellor, clinical psychologist
Conventional — Prefers rule-regulated, orderly, and unambiguous activities	Conforming, efficient, practical, unimaginative, inflexible	Accountant, corporate manager, bank teller, file clerk
Enterprising — Prefers verbal activities where there are opportunities to influence others and attain power	Self-confident, ambitious, energetic, domineering	Lawyer, real estate agent, public relations specialist, small business manager
Artistic — Prefers ambiguous and unsystematic activities that allow creative expression	Imaginative, disorderly, idealistic, emotional, impractical	Painter, musician, writer, interior decorator

Exhibit 10-3   Holland's Typology of Personality and Sample Occupations

Source: Reproduced by special permission of the publisher, Psychological Assessment Resources, Inc., *Making Vocational Choices*, copyright 1973, 1985 by Psychological Assessment Resources, Inc. All rights reserved.

Holland's research strongly supports the hexagonal diagram in Exhibit 10-4.[23] This exhibit shows that the closer two fields or orientations are in the hexagon, the more compatible they are. Adjacent categories are quite similar, while those diagonally opposite are highly dissimilar.

What does all this mean? The theory argues that satisfaction is highest and turnover lowest where personality and occupation are in agreement. Social individuals should be in social jobs, conventional people in conventional jobs, and so forth. A realistic person in a realistic job is in a more congruent situation

Exhibit 10-4   Relationship among Occupational Personality Types

Source: Reproduced by special permission of the publisher, Psychological Assessment Resources, Inc., *Making Vocational Choices*, copyright 1973, 1985 by Psychological Assessment Resources, Inc. All rights reserved.

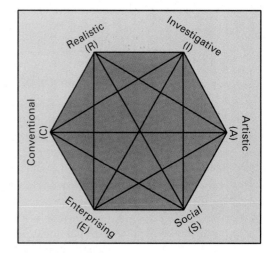

than is a realistic person in an investigative job. A realistic person in a social job is in the most incongruent situation possible. The key points of this model are that (1) there do appear to be intrinsic differences in personality among individuals, (2) there are different types of jobs, and (3) people in job environments congruent with their personality types will probably be more satisfied and less likely to resign voluntarily than will people in incongruent jobs.

Brian Scudamore: The Rubbish Boys

The Rubbish Boys, founded by Brian Scudamore, charges affordable rates to pick up large garbage items that the city's trucks won't take. The company has grown from one truck to a dozen, and now employs 40 people in Vancouver and Victoria.

How Can an Understanding of Personality Help Managers Be More Effective?

The major value of a manager's understanding personality differences probably lies in selection. Managers are likely to have higher-performing and more satisfied employees if consideration is given to matching personality types with compatible jobs. In addition, there may be other benefits. For instance, managers can expect that individuals with an external locus of control may be less satisfied with their jobs than may internals, and also that they may be less willing to accept responsibility for their actions.

Do Personality Attributes Differ Among National Cultures?

There are certainly no common personality types for a given country. You can, for instance, find high risk takers and low risk takers in almost any culture. Yet a country's culture influences the dominant personality characteristics of its population. We can see this by looking at two personality traits—locus of control and authoritarianism.

National cultures differ in terms of the degree to which people believe they control their environment. North Americans, for example, believe that they can dominate their environment, while other societies, such as Middle Eastern countries, believe that life is essentially preordained. Notice the close parallel to internal and external locus of control. We can expect a larger proportion of internals in the Canadian and U.S. workforces than in the workforces of Saudi Arabia or Iran.

Authoritarianism is closely related to the concept of power distance. In high power-distance societies, such as Mexico or Venezuela, there should be a large proportion of individuals with authoritarian personalities, especially among the ruling class. In contrast, because Canada rates below average on this dimension, we'd expect authoritarian personalities to be less prevalent here than in the high power-distance countries.

Perception

Perception is a process by which individuals organize and interpret their sensory impressions to give meaning to their environment. Research on perception consistently demonstrates that individuals may look at the same thing yet perceive it differently. One manager, for instance, can interpret the fact that her assistant regularly takes several days to make important decisions as evidence that the assistant is slow, disorganized, and afraid to make decisions. Another manager, with the same assistant, might interpret the same action as evidence that the assistant is thoughtful, thorough, and deliberate. The first manager would probably evaluate her assistant negatively, while the second manager would probably evaluate the person positively. The point is that none of us actually sees reality. We interpret what we see and call it reality. And, of course, as the above example illustrates, we act according to our perceptions.

perception
The process of organizing and interpreting sensory impressions to give meaning to the environment.

What Influences Perception?

How do we explain the fact that people can perceive the same thing differently? A number of factors operate to shape and sometimes distort perception. These factors can reside in the perceiver; in the object, or target, being perceived; or in the context of the situation in which the perception is made.

When an individual looks at a target and attempts to interpret what she sees, the individual's personal characteristics are going to influence heavily the interpretation. These personal characteristics include attitudes, personality, motives, interests, past experiences, and expectations.

The characteristics of the target being observed can also affect what is perceived. Loud people are more likely than quiet people to be noticed in a group. So, too, are extremely attractive or unattractive individuals. Because targets are not looked at in isolation, the relationship of a target to its background also influences perception (see Exhibit 10-5), as does our tendency to group close things and similar things together.

The context in which we see objects or events is also important. The time at which an object or event is seen can influence attention, as can location, light, heat, and any number of other situational factors.

How Do Managers Judge Employees?

Much of the research on perception is directed at inanimate objects. Managers, though, are more concerned with human beings. So our discussion of perception should focus on "person" perception. Our perceptions of people differ from our perceptions of such inanimate objects as desks, machines, or buildings because we make inferences about the actions of people that we don't make about inanimate objects. Nonliving objects have no beliefs, motives, or intentions; people do. The result is that when we observe people, we attempt to develop explanations of why they behave in certain ways. Our perception and judgment of a person's actions, therefore, will be significantly influenced by the assumptions we make about the person's internal state. Many of these assumptions have led researchers to develop attribution theory.

What Is Attribution Theory?

attribution theory
A theory used to develop explanations of how we judge people differently depending on the meaning we attribute to a given behaviour.

Attribution theory has been proposed to develop explanations of how we judge people differently depending on what meaning we attribute to a given behaviour.[24] Basically, the theory suggests that when we observe an individual's behaviour, we attempt to determine whether it was internally or externally caused. Internally caused behaviours are those that are believed to be under the personal control of the individual. Externally caused behaviour results from outside causes; that is, the person is seen as forced into the behaviour by the situation. That determination, however, depends on three factors: (1) distinctiveness, (2) consensus, and (3) consistency.

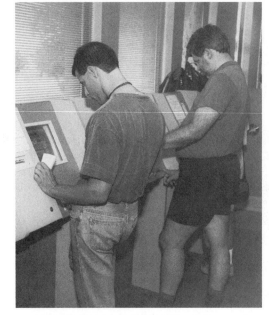

Why are these individuals unemployed? Is it because they are lazy and can't keep a job? Or was it the economic downturn and just bad luck? Your response will depend on what you believe caused the unemployment. That's precisely what attribution theory tells us.

Distinctiveness refers to whether an individual displays a behaviour in many situations or whether it is particular to one situation. Is the employee who arrives late today also the source of complaints by coworkers for being a "goof-off"? What we want to know is whether this behaviour is unusual. If it is, the observer is likely to give the behaviour an external attribution. If this action is not unique, it will probably be judged as internal.

If everyone who is faced with a similar situation responds in the same way, we can say the behaviour shows consensus. Our tardy employee's behaviour would meet this criterion if all employees who took the same route to work were also late. From an attribution perspective, if consensus is high you would be expected to give an external attribution to the employee's tardiness; whereas if other employees who took the same route made it to work on time, your conclusion for causation would be internal.

Finally, an observer looks for consistency in a person's actions. Does the person engage in the behaviours regularly and consistently? Does the person respond the same way over time? Coming in 10 minutes late for work is not perceived in the same way if for one employee it represents an unusual case (she hasn't been late for several months), while for another it is part of a routine pattern (she is regularly late two or three times a week). The more consistent the behaviour, the more the observer is inclined to attribute it to internal causes.

Exhibit 10-5 summarizes the key elements in attribution theory. It would tell us, for instance, that if an employee—let's call her Ms. Parker—generally performs at about the same level on other related tasks as she does on her current task (low distinctiveness), if other employees frequently perform differently—better or worse—

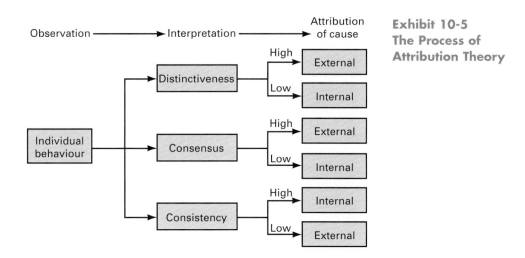

**Exhibit 10-5
The Process of
Attribution Theory**

than Ms. Parker does on that current task (low consensus), and if Ms. Parker's performance on this current task is consistent over time (high consistency), her manager or anyone else who is judging Ms. Parker's work is likely to hold her primarily responsible for her task performance (internal attribution).

Can Attributions Be Distorted?

One of the more interesting findings drawn from attribution theory is that there are errors or biases that distort attributions. For instance, there is substantial evidence to support that when we make judgments about the behaviour of other people, we have a tendency to underestimate the influence of external factors and overestimate the influence of internal or personal factors.[25] This is called the **fundamental attribution error** and can explain why a sales manager may be prone to attribute the poor performance of her sales agents to laziness rather than to the innovative product line introduced by a competitor. There is also a tendency for individuals to attribute their own successes to internal factors such as ability or effort while putting the blame for failure on external factors such as luck. This is called the **self-serving bias** and suggests that feedback provided to employees in performance reviews will be predictably distorted by recipients depending on whether it is positive or negative.

What Shortcuts Do Managers Use in Judging Others?

Managers use a number of shortcuts to judge others. Perceiving and interpreting what others do is burdensome. As a result, individuals develop techniques for making the task more manageable. These techniques are frequently valuable; they allow us to make accurate perceptions rapidly and provide valid data for making predictions. However, they are not foolproof. They can and do get us into trouble. An understanding of these shortcuts can be helpful as a step toward recognizing when they can result in significant distortions (see Exhibit 10-6).

Individuals cannot assimilate all they observe, so they engage in **selectivity**. They take in bits and pieces. These bits and pieces are not chosen randomly; rather, they are selectively chosen depending on the interests, background, experience, and attitudes of the observer. Selective perception allows us to "speed read" others, but not without the risk of drawing an inaccurate picture.

fundamental attribution error
The tendency to underestimate the influence of external factors and overestimate the influence of internal factors when making judgments about the behaviour of others.

self-serving bias
The tendency for individuals to attribute their own successes to internal factors while putting the blame for failures on external factors.

selectivity
The process by which people assimilate certain bits and pieces of what they observe, depending on their interests, background, experience, and attitudes.

assumed similarity
The belief that others are like yourself.

It is easy to judge others if we assume that they are similar to us. In **assumed similarity**, or the "like me" effect, the observer's perception of others is influenced more by the observer's own characteristics than by those of the person observed. For example, if you want challenge and responsibility in your job, you will assume that others want the same. People who assume that others are like them can, of course, be right, but most of the time they're wrong.

stereotyping
Judging a person on the basis of one's perception of a group to which she belongs.

When we judge someone on the basis of our perception of a group to which she belongs, we are using the shortcut called **stereotyping**. "Married people are more stable employees than singles" and "union people expect something for nothing" are examples of stereotyping. To the degree that a stereotype is based on fact, it may produce accurate judgments. However, many stereotypes have no foundation in fact. In such cases, stereotypes distort judgments.

halo effect
A general impression of an individual based on a single characteristic.

When we form an impression about an individual based on a single characteristic such as intelligence, sociability, or appearance, we are being influenced by the **halo effect**. This effect frequently occurs when students evaluate their classroom instructor. Students may isolate a single trait such as enthusiasm and allow their entire evaluation to be tainted by their perception of this one trait. An instructor might be quiet, assured, knowledgeable, and highly qualified, but if his style lacks zeal, he will be rated lower on a number of other characteristics.

Exhibit 10-6
Distortions in Shortcut Methods of Judging Others

SHORTCUT	WHAT IT IS	DISTORTION
Selectivity	People assimilate certain bits and pieces of what they observe depending on their interests, background, experience, and attitudes	By "speed reading" others, may draw an inaccurate picture
Assumed Similarity	People assume others are like themselves	May fail to take into account individual differences resulting in incorrect similarities
Stereotyping	People judge others based on their perception of a group to which others belong	May result in distorted judgments because many stereotypes have no factual foundation
Halo Effect	People form an impression of others based on a single trait	Fails to take into account the "total" picture of what an employee has done

How Can an Understanding of Perceptions Help Managers Be More Effective?

Managers need to recognize that their employees react to perceptions, not reality. So whether a manager's appraisal of an employee is actually objective and unbiased or whether the organization's wage levels are actually among the highest in the industry is less relevant than what employees perceive them to be. If individuals perceive appraisals to be biased or wage levels as low, they will behave as if these conditions actually exist. Employees organize and interpret what they see; this creates the potential for perceptual distortion.

The message to managers should be clear: Close attention needs to be paid to how employees perceive both their jobs and management practices. Remember, the valuable employee who quits because of an incorrect perception is just as great a loss to an organization as the valuable employee who quits for a valid reason.

Learning never stops. These employees are continuing their education by attending seminars on techniques for sales presentation graphics.

Learning

The last individual behaviour concept we want to introduce in this chapter is learning. It is included for the obvious reason that almost all complex behaviour is learned. If we want to explain and predict behaviour, we need to understand how people learn. What is **learning**? A psychologist's definition is considerably broader than the layperson's view that "it's what we did when we went to school." In actuality, each of us is continuously "going to school." Learning occurs all the time. We continually learn from our experiences. A workable definition of learning is, therefore, any relatively permanent change in behaviour that occurs as a result of experience.

learning
Any relatively permanent change in behaviour that occurs as a result of experience.

What Is Operant Conditioning?

Operant conditioning argues that behaviour is a function of its consequences. People learn to behave to get something they want or to avoid something they don't want. Operant behaviour means voluntary or learned behaviour in contrast to reflexive or unlearned behaviour. The tendency to repeat such behaviour is influenced by the reinforcement or lack of reinforcement brought about by the consequences of the behaviour. Reinforcement, therefore, strengthens a behaviour and increases the likelihood that it will be repeated.

operant conditioning
A type of conditioning in which desired voluntary behaviour leads to a reward or prevents a punishment.

Building on earlier work in the field, the late Harvard psychologist B.F. Skinner's research has extensively expanded our knowledge of operant conditioning.[26] Even his staunchest critics, who represent a sizeable group, admit that his operant concepts work.

Behaviour is assumed to be determined from without—that is, learned—rather than from within—reflexive or unlearned. Skinner argued that by creating pleasing consequences to follow specific forms of behaviour, the frequency of that behaviour will increase. People will most likely engage in desired behaviours if they are positively reinforced for doing so. Rewards, for example, are most effective if they immediately follow the desired response. Also, behaviour that is not rewarded, or is punished, is less likely to be repeated.

You see illustrations of operant conditioning everywhere. For example, any situation in which it is either explicitly stated or implicitly suggested that reinforcements are contingent on some action on your part involves the use of operant learning. Your instructor says that if you want a high grade in the course you must supply correct answers on the test. A commissioned salesperson wanting to earn a sizeable income finds that this is contingent on generating high sales in her territory. Of course, the linkage can also work to teach the individual to engage in behaviours that work against the best interests of the organization. Assume that your boss tells you that if you will work overtime during the next three-week busy season, you will be compensated for it at the next performance appraisal. However, when performance appraisal time comes, you find that you are given no positive reinforcement for your overtime work. The next time your boss asks you to work overtime, what will you do? You will probably decline! Your behaviour can be explained by operant conditioning: If a behaviour fails to be positively reinforced, the probability that the behaviour will be repeated declines.

What Is Social Learning Theory?

Individuals can also learn by observing what happens to other people and just by being told about something, as well as by direct experiences. So, for example, much of what we have learned comes from watching models—parents, teachers, peers, television and movie performers, bosses, and so forth. This view that we can learn both through observation and direct experience has been called **social learning theory**.[27]

social learning theory
People can learn through observation and direct experience.

While social learning theory is an extension of operant conditioning—that is, it assumes that behaviour is a function of consequences—it also acknowledges the existence of observational learning and the importance of perception in learning. People respond to how they perceive and define consequences, not to the objective consequences themselves.

The influence of models is central to the social learning viewpoint. Four processes have been found to determine the influence that a model will have on an individual:

▶ **1. Attentional processes** People learn from a model only when they recognize and pay attention to its critical features. We tend to be most influenced by repeatedly available models that we think are attractive, important, or similar to us.

▶ **2. Retention processes** A model's influence will depend on how well the individual remembers the model's action, even after the model is no longer readily available.

▶ **3. Motor reproduction processes** After a person has seen a new behaviour by observing the model, the watching must be converted to doing. This process then demonstrates that the individual can perform the modelled activities.

▶ **4. Reinforcement processes** Individuals will be motivated to exhibit the modelled behaviour if positive incentives or rewards are provided. Behaviours that are reinforced will be given more attention, learned better, and performed more often.

How Can Managers Shape Behaviour?

Because learning takes place on the job as well as prior to it, managers will be concerned with how they can teach employees to behave in ways that most benefit the organization. Thus, managers will often attempt to mould individuals by guiding their learning in graduated steps. This process is called **shaping behaviour** (see Developing Management Skills).

shaping behaviour
Systematically reinforcing each successive step that moves an individual closer to the desired response.

Consider the situation in which an employee's behaviour is significantly different from that sought by management. If management only reinforced the individual when

DEVELOPING MANAGEMENT SKILLS

▼

SHAPING BEHAVIOUR SKILLS

▲

▶ **1. Identify the critical behaviours that have a significant impact on an employee's performance.** Not everything employees do on the job is equally important in terms of performance outcomes. A few critical behaviours may, in fact, account for the majority of one's performance. It is these high-impact behaviours that need identifying.

▶ **2. Establish a base line of performance.** This is obtained by determining the number of times the identified behaviours occur under the employee's current job conditions.

▶ **3. Analyse contributing factors to performance and their consequences.** A number of factors, such as the norms of a group, may be contributing to the base line performance. Identify these factors and their effect on performance.

▶ **4. Develop a "shaping" strategy.** The change that may occur will entail changing some element of performance—structure, processes, technology, groups, or the task. The purpose of the strategy is to strengthen the desirable behaviours and weaken the undesirable ones.

▶ **5. Apply the appropriate strategy**. Once the strategy has been developed, it needs to be implemented. In this step, the intervention occurs.

▶ **6. Measure the change that has occurred.** The intervention should produce desired results in performance behaviours. Evaluate the number of times the identified behaviours now occur. Compare these with the base line evaluation in step 2.

▶ **7. Reinforce desired behaviours.** If the intervention has been successful and the new behaviours are producing the desired results, maintain these behaviours through reinforcement mechanisms.

he showed desirable responses, there might be very little reinforcement taking place. In such a case, shaping offers a logical approach toward achieving the desired behaviour.

We shape behaviour by systematically reinforcing each successive step that moves the individual closer to the desired response. If an employee who has chronically been 30 minutes late for work comes in only 20 minutes late, we can reinforce this improvement. Reinforcement would increase as responses more closely approximate the desired behaviour.

There are four ways in which to shape behaviour: positive reinforcement, negative reinforcement, punishment, or extinction. When a response is followed with something pleasant, such as when a manager praises an employee for a job well done, it is called positive reinforcement. Rewarding a response with the termination or withdrawal of something unpleasant is called negative reinforcement. Managers who habitually criticize their employees for taking extended coffee breaks are using negative reinforcement. The only way these employees can stop the criticism is to shorten their breaks. Punishment penalizes undesirable behaviour. Suspending an employee for two days without pay for showing up drunk is an example of punishment. Eliminating any reinforcement that is maintaining a behaviour is called extinction. When the behaviour is not reinforced, gradually it tends to be extinguished. In meetings, managers who wish to discourage employees from continually asking distracting or irrelevant questions can eliminate this behaviour by ignoring these employees when they raise their hands to speak. Hand raising will become extinct when it is invariably met with an absence of reinforcement.

ETHICAL DILEMMAS IN MANAGEMENT

▼

IS SHAPING BEHAVIOUR A FORM OF CONTROL?

▲

Animal trainers use rewards—typically food—to get dogs, porpoises, and whales to perform extraordinary stunts. Behavioural psychologists have put rats through thousands of experiments by manipulating their food supply. These trainers and researchers have shaped the behaviour of these animals by controlling consequences. Such learning techniques may be appropriate for animals performing in zoos, circuses, or laboratories, but are they appropriate for managing the behaviour of people at work?

Critics argue that human beings are not rats in an experiment. Human beings should be treated with respect and dignity. To explicitly use rewards as a learning device—to encourage the repetition of desired behaviours—is manipulative. Human beings in organizations should act of free will and not be subjected to manipulative control techniques by their bosses.

No well-schooled behavioural scientist would argue that shaping isn't a powerful tool for controlling behaviour. But when used by managers, is it a form of manipulation? If an employee engages in behaviours that the organization later judges wrong but that were motivated by a manager's control of rewards, is that employee any less responsible for her actions than if such rewards were not involved? What do you think?

Both positive and negative reinforcement result in learning. They strengthen a desired response and increase the probability of repetition. Both punishment and extinction also result in learning; however, they weaken behaviour and tend to decrease its subsequent frequency (see Ethical Dilemmas in Management).

How Can an Understanding of Learning Help Managers Be More Effective?

Managers can undoubtedly benefit from understanding the learning process. Because employees continually learn on the job, the only issue is whether managers are going to let employee learning occur randomly or whether they are going to manage learning through the rewards they allocate and the examples they set. If marginal employees are rewarded with pay raises and promotions, they will have little reason to change their behaviour. If managers want a certain type of behaviour but reward a different type of behaviour, it shouldn't surprise them to find employees learning to engage in the other type of behaviour. Similarly, managers should expect that employees will look to them as models. Managers who are constantly late to work, or take two hours for lunch, or help themselves to company office supplies for personal use should expect employees to read the message they're sending and model their behaviour accordingly.

Summary

This summary is organized by the chapter Learning Objectives found on page 264.

1. The field of organizational behaviour is concerned with the actions of people—managers and operatives alike—in organizations. By focusing on individual- and group-level concepts, OB seeks to explain and predict behaviour. Because they get things done through other people, managers will be more effective leaders if they have an understanding of behaviour.

2. Attitudes are made up of three components. The cognitive component is the beliefs, opinions, knowledge, or information held by the person. The affective component is the emotional or feeling segment of the individual. The behavioural component of an attitude is one's intention to behave in a certain manner toward someone or something.

3. People seek consistency among their attitudes and between their attitudes and their behaviour. They seek to reconcile divergent attitudes and align their attitudes and behaviour so they appear rational and consistent.

4. Cognitive dissonance, proposed by Leon Festinger in the late 1950s, explains the relationship between attitudes and behaviour. Cognitive dissonance refers to any incompatibility that an individual might perceive between two or more attitudes or between behaviour and attitudes.

5. Companies use attitude surveys to elicit responses from employees about how they feel about their jobs, work groups, supervisors, and the organization.

6. Six personality traits have been linked to organizational behaviour. These are locus of control, authoritarianism, Machiavellianism, self-esteem, self-monitoring, and risk propensity.

7. Holland identified six basic personality types and six sets of congruent occupations. He found that when individuals were properly matched with occupations that were congruent with their personality types, they experienced high satisfaction with their job and lower turnover rates.

8. Perception is the process of organizing and interpreting sensory impressions to give meaning to the environment. Several factors operate to shape and sometimes distort perceptions. These factors can reside in the perceiver, in the target being perceived, or in the context of the situation in which the perception is being made.

9. Attribution theory proposes that we judge people differently depending on whether we attribute their behaviour to internal or external causation. This determination, in turn, depends on three factors: distinctiveness, consensus, and consistency.

10. Managers can shape or mould employee behaviour by systematically reinforcing each successive step that moves the employee closer to the response desired by the manager.

Review and Discussion Questions

1. How is an organization like an iceberg? Use the iceberg metaphor to describe the field of organizational behaviour.

2. What are the three components of an attitude?

3. Clarify how individuals reconcile inconsistencies between attitudes and behaviours.

4. What are attitude surveys and how do they help managers?

5. What behavioural predictions might you make if you knew that an employee had (a) an external locus of control? (b) a low Mach score? (c) low self-esteem? (d) high self-monitoring tendencies?

6. How could you use personality traits to improve employee selection?

7. What factors do you think might create the fundamental attribution error?

8. Name four shortcuts used in judging others. What effect does each of these have on perception?

9. What is the self-serving bias?

10. What is social learning theory? What are its implications for managing people at work?

Testing Your Comprehension

Circle the correct answer, then check yourself on page 472.

1. The hidden aspects of organizations refers to
   a) the strategies and objectives, which are useless to most employees
   b) the attitudes, perceptions, and group dynamics
   c) the behaviours that are restricted by authoritarian managers
   d) any illegal activities of some department of an organization

2. OB essentially seeks to _____ and _____ behaviour.
   a) explain; manage
   b) predict; manipulate
   c) predict; manage
   d) explain; predict

3. The cognitive component of an attitude refers to
   a) the intention to behave a certain way
   b) the emotional feeling associated with an attitude
   c) the factors such as opinions, beliefs, and knowledge
   d) the desires, wishes, and dreams of employees

4. Which of the following statements is TRUE regarding the satisfaction-productivity controversy?
   a) There is a strong positive relationship; satisfied employees are more productive employees.
   b) The satisfaction-productivity relationship is stronger when an employee's behaviour is constrained by outside forces.
   c) Successful job performance always leads to things that satisfy employees.
   d) None of the above.

5. Individuals who believe that their lives are in the hands of fate and generally beyond their control have
   a) an internal locus of control
   b) an external locus of control
   c) high risk-taking propensity
   d) Machiavellian characteristics

6. A major contribution of Holland's personality–job fit theory is the idea that
   a) congruency between personality traits and occupations should improve job satisfaction
   b) changing jobs to fit one's personality increases productivity
   c) personality must adapt to different jobs
   d) ability to assert will enhances job satisfaction

7. The process by which people assimilate parts of what they observe, depending on characteristics of the observer, is known as
   a) self-serving bias
   b) fundamental attribution error
   c) stereotyping
   d) selectivity

8. The tendency for individuals to attribute their own successes to internal factors while putting the blame for failures on external factors is known as
   a) selectivity
   b) self-serving bias
   c) halo effect
   d) fundamental attribution error

9. The halo effect is
   a) an attempt by managers to identify good behaviours
   b) judging someone on the basis of a single personality trait
   c) judging someone on the basis of the group to which the person belongs
   d) a model to predict group behaviour

10. The fact that several people can see the same crime being committed and yet give different descriptions of the suspect is explained by
    a) the halo effect
    b) assumed similarity
    c) perception
    d) sterotyping

11. "Behaviour is a function of its consequences" demonstrates
    a) operant conditioning
    b) the halo effect
    c) assumed similarity
    d) modelling

12. A new employee can't recall how a job that was demonstrated yesterday was done. The employee is experiencing
    a) one of the drawbacks of classical conditioning
    b) a breakdown in the motor reproduction process of the social learning theory
    c) one of the drawbacks of operant conditioning
    d) a breakdown in the retention process of the social learning theory

13. The first step in shaping behaviour is
    a) developing a "shaping" strategy
    b) reinforcing desired behaviours
    c) analysing contributing factors to performance and their consequences
    d) identifying the critical behaviours that have a significant impact on an employee's performance

14. Managers who question the validity of employees' bathroom breaks, with questions such as "where have you been all this time?", are using

a) negative reinforcement

b) punishment

c) positive reinforcement

d) extinction

Self-Assessment Exercise

Who Controls Your Life?

Instructions: Read the following statement and indicate whether you agree more with choice A or choice B.

A	B	
1. Making a lot of money is largely a matter of getting the right breaks.	1. Promotions are earned through hard work and persistence.	____
2. I have noticed that there is usually a direct connection between how hard I study and the grades I get.	2. Many times the reactions of teachers seem haphazard to me.	____
3. The number of divorces indicates that more and more people are not trying to make their marriages work.	3. Marriage is largely a gamble.	____
4. It is silly to think that one can really change another person's basic attitudes.	4. When I am right I can convince others.	____
5. Getting promoted is really a matter of being a little luckier than the next person.	5. In our society a person's future earning power depends upon her ability.	____
6. If one knows how to deal with people, they are really quite easily led.	6. I have little influence over the way other people behave.	____
7. The grades I make are the result of my own efforts; luck has little or nothing to do with it.	7. Sometimes I feel that I have little to do with the grades I get.	____
8. People like me can change the course of world affairs if we make ourselves heard.	8. It is only wishful thinking to believe that one can really influence what happens in our society.	____
9. A great deal that happens to me is probably a matter of chance.	9. I am the master of my fate.	____
10. Getting along with people is a skill that must be practised.	10. It is almost impossible to figure out how to please some people.	____

Turn to page 467 for scoring directions and key.

Source: Adapted from Julian B. Rotter, "External Control and Internal Control," *Psychology Today*, June 1971, p. 42. Copyright 1971 by the American Psychological Association. Adapted with permission.

Class Exercise

Salary Increase Request

Objectives:

1. To illustrate how perceptions can influence decisions.
2. To illustrate the effects of shortcuts used in evaluating others.

Situation:

You will be given a composite of an employee who is submitting a salary increase request for consideration. Your instructor will hand these out. You are to read this scenario and make a recommendation to HRM (either favourably or unfavourably) about the raise.[28]

1. Divide yourselves into groups of five to seven and take the role of manager making the salary increase decision.
2. Each group should identify its perceptions about the employee, work habits, etc., in support of its decision.
3. Reassemble the class and hear each group's recommendations and explanations.

Case Application

The Entrepreneurial Spirit of Japanese Women

In many discussions about comparing work life in Japan with that in Canada, one factor is frequently mentioned: workers in Japan often have the luxury of a job for life. That is, once a Japanese citizen is hired by an organization, she can be somewhat certain of having that job until retirement. On face value that may appear to be an important work benefit. Compared with what is happening in Canada with respect to downsizing, reengineering, and the like, the security of a job for life may sound appealing. Of course, it comes with some strings attached.[29]

When the economy is in recession, Japanese employers, like those here, cannot afford to keep everyone working. Some layoffs occur. The difference is that, in Japan, those layoffs are targeted toward a particular group. In their attempt to save management positions, Japanese company officials decimate their clerical staffs. Considering the fact that 99 per cent of all clerical workers are female, when layoffs occur women are the hardest hit. Women are treated as second-class employees. If a recession doesn't result in their being laid off or fired, getting married or having children probably will.

What can Japanese women do? Should they accept the culture of their society and live with the employment cycles they experience? Should they revolt against the "man's world" and fight for their rightful place in the organization? For many, such routes are impossible. The fight would be too heavy, and the rebels would be up against a societal culture that is hundreds of years old. Instead, many have opted for another choice—starting their own business. Of those started in the early 1990s, most have been exceptionally successful.

Questions

1. In terms of locus of control, Machiavellianism, self-esteem, and risk taking, discuss Japanese women who start their own businesses.
2. Identify how men's cognitive, affective, and behavioural components of attitude are evident in the case of women in Japan.
3. Are there different attitudes in Canada that prevent women from being expendable workers in our organizations? Explain your position.

chapter

11

Understanding Groups and Teams

Learning Objectives

What will I be able to do after I finish
this chapter?

1 • Contrast formal and informal groups.

2 • Explain why people join groups.

3 • State how roles and norms influence an employee's behaviour.

4 • Explain how norms affect group performance.

5 • Describe how group size affects group behaviour.

6 • Explain the increased popularity of work teams in organizations.

7 • Describe the characteristics of effective teams.

8 • Identify the obstacles that exist for creating effective teams.

9 • Describe the role of teams in TQM.

There have been few examples of the benefits of self-directed work teams so outstandingly impressive as that of Algoma Steel. The company was a division of Dofasco up until 1991, and it was being run into the ground by poor management. Algoma was floundering under an $800-million debt, and the only way the plant would be kept open by Dofasco was if the workers agreed to major wage concessions. The union rejected this proposal, but it countered with an unexpected one: the workers would take a $10-million wage cutback in return for 60-per-cent ownership in Algoma, along with a government-backed restructuring of the company's debt.[1]

Restructuring the debt and lowering labour costs within a company are greatly beneficial to turning around losses, but a lot more had to be changed to make Algoma profitable. The Steelworkers Union decided that while it would have four directors on the 13-member board, it did not want to actually manage Algoma. Steve Boniferro, a union leader, commented, "Somebody has to be looking after the business, and, quite frankly, we aren't trained, prepared, or interested in looking after the business. We want to balance what's best for the company with what's best for the workers." Management philosophy has changed at Algoma to recognize that its success is based on the balance of a "strong independent union, and a strong, independent management."

Today, self-directed work groups have replaced the old command-and-control structure (so, for instance, at No. 1 Ladle Transfer Station, where once there were three foremen, there are now none; and where there were 20 workers per shift, there are now seven). These work teams are empowered to deal with everything from determining their own vacation schedules to redesigning their workplaces.

Costs have been cut, productivity has increased, and the workforce has actually grown. Algoma, after nearly being written off as bankrupt in 1991, was, by 1997, a company showing profits of roughly $70 million.

Algoma provides a great example of what can be accomplished through the use of teams.

Algoma Steel's organization is no longer unique. Thousands of organizations have recently made the move to restructure work around groups and teams and empowered individuals. Why has this occurred? What do these teams look like? How can interested managers build effective teams? We'll answer these questions in this chapter. First, however, let's begin by developing our understanding of group behaviour.

ALGOMA STEEL INC.
www.algoma.com/ trade.html

Understanding Group Behaviour

The behaviour of individuals in groups is not the same as the sum total of each individual's behaviour. This is because individuals act differently in groups than they do when they are alone. Therefore, if we want to understand organizational behaviour more fully, we need to study groups.

What Is a Group?

group
Two or more interacting
and interdependent indi-
viduals who come together
to achieve particular
objectives.

A **group** is defined as two or more interacting and interdependent individuals who come together to achieve particular objectives. Groups can be either formal or informal. Formal groups are work groups established by the organization and have designated work assignments and established tasks. In formal groups, the behaviours in which one should engage are stipulated by and directed toward organizational goals. Exhibit 11-1 provides some examples of different types of formal groups used in organizations today.

In contrast, informal groups are of a social nature. These groups are natural formations that appear in the work environment in response to the need for social contact. Informal groups tend to form around friendships and common interests.

Why Do People Join Groups?

There is no single reason why individuals join groups. Because most people belong to a number of groups, it's obvious that different groups provide different benefits to their members. Most people, then, join a group out of needs for security, status, self-esteem, affiliation, power, or goal achievement.

Security reflects a strength in numbers. By joining a group, individuals can reduce the insecurity of "standing alone," which results in feeling stronger, having fewer self-doubts, and being more resistant to threats. Status indicates a prestige that comes from belonging to a particular group. Inclusion in a group that others view as important provides recognition and status for its members. Self-esteem conveys people's feelings of self-worth. That is, in addition to conveying status to those outside the group, membership can also raise feelings of self-esteem as the individual is accepted into a highly valued group.

Command Groups	These are the basic, traditional work groups determined by formal authority relationships and depicted on the organizational chart. They typically include a manager and those subordinates who report directly to him.
Cross-functional Teams	These bring together the knowledge and skills of individuals from various work areas in order to come up with solutions to operational problems. Cross-functional teams also include groups whose members have been trained to do each other's jobs.
Self-managed Teams	These are essentially independent groups that in addition to doing their operating jobs take on traditional management responsibilities such as hiring, planning and scheduling, and performance evaluations.
Task Forces	These are temporary groups created to accomplish a specific task. Once the task is completed, the group is disbanded.

**Exhibit 11-1
Examples of
Formal Groups**

Affiliation with groups can fulfil one's social needs. People enjoy the regular interaction that comes with group membership. For many people, these on-the-job interactions are their primary means of fulfilling their need for affiliation. For almost all people, work groups significantly contribute to fulfilling their need for friendships and social relations. One of the appealing aspects of groups is that they represent power. What often cannot be achieved individually becomes possible through group action. Of course, this power might not be sought only to make demands on others. It might be desired merely as a countermeasure. To protect themselves from unreasonable demands by management, individuals may align with others. Informal groups additionally provide opportunities for individuals to exercise power over others. For individuals who desire to influence others, groups can offer power without a formal position of authority in the organization. As a group leader, you might be able to make requests of group members and obtain compliance without any of the responsibilities that traditionally go with formal managerial positions. For people with a high power need, groups can be a vehicle for fulfilment. Finally, people may join a group for goal achievement. There are times when it takes more than one person to accomplish a particular task, when there is a need to pool talents, knowledge, or power in order to get a job completed. In such instances, management will rely on the use of a formal group.

YOUNG CANADIANS

Terry Hui: BurCon Properties Ltd.

Terry Hui's accomplishments are impressive. In his early thirties, he is president of a real estate development company involved in multi-billion-dollar projects, BurCon Properties Ltd. But Hui's young age had nothing to do with his being featured on the cover of *The Financial Post Magazine*. That was simply the result of his phenomenal leadership abilities. Hui is also founder/chairman of Vancouver-based MultiActive Technologies Inc., and chairman and principal of Maximizer Technologies.

What Are the Basic Concepts for Understanding Group Behaviours?

The basic foundation for understanding group behaviour includes roles, norms and conformity, status systems, and group cohesiveness. Let's take a closer look at each of these concepts.

What Are Roles? We introduced the concept of roles in Chapter 1 when we discussed what managers do. Of course, managers are not the only individuals in an organization who have roles. The concept of roles applies to all employees in organizations and to their life outside the organization as well.

A **role** refers to a set of expected behaviour patterns attributed to someone who occupies a given position in a social unit. Individuals play multiple roles, adjusting their roles to the group to which they belong at the time. In an organization, employees attempt to determine what behaviours are expected of them. They'll read their job descriptions, get suggestions from their boss, and watch what their coworkers do. An individual who is confronted by divergent role expectations experiences role conflict. Employees in organizations often face such role conflicts. The credit manager expects her credit analysts to process a minimum of 30 applications a week, but the work group pressures members to restrict output to 20 applications a week so that everyone has

role
A set of behaviour patterns expected of someone occupying a given position in a social unit.

work to do and no one gets laid off. A young university instructor's colleagues want him to give out very few high grades in order to maintain the department's "tough standards" reputation, whereas students want him to give out lots of high grades to enhance their grade-point averages. To the degree that the instructor sincerely seeks to satisfy the expectations of both his colleagues and his students, he faces role conflict.

How Do Norms and Conformity Affect Group Behaviour? All groups have established **norms**, or acceptable standards that are shared by the group's members. Norms dictate things such as output levels, absenteeism rates, promptness or tardiness, and the amount of socializing allowed on the job.

norms
Acceptable standards shared by a group's members.

Norms, for example, dictate the "dress code" among customer service representatives at one national health insurance company. Most workers who have little face-to-face customer contact come to work dressed very casually. However, on occasion, a newly hired employee will come to work the first few days dressed up in a suit. Those who do are often teased and pressured until their dress conforms to the group's standard.

Although each group will have its own unique set of norms, there are common classes of norms that appear in most organizations. These focus on effort and performance, dress, and loyalty.

Probably the most widespread norms relate to levels of effort and performance. Work groups typically provide their members with very explicit cues on how hard to work, what level of output to have, when to look busy, when it's acceptable to goof off, and the like. These norms are extremely powerful in affecting an individual employee's performance. They are so powerful that performance predictions that are based solely on an employee's ability and level of personal motivation often prove to be wrong.

Some organizations have formal dress codes. However, even in their absence, norms frequently develop to dictate the kind of clothing that should be worn to work. University seniors, interviewing for their first postgraduate job, pick up this norm quickly. Every spring on campuses throughout the country, those interviewing for jobs can usually be spotted—they're the ones walking around in the dark grey or blue pinstriped suits. They are enacting the dress norms they have learned are expected in professional positions. Of course, what connotes acceptable dress in one organization may be very different from that in another.

Few managers appreciate employees who ridicule the organization. Similarly, professional employees and those in the executive ranks recognize that most employers view those who actively look for another job unfavourably. If such people are unhappy, they know to keep their job searches secret. These examples demonstrate that loyalty norms are widespread in organizations. This concern for demonstrating loyalty, by the way, often explains why ambitious aspirants to top management positions in an organization willingly take work home at night, come in on weekends, and accept transfers to cities where they would otherwise prefer not to live.

Because individuals desire acceptance by the groups to which they belong, they are susceptible to conformity pressures. The impact that group pressures for conformity can have on an individual member's judgment and attitudes was demonstrated in the now-classic studies by Solomon Asch[2] (see Details on a Management Classic). Asch's results suggest that there are group norms that press us toward conformity. We desire to be one of the group and avoid being visibly different. We can generalize this finding further to say that when an individual's opinion of objective data differs significantly from that of others in the group, he feels extensive pressure to align his opinion to conform with those of the others.

DETAILS ON A MANAGEMENT CLASSIC

Solomon Asch and Group Conformity

Does one's desire to be accepted as part of a group leave her susceptible to conforming to the group's norms? Will the group place strong enough pressure to change a member's attitude and behaviour? In the research by Solomon Asch, the answer appears to be yes.

Asch's study involved groups of seven or eight people who sat in a classroom and were asked to compare two cards held by an investigator. One card had one line, the other had three lines of varying length. As shown in Exhibit MC11-1, one of the lines on the three-line card was identical to the line on the one-line card. Also, as shown in MC11-1, the difference in line length was quite obvious; under ordinary conditions, subjects made errors less than 1 per cent of the time. The object was to announce aloud which of the three lines matched the single line. But what happens if all the members in the group begin to give incorrect answers? Will the pressures to conform result in the unsuspecting subject (USS) altering her answers to align with the others? That was what Asch wanted to know. So he arranged the group so only the USS was unaware that the experiment was "fixed." The seating was prearranged so that the USS was the last to announce her decision.

The experiment began with two sets of matching exercises. All the subjects gave the right answers. On the third set, however, the first subject gave an obviously wrong answer—for example, saying "C" in Exhibit MC11-1. The next subject gave the same wrong answer, and so did the others until it got to the unsuspecting subject. He knew "B" was the same as "X," yet everyone had said "C." The decision confronting the USS was this: Do you state a perception publicly that differs from the preannounced position of the others? Or do you give an answer that you strongly believe is incorrect in order to have your response agree with the other group members? The results obtained by Asch demonstrated that over many experiments and many trials, subjects conformed in about 35 per cent of the trials. That is, the subjects gave answers that they knew were wrong but that were consistent with the replies of other group members.

For managers, the Asch study provides considerable insight into group behaviours. The tendency, as Asch has shown, is for individual members to go along with the "pack." To diminish the negative aspects of conformity, however, it becomes necessary for managers to create a climate of openness where employees are free to discuss problems without fear of retaliation.▼

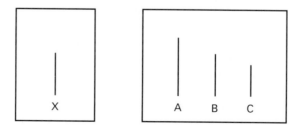

**Exhibit MC11-1
Examples of Cards Used
in the Asch Study**

status

A prestige grading, position, or rank within a group.

What Is Status and Why Is It Important? Status is a prestige grading, position, or rank within a group. As far back as scientists have been able to trace human group-ings, they have found status hierarchies: tribal chiefs and their followers, nobles and peasants, the haves and the have-nots. Status systems are an important factor in understanding behaviour. Status is a significant motivator and has behavioural con-sequences when individuals see a disparity between what they perceive their status to be and what others perceive it to be.

Status may be informally conferred by characteristics such as education, age, skill, or experience. Anything can have status value if others in the group evaluate it as such. Of course, just because status is informal does not mean that it is less impor-tant or that there is less agreement on who has it or who does not. Members of groups have no problem placing people into status categories, and they usually agree closely about who is high, low, and in the middle.

It is important for employees to believe that the organization's formal status system is congruent. That is, there should be equity between the perceived ranking of an indi-vidual and the status "symbols" she is given by the organization. For instance, incongru-ence may occur when a supervisor is earning less than her employees or when a desirable office is occupied by a lower-ranking individual. In such cases, employees may view this as a disruption to the general pattern of order and consistency in the organization.

Does Group Size Affect Group Behaviour? The size of a group has an effect on the group's behaviour. However, that effect depends on what criteria you are looking at.[3]

The evidence indicates, for instance, that small groups are faster at completing tasks than are larger ones. However, if the group is engaged in problem solving, large groups consistently get better marks than their smaller counterparts. Translating these results into specific numbers is a bit more hazardous, but we can offer some parameters. Large groups—with a dozen or more members—are good for gaining diverse input. Thus, if the goal of the group is finding facts, larger groups should be more effective. On the other hand, smaller groups are better at doing something productive with those facts. Groups of approximately five to seven members tend to be more effective for taking action.

One of the more disturbing findings related to group size is that as groups get incre-mentally larger the contribution of individual members often tends to lessen.[4] That is, while the total productivity of a group of four is generally greater than that of a group of three, the individual productivity of each group member declines as the group expands. Thus, a group of four will tend to produce at a level less than four times the average indi-vidual performance. The best explanation for this reduction of effort in groups is that dis-persion of responsibility encourages individuals to slack off. When the results of the group cannot be attributed to any single person, the relationship between an individual's input and the group's output is clouded. In such situations, individuals may be tempted to become "free riders" and coast on the group's efforts. In other words, there will be a reduction in efficiency where individuals think that their contributions cannot be mea-sured. The obvious conclusion from this finding is that when managers use work teams, they should also provide means by which individual efforts can be identified.

Are Cohesive Groups More Effective? Intuitively, it makes sense that groups in which there is a lot of internal disagreement and lack of cooperation are less effective in completing their tasks than groups in which individuals generally agree, cooperate, and like each other. Research on this position has focused on group cohesiveness, or the degree to which members are attracted to one another and share the group's goals.

The more the members are attracted to one another and the more the group's goals align with their individual goals, the greater the group's cohesiveness.

Research has generally shown that highly cohesive groups are more effective than those with less cohesiveness,[5] but the relationship between cohesiveness and effectiveness is more complex. A key moderating variable is the degree to which the group's attitude aligns with its formal goals or those of the larger organization of which it is a part.[6] The more cohesive a group is, the more its members will follow its goals. If these goals are favourable (for instance, high output, quality work, cooperation with individuals outside the group), a cohesive group is more productive than a less cohesive group. But if cohesiveness is high and attitudes are unfavourable, productivity decreases. If cohesiveness is low and goals are supported, productivity increases, but not as much as when both cohesiveness and support are high. When cohesiveness is low and goals are not supported, cohesiveness has no significant effect upon productivity. These conclusions are summarized in Exhibit 11-2.

Building Real Teams

Teams are increasingly becoming the leading means around which work is being designed. Why? Because teams typically outperform individuals when the tasks being done require multiple skills, judgment, and experience. As organizations restructure themselves to compete more effectively and efficiently, they are turning to teams as a way to better use employee talents. Teams are more flexible and thus more responsive to a changing environment than are bureaucratic groupings of employees. They also can be quickly assembled, deployed, refocused, and disbanded.

work teams
Formal groups made up of interdependent individuals, responsible for attaining a goal.

What Are Work Teams?

Work teams are formal groups, made up of interdependent individuals, responsible for attaining a goal.[7] Teams tend to fall into one of three categories based on their objectives. Some organizations use teams to provide advice. For instance, a team may be assembled to recommend ways to cut costs,

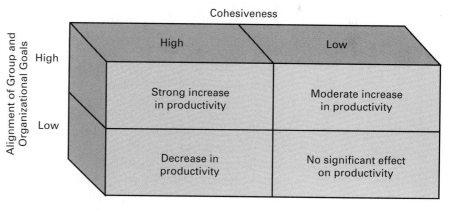

improve quality, or select a new piece of machinery (see Managers Who Made a Difference). Some teams manage. They exist at various levels to run things. For example, Thermos created a team to manage the development of a "customer-oriented, environmentally friendly" electric grill.[8] And finally, teams are created to make or do things. These would include production teams, design teams, and office teams that handle administrative work.

In this section, we'll discuss why organizations are increasingly designing work around teams rather than individuals and consider the various characteristics that are associated with effective work teams.

Exhibit 11-2
The Relationship
Between Cohesiveness
and Productivity

HEWLETT-
PACKARD
www.hp.com

Mei-Lin Cheng, Hewlett-Packard

Hewlett-Packard has long been a standard of organizational efficiency by which other companies are measured. However, a company of such mammoth size as H.P. is bound to have a few outdated aspects to its operations. Mei-Lin Cheng was given the task of identifying and dealing with one such aspect.[9]

The problem lay in the fact that when a customer order was placed, it took almost 26 days for the order to be filled. Part of the problem stemmed from the fact that this high-tech company still used some 70 computers—many being decades old—to drive its information system. This situation simply wasn't acceptable to upper management. They asked Cheng to reengineer the process.

Cheng understood immediately that Band-Aid measures would not be effective enough to cure what was ailing this process. She had to get to the heart of the matter and start from scratch, and to do this she needed complete freedom to institute any changes deemed necessary. Top management was both taken aback and impressed when Cheng proposed to have a new system operating in about nine months, and said that if she didn't succeed then she and her employees could have their funding cut off. It was a gamble, as Cheng was basically putting her own job and those of her subordinates on the line—but she was convinced that with complete autonomy to make decisions, she and her team would succeed.

When Cheng formed her team of 35 members she started with only these rules: the team would have no supervisors, no hierarchies, no titles, no job descriptions, no plans, and no step-by-step milestones. There would just be a conceptual design to develop a database that would cover customer orders, credit checks, shipping, and inventory control. She knew that this approach would create chaos, but out of that chaos she felt great things would come. The system was a complex one and had to be taken apart completely before it could be rebuilt. Cheng believed that such an arrangement would give team members a sense of personal ownership of the project, thereby increasing their commitment and making their work more meaningful to them.

The gamble paid off. The team made remarkable progress. After extensive training to get everyone up to speed in terms of team skills, the team worked ardently for the next eight months. And with one month to spare, the team reached its final and only goal. Now instead of taking 26 days to get parts to customers, it takes eight. The new process runs far more efficiently than the old one in virtually every repect. Consequently, customers are more satisfied, and Hewlett-Packard has managed to reduce its inventories by more than 20 per cent.▼

Why Use Teams?

There's no single explanation for the recent increased popularity of teams. We propose, however, that there are a number of reasons: worker morale, strategic flow, quicker decision making, workforce diversity, and better performance.

Team members expect and demand a lot from each other. In so doing, they facilitate cooperation and improve employee morale. So we find that team norms tend to encourage members to excel and, at the same time, create a climate that increases job satisfaction. The use of teams, especially self-managed ones, frees up managers to do more strategic planning. When jobs are designed around individuals, managers often spend an inordinate amount of their time supervising their people and "putting out fires." They're too busy to do much strategic thinking. Implementing work teams allows managers to redirect their energy toward bigger issues such as long-term plans. Moving decision making vertically down to teams allows the organization greater flexibility for faster decisions. Team members frequently know more about work-related problems than do managers. Moreover, team members are closer to those problems. As a result, decisions are often made more quickly when teams exist than when jobs are designed around individuals. Groups made up of individuals from different backgrounds and with different experiences often see things that homogeneous groups don't. Therefore, the use of diverse teams may result in more innovative ideas and better decisions than might arise if individuals alone made the decisions. Finally, all of the above factors can combine to make team performance higher than might be achieved by the same individuals working alone.

What Common Characteristics Exist in Effective Teams?

Teams are not automatic productivity enhancers. They can also be disappointments for management. Fortunately, recent research provides insight into the primary characteristics related to effective teams.[10] Let's take a look at these characteristics as summarized in Exhibit 11-3.

**Exhibit 11-3
Characteristics of
Effective Teams**

High-performance teams have both a clear understanding of the goal to be achieved and a belief that the goal embodies a worthwhile or important result. Moreover, the importance of these goals encourages individuals to sublimate personal concerns to these team goals. In effective teams, members are committed to the team's goals, know what they are expected to accomplish, and understand how they will work together to achieve these goals. Effective teams are composed of competent individuals. They have the necessary technical skills and abilities to achieve the desired goals and the personal characteristics required to achieve excellence while working well with others. This second point is important and often overlooked. Not everyone who is technically competent has the skills to work well as a team member. High-performing teams have members who possess both technical and interpersonal skills.

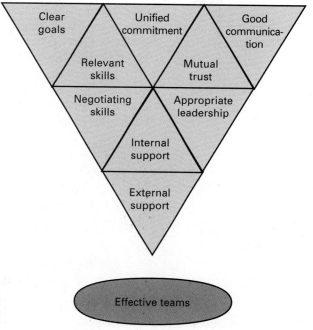

DEVELOPING MANAGEMENT SKILLS

BUILDING TRUST AMONG TEAM MEMBERS

▶ **1. Communicate with team members.** Keep team members and others informed by explaining decisions and policies and providing accurate feedback. Be candid about your own problems and limitations.

▶ **2. Be supportive of team members and their efforts.** Be available and approachable. Encourage and support team members' ideas.

▶ **3. Be respectful of team members' capabilities.** Delegate real authority to team members and listen to their ideas.

▶ **4. Be fair, equitable, and consistent.** Give credit where it's due, be objective and impartial in performance evaluations, and be generous with your praise.

▶ **5. Be predictable.** Be consistent in your daily affairs. Make good on your explicit and implied promises.

▶ **6. Demonstrate competence.** Develop the admiration and respect of team members by demonstrating technical and professional ability and good business sense.[11]

SATURN
www.saturn.com/
index.html

Supervisors of these Saturn employees give their workers the responsibility to share in decision making—deciding on everything from hiring coworkers to buying equipment. Supervisors intervene only when needed and when asked by the group.

Effective teams are characterized by high mutual trust among members. That is, members believe in the integrity, character, and ability of one another. But as you probably know from personal relationships, trust is fragile. It takes a long time to build and can be easily destroyed. The climate of trust within a group tends to be strongly influenced by the organization's culture and the actions of management. Organizations that value openness, honesty, and collaborative processes and that also encourage employee involvement and autonomy are likely to create trusting cultures (see Developing Management Skills).

Members of an effective team exhibit intense loyalty and dedication to the team. They're willing to do anything that has to be done to help their team succeed. We call this loyalty and dedication "unified commitment." Studies of successful teams have found that members identify with their teams.[12] Members redefine themselves to include membership in the team as an important aspect of the self. Unified commitment, then, is characterized by dedication to the team's goals and a willingness to expend extraordinary amounts of energy to achieve it.

Not surprisingly, effective teams are characterized by good communication. Members can convey messages to one another in a form that is readily and clearly understood. This includes nonverbal as well as spoken messages. Good communication is also characterized by a healthy dose of feedback from team members and management. This helps to guide team members and to correct misunderstandings. Like a couple who have been together for many years, members on high-performing teams are able to quickly and efficiently share ideas and feelings.

When jobs are designed around individuals, then job descriptions, rules and procedures, and other types of formal documentation clarify employee roles. Effective teams, on the other hand, tend to be flexible and continually making adjustments. This requires team members to possess adequate negotiating skills. Problems and relationships are regularly changing in teams, requiring members to confront and reconcile differences.

Effective leaders can motivate a team to follow them through the most difficult situations. How? Leaders help clarify goals. They demonstrate that change is possible by overcoming inertia. And they increase the self-confidence of team members, helping members to realize their potential more fully. Importantly, the best leaders are not necessarily directive or controlling. Increasingly, effective team leaders are taking the role of coach and facilitator. They help guide and support the team, but they don't control it. This obviously applies to self-managed teams but also increasingly applies to task forces and cross-functional teams in which the members themselves are empowered. For some traditional managers, changing their role from boss to facilitator—from giving orders to working for the team—is a difficult transition. While most managers relish the newfound shared authority or come to understand its advantages through leadership training, some hard-nosed dictatorial managers are just ill-suited to the team concept and must be transferred or replaced.

The final condition necessary to making an effective team is a supportive climate. Internally, the team should be provided with a sound infrastructure. This includes proper training, an understandable measurement system with which team members can evaluate their overall performance, an incentive program that recognizes and rewards team activities, and a supportive human resource system. The right infrastructure should support members and reinforce behaviours that lead to high levels of performance. Externally, management should provide the team with the resources needed to get the job done.

What Challenges Do Teams Present for Managers?

The idea of using teams to enhance productivity is nothing new for management. Teams have long been popular in Japan. When Canadian managers began to broadly introduce them in the late 1980s, critics warned that they were destined to fail. Why? Recall our discussion of culture in Chapter 2. Specifically, Japan could be classified as a collective society—where the "good of the whole" is dominant. Canadian culture, on the other hand, is based on individualism—taking care of oneself and one's immediate family. This led many observers to believe that Canadian workers would not diminish their needs for individual responsibility and recognition in order to be an anonymous part of a team. While the introduction of work teams in some organizations has met with resistance and disappointments, the overall picture has been encouraging. When teams are properly used in organizations and when the organization's culture is consistent with a team approach, results have been positive.

Let's look at the obstacles that may exist and review some suggestions for overcoming them.

What Can Block Team Effectiveness? Any time two or more people are brought together, there is a tendency for problems to arise. Teams are no exceptions (see Ethical Dilemmas in Management)! As managers, we must understand what may cause team effectiveness to decrease—blocking our team from becoming a high performer. These barriers can be found in a weak sense of direction, lack of organizational support, infighting, and lack of trust.

Teams perform poorly when they have a weak sense of direction. Nothing will undermine the enthusiasm for the team concept as quickly as the frustration of being on a team where the purpose, goals, or approach are unclear. Teams exist within the larger organization. They rely on that organization for a variety of resources—people,

ETHICAL DILEMMAS IN MANAGEMENT

SHOULD MANAGERS SAY THEY AGREE WITH THEIR BOSS WHEN THEY DON'T?

Asch's studies looked at how group norms press individuals toward conformity. This suggests an ethical dilemma that many managers face: whether it is ethical to outwardly agree with their boss when, in actuality, they think he is wrong.

Are managers who disagree with their boss acting unethically by claiming to agree? Are they compromising personal standards of integrity? Would it be unethical merely to suppress their disagreement? Open agreement may be the politically astute thing to do, but does it display a lack of moral character?

The norms of conformity can be very strong in an organization. Individuals who openly challenge long-condoned but questionable practices may be labelled as disloyal or lacking in commitment. Another perspective is that conformance with group and organizational norms acts to bond people together. Conformity facilitates cooperation and cohesiveness. It also contributes toward standardizing behaviour. These are qualities that can enhance organizational effectiveness. Still another argument might be that suppression of dissent and the appearance of conformity doesn't improve organizational effectiveness; it merely plants the seeds for later hostilities and conflicts.

What should a manager do when she disagrees with the boss? What can organizations do to avoid encouraging individuals to unethically conform, while at the same time maintaining cohesiveness and commitment?

money, and equipment. If those resources are lacking or insufficient, it will be difficult for teams to reach their objectives.

Team effectiveness will also decrease when there is an inordinate amount of infighting. For teams to be effective, all members do not have to like each other. Rather, team members must be willing to put aside petty differences in order to reach their goals. Closely aligned with infighting is lack of trust. Where there is trust, team members believe in the integrity, character, and ability of one another. When trust is lacking, members are unable to depend on each other. Consequently, such teams are typically short-lived.

Exhibit 11-4
Overcoming Obstacles to Effective Teams

TO OVERCOME OBSTACLES	HOW IT AFFECTS TEAMS
Create a clear purpose and goals	High-performance teams have both a clear understanding of the goals to be achieved and a belief that each goal embodies a worthwhile or important result.
Provide the necessary resources	Without necessary resources, achieving team goals is, at best, a hit-or-miss proposition. Skilful team managers will influence decision makers to provide the necessary resources.
Build mutual trust	Mutual trust creates an environment that is conducive to high-performing teams. This includes open communications, respect for team members, fair and equitable treatment, consistency in actions, follow-through on promises made, and training of team members in problem solving, communication, negotiation, conflict resolution, and group-processing skills.
Change the team's membership	Rotating team members, when team problems arise, may result in the meshing of different personalities, and better complements of skills.

How Can a Manager Overcome the Obstacles to Team Effectiveness? There are a number of things managers can do to overcome the obstacles mentioned and help their teams to reach their full potential (see Exhibit 11-4).

High-performance teams have both a clear understanding of their purpose and goals and a belief that each goal embodies a worthwhile or important result. The team must understand and believe in its mission. This mission must then be translated into specific, measurable, and realistic performance goals. In effective teams, members are committed to the team's goals, know what they are expected to accomplish, and understand how they will work together to achieve these goals.

Managers of teams need to accept the responsibility of ensuring their teams are provided with the necessary organizational resources. They must prepare their case and present it to key decision makers in the organization for tools, equipment, training, personnel, physical space, or other resources that the team needs.

Managers must also recognize that team trust is fragile. As such, they must create an environment that builds and supports mutual trust. This is accomplished by providing continuous feedback, respecting team members, being fair and objective in the treatment of the team, and holding team members accountable at both the individual and group level. Furthermore, these managers recognize that team trust and cohesiveness are not formulated overnight. Rather, it is a function of time together. Consequently, effective team managers ensure that members experience team-building training.

Finally, one must recognize that at times teams do get bogged down and some individuals just cannot work with others. In some cases, this may be the result of an incorrect mix of the technical, problem solving, or interpersonal skills that group members bring to the team. In these cases, change the team's membership. Rotating some team members may result in a "reformed" team that has a better complement of skills.

Teams and TQM

One of the central characteristics of total quality management is the use of teams. But why teams? The essence of TQM is process improvement, and employee participation is the linchpin of process improvement. In other words, TQM requires management to give employees the encouragement to share ideas and act on what they suggest. Problem-solving teams provide the natural vehicle for employees to share ideas and to implement improvements. As stated by Gil Mosard, a TQM specialist at McDonnell Douglas: "When your measurement system tells you your process is out of control, you need teamwork for structured problem-solving. Not everyone needs to know how to do all kinds of fancy control charts for performance tracking, but everybody does need to know where their process stands so they can judge if it is improving."[13]

Ford began its TQM efforts in the early 1980s with teams as the primary organizing mechanism. "Because this business is so complex, you can't make an impact on it without using a team approach," noted one Ford manager. In designing their quality problem-solving teams, Ford's management identified five goals. The teams should (1) be small enough to be efficient and effective; (2) be properly trained in the skills their members will need; (3) be allocated enough time to work on the problems they plan to address; (4) be given the authority to resolve the problems and implement corrective action; and (5) each have a designated "champion" whose job it is to help the team get around roadblocks that arise.

Consumers Packaging's glass container plant in Bramalea was a chronic under-performer in the late 1980s. Nearly all of its operations needed improvement, so the company set up 12 teams called "communication teams" to solve problems. Each of the teams is free to set its own agenda, but it must find ways to improve the plant's performance in relation to eight performance indicators set down by management. These indicators include, among other things, measures of productivity, profitability, and even absenteeism.

quality circles
Work groups that meet regularly to discuss, investigate, and correct quality problems.

Another team application to TQM is **quality circles**. These are work groups of eight to 10 employees and supervisors who share an area of responsibility. They meet regularly (typically once a week on company time and on company premises) to discuss their quality problems, investigate causes of the problems, recommend solutions, and take corrective actions. They assume responsibility for solving quality problems, and they generate and evaluate their own feedback. However, management usually makes the final decision about the implementation of recommended solutions. Exhibit 11-5 describes a typical quality circle process.

Exhibit 11-5
How a Typical Quality Circle Operates

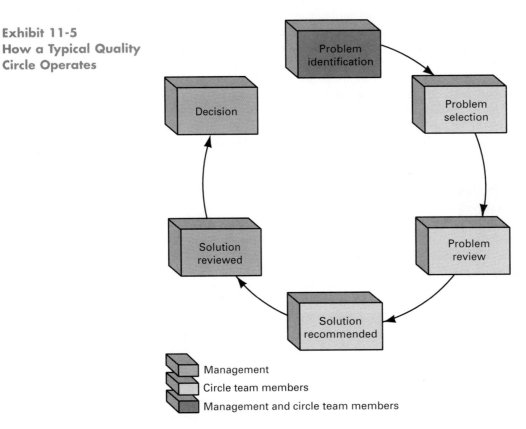

Management
Circle team members
Management and circle team members

Summary

This summary is organized by the chapter Learning Objectives found on page 290.

1. Formal groups are defined by the organization's structure, with designated work assignments establishing tasks. Informal groups are social alliances that are neither structured nor organizationally determined.

2. People join groups because of their needs for security, status, self-esteem, affiliation, power, or goal achievement.

3. A role refers to a set of behaviour patterns expected of someone occupying a given position in a social unit. At any given time, employees adjust their role behaviours to the group of which they are a part. Norms are standards shared by group members. They informally convey to employees which behaviours are acceptable and which are unacceptable.

4. Norms relate to levels of effort and performance in several ways. Work groups typically provide their members with very explicit cues on how hard to work, what level of output to have, when to look busy, when it's acceptable to goof off, and the like.

5. Group size affects group behaviour in various ways. Smaller groups are faster at completing tasks than are larger ones. However, larger groups are better for fact finding.

6. Teams have become increasingly popular in organizations because they build esprit de corps, free up management to think more strategically, permit faster decision making, facilitate workforce diversity, and usually increase performance.

7. Effective work teams are characterized by clear goals, members with relevant skills, mutual trust among members, unified commitment, good communication, adequate negotiating skills, and appropriate leadership.

8. Obstacles for creating effective work teams can be viewed from several perspectives. These can be a weak sense of direction, a lack of resources, infighting among team members, and a lack of members' trust.

9. Problem-solving teams provide a natural vehicle for employees to share ideas and to implement improvements as part of the TQM process. Teams are particularly effective for resolving complex problems.

Review and Discussion Questions

1. How can joining a group increase an individual's sense of power?

2. How might organizations create role conflicts for an employee?

3. Identify five roles you play. What behaviours do they require? Are any of these roles in conflict? If so, in what way? How do you resolve these conflicts?

4. What is the relationship between a work group and the organization of which it is a part?

5. What is the most effective size for a group?

6. What is the relationship between group cohesiveness and effectiveness?

7. Why are some groups more successful than others?

8. When might individuals, acting independently, outperform teams in an organization?

9. How do you explain the rapidly increasing popularity of work teams in Canada when our culture places such high value on individualism?

10. In what ways can the obstacles to effective teams be overcome?

11. How do you think scientific management theorists would react to the increased reliance on teams in organizations? How about the behavioural science theorists?

Testing Your Comprehension

Circle the correct answer, then check yourself on page 472.

1. Formal groups differ from informal groups in that formal groups
   a) have a leader
   b) have a purpose
   c) are organizationally sanctioned
   d) are often friendship groups

2. The motivation to join a group that others view as important and influential is
   a) affiliation
   b) status
   c) self-esteem
   d) power

3. A prestigious ranking within a group is
   a) a role
   b) a norm-conformity pattern
   c) status hierarchy
   d) indicative of cohesive groups

4. Large groups are generally superior when
   a) speed of decision making is desired
   b) more diversity is sought
   c) performing productively with predetermined facts
   d) flexibility is necessary

5. As groups get larger
   a) average performance declines
   b) total performance declines
   c) individual effort increases
   d) speed increases

6. The degree to which group members are attracted to one another and share the group's goal is
   a) a norm
   b) a role
   c) status
   d) cohesiveness

7. Willingness to do what has to be done for the team to succeed is called
   a) clear goals
   b) appropriate leadership
   c) unified commitment
   d) internal support

8. High-performance work teams gain a clearer understanding when managers
   a) create a clear purpose
   b) provide resources
   c) build mutual trust
   d) change the team's membership

9. For teams to be effective,
   a) all team members must like each other
   b) team members must resolve petty differences from the start
   c) team members cannot disagree
   d) team members must put aside differences in light of goals

10. Benefits of work teams generally do NOT include
    a) faster decision making
    b) lower costs
    c) improved performance
    d) improved morale

11. Quality circles
    a) identify problems
    b) determine their own membership
    c) investigate the causes of problems
    d) make final decisions regarding recommended solutions

12. Which of the following is NOT a result of using work teams?
    a) lower absenteeism
    b) improved morale
    c) increased productivity
    d) increased centralization

13. Which of the following is identified as a way to build trust among team members?
    a) demonstrate competence
    b) demonstrate conservative communication
    c) demonstrate creativity
    d) demonstrate flexibility

14. Readjusting work skills to fit the needs of the team is called
    a) career development
    b) job morphing
    c) skills training
    d) none of the above

Self-Assessment Exercise

How Trustworthy Are You?

Answer these eight questions using the following scale:

	Strongly Disagree								Strongly Agree
	1 2 3 4 5 6 7 8 9 10								

1. People can expect me to play fair. _____

2. People can confide in me and know that I will listen. _____

3. People can expect me to tell the truth. _____

4. People know that I would never intentionally misrepresent their points of view to others. _____

5. People can confide in me and know that I will not discuss it with others. _____

6. People know that if I promised to do them a favour, I would carry out that promise. _____

7. If I had an appointment with someone, she could count on me showing up. _____

8. If I borrowed money from someone, he could count on getting it back as soon as possible. _____

Total score = _____

Turn to page 467 for scoring directions and key.

Source: Based on Cynthia Johnson-George and Walter C. Swap, "Measurement of Specific Interpersonal Trust: Construction and Validation of a Scale to Assess Trust in a Specific Other," *Journal of Personality and Social Psychology*, December 1982, pp. 1306–17.

Class Exercise

Building an Airplane

Step 1: Get into groups of five to seven people.

Step 2: Each group will be given a piece of poster paper, a pair of scissors, a box of paper clips, a roll of tape, and a magic marker.

Step 3: You have 30 minutes to design, manufacture, and assemble your airplane.

Step 4: At the end of the assembly process, your instructor will take you to a safe place to fly the planes. You have one throw. The winner will be determined based on which group's plane flies the farthest; second place, the second farthest; and so on.

Step 5: After rankings have been determined, return to your classroom, and in your group discuss the following:

a. How much did each group member contribute to the design, manufacture, and assembly of the plane?

b. Was there a group leader? If so, how did that person become the leader?

c. Were you able to express yourself freely, especially if you disagreed with the majority of the group?

d. Using information from the text, describe what barriers your group encountered. How did the group attempt to overcome these?

Step 6: Assembling as a large group, discuss your responses to Step 5 above.

Source: This exercise was directly influenced by P.L. Hunsaker's and J.S. Hunsaker's "The Paper Towel Exercise: Experiencing Leadership and Group Dynamics," published in Stephen P. Robbins, *Organizational Behavior: Concepts, Controversies, and Applications* (Englewood Cliffs, N.J.: Prentice-Hall, Inc., 1993), p. 318.

Case Application

Is This Guy Crazy or What?

Some people might say that Eric Gershman, president and founder of Published Image, is a little off his rocker. Why? Because his career goal is eliminating his job. That's the statement he made when he organized his small Boston company into four self-managed teams.

Published Image Inc. produces newsletters and other publications for shareholders of mutual fund companies. Revenues soon hit the $4-million mark with a profit margin of 20 per cent. Gershman notes, with some pride, that most of the profit margin gain came during the fourth quarter after he implemented the teams. And the company forecasts call for continued astounding growth. Yet, prior to the radical reorganization, the situation was serious enough that the company was on the brink of failure. Employee turnover was high (around 50 per cent a year), product quality was pathetic (customers complained about numerous factual errors in the publications), and the company was losing a third of its clients every year. That's when Gershman decided he had to do something drastic.

And he did. The old company was "blown up" and in its place now are four largely autonomous work teams, each with its own clients who are serviced by staff from sales, editorial, and production. The teams set their own work schedules, prepare their own budgets, and receive bonuses on their team's performances. Each team member specializes in a skill, but can perform any function to meet daily deadlines. This type of job sharing broadens each team member's perspective and improves planning.

Managers are now called *coaches*, and they offer advice and assistance rather than giving orders. Managers also rate the teams for timeliness and accuracy. A monthly score of 90 or higher on these performance measures qualifies team members to biannual bonuses, which can equal up to 15 per cent of an employee's base pay.

So, even though some people might think he's a little crazy for trying to "lose" his job, Eric Gershman feels he has found a way to better manage his company's growth.

Questions

1. Could the group behaviour model be used in managing these teams? Explain.
2. What did teams do for Published Image Inc. that the previous structure couldn't?
3. What problems should Eric be prepared for as a result of the changes he's made?

Source: Based on Michael Seliz, "Testing Self-Managed Teams, Entrepreneur Hopes to Lose Job," *Wall Street Journal*, January 11, 1994, pp. B1+.

c h a p t e r   12

Motivating Employees

Learning Objectives

What will I be able to do after I finish
this chapter?

1 • Describe the motivation process.

2 • Define needs.

3 • Explain the hierarchy of needs theory.

4 • Differentiate Theory X from Theory Y.

5 • Explain the motivational implications of the motivation-
hygiene theory.

6 • Identify the characteristic that high achievers seek in a job.

7 • Describe the motivational implications of equity theory.

8 • Explain the key relationships in expectancy theory.

PCL Construction Group Inc. operates out of Edmonton and is one of the 10 biggest general construction contractors in North America. The company did $1.8 billion worth of business in 1996. PCL's stakeholder strategy makes it stand out in the industry—the company's shares are owned by its employees. Some 750 employees out of 1,300 working for PCL have shares in the company, while no one employee is allowed more than 10 per cent of the company's stock. The idea for employee-ownership was devised by Robert Stollery in 1977, as part of the financing package he put together to buy the company from its existing owners. Stollery remained CEO of PCL until 1993, by which point the company had become completely owned by its employees. Today Ross Grieve is CEO of PCL, succeeding to the post from Joseph Thompson—both men were put in line for their positions by Stollery.[1]

The ownership structure makes it very easy for employees to remain motivated. All salaried employees benefit from a profit-sharing plan (10 to 20 per cent of pre-tax profits are distributed among employees) as well as receiving dividends on their shares. Also, a rule is enforced mandating that employees at all levels of management must divest themselves of all shares when they reach age 64. This allows shares to continually recycle through to younger employees, keeping PCL constantly rejuvenated. Not only does this policy serve to motivate employees, but it also keeps upper management on its toes. As Ross Grieve says, "There are 750 sets of eyes watching that we're doing a good job."

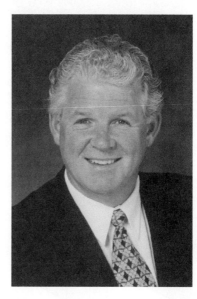

As CEO of PCL Construction Group Inc., Ross Grieve's job of keeping employees motivated is made much easier by the organization's ownership structure.

PCL CONSTRUCTION GROUP
www.pcl.ca

Motivation and Individual Needs

To understand what motivation is, let us begin by pointing out what motivation isn't. Why? Because many people incorrectly view motivation as a personal trait—that is, some have it and others don't. In practice, this would characterize the manager who labels a certain employee as unmotivated. Our knowledge of motivation, though, tells us that this just isn't true. What we know is that motivation is the result of the interaction between the individual and the situation. Certainly, individuals differ in motivational drive, but overall motivation varies from situation to situation. As we analyse the concept of motivation, keep in mind that level of motivation varies both between individuals and within individuals at different times.

We'll define **motivation** as the willingness to exert high levels of effort to reach organizational goals, conditioned by the effort's ability to satisfy some individual need. While general motivation refers to effort toward any goal, here it will refer to organizational goals because our focus is on work-related behaviour. The three key elements in our definition are effort, organizational goals, and needs.

The effort element is a measure of intensity. When someone is motivated, he tries hard. But high levels of effort are unlikely to lead to favourable job performance

motivation
The willingness to exert high levels of effort to reach organizational goals, conditioned by the effort's ability to satisfy some individual need.

outcomes unless the effort is channelled in a direction that benefits the organization.[2] Therefore, we must consider the quality of the effort as well as its intensity. Effort that is directed toward, and consistent with, the organization's goals is the kind of effort that we should be seeking. Finally, we will treat motivation as a need-satisfying process. This is depicted in Exhibit 12-1.

YOUNG CANADIANS

John Curkan: Renaissance Energy

John Curkan is a vice-president of Renaissance Energy, one of Canada's biggest companies. Curkan began in the business working summer jobs. Today he is responsible for the marketing division at Renaissance, the fastest-growing company in Canada's top 50 profit earners.

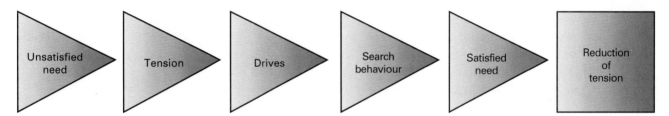

Exhibit 12-1   The Motivation Process

need
An internal state that makes certain outcomes appear attractive.

A **need**, in our terminology, means some internal state that makes certain outcomes appear attractive. An unsatisfied need creates tension that stimulates drives within an individual. These drives generate a search behaviour to find particular goals that, if attained, will satisfy the need and reduce the tension.

We can say that motivated employees are in a state of tension. To relieve this tension, they exert effort. The greater the tension, the higher the effort level. If this effort successfully leads to the satisfaction of the need, it reduces tension. Since we are interested in work behaviour, this tension-reduction effort must also be directed toward organizational goals. Therefore, inherent in our definition of motivation is the requirement that the individual's needs be compatible and consistent with the organization's goals. When this does not occur, individuals may exert high levels of effort that run counter to the interests of the organization. Incidentally, this is not so unusual. Some employees regularly spend a lot of time talking with friends at work in order to satisfy their social needs. There is a high level of effort, but it's being unproductively directed.

Early Theories of Motivation

The 1950s were a fruitful time for the development of motivation concepts. Three specific theories were formulated during this period that although heavily attacked and now considered questionably valid are probably still the best-known explanations for employee motivation. These are the hierarchy of needs theory, Theories X and Y, and the motivation-hygiene theory. While more valid explanations of motivation have been developed, you should know these theories for at least two reasons: (1) They represent the foundation from which contemporary theories grew; and (2) practising managers regularly use these theories and their terminology in explaining employee motivation.

What Is Maslow's Hierarchy of Needs Theory?

The best-known theory of motivation is probably Abraham Maslow's **hierarchy of needs theory**.[3] He imagined that within every human being there exists a hierarchy of five needs:

► 1. **Physiological needs:** food, drink, shelter, sexual satisfaction, and other bodily requirements
► 2. **Safety needs:** security and protection from physical and emotional harm
► 3. **Social needs:** affection, belongingness, acceptance, and friendship
► 4. **Esteem needs:** internal esteem factors such as self-respect, autonomy, and achievement; and external esteem factors such as status, recognition, and attention
► 5. **Self-actualization needs:** growth, achieving one's potential, and self-fulfilment; the drive to become what one is capable of becoming

As each need is substantially satisfied, the next need becomes dominant. In terms of Exhibit 12-2, the individual moves up the hierarchy. From a motivation viewpoint, the theory says that although no need is ever fully gratified, a substantially satisfied need no longer motivates. If you want to motivate someone, according to Maslow, you need to understand where that person is in the hierarchy and focus on satisfying needs at or above that level.

Maslow's needs theory has received wide recognition, particularly among practising managers. This can be attributed to the theory's intuitive logic and ease of understanding. Unfortunately, however, research does not generally validate the theory. Maslow provided no empirical substantiation for his theory, and several studies that sought to validate it found no support.[4]

hierarchy of needs theory
Maslow's theory is that there is a hierarchy of five human needs: physiological, safety, social, esteem, and self-actualization. As each need is substantially satisfied, the next becomes dominant.

physiological needs
Basic food, drink, shelter, and sexual needs.

safety needs
A person's needs for security and protection from physical and emotional harm.

social needs
A person's needs for affection, belongingness, acceptance, and friendship.

esteem needs
Internal factors such as self-respect, autonomy, and achievement; and external factors such as status, recognition, and attention.

self-actualization needs
A person's drive to become what he is capable of becoming.

Abraham Maslow believed that motivation stemmed from fulfilling successively higher-level needs, such as physiological, safety, social, esteem, and self-actualization needs.

**Exhibit 12-2
Maslow's Hierarchy
of Needs**

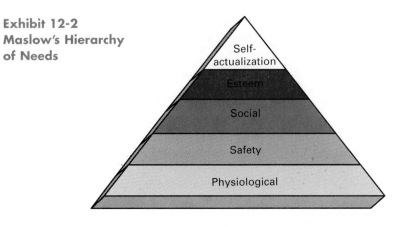

What Are McGregor's Theory X and Theory Y?

Theory X
The assumption that employees dislike work, are lazy, seek to avoid responsibility, and must be coerced to perform.

Theory Y
The assumption that employees are creative, seek responsibility, and can exercise self-direction.

Douglas McGregor proposed two distinct views of the nature of human beings: a basically negative view, labelled **Theory X**, and a basically positive view, labelled **Theory Y**.[5] After viewing the way managers dealt with employees, McGregor concluded that a manager's view of human nature is based on a group of assumptions, either positive or negative (see Exhibit 12-3), and that the manager moulds her behaviour toward employees according to these suppositions.

What does McGregor's analysis imply about motivation? The answer is best expressed in the framework presented by Maslow. Theory X assumes that physiological and safety needs dominate the individual. Theory Y assumes needs like social and esteem are dominant. McGregor himself believed that the assumptions of Theory Y were more valid than those of Theory X. Therefore, he proposed that participation in decision making, responsible and challenging jobs, and good group relations would maximize work effort.

Unfortunately, there is no evidence to confirm that either set of assumptions is valid or that accepting Theory Y assumptions and altering one's actions accordingly will make one's employees more motivated. In the real world, there are examples of effective managers who make Theory X assumptions. For instance, Bob McCurry, vice-president of Toyota's U.S. marketing operations, essentially follows Theory X. He drives his staff hard and uses a "crack-the-whip" style. Yet he has been extremely successful at increasing Toyota's market share in a highly competitive environment.

What Is Herzberg's Motivation-Hygiene Theory?

motivation-hygiene theory
The theory that intrinsic factors are related to job satisfaction, while extrinsic factors are associated with dissatisfaction.

The **motivation-hygiene theory** was proposed by psychologist Frederick Herzberg.[6] Believing that an individual's relation to his work is a basic one and that his attitude toward work can very well determine success or failure, Herzberg investigated the question, "What do people want from their jobs?" He asked people to describe in detail situations in which they felt exceptionally good or bad about their jobs. These responses were then tabulated and categorized. Exhibit 12-4 represents Herzberg's findings.

From analysing the responses, Herzberg concluded that the replies people gave when they felt good about their jobs were significantly different from the replies given when they felt bad. As seen in Exhibit 12-4, certain characteristics were consistently related to job satisfaction (factors on the left side of the figure) and others to job dissatisfaction (the right side of the figure). Intrinsic factors such as achievement,

Theory X: A manager who views employees from a Theory X (negative) perspective, believes:

▶ **1.** Employees inherently dislike work and, whenever possible, will attempt to avoid it

▶ **2.** Because employees dislike work, they must be coerced, controlled, or threatened with punishment to achieve desired goals

▶ **3.** Employees will shirk responsibilities and seek formal direction whenever possible

▶ **4.** Most workers place security above all other factors associated with work and will display little ambition

Theory Y: A manager who views employees from a Theory Y (positive) perspective believes:

▶ **1.** Employees can view work as being as natural as rest or play

▶ **2.** Men and women will exercise self-direction and self-control if they are committed to the objectives

▶ **3.** The average person can learn to accept, even seek, responsibility

▶ **4.** The ability to make good decisions is widely dispersed throughout the population and is not necessarily the sole province of managers

**Exhibit 12-3
Theory X and
Theory Y Premises**

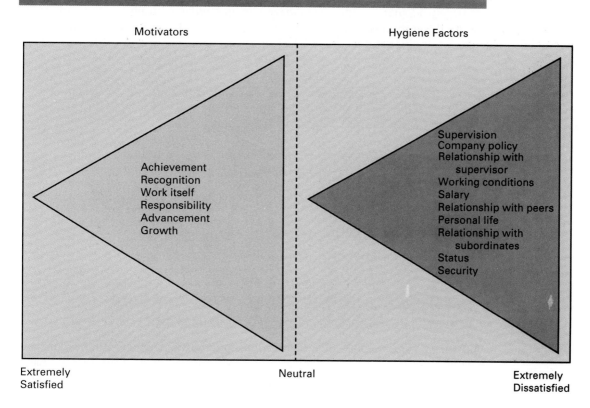

Exhibit 12-4   Herzberg's Motivation-Hygiene Theory

recognition, and responsibility were related to job satisfaction. When those questioned felt good about their work, they tended to attribute these characteristics to themselves. On the other hand, when they were dissatisfied, they tended to cite extrinsic factors such as company policy and administration, supervision, interpersonal relationships, and working conditions.

The data suggest, said Herzberg, that the opposite of satisfaction is not dissatisfaction, as was traditionally believed. Removing dissatisfying characteristics from a job does not necessarily make the job satisfying. As illustrated in Exhibit 12-5, Herzberg proposed that his findings indicate the existence of a dual continuum: The opposite of "satisfaction" is "no satisfaction," and the opposite of "dissatisfaction" is "no dissatisfaction."

According to Herzberg, the factors leading to job satisfaction are separate and distinct from those that lead to job dissatisfaction. Therefore, managers who seek to eliminate factors that create job dissatisfaction can bring about peace but not necessarily motivation. They are placating their workforce rather than motivating it. Because they don't motivate employees, the factors that eliminate job dissatisfaction were characterized by Herzberg as **hygiene factors**. When these factors are adequate, people will not be dissatisfied; however, neither will they be satisfied. To motivate people on their jobs, Herzberg suggested emphasizing **motivators**, the factors that increase job satisfaction.

The motivation-hygiene theory is not without its detractors. The criticisms of the theory include the methodology Herzberg used to collect data and his failure to account for situational variables.[7] Regardless of any criticism, Herzberg's theory has been widely popularized and few managers are unfamiliar with his recommendations. Much of the enthusiasm for job enrichment, cited in Chapter 7, can be attributed to Herzberg's findings and recommendations.

hygiene factors
Factors that eliminate dissatisfaction.

motivators
Factors that increase job satisfaction.

**Exhibit 12-5
Contrasting Views
of Satisfaction and
Dissatisfaction**

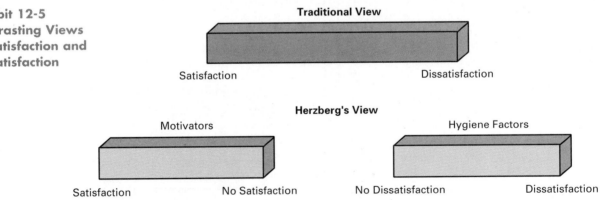

Contemporary Theories of Motivation

While the previous theories are well known, they unfortunately have not held up well under close examination. However, all is not lost. Some contemporary theories have one thing in common: each has a reasonable degree of valid supporting documentation. The following theories represent the current "state-of-the-art" explanations of employee motivation.

What Is McClelland's Three-Needs Theory?

David McClelland and others have proposed the **three-needs theory**, which maintains that there are three major relevant motives or needs in work situations:

▶ 1. **Need for achievement (*nAch*):** the drive to excel, to achieve in relation to a set of standards, to strive to succeed
▶ 2. **Need for power (*nPow*):** the need to make others behave in a way that they would not have behaved otherwise
▶ 3. **Need for affiliation (*nAff*):** the desire for friendly and close interpersonal relationships[8]

three-needs theory
The needs for achievement, power, and affiliation are major motives in work.

need for achievement
The drive to excel, to achieve in relation to a set of standards, to strive to succeed.

This is a sample of the test McClelland used to measure achievement. Individuals looked at ambiguous pictures and created stories based on what they saw. McClelland and his associates then analysed the story to assess the degree of achievement the individuals projected.

Some people have a compelling drive to succeed, but they are striving for personal achievement rather than for the rewards of success per se (*nAch*). They have a desire to do something better or more efficiently than it has been done before. This drive is the need for achievement. From research concerning the achievement need, McClelland found that high achievers differentiate themselves from others by their desire to do things better.[9] They seek situations in which they can attain personal responsibility for finding solutions to problems, in which they can receive rapid and unambiguous feedback on their performance in order to tell whether they are improving, and in which they can set moderately challenging goals (see Details on a Management Classic). High achievers are not gamblers; they dislike succeeding by chance. They prefer the challenge of working at a problem and accepting the personal responsibility for success or failure, rather than leaving the outcome to chance or the actions of others. An important point is that they avoid what they perceive to be very easy or very difficult tasks.

The need for power (*nPow*) is the desire to have impact and to be influential. Individuals high in nPow enjoy being "in charge," strive for influence over others, and prefer to be in competitive and status-oriented situations. The third need isolated by McClelland is affiliation (*nAff*), which is the desire to be liked and accepted by others. This need has received the least attention by researchers. Individuals with high nAff strive for friendships, prefer cooperative situations rather than competitive ones, and desire relationships involving a high degree of mutual understanding.

need for power
The need to make others behave in a way that they would not have behaved otherwise.

need for affiliation
The desire for friendly and close interpersonal relationships.

David McClelland and the Three-Needs Theory

David McClelland's work in helping to understand motivation in organizational settings focused on aspects of personality characteristics. Much of his research centred on achievement, power, and affiliation orientations. Of the three needs, McClelland found that some people have a compelling drive to succeed for personal achievement rather than rewards of success per se. The question then is how do you find out if someone is, for instance, a high achiever. And what effect can that have on an organization?

In his research, McClelland would give individuals a projective test in which subjects responded to a set of pictures. Each picture was briefly shown to a subject who then wrote a story based on the picture. Those responses generated were then classified by McClelland as focusing on a need for achievement, power, or affiliation. Those who had a high need for achievement, however, shared some similar attributes.

High achievers perform best when they perceive their probability of success as being 0.5—that is, when they estimate they have a fifty-fifty chance of success. They dislike gambling when the odds are high because they get no achievement satisfaction from happenstance success. Similarly, they dislike low odds (high probability of success) because then there is no challenge to their skills. They like to set goals that require stretching themselves a little. When there is an approximately equal chance of success or failure, there is optimum opportunity to experience feelings of successful accomplishment and satisfaction in their efforts.

Based on an extensive amount of research, some reasonably well-supported predictions can be made between the relationship of the achievement need and job performance. Though less research has been done on power and affiliation needs, there are consistent findings here, too. First, individuals with a high need to achieve prefer job situations with personal responsibility, feedback, and an intermediate degree of risk. When these characteristics are prevalent, high achievers are strongly motivated. The evidence consistently demonstrates, for instance, that high achievers are successful in entrepreneurial activities like running their own business, managing a self-contained unit within a large organization, and many sales positions.[10] Second, a high need to achieve does not necessarily lead to being a good manager, especially in large organizations. A high nAch salesperson at Pfizer does not necessarily make a good sales manager, and good managers in large organizations like Exxon, AT&T, or Sears do not necessarily have a high need to achieve.[11] Third, the needs for affiliation and power are closely related to managerial success.[12] The best managers are high in the need for power and low in the need for affiliation. Last, employees can be trained successfully to stimulate their achievement need.[13] If a job calls for a high achiever, management can select a person with a high nAch or develop their own candidate through achievement training.▼

How Does Adams's Equity Theory Help Explain Employee Motivation?

Employees don't work in a vacuum. They make comparisons. If someone offered you $60,000 a year on your first job upon graduation from university, you'd probably grab the offer and report to work enthusiastic and certainly satisfied with your pay. How would you react if you found out a month or so into the job that a coworker—another recent graduate, your age, with comparable grades from a comparable university—was getting $70,000 a year? You would probably be upset! Even though, in absolute terms, $60,000 is a lot of money for a new graduate to make (and you know it!), that suddenly would not be the issue. The issue would now centre on relative rewards and what you believe is fair. There is considerable evidence that employees make comparisons of their job inputs and outcomes relative to others and that inequities influence the degree of effort that employees exert.[14]

Developed by J. Stacey Adams, **equity theory** says that employees perceive what they get from a job situation (outcomes) in relation to what they put into it (inputs) and then compare their inputs-outcomes ratio with the inputs-outcomes ratio of relevant others. This is shown in Exhibit 12-6. If they perceive their ratio to be equal to those of the relevant others with whom they compare themselves, a state of equity exists. They perceive that their situation is fair—that justice prevails. If the ratios are unequal, inequity exists; that is, they view themselves as underrewarded or over-rewarded. When inequities occur, employees attempt to correct them.

The **referent** with whom employees choose to compare themselves is an important variable in equity theory.[15] The three referent categories have been classified as "other," "system," and "self." The "other" category includes other individuals with similar jobs in the same organization and also includes friends, neighbours, or professional associates. On the basis of information they receive through word of mouth, newspapers, and magazine articles on issues such as executive salaries or a recent union contract, employees compare their pay with that of others (see Ethical Dilemmas in Management).

equity theory
The theory that an employee compares her job's inputs-outcomes ratio to that of relevant others and then corrects any inequity.

referents
The persons, systems, or selves against which individuals compare themselves to assess equity.

PERCEIVED RATIO COMPARISON*		EMPLOYEE'S ASSESSMENT
$\dfrac{\text{Outcomes A}}{\text{Inputs A}} <$	$\dfrac{\text{Outcomes B}}{\text{Inputs B}}$	Inequity (underrewarded)
$\dfrac{\text{Outcomes A}}{\text{Inputs A}} =$	$\dfrac{\text{Outcomes B}}{\text{Inputs B}}$	Equity
$\dfrac{\text{Outcomes A}}{\text{Inputs A}} >$	$\dfrac{\text{Outcomes B}}{\text{Inputs B}}$	Inequity (overrewarded)

**Exhibit 12-6
Equity Theory Relationships**

*Person A is the employee, and Person B is a relevant other or referent.

The "system" category considers organizational pay policies and procedures and the administration of this system. It considers organization-wide pay policies, both implied and explicit. Patterns by the organization in terms of allocation of pay are major determinants in this category.

The "self" category refers to inputs-outcomes ratios that are unique to the individual. It reflects past personal experiences and contacts. This category is influenced by criteria such as past jobs or family commitments.

The choice of a particular set of referents is related to the information available about referents as well as to their perceived relevance. On the basis of equity theory, when employees perceive an inequity, they might (1) distort either their own or others'

ETHICAL DILEMMAS IN MANAGEMENT

▼
THE ETHICS OF CEO COMPENSATION
▲

We have already noted (in Chapter 1) that the average pay for the top-25 Canadian CEOs in 1996 was more than $6 million.

Critics would describe the astronomical pay packages of some CEOs as being indicative of nothing but pure greed. In the U.S., executive pay can reach phenomenal heights, as illustrated by Michael Eisner's (CEO of Walt Disney Co.) 1996 take in salary, bonuses, and stock-based incentive plans: $204.2 million (U.S.)—and no, that's not a typographical error on our part.

The chief executive officers of some of Canada's largest companies earn multimillion-dollar compensation packages a year, hundreds of times as much as the typical blue-collar worker.

Some say this represents a classic economic response to a situation in which the demand is great for high-quality top-executive talent and the supply is low. Other arguments in favour of paying CEOs $1 million a year or more include the need to compensate people for the tremendous responsibilities and stress that go with such jobs, the motivating potential that seven- and eight-figure annual incomes provide to both the CEOs and those who might aspire to the position, and the CEOs' influence on their companies' bottom lines.

Executive pay is considerably higher in the United States than in most other countries. American CEOs typically make two or three times as much as their counterparts in Canada and Europe. In Japan, CEOs earn only 17 times the pay of an ordinary worker.

Critics of executive pay practices argue that CEOs choose board members who can be counted on to support ever-increasing pay for top management. If board members fail to "play along," they risk losing their positions, their fees, and the prestige and power inherent in board membership.

Does the blame for the problem lie with CEOs or with the shareholders and boards that knowingly allow the practice?

Are CEOs greedy? Are these CEOs acting unethically? What do you think?

inputs or outcomes; (2) behave in some way to induce others to change their inputs or outcomes; (3) behave in some way to change their own inputs or outcomes; (4) choose a different comparison referent; and/or (5) quit their jobs.

Equity theory recognizes that individuals are concerned not only with the absolute rewards they receive for their efforts but also with the relationship of these rewards to what others receive. They make judgments concerning the relationship between their inputs and outcomes and the inputs and outcomes of others. On the basis of one's inputs, such as effort, experience, education, and competence, one compares outcomes such as salary levels, raises, recognition, and other factors. When people perceive an imbalance in their inputs-outcomes ratio relative to those of others, they experience tension. This tension provides the basis for motivation as people strive for what they perceive as equity and fairness.

The theory establishes the four propositions relating to inequitable pay. These propositions listed in Exhibit 12-7 have generally proven to be correct.[16] A review of the research consistently confirms the equity thesis: employee motivation is influenced significantly by relative rewards as well as by absolute rewards. Whenever employees perceive inequity, they will act to correct the situation.[17] The result might be lower or higher productivity, improved or reduced quality of output, increased absenteeism, or voluntary resignation.

From the discussion above, however, we should not conclude that equity theory is without problems. The theory leaves some key issues still unclear.[18] For instance, how do employees define inputs and outcomes? How do they combine and weigh their inputs and outcomes to arrive at totals? When and how do the factors change over time? Regardless of these problems, equity theory has an impressive amount of research support and offers us some important insights into employee motivation.

Exhibit 12-7
Equity Theory
Propositions

▶ **1. Given payment by time, overrewarded employees will produce more than equitably paid employees.** Hourly and salaried employees will generate a high quantity or quality of production in order to increase the input side of the ratio and bring about equity.

▶ **2. Given payment by quantity of production, overrewarded employees will produce fewer but higher-quality units than equitably paid employees.** Individuals paid on a piece-rate basis will increase their effort to achieve equity, which can result in greater quality or quantity. However, increases in quantity will only increase inequity, since every unit produced results in further overpayment. Therefore, effort is directed toward increasing quality rather than quantity.

▶ **3. Given payment by time, underrewarded employees will produce less or poorer-quality output.** Effort will be decreased, which will bring about lower productivity or poorer-quality output than equitably paid subjects.

▶ **4. Given payment by quantity of production, underrewarded employees will produce a large number of low-quality units in comparison with equitably paid employees.** Employees on piece-rate pay plans can bring about equity because trading off quality of output for quantity will result in an increase in rewards with little or no increase in contributions.

Why Is Vroom's Expectancy Theory Considered a Comprehensive Theory of Motivation?

The most comprehensive explanation of motivation is Victor Vroom's **expectancy theory**.[19] Though it has its critics,[20] most of the research evidence supports the theory.[21]

The expectancy theory states that an individual tends to act in a certain way based on the expectation that the act will be followed by a given outcome and on the attractiveness of that outcome to the individual. It includes three variables or relationships:

▶ **1. Effort-performance linkage:** the probability perceived by the individual that exerting a given amount of effort will lead to performance

▶ **2. Performance-reward linkage:** the degree to which the individual believes that performing at a particular level will lead to the attainment of a desired outcome

▶ **3. Attractiveness:** the importance that the individual places on the potential outcome or reward that can be achieved on the job. This considers the goals and needs of the individual[22]

While this might sound complex, it really is not that difficult to visualize. It can be summed up in several questions: How hard do I have to work to achieve a certain

expectancy theory
The theory that an individual tends to act in a certain way based on the expectation that the act will be followed by a given outcome and on the attractiveness of that outcome to the individual.

effort-performance linkage
An individual's perceived probability that exerting a given amount of effort will lead to performance.

performance-reward linkage
The degree to which the individual believes that performing at a particular level will lead to the attainment of a desired outcome.

attractiveness
The importance that the individual places on the potential outcome or reward that can be achieved on the job.

level of performance and can I actually achieve that level? What reward will performing at that level get me? How attractive is this reward to me and does it help achieve my goals? Whether one has the desire to produce at any given time depends on one's particular goals and one's perception of the relative worth of performance as a path to the attainment of these goals.

How Does Expectancy Theory Work? Exhibit 12-8 shows a very simple version of the expectancy theory that expresses its major contentions. The strength of a person's motivation to perform (effort) depends on how strongly that individual believes that she can achieve what is being attempted. If this goal is achieved (performance), will she be adequately rewarded by the organization? If so, will the reward satisfy her individual goals? Let us consider the four steps inherent in the theory and then attempt to apply it.

First, what perceived outcomes does the job offer the employee? Outcomes may be positive: pay, security, companionship, trust, employee benefits, a chance to use talent or skills, or congenial relationships. On the other hand, employees may view the outcomes as negative: fatigue, boredom, frustration, anxiety, harsh supervision, or threat of dismissal. Reality is not relevant here; the critical issue is what the individual employee perceives the outcome to be, regardless of whether her perceptions are accurate.

Second, how attractive do employees consider these outcomes to be? Are they valued positively, negatively, or neutrally? This obviously is an internal issue and considers the individual's personal attitudes, personality, and needs. The individual who finds a particular outcome attractive—that is, values it positively—would rather attain it than not attain it. Others may find it negative and therefore prefer not attaining it to attaining it. Still others may be neutral.

Third, what kind of behaviour must the employee exhibit to achieve these outcomes? The outcomes are not likely to have any effect on an individual employee's performance unless the employee knows, clearly and unambiguously, what he must do to achieve them. For example, what is "doing well" in terms of performance appraisal? What criteria will be used to judge the employee's performance?

Fourth and last, how does the employee view his chances of doing what is asked? After the employee has considered his own competencies and ability to control those variables that will determine success, what is his probability of successful attainment?[23]

How Can Expectancy Theory Be Applied? Let's use a classroom analogy as an illustration of how one can use the expectancy theory to explain motivation.

Most students prefer an instructor who tells them what is expected of them in the course. They want to know what the assignments and examinations will be like, when they are due or to be taken, and how much weight each carries in the final term grade. They also like to think that the amount of effort they exert in attending classes, taking notes, and studying will be reasonably related to the grade they will make in the course. Let us assume that you, as a student, feel this way. Consider that five weeks into a class you are really enjoying (we'll call it MNGT 301), an examination is given back to you. You studied hard for this examination, and you have consistently made As and Bs on examinations in other courses for which you have expended similar effort. The reason you work so hard is to make top grades, which you believe are important for getting a good job upon graduation. Also, you are not sure, but you might want to go on to graduate school. Again, you think grades are important for getting into a good graduate school.

YOUNG CANADIANS

Antoine Paquin: Skystone Systems

Antoine Paquin's company, Skystone Systems, was founded in his basement. With an innovative product—technology to carry data in optical networks—Paquin and his partner, Stefan Dralski, hand-picked the company's 50 employees, creating a highly effective team by instilling a shared vision, as well as by offering members the opportunity to share in the profit. In three years, still with sales of only $4 million, the company was seen to be so promising that the U.S. giant Cisco Systems paid $150 million for it.

SKYSTONE
SYSTEMS
www.skystone.com/

Well, the results of that five-week examination are in. The class median was 74. Ten per cent of the class scored an 85 or higher and got an A. Your grade was 46; the minimum passing mark was 50. You're mad. You're frustrated. Even more, you're perplexed. How could you possibly have done so poorly on the examination when you usually score in the top range in other classes by preparing as you did for this one?

Several interesting things are immediately evident in your behaviour. Suddenly, you are no longer driven to attend MNGT 301 classes regularly. You find that you do not study for the course, either. When you do attend classes, you daydream a lot—the result is an empty notebook instead of several pages of notes. One would probably be correct in describing you as "lacking in motivation" in MNGT 301. Why did your motivation level change? You know and I know, but let's explain it in expectancy terms.

If we use Exhibit 12-8 to understand this situation, we might say the following: Studying for MNGT 301 (effort) is conditioned by the resulting correct answers on the examination (performance), which will produce a high grade (reward), which will lead, in turn, to the security, prestige, and other benefits that accrue from obtaining a good job (individual goal).

The attractiveness of the outcome, which in this case is a good grade, is high. But what about the performance-reward linkage? Do you feel that the grade you received truly reflects your knowledge of the material? In other words, did the test fairly measure what you know? If the answer is yes, then this linkage is strong. If the answer is no, then at least part of the reason for your reduced motivational level is your belief that the test was not a fair measure of your performance. If the test was an essay type, maybe you believe that the instructor's grading method was poor. Was too much weight placed on a question that you thought was trivial? Maybe the instructor does not like you and was biased in grading your paper. These are examples of perceptions that influence the performance-reward linkage and your level of motivation.

Another possible demotivating force may be the effort-performance relationship. If, after you take the examination, you believe that you could not have passed it regardless of the amount of preparation you had done, then your desire to study will

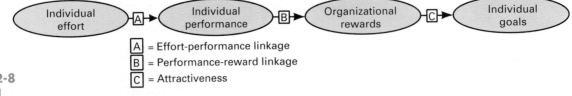

**Exhibit 12-8
Simplified
Expectancy Theory**

drop. Possibly the instructor wrote the examination under the assumption that you had a considerably broader background in the subject matter. Maybe the course had several prerequisites that you did not know about, or possibly you had the prerequisites but took them several years ago. The result is the same: You place a low value on your effort leading to answering the examination questions correctly; hence, your motivational level decreases, and you lessen your effort.

Given our classroom analogy, can we relate this to a work setting? In other words, what does expectancy theory say that can help us motivate our employees? To answer that question, let's summarize some of the issues surrounding the theory. First, expectancy theory emphasizes payoffs, or rewards. As a result, managers have to believe that the rewards they offer will align with what the employee wants. As such, it is a theory based on self-interest, wherein each individual seeks to maximize her expected satisfaction. Second, expectancy theory stresses that managers understand why employees view certain outcomes as attractive or unattractive. They will want to reward individuals with things they value positively. Third, expectancy theory emphasizes expected behaviours. Do individuals know what is expected of them and how they will be appraised? Unless employees see this connection between performance and rewards, organizational goals may not be met. Finally, the theory is concerned with perceptions. What is realistic is irrelevant. An individual's own perceptions of performance, reward, and goal-satisfaction outcomes will determine her level of effort, not the objective outcomes themselves. Accordingly, there must be continuous feedback to align perceptions with reality.

How Can We Integrate the Contemporary Theories of Motivation?

We have presented several motivation theories in this chapter. There is a tendency, at this point, to view them independently. This is a mistake. The fact is that many of the ideas underlying the theories are complementary, and your understanding of how to motivate people is maximized when you see how the theories fit together.[24]

Exhibit 12-9 presents a model that integrates much of what we know about motivation. Its basic foundation is the simplified expectancy model shown in Exhibit 12-8. Let's work through Exhibit 12-9, beginning at the left.

The individual effort box has an arrow leading into it. This arrow flows out of the individual's goals. This goals-effort loop is meant to remind us that goals direct behaviour.

Expectancy theory predicts that an employee will exert a high level of effort if he perceives that there is a strong relationship between effort and performance, performance and rewards, and rewards and satisfaction of personal goals. Each of these relationships, in turn, is influenced by certain factors. For effort to lead to good performance, the individual must have the requisite ability to perform, and the performance-evaluation system that measures the individual's performance must be

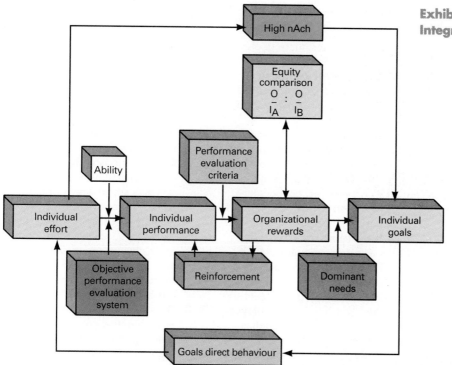

Exhibit 12-9
Integrating Theories of Motivation

perceived as being fair and objective. The performance-reward relationship will be strong if the individual perceives that it is performance (rather than seniority, personal favourites, or other criteria) that is rewarded. Thus, if management has designed a reward system that is seen by employees as "paying off" for good performance, the rewards will reinforce and encourage continued good performance.

The final link in expectancy theory is the rewards-goals relationship. Need theories would come into play at this point. Motivation would be high to the degree that the rewards an individual received for his high performance satisfied the dominant needs consistent with his individual goals.

A closer look at Exhibit 12-9 will also reveal that the model considers the need for achievement and equity theories. The high achiever is not motivated by the organization's assessment of his performance or by organizational rewards, hence the jump from effort to individual goals for those with a high nAch. Remember that high achievers are internally driven as long as the jobs they are doing provide them with personal responsibility, feedback, and moderate risks. They are not concerned with the effort-performance, performance-rewards, or rewards-goal linkages. Finally, rewards also play a key part in equity theory. Individuals will compare the rewards (outcomes) they receive from the inputs they make with the inputs-outcomes ratio of relevant others (O/IA:O/IB), and inequities may influence the effort expended.

If you're a manager concerned with motivating your employees, what specific recommendations can you draw from this integration? While there is no simple, all-encompassing set of guidelines, we offer the following suggestions that draw on the essence of what these theories have taught us about motivating employees (see Developing Management Skills).

DEVELOPING MANAGEMENT SKILLS

▼

GETTING THE MOST FROM EMPLOYEES

▲

▶ **1. Recognize individual differences.** Almost every contemporary motivation theory recognizes that employees are not homogeneous. They have different needs. They also differ in terms of attitudes, personality, and other important individual variables.

▶ **2. Match people to jobs.** There is a great deal of evidence showing the motivational benefits of carefully matching people to jobs. People who lack the necessary skills to perform successfully will be disadvantaged.

▶ **3. Use goals.** Managers should ensure that employees have hard, specific goals and feedback on how well they are doing in pursuit of those goals.

In many cases, these goals should be participatively set.

▶ **4. Ensure that goals are perceived as attainable.** Regardless of whether goals are actually attainable, employees who see these goals as unattainable will reduce their effort. Managers must be sure, therefore, that employees feel confident that increased efforts can lead to performance goals.

▶ **5. Individualize rewards.** Because employees have different needs, what acts as a reinforcer for one may not for another. Managers should use their knowledge of employee differences to individualize the rewards over which they have control. Some of the more obvious rewards that managers allocate include pay, promotions, autonomy, and the opportunity to participate in goal setting and decision making.

▶ **6. Link rewards to performance.** Managers need to make rewards contingent on

performance. Rewarding factors other than performance will only reinforce those other factors. Key rewards such as pay increases and promotions should be given for the attainment of employees' specific goals.

▶ **7. Check the system for equity.** Employees should perceive that rewards or outcomes are equal to the inputs given. On a simplistic level, experience, ability, effort, and other obvious inputs should explain differences in pay, responsibility, and other obvious outcomes.

▶ **8. Don't ignore money.** It's easy to get so caught up in setting goals, creating interesting jobs, and providing opportunities for participation that one forgets that money is a major reason why most people work. Thus, the allocation of performance-based wage increases, piece-work bonuses, and other pay incentives is important in determining employee motivation.

Are Theories of Motivation Transferable Across National Cultures?

The theories of motivation we have been studying were developed largely by U.S. psychologists and validated through studies of American workers. These theories, however, need to be modified for different cultures.[25]

The self-interest concept is consistent with capitalism and the extremely high value placed on individualism in North America. Because almost all the motivation theories presented in this chapter are based on the self-interest motive, they should be applicable to organizations in such countries as Great Britain and Australia, where capitalism and individualism are highly valued. In more collectivist nations—Venezuela, Singapore, Japan, and Mexico—the link to the organization is the individual's loyalty to the organization or society, rather than her self-interest. Employees in collectivist cultures should be more receptive to team-based job design, group goals, and group-performance evaluations. Reliance on the fear of being fired in such cultures is likely to be less effective, even if the laws in these countries allow managers to fire employees.

The need for achievement concept provides another example of a motivation theory with a North American bias. The view that a high need for achievement acts as an internal motivator presupposes the existence of two cultural characteristics: a willingness to accept a moderate degree of risk and a concern with performance. These characteristics would exclude countries with high uncertainty-avoidance scores and high quality-of-life ratings. The remaining countries are exclusively Anglo-American countries such as New Zealand, South Africa, Ireland, the United States, and Canada.

Motivating a Diversified Workforce

To maximize motivation among today's diversified workforce, management needs to think in terms of flexibility (see Managers Who Made a Difference). For instance, studies tell us that men place considerably more importance on having a lot of autonomy in their jobs than do women. In contrast, the opportunity to learn, convenient work hours, and good interpersonal relations are more important to women than to men.[26] Managers need to be aware that what motivates the single mother with two dependent children who's working full time to support her family may be very different from the needs of a young, single, part-time worker or the older employee who is working to supplement his pension income. The following examples, which link the issue of motivation with our previous discussion of job design in Chapter 7, illustrate the importance of designing flexible work schedules and benefit programs to respond to employees' varied needs.

Ann works for Merck Pharmaceuticals. As a mother of two preschool children, she finds that the company's family-friendly benefits—day care, flextime, job sharing, flexible benefits, and personal leaves of absence—increase her commitment to her job and to Merck.

Mark also works for Merck. He is among the company's 2,000 or so employees who work part time. This Merck option allows Mark to gain valuable experience and meet his financial obligations, while at the same time allowing him to pursue his graduate studies in chemistry.

Jack is 72 years old. Because his pension cheque provides an inadequate income, Jack works full time at a local McDonald's. One of the franchise's hardest-working and most enthusiastic employees, he regularly praises the hamburger chain for providing him with flexible work hours and an excellent health plan.

MERCK
PHARMACEUTICALS
www.merck.com

MANAGERS WHO MADE A DIFFERENCE

Frank Delfino: Teknion Furniture Systems

TEKNION
www.tekus.com/

Frank Delfino has a very solid understanding of the unstable nature of his business. The furniture manufacturing industry is a cyclical one, with the market fluctuating between boom times and drought. The double-shot of Free Trade opening the doors to U.S. competitors, followed by the Recession, caused major upheaval in the Canadian furniture-making industry. More than 500 manufacturers went under during this period. Teknion weathered the crisis much more successfully—they looked to new markets worldwide and even managed to add to their workforce.[27]

Teknion's chief operating officer attributes the company's continuing success to its handling of employees. Delfino says, "People are not an expendable resource. When you lay off, you lose skill sets, morale, and, most important, trust." This attitude—paying close attention to the morale and indeed loyalty of the workforce—translates to a well-motivated employee base. Trust is a two-way street. Teknion can rest assured that it will keep its highly skilled workforce loyal by making it clear that their needs are held in high priority by the company.

Job security is a precious commodity in a business such as this where layoffs are commonplace. When orders for furniture lessen in this ever-changing marketplace, Teknion does not send workers home. Instead the company finds something for its employees to do while it rides out the bad times. For instance, Delfino recently chose to react to a slowdown in production by taking his workers off their normal tasks and utilizing them in different areas, such as cleaning and painting storage areas and machinery. When employees know that their employer appreciates their work, wants to retain their skills, and would lay them off only as a very last resort, their work will reflect their contentment.▼

Summary

This summary is organized by the chapter Learning Objectives found on page 310.

1. Motivation is the willingness to exert high levels of effort toward organizational goals, conditioned by the effort's ability to satisfy some individual need. The motivation process begins with an unsatisfied need, which creates tension and drives an individual to search for goals that, if attained, will satisfy the need and reduce the tension.

2. A need is some internal state that makes certain outcomes appear attractive.

3. The hierarchy of needs theory states that there are five needs—physiological, safety, social, esteem, and self-actualization—that individuals attempt to satisfy in a steplike progression. A substantially satisfied need no longer motivates.

4. Theory X is basically a negative view of human nature, assuming that employees dislike work, are lazy, seek to avoid responsibility, and must be coerced to perform. Theory Y is basically positive, assuming that employees are creative, seek responsibility, and can exercise self-direction.

5. The motivation-hygiene theory states that not all job factors can motivate employees. The presence or absence of certain job characteristics, or hygiene factors, can only placate employees and cannot lead to satisfaction or motivation. Factors that people find intrinsically rewarding, such as achievement, recognition, responsibility, and growth, act as motivators and produce job satisfaction.

6. High achievers prefer jobs that offer personal responsibility, feedback, and moderate risks.

7. In equity theory, individuals compare their job's inputs-outcomes ratio to those of relevant others. If they perceive that they are underrewarded, their work motivation declines. When individuals perceive that they are overrewarded, they often are motivated to work harder to justify their pay.

8. The expectancy theory states that an individual tends to act in a certain way based on the expectation that the act will be followed by a given outcome and on the attractiveness of that outcome to the individual. Its prime components are the relationships between effort and performance, performance and rewards, and rewards and individual goals.

Review and Discussion Questions

1. What role do needs play in motivation?

2. What role would money play in (a) the hierarchy of needs theory, (b) motivation-hygiene theory, (c) equity theory, (d) expectancy theory, and (e) employees with a high nAch?

3. Contrast lower-order and higher-order needs in Maslow's need hierarchy.

4. If you accept Theory Y assumptions, how would you be likely to motivate employees?

5. Describe the three needs in the three-needs theory.

6. Would an individual with a high nAch be a good candidate for a management position? Explain.

7. What are some of the possible consequences of employees perceiving an inequity between their inputs and outcomes and those of others?

8. What difficulties do you think workforce diversity causes for managers trying to use equity theory?

9. What role does perception play in (a) expectancy theory, (b) equity theory, and (c) reinforcement theory?

10. Explain the motivation implications of expectancy theory for management practice.

Testing Your Comprehension

Circle the correct answer, then check yourself on page 472.

1. A state within an individual that results in an outcome's appearing attractive is called

   a) a reward

   b) a hygiene factor

   c) perception

   d) a need

2. Which of the following BEST describes a highly motivated employee?

   a) an employee who spends company time raising funds for the Red Cross

   b) an employee who is working hard at increasing her department's profits

   c) an employee who just received his annual cost-of-living raise

   d) an employee who puts out only as much effort as is necessary

3. Unsatisfied needs create

   a) tension

   b) aggravation

   c) frustration

   d) aggression

4. The motto "Let each become all he or she is capable of being" BEST illustrates

   a) the expectancy theory of motivation

   b) the relationship between needs and tension

   c) self-actualization needs

   d) Theory Y

5. According to Maslow, when does a need stop motivating?

   a) when it is substantially satisfied

   b) never

   c) when the person returns to a lower-level need

   d) when the situation changes

6. The Theory Y manager would

   a) monitor and continually prompt her employees to keep them working

   b) use threats and punishment to ensure performance

   c) obtain more desirable results with subordinates who had a predominately external locus of control

   d) delegate and use participative management techniques more than would a Theory X manager

7. Factors that eliminate dissatisfaction are
   a) motivators
   b) hygiene factors
   c) referents
   d) eliminators

8. When an individual is characterized by a need to constantly do better, to accomplish rather difficult goals, and to succeed, he has
   a) a high nAch
   b) an external locus of control
   c) an unfulfilled need for hygiene factors
   d) a high nAff

9. According to the equity theory, individuals are constantly perceiving the
   a) cost-benefit ratio
   b) efficiency-effectiveness trade-off
   c) quantity-quality trade-off
   d) inputs-outcomes ratio

10. If a salaried employee is overpaid, one would expect from the equity theory assumptions that
    a) quantity will increase and quality will decrease
    b) quantity and quality will decrease
    c) quantity and quality will increase
    d) quantity will decrease and quality will increase

11. The "self," "other," and "system" are categories of
    a) motivation
    b) hygiene factor
    c) McClelland's three-needs theory
    d) referents

12. The degree to which an individual believes that working at a particular level will generate a desired outcome is defined by the expectancy theory as
    a) attractiveness
    b) performance-reward linkage
    c) effort-performance linkage
    d) value or valence

13. Which of the following concepts is INCONSISTENT with the expectancy theory of motivation?
    a) self-interest
    b) relative worth of rewards
    c) knowledge of performance criteria
    d) one's inputs and outputs compared with another's

14. Motivation theories

     a) are universal

     b) are specific to the United States

     c) need to be modified for different cultures

     d) rarely work today

15. The key to motivating today's diversified workforce lies in

     a) creativity

     b) goal setting

     c) support

     d) flexibility

Self-Assessment Exercise

What Needs Are Most Important to You?

Instructions: Rank your responses for each of the following questions. The response that is most important or most true for you should receive a 5; the next should receive a 4; the next a 3; the next a 2; and the least important or least true should receive a 1.

Example

The work I like best involves:

A ____ Working alone.

B ____ A mixture of time spent with people and time spent alone.

C ____ Giving speeches.

D ____ Discussion with others.

E ____ Working outdoors.

1. Overall, the most important thing to me about a job is whether or not:

     A ____ The pay is sufficient to meet my needs.

     B ____ It provides the opportunity for fellowship and good human relations.

     C ____ It is a secure job with good employee benefits.

     D ____ It allows me freedom and the chance to express myself.

     E ____ There is opportunity for advancement based on my achievements.

2. If I were to quit a job, it would probably be because:

     A ____ It was a dangerous job, such as working with inadequate equipment or poor safety procedures.

     B ____ Continued employment was questionable because of uncertainties in business conditions or funding sources.

C ____ It was a job people looked down on.

D ____ It was a one-person job, allowing little opportunity for discussion and interaction with others.

E ____ The work lacked personal meaning to me.

3. For me, the most important rewards in working are those that:

     A ____ Come from the work itself—important and challenging assignments.

     B ____ Satisfy the basic reasons why people work—good pay, a good home, and other economic needs.

     C ____ Are provided by fringe benefits—such as hospitalization insurance, time off for vacations, security for retirement, etc.

     D ____ Reflect my ability—such as being recognized for the work I do and knowing I am one of the best in my company or profession.

     E ____ Come from the human aspects of working—that is, the opportunity to make friends and to be a valued member of a team.

4. My morale would suffer most in a job in which:

     A ____ The future was unpredictable.

     B ____ Other employees received recognition, when I didn't, for doing the same quality of work.

C _____ My coworkers were unfriendly or held grudges.

D _____ I felt stifled and unable to grow.

E _____ The job environment was poor—no air conditioning, inconvenient parking, insufficient space and lighting, primitive toilet facilities.

5. In deciding whether or not to accept a promotion, I would be most concerned with whether:

A _____ The job was a source of pride and would be viewed with respect by others.

B _____ Taking the job would constitute a gamble on my part, and I could lose more than I gained.

C _____ The economic rewards would be favourable.

D _____ I would like the new people I would be working with, and whether or not we would get along.

E _____ I would be able to explore new areas and do more creative work.

6. The kind of job that brings out my best is one in which:

A _____ There is a family spirit among employees and we all share good times.

B _____ The working conditions—equipment, materials, and basic surroundings—are physically safe.

C _____ Management is understanding and there is little chance of losing my job.

D _____ I can see the returns on my work from the standpoint of personal values.

E _____ There is recognition for my achievement.

7. I would consider changing jobs if my present position:

A _____ Did not offer security and fringe benefits.

B _____ Did not provide a chance to learn and grow.

C _____ Did not provide recognition for my performance.

D _____ Did not allow close personal contacts.

E _____ Did not provide economic rewards.

8. The job situation that would cause the most stress for me is:

A _____ Having a serious disagreement with my coworkers.

B _____ Working in an unsafe environment.

C _____ Having an unpredictable supervisor.

D _____ Not being able to express myself.

E _____ Not being appreciated for the quality of my work.

9. I would accept a new position if:

A _____ The position would be a test of my potential.

B _____ The new job would offer better pay and physical surroundings.

C _____ The new job would be secure and offer long-term fringe benefits.

D _____ The position would be respected by others in my organization.

E _____ Good relationships with coworkers and business associates were probable.

10. I would work overtime if:

A _____ The work is challenging.

B _____ I need the extra income.

C _____ My coworkers are also working overtime.

D _____ I must do it to keep my job.

E _____ The company recognizes my contribution.

Turn to page 467 for scoring directions and key.

Source: George Manning and Kent Curtis, *Human Behaviour: Why People Do What They Do* (Cincinnati, Ohio: Vista Systems/SouthWestern Publishing, 1988), pp. 17–20. With permission.

Class Exercise

How Can We Motivate Others?

This exercise is designed to help increase your awareness of how and why we motivate others and to help focus on the needs of those we are attempting to motivate.

Step 1: Break into groups of five to seven people. Each group member is to individually respond to the following:

Situation 1: You are the owner and president of a 50-employee organization. Your goal is to motivate all 50 employees to their highest effort level.

Task 1: On a separate piece of paper, list the factors you would use to motivate your employees. Avoid general statements like *give them a raise*. Rather, be as specific as possible.

Task 2: Rank order (from highest to lowest) all the factors listed in task one above.

Situation 2: Consider now that you are one of the 50 employees who has been given input into what motivates you.

Task 3: As an employee, list factors that would most effectively motivate you. Again, be as specific as possible.

Task 4: Rank order (from highest to lowest) those factors listed in task three above.

Step 2: Each member should share his prioritized lists (both lists from tasks 2 and 4 above) with the other members of the group.

Step 3: After each member has presented her lists, the group should respond to the following questions:

1. Are each individual's lists (task 2 and task 4) more similar or dissimilar? What does this mean to you?

2. What have you learned about how and why to motivate others and how can you apply these data?

Step 4: Each group should appoint a spokesperson to present its answers from step 3 to the class.

Source: Adapted from B.E. Smith, "Why Don't They Respond: A Motivational Experience," *Organizational Behavior Teaching Review*, Vol. X, No. 2 (1985–86), pp. 98–100.

Case Application

Workers of the World Unite! (with Management)

Avcorp Industries of Richmond, British Columbia, is a manufacturer of aircraft parts that has pulled off a phenomenal corporate turnaround. In both 1992 and 1993, Avcorp posted losses of more than $3 million. In 1995 Avcorp had bounced back to bring in a net profit of $3.5 million, but not without facing huge obstacles, not the least of which was keeping its workforce onside. When sales dropped by $10 million in two years, Avcorp knew it was about to face its greatest challenge to keep the company alive. This is when they placed Peter Jeffrey at the helm of the sinking ship. By the time Jeffrey was made CEO, the workforce had already borne the brunt of its layoffs due to the decrease in sales. But things looked bleak at the company and workers were far from confident that they would be keeping their jobs.

It was a classic case of labour-management distrust, and it was essential for Avcorp to overcome this if it was to survive. Everyone waited for news of heavy cutbacks and layoffs as Jeffrey took control. But this was not in the new CEO's game plan. There were job cuts, but to the surprise of the union, they were in middle management. Still, only 30 of the 250-strong staff were let go, and they were supervisors and account executives. Perhaps some people breathed easier on the shop floor, but it seemed that this was likely just a taste of what was to come.

Jeffrey now had to deal with the union, and he had to tread very lightly. As he says, "It takes five minutes to create a credibility gap between labour and management and five years to close it again." Credibility was not going to be an easy thing to come by in a company such as Avcorp, where one union representative depicts past management as being "very adversarial, very confrontational." So, Jeffrey decided that his only course of action was to be up front with his workforce. He put together a meeting between union representatives and the bankers in order to let the union see first-hand just how bad things were. The employees at Avcorp agreed to accept a 6-per-cent rollback in their wages—a sign of faith for Jeffrey.

Then the real work began. To truly give employees a sense of belonging in their positions, the Continuous Improvement Program came into effect. Through this program, each employee at Avcorp now receives intensive training in every aspect of the business: production, billing, bidding, and everything in between. This kind of initiative can close a labour-management credibility gap quickly. For Jeffrey, the reasons behind this move were simple. He says: "We wanted everyone to understand where they fit in the system."

Then the factory was reengineered, and the real employee empowerment came into effect. About empowerment, Jeffrey says, "This management believes that the best solution to a problem on the shop floor comes from the shop floor." To put this belief into practice, Avcorp instituted a shop-floor system called the Red Flag System which tracks the progression of any given project as it goes through the various stages at the plant. Workers use red flags any time a problem occurs at their station, and in conjunction with supervisors, attempt to find a quick remedy. If it takes more than three minutes to correct a problem, the worker and supervisor involved make up a report detailing the problem, and this is entered into Avcorp's computer system. Anyone working on the project at hand has access to this information and can suggest possible solutions: Democracy in the workplace. This fosters a feeling among workers of belonging to a team, as well as letting people know that their input is appreciated, and that their positions are important in the overall scheme.

These radical changes at Avcorp have led to much easier relations between labour and management. The new contract with the union provides for flexibility rather than set job descriptions for the workers. Promotions and wage increases are now based more heavily on skills-training and self-motivation than time-earned seniority. Bonuses will soon come in the form of profit-sharing programs. And an apprenticeship program will provide the opportunity for advancement among workers.

These are major changes, and they have worked wonders for this company, which many people believed would never crawl back out of the hole. And when a giant company such as Boeing in Seattle decides to do business with you because they believe your management techniques are more advanced than their own, you know you're doing something right. Avcorp's success lies in its ability to be farsighted enough to understand the importance of labour relations, and to have the courage to make sweeping changes in order to make these relations work.

Questions

1. What other motivation techniques could Avcorp implement to further enhance employee performance?

2. Compare and contrast the conditions for workers at Avcorp before its reengineering and after. How do you think employee satisfaction would vary between the two periods?

3. In a situation such as Avcorp is in now, how do you think a sense of teamwork serves to help motivate employees?

Source: Richard Littlemore, "The President's Choice," *The Financial Post Magazine*, April 1996, pp. 71-78.

chapter 13

Leadership and Supervision

Learning Objectives

What will I be able to do after I finish this chapter?

1 • Explain the difference between managers and leaders.

2 • Summarize the conclusions of trait theories.

3 • Identify the two underlying leadership styles in the managerial grid.

4 • Describe the Fiedler contingency model.

5 • Summarize the path-goal model.

6 • Explain when leaders may not be that important.

7 • Identify the key characteristics of charismatic leaders.

8 • Contrast transactional and transformational leadership.

9 • Describe the unique characteristics of being a first-line supervisor.

10 • Explain how the supervisor's role is changing in today's organizations.

Laurent Beaudoin was a young man when he was given control of his father-in-law's business, Bombardier Inc. of Montreal. It was the 1960s, Beaudoin was 28, and snowmobile inventor and company founder Joseph-Armand Bombardier decided it was time to hand over the reins. Since then Laurent Beaudoin has proved himself to be one of the greatest business leaders this country has ever seen. With decisive strategies and barely a misstep in more than three decades as CEO, Beaudoin has built Bombardier into a world leader in three separate industries.[1]

Beaudoin's first dramatic manoeuvre came in 1973 when the company's snowmobile sales took a heavy hit due to the oil crisis. Beaudoin decided that a shift to manufacturing subway and railway cars would be profitable. Major contracts in Montreal and then New York City started Bombardier off on its new course. This proved to be a highly lucrative business for Bombardier, and things were going so well that a foray into yet another industry in 1986 was met with shock and scepticism by the public. Why risk a highly profitable enterprise with a move into an industry that seems to crush companies regularly? But of course Laurent Beaudoin knew what he was doing when he moved into the aerospace industry. Beaudoin saw a niche in the regional and business plane market, and purchased Canadair from the government. Subsequently Bombardier bought Short Bros. (1989), Learjet (1990), half of De Havilland in 1992, and the remaining half in 1997.

These moves have paid off handsomely. The three divisions are each generating substantial revenues, combining for more than $7 billion in sales in 1996. The Ski-Doo unit has added the Sea-Doo to its production, and both products are steadily increasing their worldwide markets: Bombardier currently controls nearly 30 per cent of the snowmobile market and 50 per cent of the personal watercraft market. In 1997 Bombardier's rail and subway division had amongst its contracts a $1.3-billion deal to build subway cars for New York, and a $600-million project for a high-speed train between Boston and Washington. And the aerospace division is the company's star performer.

Laurent Beaudoin's leadership capabilities earned Bombardier the status of the most-respected corporation in Canada, in a CEO poll.

But if leadership is so important, it's only natural to ask: Are leaders born or made? What differentiates leaders from nonleaders? What can you do if you want to be seen as a leader? In this chapter we'll try to answer such questions.

SKI-DOO
www.ski-doo.com/

SEA-DOO
www.sea-doo.com/

Managers versus Leaders

Let's begin by clarifying the distinction between managers and leaders. Writers frequently confuse the two, although they are not necessarily the same.

Managers are appointed. They have legitimate power that allows them to reward and punish. Their ability to influence is based on the formal authority inherent in their positions. In contrast, leaders may either be appointed or emerge from within a group. Leaders can influence others to perform beyond the actions dictated by formal authority.

Should all managers be leaders? Conversely, should all leaders be managers? Because no one yet has been able to demonstrate through research or logical argument that leadership ability is a handicap to a manager, we can state that all managers should ideally be leaders. However, not all leaders necessarily have the capabilities to carry out other managerial functions, and thus not all should hold managerial positions. The fact that an individual can influence others does not indicate whether she can also plan, organize, and control. Given (if only ideally) that all managers should be leaders, we will pursue the subject from a managerial perspective. Therefore, **leaders** in this chapter mean those who are able to influence others and who possess managerial authority.

leaders
Those who are able to influence others and who possess managerial authority.

Trait Theories of Leadership

Ask the average person on the street what comes to mind when she thinks of leadership. You're likely to get a list of qualities such as intelligence, charisma, decisiveness, enthusiasm, strength, bravery, integrity, and self-confidence. These responses represent, in essence, **trait theories** of leadership. The search for traits or characteristics that differentiate leaders from nonleaders, though done in a more sophisticated manner than our on-the-street survey, dominated the early research efforts in the study of leadership.

trait theories
Theories isolating characteristics that differentiate leaders from nonleaders.

Is it possible to isolate one or more traits in individuals who are generally acknowledged to be leaders—for instance, Pierre Trudeau, Winston Churchill, Joan of Arc, Nelson Mandela, Mahatma Gandhi, Margaret Thatcher—that nonleaders do not possess? We may agree that these individuals meet our definition of a leader, but they represent individuals with utterly different characteristics. If the concept of traits was to prove valid, all leaders would have to possess specific characteristics.

Research efforts at isolating these traits resulted in a number of dead ends. Attempts failed to identify a set of traits that would always differentiate leaders from followers and effective leaders from ineffective leaders. Perhaps it was a bit optimistic

SNC-LAVALIN
www.snc-lavalin.com/
snc/index.htm

to believe that a set of consistent and unique personality traits could apply across the board to all effective leaders, whether they were in charge of the Hell's Angels, Montreal Expos, Federal Express, Petro-Canada, Vancouver General Hospital, or the Anglican Church of Canada.

However, attempts to identify traits consistently associated with leadership have been more successful. Six traits on which leaders are seen to differ from nonleaders include drive, the desire to lead, honesty and integrity, self-confidence, intelligence, and job-relevant knowledge.[2] These traits are briefly described in Exhibit 13-1.

Yet traits alone are not sufficient to explain leadership. Explanations based solely on traits ignore situational factors. Possessing the appropriate traits only makes

What traits characterize leaders like SNC-Lavalin CEO Guy Saint-Pierre? Research has identified six: drive, the desire to lead, honesty and integrity, self-confidence, intelligence, and job-related knowledge.

► **1. Drive.** Leaders exhibit a high effort level. They have a relatively high desire for achievement, they're ambitious, they have a lot of energy, they're tirelessly persistent in their activities, and they show initiative.

► **2. Desire to lead.** Leaders have a strong desire to influence and lead others. They demonstrate the willingness to take responsibility.

► **3. Honesty and integrity.** Leaders build trusting relationships between themselves and followers by being truthful or nondeceitful and by showing high consistency between word and deed.

► **4. Self-confidence.** Followers look to leaders for an absence of self-doubt. Leaders, therefore, need to show self-confidence in order to convince followers of the rightness of goals and decisions.

► **5. Intelligence.** Leaders need to be intelligent enough to gather, synthesize, and interpret large amounts of information; and to be able to create visions, solve problems, and make correct decisions.

► **6. Job-relevant knowledge.** Effective leaders have a high degree of knowledge about the company, industry, and technical matters. In-depth knowledge allows leaders to make well-informed decisions and to understand the implications of those decisions.

**Exhibit 13-1
Six Traits That Differentiate Leaders from Nonleaders**

Source: Shelly A. Kirkpatrick and Edwin A. Locke, "Leadership: Do Traits Really Matter?," *Academy of Management Executive*, May 1991, pp. 48–60.

it more likely that an individual will be an effective leader. She still has to take the right actions. And what is right in one situation is not necessarily right for a different situation. So while there has been some resurgent interest in traits during the past decade, a major movement away from trait theories began as early as the 1940s. Leadership research from the late 1940s through the mid-1960s emphasized the preferred behavioural styles that leaders demonstrated.

Behavioural Theories of Leadership

The inability to explain leadership solely from traits led researchers to look at the behaviour that specific leaders exhibited. Researchers wondered whether there was something unique in the behaviour of effective leaders. For example, do leaders tend to be more democratic than autocratic?

It was hoped that the **behavioural theories** would not only provide more definitive answers about the nature of leadership but, if successful, would also have practical implications quite different from those of the trait approach. If trait research had been successful, it would have provided a basis for selecting the "right" people to assume formal positions in organizations requiring leadership. In contrast, if behavioural studies were to turn up critical behavioural determinants of leadership, we could train people to be leaders.

A number of studies looked at behavioural styles. We shall briefly review the two most popular ones: the Ohio State University group and the University of Michigan group. Then we shall see how the concepts that these studies developed could be used to create a grid for looking at and appraising leadership styles.

behavioural theories
Theories identifying behaviours that differentiate effective from ineffective leaders.

What Was the Importance of the Ohio State Studies?

The most comprehensive and replicated of the behavioural theories resulted from research that began at Ohio State University in the late 1940s.[3] These studies sought to identify independent dimensions of leader behaviour. Beginning with more than 1,000 dimensions, they eventually narrowed down the list to two categories that accounted for most of the leadership behaviour described by employees. They called these two dimensions *initiating structure* and *consideration*.

initiating structure
The extent to which a leader defines and structures his role and those of employees to attain goals.

Initiating structure refers to the extent to which a leader is likely to define and structure his role and those of employees in the search for goal attainment. It includes behaviour that attempts to organize work, work relationships, and goals. For example, the leader who is characterized as high in initiating structure assigns group members to particular tasks, expects workers to maintain definite standards of performance, and emphasizes meeting deadlines.

consideration
The extent to which a person has job relationships characterized by mutual trust, respect for employees' ideas, and regard for their feelings.

Consideration is defined as the extent to which a person has job relationships characterized by mutual trust and respect for employees' ideas and feelings. A leader who is high in consideration helps employees with personal problems, is friendly and approachable, and treats all employees as equals. He shows concern for his followers' comfort, well-being, status, and satisfaction.

Extensive research based on these definitions found that a leader who is high in initiating structure and consideration (a "high-high" leader) achieved high employee performance and satisfaction more frequently than one who rated low on either consideration, initiating structure, or both. However, the high-high style did not always yield positive results. For example, leader behaviour characterized as high on initiating structure led to greater rates of grievances, absenteeism, and turnover and lower levels of job satisfaction for workers performing routine tasks. Other studies found that high consideration was negatively related to performance ratings of the leader by her manager. In conclusion, the Ohio State studies suggested that the high-high style generally produced positive outcomes, but enough exceptions were found to indicate that situational factors needed to be integrated into the theory (see Managers Who Made a Difference).

SURVEY
RESEARCH
CENTRE
(UNIVERSITY
OF MICHIGAN)
www.isr.umich.edu/src/

What Were the Leadership Dimensions of the University of Michigan Studies?

Leadership studies undertaken at the University of Michigan's Survey Research Center, at about the same time as those being done at Ohio State, had similar research objectives: to locate behavioural characteristics of leaders that were related to performance effectiveness. The Michigan group also came up with two dimensions of leadership behaviour, which they labelled *employee oriented* and *production oriented*.[4]

employee oriented
Leadership style that emphasizes interpersonal relations.

Leaders who were **employee oriented** were described as emphasizing interpersonal relations; they took a personal interest in the needs of their employees and accepted individual differences among members. The **production-oriented** leaders, in contrast, tended to emphasize the technical or task aspects of the job, were concerned mainly with accomplishing their group's tasks, and regarded group members as a means to that end.

production oriented
Leadership style that emphasizes technical aspects of the job.

The conclusions of the Michigan researchers strongly favoured leaders who were employee oriented. Employee-oriented leaders were associated with higher group productivity and higher job satisfaction. Production-oriented leaders were associated with lower group productivity and lower worker satisfaction.

MANAGERS WHO MADE A DIFFERENCE

Douglas Hallett: ELI Eco Logic

ELI ECO
LOGIC
INTERNATIONAL
INC.
www.eco-logic-
intl.com/

Great ideas sometimes come upon us in strange forms. For Doug Hallett, at the time a senior scientist for the government, a great idea came in a dream. Hallett's view of the occurrence is straightforward: "Musicians dream in melody. I'm a chemist, so I dream in equations." What he dreamed was a technique for the disposal of toxic waste, a technique David Suzuki has described as "stunningly and elegantly simple." Leaving his job with the Canadian government, Hallett developed a machine he calls a Destructor. This machine (price tag: $10 million) has the ability to destroy a wide array of hazardous wastes without incinerating them and without producing uncontrolled emissions. Moreover, the Destructor can perform at a cost that is competitive with incineration, while being a completely portable technology.[5]

But the process of getting ELI Eco Logic up and running was not so simple. Hallett discovered, as many entrepreneurs do, that having a dream and bringing it to fruition are two very different things. Funding for a prototype was hard to find. The banks would not touch a project involving such unproven technology. Environment Canada even refused to provide research money. At this point Hallett cleverly took a good look at his business and the environment in which it was operating. He discovered that "95 per cent of the research money available in Canada is spent on defence." The solution: become a defence contractor.

Now with the Destructor fully developed, Hallett can move into a multitude of markets. The Destructor is unbelievably efficient. In 1996, a machine destroyed 99.999999 per cent of toxins (nerve gas and chemical agents) fed into it by U.S. army personnel. The technology has produced similar results dealing with toxic sediment (containing coal tar and PCBs) from Hamilton harbour, as well as a PCB-ridden dump in Bay City, Michigan.

ELI Eco Logic, still a relatively small company based in Rockwood, Ontario, recognizes its phenomenal growth potential. Virtually anywhere there is industry, there is chemical waste. At this point ELI Eco Logic is involved in discussions with companies in Spain, South Africa, and the Middle East. But as sad as it is to admit, there is enough work to be done in North America to keep Doug Hallett busy for a long time.▼

What Is the Managerial Grid?

managerial grid
A two-dimensional portrayal of leadership based on concerns for people and for production.

The **managerial grid** is a two-dimensional view of leadership style developed by Robert Blake and Jane Mouton.[6] They proposed a managerial grid based on the styles of "concern for people" and "concern for production," which essentially represent the Ohio State dimensions of consideration and initiating structure and the Michigan dimensions of employee orientation and production orientation.

The grid, depicted in Exhibit 13-2, has nine possible positions along each axis, creating 81 different positions into which a leader's style may fall. The grid does not show the results produced but rather the dominating factors in a leader's thinking in regard to getting results. That is, although there are 81 positions on the grid, the five key positions identified by Blake and Mouton focus on the four corners of the grid and a middle-ground area.

From their findings, Blake and Mouton concluded that managers perform best using a 9,9 style. Unfortunately, the grid offers no answers to the question of what makes a manager, just a framework for conceptualizing leadership style. In fact, there is little substantive evidence to support the conclusion that a 9,9 style is most effective in all situations.[7]

Exhibit 13-2   The Managerial Grid

Source: Reprinted by permission of *Harvard Business Review*. An exhibit from "Breakthrough in Organization Development" by Robert R. Blake, Jane S. Mouton, Louis B. Barnes, and Larry E. Greiner, November–December 1964, p. 136. Copyright © 1964 by the President and Fellows of Harvard College; all rights reserved.

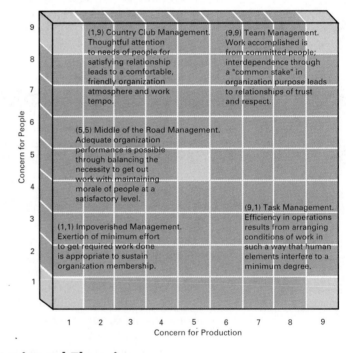

What Did the Behavioural Theories Teach Us About Leadership?

We have described the most popular and important attempts to explain leadership in terms of behaviour. Obviously there were other efforts,[8] but they faced the same problem that confronted the Ohio State and Michigan researchers: they had very little success in identifying consistent relationships between patterns of leadership behaviour and successful performance. General statements could not be made because results would vary over different ranges of circumstances. What was missing was consideration of the situational factors that influence success or failure. For example, would we be inclined to put up with Mackenzie King if his time had been in the 1990s? Without hockey's existence would Wayne Gretzky have stood out so distinctly in another field? Would Bill Gates have risen to prominence in the 1960s? It seems quite unlikely, yet the behavioural approaches we have described could not clarify such situational factors.

Contingency Theories of Leadership

It became increasingly clear to those studying the leadership phenomenon that predicting leadership success involved something more complex than isolating a few traits or preferable behaviours. The failure to obtain consistent results led to a new focus on situational influences. The relationship between leadership style and effectiveness suggested that under condition *a*, style *X* would be appropriate, whereas style Y would be more suitable for condition *b*, and style *Z* for condition *c*. But what were the conditions *a*, *b*, *c*, and so forth? It was one thing to say that leadership effectiveness depended on the situation and another to be able to isolate those situational conditions.

Several approaches to isolating key situational variables have proven more successful than others and, as a result, have gained wider recognition. We shall consider three of these: the Fiedler model, path-goal theory, and the leader-participation model.

What Is the Fiedler Model?

The first comprehensive contingency model for leadership was developed by Fred Fiedler.[9] The **Fiedler contingency model** proposes that effective group performance depends upon the proper match between the leader's style of interacting with her employees and the degree to which the situation gives control and influence to the leader. Fiedler developed the **least-preferred coworker (LPC) questionnaire** that purports to measure whether a person is task or relationship oriented. Further, he isolated three situational criteria—**leader-member relations**, **task structure**, and **position power**—that he believes can be manipulated to create the proper match with the behavioural orientation of the leader. In a sense the Fiedler model is an outgrowth of trait theory, since the LPC questionnaire is a simple psychological test. However, Fiedler goes significantly beyond trait and behavioural approaches by isolating situations, relating an individual's personality to the situation, and then predicting leadership effectiveness as a function of the two.

Fiedler believes a key factor in leadership success to be an individual's basic leadership style. Thus, he first tries to find out what that basic style is. Fiedler created the LPC questionnaire for this purpose. As shown in Exhibit 13-3, it contains 16 pairs of contrasting adjectives. Respondents are asked to think of all the coworkers they have ever had and to describe the one person they least enjoyed working with by rating him on a scale of 1 to 8 for each of the 16 sets of adjectives. Fiedler believes that on the basis of the respondents' answers to this LPC questionnaire, one can determine most people's basic leadership style.

If the least-preferred coworker is described in relatively positive terms (a high LPC score), then the respondent is primarily interested in good personal relations with this coworker. That is, if you describe the person you are least able to work with in favourable terms, Fiedler would label you relationship oriented. In contrast, if you see the least-preferred coworker in relatively unfavourable terms (a low LPC score), you are primarily interested in productivity and thus would be labeled task oriented.

Fiedler contingency model
The theory that effective groups depend on a proper match between a leader's style of interacting with employees and the degree to which the situation gives control and influence to the leader.

least-preferred coworker (LPC) questionnaire
A questionnaire that measures whether a person is task or relationship oriented.

leader-member relations
The degree of confidence, trust, and respect subordinates have in their leader.

task structure
The degree to which the job assignments are procedurized.

position power
The degree of influence a leader has over power variables such as hiring, firing, discipline, promotions, and salary increases.

Exhibit 13-3
Fiedler's LPC Scale

Source: From Fred E. Fiedler and Martin M. Chemers, *Leadership and Effective Management* (Glenview, IL: Scott, Foresman & Co., 1974). Reprinted by permission of authors.

	8	7	6	5	4	3	2	1	
Pleasant	8	7	6	5	4	3	2	1	Unpleasant
Friendly	8	7	6	5	4	3	2	1	Unfriendly
Rejecting	1	2	3	4	5	6	7	8	Accepting
Helpful	8	7	6	5	4	3	2	1	Frustrating
Unenthusiastic	1	2	3	4	5	6	7	8	Enthusiastic
Tense	1	2	3	4	5	6	7	8	Relaxed
Distant	1	2	3	4	5	6	7	8	Close
Cold	1	2	3	4	5	6	7	8	Warm
Cooperative	8	7	6	5	4	3	2	1	Uncooperative
Supportive	8	7	6	5	4	3	2	1	Hostile
Boring	1	2	3	4	5	6	7	8	Interesting
Quarrelsome	1	2	3	4	5	6	7	8	Harmonious
Self-assured	8	7	6	5	4	3	2	1	Hesitant
Efficient	8	7	6	5	4	3	2	1	Inefficient
Gloomy	1	2	3	4	5	6	7	8	Cheerful
Open	8	7	6	5	4	3	2	1	Guarded

How effective will the leader of this group be? According to the Fiedler contingency model, based on the individual's LPC, effective leadership will be contingent on the situation he leads. That is, an effective leader is one whose leadership style fits the job situation.

Using the LPC instrument, Fiedler is able to place most respondents into one or the other of these two leadership styles (see Details on a Management Classic).

Once an individual's basic leadership style has been assessed through the LPC, it is necessary to evaluate the circumstances and match the leader with the situation. Fiedler has identified three contingency dimensions that, he argues, define the key situational factors for determining leadership effectiveness. These are leader-member relations (the degree of confidence, trust, and respect employees have in their leader); task structure (the degree to which the job assignments are structured or unstructured); and position power (the degree of influence a leader has over power variables such as hiring, firing, discipline, promotions, and salary increases). These situational dimensions are then evaluated. Leader-member relations are either good or poor, task structure either high or low, and position power either strong or weak. Altogether, by mixing the three contingency variables, there are potentially eight different situations or categories in which a leader could find herself.

DETAILS ON A MANAGEMENT CLASSIC

Fred Fiedler and the Fiedler Contingency Model of Leadership

The Fiedler model proposes matching an individual's LPC and an assessment of the three contingency variables to achieve maximum leadership effectiveness. In his studies of more than 1,200 groups, in which he compared relationship- versus task-oriented leadership styles in each of the eight situational categories, Fiedler concluded that task-oriented leaders tended to perform better in situations that were very favourable to them and in situations that were very unfavourable (see Exhibit MC13-1). Fiedler would predict that when faced with a category I, II, III, VII, or VIII situation, task-oriented leaders perform better. Relationship-oriented leaders, however, perform better in moderately favourable situations—categories IV through VI.

Remember that according to Fiedler an individual's leadership style is fixed. Therefore, there are really only two ways in which to improve leader effectiveness. First, you can change the leader to fit the situation. For example, if a group situation rates as highly unfavourable but is currently led by a relationship-oriented manager, the group's performance could be improved by replacing that manager with one who is task-oriented. The second alternative would be to change the situation to fit the leader. That could be done by restructuring tasks or increasing or decreasing the power that the leader has to control factors such as salary increases, promotions, and disciplinary actions.

As a whole, reviews of the major studies undertaken to test the overall validity of the Fiedler model show there is considerable evidence to support it.[10] But there are problems with the LPC and the practical use of the model that need to be addressed.[11] Nonetheless, Fiedler has made an important contribution toward understanding leadership effectiveness. His work continues to be a dominant input in the development of contingency explanations of leadership effectiveness.▼

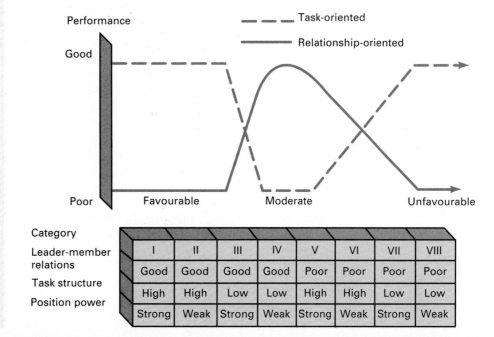

**Exhibit MC13-1
The Findings of
the Fiedler Model**

Category	I	II	III	IV	V	VI	VII	VIII
Leader-member relations	Good	Good	Good	Good	Poor	Poor	Poor	Poor
Task structure	High	High	Low	Low	High	High	Low	Low
Position power	Strong	Weak	Strong	Weak	Strong	Weak	Strong	Weak

It's important to note that Fiedler assumes that an individual's leadership style is fixed. This means that if a situation requires a task-oriented leader and the person in that leadership position is relationship oriented, either the situation has to be modified or the leader has to be removed and replaced if optimum effectiveness is to be achieved. Fiedler argues that leadership style is innate—you can't change your style to fit changing situations!

How Does Path-Goal Theory Operate?

path-goal theory
The theory that a leader's behaviour is acceptable to employees insofar as they view it as a source of either immediate or future satisfaction.

Currently, one of the most respected approaches to leadership is **path-goal theory**. Developed by Robert House, path-goal theory is a contingency model of leadership that extracts key elements from the Ohio State leadership research and the expectancy theory of motivation.[12]

The essence of the theory is that it's the leader's job to assist his followers in attaining their goals and to provide the necessary direction and support to ensure that their goals are compatible with the overall objectives of the group or organization. The term "path-goal" is derived from the belief that effective leaders clarify the path to help their followers get from where they are to the achievement of their work goals, and make the journey along the path easier by reducing roadblocks and pitfalls.

According to path-goal theory, a leader's behaviour is acceptable to employees to the degree that they view it as an immediate source of satisfaction or as a means of future satisfaction. A leader's behaviour is motivational to the degree that it (1) makes employee need-satisfaction contingent on effective performance, and (2) provides the coaching, guidance, support, and rewards that are necessary for effective performance. To test these statements, House identified four leadership behaviours. The directive leader lets employees know what is expected of them, schedules work to be done, and gives specific guidance as to how to accomplish tasks. This type of leadership closely parallels the Ohio State dimension of initiating structure. The supportive leader is friendly and shows concern for the needs of employees. This type of leadership is essentially synonymous with the Ohio State dimension of consideration. The participative leader consults with employees and uses their suggestions before making a decision. The achievement-oriented leader sets challenging goals and expects employees to perform at their highest level. In contrast to Fiedler's view of a leader's behaviour, House assumes that leaders are flexible. Path-goal theory implies that the same leader can display any or all of these leadership styles depending on the situation.

As Exhibit 13-4 illustrates, path-goal theory proposes two classes of situational or contingency variables that moderate the leadership behaviour-outcome relationship—those in the environment that are outside the control of the employee (task structure, the formal authority system, and the work group) and those that are part of the personal characteristics of the employee (locus of control, experience, and perceived ability). Environmental factors determine the type of leader behaviour required as a complement if subordinate outcomes are to be maximized, while personal characteristics of the subordinate determine how the environment and leader behaviour are interpreted. The theory proposes that leader behaviour will be ineffective when it is redundant with sources of environmental structure or incongruent with subordinate characteristics.

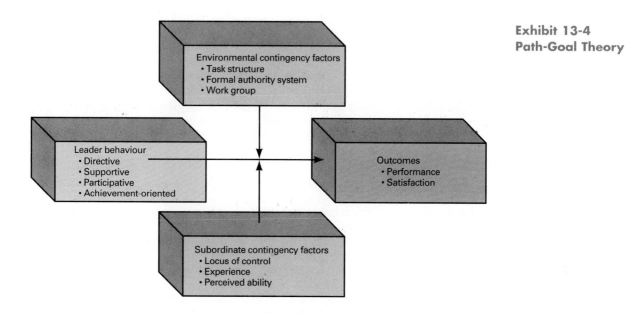

Exhibit 13-4
Path-Goal Theory

What Is the Leader-Participation Model?

Back in 1973, Victor Vroom and Phillip Yetton developed a **leader-participation model** that related leadership behaviour and participation to decision making.[13] Recognizing that task structures have varying demands for routine and nonroutine activities, these researchers argued that leader behaviour must adjust to reflect the task structure. Vroom and Yetton's model was normative; it provided a sequential set of rules that should be followed in determining the form and amount of participation in decision making, as determined by different types of situations. The model was a decision tree incorporating seven contingencies (whose relevance could be identified by making yes or no choices) and five alternative leadership styles.

More recent work by Vroom and Arthur Jago has resulted in a revision of this model.[14] The new model retains the same five alternative leadership styles but expands the contingency variables to 12—from the leader making the decision completely by herself, to sharing the problem with the group and developing a consensus decision. These are listed in Exhibit 13-5.

Research testing the original leader-participation model was very encouraging.[15] But unfortunately, the model is far too complex for the typical manager to use regularly. In fact, Vroom and Jago have developed a computer program to guide managers through all the decision branches in the revised model. Although we obviously cannot do justice to the model's sophistication in this discussion, the model has provided us with some solid, empirically supported insights into contingency variables of leadership. For instance, the leader-participation model confirms that leadership research should be directed at the situation rather than at the person. It probably makes more sense to talk about autocratic and participative situations rather than autocratic and participative leaders. As did House in his path-goal theory, Vroom, Yetton, and Jago argue against the notion that leader behaviour is inflexible. The leader-participation model assumes that the leader can adapt his style to different situations.

leader-participation model
A leadership theory that provides a set of rules to determine the form and amount of participative decision making in different situations.

QR:	Quality Requirement:	How important is the technical quality of this decision?
CR:	Commitment Requirement:	How important is employee commitment to the decision?
LI:	Leader Information:	Do you have sufficient information to make a high-quality decision?
ST:	Problem Structure:	Is the problem well-structured?
CP:	Commitment Probability:	If you were to make this decision by yourself, is it reasonably certain that your employees would be committed to the decision?
GC:	Goal Congruence:	Do employees share the organizational goals to be attained in solving this problem?
CO:	Employee Conflict:	Is conflict among employees over preferred solutions probable?
SI:	Employee Information:	Do employees have sufficient information to make a high-quality decision?
TC:	Time Constraint:	Does a critically severe time constraint limit your ability to involve employees?
GD:	Geographical Dispersion:	Are the costs involved in bringing together geographically dispersed employees prohibitive?
MT:	Motivation Time:	How important is it to you to minimize the time it takes to make the decision?
MD:	Motivation-Development:	How important is it to you to maximize the opportunities for employee development?

Exhibit 13-5 Contingency Variables in the Revised Leader-Participation Model

Source: V.H. Vroom and A.G. Jago, *The New Leadership: Managing Participation in Organizations* (Englewood Cliffs, N.J.: Prentice Hall, Inc., 1988), pp. 111–12. With permission.

Is Leadership Ever Irrelevant?

In keeping with the contingency spirit, we want to conclude this section by offering this notion: The belief that some leadership style will always be effective regardless of the situation may not be true. Leadership may not always be important. Data from numerous studies demonstrate that in many situations any behaviours a leader exhibits are irrelevant. Certain individual, job, and organizational variables can act as "substitutes for leadership," negating the influence of the leader.[16]

For instance, characteristics of employees such as experience, training, "professional" orientation, or need for independence can neutralize the effect of leadership. These characteristics can replace the need for a leader's support or ability to create structure and reduce task ambiguity. Similarly, jobs that are inherently unambiguous and routine or that are intrinsically satisfying may place fewer demands on the leadership variable. Finally, such organizational characteristics as explicit formalized goals, rigid rules and procedures, or cohesive work groups can act in the place of formal leadership.

Canadians have made some important contributions to leadership thinking. Bill Reddin, a former professor at the University of New Brunswick, developed a contingency approach to leadership in 1970 that was based on the idea that "the effectiveness of any behaviour depends on the situation in which it is used."[17] He argued that a manager must be able to read a situation in order to know how best to manage it. Effectiveness is not simply a matter of leadership style, it's a matter of using a particular style at the right time. Reddin's 3-D theory of management looks at how using a particular style of leadership in one situation can be ineffective, while using it in another situation can be effective. So leaders must have a sensitivity to the situation in which they find themselves. Reddin's theory helps to explain why leaders can turn from being highly successful to being failures while still doing the same sorts of things. General George Patton is a good example—the right man for the moment, but ineffective once the need for his skills was over. IBM and General Motors both encountered huge problems because their leadership style remained constant while the situation changed around them.

Rick Roskin, a professor at Memorial University in Newfoundland, has also made a significant contribution to thinking on leadership with his M.ach One theory.[18] Roskin looked at the data on which the Ohio State model was based and found that while the findings showed clusters that could be interpreted as structure and consideration, there was a lot of the basic data that remained unexplained. He examined it more closely and recognized that there was indeed a *third* type of behaviour in which managers engage: bringing together the diverse activities and outputs of the people who report to them. This is the function of *integration* and *coordination*. Roskin's model is three-dimensional. And, like Reddin, he has developed a method of analysing the situational demands of a job, which means that managers can determine the optimal leadership style behaviour for a particular job.

YOUNG CANADIANS

Jeff Spencer: Tim Hortons

Jeff Spencer had not worked for Tim Hortons in years when he was given a great opportunity—to try to turn around a struggling store in Lloydminster, Alberta. He and his friend Dave (who now manages eight Tim Hortons in Nova Scotia) put in long, long hours to get the store back on its feet. In a few years, Jeff was offered the chance to buy the store. It meant a major bank loan, but Jeff became the youngest Tim Hortons franchise owner in Canada, at the age of 26. Today the store continually breaks sales and profit records.

Emerging Approaches to Leadership

We conclude our review of leadership theories by presenting two emerging approaches to the subject: charismatic leadership and transactional versus transformational leadership. If there is one theme that underlies these approaches, it is that they take a more practical view of leadership than have previous theories (with the exception of trait theories, of course). That is, both approaches look again at leadership the way the average "person on the street" does.

What Is Charismatic Leadership Theory?

charismatic leadership theory
Followers make attributions of heroic or extraordinary leadership abilities when they observe certain behaviours.

In Chapter 10, we discussed attribution theory in relation to perception. **Charismatic leadership theory** is an extension of that theory. It says that followers make attributions of heroic or extraordinary leadership abilities when they observe certain behaviours.[19] Studies on charismatic leadership have, for the most part, been directed at identifying behaviours that differentiate charismatic leaders—the Pierre Trudeaus and Ronald Reagans of the world—from their noncharismatic counterparts.

Several authors have attempted to identify personal characteristics of the charismatic leader. Robert House (of path-goal fame) has identified three: extremely high confidence, dominance, and strong convictions.[20] Warren Bennis, after studying 90 of the most effective and successful leaders in the United States, found that they had four common competencies: they had a compelling vision or sense of purpose; they could communicate that vision in clear terms that their followers could readily identify with; they demonstrated consistency and focus in the pursuit of their vision; and they knew their own strengths and capitalized on them.[21] The most recent and comprehensive analysis, however, has been completed by Jay Conger and Rabindra Kanungo at McGill University.[22] Among their conclusions, they propose that charismatic leaders have an idealized goal that they want to achieve and a strong personal commitment to that goal, are perceived as unconventional, are assertive and self-confident, and are perceived as agents of radical change rather than managers of the status quo. Exhibit 13-6 summarizes the key characteristics that appear to differentiate charismatic leaders from noncharismatic ones.

What can we say about the charismatic leader's effect on his followers? There is an increasing body of research that shows impressive correlations between charismatic leadership and high performance and satisfaction among followers.[23] People working for charismatic leaders are motivated to exert extra work effort and, because they like their leader, express greater satisfaction.

On the contrary, charismatic leadership may not always be needed to achieve high levels of employee performance. It may be most appropriate when the follower's task has an ideological component.[24] This may explain why, when charismatic leaders surface, it is more likely to be in politics, religion, or a business firm that is introducing a radically new product or facing a life-threatening crisis. Such conditions tend to involve ideological issues. Second, charismatic leaders may be ideal for pulling an organization through a crisis but become a liability to an organization once the crisis and need for dramatic change subsides.[25] Why? Because the charismatic leader's overwhelming self-confidence often becomes problematic. She is unable to listen to others, becomes uncomfortable when challenged by aggressive employees, and begins to hold an unjustifiable belief in her "rightness" on issues.

How Do Transactional Leaders Differ from Transformational Leaders?

transactional leaders
Leaders who guide or motivate their followers in the direction of established goals by clarifying role and task requirements.

The second section of research we'll touch on is the recent interest in differentiating transformational leaders from transactional leaders.[26] As you'll see, because transformational leaders are also charismatic, there is some overlap between this topic and our discussion above on charismatic leadership.

Most of the leadership theories presented in this chapter—for instance, the Ohio State studies, Fiedler's model, path-goal theory, and the leader-participation model—have been addressing **transactional leaders**. These leaders guide or motivate their followers

▶ 1. **Self-confidence.** Charismatic leaders have complete confidence in their judgment and ability.

▶ 2. **Vision.** They have an idealized goal that proposes a future better than the status quo. The greater the disparity between this idealized goal and the status quo, the more likely that followers will attribute extraordinary vision to the leader.

▶ 3. **Ability to articulate the vision.** They are able to clarify and state the vision in terms that are understandable to others. This articulation demonstrates an understanding of the followers' needs and, hence, acts as a motivating force.

▶ 4. **Strong convictions about the vision.** Charismatic leaders are perceived as being strongly committed and willing to take on high personal risk, incur high costs, and engage in self-sacrifice to achieve their vision.

▶ 5. **Behaviour that is out of the ordinary.** They engage in behaviour that is perceived as being novel, unconventional, and counter to norms. When successful, these behaviours evoke surprise and admiration in followers.

▶ 6. **Appearance as a change agent.** Charismatic leaders are perceived as agents of radical change rather than as caretakers of the status quo.

▶ 7. **Environmental sensitivity.** They are able to make realistic assessments of the environmental constraints and resources needed to bring about change.

**Exhibit 13-6
Key Characteristics of
Charismatic Leaders**

Source: Based on Jay A. Conger and R.N. Kanungo, "Behavioral Dimensions of Charismatic Leadership," in Jay A. Conger and R.N. Kanungo, *Charismatic Leadership* (San Francisco: Jossey-Bass, 1988), p. 91.

in the direction of established goals by clarifying role and task requirements. But there is another type of leader who inspires followers to transcend their own self-interests for the good of the organization and is capable of having a profound and extraordinary effect on his followers. These are **transformational leaders**. They pay attention to the concerns and developmental needs of individual followers; they change followers' awareness of issues by helping those followers to look at old problems in new ways; and they are able to excite, arouse, and inspire followers to put extra effort into achieving group goals.

transformational leaders
Leaders who provide individualized consideration, intellectual stimulation, and possess charisma.

Transactional and transformational leadership should not be viewed as opposing approaches to getting things done.[27] Transformational leadership is built on top of transactional leadership. Transformational leadership produces levels of employee effort and performance that go beyond what would occur with a transactional approach alone. Moreover, transformational leadership is more than charisma. "The purely charismatic [leader] may want followers to adopt the charismatic's world view and go no further; the transformational leader will attempt to instill in followers the ability to question not only established views but eventually those established by the leader."[28]

The evidence supporting the superiority of transformational leadership over the transactional variety is overwhelmingly impressive (see Ethical Dilemmas in Management). For instance, a number of studies with U.S., Canadian, and German military officers found, at every level, that transformational leaders were evaluated as being more effective than their transactional counterparts.[29] Managers at Federal Express who were rated by their followers as exhibiting more transformational leadership were evaluated by their immediate supervisors as higher performers and as more promotable.[30] In summary, the overall evidence indicates that transformational, as compared with transactional, leadership is more strongly correlated with lower turnover rates, higher productivity, and higher employee satisfaction.[31]

ETHICAL DILEMMAS IN MANAGEMENT

IS IT UNETHICAL TO CREATE CHARISMA?

In 1998, no list of charismatic Canadian business leaders would have been complete without names such as Michael Cowpland, Conrad Black, and Edgar Bronfman Jr. They personified the contemporary idea of charisma in the corporate world. But are these men authentically charismatic figures or self-created images?

Each of these men employs a public relations firm or has public relations specialists on his staff to shape and hone his image. Conrad Black relishes his reputation as a media mogul, buying newspapers the world over. Edgar Bronfman Jr. is seen in the press as a stylish, shrewd, in-charge CEO—a major force in Hollywood (though his company's quality liquor-producing division is not such popular media fodder).

One view of these men is that they are authentically charismatic leaders whose actions and achievements have caught the fancy of the media. This view assumes that these leaders couldn't hide their charismatic qualities. It was just a matter of time before they were found out and gained the public's eye. Another view—certainly a more cynical one—proposes that these men consciously created an image that they wanted to project and then purposely went about doing things that would draw attention to, and confirm, that image. They are not inherently charismatic individuals but rather highly astute manipulators of symbols, circumstances, and the media. In support of this latter position, one can identify leaders such as Laurent Beaudoin at Bombardier, Bobbie Gaunt at Ford Canada, and Clayton Woitas at Calgary's Renaissance Energy, who are widely viewed as charismatic in their firms and industries but are relatively unknown in the popular press.

Is charismatic leadership an inherent quality within a person, a label thrust upon an individual, or a purposely and carefully moulded image? If charisma can be derived from the media, is it unethical for a person to engage in practices whose primary purposes are to create or enhance this perception? Is it unethical to "create" charisma? What do you think?

A Special Case of Leadership: First-line Supervision

Supervision is often conveniently lumped together with all levels in the managerial hierarchy, yet this camouflages the fact that supervisors are uniquely different from all other managers. This difference, together with the growing recognition that the job of supervisor is undergoing rapid change, justifies a separate discussion. In the following pages, we will highlight the factors that make the supervisory position a special case of leadership, show how the supervisor's role suffers from ambiguous interpretations, and demonstrate how the supervisor's job is likely to change in the near term.

Why Are Supervisors Considered First-level Managers?

supervision
First-level management task of directing the activities of immediate employees.

The term **supervision** is often used to refer to the activity of directing the immediate activities of employees. In such a context, it can occur at all levels. However, we use a narrower perspective. We consider supervision to be a first-level management task and supervisors to be first-level managers. That is, counting from the bottom of the traditional pyramid-shaped organization, they represent the first, or lowest, level in the management hierarchy.

As first-level managers, supervisors must, by definition, occupy the only level of management charged with the responsibility of directing the work of nonmanagerial employees. It is true, of course, that all managers may direct activities of their staff, but the direct responsibility of nonsupervisory managers is to work for other managers. Therefore, only supervisors are directly responsible for the daily activities of operative employees.

What's Unique About Being a Supervisor?

We have already noted one of the unique characteristics of supervisors—they don't direct activities of other managers. In addition, there are specific distinctive characteristics that create problems peculiar to first-level managers. These arise from the supervisor relying heavily on technical expertise; having to communicate to both managers and operative employees; coping with role conflict; coping with constrained authority; and being management's representative to operative employees (see Exhibit 13-7).

How Is the Supervisor's Role Different?

Interpretations of the supervisor's role in an organization have been very inconsistent. The position has been described as everything from the "critical link" in an organization to a "necessary evil." A synthesis of five such descriptions of the supervisor's role is shown in Exhibit 13-8.[32]

**Exhibit 13-7
Unique Characteristics
of Being a Supervisor**

▶ **1. Relying heavily on technical expertise.** Supervisors are required to know the job they supervise. Unlike other managers who are heavily oriented toward planning and controlling, supervisors spend a large portion of their time leading and overseeing the activities of operative employees.

▶ **2. Communicating to both managers and operative employees.** Communications is a problem at all levels in the organization. However, it is particularly a problem for supervisors. Middle- and top-level managers converse with managers both above and below them, in many cases with people who share their educational backgrounds, experiences, and needs. On the other hand, supervisors are required to communicate with two distinct groups—managers and workers. Therefore, they must be able to blend the experiences, expectations, and needs of these divergent groups.

▶ **3. Coping with role conflict.** Supervisors are neither fish nor fowl. They're not operatives, and although they are officially classified as management, they are often not accepted by other managers. A supervisor may be assumed to be like any other manager, but her activities, status, and security are quite different.

▶ **4. Coping with constrained authority.** Sixty years ago, supervisors had complete authority. In the production area, for example, the foreman was the biggest, meanest, and toughest. His word was law. Today, however, key personnel decisions are determined by the conditions of the labour-management collective bargaining agreement or have been centralized in HRM departments.

▶ **5. Being management's representative.** The final problem unique to supervisors is that to the operatives they are *the organization*. Rules, policies, procedures, and other dictates from above are implemented at the supervisory level. So when operatives think of management, their main point of reference is their supervisors.

Exhibit 13-8
Different Views of the Supervisor's Role

Source: Adapted from Keith Davis, *Human Behavior at Work: Organizational Behavior*, 6th ed. (New York: McGraw-Hill, 1981), p. 142. With permission.

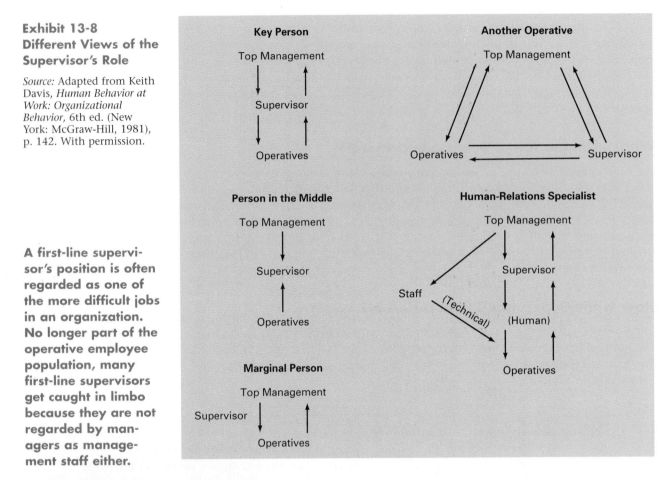

A first-line supervisor's position is often regarded as one of the more difficult jobs in an organization. No longer part of the operative employee population, many first-line supervisors get caught in limbo because they are not regarded by managers as management staff either.

A supervisor may be viewed as the key person in getting the work done. She is the hub in the communication wheel, with every crucial organizational activity related to generating the final product or service revolving around her. However, a supervisor may be seen as the person in the middle. She is forced to interact with, and reconcile, the different frames of references, experiences, and needs of managers and operative employees—thus serving as a buffer between the two groups.

At times, however, supervisors can be viewed as being marginal people. This stigma may derive from being powerless in the organizational hierarchy, left out of, or on the margin of, the principal decisions and influences that affect their unit. This marginal status is often reinforced by their being held accountable for their units' performance but with authority that is often extremely confining. For instance, they may be bypassed on union matters, which are negotiated above them, or constrained by the grievance procedure that subjects their decision to review. Such constraints, plus the abundance of rules and procedures, frequently make supervisors powerless in dealing with both operative employees and nonsupervisory managers.

Supervisors may also be viewed as glorified operative employees. This can be reinforced because supervisors frequently lack authority, implement other people's decisions, and strictly follow instructions. However, the legal interpretation since the 1940s has been that supervisors are members of the management team. Unfortunately, the way they are treated is frequently at odds with their legal status.

A final view of the supervisor's role is that of a staff specialist concerned with caring for the human or people side of the operations—a human relations specialist. They must deal with everyday problems that employees may have. As such, it can be said that supervisors get the work done best by getting along with others and by gaining cooperation and compliance from their operative employees.

It is difficult to accept any of the descriptions above as characteristic of all supervisors, but there is some truth in each of them. We have not presented these five roles to arrive at a universal description of the supervisor but to show the differing perceptions of the supervisor's position. The supervisor truly holds a unique position in the managerial hierarchy—one that is unlike any other management position. Of course, that position continues to change today!

Todd McFarlane: Spawn

Calgary-born Todd McFarlane's comic-book creation Spawn has been the number-one seller in North America since its beginnings in 1992. In 1997, *Spawn*, the movie, went to number one at the box office. McFarlane has not only retained control of his creation, he has also overseen the development of action figures, CD-ROM and video games, and a cartoon TV show. McFarlane runs what he calls The Spawn Empire at home in an office above his garage.

How Is the Supervisor's Role Changing in Today's Organizations?

A number of forces are reshaping the supervisor's job in today's organizations. Primary among them are changing technology in the workplace, new organizational designs, and ideas about appropriate leadership styles.

What Effect Does Changing Technology Have on Supervisory Roles?
Computer-based technology is changing the work of both blue- and white-collar employees. This, in turn, is changing the supervisor's role.

More and more white-collar workers are performing clerical tasks and data analyses at a video display terminal. Supervisors of these employees are thus confronted with new challenges. They have to understand the capabilities of the software programs that their employees use in order to teach new employees and to respond to problems as they occur. They also have to deal with the increasingly difficult problems of coordinating integrated office systems. Computers are now linking data entry equipment, printers, reproduction machines, telecommunications systems, and the like. Today, when problems occur in the office, they are more difficult to identify and broader in impact than they were when various office activities were separate and independent.

Among blue-collar workers, changing technology has introduced things such as robotics to assembly lines and computer-controlled production flows. In many cases, such innovations have reduced the need for supervisors to directly monitor and control operating activities.

In both offices and factories, computerized information systems will increasingly substitute for direct supervision. These systems will make it possible for management to obtain information about workers' quantity of output, quality level, ability to meet deadlines, and similar performance standards—without going to their supervisors.

Will New Organizational Designs Eliminate the Need for Supervisors? In Chapter 7, we introduced boundary-free organizations and self-managed work teams. One of the important characteristics of these groups is that they are self-governing; that is, they eliminate the need for the traditional supervisor.

There is no current evidence to suggest any imminent wholesale replacement of traditional supervised work groups with self-governing groups. However, to the degree that self-managed work teams increase in popularity, they represent a direct threat to the traditional authority of the supervisor. The supervisor's role in a self-governing group becomes predominately that of a coach and mentor responsible for developing members' roles, which many supervisors find unfamiliar (see Developing Management Skills).

How Are Supervisory Leadership Styles Changing? Old-style effective supervisors tended to be seen as hard-nosed disciplinarians who closely watched over their employees. This fit with the assumption that employees were low in intelligence, modestly skilled, and prone to goof off. It was the supervisor's job, therefore, to autocratically tell employees what to do and closely monitor their work. When performance wasn't satisfactory, supervisors were expected to take appropriate disciplinary actions.

Those assumptions no longer hold. Today's operative employees are better educated and skilled than those of previous generations. Moreover, these employees, and society as a whole, have changed their expectations of the supervisor's leadership behaviour. Supervisors are expected to exhibit a more "worker-sensitive" style. They should listen to what workers have to say and use the workers' ideas. The supervisor is now seen as a coach—the person who helps employees set goals, provides general direction for their attainment, and supports rather than intimidates. Not surprisingly, many old-line and experienced supervisors are having a difficult time accepting these changing expectations.

DEVELOPING MANAGEMENT SKILLS

▼

COACHING SKILLS

▲

► **1. Show genuine interest in the person as an individual, not merely as "an employee."** During times when people need assistance, they need to know you care. Give the individual your undivided attention.

► **2. Listen to the employee to better understand his world.** Don't interrupt the employee so you can talk. Concentrate on what is being said, and if you aren't sure about something said, ask for clarification.

► **3. Create a climate that contributes to a free and open exchange of ideas.** Do not judge what is being said. The minute you evaluate a statement or concern from an employee, she will probably "clam up."

► **4. Offer help and assistance when asked.** Don't dictate to the employee what to do. If help is asked for, be prepared and willing to assist.

► **5. Encourage your employees by being positive and upbeat.** Nothing can "motivate" a person more than having a genuinely positive and upbeat supervisor. The "yes you can" attitude can be the strength or nudge some employees need.

► **6. Focus on mistakes as learning opportunities.** We all make mistakes. Hopefully, though, we learn from them. Point out what was done incorrectly and how the employee can prevent it from occurring again. In this way, the mistake will lead to personal growth.

► **7. Reduce any obstacles that might hinder the employee from improving his performance.** Many variables can be contributing factors in a performance issue. For example, if the employee's computer system is outdated, and unable to speedily process the necessary statistics, no effort by the employee is likely to help. Such obstructions must be eliminated!

► **8. Express to the employee the value of her contribution to the department's goals.** Reinforce to the employee that she is valuable to the department. Each employee contributes in some significant way. Sometimes this is not fully understood by the employee.

► **9. Recognize and reward small improvements.** When efforts are being made by the employee, give credit. Don't expect a major turnaround overnight. It takes time and a lot of encouragement on your part. As the saying goes, How do you eat an elephant? One bite at a time!

► **10. Use a collaborative style.** Engage your employee in joint problem solving. Let him have a role in developing methods for correcting the problem. This increases the employee's commitment to the "new" requirements.

► **11. Model the qualities that you expect from your employees.** Don't have employees do as you say, have them do as you do. In the 1990s, it's called "walking the talk." The best teacher is a good example.

Summary

This summary is organized by the chapter Learning Objectives found on page 336.

1. Managers are appointed. They have legitimate power that allows them to reward and punish. Their ability to influence is founded upon the formal authority inherent in their positions. In contrast, leaders may either be appointed or emerge from within a group. Leaders can influence others to perform beyond the actions dictated by formal authority.

2. Six traits have been found on which leaders differ from nonleaders—drive, the desire to lead, honesty and integrity, self-confidence, intelligence, and job-relevant knowledge. Yet possession of these traits is no guarantee of leadership because it ignores situational factors.

3. The managerial grid focuses on two leader styles: concern for people and concern for production.

4. Fiedler's contingency model identifies three situational variables: leader-member relations, task structure, and position power. In situations that are highly favourable or highly unfavourable, task-oriented leaders tend to perform best. In moderately favourable or unfavourable situations, relations-oriented leaders are preferred.

5. The path-goal model proposes two classes of contingency variables—those in the environment and those that are part of the personal characteristics of the subordinate. Leaders select a specific behaviour—directive, supportive, participative, or achievement-oriented—that is congruent with the demands of the environment and the characteristics of the subordinate.

6. Leaders might not be important when individual variables replace the need for a leader's support or ability to create structure and reduce task ambiguity; when jobs are unambiguous, routine, or intrinsically satisfying; or when such organizational characteristics as explicit goals, rigid rules and procedures, or cohesive work groups act in place of formal leadership.

7. Charismatic leaders are self-confident, possess a vision of a better future, have a strong belief in that vision, engage in unconventional behaviours, and are perceived as agents of radical change.

8. Transactional leaders guide their followers in the direction of established goals by clarifying role and task requirements. Transformational leaders inspire followers to transcend their own self-interests for the good of the organization and are capable of having a profound and extraordinary effect on their followers.

9. Unique characteristics of being a supervisor include not directing the activities of other managers; a heavy reliance on technical expertise; having to communicate to both managers and operative employees; coping with role conflict; coping with constrained authority; and being management representative to the employees.

10. Supervisors' roles are changing in today's organizations due to technology changes, new organizational designs, and expectations for leadership styles.

Review and Discussion Questions

1. "All managers should be leaders, but not all leaders should be managers." Do you agree or disagree with this statement? Support your position.

2. Discuss the strengths and weaknesses of the trait theory of leadership.

3. What is the managerial grid? Contrast its approach to leadership with that of the Ohio State and Michigan groups.

4. Is "high-high" the most effective leadership style? Explain.

5. What similarities, if any, can you find among all the behavioural theories?

6. How is a least-preferred coworker determined? What is the importance of one's LPC for the Fiedler theory of leadership?

7. What are the contingencies in the path-goal theory of leadership?

8. What is charismatic leadership? Can people learn to be charismatic leaders? Explain.

9. "Charismatic leadership is always appropriate in organizations." Do you agree or disagree? Support your position.

10. Contrast transactional and transformational leaders.

11. What is a first-line supervisor? Why is that job unique in management?

12. "First-line supervision will become tomorrow's dinosaur. With the rapid changes in American businesses, there will be little need for supervisors for tomorrow's organizations." Do you agree or disagree with this statement? Explain.

Testing Your Comprehension

Circle the correct answer, then check yourself on page 472.

1. Which of the following BEST describes a leader?
   a) Being a leader means also being a manager.
   b) A leader always emerges from within the group.
   c) Leaders are appointed to their positions.
   d) Leaders can influence others beyond the formal authority of their position.

2. Theories of leadership isolating characteristics that differentiate leaders from nonleaders are called
   a) behavioural theories of leadership
   b) trait theories of leadership
   c) contingency theories of leadership
   d) situational theories of leadership

3. Which of the following is LEAST accurate about the Ohio State studies?
   a) "High-high" leaders generally had superior subordinate performance.
   b) High initiating structure is positively related to grievances.
   c) High consideration is positively related to managers' favourable performance evaluations.
   d) "High-high" style sometimes had negative leadership results.

4. The University of Michigan researchers concluded that
   a) production-oriented leaders were associated with lower employee satisfaction
   b) production-oriented leaders were associated with higher productivity
   c) employee-oriented leaders had lower productivity
   d) employee-oriented leaders had higher productivity

5. The managerial grid was an attempt by Blake and Mouton to
   a) discredit the University of Michigan and Ohio State University studies
   b) explain leadership success using a decision tree
   c) describe leadership style using dimensions similar to the University of Michigan and Ohio State studies
   d) predict managerial success using a production versus a people orientation

6. Which of the following statements is MOST correct?
   a) If has been proved conclusively that physical stature and leadership are positively related.
   b) Behaviour theories of leadership research findings are confusing and do not allow for significant generalizations.
   c) The trait view of leadership is accepted by Fiedler.
   d) The Ohio State researchers originally began with a contingency model.

7. If a leader describes his least-preferred coworker in relatively unfavourable terms, according to Fiedler,
   a) the leader would be classified as task oriented
   b) the leader would be classified as relationship oriented
   c) the leader would be classified as authoritarian
   d) none of the above

8. In which of the following situations would the path-goal model suggest a consideration style of leadership?
   a) when employees have an external locus of control
   b) when employees have low skill levels
   c) when employees work in an organizational culture characterized as authoritarian
   d) when employees have well-structured tasks

9. According to the leader-participation model of leadership, when goal congruence between the employees and the organization is low,
   a) an autocratic style is more appropriate
   b) a group style of leadership is more appropriate
   c) a consultative style of leadership is more appropriate
   d) a democratic style of leadership is more appropriate

10. A leader who looks beyond her own self-interest, and instead places the goals of the organization first, is called a _____ leader.
    a) transactional
    b) authoritarian
    c) transformational
    d) situational

11. Which of the following is NOT true for a charismatic leader?
    a) A charismatic leader is usually participative and is willing to listen to the opinions of employees.
    b) A charismatic leader might not always be needed to achieve high levels of employee performance.
    c) It is not unusual for a charismatic leader to pull an organization through a crisis but to perform poorly after the crisis subsides.
    d) It is more important to have a charismatic leader when the followers' tasks have an ideological component.

12. What is the main difference between first-line supervisors and other managers?
    a) First-line supervisors are concerned with local issues; managers are concerned with global issues.
    b) First-line supervisors oversee operative employees.
    c) First-line supervisors are not considered "real" managers.
    d) There is no difference between first-line supervisors and other managers.

Self-Assessment Exercise

What Kind of Leader Are You?

Instructions: The following items describe aspects of leadership behaviour. Respond to each item according to the way you would be most likely to act if you were the leader of a work group. Circle whether you would be likely to behave in the described way Always (A), Frequently (F), Occasionally (O), Seldom (S), or Never (N).

If I were the leader of a work group . . .

A F O S N _____ 1. I would most likely act as the spokes-person of the group.

A F O S N _____ 2. I would encourage overtime work.

A F O S N _____ 3. I would allow members complete freedom in their work.

A F O S N _____ 4. I would encourage the use of uniform procedures.

A F O S N _____ 5. I would permit the members to use their own judgment in solving problems.

A F O S N _____ 6. I would stress being ahead of competing groups.

A F O S N _____ 7. I would speak as a representative of the group.

A F O S N _____ 8. I would needle members for greater effort.

A F O S N _____ 9. I would try out my ideas in the group.

A F O S N _____ 10. I would let the members do their work the way they think best.

A F O S N _____ 11. I would be working hard for a promotion.

A F O S N _____ 12. I would be able to tolerate postponement and uncertainty.

A F O S N _____ 13. I would speak for the group when visitors were present.

A F O S N _____ 14. I would keep the work moving at a rapid pace.

A F O S N _____ 15. I would turn the members loose on a job and let them go to it.

A F O S N _____ 16. I would settle conflicts when they occur in the group.

A F O S N _____ 17. I would get swamped by details.

A F O S N _____ 18. I would represent the group at outside meetings.

A F O S N _____ 19. I would be reluctant to allow the members any freedom of action.

A F O S N _____ 20. I would decide what shall be done and how it shall be done.

A F O S N _____ 21. I would push for increased production.

A F O S N _____ 22. I would let some members have authority that I could keep.

A F O S N _____ 23. Things would usually turn out as I predict.

A F O S N _____ 24. I would allow the group a high degree of initiative.

A F O S N _____ 25. I would assign group members to particular tasks.

A F O S N _____ 26. I would be willing to make changes.

A F O S N _____ 27. I would ask the members to work harder.

A F O S N _____ 28. I would trust the group members to exercise good judgment.

A F O S N _____ 29. I would schedule the work to be done.

A F O S N _____ 30. I would refuse to explain my actions.

A F O S N _____ 31. I would persuade others that my ideas are to their advantage.

A F O S N _____ 32. I would permit the group to set its own pace.

A F O S N _____ 33. I would urge the group to beat its previous record.

A F O S N _____ 34. I would act without consulting the group.

A F O S N _____ 35. I would ask that group members follow standard rules and regulations.

Turn to page 468 for scoring directions and key.

Source: From J. William Pfeiffer and John E. Jones, eds., *A Handbook of Structural Experiences for Human Relations Training,* Vol. 1 (San Diego, Calif.: University Associates, Inc., 1974). With permission.

Class Exercise

The Pre-Post Leadership Assessment

Objective: To compare characteristics intuitively related to leadership with leadership characteristics found in leadership theory.

Time: Part I takes approximately 10 minutes.
Part II takes about 25 minutes.

Procedure: Part I is to be completed prior to reading Chapter 13. Identify three people (i.e., friends, relatives, previous boss, public figures, etc.) whom you consider to be outstanding leaders. For each one of these individuals, make a list of reasons you feel they are good leaders. Compare your lists of the three individuals. Which traits, if any, are common to all three?

Part II is to be completed after the lecture on the material in Chapter 13. Your instructor will lead the class in a discussion of leadership characteristics based on your lists developed in Part I. Students will call out what they identified and your instructor will write the traits on the chalkboard. When all students have shared their lists, class discussion will focus on the following:

1. What characteristics consistently appeared on students' lists?
2. Were these characteristics more trait oriented or behaviour oriented?
3. Under what situations were these characteristics useful?
4. What, if anything, does this exercise suggest about leadership attributes?

Case Application

Roger Gruben of The Aboriginal Global Investment Corp.

Roger Gruben is an Inuvialuk who runs a global investment fund—The Aboriginal Global Investment Corp.—worth about a billion dollars. It owns an airline, a food company, a food store, as well as a number of international investments. Its portfolio includes 56,000 square kilometres of land, an oil company, and real estate in Vancouver.[33]

Gruben is a man with a vision of what can be achieved in the Northwest Territories. He's been described as part politician and part businessman, and while he isn't a "formal" leader with impressive titles and hundreds of staff, he's an example of a transformational leader—helping people look at old problems in new ways, and exciting and inspiring people to achieve goals they would not normally have thought possible. He's full of energy and ideas, and he's always on the move, meeting with people across the country and internationally.

The Inuvialuit got a $170-million land claim settlement, and Roger Gruben has increased its worth by more than 40 per cent through investment. But his vision is not limited to managing the Inuvialuit funds; by next year native land claim settlements could total $7 billion, and Gruben recognizes the incredible potential for pooling a large percentage of that money in a global investment fund. His interest is in setting up something that is enduring and that will help native peoples to develop their economies and cultures in a sustained manner over the long term. So, as well as managing investments, Gruben is also involved in negotiating on behalf of various Inuit groups for participation in projects in the North. For instance, he has negotiated to have native firms and native people take part in the federal government's $50-million maintenance contract for the North Warning System.

When the Northwest Territories is divided, creating new entities with their own governments, structures, and cultures, money alone will not ensure that the native cultures of the North remain strong. Leadership from a variety of sectors and people is needed. Individuals with vision and drive, like Roger Gruben, can make a big difference.

Questions

1. Compare Roger Gruben, as a leader, with Laurent Beaudoin (Bombardier). They manage in quite different situations. How does that affect the way they need to operate to be effective?

2. What are the three main things Roger Gruben should focus on in order to be an effective leader?

3. Transformational leaders often appear to be driven. They believe deeply in what they're doing and at times their ideas can get ahead of the thinking of others around them. Would you like to work with such a person? Why? Why not?

c h a p t e r

14

Communication and Conflict Management

Learning Objectives

What will I be able to do after I finish this chapter?

1 • Define communication and explain why it is important to managers.

2 • Describe the communication process.

3 • Identify the more popular methods of communication.

4 • Describe the barriers that exist to effective communication.

5 • List techniques for overcoming communication barriers.

6 • Define conflict.

7 • Explain the three views of conflict.

8 • Describe how conflict can be positive.

9 • List the more popular conflict-resolution skills.

10 • Describe how managers can stimulate conflict.

At 7:40 p.m. on January 25, 1990, Avianca Flight 52 was cruising at 37,000 feet above the southern New Jersey coast.[1] The aircraft had enough fuel to last nearly two hours—a healthy cushion considering the plane was less than half an hour from touchdown at New York's Kennedy Airport. Then a series of delays began. First, at 8:00, the air traffic controllers at Kennedy told the pilots on Flight 52 that they would have to circle in a holding pattern because of heavy traffic. At 8:45, the Avianca copilot advised Kennedy that they were "running low on fuel." The controller at Kennedy acknowledged the message, but the plane was not cleared to land until 9:24. In the interim, the Avianca crew relayed no information to Kennedy that an emergency was imminent, yet the cockpit crew spoke worriedly among themselves about their dwindling fuel supplies.

Flight 52's first attempt to land at 9:24 was aborted. The plane had come in too low and poor visibility made a safe landing uncertain. When the Kennedy controllers gave Flight 52's pilot new instructions for a second attempt, the crew again mentioned that they were running low on fuel, but the pilot told the controllers that the newly assigned flight path was OK. At 9:32, two of Flight 52's engines lost power. A minute later, the other two cut off. The plane, out of fuel, crashed on Long Island at 9:34. All 73 people on board were killed.

When investigators reviewed the cockpit tapes and talked with the controllers involved, they learned that a communication breakdown caused this tragedy. A closer look at the events of that evening help to explain why a simple message was neither clearly transmitted nor adequately received.

First, the pilots kept saying they were "running low on fuel." Traffic controllers told investigators that it is fairly common for pilots to use this phrase. In times of delay, controllers assume that everyone has a fuel problem. However, had the pilots uttered the words "fuel emergency," the controllers would have been obligated to direct the jet ahead of all others

and clear it to land as soon as possible. As one controller put it, if a pilot "declares an emergency, all rules go out the window and we get the guy to the airport as quickly as possible." Unfortunately, the pilots of Flight 52 never used the word "emergency," so the people at Kennedy never understood the true nature of the pilots' problem.

Second, the vocal tone of the pilots on Flight 52 didn't convey the severity or urgency of the fuel problem to the air traffic controllers. Many of these controllers are trained to pick up subtle tones in a pilot's voice in such situations. While the crew of Flight 52 expressed considerable concern among themselves about the fuel problem, their voice tones in communicating to Kennedy were cool and professional.

Air traffic controllers are responsible for keeping all air traffic in its proper flight routes. Doing so requires constant and precise communications.

Finally, the culture and traditions of pilots and airport authorities may have made the pilot of Flight 52 reluctant to declare an emergency. A pilot's expertise and pride can be at stake in such a situation. Declaration of a formal emergency requires the pilot to complete a wealth of paperwork. Moreover, if a pilot has been found to be negligent in calculating how much fuel was needed for a flight, the Federal Aviation Administration can suspend his licence. These negative reinforcers strongly discourage pilots from calling an emergency.

 FEDERAL AVIATION ADMINISTRATION   www.faa.gov/

The Avianca Flight 52 disaster illustrates an important point: communication is fundamentally linked to successful performance.[2] In this chapter, we will present basic concepts in interpersonal communication. We'll explain the communication process, methods of communicating, barriers to effective communication, and ways to overcome those barriers. Additionally, we'll also use this chapter to review a basic interpersonal skill—managing conflict—in which every manager needs to become proficient.

Understanding Communication

The main purpose of communications is to get the message across the way it is intended. International symbols, such as this no smoking sign, clearly transfer meaning and understanding. As a result, effective communications occur.

The importance of effective communication for managers can't be overemphasized for one specific reason: everything a manager does involves communicating. Not some things, but everything! A manager can't make a decision without information. That information has to be communicated. Once a decision is made, communication must again take place. Otherwise, no one will know that a decision has been made. The best idea, the most creative suggestion, or the finest plan cannot take form without communication. Managers therefore need effective communication skills. We are not suggesting, of course, that good communication skills alone make a successful manager. We can say, however, that ineffective communication skills can lead to a continuous stream of problems for the manager.

What Is Communication?

Communication involves the transfer of meaning. If no information or ideas have been conveyed, communication has not taken place. The speaker who is not heard or the writer who is not read does not communicate. The philosophical question, "If a tree falls in a forest and no one hears it, does it make any noise?" must, in a communicative context, be answered negatively.

communication
The transferring and understanding of meaning.

However, for communication to be successful, the meaning must be not only imparted but also understood. A letter addressed to us but written in Farsi (a language of which we are totally ignorant) cannot be considered a communication until we have it translated. **Communication** is the transferring and understanding of meaning (see Managers Who Made a Difference). Perfect communication, if such a thing were possible, would exist when a transmitted thought or idea was perceived by the receiver exactly as it was envisioned by the sender.

Another point to keep in mind is that good communication is often erroneously defined by the communicator as agreement, instead of clarity of understanding.[3] If someone disagrees with us, many of us assume that the person just didn't fully understand our position. In other words, many of us define good communication as having someone accept our views. But I can understand very clearly what you mean and not agree with what you say. In fact, when observers conclude that a lack of communication must exist because a conflict has continued for a prolonged time, a close examination often reveals that there is plenty of effective communication going on. Each fully understands the other's position. The problem is one of equating effective communication with agreement.

MANAGERS WHO MADE A DIFFERENCE

**MCDONALD'S
RESTAURANTS**
www.mcdonalds.com

George Cohon of McDonald's

George Cohon is a Canadian who made world history. He is the man who brought McDonalds to the former Soviet Union, a project that took 14 years to bring to fruition. There were many, many critics of the idea, and (let's face it) who would believe that during the Cold War someone could establish a McDonald's—an icon of Western capitalism—near Red Square?[4]

Well, George Cohon achieved that feat, but not before having to overcome many bureaucratic, cultural, and economic obstacles. Discussions with the various levels of government seemed at times to be going in circles. When an agreement finally seemed to be within reach, the negotiations began to become increasingly intense, with the Soviet delegates flatly demanding consent on such issues as rates for land and the percentage of sales to be paid to the Canadian company. Negotiating in a foreign language is one thing, but dealing with a totalitarian government as a prospective partner is a whole different ball game. This was a communications challenge straight from hell.

Once the agreement had been reached, the struggles became faster paced. Suppliers had to be found, and at the time the agricultural industry in the U.S.S.R. was dismal, with constant crop failures and poor management. Moreover, a staff had to be hired and trained. In North America, the McDonald's corporate culture is very much ingrained. But how easily could this culture be adapted to Russian workers? As Cohon said in his book which came out in the fall of 1997: "When we began our training, most of our crew and our Soviet managers had never actually tasted a hamburger, much less made or served one." The Soviet managers were trained in Toronto, at the Canadian Institute of Hamburgerology. The rest of the staff had to be trained on-site.

On its first day, the Moscow McDonald's served 30,567 people. Since then the chain has expanded throughout Russia. It was an accomplishment of serious magnitude that George Cohon managed to create a reliable system of suppliers, overcome government bureaucracy, and train his employees to function at the regimented level demanded by McDonald's—in a country that was going through one of its greatest periods of upheaval. This is an impressive lesson in the fine art of managing communication and conflict.▼

interpersonal communication
Communication between two or more people in which the parties are treated as individuals rather than as objects.

message
A purpose to be conveyed.

encoding
Converting a message into symbols.

channel
The medium by which a message travels.

decoding
Retranslating a sender's message.

communication process
The seven stages by which meaning is transmitted and understood.

noise
Disturbances that interfere with the transmission of a message.

A final point before we move on: Our attention in this chapter will be on **interpersonal communication**. This is communication between two or more people in which the parties are treated as individuals rather than as objects. Organization-wide communication—which encompasses topics such as the development of management information systems—will be covered in our discussion of information control systems in Chapter 16.

How Does the Communication Process Work?

Before communication can take place, a purpose, expressed as a **message** to be conveyed, must exist. It passes between a source (the sender) and a receiver. The message is converted to symbolic form (called **encoding**) and passed by way of some medium (**channel**) to the receiver, who retranslates the sender's message (called **decoding**). The result is the transfer of meaning from one person to another.[5]

Exhibit 14-1 depicts the **communication process**. This model is made up of seven stages: (1) the communication source, (2) the message, (3) encoding, (4) the channel, (5) decoding, (6) the receiver, and (7) feedback. In addition, the entire process is susceptible to **noise**—that is, disturbances that interfere with the transmission of the message (depicted in Exhibit 14-1 as lightning bolts). Typical examples of noise include illegible print, telephone static, inattention by the receiver, or the background sounds of machinery on the production floor. Remember that anything that interferes with understanding—whether internal (such as the low speaking voice of the speaker/sender) or external (like the loud voices of coworkers talking at an adjoining desk)—represents noise. Noise can create distortion at any point in the communication process. Because the impact of external noise on communication effectiveness is self-evident, let's look at some potential internal sources of distortion.

A source initiates a message by encoding a thought. Four conditions affect the encoded message: skills, attitudes, knowledge, and the social-cultural system.

If textbook authors are without the requisite skills, their message will not reach students in the form desired. Our success in communicating to you depends on our writing skills. One's total communicative success also includes speaking, reading, listening, and reasoning skills. As we discussed in Chapter 10, our attitudes influence our behaviour. We hold preformed ideas on numerous topics, and these ideas affect our communications. Furthermore, we are restricted in our communicative activity by the

**Exhibit 14-1
The Communication Process**

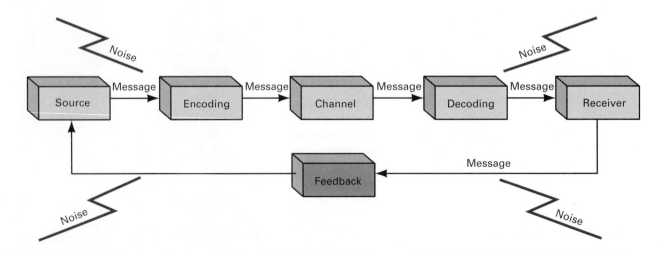

extent of our knowledge of a particular topic. We cannot communicate what we do not know; and should our knowledge be too extensive, it is possible that our receiver will not understand our message. Clearly, the amount of knowledge we have about a subject affects the message we seek to transfer. Finally, just as our attitudes influence our behaviour, so does our position in the social-cultural system in which we exist. Our beliefs and values (all part of our culture) act to influence us as communication sources.

YOUNG CANADIANS

Frances Oliver and Greg Miller: Fresherb

When Frances Oliver and Greg Miller set out to grow herbs indoors to sell to grocers, real estate agents had their doubts about whether to lease space in a factory for a hydroponic setup in the basement—the legality of what they would be growing seemed dubious. But the couple prevailed and their company Fresherb, in Lachine, Quebec, has been growing quickly. The pair hope to continue to capture more of the market, focusing on close customer relations.

The message itself can cause distortion in the communication process, regardless of the supporting apparatus used to convey it. Our message is the actual physical product encoded by the source. "When we speak, the speech is the message. When we write, the writing is the message. When we paint, the picture is the message. When we gesture, the movements of our arms, the expressions on our face are the message."[6] Our message is affected by the code or group of symbols we use to transfer meaning, the content of the message itself, and the decisions that the source makes in selecting and arranging both codes and content. Each of these three segments can act to distort the message.

The channel is the medium through which the message travels. It is selected by the sender. Common channels are air for the spoken word and paper for the written word. If you decide to convey to a friend something that happened to you during the day in a face-to-face conversation, you're using spoken words and gestures to transmit your message. But you have choices. A specific message—an invitation to a party, for example—can be communicated orally or in writing. In an organization, certain channels are more appropriate for certain messages. Obviously, if the building is on fire, a memo to convey the fact is inappropriate! If something is important, such as an employee's performance appraisal, a manager might want to use multiple channels—for instance, an oral review followed by a summary letter. This decreases the potential for distortion.

The receiver is the individual to whom the message is directed. But before the message can be received, the symbols in it must be translated into a form that can be understood by the receiver. This is the decoding of the message. Just as the encoder was limited by her skills, attitudes, knowledge, and social-cultural system, so is the receiver equally restricted. Just as the source must be skilful in writing or speaking, the receiver must be skilful in reading or listening, and both must be able to reason. A person's level of knowledge influences her ability to receive, just as it does her ability to send. Moreover, the receiver's preformed attitudes and cultural background can distort the message being transferred.

The final link in the communicative process is a feedback loop. "If a communication source decodes the message that he encodes, if the message is put back into the system, we have feedback."[7] That is, feedback returns the message to the sender and provides a check on whether understanding has been achieved.

What is Oral Communication?

People communicate with each other most often by talking, or oral communication. Popular forms of oral communication include speeches, formal one-on-one and group discussions, informal discussions, and the rumour mill or grapevine.

The advantages of oral communication are quick transmission and quick feedback. A verbal message can be conveyed and a response received in a minimum amount of time. If the receiver is unsure of the message, rapid feedback allows the sender to detect the uncertainty and to correct it.

The major disadvantage of oral communication surfaces whenever a message has to be passed through a number of people. The more people who are involved, the greater the potential for distortion. Each person interprets the message in his own way. The message's content, when it reaches its destination, is often very different from the original. In an organization where decisions and other communiqués are verbally passed up and down the authority hierarchy, considerable opportunity exists for messages to become distorted.

Are Written Communications More Effective?

Written communications include memos, letters, organizational periodicals, bulletin boards, or any other device that transmits written words or symbols. Why would a sender choose to use written communications? Because they're permanent, tangible, and verifiable. Typically, both sender and receiver have a record of the communication. The message can be stored for an indefinite period of time. If there are questions about the content of the message, it is physically available for later reference. This is particularly important for complex or lengthy communications. For example, the marketing plan for a new product is likely to contain a number of tasks spread out over several months. By putting it in writing, those who have to initiate the plan can readily refer to it over the life of the plan. A final benefit of written communication comes from the process itself. Except in rare instances, such as when presenting a formal speech, more care is taken with the written word than with the oral word. Having to put something in writing forces a person to think more carefully about what he wants to convey. Therefore, written communications are more likely to be well thought out, logical, and clear.

Of course, written messages have their drawbacks. While writing may be more precise, it also consumes a great deal more time. You could convey far more information to your instructor in a one-hour oral exam than in a one-hour written exam. In fact, you could probably say the same thing in ten to 15 minutes that takes you an hour to write. The other major disadvantage is feedback or lack of it. Oral communications allow the receivers to respond rapidly to what they think they hear. However, written communications do not have a built-in feedback mechanism. The result is that sending a memo is no assurance that it will be received; if it is received, there is no guarantee that the recipient will interpret it as the sender meant. The latter point is also relevant in oral communiqués, except that it's easier in such cases merely to ask the receiver to summarize what you've said. An accurate summary presents feedback evidence that the message has been received and understood.

How Do Nonverbal Cues Affect Communication?

Some of the most meaningful communications are neither spoken nor written. These are **nonverbal communications**. A loud siren or a red light at an intersection tells you something without words. A university instructor doesn't need words to know that students are bored when their eyes get glassy or they begin to read the school newspaper during class. Similarly, when papers start to rustle and notebooks begin to close, the message is clear: class time is about over. The size of a person's office and desk or the clothes a person wears also convey messages to others. However, the best-known areas of nonverbal communication are body language and verbal intonation.

Body language refers to gestures, facial configurations, and other movements of the body. A snarled face, for example, says something different from a smile. Hand motions, facial expressions, and other gestures can communicate emotions or temperaments such as aggression, fear, shyness, arrogance, joy, and anger. **Verbal intonation** refers to the emphasis someone gives to words or phrases. To illustrate how intonations can change the meaning of a message, consider the student who asks the instructor a question. The instructor replies, "What do you mean by that?" The student's reaction will vary, depending on the tone of the instructor's response. A soft, smooth tone creates a different meaning from one that is abrasive and puts a strong emphasis on the last word. Most of us would view the first intonation as coming from someone who sincerely sought clarification, whereas the second suggests that the person is aggressive or defensive.

The fact that every oral communication also has a nonverbal message cannot be overemphasized. Why? Because the nonverbal component is likely to carry the greatest impact. One researcher found that 55 per cent of an oral message is derived from facial expression and physical posture, 38 per cent from verbal intonation, and only 7 per cent from the actual words used.[8] Most of us know that animals respond to how we say something rather than what we say. Apparently, people aren't much different.

Is the Wave of the Future Electronic Media?

Today we rely on a number of sophisticated electronic media to carry our communications. In addition to the more common media—the telephone and public address system—we have closed-circuit television, voice-activated computers, xerographic reproduction, fax machines, and a host of other electronic devices that we can use in conjunction with speech or paper to create more effective communication. Maybe the fastest growing is **electronic mail**. Electronic mail allows individuals to instantaneously transmit written messages on computers that are linked with the appropriate software. Messages sit at the receiver's terminal to be read at the receiver's convenience. Electronic mail is fast and cheap and can be used to send the same message to dozens of people at the same time. Its other strengths and weaknesses generally parallel those of written communications.

nonverbal communication
Communication transmitted without words.

body language
Gestures, facial configurations, and other movements of the body that convey meaning.

verbal intonation
An emphasis given to words or phrases that conveys meaning.

electronic mail
Instantaneous transmission of written messages on computers that are linked.

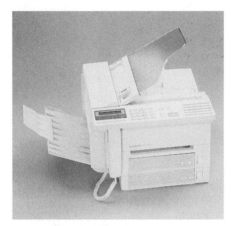

Years ago, we relied on Canada Post and mail couriers to deliver our written messages. Then companies like Federal Express helped us with overnight deliveries. Now with the fax machine and the Internet, documentation can quickly be sent anywhere in the world.

What Barriers Exist to Effective Communication?

In our discussion of the communication process, we noted the consistent potential for distortion. What causes such distortions? In addition to the general distortions identified in the communication process, there are other barriers to effective communication. These are presented below and are summarized in Exhibit 14-2.

Filtering is the deliberate manipulation of information to make it appear more favourable to the receiver. For example, when a manager tells her boss what the boss wants to hear, the manager is filtering information. The extent of filtering tends to be a function of the height of the structure and the organizational culture. The more vertical levels there are in an organization's hierarchy, the more opportunities there are for filtering. The organizational culture encourages or discourages filtering by the type of behaviour it emphasizes through rewards. The more rewards emphasize style and appearance, the more managers are motivated to alter communications in their favour.

The second barrier can be identified as selective perception. We've mentioned selective perception several times throughout this book. The receiver in the communication process selectively sees and hears communications depending on his needs, motivation, experience, background, and other personal characteristics. The receiver also projects his interests and expectations into communications in decoding them. The employment interviewer who expects a female job candidate to put family before career is likely to see that in all female candidates, regardless of whether the candidates feel that way. As we said in Chapter 10, we don't see reality; instead, we interpret what we see and call it reality (see Ethical Dilemmas in Management).

Another obstruction in communications comes from people's emotions. How the receiver feels when a message is received influences how he interprets it. Extreme emotions such as jubilation or depression are most likely to hinder effective communication. In such instances, we often disregard our rational and objective thinking processes and substitute emotional judgments.

Exhibit 14-2
Barriers to Effective
Communication

Filtering:	The deliberate manipulation of information to make it appear more favourable to the receiver.
Selective Perception:	Receiving communications based on what one selectively sees and hears depending on his needs, motivation, experience, background, and other personal characteristics.
Emotions:	Messages will often be interpreted differently depending on how happy or sad one is when the message is being communicated.
Language:	Words have different meanings to different people. As such, receivers will use their definition of words communicated, which may be different from what the sender intended.
Nonverbal Cues:	Body language or intonation that sends the receiver another message. When the two are not aligned, communication is distorted.

ETHICAL DILEMMAS IN MANAGEMENT

▼

IS IT UNETHICAL TO PURPOSELY DISTORT INFORMATION?

▲

The issue of ethics was introduced in Chapter 2. Since then, you've had ample time to think about this issue. Because lying is such a broad concern and so closely intertwined with interpersonal communication, this might be a good time to think again about dilemmas that managers face relating to the intentional distortion of information.

You have just seen your division's sales report for last month. Sales are down considerably. Your boss, who works 2,000 miles away in another city, is unlikely to see last month's sales

figures. You're optimistic that sales will pick up this month and next so that your overall quarterly numbers will be acceptable. You also know that your boss is the type of person who hates to hear bad news. You're having a phone conversation today with your boss. He happens to ask, in passing, how last month's sales went. Do you tell him the truth?

An employee asks you about a rumour she's heard that your department and all its employees will be transferred from Vancouver to Toronto. You know the rumour to be true, but you would rather not let the information out just yet. You're fearful that it could hurt departmental morale and lead to premature resignations. What do you say to your employee?

These two incidents illustrate dilemmas that managers face relating to evading the truth, distorting facts, or lying to others.

It might not always be in a manager's best interest or that of her unit to provide full and complete information. In fact, a strong argument can be made for managers to purposely keep their communications vague and unclear.[9] Keeping communications fuzzy can cut down on questions, permit faster decision making, minimize objections, reduce opposition, make it easier to deny one's earlier statements, preserve the freedom to change one's mind, permit one to say no diplomatically, help to avoid confrontation and anxiety, and provide other benefits that work to the advantage of the manager.

Is it unethical to purposely distort communications to get a favourable outcome? Is distortion acceptable, but lying not? What about "little white lies" that really don't hurt anybody? What do you think?

Words, too, mean different things to different people. Age, education, and cultural background are three of the more obvious variables that influence the language a person uses and the definitions she gives to words. The language of George Will is clearly different from that of the typical high-school-educated factory worker. The latter, in fact, would undoubtedly have trouble understanding much of Will's vocabulary. In an organization, employees usually come from diverse backgrounds. And this diversity may mean that you will work with people who don't speak your language. But even if they did, our use of that language is far from uniform. A knowledge of how each of us modifies the language would minimize communication difficulties. The problem is that members in an organization usually don't know how others with whom they interact have modified the language. Senders tend to assume that their words and terms will be appropriately interpreted by the receiver. This, of course, is often incorrect and creates communication difficulties.

Finally, barriers to effective communications can come from nonverbal cues. Earlier, we noted that nonverbal communication is an important way in which people convey messages to others. But nonverbal communication is almost always accompanied by oral communication. As long as the two are in agreement, they act to reinforce each other.

YOUNG CANADIANS

Greg Kalinin and Bob MacKalski: Stria Communications

Greg Kalinin and Bob MacKalski are two McGill University MBA grads who started their own company, Stria Communications, when they saw opportunities in electronic commerce and Internet markets. The company has set up Canada's first online supermarket for AM Foodfare Ltd., a chain of grocers in Manitoba and Saskatchewan, and has gone on to develop a network of online grocers called The Peachtree in cities such as Toronto, Vancouver, and Montreal. Kalinin and MacKalski are partners with David Zilioli and Neil Bienstock.

STRIA COMMUNICATIONS
www.stria.ca/

How Can Managers Overcome Communication Barriers?

Given these barriers to communication, what can managers do to overcome them? The following suggestions should help to make communication more effective (see also Exhibit 14-3).

Why Use Feedback? Many communication problems can be directly attributed to misunderstandings and inaccuracies. These problems are less likely to occur if the manager uses the feedback loop in the communication process. This feedback can be verbal or nonverbal.

If a manager asks a receiver, "Did you understand what I said?", the response represents feedback. Also, feedback should include more than yes and no answers. The manager can ask a set of questions about a message in order to determine whether or not the message was received as intended. Better yet, the manager can ask the receiver to restate the message in his own words. If the manager then hears what was

**Exhibit 14-3
Overcoming Barriers to Effective Communication**

Use Feedback:	Check the accuracy of what has been communicated—or what you think you heard.
Simplify Language:	Use words that the intended audience understands.
Listen Actively:	Listen for the full meaning of the message without making premature judgments or interpretations—or thinking about what you are going to say in response.
Constrain Emotions:	Recognize when your emotions are running high. When they are, don't communicate until you have calmed down.
Watch Nonverbal Actions:	Be aware that your actions speak louder than your words. Keep the two consistent.

intended, understanding and accuracy should be enhanced. Feedback also includes subtler methods than the direct asking of questions or the summarizing of messages. General comments can give a manager a sense of the receiver's reaction to a message. In addition, performance appraisals, salary reviews, and promotions represent important forms of feedback.

Of course, feedback does not have to be conveyed in words. Actions can speak louder than words. The sales manager who sends out a directive to her staff, describing a new monthly sales report that all sales personnel will need to complete, receives feedback if some of the salespeople fail to turn in the new report. This feedback suggests that the sales manager needs to clarify the initial directive. Similarly, when you give a speech to a group of people, you watch their eyes and look for other nonverbal clues to tell you whether they are getting your message.

Why Should Simplified Language Be Used? Because language can be a barrier, managers should choose words and structure their messages in ways that will make those messages clear and understandable to the receiver. The manager should consider the audience to whom the message is directed so that the language will be tailored to the receivers. Remember, effective communication is achieved when a message is both received and understood. Understanding is improved by simplifying the language used in relation to the audience intended. This means, for example, that a hospital administrator should always try to communicate in clear, easily understood terms and that the language used in messages to the surgical staff should be different from that used with office employees. Jargon can facilitate understanding when it is used within a group of people who know what it means, but it can cause innumerable problems when used outside that group.

Why Must We Listen Actively? When someone talks, we hear. But too often we don't listen. Listening is an active search for meaning, whereas hearing is passive. In listening, two people are thinking—the receiver and the sender.

Many of us are poor listeners. Why? Because it's difficult, and it's usually more satisfying to be on the offensive. Listening, in fact, is often more tiring than talking. It demands intellectual effort. Unlike hearing, **active listening** demands total concentration. The average person speaks at a rate of about 150 words per minute, whereas we have the capacity to listen at the rate of nearly 1,000 words per minute.[10] The difference obviously leaves idle time for the brain and opportunities for the mind to wander.

Active listening is enhanced by developing empathy with the sender—that is, by placing yourself in the sender's position. Because senders differ in attitudes, interests, needs, and expectations, empathy makes it easier to understand the actual content of a message (see Developing Management Skills). An empathic listener reserves judgment on the message's content and carefully listens to what is being said. The goal is to improve one's ability to receive the full meaning of a communication without having it distorted by premature judgments or interpretations.

active listening
Listening for full meaning without making premature judgments or interpretations.

Why Must We Constrain Emotions? It would be naive to assume that managers always communicate in a fully rational manner. We know that emotions can severely cloud and distort the transference of meaning. A manager who is emotionally upset over an issue is more likely to misconstrue incoming messages and fail to express his outgoing messages clearly and accurately. What can the manager do? The simplest answer is to desist from further communication until he has regained composure.

DEVELOPING MANAGEMENT SKILLS

▼

DEVELOPING EFFECTIVE ACTIVE LISTENING SKILLS

▲

► **1. Make eye contact.** How do you feel when somebody doesn't look at you when you're speaking? If you're like most people, you're likely to interpret this as aloofness or disinterest. Making eye contact with the speaker focuses your attention, reduces the likelihood that you will become distracted, and encourages the speaker.

► **2. Exhibit affirmative nods and appropriate facial expressions.** The effective listener shows interest in what is being said through nonverbal signals. Affirmative nods and appropriate facial expressions, when added to good eye contact, convey to the speaker that you're listening.

► **3. Avoid distracting actions or gestures that suggest boredom.** The other side of showing interest is avoiding actions that suggest that your mind is somewhere else. When listening, don't look at your watch, shuffle papers, play with your pencil, or engage in similar distractions. They make the speaker feel that you're bored or uninterested, or indicate that you aren't fully attentive.

► **4. Ask questions.** The critical listener analyses what he hears and asks questions. This behaviour provides clarification, ensures understanding, and assures the speaker that you're listening.

► **5. Paraphrase using your own words.** The effective listener uses phrases such as: "What I hear you saying is…" or "Do you mean…?" Doing so is an excellent control device to check on whether you're listening carefully and to verify that what you heard is accurate.

► **6. Avoid interrupting the speaker.** Let the speaker complete her thought before you try to respond. Don't try to second-guess where the speaker's thoughts are going. When the speaker is finished, you'll know it.

► **7. Don't overtalk.** Most of us would rather speak our own ideas than listen to what someone else says. While talking might be more fun and silence might be uncomfortable, you can't talk and listen at the same time. The good listener recognizes this fact and doesn't overtalk.

► **8. Make smooth transitions between the roles of speaker and listener.** The effective listener makes transitions smoothly from speaker to listener and back to speaker. From a listening perspective this means concentrating on what a speaker has to say and practising not thinking about what you're going to say as soon as you get your chance.

Why the Emphasis on Nonverbal Cues? If actions speak louder than words, then it's important to watch your actions to make sure that they align with and reinforce the words that go along with them. We noted that nonverbal messages carry a great deal of weight. Given this fact, the effective communicator watches her nonverbal cues to ensure that they too convey the desired message.

Cross-cultural Insights into Communication Processes

Interpersonal communication is not conducted in the same way around the world. For example, compare countries that place a high value on individualism (such as Canada) with countries where the emphasis is on collectivism (such as Japan).[11]

Owing to the emphasis on the individual in countries such as Canada, communication patterns here are individual oriented and rather clearly spelled out. For instance, Canadian managers rely heavily on memoranda, announcements, position papers, and other formal forms of communication to stake out their positions in intra-organizational negotiations. Supervisors in Canada often hoard secret information in an attempt to promote their own advancement and as a way of inducing their employees to accept decisions and plans. For their own protection, lower-level employees also engage in this practice.

In collectivist countries such as Japan, there is more interaction for its own sake and a more informal manner of interpersonal contact. The Japanese manager, in contrast to Canadian managers, will engage in extensive verbal consultation over an issue first and only draw up a formal document later to outline the agreement that was made. Face-to-face communication is encouraged. Additionally, open communication is an inherent part of the Japanese work setting. Work spaces are open and crowded with individuals at different levels in the work hierarchy. Canadian organizations emphasize authority, hierarchy, and formal lines of communication.

Conflict Management Skills

The ability to manage conflict is undoubtedly one of the most important skills a manager needs to possess. A study of middle- and top-level executives by the American Management Association revealed that the average manager spends approximately 20 per cent of his time dealing with conflict.[12] The importance of conflict management is reinforced by a survey of what topics practising managers consider most important in management development programs; conflict management was rated as being more important than decision making, leadership, or communication skills.[13] In further support of our claim, one researcher studied a group of managers and looked at 25 skill and personality factors to determine which, if any, were related to managerial success (defined in terms of ratings by one's boss, salary increases, and promotions).[14] Of the 25 measures, only one—the ability to handle conflict—was positively related to managerial success.

AMERICAN
MANAGEMENT
ASSOCIATION
www.amanet.org/

Exhibit 14-4
Three Views of
Conflict

Traditional View:	The early approach assumed that conflict was bad and would always have a negative impact on an organization. Conflict became synonymous with violence, destruction, and irrationality. Because conflict was harmful, it was to be avoided. Management had a responsibility to rid the organization of conflict. This traditional view dominated management literature during the late nineteenth century and continued until the mid-1940s.
Human Relations View:	The human relations position argued that conflict was a natural and inevitable occurrence in all organizations. Because conflict was inevitable, the human relations approach advocated acceptance of conflict. This approach rationalized the existence of conflict; conflict cannot be eliminated, and there are times when it may even benefit the organization. The human relations view dominated conflict thinking from the late 1940s through the mid-1970s.
Interactionist View:	The current theoretical perspective on conflict is the interactionist approach. While the human relations approach accepts conflict, the interactionist approach encourages conflict on the grounds that a harmonious, peaceful, tranquil, and cooperative organization is prone to become static, apathetic, and nonresponsive to needs for change and innovation. The major contribution of the interactionist approach, therefore, is that it encourages managers to maintain an ongoing minimum level of conflict—enough to keep units viable, self-critical, and creative.

What Is Conflict?

conflict
Perceived incompatible differences that result in interference or opposition.

When we use the term **conflict**, we are referring to perceived incompatible differences resulting in some form of interference or opposition. Whether the differences are real or not is irrelevant. If people perceive that differences exist, then a conflict state exists. In addition, our definition includes the extremes, from subtle, indirect, and highly controlled forms of interference to overt acts such as strikes, riots, and wars.

traditional view of conflict
The view that all conflict is bad and must be avoided.

Over the years, three differing views have evolved toward conflict in organizations[15] (see Exhibit 14-4). One argues that conflict must be avoided, that it indicates a malfunctioning within the organization. We call this the **traditional view of conflict**. A second, the **human relations view of conflict**, argues that conflict is a natural and inevitable outcome in any organization and that it need not be evil but, rather, has the potential to be a positive force in contributing to an organization's performance. The third and most recent perspective proposes not only that conflict can be a positive force in an organization but also that some conflict is absolutely necessary for an organization or units within an organization to perform effectively. We label this third approach the **interactionist view of conflict**.

human relations view of conflict
The view that conflict is a natural and inevitable outcome in any organization.

interactionist view of conflict
The view that some conflict is necessary for an organization to perform effectively.

Can Conflict Ever Be Positive?

functional conflicts
Conflicts that support an organization's goals.

The interactionist view does not propose that all conflicts are good. Rather, some conflicts support the goals of the organization; these are **functional conflicts** of a constructive form. However, some conflicts prevent an organization from achieving its goals; these are **dysfunctional conflicts** and are destructive forms.

dysfunctional conflicts
Conflicts that prevent an organization from achieving its goals.

Of course, it is one thing to argue that conflict can be valuable, but how does a manager tell whether a conflict is functional or dysfunctional? Unfortunately, the demarcation is neither clear nor precise. No one level of conflict can be adopted as acceptable or unacceptable under all conditions. The type and level of conflict that promote a healthy and positive involvement toward one department's goals may, in another department or in the same department at another time, be highly dysfunctional. Functionality or dysfunctionality, therefore, is a matter of judgment. Exhibit 14-5 illustrates the challenge facing managers. They want to create an environment within their organization or organizational unit in which conflict is healthy but not allowed

DIGITAL EQUIPMENT CORP.
www.digital.com/

Digital Equipment Corporation is one of an increasing number of firms that have learned the value of functional conflict. DEC openly encourages all employees "to push back against the system," and the company rewards those who do.

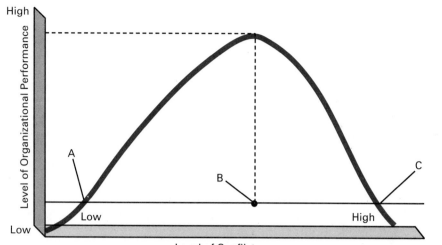

Exhibit 14-5
Conflict and
Organizational
Performance

Situation	Level of Conflict	Type of Conflict	Organization's Internal Characteristics	Level of Organizational Performance
A	Low or none	Dys-functional	Apathetic Stagnant Unresponsive to change Lack of new ideas	Low
B	Optimal	Functional	Viable Self-critical Innovative	High
C	High	Dys-functional	Disruptive Chaotic Uncooperative	Low

to run to pathological extremes. Neither too little nor too much conflict is desirable. Managers should stimulate conflict to gain the full benefits of its functional properties, yet reduce its level when it becomes a disruptive force. Because we have yet to devise a sophisticated measuring instrument for assessing whether a given conflict level is functional or dysfunctional, it remains for managers to make intelligent judgments as to whether conflict levels in their units are optimal, too high, or too low.

If conflict is dysfunctional, what can a manager do? In the following sections, we'll review conflict-resolution skills. Essentially, you need to know your basic conflict-handling style, as well as those of the conflicting parties, to understand the situation that has created the conflict and to be aware of your options.

What Is Your Underlying Conflict-Handling Style?

While most of us have the ability to vary our conflict response according to the situation, each of us has a preferred style for handling conflicts.[16] The self-assessment exercise at the end of this chapter can help you to identify your basic conflict-handling style. You might be able to change your preferred style to suit the context in which a certain conflict exists; however, your basic style tells you how you're most likely to behave and the conflict-handling approaches on which you most often rely.

Which Conflicts Do You Handle?

Not every conflict justifies your attention. Some might not be worth the effort; others might be unmanageable. Not every conflict is worth your time and effort to resolve. While avoidance might appear to be a "cop-out," it can sometimes be the most appropriate response. You can improve your overall management effectiveness, and your conflict-management skills in particular, by avoiding trivial conflicts. Choose your battles judiciously, saving your efforts for the ones that count.

Regardless of our desires, reality tells us that some conflicts are unmanageable.[17] When antagonisms are deeply rooted, when one or both parties wish to prolong a conflict, or when emotions run so high that constructive interaction is impossible, your efforts to manage the conflict are unlikely to meet with much success.

Don't be lured into the naive belief that a good manager can resolve every conflict effectively. Some aren't worth the effort. Some are outside your realm of influence. Still others may be functional and, as such, are best left alone.

Who Are the Conflict Players?

If you choose to manage a conflict situation, it's important that you take the time to get to know the players. Who is involved in the conflict? What interests does each party represent? What are each player's values, personality, feelings, and resources? Your chances of success in managing a conflict will be greatly enhanced if you can view the conflict situation through the eyes of the conflicting parties.

What Are the Sources of the Conflict?

Conflicts don't pop out of thin air. They have causes. Because your approach to resolving a conflict is likely to be determined largely by its causes, you need to determine the source of the conflict. Research indicates that while conflicts have varying causes, they can generally be separated into three categories: communication differences, structural differences, and personal differences.[18]

Communication differences are disagreements arising from semantic difficulties, misunderstandings, and noise in the communication channels. People are often quick to assume that most conflicts are caused by lack of communication but, as one author has noted, there is usually plenty of communication going on in most conflicts.[19] As we pointed out at the beginning of this chapter, the mistake many people make is equating good communication with having others agree with their views. What might at first look like an interpersonal conflict based on poor communication is usually found, upon closer analysis, to be a disagreement caused by different role requirements, unit goals, personalities, value systems, or similar factors. As a source of conflict for managers, poor communication probably gets more attention than it deserves.

As we discussed in Chapter 6, organizations are horizontally and vertically differentiated. This structural differentiation creates problems of integration. The frequent result is conflicts. Individuals disagree over goals, decision alternatives, performance criteria, and resource allocations. These conflicts are not due to poor communication or personal animosities. Rather, they are rooted in the structure of the organization itself.

The third conflict source is personal differences. Conflicts can evolve out of individual idiosyncrasies and personal value systems. The chemistry between some people makes it hard for them to work together. Factors such as background, education, experience, and training mould each individual into a unique personality with a particular set of values. The result is people who may be perceived by others as abrasive, untrustworthy, or strange. These personal differences can create conflict.

DETAILS ON A MANAGEMENT CLASSIC

Kenneth W. Thomas and Conflict-Handling Techniques

Conflict in any organization is inevitable. Whenever you put people together and arrange them into some type of structure (formal or informal) there is a good probability that some individuals will perceive that others have negatively affected, or are about to negatively affect, something that they care about. How then do we react to deal with the conflict? The research of Kenneth W. Thomas has given us some insight.

Thomas recognized that in these conflict-laden situations, one must first determine the intention of the other party. That is, one has to speculate as to the other person's purpose for causing the conflict in order to respond to that behaviour. To do so, Thomas concluded that one's response will depend on one's cooperativeness or assertiveness. Cooperativeness is the degree to which an individual attempts to rectify the conflict by satisfying the other person's concerns. On the other hand, assertiveness is the degree to which an individual will attempt to rectify the conflict to satisfy her concerns. Placing assertiveness on the "Y" axis and cooperativeness on the "X" axis (and ranging both from low to high), Thomas was able to identify four distinct conflict-handling techniques—plus one middle-of-the-road combination. These were competing (where one is assertive, but uncooperative); collaborating (assertive and cooperative); avoiding (unassertive and uncooperative); accommodating (unassertive, but cooperative); and compromising (mid-range on both assertiveness and cooperativeness). The question raised, then, is when should these be used?

Thomas recognized that one conflict-resolution method is not appropriate in all situations.[20] Rather, the situation itself must dictate the technique. For instance, competition is most appropriate when a quick decisive action is vital or against people who take advantage of noncompetitive behaviours. Collaboration is appropriate when one is attempting to merge insights from different people, and avoidance works well when the potential for disruption outweighs the benefits of resolving the conflict. Accommodation can assist in issues that are more important to others than to yourself or where harmony and stability are important to you. Finally, compromise works well in achieving temporary settlements to complex issues or reaching a solution when time constraints dictate.

Thomas's work provided us with general guidelines for dealing with conflict. Although we know that people do change their intentions because of how they currently see the issue, or in an emotional reaction to the other individual, it appears that people do prefer one of the five techniques more often than the other four. Subsequent research supports that a person's intentions can also be predicted rather well from a combination of intellectual and personality characteristics. Thus, it may be more appropriate to view individuals from their preferred style and react accordingly. That is, when confronting a conflict situation, recognize that some people want to win it all at any cost, some want to find an optimum solution, some want to run away, others want to be obliging, and still others want to "split the difference."▼

What Tools Can You Use to Reduce Conflict?

Managers essentially can draw upon five conflict-resolution options to reduce conflict when it is too high: avoidance, accommodation, forcing, compromise, and collaboration.[21] Each has particular strengths and weaknesses, and no one option is ideal for every situation. You should consider each to be a "tool" in your conflict-management "tool chest." While you might be better at using some tools than others, the skilled manager knows what each tool can do and when each is likely to be most effective (see Details on a Management Classic).

As we noted earlier, not every conflict requires an assertive action. Sometimes **avoidance**—just withdrawing from or suppressing the conflict—is the best solution. When is avoidance a desirable strategy? When the conflict is trivial, when emotions are running high and time is needed to cool them down, or when the potential disruption from a more assertive action outweighs the benefits of resolution.

The goal of **accommodation** is to maintain harmonious relationships by placing another's needs and concerns above your own. You might, for example, yield to another person's position on an issue. This option is most viable when the issue under dispute isn't that important to you or when you want to build up credits for later issues.

In **forcing**, you attempt to satisfy your own needs at the expense of the other party. In organizations, this is most often illustrated by a manager using his formal authority to resolve a dispute. Forcing works well when you need a quick resolution on important issues where unpopular actions must be taken, and when commitment by others to your solution is not critical.

A **compromise** requires each party to give up something of value. Typically this is the approach taken by management and labour in negotiating a new labour contract. Compromise can be an optimum strategy when conflicting parties are about equal in power, when it is desirable to achieve a temporary solution to a complex issue, or when time pressures demand an expedient solution.

Collaboration is the ultimate win-win solution. All parties to the conflict seek to satisfy their interests. It is typically characterized by open and honest discussion among the parties, active listening to understand differences, and careful deliberation over a full range of alternatives to find a solution that is advantageous to all. When is collaboration the best conflict option? When time pressures are minimal, when all parties seriously want a win-win solution, and when the issue is too important to be compromised.

How Does a Manager Stimulate Conflict?

What about the other side of conflict management—situations that require managers to stimulate conflict? The notion of stimulating conflict is often difficult to accept. For almost all of us the term "conflict" has a negative connotation, and the idea of purposely creating conflict seems to be the antithesis of good management. Few of us personally enjoy being in conflict situations. Yet the evidence demonstrates that there are situations in which an increase in conflict is constructive.[22] Given this reality and the fact that there is no clear demarcation between functional and dysfunctional conflict, we have listed in Exhibit 14-6 a set of questions that might help you. While there is no definitive method for assessing the need for more conflict, an affirmative answer to one or more of the questions in Exhibit 14-6 suggests a need for conflict stimulation.

---

avoidance
Withdrawal from or suppression of conflict.

accommodation
Resolving conflicts by placing another's needs and concerns above one's own.

forcing
Satisfying one's own needs at the expense of another's.

compromise
A solution to conflict in which each party gives up something of value.

collaboration
Resolving conflict by seeking a solution advantageous to all parties.

We know a lot more about resolving conflict than about stimulating it. That's only natural, because human beings have been concerned with the subject of conflict reduction for hundreds, maybe thousands, of years. The dearth of ideas on conflict-stimulation techniques reflects the very recent interest in the subject. The following are some preliminary suggestions that managers might want to use.[23]

The initial step in stimulating functional conflict is for managers to convey to employees the message, supported by actions, that conflict has its legitimate place. This may require changing the culture of the organization. Individuals who challenge the status quo, suggest innovative ideas, offer divergent opinions, and demonstrate original thinking need to be rewarded visibly with promotions, salary increases, and other positive reinforcers.

The labour mediator attempts to get both labour and management to overcome their impasse. By getting to know each side's issues, values, and the like, he is in a better position to find common ground that both parties can live with.

Politicians frequently use communication to stimulate conflict. Ministers "plant" possible policy decisions with the media through "leaks" and then assess the public reaction. This way they can test whether a tax change, a change in the health care system, welfare, unemployment, or whatever, will be acceptable to the voting public. If there is a huge outcry that the politicians judge to be representative of the voters in Canada, they simply deny the rumours, and the policy change is either dropped from the agenda or altered.

Ambiguous or threatening messages also encourage conflict. Information that a plant might close, that a department is likely to be eliminated, or that a layoff is imminent can reduce apathy, stimulate new ideas, and force reevaluation—all positive outcomes that result from increased conflict.

▶ **1.** Are you surrounded by "yes people"?

▶ **2.** Are employees afraid to admit ignorance and uncertainties to you?

▶ **3.** Is there so much concentration by decision makers on reaching a compromise that they lose sight of values, long-term objectives, or the organization's welfare?

▶ **4.** Do managers believe that it is in their best interest to maintain the impression of peace and cooperation in their unit, regardless of the price?

▶ **5.** Is there an excessive concern by decision makers for not hurting the feelings of others?

▶ **6.** Do managers believe that popularity is more important for obtaining organizational rewards than competence and high performance?

▶ **7.** Are managers unduly enamored of obtaining consensus for their decisions?

▶ **8.** Do employees show unusually high resistance to change?

▶ **9.** Is there a lack of new ideas?

▶**10.** Is there an unusually low level of employee turnover?

An affirmative answer to any or all of these questions suggests the need for conflict stimulation.

**Exhibit 14-6
Is Conflict Stimulation Needed?**

Source: From Stephen P. Robbins, "'Conflict Management' and 'Conflict Resolution' Are Not Synonymous Terms," *California Management Review*, Winter 1978, p. 71. With permission of the regents.

Another widely used method for shaking up a stagnant unit or organization is to bring in outsiders—either by hiring from outside or by internal transfer—whose backgrounds, values, attitudes, or managerial styles differ from those of current members. Many large corporations have used this technique during the last decade in filling vacancies on their boards of directors. Women, minority group members, consumer activists, and others whose backgrounds and interests differ significantly from those of the rest of the board, have been purposely selected to add a fresh perspective.

We also know that structural variables are a source of conflict. It is therefore only logical that managers look to structure as a conflict-stimulation device. Centralizing decisions, realigning work groups, increasing formalization, and increasing interdependencies between units are all structural devices that disrupt the status quo and act to increase conflict levels.

Finally, one can appoint a **devil's advocate**. A devil's advocate is a person who purposely presents arguments that run counter to those proposed by the majority, or against current practices. She plays the role of the critic, even to the point of arguing against positions with which she actually agrees. A devil's advocate acts as a check against groupthink and practices that have no better justification than "that's the way we've always done it around here." When thoughtfully listened to, the advocate can improve the quality of group decision making. On the other hand, others in the group often view advocates as time wasters, and their appointment is almost certain to delay any decision process.

devil's advocate
A person who purposely presents arguments that run counter to those proposed by the majority.

Summary

This summary is organized by the chapter Learning Objectives found on page 364.

1. Communication is the transference and understanding of meaning. It is important because everything a manager does—decision making, planning, leading, and all other activities—requires that information be communicated.

2. The communication process begins with a communication source (a sender) who has a message to convey. The message is converted to symbolic form (encoding) and passed by way of a channel to the receiver, who decodes the message. To ensure accuracy, the receiver should provide the sender with feedback as a check on whether understanding has been achieved.

3. The more popular methods of communication are oral or verbal communications, written communications, nonverbal communications, and electronic media.

4. Several barriers to communications exist. They can take many forms, such as filtering, selective perception, emotions, language, and nonverbal cues.

5. Some techniques for overcoming communication barriers include using feedback, simplifying language, listening actively, constraining emotions, and watching nonverbal cues.

6. Conflict is the perceived incompatible differences that result in interference or opposition.

7. The three views of conflict are the traditional view that holds that all conflict should be avoided; the human relations view that holds that conflict is natural and inevitable in any organization; and the interactionist view that holds that some conflict is necessary for an organization to perform effectively.

8. Conflict can be positive when it leads to high levels of organizational performance that support an organization's goals.

9. The more popular conflict-resolution techniques are understanding one's conflict-handling style; determining which conflicts to handle; evaluating the conflict players; assessing the source of the conflict; and understanding the options one has for dealing with the conflict (avoidance, accommodation, forcing, compromise, or collaboration).

10. A manager can stimulate conflict by changing the organization's culture through the use of communications, by bringing in outsiders, by restructuring the organization, or by appointing a devil's advocate.

Review and Discussion Questions

1. Why isn't effective communication synonymous with agreement?

2. Where in the communication process is distortion likely to occur?

3. "Ineffective communication is the fault of the sender." Do you agree or disagree with this statement? Support your position.

4. What are the most popular communication methods used by people in organizations?

5. Why are effective communication skills so important to a manager's success?

6. What is conflict?

7. Contrast the traditional, human relations, and interactionist views of conflict.

8. What view of conflict—traditional, human relations, or interactionist—do you think most managers have? Do you think this view is appropriate?

9. What are the five primary conflict-resolution techniques?

10. Why might a manager want to stimulate conflict?

Testing Your Comprehension

Circle the correct answer, then check yourself on page 472.

1. Good communication does NOT require

   a) transference

   b) agreement

   c) understanding

   d) meaning

2. The encoding step in the communication process

   a) is not necessary for verbal communications

   b) enables the sender to keep the message from everyone except the intended receiver

   c) involves converting the message into some type of symbol

   d) follows the transmission of the message to the receiver

3. Before communication in any form can occur, which of the following is required?

   a) a sender

   b) a receiver

   c) a message

   d) a purpose

4. Which of the following is an advantage of oral communication?

   a) permanent record of the communication

   b) accurate when passing through many people

   c) chance for timely feedback

   d) more likely to be well thought out

5. The GREATEST value of feedback is that it

   a) improves communication by reducing the chance of misunderstandings

   b) allows for further discussions between the sender and receiver

   c) is not necessary in written communications because the message is tangible and verifiable

   d) forces the sender to think twice about what is communicated

6. A major disadvantage to written communication is

   a) only the recipient of the communication gets a written record

   b) lack of thought and precision

   c) the double meanings often accompanying written communication

   d) the minor role feedback plays in the process

7. Intentional distortion of information to enhance its appearance is

   a) more likely to occur in simple organizational structures

   b) called shaping communication

   c) consistent with cultures that reward performance

   d) called filtering

8. Communication is distorted when

   a) body language and verbal intonations are used

   b) e-mail, which lacks feedback opportunities, is used

   c) body language and information are not aligned

   d) the information is complex

9. Which of the following is NOT true regarding paraphrasing in active listening?

   a) Paraphrasing distorts efforts required for effective active listening.

   b) Paraphrasing is a control device that a listener uses to be sure she is listening carefully.

   c) Paraphrasing is a feedback mechanism.

   d) none of the above

10. What should active listeners do with idle brain time?

    a) summarize and integrate what has been said

    b) organize their schedules for the next few hours

    c) plan how to ask questions of the speaker

    d) rest and prepare to receive future communication

11. According to the interactionist view of conflict

    a) very low levels of conflict indicate the optimal state

    b) managers may need to stimulate dysfunctional conflict

    c) some conflict keeps the group critical of itself

    d) managers may need to stifle dysfunctional conflict

12. Which of the following LEAST suggests the need for a manager to stimulate conflict?

    a) when a manager is surrounded by "yes people"

    b) when employees in a department lack specific expertise

    c) when the work environment is peaceful and cooperative

    d) when creativity and innovation are lacking

13. Which of the following conflict-handling orientations represents a desire to maximize the joint outcomes of the two parties involved in the conflict?

    a) avoidance

    b) collaboration

    c) accommodation

    d) compromise

14. To achieve a compromise approach, one needs to

    a) avoid overt disagreement

    b) value openness and trust

    c) dominate the other conflicting party

    d) give up something of value

15. A person who purposely presents arguments that run counter to those proposed by the majority or against current practices is called

    a) a conflict stimulator

    b) a devil's advocate

    c) an external consultant

    d) all of the above

Self-Assessment Exercise

Conflict-Handling Style Questionnaire

Indicate how often you do the following when you differ with someone.

When I differ with someone:	Usually	Sometimes	Seldom
1. I explore our differences, not backing down, but not imposing my view either.	☐	☐	☐
2. I disagree openly, then invite more discussion about our differences.	☐	☐	☐
3. I look for a mutually satisfactory solution.	☐	☐	☐
4. Rather than let the other person make a decision without my input, I make sure I am heard and also that I hear the other out.	☐	☐	☐
5. I agree to a middle ground rather than look for a completely satisfying solution.	☐	☐	☐
6. I admit I am half wrong rather than explore our differences.	☐	☐	☐
7. I have a reputation for meeting a person halfway.	☐	☐	☐
8. I expect to get out about half of what I really want to say.	☐	☐	☐
9. I give in totally rather than try to change another's opinion.	☐	☐	☐
10. I put aside any controversial aspects of an issue.	☐	☐	☐
11. I agree early on, rather than argue about a point.	☐	☐	☐
12. I give in as soon as the other party gets emotional about an issue.	☐	☐	☐
13. I try to win the other person over.	☐	☐	☐
14. I work to come out victorious, no matter what.	☐	☐	☐
15. I never back away from a good argument.	☐	☐	☐
16. I would rather win than end up compromising.	☐	☐	☐

Turn to page 469 for scoring directions and key.

Source: Reprinted with the permission of Macmillan College Publishing from *Supervision: Managerial Skills for a New Era* by Thomas Von Der Embse. Copyright © 1987 by Macmillan College Publishing, Inc.

Class Exercise

Active Listening

Purpose:
To reinforce that good listening skills are necessary for managers and that as communicators we can motivate listeners to actively listen.

Time Required:
Approximately 30 minutes

Instructions:
Most of us are pretty poor listeners. This is probably because active listening is very demanding. This exer-

cise is specifically designed to dramatize how difficult it is to listen actively and to accurately interpret what is being said. It also points out how emotions can distort communication.

Your instructor will read you a story and ask you some follow-up questions. You'll need paper and pencil.

Source: Adopted from Bonnie L. McNeely, "A Fun Exercise in Listening: The Neglected Managerial Skill," *The Organizational Behavior Teaching Review*, Vol. XIII, No. 4 (1988–1989), pp. 126–29.

Case Application

WordPerfect

Today's communication patterns have drastically changed. More and more of us are faced with electronic media that are designed to enhance communications effectiveness and make our lives "easier." But do such systems really support the basic premise that communication implies an understanding between two or more people?

Consider when you have had to contact an organization—especially one with an 800 number. These companies provide toll-free lines to assist us in obtaining the information we want, whether it's ordering a product, seeking advice, or attempting to get some help with a product we purchased. And while this is a cost-saving service to customers, what do we typically find? A response that all operators are currently busy, so please hold the line for the next available customer service representative. Then to top it off, we have to listen to "elevator music" while waiting for our turn in the queue. How dehumanizing!

WordPerfect (WP) recognized this. In its business, many people call for technical assistance, but instead of listening to electronically enhanced directions, they listen to "hold jockeys." Barbara Lee and Dave Webb share these duties. What do they do? Trained as disc jockeys, they give customers on hold a "live" person to relate to. Using 16 monitors in their studio to determine the backup for the 50-plus support lines that WP currently has, they create an atmosphere that entertains customers who are waiting for service. This is done by introducing and playing pop music, interspersed with "traffic update" messages that provide the caller with the "detour" they may encounter. For example, one of these two hold jockeys may announce "a three-call delay for Windows installation support," interjecting to the customer next in line that they are about to be waved through the "call jam."

One would expect an organization in the software industry to provide more automated support. But feedback from callers indicates their appreciation for this "more caller-friendly" approach. In fact, it's gotten so much praise that competitors like Lotus and Microsoft have removed some of their automated lines and hired hold jockeys.

Questions

1. Analyse how hold jockeys at WP help to enhance communications between the company and customers.

2. Considering that the electronic media is the "wave of the future," what potential barriers for effective communications does this create?

3. "Efforts at companies like WordPerfect, Lotus, and Microsoft to hire hold jockeys are reversing a trend in telephone customer service operations—going from automated systems back to people-run operations." Do you agree or disagree with this statement. Support your position.

Source: Mark D. Fefer, "Taking the Pain Out of Holding Patterns," *Fortune*, January 10, 1994, p. 20.

Gender Problems at CIBC: Men and Women Working Together

CBC ⊛

Research into the differences between men and women shows that women are socialized to value affiliation and attachment, men to value power and competition. This difference has major consequences when they work together and try to understand one another. Deborah Tannen, who has studied the way men and women communicate (or don't communicate), says that men talk to emphasize status and women talk to create communication. This discrepancy creates cultures in the workplace.

The CIBC is trying to deal with the differences and difficulties and make the bank a place that both men and women find attractive to work in. Women occupy only 14 per cent of senior management positions in the bank, but hold more than 50 per cent of middle management jobs. Female managers interviewed at the bank state that they tend to find the environment blocks their ability to grow and to contribute at the level they feel they are capable of. They get turned off by the traditional male culture.

At a two-day seminar for 15 CIBC middle managers from across Ontario, the differences were highlighted in comments from the group. "Men don't listen." "Women take everything personally." "When men say yes they mean 'I agree with you'; when women say yes they mean 'I'm following what you're saying.'" "Women use talking to focus thoughts; men get straight to the issues." Barbara Annis, a consultant working with the CIBC, notes that both men and women get angry and defensive about their positions, and it is this defensiveness that gets in the way of real communication. The truth is, she says, that both sides are right, but unless they get beyond the aggression and defensiveness, they can't make any progress.

Deborah Tannen points out that women speak and hear a language of connection and intimacy; men speak and hear one of status and independence. For many men, conversations are primarily a means to preserve independence and maintain status in a hierarchical social order. For many women, conversations are negotiations for closeness in which people try to speak and give confirmation and support. For example, men frequently criticize women for talking about their problems; what's happening is that when men hear problems, they frequently assert their need for independence and control by providing solutions. Many women, however, view talking about a problem as a means to promote closeness. They present the problem to gain support and connection, not to get a man's advice.

Questions

1. "The fact that women have better honed senses, are less aggressive, and use communication to facilitate connection rather than competition tends to suggest they have superior qualities to those of men for managing in the 1990s." Agree or disagree? Support your position.

2. If managers can shape behaviour, how can organizations shape male and female behaviour so that men and women work more effectively together?

3. How can an understanding of perception improve the way women and men judge one another and react to one another?

Video Resource: "Men/Women," *Venture* 480 (March 20, 1994).

Additional Source: Deborah Tannen, *You Just Don't Understand: Women and Men in Conversation* (New York: Ballantine Books, 1991).

Understanding the Importance of the Workforce

CBC

As this chapter has shown, keeping a well-motivated and content workforce is a key to managing a successful operation. By offering job security and a system of bonuses based on production, Frank Hasenfratz at Guelph, Ontario's Linamar Corp. has built a solid, skilled, motivated employee base. Giving employees autonomy in their work also builds a greater sense of importance in the firm, and boosts morale. As Linamar's president Larry Pearson has said, "We're aggressive about training employees and providing the right tools to do the job." Teamwork is the key at Linamar. "I lead by pulling, not pushing," Hasenfratz has said. This managerial attitude has led to consistent success for Linamar, which now has more than 4,300 employees, and annual revenues of more than $600 million.

Sony Music Canada's CEO Rick Camilleri has brought about major changes in the company. Since Camilleri—young enough to qualify for this textbook's Young Canadians section, and a lawyer trained at Toronto's Osgoode Hall—took over the reigns in 1993, the company has seen profits grow by more than 150 per cent. Sony Canada is currently the top-performing division of the company in the world. And Camilleri would be the first to admit that hiring and keeping an excellent staff has been an integral part of this success. Apart from excellent job security—the company has been growing steadily, even through the lean years in the early- to mid-1990s when lay-offs abounded in all industries—Sony Canada is a very employee-friendly place to work. Camilleri has overseen additions such as a gourmet cafeteria, artwork-a-plenty, and more than 100 stereo systems throughout the company.

The stunning growth of both these companies is a testament to the power of a well-motivated workforce. And there are many more examples in the Canadian business world.

SONY MUSIC CANADA
www.music.sony.com/Canada/

Questions

1. Why do you think a Theory Y manager, such as Hasenfratz or Camilleri, might be more successful than a Theory X manager?

2. In what ways could Hasenfratz promote Theory Y ideals in the workplace? How could Camilleri do so?

3. How could Hasenfratz's policy of training every employee on different jobs—as seen in the video where a human resources manager was operating a machine—allow them to function better in their normal tasks? How might this process serve to motivate employees?

Video Resource: "Growth," *Venture* 587 (April 21, 1996).

Additional Sources: Report on Business Magazine, "The Top 1000," July 1997, p. 108; Brian Higgins, "Manufacturing Entrepreneur," *Profit*, December 1994, p. 21; *The Financial Post Magazine*, "Spin Master," April 1997, p. 18.

chapter

15

Foundations
of Controlling

Learning Objectives

What will I be able to do after I finish
this chapter?

1 • Define control.

2 • Explain why control is important.

3 • Describe the control process.

4 • Distinguish between the three types of control.

5 • Describe the qualities of an effective control system.

6 • Identify the contingency factors in the control process.

7 • Explain how controls can become dysfunctional.

MDS Laboratory Services is a diversified health services company based in Toronto. MDS operates the largest medical testing lab in Canada, their Toronto reference lab. A few years ago this lab—along with MDS's other labs—was operating very inefficiently. Thousands of medical samples were being analysed, but each type of sample test was handled individually by technicians who worked in their own separate groups. Therefore, each specimen would be sent to a specific area where it would be put through a series of tests, and then sent on to another area for more testing. The problem with this system was that highly skilled technicians would find their time taken up by menial tasks such as loading, unloading, and moving around trays of specimens, and waiting for results. Clearly there was need for improvement in the processing, considering that up to three-quarters of technicians' time was spent on unskilled tasks.[1]

A completely new approach was instituted. A bar-code system was put in place, where samples are loaded onto conveyer belts and moved through the entire facility (the walls were done away with at the suggestion of employees). A software system was developed whereby the information that was once gathered on worksheets was now collected by computers scanning bar codes. A control centre keeps track of where each specimen has been sent and the results of various tests done on the specimen.

Within two-and-a-half years, efficiency at the lab was improved to the extent that three times the number of samples were being completed. Productivity increases led to increases in revenue and by 1997 higher revenue had more than paid for the $25-million costs of developing the new system. Now MDS wants to take its control system to the world. The company's AutoLab Systems division is marketing the new technology internationally, and the system could come to account for a large part of MDS's revenues.

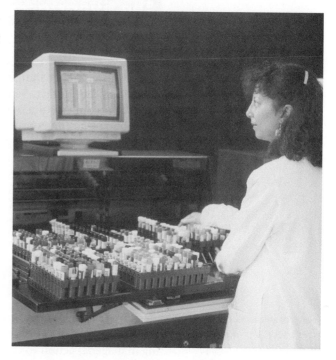

At MDS Laboratory Services control measures have made significant contributions to productivity and profitability.

The MDS example illustrates what can happen when an organization has effective controls. Regardless of the thoroughness of the planning, an idea still may be poorly or improperly implemented without a satisfactory control system. Effective management, therefore, needs to consider the benefits of a well-designed control system.

MDA LABORATORY SERVICES
www.mdslabs.com/

What Is Control?

Control can be defined as the process of monitoring activities to ensure that they are being accomplished as planned, and of correcting any significant deviations. All managers should be involved in the control function even if their units seem to be performing as planned. Managers cannot really know whether their units are performing

control
The process of monitoring activities to ensure they are being accomplished as planned, and of correcting any significant deviations.

properly until they have evaluated what activities have been done and have compared the actual performance with the desired standard.[2] An effective control system ensures that activities are completed in ways that lead to the attainment of the organization's goals. The criterion that determines the effectiveness of a control system is how well it facilitates goal achievement. The more it helps managers achieve their organization's goals, the better the control system.[3]

The Importance of Control

Planning can be done, an organization structure can be created to efficiently facilitate the achievement of objectives, and employees can be directed and motivated. Still, there is no assurance that activities are going as planned and that the goals managers are seeking are, in fact, being attained. Control is important, therefore, because it is the final link in the functional chain of management. However, the value of the control function lies predominantly in its relation to planning and delegating activities.

In Chapter 3, we described objectives as the foundation of planning. Objectives give specific direction to managers. However, just stating objectives or having employees accept your objectives is no guarantee that the necessary actions have been accomplished. The effective manager needs to follow up to ensure that the actions that others are supposed to take and the objectives they are supposed to achieve are, in fact, being taken and achieved.

The Control Process

control process
The process of measuring actual performance, comparing it against a standard, and taking managerial action to correct deviations or inadequate standards.

The **control process** consists of three separate and distinct steps: (1) measuring actual performance; (2) comparing actual performance against a standard; and (3) taking managerial action to correct deviations or inadequate standards (see Exhibit 15-1). Before we consider each step in detail, you should be aware that the control process assumes that standards of performance already exist. These standards are the specific objectives against which progress can be measured. They are created in the planning function. If managers use some variation of mutual goal setting, then objectives are, by definition, tangible, verifiable, and measurable. In such instances, these objectives are the standards against which progress is measured and compared. If "goal setting" is not practised, then standards are the specific performance indicators that management uses. Our point is that these standards are developed in the planning function; planning must precede control.

What Is Measuring?

To determine what actual performance is, a manager must acquire information about it. The first step in control, then, is measuring. Let us consider *how* we measure and *what* we measure.

How Do Managers Measure? Four common sources of information, frequently used by managers to measure actual performance, are personal observation, statistical

Exhibit 15-1
The Control Process

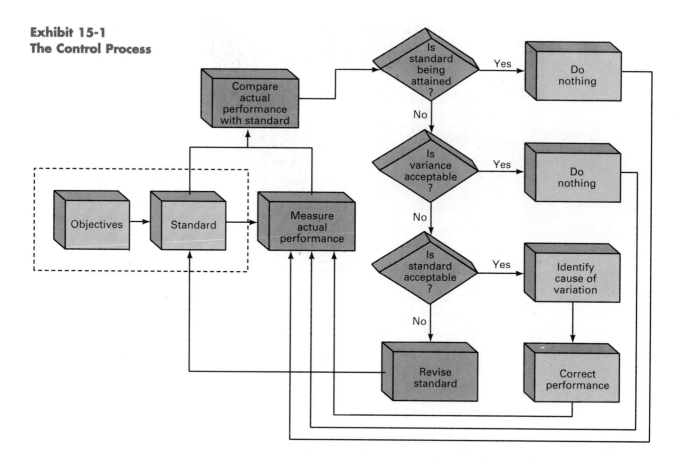

reports, oral reports, and written reports. Each has particular strengths and weaknesses; however, a combination of them increases both the number of input sources and the probability of receiving reliable information.

Personal observation provides firsthand, intimate knowledge of the actual activity—information that is not filtered through others. It permits intensive coverage because minor as well as major performance activities can be observed, and it provides opportunities for the manager to "read between the lines." Management-by-walking-around can pick up omissions, facial expressions, and tones of voice that may be missed by other sources. Unfortunately, in a time when quantitative information suggests objectivity, personal observation is often considered an inferior information source. It is subject to perceptual biases—what one manager sees, another might not. Personal observation also consumes a good deal of time. Finally, this method suffers from obtrusiveness. Employees might interpret a manager's overt observation as a sign of a lack of confidence in them or of mistrust.

The current wide use of computers in organizations has made managers rely increasingly on statistical reports for measuring actual performance. This measuring device, however, is not limited to computer outputs. It also includes graphs, bar charts, and numerical displays of any form that managers may use for assessing performance. Although statistical data are easy to visualize and effective for showing relationships, they provide limited information about an activity. Statistics report on only a few key areas and often ignore other important factors.

YOUNG CANADIANS

Kevin Cuthbertson: Joey Tomatoes

Kevin Cuthbertson is quality control leader for Joey Tomatoes restaurants in Alberta. Having been a kitchen manager for Earls, he has quickly moved up in the organization to his present position wherein he is in charge of operations for seven restaurants. In this capacity Kevin tries to sit down with workers to come up with solutions to the various problems that inevitably occur.

Information can also be acquired through oral reports—that is, through conferences, meetings, one-to-one conversations, or telephone calls. The advantages and disadvantages of this method of measuring performance are similar to those of personal observation. Although the information is filtered, it is fast, allows for feedback, and permits language expression and tone of voice, as well as words themselves, to convey meaning. Historically, one of the major drawbacks of oral reports was the problem of documenting information for later reference. However, our technological capabilities have progressed in the last couple of decades to the point that oral reports can be efficiently taped and become as permanent as if they were written.

Actual performance may also be measured by written reports. As with statistical reports, written are slower yet more formal than first- or second-hand oral measures. This formality also often means greater comprehensiveness and conciseness than is found in oral reports. In addition, written reports are usually easy to catalogue and reference.

Given the varied advantages and disadvantages of each of these four measurement techniques, comprehensive control efforts by managers should use all four.

How do you measure the performance of this grade school teacher? Often his activities are not easily quantified. Thus, his principal must determine what value he adds to the school and translate that into job standards.

What Do Managers Measure? *What* we measure is probably more critical to the control process than *how* we measure. The selection of the wrong criteria can result in serious dysfunctional consequences. Besides, what we measure determines, to a great extent, what people in the organization will attempt to excel at.[4] For example, assume your instructor has assigned a 20-page term paper on your syllabus for this course. In the grade computation section of the syllabus, you notice that the term paper is not scored. In fact, when you ask your professor if that is a mistake, she says no; the term paper is for your own enlightenment and has no grade consequence for the course. Grades are solely a function of how well you perform on the three exams in the course. Accordingly, we can expect most, if not all, your effort will be geared toward preparing for and taking the three exams.

For the most part, controls are directed at one of several areas: information, operations, finances, or people (we'll explore these areas in more detail in the next chapter). Some control criteria, however, are applicable to any management situation. For instance, because all managers, by definition, direct the activities of others, criteria such as employee satisfaction or turnover and absenteeism rates can be measured. Most managers have budgets for their area of responsibility set in dollar costs. Keeping costs within budget is therefore a fairly common control measure. However, any comprehensive control system needs to recognize the diversity of activities among managers. A production manager in a manufacturing plant might use measures of the quantity of units produced per day, units produced per labour hour, scrap per unit of output, or percentage of rejects returned by customers. The manager of an administrative unit in a government agency might use number of document pages typed per day, number of orders processed per hour, or average time required to process service calls. Marketing managers often use measures such as percentage of market captured, average dollar value per sale, or number of customer visits per salesperson.

The performance of some activities is difficult to measure in quantifiable terms. It is more difficult, for instance, for an administrator to measure the performance of a research chemist or an elementary school teacher than of a person who sells life insurance. But most activities can be broken down into objective segments that allow for measurement. The manager needs to determine what value a person, department, or unit contributes to the organization and then convert the contribution into standards.

Most jobs and activities can be expressed in tangible and measurable terms. When a performance indicator cannot be stated in quantifiable terms, managers should look for and use subjective measures. Certainly, subjective measures have significant limitations. Still, they are better than having no standards at all and ignoring the control function. If an activity is important, the excuse that it is difficult to measure is inadequate. In such cases, managers should use subjective performance criteria. Of course, any analysis or decisions made based on subjective criteria should recognize the limitations of the data.

How Do Managers Determine Variations Between Actual Performance and Planned Goals?

Managers determine the variation between actual performance and the standard through a process called comparing. The comparing step determines the degree of variation between actual performance and the standard. Some variation in performance can be expected in all activities; it is therefore critical to determine the acceptable **range of variation** (see Exhibit 15-2). Deviations in excess of this range become significant and receive the manager's attention. In the comparison stage, managers are particularly concerned with the size and direction of the variation. An example should help make this clearer.

range of variation
The acceptable parameters of variance between actual performance and the standard.

Julie Black is sales manager for CanuckBrew, a distribution company that supplies bars in Manitoba with beers from across the rest of the country. Julie prepares a report during the first week of each month that describes sales for the previous month, classified by brand name. Exhibit 15-3 displays both the standard and actual sales figures (in hundreds of cases) for the month of July.

The deviation on several brands is very small and undoubtedly not worth special attention. Are the shortages for La Maudite and St. Ambroise significant? That's a judgment Julie must make. Alexander Keith's sales were 15 per cent below her goal. This demands attention. She should look for a cause. In this case Julie attributed the

**Exhibit 15-2
Defining an
Acceptable Range
of Variation**

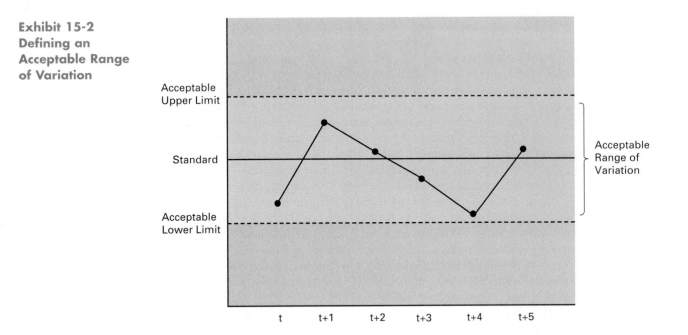

**Exhibit 15-3
CanuckBrew's Sales
Performance for July
(in cases)**

BRAND	STANDARD	ACTUAL	OVER (UNDER)
Alexander Keith's I.P.A.	1075	913	(162)
Big Rock Warthog Ale	630	634	4
Okanagan Spring Pale Ale	800	912	112
Moosehead Export	620	622	2
Olands Export Ale	540	672	132
McAuslan's St. Ambroise	160	140	(20)
Granville Island Lager	225	220	(5)
Unibroue's La Maudite	80	65	(15)
Nelson After Dark	170	286	116
TOTAL CASES	4300	4464	164

loss to aggressive advertising and promotion programs by the big domestic producers, Labatt and Molson. Since Keith's is CanuckBrew's number-one seller, it is most vulnerable to the promotion clout of the big breweries. If the decline in Keith's is more than a temporary slump, Julie will need to reduce her orders with the brewery and lower her inventory stock until she can boost the numbers back up.

An error in understating sales can be as troublesome as can overstatement. For instance, is the surprising popularity of Nelson a one-month aberration, or is this brand increasing its market share? Our CanuckBrew example illustrates that both overvariance and undervariance require managerial attention.

What Managerial Action Can Be Taken?

The third and final step in the control process is taking managerial action. Managers can choose among three courses of action: they can do nothing; they can correct the actual performance; or they can revise the standard. Because "doing nothing" is fairly self-explanatory, let's look more closely at the latter two.

If the source of the variation has been deficient performance, the manager will want to take corrective action. Examples of such corrective action might include changes in strategy, structure, compensation practices, or training programs; the redesign of jobs; or the replacement of personnel.

A manager who decides to correct actual performance has to make another decision: should she take immediate or basic corrective action? **Immediate corrective action** corrects problems at once and gets performance back on track. **Basic corrective action** asks how and why performance has deviated and then proceeds to correct the source of deviation. It is not unusual for managers to rationalize that they do not have the time to take basic corrective action and therefore must be content to perpetually "put out fires" with immediate corrective action. Effective managers, however, analyse deviations and, when the benefits justify it, take the time to permanently correct significant variances between standard and actual performance.

To return to our example of CanuckBrew, Julie Black might take basic corrective action on the negative variance for Alexander Keith's. She might increase promotion efforts, increase the advertisement budget for this brand, or reduce future orders with the manufacturer. The action she takes will depend on her assessment of each brand's potential effectiveness.

It is also possible that the variance was a result of an unrealistic standard—that is, the goal may be too high or too low. In such cases it's the standard that needs corrective attention, not the performance. In our example, the sales manager might need to raise the standard for Nelson to reflect its increasing popularity. This frequently happens in sports when athletes adjust their performance goals upward during a season if they achieve their season goal early.

immediate corrective action
Correcting an activity at once to get performance back on track.

basic corrective action
Determining how and why performance has deviated and correcting the source of deviations.

D I G I T A L
R E N A I S S A N C E
I N C .
www.digital-ren.com/

YOUNG CANADIANS

Keith Kocho:
Digital Renaissance Inc.

In 1991, at the age of 21, Keith Kocho thought to himself, "I've got a credit card and I'll go conquer the world." Maxing out his few-hundred-dollar limit, Kocho started Digital Renaissance Inc., a producer of multimedia programs. By 1998 the company had offices in Toronto, Ottawa, Saint John, and Boston.

The more troublesome problem is the revising of a performance standard downward. If an employee or unit falls significantly short of reaching its target, the natural response is to shift the blame for the variance to the standard. For instance, students who make a low grade on a test often attack the grade cutoff points as too high. Rather than accept the fact that their performance was inadequate, students argue that the standards are unreasonable. Similarly, salespeople who fail to meet their monthly quota may attribute the failure to an unrealistic quota. It may be true that standards are too high, resulting in a significant variance and acting to demotivate employees being assessed against it. But keep in mind that if employees or managers don't meet the standard, the first thing they are likely to attack is the standard itself. If you believe the standard is realistic, hold your ground. Explain your position, reaffirm to the employee or manager that you expect future performance to improve, and then take the necessary corrective action to turn that expectation into reality.

Types of Control

Management can implement controls before an activity commences, while the activity is going on, or after the activity has been completed. The first type is called feedforward control, the second is concurrent control, and the last is feedback control (see Exhibit 15-4).

What Is Feedforward Control?

feedforward control
Control that prevents anticipated problems.

The most desirable type of control—**feedforward control**—prevents anticipated problems. It is called feedforward control because it takes place in advance of the actual activity. It is future-directed.[5] For instance, managers at Westinghouse Corporation may hire additional personnel as soon as the government announces that the firm has won a major defence contract. The hiring of personnel ahead of time prevents potential delays. The key to feedforward control, therefore, is taking managerial action before a problem occurs.

Feedforward controls are desirable because they allow management to prevent problems rather than having to cure them later. Unfortunately, these controls require timely and accurate information that is often difficult to develop. As a result, managers frequently have to use one of the other two types of control.

**Exhibit 15-4
Types of Control**

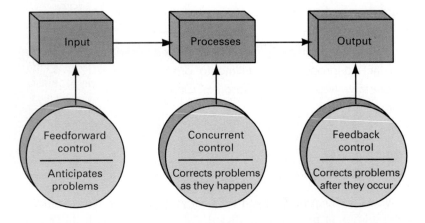

When Is Concurrent Control Used?

Concurrent control, as its name implies, takes place while an activity is in progress. When control is enacted while the work is being performed, management can correct problems before they become too costly.

The best-known form of concurrent control is direct supervision. When a manager directly oversees the actions of an employee, the manager can concurrently monitor the employee's actions and correct problems as they occur. While there is obviously some delay between the activity and the manager's corrective response, the delay is minimal. Technical equipment can be designed to include concurrent controls. Most computers, for instance, are programmed to provide operators with immediate response if an error is made. If you input the wrong command, the program's concurrent controls reject your command and may even tell you why it is wrong.

Why Is Feedback Control So Popular?

The most popular type of control relies on feedback. The control takes place after the action. The control report that Julie Black used for assessing beer sales is an example of a **feedback control**.

The major drawback of this type of control is that by the time the manager has the information, the damage is already done. It's analogous to the proverbial closing of the barn door after the horse has been stolen. But for many activities, feedback is the only viable type of control available.

We should note that feedback has two advantages over feedforward and concurrent control.[6] First, feedback provides managers with meaningful information on the effectiveness of their planning effort. If feedback indicates little variance between standard and actual performance, this is evidence that planning was generally on target. If the deviation is great, a manager can use this information when formulating new plans to make them more effective. Second, feedback control can enhance employee motivation. People also want information on how well they have performed. Feedback control provides that information (see Developing Management Skills.)

Good news for the parking cops, bad news for us. Meter-vision of Fredericton, N.B., has designed a wireless information system for municipal metered parking and public safety. It registers when a car pulls into a spot and doesn't pay, then sends a signal to the nearest parking enforcement personnel.

concurrent control
Control that occurs while an activity is in progress.

feedback control
Control imposed after an action has occurred.

This Motorola manager works with company suppliers to teach them how Motorola's control process operates. In running such seminars, and increasing supplier understanding of what Motorola wants, quality of goods supplied has increased. So, too, has there been a reduction in the suppliers' time taken to ship the parts.

DEVELOPING MANAGEMENT SKILLS

▼

PROVIDING FEEDBACK

▲

▶ **1. Focus on specific rather than general behaviours.** Feedback should be specific rather than general. General statements are vague and provide little useful information which the recipient can use to "correct" the problem.

▶ **2. Support negative feedback with hard data.** Tell the recipient precisely why you are being critical and on what basis you concluded that a "good job" was not com-pleted. Hard data also help the recipient to identify where she erred and what behaviours should be avoided in the future.

▶ **3. Keep comments impersonal and job related.** Feedback, particularly the negative kind, should be descriptive rather than judgmental or evaluative. No matter how upset you are, keep the feedback job-related and never criticize someone personally because of an inappropriate action. You are censuring job-related behaviour, not the person!

▶ **4. Ensure the recipient has clear and full understanding of the feedback.** Feedback must be concise and complete enough so that the recipient clearly and fully understands your communications. Consistent with active listening techniques, have the recipient rephrase the content of your feedback to check whether it fully captures your meaning.

▶ **5. Direct the negative feedback toward behaviour that is controllable by the recipient.** Negative feedback should be directed toward behaviour that the recipient can do something about. Indicate what the recipient can do to improve the situation. This helps to take the sting out of the criticism and offers guidance to those who understand the problem but don't know how to resolve it.

Qualities of an Effective Control System

Effective control systems tend to have certain qualities in common.[7] The importance of these qualities varies with the situation, but we can generalize that the following characteristics should make a control system more effective.

▶ **1. Accuracy** A control system that generates inaccurate information can result in management failing to take action when it should or responding to a problem that doesn't exist. An accurate control system is reliable and produces valid data.

▶ **2. Timeliness** Controls should call management's attention to variations in time to prevent serious infringement on a unit's performance. The best information has little value if it is dated. Therefore, an effective control system must provide timely information.

▶ **3. Economy** A control system must be economically reasonable to operate. Any system of control has to justify the benefits that it gives in relation to the costs it incurs. To minimize costs, management should try to impose the least amount of control that is necessary to produce the desired results.

▶ **4. Flexibility** Effective controls must be flexible enough to adjust to adverse change or to take advantage of new opportunities. Few organizations face environments so stable that there is no need for flexibility. Even highly mechanistic structures require controls that can be adjusted as times and conditions change.

▶ **5. Understandability** Controls that cannot be understood have no value. It is sometimes necessary, therefore, to substitute less complex controls for sophisticated devices. A control system that is difficult to understand can cause unnecessary mistakes, frustrate employees, and eventually be ignored.

▶ **6. Reasonable criteria** Control standards must be reasonable and attainable. If they are too high or unreasonable, they no longer motivate. Because most employees don't want to risk being labelled incompetent by accusing superiors of asking too much, employees may resort to unethical or illegal shortcuts. Controls should, therefore, enforce standards that challenge and stretch people to reach higher performance levels without being demotivating or encouraging deception.

▶ **7. Strategic placement** Management can't control everything that goes on in an organization (see Managers Who Made a Difference). And in any case, the benefits couldn't justify the costs. As a result, managers should place controls on factors that are strategic to the organization's performance. Controls should cover the critical activities, operations, and events within the organization. That is, they should focus on places where variations from standard are most likely to occur or where a variation would do the greatest harm. In a department where labour costs are $20,000 a month and postage costs are $50 a month, a 5-per-cent overrun in the former is more critical than a 20-per-cent overrun in the latter. Hence, we should establish controls for labour and a critical dollar allocation, whereas postage expenses would not appear to be critical.

Managers at the Goodyear Tire and Rubber Company would pay particular attention to the demands of suppliers of critical petroleum products used in the tire manufacturing process; officials at banks where the company has sizeable short-term loans; government regulatory agencies that grade tires and inspect facilities; security analysts at major brokerage firms who specialize in the tire and rubber industry; regional tire jobbers and distributors; and purchasing agents responsible for the acquisition of tires at Ford, Mack Truck, Caterpillar, and other vehicle manufacturers.

▶ **8. Emphasis on the exception** Because managers can't control all activities, they should place their strategic control devices where those devices can call attention only to the exceptions. An exception system ensures that a manager is not overwhelmed by information on variations from standard. For instance, if management policy gives supervisors the authority to give annual raises up to $200 a month, approve individual expenses up to $500, and make capital expenditures up to $5,000, then only deviations above these amounts require approval from higher levels of management. These checkpoints become controls that are part of the authority constraints and free higher levels of management from reviewing routine expenditures.

▶ **9. Multiple criteria** Managers and employees alike will seek to "look good" on the criteria that are controlled. If management controls by using a single measure such as unit profit, effort will be focused only on looking good on this standard. Multiple measures of performance decrease this narrow focus. Multiple criteria have a dual positive effect. Because they are more difficult to manipulate than a single measure, they can discourage employee efforts to merely look good. And because performance can rarely be objectively evaluated from a single indicator, multiple criteria make possible more accurate assessments of performance.

▶ **10. Corrective action** An effective control system not only indicates when a significant deviation from standard occurs but also suggests what action should be taken to correct the deviation. That is, it ought to both point out the problem and specify the solution. This is frequently accomplished by establishing if-then guidelines; for instance, if unit revenues drop more than 5 per cent, then unit costs should be reduced by a similar amount.

Contingency Factors of Control

While the generalizations above about effective control systems provide guidelines, their validity is influenced by situational factors. These include size of the organization, position in the organization's hierarchy, degree of decentralization, organizational culture, and importance of an activity (see Exhibit 15-5).

Control systems should vary to reflect the size of the organization. A small business relies on informal and more personal control devices. Concurrent control through direct supervision is probably most cost effective. As organizations increase in size, direct supervision is likely to be supported by an expanding formal system. Very large organizations will typically have highly formalized and impersonal feed-forward and feedback controls.

The higher one moves in the organization's hierarchy, the greater the need for multiple sets of control criteria, tailored to the unit's goals. This reflects the increased ambiguity in measuring performance as a person moves up the hierarchy. Conversely, lower-level jobs have clearer definitions of performance that allow for a more narrow interpretation of job performance.

The greater the degree of decentralization, the more managers will need feedback on the performance of subordinate decision makers. Since managers who delegate authority are ultimately responsible for the actions of those to whom it is delegated, managers will want proper assurances that their employees' decisions are both effective and efficient.

George Melville and Jim Treliving of the Western Professional Hockey League

WESTERN PROFESSIONAL HOCKEY LEAGUE
www.wphlhockey. com/

How's this for a gamble: hockey in New Mexico and Texas? The very idea of ice hockey being played in these arid states seems crazy, let alone the logistics of forming a professional league. But for Jim Treliving and George Melville, it's an idea that has paid off well. The two men formed a partnership long ago that gradually became the franchise chain of Boston Pizza (headquartered in Vancouver in spite of the name) which now boasts over 100 outlets in western Canada. The desire to buy a minor-league team turned out to be too expensive, so they decided to transfer their knowledge of franchising from pizza outlets to a hockey league.[8]

The Western Professional Hockey League began with an initial investment of $300,000 (U.S.) from the two partners. This quickly proved to be a lucrative investment as they sold the original six teams for $100,000 each. The unique aspect of this league—apart from being located in the U.S. southwest—is that each team is a franchise. Whereas with all other professional hockey leagues the teams are individually owned and operated, in the WPHL teams are purchased as franchises from the league. For Melville and Treliving this business structure allows them one crucial advantage—control. The league has been extremely successful, with all six original teams passing the $1.5 million mark in gross revenue (WPHL gets 5 per cent of this) for the first season. The following season six new teams came aboard, this time at a cost of $250,000 each for the franchise rights. The game is fast, allowing two-line passes, and the fans seem to be taking to it quickly. Apart from the start-up costs which each franchise is responsible for (and these can be hefty, building a hockey rink in cattle country), the overhead for each team is fairly low, and therefore the investment can be very profitable.

Treliving and Melville want to keep things that way. Success for the franchises translates to success for the league. Therefore the two men are obsessive about control. And the franchise arrangement allows them the ability to exercise strict control measures. Think of Tim Hortons or McDonald's—in these businesses the head office controls almost every aspect of the individual franchises' operations. For the WPHL, franchises pick their rosters from player lists supplied by head office, and a salary cap is strictly enforced. This, along with other measures, keeps costs down. Auditors from head office are periodically sent to check up on the individual franchises. The WPHL also has a marketing manager who controls the marketing for all of the franchises—allowing the league to retain complete control of its overall image. With control techniques such as these, the WPHL should remain profitable for quite some time.▼

**Exhibit 15-5
Contingency Factors
in the Design of
Control Systems**

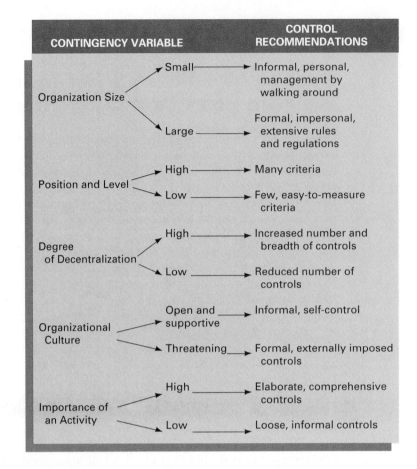

The organizational culture may be one of trust, autonomy, and openness, or fear and reprisal. In the former, we can expect to find more informal self-control and, in the latter, more externally imposed and formal control systems to ensure that performance is within standards. As with leadership styles, motivation techniques, organizational structuring, conflict-management techniques, and the extent to which organizational members participate in decision making, the type and extent of controls should be consistent with the organization's culture.

Finally, the importance of an activity influences whether, and how, it will be controlled. If control is costly and the repercussions from error small, the control system is not likely to be elaborate. However, if an error can be highly damaging to the organization, extensive controls are likely to be implemented—even if the cost is high.

Adjusting Controls for National Differences

Methods of controlling people and operations can be quite different in foreign countries. For the multinational corporation, managers of foreign operations tend to be less closely controlled by the head office, if for no other reason than that distance precludes direct controls. The head office of a multinational must rely on extensive formal reports to maintain control. But collecting data that are comparable between countries introduces problems for multinationals. A company's factory in Mexico might produce the same products as its factory in Canada. The Mexican factory, however, might be much more labour intensive than its counterpart in Canada (to take advantage of low labour costs in Mexico). If headquarters' executives were to control costs by, for example, calculating labour costs per unit or output per worker, the figures would not be comparable. Therefore, distance creates a tendency to formalize controls, and technological differences often make control data uncomparable.

Technology's impact on control is most evident in comparing technologically advanced nations with more primitive countries. Organizations in technologically advanced nations such as the United States, Japan, Canada, Great Britain, Germany, and Australia use indirect control devices—particularly computer-related reports and analyses—in addition to standardized rules and direct supervision, to ensure that activities are going as planned. In Tanzania, Zambia, Lebanon, and other less advanced countries, direct supervision, and highly centralized decision making are the basic means of control.

Constraints on managerial corrective action may also affect managers in foreign countries. For example, laws in some countries do not allow management the options of closing plants, laying off personnel, taking money out of the country, or bringing in a new management team from outside the country.

The Dysfunctional Side of Controls

Here are actual instances of controls taken too far. Fortunately they didn't happen in Canada, but the negative aspects of what we criticize as "bureaucratic procedures" taken to the extreme are well illustrated by the examples, and we, as Canadians, are no more immune to them than is any other culture. Larry Boff called the Dallas Fire Department's emergency number to get immediate help for his stepmother, who was having trouble breathing.[9] The nurse/dispatcher spent 15 minutes arguing with Boff because he wouldn't bring his stepmother to the phone. He told the dispatcher that his stepmother was in the bedroom and couldn't speak. The dispatcher insisted that she was required to talk to the person in question so she could determine if the situation was a true emergency. Boff insisted that his stepmother was unable to speak on the phone and pleaded with the dispatcher to send an ambulance. The dispatcher continually responded that she could not send an ambulance until she spoke to Boff's stepmother. After getting nowhere for 15 minutes, Boff hung up the phone. His stepmother was dead.

Three managers at a big General Motors truck plant installed a secret control box in a supervisor's office to override the control panel that governed the speed of the assembly line.[10] The device allowed the managers to speed up the assembly line—a serious violation of GM's contract with the United Auto Workers. When caught, the managers explained that while they knew that what they had done was wrong, the pressure from higher-ups to meet unrealistic production goals was so great that they felt the secret control panel was the only way they could meet their targets. As described by one manager, senior GM executives would say, "I don't care how you do it—just do it."

Did you ever notice that the people who work in the college registrar's office often don't seem to care much about students' problems? They become so fixated on ensuring that every rule is followed that they lose sight of the fact that their job is to serve students, not hassle them!

These examples illustrate what can happen when controls are inflexible or control standards are unreasonable. People lose sight of the organization's overall goals.[11] Instead of the organization running the controls, sometimes the controls run the organization.

Because any control system has imperfections, problems occur when individuals or organizational units attempt to look good exclusively in terms of the control devices. The result is dysfunctional in terms of the organization's goals. More often than not, this dysfunctionality is caused by incomplete measures of performance. If the control system evaluates only the quantity of output, people will ignore quality. Similarly, if the system measures activities rather than results, people will spend their time attempting to look good on the activity measures.

To avoid being reprimanded by managers because of the control system, people can engage in behaviours that are designed solely to influence the information sys-

ETHICAL DILEMMAS IN MANAGEMENT

▼

CONTROL AND EMPLOYEES' RIGHT TO PRIVACY

▲

When do management's efforts to control the actions of its employees become an invasion of privacy? In the United States workers will go to great lengths to evade being caught-out by drug testing. Employees may drink gallons of fluids before testing and take some vitamin B-2 to give their diluted urine a natural yellow colouration. Dehydrated urine is a big seller, and sneaking baggies of drug-free urine into testing booths is so common as to be almost routine. This raises the question, does management have the right to tell employees how they can or cannot spend their time off the job?

In Canada it is not so simple to dismiss an employee due to his or her off-the-job behaviour. A recent case in Ontario involved a sales executive who had been transferred to a new post in his organization. The man met an old client for lunch to thank him for his patronage. The two drank heavily and proceeded to get into a physical fight. The employee then drove a company vehicle—obviously against company policy when under the influence of alcohol. The man was fired, and he then sued for wrongful dismissal. The courts found in his favour, citing his 27 years of good service to the company. While it is quite common for an employee to have a couple of drinks with a client during working hours, the extreme nature of this case would seem to justify the company's actions.[12]

The Sheraton Hotel in Boston was recently sued by an employee for videotaping the men's dressing room—the company was trying to ferret out possible drug dealing. So, when does management overstep the bounds of decency and privacy by silently (even covertly) scrutinizing the behaviour of its employees?

How does management defend such practices? The argument is essentially based on keeping medical costs down. With corporate insurance plan premiums rising, companies wish to limit the amount of claims, and this means cracking down on employees who drink, smoke, and engage in other activities generally deemed unhealthy.

Nearly two-thirds of U.S. employers record employees' voice mail, e-mail, or phone calls, and review computer files and videotapes of the workplace. The reason for this is ostensibly to help employees do their jobs better. Managers can review employee performance and provide feedback that can improve the quality of the employee's work.

But once management starts regulating off-the-job behaviour, where does it stop? What about employees who eat lots of greasy food? Is that grounds for disciplinary action? Similarly, when does management's need for more information about employee performance cross over the line and interfere with a worker's right to privacy? What do you think?

tem's data output during a given control period. Rather than actually performing well, employees can manipulate measures to give the appearance that they are performing well. Evidence indicates that the manipulation of control data is not a random phenomenon. It depends on the importance of an activity. Organizationally important activities are more likely to make a difference in a person's rewards; therefore, there is a greater incentive to look good on these particular measures.[13] When rewards are at stake, individuals tend to manipulate data to appear in a favourable light by, for instance, distorting actual figures, emphasizing successes, and suppressing evidence of failures. On the other hand, only random errors occur when the distribution of rewards is unaffected.[14]

Our conclusion is that controls have both an up side and a down side (see Ethical Dilemmas in Management). Failure to design flexibility into a control system can create problems more severe than those the controls were implemented to prevent.

Summary

This summary is organized by the chapter Learning Objectives found on page 392.

1. Control is the process of monitoring activities to ensure that they are being accomplished as planned, and of correcting any significant deviations.

2. Control is important because it monitors whether objectives are being accomplished as planned and whether delegated authority is being abused.

3. In the control process, management must first have standards of performance from the objectives it formed in the planning stage. Management must then measure actual performance and compare that performance to the standards. If a variance exists between standards and performance, management must either adjust performance, adjust the standards, or do nothing, according to the situation.

4. There are three types of control: feedforward control is future-directed and prevents anticipated problems; concurrent control takes place while an activity is in progress; feedback control takes place after the activity.

5. An effective control system is accurate, timely, economical, flexible, and understandable. It uses reasonable criteria, has strategic placement, emphasizes the exception, uses multiple criteria, and suggests corrective action.

6. The contingency factors in control systems include the size of the organization; the level in the organization's hierarchy; the degree of decentralization; the organization's culture; and the importance of the activity.

7. Controls can be dysfunctional when they redirect behaviour away from an organization's goals. This can occur as a result of inflexibility or unreasonable standards. Also, when rewards are at stake, individuals are more likely to manipulate data so that their performance will be perceived positively.

Review and Discussion Questions

1. What is the role of control in management?

2. How are planning and control linked?

3. In Chapter 9 we discussed the white water rapids view of change. Do you think it's possible to establish and maintain effective standards and controls in this type of atmosphere?

4. Why is *what* is measured in the control process probably more critical to the control process than *how* it is measured?

5. Name four methods that managers can use to acquire information about actual performance.

6. Contrast immediate and basic corrective action.

7. What are the advantages and disadvantages of feedforward control?

8. Why is feedback control the most popular type of control?

9. What can management do to reduce the dysfunctionality of controls?

10. Do you think goal setting and TQM programs facilitate the control process? Explain your answer.

Testing Your Comprehension

Circle the correct answer, then check yourself on page 472.

1. Which of the following would be indicative of a POOR control system?
   a) a frequent goal conflict that leads to suboptimization of goals
   b) the discovery that results are significantly below plans
   c) a change in structure recommended by the control system to improve an inefficient process
   d) the establishment of an adherence to goals prior to controlling

2. The ultimate criterion of control is the extent to which activities are completed in ways that lead to
   a) cost effectiveness
   b) cost efficiencies
   c) more profits
   d) goal attainment

3. Which of the following is NOT a reason for the importance of control?
   a) It allows managers to delegate.
   b) It helps establish hierarchical relationships.
   c) It ensures that the organization is moving toward established goals.
   d) It is related to planning.

4. The MOST important distinguishing feature of personal observation as a measurement method is that
   a) it works for individuals as well as groups
   b) it can be done on a daily basis so the time involved is minimal
   c) firsthand information is not subject to others' biases and filtering
   d) it adds a necessary degree of objectivity

5. A disadvantage of personal observation as a method for measuring performance is
   a) the time involved
   b) the limited level of coverage of performance activities
   c) others' biases
   d) infrequency

6. Once actual results have been measured, the next step in the control process is
   a) determination of goals consistent with organizational objectives
   b) taking action to correct unfavourable variations from the plan
   c) comparisons between the plan and results
   d) checking measurements against established legal standards

7. If a manager's response to a key employee's repeated absence is to perform that subordinate's job for the day, the manager is
   a) performing immediate corrective action
   b) performing basic corrective action
   c) demonstrating delegation
   d) illustrating the role of an effective manager

8. When would it be appropriate for a manager to do nothing when a variance is detected in actual performance compared against a standard?
   a) when people may take offense at efforts to change their behaviour
   b) when the variance is not significant
   c) when the standard is obviously incorrect
   d) it is never appropriate for a manager to "do nothing"

9. The MAJOR problem with feedback controls is that they
   a) are costly to implement
   b) are time-consuming to implement
   c) indicate a problem only after it has occurred
   d) require information that is often difficult or impossible to obtain

10. Which of the following statements is MOST accurate?
    a) The type of control most widely used is feedback control.
    b) The best-known form of feedback control is direct supervision.
    c) Feedback controls are designed to detect problems before they occur.
    d) Feedback controls have the greatest impact on motivation.

11. The BIGGEST problem with feedback controls is that
    a) they are of little use as a motivational tool
    b) it is difficult, if not impossible, to obtain the necessary information
    c) when significant deviations are detected, the damage has already been done
    d) they do not provide the type of information needed to judge the accuracy of the planning process

12. The BEST-KNOWN form of concurrent control is
    a) internal selection
    b) direct supervision
    c) feedback
    d) decentralization

13. Reviewing reports is a form of
    a) consecutive control
    b) concurrent control
    c) feedback control
    d) feedforward control

14. Controls should be placed
    a) where they are cost-effective
    b) on all activities
    c) where there are problem areas
    d) on the single most important factor

15. Because management cannot control all activities, controls should be placed on _____ activities.
    a) risky
    b) risk-free
    c) critical
    d) complex

16. Informal controls are recommended when
    a) decentralization is high
    b) organizational culture is threatening
    c) organizational size is large
    d) importance of an activity is low

Self-Assessment Exercise

How Willing Are You to Give Up Control?

Instructions: You can get a good idea of whether you are willing to give up enough control to be effective in delegating by responding to the following items. If you have limited work experience, base your answers on what you know about yourself and your personal beliefs. Indicate the extent to which you agree or disagree by circling the number following each statement.

	Strongly Agree				Strongly Disagree
1. I'd delegate more, but the jobs I delegate never seem to get done the way I want them to be done.	5	4	3	2	1
2. I don't feel I have the time to delegate properly.	5	4	3	2	1
3. I carefully check on subordinates' work without letting them know I'm doing it, so I can correct their mistakes if necessary before they cause too many problems.	5	4	3	2	1
4. I delegate the whole job—giving the opportunity for the subordinate to complete it without any of my involvement. Then I review the result.	5	4	3	2	1
5. When I have given clear instructions and the task isn't done right, I get upset.	5	4	3	2	1
6. I feel the staff lacks the commitment that I have. So any task I delegate won't get done as well as I'd do it.	5	4	3	2	1
7. I'd delegate more, but I feel I can do the task better than the person I might delegate it to.	5	4	3	2	1
8. I'd delegate more, but if the individual I delegate the task to does an incompetent job, I'll be severely criticized.	5	4	3	2	1
9. If I were to delegate a task, my job wouldn't be nearly as much fun.	5	4	3	2	1
10. When I delegate a task, I often find that the outcome is such that I end up doing the task over again myself.	5	4	3	2	1
11. I have not really found that delegation saves any time.	5	4	3	2	1
12. I delegate a task clearly and concisely, explaining exactly how it should be accomplished.	5	4	3	2	1
13. I can't delegate as much as I'd like to because my subordinates lack the necessary experience.	5	4	3	2	1
14. I feel that when I delegate I lose control.	5	4	3	2	1
15. I would delegate more but I'm pretty much a perfectionist.	5	4	3	2	1
16. I work longer hours than I should.	5	4	3	2	1
17. I can give subordinates the routine tasks, but I feel I must do nonroutine tasks myself.	5	4	3	2	1
18. My own boss expects me to keep very close to all details of my job.	5	4	3	2	1

Turn to page 470 for scoring directions and key.

Reprinted by permission of publisher from *Management Review*, May 1982. © 1982 American Management Association, New York. All rights reserved.

Class Exercise

Paper Plane Corporation

Purpose

1. To integrate the management functions.
2. To apply planning and control concepts specifically to improve organizational performance.

Required Knowledge
Planning, organizing, and controlling concepts.

Time Required
Approximately one hour.

Instructions for aircraft assembly

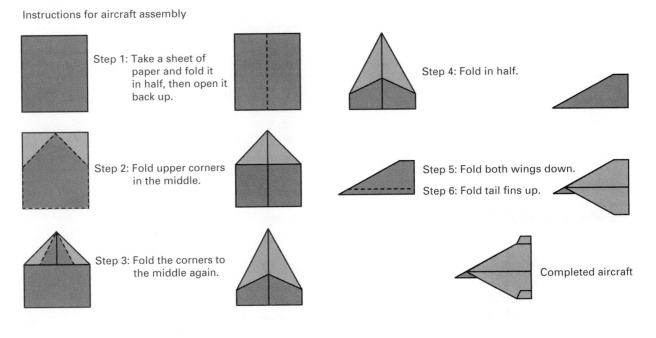

Step 1: Take a sheet of paper and fold it in half, then open it back up.

Step 2: Fold upper corners in the middle.

Step 3: Fold the corners to the middle again.

Step 4: Fold in half.

Step 5: Fold both wings down.

Step 6: Fold tail fins up.

Completed aircraft

Summary Sheet

Round 1:
Bid: _____ Aircraft @ $20,000.00 per aircraft = _____
Result: _____ Aircraft @ $20,000.00 per aircraft = _____
Less: $300,000.00 overhead
_____ × $3,000 cost of raw materials
_____ × $25,000 penalty
Profit: _____

Round 2:
Bid: _____ Aircraft @ $20,000.00 per aircraft = _____
Result: _____ Aircraft @ $20,000.00 per aircraft = _____
Less: $300,000.00 overhead
_____ × $3,000 cost of raw materials
_____ × $25,000 penalty
Profit: _____

Round 3:
Bid: _____ Aircraft @ $20,000.00 per aircraft = _____
Result: _____ Aircraft @ $20,000.00 per aircraft = _____
Less: $300,000.00 overhead
_____ × $3,000 cost of raw materials
_____ × $25,000 penalty
Profit: _____

Exhibit CE15-1
Paper Plane Corporation: Data Sheet

Source: Based on an exercise in James H. Donnelly, Jr., James L. Gibson, and John M. Ivancevich. *Fundamentals of Management,* 8th ed. (Burr Ridge, IL: Irwin, 1992), pp. 285–89. With permission.

Instructions

Any number of groups of six participants each are used in this exercise. These groups may be directed simultaneously in the same room. Each person should have assembly instructions (Exhibit CE15-1) and a summary sheet, plus ample stacks of paper (8-1/2 by 11 inches). The physical setting should be a room that is large enough that individual groups of six can work without interference from other groups. A working space should be provided for each group.

▶ The participants are doing an exercise in production methodology.

▶ Each group must work independently of the other groups.

▶ Each group will choose a manager and an inspector, and the remaining participants will be employees.

▶ The objective is to make paper airplanes in the most profitable manner possible.

▶ The facilitator will give the signal to start. This is a 10-minute, timed event utilizing competition among the groups.

▶ After the first round, each group should report its production and profits to the entire group. Each group reports the manner in which it planned, organized, and controlled for the production of the paper airplanes. This same procedure is followed for as many rounds as there is time.

Your group is the complete workforce for Paper Plane Corporation. Established in 1943, Paper Plane has led the market in paper plane production. Currently under new management, the company is contracting to make aircraft for the U.S. Air Force. You must establish a plan and organization to produce these aircraft. You must make your contract with the Air Force under the following conditions:

1. The Air Force will pay $20,000 per airplane.

2. The aircraft must pass a strict inspection.

3. A penalty of $25,000 per airplane will be subtracted for failure to meet the production requirements.

4. Labour and other overhead will be computed at $300,000.

5. Cost of materials will be $3,000 per bid plane. If you bid for 10 but make only eight, you must pay the cost of materials for those you failed to make or that did not pass inspection.

Case Application

Control Measures at Frito-Lay

All day long, each working day of the week, salespeople at Frito-Lay punch information into their hand-held computers. At the end of each workday, these salespeople download the collected information into minicomputers at local sales offices, or do it through modems in their homes. The downloaded data are then relayed to corporate headquarters. The company's CEO will have the report within 24 hours. Information on 100 Frito-Lay product lines in 400 000 stores is available on his computer screen in easy-to-read, colour-coded charts. This system allows problems to be quickly identified and corrected.[15]

Frito-Lay's control system helped the company solve a recent problem in two regional markets where sales were slumping in area supermarkets. The CEO turned on his computer, called up data for the areas, and quickly isolated the cause. A regional competitor had introduced a new white-corn tortilla chip. The product was getting good word-of-mouth advertising, and store managers were giving it more shelf space than Frito-Lay's traditional Tostitos tortilla chips. Using this information, the CEO sprang into action. He immediately directed his product development team to produce a white-corn version of Tostitos. Within three months their new product was on the shelves, and the company successfully won back lost market share.

This control mechanism at Frito-Lay is relatively new. Before its installation, the CEO would have needed at least three months just to pinpoint the problem. But this new system gathers data daily from supermarkets, scans it for important clues about local trends, and warns executives about problems and opportunities in all of Frito-Lay's markets.

 FRITO-LAY
www.fritolay.com/

Questions

1. Describe possible instances when Frito-Lay could use feedforward, concurrent, and feedback controls.

2. Describe how the company's control measures are helping it enhance organizational performance.

3. Could a small company such as CanuckBrew use this type of computer-aided control? How would it help operations?

chapter 16

Control Tools and Techniques

Learning Objectives

What will I be able to do after I finish this chapter?

1 • Explain the purpose of a management information system (MIS).

2 • Differentiate between data and information.

3 • Describe how an MIS affects decision making.

4 • Explain the role of information systems in control.

5 • Define the role of the transformation process in operations management.

6 • Explain the relationship between cost centres, direct costs, and indirect costs.

7 • Identify three approaches to maintenance control.

8 • Contrast TQM and quality control.

9 • Distinguish between external and internal audits.

10 • Explain how cost-benefit analysis can improve financial control.

11 • Identify six performance appraisal methods.

12 • Explain the "hot stove" rule of discipline.

learly Canadian Beverage Corp. of Vancouver found itself in a situation in which new markets for its line of specialty beverages were being added at a rapid rate. This growth forced the company to look at instituting a new comprehensive control system that would increase efficiency in both production and distribution. Management decided that a central control system would have to be implemented. The software system that was put in place completely revolutionized the manufacturing and distribution procedures at Clearly Canadian. Production information is plugged into the computer—for example, the need for 100,000 bottles of a certain beverage—and the software determines what ingredients are needed. The system then sends orders to suppliers, and tracks the shipping of those orders. At the bottling plant the system controls the manufacturing process, keeping tabs on every facet of production, such as ensuring the labels for orders meet the provincial or state requirements of their destinations. The control system then routes the orders to the various distributors, while at the same time sending financial information to the accounting system.

This control system has had a significant effect on the bottom line, greatly cutting costs for Clearly Canadian. The order cycle has been cut down from 30 days to just two, while inventory costs have been slashed. Best of all, the central system in Vancouver can control operations at every one of Clearly Canadian's plants, in Toronto, St. Louis, and California.

Clearly Canadian has instituted control systems to improve productivity.

In this chapter, we want to take a closer look at control tools and techniques. Specifically, we want to address four primary areas that require effective controls: information, operations, finances, and employee behaviour.

Today's organizations are information-processing "machines." With new technologies available to managers such as those at Clearly Canadian, they need to understand how to best use this information and to ensure organizational activities are proceeding as planned. With the greater importance placed on efficiency, effectiveness, and productivity, managers must develop well-designed operating systems and tight controls to survive in the global village. In addition, managers need to monitor the financial side of the organization to ensure budgets and costs are kept in line. Finally, since achieving organizational objectives greatly depends on management's ability to effectively use people, it makes good sense to understand the control mechanisms available for monitoring their performance.

Technologically advanced systems such as this one at Dell Computer handle customer requests efficiently. Cassye Ewald (pictured) takes an order. By having production schedules at her disposal, Cassye is able to tell the customer that his specifically designed computer will be delivered within five working days.

DELL COMPUTER
www.dell.com/

Information Control Systems

How does management control the rapid, ongoing information about all the major activities in the organization? And how are the techniques for controlling and using this information changing the way managers manage? In this section, we'll address these two issues.

What Is a Management Information System (MIS)?

While there is no universally agreed-upon definition for a **management information system (MIS)**, we'll define the term as a system used to provide management with needed information on a regular basis.[1] In theory, this system can be manual or computer based, although all current discussions—including ours—focus on computer-supported applications.

The term "system" in MIS implies order, arrangement, and purpose. Further, an MIS focuses specifically on providing management with information, not merely data. These two points are important and require elaboration.

A library provides a good analogy. Although it can contain millions of volumes, a library doesn't do users much good if they can't quickly find what they want. That's why libraries spend a lot of time cataloguing their collections and ensuring that volumes are returned to their proper locations. Organizations today are like well-stocked libraries. There are no lack of data. There is, however, a lack of ability to process those data so that the right information is available to the right person when he needs it.[2] A library is almost useless if it has the book you want, but either you can't find it or the library takes a week to retrieve it from storage. An MIS, on the other hand, has organized data in some meaningful way and can access the information in a reasonable amount of time. **Data** are raw, unanalysed facts, such as numbers, names, or quantities. But as data, these facts are relatively useless to managers.[3] When data are analysed and processed, they become **information**. An MIS collects data and turns them into relevant information for managers to use. Exhibit 16-1 summarizes these observations.

management information system (MIS)
A system that provides management with needed information on a regular basis.

data
Raw, unanalysed facts

information
Analysed and processed data.

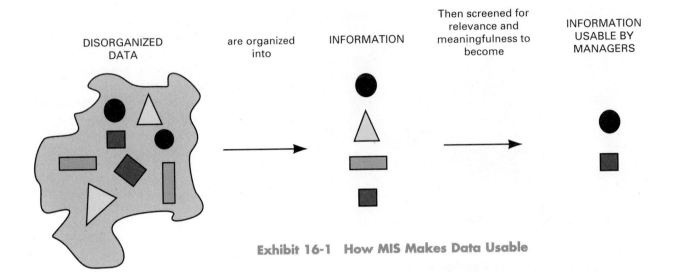

Exhibit 16-1   How MIS Makes Data Usable

Why Are End-users Replacing Centralized Systems?

end-user
The person who uses information and assumes responsibility for its control.

network
Linking computers so that they can communicate with each other.

MIS has come a long way in the last four-plus decades. Most of this progress is a direct result of improvements in computing power. The trend has been toward smaller, faster, and cheaper technology. For example, in 1946, there was one computer in the United States. It weighed 30 tons and had 18,000 vacuum tubes and 70,000 resistors. The computing power that in 1966 took a roomful of equipment and cost $15 million is available today on a $10 microprocessor chip that's only a quarter of an inch square.[4] The results of technological advancements have fostered the decentralization of information control—meaning that managers are now becoming **end-users**.

When a manager becomes an end-user, she takes responsibility for information control (also see Ethical Dilemmas in Management).[5] It is no longer delegated to some other department or staff assistant. As end-users, managers have to become knowledgeable about their own needs and the systems that are available to meet those needs—and to accept responsibility for their systems' failures. Accordingly, if they don't have the information they want, there is no one to blame but themselves.

Managers have come to realize that they now have a better information base from which to make more timely decisions and to improve managerial control. By developing their computer skills and judiciously selecting the right software, managers are able to get the exact information they want, literally in seconds.

A final outcome of today's MIS is the creation and implementation of mechanisms to link end-users. By means of an interactive **network**, a manager's computer can communicate with other computers.[6] That is, the user of a personal computer can communicate with other personal computers, turn the computer into a terminal and gain access to an organization's mainframe system, share the use of expensive printers, and tap into outside databases.

Is this a picture of the war room at the Pentagon? No! It's EDS's command post, its MIS centre. This centre provides data support and computer information to the organization's worldwide operations.

ETHICAL DILEMMAS IN MANAGEMENT

▼

WHAT'S WRONG WITH PIRATING SOFTWARE?

▲

The court officers and lawyers walked into the Milan headquarters of Montedison, Italy's chemical giant. Employees at computer work stations were ordered to step away from their keyboards while the investigators punched in commands to test the programs. Their suspicions were confirmed. The employees were using pirated copies of Lotus 1-2-3, the popular spreadsheet program.

The duplicating of software programs has become a widespread practice. It's been estimated that in the United States about 40 per cent of all software used is pirated,[7] cheating software developers of approximately $1.5 billion. Go worldwide, and that number increases to $12 billion a year. Yet almost all these duplicated programs are protected by copyright law. Copying them is punishable by fines of up to $100,000 and five years in jail. How is it, then, that this lawbreaking has become such a common practice? Part of the answer is cultural differences. A lot of piracy occurs in places such as Hong Kong and Singapore, where copyright laws don't apply and sharing rather than protecting creative work is the norm. In the United States, employees and managers who pirate software defend their behaviour by giving such answers as: "Everybody does it!" "I won't get caught!" "The law isn't enforced!" "No one really loses!" or "Our departmental budget isn't large enough to handle buying dozens of copies of the same program!"

Contrast software to other forms of intellectual property. Ask the same employees who copy software if it is similarly acceptable to steal a book from the library or a tape from a video store. Most are quick to condemn such practices. However, some think that there's nothing wrong with checking out a video, making a copy, and returning it—despite the copyright statement at the beginning of the tape that specifically states that the act of copying that tape is in violation of the law.

Is reproducing copyrighted software ever an acceptable practice? Is it wrong for employees of a corporation, but permissible for struggling college students? What do you think?

How Can MIS Enhance Planning?

As we discussed in Chapter 3, managers seek to develop organization-wide strategies that will give them an advantage over their competition. We talked about gaining a competitive advantage through strategies such as being the cost leader in a given market or by carefully differentiating your product from that of the competition. In recent years, managers at a number of organizations have realized that information systems can be used as a tool to give their firms a competitive advantage.[8]

A 1997 survey of 150 Canadian companies found that 58 per cent of them had a customer database.[9] However, only 48 per cent of those companies with databases had a structure in place to respond to different customer needs. Without the ability to capitalize on it, the information is simply ineffectual. Companies that organize their business procedures to respond to customer information have an edge.

Once an information system has been put in place and management gains a leg up on its competition, the trick—as with any competitive advantage—is to sustain that advantage. Kmart, for instance, has recently invested in an information system that seeks to duplicate the one at Wal-Mart. Similarly, Federal Express was able to deliver packages faster and with more detailed tracking than could its competition for many years because it was the first to completely computerize the process. But as UPS,

KMART
www.kmart.com/

WAL-MART
www.wal-mart.com/

FEDERAL EXPRESS
www.fedex.com/

Canada Post, and other competitors introduced comparable systems, Federal Express's on-time delivery advantage based on its MIS all but disappeared. So while MIS can provide a competitive edge, that edge is not permanent. The system must be regularly modified and updated if it is to give an organization a sustainable advantage.

What Effect Does MIS Have on Decision Making?

We know that managers rely on information to make decisions. Because a sophisticated MIS significantly alters the quantity and quality of information (see Managers Who Made a Difference), as well as the speed with which it can be obtained, an effective MIS will improve management's decision-making capability.[10]

The effect will be seen in establishing the need for a decision, in the development and evaluation of alternatives, and in the final selection of the best alternative. On-line, real-time systems allow managers to identify problems almost as they occur. Gone are the long delays between the appearance of a serious discrepancy and a manager's ability to find out about it. Easy access to large databases allows managers to look things up or get to the facts without either going to other people or digging through piles of paper. This reduces a manager's dependence on others for data and makes fact gathering far more efficient. Today's manager can identify alternatives quickly, evaluate those alternatives by posing a series of what-if questions based on financial data, and finally select the best alternative on the basis of answers to those questions.

How Does MIS Affect an Organization's Structure?

When organizations introduce sophisticated, computer-based management information systems, they are changing the technology component of organizational structure (see Chapter 6). For instance, a computer-based MIS lessens the need to depend on direct supervision and staff reports as control mechanisms. A senior executive can monitor what's occurring on the shop floor or in the accounts payable department by simply pushing a few keys on her desk terminal. And such changes in technology have a very real effect on the organization's structure. For instance, traditional departmental boundaries are becoming less confining as networks cut across departments, divisions, geographic locations, and levels in the organization. But the most evident change is probably that MIS is making organizations flatter and more organic.[11]

Managers can now handle more employees. Why? Because computer control substitutes for personal supervision. As a result, there are wider spans of control and fewer levels in the organization. The need for staff support is also reduced with an MIS. By being an end-user, managers can obtain information directly. Thus, large staff support groups, which traditionally compiled, tabulated, and analysed data, become redundant.[12] Both forces—wider spans and reduced staff—lead to flatter organizations.

One of the more interesting phenomena created by sophisticated information systems is that they have allowed management to make organizations more organic without any loss in control.[13] Management can lessen formalization and become more decentralized—thus making their organizations more organic—without giving up control. How? MIS substitutes computer control for rules and decision discretion. Computer technology rapidly informs top managers of the consequences of any decision and allows them to take corrective action if the decision is not to their liking. Thus, there's the appearance of decentralization without any commensurate loss of control.

MANAGERS WHO MADE A DIFFERENCE

Robert Cullen at Mount Sinai Hospital

A hospital like Mount Sinai in Toronto needs a constant flow of medical supplies. It buys about 600 different medical and surgical items from 60 vendors, which means that 60 deliveries have to arrive at the hospital, many of them at the same time. That can amount to major traffic congestion at the delivery doors, making it impossible for a hospital in a downtown location like Mount Sinai's to consider a traditional just-in-time inventory system with each of its suppliers. So it did what most Canadian hospitals do: it stocked all the myriad items needed in the daily running of a hospital and bore the cost of doing that as part of its annual budget.

Staffing a department to handle supplies—ordering them, paying for them, maintaining inventory control of them, tracking them, handling them, etc.—cost Mount Sinai about $5 million a year. Medical and surgical supplies account for about $6 million of the overall supplies budget. Under the old system of buying, inventorying, and transferring to various departments, some items in the hospital could be handled as many as 20 times before being used on a patient. That is, until Robert Cullen, the hospital's director of materials management, had a better solution.

The solution was to find a single sourcing agent for medical and surgical supplies—Livingston Healthcare Services Inc., of Oakville, Ontario. What Livingston does is take orders, by user department or work station, pack them, and deliver them the same day directly to the part of the hospital where they are used. Of course, technology is needed to make the system work. First, all items are bar-coded. A clerk daily scans the inventory at each work station and feeds the information into a computer, which assembles the data and transmits an order to Livingston. Livingston then packs boxes of supplies for each work station and delivers them that night to the hospital, with each box labelled for its final destination.

The hospital's inventory is now much smaller, but controls in the system can indicate where materials are elsewhere in the hospital if one work station should somehow run out. And if there is a real pinch, Livingston can deliver in one hour. Materials costs are also controlled through a process whereby Mount Sinai puts its annual needs for each item out to tender, with the understanding that items are to be delivered to Livingston Healthcare. In 1993, Mount Sinai saved $200,000 with the program. The hospital has also freed up 5,000 square feet of space, which, at $150 a foot, means that the hospital could expand its facilities without paying $750,000 for the new space. With increasing pressure on the cost of health care, making a difference will focus more and more on solutions of this kind.[14]▼

Does MIS Change Communication Patterns in Organizations?

Improvements in information technology—specifically, progress made in MIS that has enhanced our ability to gather, synthesize, organize, monitor, and disseminate information—are significantly changing the way communication takes place in organizations.[15] Traditional discussions of organizational communication focused on upward and downward communication. The primary flow of formal communication was vertical. The MIS, however, permits more lateral and diagonal communication on a formal basis.

Employees using internal networks can get their work done more efficiently by jumping levels in the organization and avoiding the obstacles involved in "going through channels." The direct accessing of data, rather than the traditional sequential passing of data up and down the hierarchy, also decreases the historical problem of distortion and filtering of information. Breaking down sequential communication patterns allows managers to formally monitor information across the organization that previously was limited to informal channels such as the grapevine.

What Effect Does MIS Have on Controlling?

Inherent in the control function is a manager's need to assess how the work is being performed and compare those data with the plan. MIS makes it possible to obtain more complete and accurate information in the measuring phase of controlling. Furthermore, the sophistication of the system may also permit managers to focus precisely on what they want to know. For example, suppose a manager at Hershey-Pasta wants to confirm that the long-noodle spaghetti production is on schedule to fill a major grocery chain order that is to be shipped by 4:00 P.M. that day. By entering the MIS system and directing the inquiry to the computer controlling the long-noodle production run, she can obtain the specific information she needs. Accordingly, MIS assists managers in obtaining timely information about workers' quantity of output, quality level, and other performance data. And because the data are directly assessed, many of the potential distortions that may arise when information is obtained "through channels" are avoided.

But accurate, timely, and complete information is only half the issue here. With controlling, when a significant variance is determined, managers must take some action. By obtaining the precise information one seeks, and getting it faster, a manager can correct a problem sooner. Thus, MIS enables managers to be more efficient and more effective in the controlling function.

Operations Controls

In this section, we want to focus on the importance of efficiency and productivity in the operations' side of the organization. Effective control systems allow organizations to produce higher-quality products and services at prices that meet or beat those of their rivals.

What Is the Transformation Process?

transformation process
The process through which an organization produces goods or services.

All organizations produce goods or services—through a means called the **transformation process**. Exhibit 16-2 portrays, in a simplified fashion, the fact that every

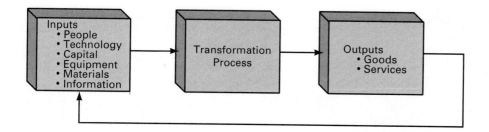

Exhibit 16-2
The Transformation
Process

organization has an operations system that creates value by transforming inputs into outputs. The system takes inputs—people, capital, equipment, materials—and transforms them into desired finished goods and services.

The transformation process is readily applicable to the manufacturing process. But what about a service organization—such as a university? University administrators bring together instructors, books, journals, audio-visual materials, and similar resources to transform "unenlightened" students into educated and skilled individuals. Our conclusion: the transformation process is as relevant to service organizations as it is to those in manufacturing. The study and application of this transformation process to organizations is called **operations management**.

Because organizational survival may very well rest on how successful operations management is, managers need to develop control techniques to monitor their productive processes. We will focus our discussion on four primary operations subsystems: cost controls, inventories, maintenance, and quality controls.

operations management
The design, operation, and control of the transformation process that converts resources into finished goods and services.

How Can Managers Control Costs?

An automobile industry analyst has compared the U.S. and Japanese approaches to cost control: "The Japanese regard cost control as something you wake up every morning and do. Americans have always thought of it as a project. You cut costs 20 per cent and say: 'Whew! That's over.' We can't afford to think that way anymore."[16]

U.S. managers have often treated cost control as an occasional crusade that is initiated and controlled by the accounting staff. Accountants establish cost standards per unit, and, if deviations occur, management looks for the cause. Have material prices increased? Is labour being used efficiently? Do employees need additional training? Cost control, nonetheless, needs to play a central part in the design of an operating system, and it needs to be a continuing concern of every manager.

Many organizations have adopted the **cost-centre approach** to controlling costs. Work areas, departments, or plants are identified as distinct cost centres, and their managers are held responsible for the cost performance of these units. Any unit's total costs are made up of two types of costs: direct and indirect. **Direct costs** are costs incurred in proportion to the output of a particular good or service. Labour and materials typically fall into this category. On the other hand, indirect costs are largely unaffected by changes in output. Insurance expenses and the salaries of staff are examples of typical indirect costs. This direct-indirect distinction is important. While cost-centre managers are held responsible for all direct costs in their units, **indirect costs** are not necessarily within their control. However, because all costs are controllable at some level in the organization, top managers should identify where the control lies and hold lower managers accountable for costs that are under their control.[17]

cost-centre approach
Managers are held responsible for costs within their unit.

direct costs
Costs incurred in proportion to the output of a particular good or service.

indirect costs
Costs that are largely unaffected by changes in output.

Computer-aided design allows manufacturers to create and view a model in a fraction of the time it would have taken to prepare a preproduction sample for customer inspection. That translates into significant cost savings.

How Can Managers Minimize Purchasing Costs?

It has been said that human beings are what they eat. Metaphorically, the same applies to organizations. Their processes and outputs depend on the inputs they "eat." It's difficult to make quality products out of inferior inputs. Gas station operators depend on a regular and dependable inflow of certain octane-rated gasolines from their suppliers in order to meet their customers' demands. If the gas isn't there, they can't sell it. If the gasoline is below the specified octane rating, customers may be dissatisfied and take their business elsewhere. Management must therefore monitor the delivery, performance, quality, quantity, and price of inputs from suppliers. Purchasing control seeks to ensure availability, acceptable quality, continued reliable sources, and, at the same time, reduced costs.

What can managers do to facilitate control of inputs? They need to gather information on delivery dates and conditions in which supplies arrive. They need to gather data about the quality of supplies and the compatibility of those supplies with operations processes. Finally, they need to obtain data on supplier price performance. Are the prices of the delivered goods the same as those that were quoted when the order was placed?

This information can be used to rate suppliers, identify problem suppliers, and guide management in choosing future suppliers. Trends can be detected. Suppliers can be evaluated, for instance, on responsiveness, service, reliability, and competitiveness.

Why Should an Organization Build Close Links with Suppliers? A rapidly growing trend in manufacturing is turning suppliers into partners.[18] Instead of using 10 or 12 vendors and forcing them to compete against each other to gain the firm's business, manufacturers are using only two or three vendors and working closely with them to improve efficiency and quality.

Motorola, for instance, sends its design-and-manufacturing engineers to suppliers to help with any problems.[19] Other firms now routinely send inspection teams to rate suppliers' operations. They're assessing these suppliers' manufacturing and delivery techniques, statistical process controls that identify causes of defects, and ability to handle data electronically. Companies in Canada and around the world are doing what has long been a tradition in Japan—that is, they are developing long-term relationships with suppliers. As collaborators and partners, rather than adversaries, firms are finding that they can achieve better quality of inputs, fewer defects, and lower costs. Furthermore, when problems arise with suppliers, open communication channels facilitate quick resolutions.

What is the Economic Order Quantity Model? One of the best-known techniques for mathematically deriving the optimum quantity for a purchase order is the **economic order quantity model (EOQ)** (see Exhibit 16-3). The EOQ model seeks to balance four costs involved in ordering and carrying inventory: the purchase costs (purchase price plus delivery charges less discounts); the ordering costs (paperwork, follow-up, inspection when the item arrives, and other processing costs); carrying costs (money tied up in inventory, storage, insurance, taxes, and so forth); and stockout costs (profits foregone from orders lost, the cost of reestablishing goodwill, and additional expenses incurred to expedite late shipments). When these four costs are known, the model identifies the optimal order size for each purchase. Readers interested in the detailed mathematics of the EOQ model are encouraged to research the model in a current production/operations management textbook.

economic order quantity model (EOQ)
A technique for balancing purchase, ordering, carrying, and stockout costs to derive the optimum quantity for a purchase order.

What Are Inventory Ordering Systems? In many chequebooks, after you use up about 80 per cent of the cheques, you find a reorder form included among the few that remain; it reminds you that it's time to reorder. This is an example of a **fixed-point reordering system**. At some preestablished point in the operations process, the system is designed to "flag" the fact that the inventory needs to be replenished. The flag is triggered when the inventory reaches a certain point, or the safety stock level (see Exhibit 16-4).

fixed-point reordering system
A system that "flags" the fact that inventory needs to be replenished when it reaches a certain level.

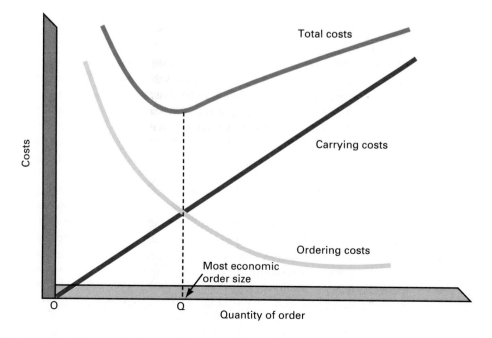

Exhibit 16-3 Determining the Most Economic Order Quantity

**Exhibit 16-4
Inventory Cycle
with Safety Stock**

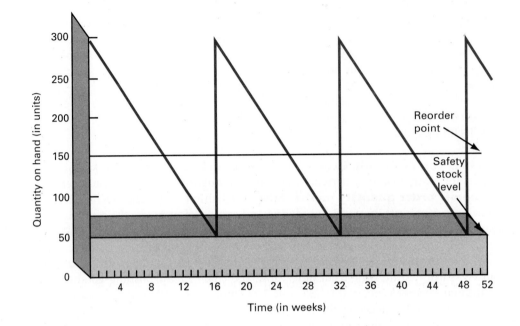

**fixed-interval
reordering system**
A system that uses time as
the determining factor for
reviewing and reordering
inventory items.

Another common inventory system is the **fixed-interval reordering system**. The fixed-interval system uses time as the determining factor for inventory control. At a predetermined time—say, once a week, or every 90 days—the inventory is counted, and an order is placed for the number of items necessary to bring the inventory back to the desired level. The desired level is established so that if demand and ordering lead time are average, consumption will draw the inventory down to zero (or some safety lead time can be added) just as the next order arrives. This system may have some transportation economies and quantity discount economies over the fixed-point system. For example, it may allow us to consolidate orders from one supplier if we review all the items we purchase from this source at the same time. This is not possible in the fixed-point reordering system.

What Is a Just-In-Time Inventory Practice? Arguably the fastest-growing control technique for minimizing inventory costs is the **just-in-time (JIT) inventory**. With JIT, inventory items arrive when they are needed in the production process instead of being stored in stock. The ultimate goal of JIT is to have only enough inventory on hand to complete the day's work—reducing a company's inventory, and its associated costs, to zero. Organizations using JIT methods range from small operations such as Fred Deeley Imports in Toronto (a Harley Davidson distributor for Canada) to huge operations such as Xerox Canada.

**just-in-time (JIT)
inventory**
A system in which inventory items arrive when
they are needed in the
production process instead
of being stored in stock.

JIT attempts to eliminate raw material inventories by precisely coordinating production and supply deliveries. When the system works as designed, it results in a number of positive benefits for a manufacturer. These include reduced inventories, reduced setup time, better work flow, shorter manufacturing time, less space consumption, and even higher quality. Of course, suppliers must be found who can be depended on to deliver quality materials on time. Because there are no inventories, there is no slack in the system to absorb defective materials or delays in shipment.

What Is Maintenance Control?

Delivering goods or services in an efficient and effective manner requires operating systems with high equipment utilization and a minimum amount of downtime. Therefore, managers need to be concerned with maintenance control. The importance of maintenance control, however, depends on the process technology used. For example, if a standardized assembly line process breaks down, it can affect hundreds of employees. On an automobile or dishwasher assembly line, it's not unusual for a serious breakdown on one machine to bring an entire plant to a halt. In contrast, most systems using more general-purpose and redundant processes have less interdependency between activities; therefore, a machine breakdown is likely to have less of an impact. Nevertheless, an equipment breakdown—like an inventory stockout—may mean higher costs, delayed deliveries, or lost sales.

YOUNG CANADIANS

Claude Mongeau: CN

Claude Mongeau's work at Imasco impressed CN enough to coax the then 32-year-old manager over to the Crown corporation as it was preparing to go private. Mongeau's challenge was to create a more appealing balance sheet for potential buyers of CN. Mongeau's cost-cutting and efficiency-improvement measures bolstered CN's worth up to a $2-billion value, making the privatization the most successful in Canadian history.

There are three approaches to maintenance control.[20] **Preventive maintenance** is performed before a breakdown occurs. **Remedial maintenance** is a complete overhaul, replacement, or repair of the equipment when it breaks down. **Conditional maintenance** refers to overhaul or repair in response to an inspection and measurement of the equipment's state. When British Airways tears down its planes' engines every 1,000 hours, it is engaging in preventive maintenance. When it inspects the planes' tires every 24 hours and changes them when conditions warrant, it is performing conditional maintenance. Finally, if British Airways' operations policy is to repair lavatory equipment on board its planes only after the equipment breaks down, then it is using remedial maintenance practices.

The British Airways example points out that the type of maintenance control depends on the costs of a breakdown. The greater the cost in terms of money, time, liability, or loss of goodwill, the greater the benefits of preventive maintenance.

Maintenance control should also be considered in the design of equipment. If downtime is highly inconvenient or costly, reliability can be increased by designing

preventive maintenance
Maintenance performed before a breakdown occurs.

remedial maintenance
Maintenance that calls for the overhaul, replacement, or repair of equipment when it breaks down.

conditional maintenance
Maintenance that calls for an overhaul or repair in response to an inspection.

**H O M E
H A R D W A R E**
www.homehardware
dealers.com/

redundancy into the equipment. Nuclear power plants, for example, have elaborate backup systems built in. Home Hardware has a fibre-optic cable link that duplicates all information going into the corporate data centre in St. Jacobs, Ontario, at a backup centre 12 kilometres away. Therefore, if the primary centre's system fails, information is safe at another facility and operations can continue.[21]

Similarly, equipment can be designed to facilitate fast or low-cost maintenance. Equipment that has fewer parts has fewer things to go wrong. High-failure items can also be placed in locations that are easily accessible or in independent modular units that can be quickly removed and replaced. Cable-television operators follow these guidelines. Breakdowns infuriate customers, so when they occur, management wants to be able to correct them quickly. Speed is facilitated by centralizing equipment in easy-access locations and making extensive use of modular units. If a piece of equipment fails, the whole module of which it is a part can be pulled or replaced in just a few minutes. Television service is resumed rapidly, and the pulled modular unit can be taken to the shop and repaired without time pressures.

Are TQM and Quality Control the Same Thing?

We've discussed total quality management throughout this book, describing it as a comprehensive, customer-focused program to continuously improve the quality of the organization's processes, products, and services. While TQM emphasizes actions to prevent mistakes, **quality control** emphasizes identifying mistakes that may have already occurred.

So what do we mean by quality control? It refers to monitoring quality—weight, strength, consistency, colour, taste, reliability, finish, or any one of a myriad of characteristics—to ensure that it meets some preestablished standard. Quality control will

quality control
Ensuring that what is produced meets some preestablished standard.

probably be needed at one or more points beginning with the receipt of inputs. It will continue with work in process and all steps up to the final product. Assessments at intermediate stages of the transformation process typically are part of quality control. Early detection of a defective part or process can save the cost of further work on the item.

In imposing quality control, managers should begin by asking whether they expect to examine 100 per cent of the items or whether a sample can be used. The inspection of each item makes sense if the cost of continuous evaluation is very low or if the consequences of a statistical error are very high (as in the manufacture of a drug used in open-heart surgery). Statistical samples are usually less costly, and sometimes they are the only viable option. For example, if the quality test destroys the product— as happens with bombs or flashbulbs—

**D A E W O O   M O T O R
C O M P A N Y**
www.dm.co.kr/english/
english.htm

These Daewoo Company employees perform several inspections of railroad cars at their Korea plant to ensure that no defects exist. This is all part of the company's quality control program.

then sampling has to be used. There are two categories of statistical quality control procedures: acceptance sampling and process control. **Acceptance sampling** refers to the evaluation of purchased or manufactured materials or products that already exist. A sample is taken; then the decision to accept or reject the whole lot is based on a calculation of sample risk error. **Process control** refers to sampling items during the transformation process to see whether the transformation process itself is under control.

A final consideration in quality control relates to whether the test is done by examining attributes or variables. The inspection and classification of items as acceptable or unacceptable is called **attribute sampling**. An inspector compares the items against some standard and rates their quality as acceptable or not acceptable. In contrast, **variable sampling** involves taking a measurement to determine how much an item varies from the standard. It involves a range rather than a dichotomy. Management typically identifies the standard and an acceptable deviation. Any sample that measures within the range is accepted, and those outside are rejected.

Before we leave the issue of quality control, there is an important issue before us. That is, who's really responsible for increasing the quality of our goods and services produced? We know that quality is a function of both operations and people variables. Of course, management needs to focus on both.

A lot of our discussion above has focused on the "operations" side. Management must ensure that it has a productive transformation process. From the people side, techniques we have discussed in previous chapters should be considered. Empowerment, management by objectives, team-based work groups, and equitable pay systems are examples of people-oriented approaches toward quality enhancement. But much of the people side of the equation focuses on operative employees—those actually performing the work. The late management consultant and quality expert W. Edwards Deming, however, shifted that primary responsibility to managers. Exhibit 16-5 outlines Deming's 14 points for improving quality.

A closer look at Exhibit 16-5 reveals Deming's understanding of the interplay between people and operations. High quality cannot come solely from good "people management." Rather, the truly effective organization will maximize quality and ultimately productivity by successfully integrating people into the overall operations system. This can explain, for instance, why in one recent year U.S. companies spent $17 billion on computers and new process-control equipment.[22] Increased capital investment will make facilities more modern and efficient.

Financial Controls

In Chapter 4, we introduced budgets as both a planning and control device. Now, we turn to financial analyses, which serve as feedback controls. We know that investors and stock analysts regularly use an organization's financial documents to assess its worth. These same documents can be analysed by managers as internal controls, which include ratio analyses, audits, cost-benefit analyses, and activity-based accounting.

What Are the More Popular Ratio Analyses?

Managers often want to examine their organization's balance and income statements to analyse key ratios; that is, compare two significant figures from the financial state-

acceptance sampling
A quality control procedure in which a sample is taken and a decision to accept or reject a whole lot is based on a calculation of sample risk error.

process control
A quality control procedure in which sampling is done during the transformation process to determine whether the process itself is under control.

attribute sampling
A quality control technique that classifies items as acceptable or unacceptable on the basis of a comparison to a standard.

variable sampling
A quality control technique in which a measurement is taken to determine how much an item varies from the standard.

Exhibit 16-5
Deming's 14 Points
for Improving Quality

Source: W. Edwards Deming,
"Improvement of Quality
and Productivity Through
Action by Management,"
National Productivity Review,
Winter 1981–82, pp. 12–22.
With permission.
Copyright 1981 by
Executive Enterprises, Inc.,
22 West 21st St., New York,
N.Y. 10010-6904. All
rights reserved.

► **1.** Plan for the long-term future, not for next month or next year.

► **2.** Never be complacent concerning the quality of your product.

► **3.** Establish statistical control over your production processes and require your suppliers to do so as well.

► **4.** Deal with the fewest number of suppliers—the best ones, of course.

► **5.** Find out whether your problems are confined to particular parts of the production process or stem from the overall process itself.

► **6.** Train workers for the job that you are asking them to perform.

► **7.** Raise the quality of your line supervisors.

► **8.** Drive out fear.

► **9.** Encourage departments to work closely together rather than to concentrate on departmental or divisional distinctions.

►**10.** Do not be sucked into adopting strictly numerical goals, including the widely popular formula of "zero defect."

►**11.** Require your workers to do quality work, not just to be at their stations from 9 to 5.

►**12.** Train your employees to understand statistical methods.

►**13.** Train your employees in new skills as the need arises.

►**14.** Make top managers responsible for implementing these principles.

ments and express them as a percentage or ratio. This practice allows managers to compare current financial performance with that of previous periods and against other organizations in the same industry. Some of the more useful ratios evaluate liquidity, leverage, operations, and profitability.

What Are Liquidity Ratios? Liquidity is a measure of the organization's ability to convert assets into cash in order that debts can be met. The most popular liquidity ratios are the current ratio and the acid test ratio.

current ratio
An organization's current assets divided by its current liabilities.

The **current ratio** is defined as the organization's current assets divided by its current liabilities. Although there is no magic number that is considered safe, the accountant's rule of thumb for the current ratio is 2:1. A significantly higher ratio usually suggests that management is not getting the best return on its assets. A ratio at or below 1:1 indicates potential difficulty in meeting short-term obligations (accounts payable, interest payments, salaries, taxes, and so forth).

acid test ratio
An organization's current assets, minus inventories, divided by its current liabilities.

The **acid test ratio** is the same as the current ratio except that current assets are reduced by the dollar value of inventory held. When inventories turn slowly, or are difficult to sell, the acid test ratio may more accurately represent the organization's true liquidity. That is, a high current ratio that is heavily based on an inventory that is difficult to sell overstates the organization's true liquidity. Accordingly, accountants typically consider an acid test ratio of 1:1 to be reasonable.

leverage
Refers to the use of borrowed funds to operate and expand an organization.

What Are Leverage Ratios? Leverage refers to the use of borrowed funds to operate and expand an organization. The advantage of leverage occurs when funds can be used to earn a rate of return well above the cost of those funds. For instance, if management can borrow money at 7 per cent and can earn 12 per cent on it internally, it makes good sense to borrow. But there are risks to overleveraging. The interest on the debt can be a drain on the organization's cash resources and can, at the extreme, drive an organization into bankruptcy. The objective, therefore, is to use debt wisely. Leverage ratios such as **debt-to-assets ratio** (computed by dividing total debt by total assets) or the **times-interest-earned ratio** (computed as profits before taxes divided by total interest charges) can help managers control debt levels.

What Are Operating Ratios? Operating ratios describe how efficiently management is using the organization's resources. Probably the most popular operating ratios are inventory turnover and total assets turnover.

The **inventory turnover ratio** is defined as revenue divided by inventory. The higher the ratio, the more efficiently inventory assets are being used. Revenue divided by total assets represents an organization's **total assets turnover ratio**. It measures what assets are needed to generate the organization's revenue. The fewer assets used to achieve a given level of revenue, the more efficiently management is using the organization's total assets.

What Are Profitability Ratios? Profit-making organizations want to measure their effectiveness and efficiency. Profitability ratios serve such a purpose. The better known of these are profit-margin-on-revenues and return-on-investment ratios.

Managers of organizations that have a variety of products want to put their efforts into products that are most profitable. The **profit-margin-on-revenues ratio**, computed as net profit after taxes divided by total revenues, is a measure of profits-per-dollar revenues.

One of the most widely used measures of a business firm's profitability is the **return-on-investment ratio**. It's calculated by multiplying [revenues/investments] times [profit/revenues]. This percentage recognizes that absolute profits must be placed in the context of assets required to generate those profits.

debt-to-assets ratio
Total debt divided by total assets.

times-interest-earned ratio
Profits before taxes divided by total interest charges.

inventory turnover ratio
Revenue divided by total inventory.

total assets turnover ratio
Revenue divided by total assets.

profit-margin-on-revenues ratio
Net profit after taxes divided by total revenues.

return-on-investment ratio
[Revenues/investments] times [profit/revenues].

HOSPITAL FOR
SICK CHILDREN
www.sickkids.on.ca/

YOUNG CANADIANS

Mary Federau: Hospital for Sick Children

When Mary Federau arrived at Toronto's Hospital for Sick Children, MBA from U.W.O. in hand, the hospital was a mess—administratively speaking. The institution provided excellent medical care, but lacked decent management. Federau has instituted budget control, has created an environment in which hospital staff and administration work together more harmoniously, and has brought the essential aspect of planning into the management of the hospital.

audit
Formal verification of an organization's financial statements.

What Are Audits? An **audit** is a formal verification of an organization's accounts, records, operating activities, or performance. It is essentially designed to check an organization's control mechanisms. Audits can generally be characterized as either external or internal.

external audit
Formal verification of an organization's financial statements by an outside and independent source.

What's the Difference Between External and Internal Audits? An **external audit** is a verification of an organization's financial statements by an outside and independent accounting firm. The organization creates its own financial statements using its own accountants. The external auditor's job then is to review the various accounts on the financial statements with respect to their accuracy and conformity with generally accepted accounting practices.

internal audit
Evaluation of an organization's financial statements, processes, operations, procedures, and policies by internal financial staff members.

The **internal audit**, as its name implies, is done by an organization's own financial or accounting staff. It encompasses verifying the financial statements, just as does the external audit, but also includes an evaluation of the organization's operations, procedures, and policies, plus any recommendations for improvement.

How Can Internal Audits Be Useful as a Managerial Control Tool? Internal audits go beyond verifying financial statements. They seek to uncover inefficiencies in the organization's processes and to suggest actions for their corrections. Specifically, managers can use internal audits to identify problems and ensure organizational activities are progressing as planned. For example, in our discussion of PERT networks in Chapter 4, we discussed the need to place controls on critical activities. Internal audits, in a like fashion, key into similar activities to ensure the processes are operating as needed. These preventive measures, then, can be implemented before a major "breakdown" is experienced.

What Role Does Cost-benefit Analysis Play in Control?

Some organizational activities do not lend themselves to objective financial evaluation techniques. Rather, they compare costs against objectives and use the result to prioritize and evaluate activities. When managers perform this activity, we say they are conducting a **cost-benefit analysis**. Cost-benefit analysis is useful when the amount of costs is known, but the standard against which these costs must be compared is ambiguous or difficult to measure. This is particularly the case, for example, when evaluating the effectiveness of such programs as defence projects, welfare programs, or educational systems. Cost-benefit expresses all the relevant benefits that accrue from an activity in the common denominator of money, so that they can be added together and their costs subtracted. This helps managers to determine if funds spent by their organizations on a number of activities are achieving benefits in excess of the amount spent.

cost-benefit analysis
Evaluating an activity where costs are known, but where the standard against which these costs must be compared is ambiguous or difficult to measure.

Cost-benefit analysis is probably more applicable and effective as an informal measuring concept than as a formal control technique. The reason for this is that it is difficult to objectively quantify subjective qualitative factors. Thus, cost-benefit gives no final answer as to whether a program or activity is "justified" or "good," or whether it should be expanded or contracted. Rather, it merely suggests how well an activity is operating when viewed in a specific manner.

What Is Activity-based Accounting?

activity-based accounting (ABC)
An accounting procedure whereby costs are allocated based on activities performed and resources used.

Activity-based accounting (ABC) is an accounting procedure whereby costs for producing a good or service are allocated based on the "activities performed and resources employed."[23] That is, the purpose of ABC is to reflect production costs more accurately. It is gaining an increasingly wide following in all types of businesses and not-for-profit organizations.

For instance, consider the operating room costs at a regional hospital associated with two medical procedures—tonsillectomy and heart bypass surgeries. Indeed, the latter operation is the more serious one. But what should the heart bypass operating room cost be in relation to that of the tonsillectomy? If hospital records show that a tonsillectomy is a one-hour operation, and the heart bypass a two-hour procedure, should the operating room charge be twice as much for the heart operation? Probably not. Why? Because the heart bypass requires that much more medical equipment be used. For example, a heart and lung machine, which keeps the patient breathing and blood circulating during the bypass surgery, is not used in tonsillectomies. There will also be extra costs associated with more medical apparatus and supplies. Accordingly, a simple "two-times" pricing mechanism may not reflect the true costs.

The concept of ABC is relatively simple. Allocate costs based solely on usage! Instead of spreading costs evenly or on a percentage basis to jobs as more traditional accounting methods utilize, ABC focuses on the specific costs incurred in the production of a good or service and charges them directly to the task. Thus, the tonsillectomy patient won't be charged a flat rate that overstates the costs of the operation. In this manner, organizations, like hospitals, are better able to set accurate prices, which ultimately could lead to the development of a competitive advantage.

Behavioural Controls

Managers accomplish things by working through other people. They need and depend on employees to achieve their unit goals. It's important, therefore, for managers to get their employees to behave in ways that management considers desirable. But how do managers ensure that employees are performing as they are supposed to? In organizations, the formal means of assessing the work of employees is through a systematic performance appraisal process.

What Is a Performance Appraisal?

Performance appraisal is a process of evaluating individuals' work performance in order to arrive at objective human resource decisions. Organizations use performance appraisals to make a number of employee decisions such as pay increases, training needs, as well as providing documentation to support termination decisions. Consequently, appraisals serve as control mechanisms.

Undoubtedly, performance appraisals are important. But how do you evaluate an employee's performance? That is, what are the specific techniques for appraisal? We have listed them in Exhibit 16-6.[24]

The **written essay** requires no complex forms or extensive training to complete. However, a "good" or "bad" appraisal may be determined as much by the evaluator's writing skill as by the employee's actual level of performance. The use of **critical incidents** focuses the evaluator's attention on critical or key behaviours that separate effective from ineffective job performance. The appraiser writes down little anecdotes that describe what the employee did that was especially effective or

performance appraisal
The evaluation of an individual's work performance in order to arrive at objective personnel decisions.

written essay
A performance appraisal technique in which an evaluator writes out a description of an employee's strengths, weaknesses, past performance, and potential, and then makes suggestions for improvement.

critical incidents
A performance appraisal technique in which an evaluator lists key behaviours that separate effective from ineffective job performance.

METHOD	ADVANTAGE	DISADVANTAGE
Written Essay	Simple to use	Evaluation of writer's ability as opposed to actual performance
Critical Incidents	Rich examples behaviourally based	Time consuming; lack quantification
Graphic Rating Scales	Provide quantitative data; less time-consuming	Do not provide depth of job behaviour assessed
BARS	Focus on specific and measurable job behaviours	Time-consuming; difficulty in developing measures
Multiperson	Compares employees to one another	Unwieldy with large number of employees
MBO	Focuses on end goals; results-oriented	Time-consuming

Exhibit 16-6   Performance Appraisal Methods—Advantages and Disadvantages

graphic rating scales
A performance appraisal technique in which an evaluator rates a set of performance factors on an incremental scale.

behaviourally anchored rating scales (BARS)
A performance appraisal technique in which an evaluator rates employees on specific job behaviours derived from performance dimensions.

multiperson comparison
A performance appraisal technique in which individuals are compared to one another.

group order ranking
A performance appraisal approach that groups employees into ordered classifications.

ineffective. The key here is that only specific behaviours are cited, not vaguely defined personality traits. One of the oldest and most popular methods of appraisal is **graphic rating scales**. This method lists a set of performance factors such as quantity and quality of work, job knowledge, cooperation, loyalty, attendance, honesty, and initiative. The evaluator then goes down the list and rates each on an incremental scale. Finally, an approach that has received a great deal of attention in recent years involves **behaviourally anchored rating scales (BARS)**.[25] These scales combine major elements from the critical incident and graphic rating scale approaches: the appraiser rates an employee according to items along a numerical scale, but the items are examples of actual behaviour on a given job rather than general descriptions or traits.

This is a very important point. It is essential that *specific behaviours* are being analysed, not *vaguely defined personality traits*. A recent case in Hamilton, Ontario, demonstrated the possible dangers involved in aptitude testing. Bill Robertson, an ambulance dispatcher, was given an aptitude test by his employer, the Ministry of Health. He was informed on his next shift that he had been laid off. Twenty years of excellent service had been brushed aside as a result of one test. What the Ministry was in effect saying was that Bill could not do his job because an exam had said so. So what had he been doing for the past two decades? Bill eventually got his job back with back-pay and a formal apology, and experienced dispatchers were no longer required to take the test. Where does the problem lie in such a case—with the testee or with the test? Obviously the latter.[26]

Should We Compare People to One Another Instead of Against Some Set Standards? The methods identified above have one thing in common. They require us to evaluate employees based on how well their performance matches established or absolute criteria. **Multiperson comparisons**, on the other hand, compare one person's performance to that of one or more individuals. Thus, it is a relative, not an absolute, measuring device. The three most popular uses of this method are group order ranking, individual ranking, and paired comparison.

The **group order ranking** requires the evaluator to place employees into a particular classification such as "top one-fifth" or "second one-fifth." When this method is used to appraise employees, managers rank all their employees. If a rater has 20 employees, only four can be in the top fifth, and, of course, four must be relegated to the bottom fifth. The **individual ranking** approach requires the evaluator merely to list the employees in order from highest to lowest. Only one can be "best." In an appraisal of 30 employees, the difference between the first and second employee is assumed to be the same as that between the twenty-first and twenty-second. Even though some employees may be closely grouped, there can be no ties. In the **paired comparison** approach, each employee is compared to every other employee in the comparison group and rated as either the superior or weaker member of the pair. After all paired comparisons are made, each employee is assigned a summary ranking based on the number of superior scores she achieved. While this approach ensures that each employee is compared against every other, it can become unwieldy when large numbers of employees are being assessed.

Isn't MBO an Appraisal Approach, too? We previously introduced management by objectives during our discussion of planning in Chapter 3. MBO, however, is also a mechanism for appraising performance. In fact, it is the preferred method for assessing managers and professional employees.[27]

With MBO, employees are evaluated on how well they accomplish a specific set of objectives that have been determined to be critical in the successful completion of their jobs. As you'll remember from our discussion in Chapter 3, these objectives need to be tangible, verifiable, and measurable.

MBO's popularity among managerial personnel is probably due to its focus on end goals. Managers tend to emphasize such results-oriented outcomes as profit, sales, and costs. This emphasis aligns with MBO's concern with quantitative measures of performance. Because MBO emphasizes ends rather than means, this appraisal method allows managers the discretion to choose the best path for achieving their goals.

What Is Discipline?

So far our discussion on behavioural controls has focused on the performance appraisal process. And while that is the dominant form of behavioural control, we need to ask ourselves an important question: if we find that an employee cannot perform in a satisfactory manner (even with our coaching) or, worse, violates organizational rules or policies, what can a manager do? In such cases, the manager may have no other recourse than to take the employee through the disciplinary process.

What specifically do we mean when we use the term **discipline**? It refers to actions taken by a manager to enforce the organization's standards and regulations. It generally follows a typical sequence of four steps: oral warning, written warning, suspension, and dismissal (see Exhibit 16-7). This progressive order, however, may be cir-

individual ranking
A performance appraisal approach that ranks employees in order from highest to lowest.

paired comparison
A performance appraisal approach in which each employee is compared to every other employee and rated as either the superior or weaker member of the pair.

discipline
Actions taken by a manager to enforce the organization's standards and regulations.

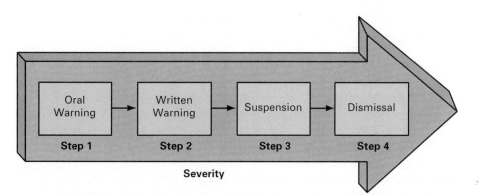

**Exhibit 16-7
The Discipline Process**

"hot stove" rule
Discipline should immediately follow an infraction, provide ample warning, be consistent, and be impersonal.

cumvented if the behaviour variance is extremely severe. For example, stealing or attacking another employee with intent to inflict serious harm may result in an immediate suspension or dismissal. Regardless of any action taken, discipline should be fair and consistent. The punishment should fit the "crime," similar violations should be treated in a like manner, and discipline should follow the "hot stove" rule.

The **"hot stove" rule** is a frequently cited set of principles that can guide you in effectively disciplining an employee.[28] The name comes from the similarities between touching a hot stove and administering discipline. Both are painful, but the analogy goes further. When you touch a hot stove, you get an immediate response. The burn you receive is instantaneous, leaving no doubt in your mind about the relation between cause and effect. You have ample warning. You know what happens if you touch a hot stove. Furthermore, the result is consistent. Every time you touch a hot stove, you get the same result—you get burned. Finally, the result is impersonal. Regardless of who you are, if you touch a hot stove, you will be burned (see Developing Management Skills).

**Exhibit 16-8
The Behavioural
Control Process**

Are There Substitutes for Direct Behavioural Control?

The likelihood that an employee's performance will prove unsatisfactory and require direct managerial control is moderated by several factors. Exhibit 16-8 illustrates that an

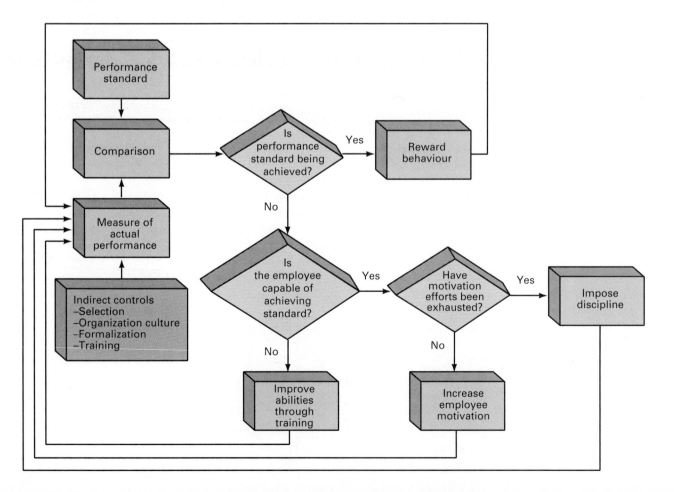

DEVELOPING MANAGEMENT SKILLS

▼

DISCIPLINING EMPLOYEES

▲

▶ **1. Before you accuse anyone, do your homework.** If you didn't personally see the infraction, investigate to determine what happened. Document date, time, place, individual involved, mitigating circumstances, and the like.

▶ **2. Ensure ample warning was provided.** Before any formal action is taken, be sure you've provided the employee with reasonable previous warnings and that those warnings have been documented.

▶ **3. Act in a timely fashion.** When you become aware of an infraction, and it has been supported by your investigation, do something, and do it quickly.

▶ **4. Conduct the discipline session in private.** Praise employees in public, but keep

punishment private. Public reprimands embarrass and humiliate the employee and may not lead to the behaviour change you desire.

▶ **5. Adopt a calm and serious tone.** Administering discipline should not be facilitated in a loose, informal, and relaxed manner. Avoid anger or other emotional responses, and convey your comments in a calm and serious tone.

▶ **6. Be specific about the problem.** Define the violation in exact terms instead of citing ambiguous regulations. Explain why the behaviour cannot continue by showing how it affects the employee's job performance, the unit's effectiveness, and the employee's colleagues.

▶ **7. Keep it impersonal.** Focus on the employee's behaviour, not the employee. The discussion should be on objective information, not some subjective or evaluative statement.

▶ **8. Get the employee's side of the story.** Due process

demands that you give the employee the opportunity to explain her position regarding what happened. If significant deviations occur, you may need to do more investigating. Active listening is critical here to ensure you have all the relevant facts.

▶ **9. Keep control of the discussion.** Disciplining an employee, by definition, is an authority-based act. You are enforcing the organization's standards and regulations. Yes, ask the employee for her side of the story and get the facts. But don't let the employee interrupt you or divert you from your objective.

▶**10. Agree on how mistakes can be prevented next time.** Discipline should include guidance and direction for correcting the problem. Have the employee draft a step-by-step plan to change the problem behaviour. Then set a timetable, with follow-up meetings in which progress can be evaluated.

effective selection process, acceptance of the organization's culture, a high degree of formalization, and employee training will all reduce the probability that an employee's actual performance will deviate from the performance standard. These subtle, but powerful, indirect control mechanisms substitute for the more overt forms of direct control.[29]

How Can the Selection Process Substitute for Behavioural Control? As we discussed in Chapter 8, managers do not choose employees at random. Rather, job applicants are processed through a series of selection devices to differentiate those who are likely to be successful performers from those who aren't. Accordingly, an effective selection process should be designed to determine if job candidates "fit" into the organization. Fit, here, implies not only the ability to do the job but also the personality, work habits, and attitudes that the organization desires. Consequently, selection should be recognized as one of the most widely used techniques by which management can control employee behaviour. That is, the selection process should screen out those who think and act in ways that management considers undesirable or inappropriate for successful performance.

In What Ways Does an Organization's Culture Substitute for Behavioural Control? The more that employees accept the values and norms of the organization's culture, the greater the likelihood that their behaviour will conform to that which management desires. Organizational culture, to the degree to which it is accepted by employees, acts to constrain and control their behaviour. Since employees who don't accept the organization's culture are not likely to stay employed long, culture is a relevant influence on all continuing employees.

To What Extent Does Formalization Substitute for Behavioural Control? Management provides most employees with a job description to clarify what their job encompasses, who they are responsible to, and what is and is not within their authority. This document formalizes behaviour and, of course, also controls behaviour. Since employees modify their behaviour to align with their job description, the job description acts as a control device. Furthermore, since management defines each individual's job description, management controls employee behaviour through it.

The job description, however, is not the only dimension of formalization that acts as a constraint on employee behaviour. Rules, procedures, and policies are other formalized controls.

How Can Employee Orientation and Training Substitute for Behavioural Control? When management provides employees with training, its intention is to instil in them preferred work behaviours and attitudes. This may be most obvious during a new employee's orientation.

New employees are often required to undergo a brief orientation program to familiarize them with the organization's objectives, history, philosophy, and rules. In many cases, this is followed by specific job training. The stated efforts of these orientation and training efforts are typically to help the new employee adjust to his new job. Another way of looking at this, however, is that orientation and training help to mould and eventually control the employee's behaviour.

Summary

This summary is organized by the chapter Learning Objectives found on page 417.

1. The purpose of an MIS is to provide managers with accurate and current information for decision making and control.

2. Data are raw, unanalysed facts. Information is data that have been organized into a usable form.

3. An MIS significantly alters the speed, quantity, and quality of information from which managers will make a decision. With an MIS, managers can identify problems more quickly, gather appropriate facts more efficiently, test alternatives through what-if questions, and select the best alternative-based answers to those questions.

4. An MIS makes it possible to obtain more complete and accurate information in the measuring phase of controlling. It also permits managers to focus precisely on what they want to know.

5. Operations management takes inputs, including people and materials, and then acts on them by transforming them into finished goods and services. This applies in service organizations as well as in manufacturing firms.

6. A cost centre is a unit in which managers are held responsible for all associated costs. These costs incurred are direct (costs incurred in proportion to the output of a particular good or service) or indi-

rect (costs that are largely unaffected by changes in output). In a cost centre, managers are generally held responsible for all direct costs, but not the indirect costs that are not within their control.

7. The three types of maintenance control are preventive, remedial, and conditional. Preventive maintenance is performed before a breakdown occurs. Remedial maintenance is performed when the equipment breaks down. Conditional maintenance is a response to an inspection.

8. Total quality management emphasizes actions that an organization can take to prevent mistakes from happening. Quality control emphasizes identifying mistakes that may have already occurred in the production of goods and services.

9. An external audit is a verification of an organization's financial statements by an outside and independent accounting firm. An internal audit is performed by an organization's own financial staff. It also verifies financial data, and includes an evaluation of the organization's operations, procedures, and policies.

10. A cost-benefit analysis is a tool for evaluating the benefits from activities whose benefits are ambiguous or subjective. It expresses all relevant benefits of an activity in the common term of money so they can be added together and their costs subtracted.

11. Six performance appraisal methods are (a) written essays—written descriptions of an employee's strengths, weaknesses, past performance, potential, and areas in need of improvement; (b) critical incidents—lists of key behaviours that separate effective from ineffective job performances; (c) graphic rating scales—ratings of performance factors on an incremental scale; (d) BARS—ratings of employees on performance factors derived from performance dimensions of the job; (e) multiperson comparisons—comparison of individual employees against one another; and (f) objectives—evaluation of employees against tangible, verifiable, and measurable objectives.

12. The "hot stove" rule of disciplining proposes that effective discipline should be equivalent to touching a hot stove. The response should be immediate, there should be ample warning, and enforcement of rules should be consistent and impersonal.

Review and Discussion Questions

1. How can an MIS assist a manager in the control function?

2. In what ways is information a unique resource for organizations? Give examples.

3. How can an MIS create a flatter organization while simultaneously giving managers more control over the organization's operations?

4. Does the use of MIS empower all employees, all managers, or only a select few individuals in the organization? Discuss.

5. What is the transformation process?

6. Contrast acceptance sampling and process control.

7. Which is more critical for success in organizations—total quality management or quality control? Support your position.

8. What are the more popular financial ratios and how are they calculated?

9. "Cost-benefit analysis is better than no analysis at all. If the data are subjective and do lend themselves to objective analyses, cost-benefit provides at least a 'good enough' response." Do you agree or disagree with the statement? Explain.

10. What qualities would characterize an effective disciplinary process?

Testing Your Comprehension

Circle the correct answer, then check yourself on page 472.

1. Which of the following is MOST accurate regarding MIS?
   a) It is used sporadically by management.
   b) It usually results in a narrow span of control.
   c) It renders data into information.
   d) It must be computer based.

2. Increased use of MIS will change the role of managers by
   a) reducing their workload
   b) making managers more dependent on the organization's computer department
   c) increasing the importance of mid-managers at the expense of first-line supervisors
   d) enhancing the effective decision-making capability of managers

3. Most operations managers have considerable influence over
   a) direct costs
   b) indirect costs
   c) fixed costs
   d) overhead costs

4. Reordering goods at some preestablished point in the operations process is reflective of
   a) distribution requirements planning
   b) a fixed-point reorder system
   c) a fixed-interval reorder system
   d) the ABC system

5. When sales are recorded in a computer and the system is preprogrammed to originate a purchase order when a minimal level remains, the system is called
   a) MIS
   b) ABC
   c) fixed-point
   d) fixed-interval

6. A JIT inventory system is MOST appropriate when
   a) a highly flexible production schedule exists
   b) suppliers are dispersed geographically
   c) reliable transportation and physical distribution systems exist between supplier and buyer
   d) a dynamic distribution system exists

7. A large interstate motor carrier company that rebuilds a diesel engine after it failed a compression test is using
   a) preventive maintenance
   b) conditional maintenance
   c) remedial maintenance
   d) systems maintenance

8. When Budget Rent-a-Car establishes a policy for oil changes at 5,000 kilometres for its fleet, it is practising
   a) remedial maintenance
   b) conditional maintenance
   c) preventive maintenance
   d) backup systems maintenance

9. Sampling items during the transformation process to see if the process is under control is called
   a) acceptance sampling
   b) variable sampling
   c) attribute sampling
   d) process control

10. An examination of some number of materials or products to determine if a lot should be accepted or rejected on the basis of the calculation of sample risk error is called
    a) acceptance sampling
    b) variable sampling
    c) attribute sampling
    d) process control

11. A quality control technique in which items are accepted or rejected on the basis of some measurement is called
    a) acceptance sampling
    b) variable sampling
    c) attribute sampling
    d) process control

12. Formal verification of an organization's accounts, records, operating activities, or performance is
    a) an acid test
    b) a ratio
    c) an audit
    d) a comparison

13. The acid test ratio is
    a) the same as the current ratio
    b) the current ratio plus inventories, divided by its current liabilities
    c) debt-to-assets minus current liabilities
    d) current assets, minus inventories, divided by current liabilities

Self-Assessment Exercise

Testing Your Understanding of Computers

The following questionnaire has been developed to determine your computer understanding. For each definition in Column A (three questions to a segment), choose the term from Column B (five possible choices) that appropriately matches.

Column A Definitions	Column B Terms
_____ **1.** Has four functional parts: input, processing, storage (programs and data), and output.	A. Arithmetic/logical unit
_____ **2.** Performs the mathematic operations and any comparisons required.	B. Computer system
_____ **3.** Physical parts of a computer.	C. CPU
	D. Firmware
	E. Hardware
_____ **4.** Standard method of representing a character with a number inside the computer.	A. Alphanumeric
_____ **5.** The base 2 numbering system that uses digits 0 and 1.	B. ASCII
_____ **6.** Number system that uses the 10 digits 0 through 9 and the six letters A through F to represent values in base 16.	C. Binary
	D. Hexadecimal
	E. Numeric data
_____ **7.** Technique for opening folders with a mouse.	A. Double-clicking
_____ **8.** Technique for moving an icon with a mouse.	B. Dragging
_____ **9.** Pointer similar to arrows.	C. Highlighting
	D. I-beam
	E. Scroll bar
_____ **10.** A read-only memory whose contents are alterable by electrical means.	A. Access
_____ **11.** Internal memory that is erased when the computer's power is shut off.	B. Clockrate
_____ **12.** Time it takes to find data stored externally.	C. Memory
	D. PROM
	E. RAM
_____ **13.** Number of characters printed per horizontal inch of space.	A. Font
_____ **14.** Set of characters in one typeface, style, and size.	B. Kerning
_____ **15.** Narrows the spacing between letters.	C. Leading
	D. Pitch
	E. Points
_____ **16.** Operator that describes the quality that connects two data or expressions such as greater than, less than, or equal to.	A. Commands
_____ **17.** Messages the user sends to the computer that make it perform specific operations.	B. Distributed
_____ **18.** The ability to run more than one program at one time without interrupting the execution of another program.	C. Execute
	D. Multitasking
	E. Relational operator
_____ **19.** Place to enlarge or shrink a window.	A. Active window
_____ **20.** Place documents are saved.	B. Dialog box
_____ **21.** Place you are typing.	C. Folders
	D. Record box
	E. Zoom box

_____ **22.**	A term that refers to memory in which data or software is lost when the computer is turned off.	A. Crash
_____ **23.**	Program that moves the read/write head to a section of the disk that has no data.	B. Erasable
_____ **24.**	Read/write comes into contact with the disk's surface.	C. Pack
		D. Park
		E. Volatile

_____ **25.**	The smallest piece of data that can be recognized by computers.	A. Bit
_____ **26.**	Basic unit of measure of computer's storage.	B. Byte
_____ **27.**	Placed in a microcomputer to take the burden of manipulating numbers off the CPU.	C. Chip
		D. Control unit
		E. Coprocessor

_____ **28.**	Program that translates the mnemonics and symbols of low-level language into the opcodes and operands of machine language.	A. Assembler
		B. Compiler
_____ **29.**	Software that translates a whole program into machine language.	C. Interpreter
_____ **30.**	Language designed so that machines and human beings can interact easily.	D. Natural
		E. Pascal

Turn to page 470 for scoring directions and key.

Source: Based on the "Computer Literacy Questionnaire," developed by Floyd Brock and Wayne Thomsen, Department of Management/MIS, University of Nevada at Las Vegas. With permission.

Class Exercise

Financial Controls

The purpose of this exercise is to provide you with an opportunity to calculate financial ratios given typical financial statements of companies. Using the information from the statements below, individually calculate the following: current ratio, acid test ratio, debt-to-assets ratio, times-interest-earned ratio, inventory turnover ratio, total assets turnover ratio, profit-margin-on-revenues ratio, and return-on-investment ratio. You may want to refer to this chapter for the formulas used in calculating these ratios.

When you have completed your calculations, get into groups of four to five individuals. Compare your ratios. If differences exist, recalculate them until each group member has the same number. Then, with your group, determine what these ratios mean. For example, if you were deciding to invest in one of the two companies listed in the financial statements, which one would you choose? Why? When all groups have made these determinations, your professor will ask each group to share its results and support for its decision.

BALANCE SHEET

ASSETS	WOLLENBURG MEDIA INC. (000s omitted)	CMT RESEARCH INTERNATIONAL (000s omitted)
Current Assets		
Cash	4,123	71,000
Market Securities (short-term investments)	4,236	-0-
Receivables, net	6,331	137,000
Inventories	5,840	202,000
Prepaid Expenses	3,830	16,000
Total Current Assets	24,360	426,000
Net Property, etc.	35,330	159,000
Investments (long-term)	23,346	10,005
Other Assets	10,493	19,460
TOTAL ASSETS	93,529	614,465
LIABILITIES AND STOCKHOLDER EQUITY		
Current Liabilities		
Notes Payable	1,244	16,438
Accounts Payable	13,851	159,219
Other Liabilities	5,822	30,343
Total Current Liabilities	20,917	206,000
Long-Term Debt	22,195	119,000
Capital Lease Obligations	24,296	20,548
Deferred Income	2,211	9,917
Stockholder Equity	23,910	259,000
TOTAL LIABILITIES AND EQUITY	93,529	614,465

....

INCOME STATEMENT	(000s omitted)	(000s omitted)
Total Revenue	148,889	462,000
Cost of Products Sold	(114,335)	(229,000)
Administrative Costs	(23,475)	(136,000)
Total Costs	(137,810)	(365,000)
Earnings from Operations	11,079	97,000
Interest Expense	(5,771)	(21,000)
Earnings Before Taxes	5,308	76,000
Income Taxes	(1,713)	(30,000)
Net Income (Earnings)	3,595	46,000

Source: Adapted from Charles T. Horngren and Walter T. Harrison, Jr., *Accounting* (Englewood Cliffs, N.J.: Prentice-Hall, Inc., 1989), pp. 762–77. Used with permission.

Case Application

MIS at Comp-U-Card

Just how far can an inspired entrepreneur go in the information age? Can today's technology allow a company to stock no inventory, yet sell everything? Walter Forbes, CEO of Comp-U-Card International (CUC) thinks so. In fact, he has built a $1-billion business around what he calls his "virtual-reality inventory."[30]

CUC is a shopping service company whose mission is relatively simple: to provide appropriate information to customers about products they want, when they want them. Forbes realized several years ago that customers' shopping habits were changing. Today's shoppers have busy lives, and associated time constraints are reflected in their buying habits. Many purchase goods from mail-order catalogues, while others tune in to cable television programs such as the Canadian Home Shopping Network. But one missing element, according to Forbes, is that these customers still want to make informed purchasing decisions. For instance, in the past, making an informed decision meant researching product information in such magazines as *Consumer Reports*. In many cases, doing this research meant a special trip to the local library. Today's average shopper can't afford the luxury of gathering the pertinent data. Therein lies CUC's niche.

CUC maintains an information database on some 250,000 products encompassing 1,700 brands—from cars and air conditioners to computers and sophisticated electronic equipment. Customers can contact CUC either over the Internet or through its 1-800 number. By connecting with a CUC customer representative, individuals can obtain immediate information on any item they desire, complete with details on how the product compares with others on the market. Thus, a customer can obtain "the information necessary to comparison shop" and make an informed decision.

Providing helpful information, however, was not enough for Forbes. He also wanted to make it easier for CUC's subscribers to order their products. That is, after customers have had an opportunity to gather all the requisite data, they can immediately place their order. CUC, in cooperation with suppliers, can then have the item delivered. CUC becomes a one-stop information and shopping source for the consumer, and that consumer never has to leave his living room.

Questions

1. Describe the transformation process at Comp-U-Card. What inputs does it use and what outputs does it create?

2. How do you think CUC's operations affect customer decision making? Cite specific examples.

3. Do you think that virtual inventory systems could be applicable to organizations such as General Motors or Mount Sinai Hospital? How do you anticipate that they would work? Explain your position.

Corel: Michael Cowpland vs. Bill Gates

CBC ⬤

When Corel's founder and CEO, Michael Cowpland, says in this *Venture* program that his company is now going "toe to toe with Microsoft," he may be exaggerating the situation somewhat. For Corel, Microsoft is now the main focus and prime competitor. But it would be more realistic to say that, at least from Microsoft's viewpoint, Corel is "nipping at the heels"of the U.S. giant. Microsoft controls 90 per cent of the worldwide market for word processing programs, and Corel is just a newcomer to this area.

While Corel faced no competition when it developed CorelDraw, its flagship product (CorelDraw was developed for IBM-compatible machines, while Apple dominated the graphics market), this time it faces a company 25 times its size. The purchase of WordPerfect was indeed a gutsy move by Cowpland. With a promotions budget of $100 million (U.S.) to bolster its CorelDraw and WordPerfect office software, Corel is gambling heavily in its new market. After purchasing WordPerfect as recently as 1996, Corel has not had a lot of time to get its feet wet in the marketplace for word processing and office suite packages. With attempted forays into such leading-edge technologies as Java-based software (see Chapter 9), and intercorporate transactions based on the Internet, it is apparent that Michael Cowpland does not shy away from risk, and, to his credit, his failures have been few in this industry that demands constant innovation.

Cowpland's success with CorelDraw—which currently has an astounding 80 per cent of the world's graphics software market—has proven his ability to lead a company successfully in a volatile industry. But now he faces another major test, and one involving far more risks. The next few years, one way or the other, should be the most interesting ones in the company's history.

Questions

1. Compare Michael Cowpland as a leader with Laurent Beaudoin of Bombardier, taking into account their respective situations.

2. How would you rate Michael Cowpland in terms of leadership ability?

3. Would you like to work for a transformational leader such as Michael Cowpland? State your reasons.

Video Resource: "Corel," *Venture* 614 (October 27, 1996).

Additional Sources: Patrick Berger, "Cowpland Bets the Company," *Globe and Mail*, March 8, 1997, p. B1; Bert Hill, "Business is Booming on the Internet," *The Ottawa Citizen*, May 2, 1997, p. C3; Jill Vardy, "Corel Fights Time and a Jittery Market," *The Financial Post*, March 8-10, 1997, p. 1; Donald Rumball, "The Perfect Pitch," *The Financial Post Magazine*, December 1996, pp. 24-34; Lesley Daw, "Corel Fires First in New Battle with Microsoft," *Marketing Magazine*, January 27, 1997, p. 3.

Doing Business In Cuba

The problems Glen Costello faces in doing business in Cuba simply come with the territory, as the saying goes. This is a burgeoning economy. After the 1989 collapse of the Soviet Union, Cuba lost its preferential trade arrangements, and as the video stated, one-third of its foreign trade. The workings of capitalism are new to Cuba, and even though the economy is growing at a rapid rate, the deep-seated bureaucracy and wariness of dealing with North American business practices make for a difficult business climate for Canadian firms.

In the joint-venture deals that typify doing business in Cuba, the government most often has controlling interest. While operations are generally left in the hands of the foreign investors, this situation leads to an uncommon amount of uncertainty. Since the *Venture* program was produced, Canada has become Cuba's number one trading partner, and Cuba's biggest foreign investor is Toronto-based Sherritt International Corp. Apart from the hassles of having to deal with the U.S.'s Helms-Burton bill (under which Sherritt can be sued for its current ownership of property seized from U.S. companies during the Cuban Revolution, not to mention the fact that Sherritt executives are forbidden entry into the U.S.), Sherritt and other Canadian companies have to contend with the ever-precarious issue of control of their operations. For most businesses operating in Cuba, such as Delta Hotels, everyday aspects of doing business such as hiring employees is done through state-run organizations.

Cultural differences in the workforce also contribute to difficulties faced by Canadian companies operating in Cuba. Employees are reluctant to make even small autonomous decisions—always checking with management first or simply not performing a task. On the other hand, strikes are nonexistent and labour shortages are never hard to fill.

Ian Delaney, chairman of Sherritt, has called Cuba "a business opportunity for which we believe there is no equal in this world." But to take advantage of this opportunity, foreign companies must have the patience and tenacity needed to constantly keep on top of their businesses in this unstable country.

Questions

1. In what ways and in what circumstances could companies such as Sherritt possibly use forward, concurrent, and feedback controls in their Cuban operations?

2. What kinds of control adjustments do you think a Canadian company would have to make between its operations here and in Cuba?

3. What sort of relationship do you think exists between planning and control for a Canadian company's interests in Cuba?

Video Resource: "Cuba Divers," *Venture* 576 (February 4, 1996).

Additional Sources: Richard Bingham, "Havana Hustle," *Report on Business Magazine*, September 1997, pp. 76–84; Barry Nelson, "Allure of Cuba," *Calgary Herald*, May 1, 1997, p. E1; Valerie Lawton, "Taking the Moral High Ground?," *Canadian Press*, February 25, 1997; John Heinzl, "Sherritt Chief Assails Helms-Burton Law," *The Globe and Mail*, February 25, 1997, p. B4; Peter Morton, "Fear and Loathing in America," *The Financial Post*, January 25, 1997, p. 12.

The Evolution of Management

United Parcel Service (UPS) employs 150,000 people and delivers an average of nine million packages a day to locations in 180 countries. To achieve its claim of "running the tightest ship in the shipping business," UPS's management methodically trains its employees how to do their jobs as efficiently as possible. For instance, consider the job of a delivery driver.[1]

Industrial engineers at UPS have time-studied each driver's route and set standards for each delivery, stop, and pickup. These engineers have recorded every second taken up by stoplights, traffic, detours, doorbells, walkways, stairways, and coffee breaks. Even bathroom stops are put into the standards. All of this is then fed into company computers to provide detailed time standards for every driver, every day.

To meet their objective of 130 deliveries and pickups each day, drivers must follow the engineers' procedures exactly. As they approach a delivery stop, drivers shed their seat belts, toot their horns, and cut their engines. In one seamless motion, they are required to yank up their emergency brakes and push their gearshifts into first. They're now ready for takeoff after their deliveries. The drivers slide to the ground with their clipboards under their right arms and their packages in their left hands. Their keys, teeth up, are in their right hands. They take one look at the package to fix the address in their minds. Then they walk to the customer's door at the prescribed three-feet-per-second and knock first to avoid lost seconds searching for the doorbell. After making the delivery, they do the paperwork on the way back to the truck.

Does this rigid time scheduling seem obsessive? Maybe. Does it make for high efficiency? You bet! Productivity experts describe UPS as one of the most efficient companies anywhere. As a case in point, Federal Express averages only 80 stops a day versus the UPS average of 130. And all of this seems to positively influence UPS's bottom line. Although the company is privately held, it is widely recognized as being highly profitable.

The purpose of this appendix is to demonstrate that a knowledge of management history can help you to understand theory and practice as they exist today. This appendix will introduce you to the origins of many contemporary management concepts and demonstrate how they have evolved to reflect the changing needs of organizations and society.

Historical Background

Organized activities that are overseen by people responsible for planning, organizing, leading, and controlling activities have existed for thousands of years. The Egyptian pyramids and the Great Wall of China are current evidence that projects of tremendous scope, employing tens of thousands of people, were undertaken well before modern times. The pyramids are a particularly interesting example. The construction of a single pyramid occupied more than 100,000 people for 20 years.[2] Who told each worker what he was supposed to do? Who ensured that there would be enough stones at the site to keep workers busy? The answer to questions such as these is management. The Roman Catholic Church also represents an interesting example of the practice of management. The current structure of the church was essentially established in the second century A.D. At that time, its objectives and doctrines were more rigorously defined. Final authority was centralized in Rome. A simple authority hierarchy was created, which has remained basically unchanged for nearly 2,000 years.

These examples from the past demonstrate that organizations have been with us for thousands of years and that management has been practised for an equivalent period. However, it has been only in the past several hundred years, particularly in the last century, that management has undergone systematic investigation, acquired a common body of knowledge, and become a formal discipline for study.

What Was Adam Smith's Contribution to the Field of Management?

Adam Smith's name is more typically cited in economics courses for his contributions to classical economic doctrine, but his discussion in *The Wealth of Nations*, published in 1776, included a brilliant argument on the economic advantages that organizations and society would reap from the division of labour. He used the pin-manufacturing industry for his examples. Smith noted that 10 individuals, each doing a specialized task, could among them produce about 48,000 pins a day. However, if each were working separately and independently, those 10 workers would be lucky to make 200—or even 10—pins in one day.

Smith concluded that division of labour increased productivity by increasing each worker's skill and dexterity, by saving time that is commonly lost in changing tasks, and by the creation of labour-saving inventions and machinery. The wide popularity today of job specialization—in-service jobs such as teaching and medicine as well as on assembly lines in automobile plants—is undoubtedly due to the economic advantages cited over 200 years ago by Adam Smith.

How Did the Industrial Revolution Influence Management Practices?

Possibly the most important pre-twentieth-century influence on management was the **Industrial Revolution**. Begun in the eighteenth century in Great Britain, the rev-

Industrial Revolution
The advent of machine power, mass production, and efficient transportation

olution had crossed the Atlantic to America by the end of the Civil War. Machine power was rapidly being substituted for human power. This, in turn, made it more economical to manufacture goods in factories. The advent of machine power, mass production, the reduced transportation costs that followed the rapid expansion of the railways, and almost no governmental regulation, also fostered the development of big organizations. John D. Rockefeller was putting together the Standard Oil monopoly, Andrew Carnegie was gaining control of two-thirds of the steel industry, and similar entrepreneurs were creating other large businesses that would require formalized management practices. The need for a formal theory to guide managers in running their organizations had arrived. However, it was not until the early 1900s that the first major step occurred toward developing such a theory.

A Period of Diversity

The first half of this century was a period of diversity in management thought. Scientific management looked at the field from the perspective of how to improve the productivity of operative personnel. The general administrative theorists were concerned with the overall organization and how to make it more effective. One group of writers and researchers emphasized the human resource or "people side" of management, while another group focused on developing and applying quantitative models.

In the following sections we'll present the contributions of these four approaches. Keep in mind that each is concerned with the same "animal"; the differences reflect the backgrounds and interests of the writers.

Scientific Management

If one had to pinpoint the year that modern management theory was born, one could make a strong case for 1911: the year that Frederick Winslow Taylor's *Principles of Scientific Management*[3] was published. Its contents would become widely accepted by managers throughout the world. The book described the theory of **scientific management**—the use of the scientific method to define the "one best way" for a job to be done. The studies conducted before and after the book's publication would establish Taylor as the father of scientific management.

scientific management
The use of the scientific method to define the "one best way" for a job to be done.

What Contributions Did Frederick Taylor Make?

Frederick Taylor did most of his work at the Midvale and Bethlehem Steel companies in Pennsylvania. As a mechanical engineer with a Quaker-Puritan background, he was consistently appalled at the inefficiency of workers. Employees used vastly different techniques to do the same job. Also, they were prone to "take it easy" on the job; Taylor believed that worker output was only about one-third of what was possible. Therefore, he set out to correct the situation by applying the scientific method to jobs on the shop floor. He spent more than two decades pursuing with a passion the "one best way" for each job to be done.

> ▶ **1.** Develop a science for each element of an individual's work, which replaces the old rule-of-thumb method.
>
> ▶ **2.** Scientifically select and then train, teach, and develop the worker. (Previously, workers chose their own work and trained themselves as best they could.)
>
> ▶ **3.** Heartily cooperate with the workers so as to ensure that all work is done in accordance with the principles of the science that has been developed.
>
> ▶ **4.** Divide work and responsibility almost equally between management and workers. Management takes over all work for which it is better fitted than the workers. (Previously, almost all the work and the greater part of the responsibility were thrown upon the workers.)

Exhibit A-1
Taylor's Four
Principles of
Management

It's important to understand what Taylor saw at Midvale Steel that aroused his determination to improve the way things were done in the plant. At the time, there were no clear concepts of worker and management responsibilities. Virtually no effective work standards existed. Workers purposely worked at a slow pace. Management decisions were of the "seat-of-the-pants" variety, based on hunch and intuition. Workers were placed on jobs with little or no concern for matching their abilities and aptitudes with the tasks they were required to do. Most important, management and workers considered themselves to be in continual conflict. Rather than cooperating to their mutual benefit, they perceived their relationship as a zero-sum game—any gain by one would be at the expense of the other.

Taylor sought to create a mental revolution among both the workers and management by defining clear guidelines for improving production efficiency. He defined four principles of management, listed in Exhibit A-1; he argued that following these principles would result in the prosperity of both management and workers. Workers would earn more pay, and management more profits. The current application of these principles at United Parcel Service continues to provide some support for Taylor's expectations. UPS delivery drivers earn more than $18 an hour. With overtime, they average better than $50,000 a year.[4] At the same time, management is able to generate consistently high profits.

Building on principle one, Taylor was able to define the one best way for doing each job. He could then, after selecting the right people for the job, train them to do it precisely in this one best way. To motivate workers, he favoured incentive wage plans. Overall, Taylor achieved consistent improvements in productivity in the range of 200 per cent or more. He reaffirmed the role of managers to plan and control and that of workers to perform as they were instructed. The *Principles of Scientific Management*, as well as other papers that Taylor wrote and presented, spread his ideas not only throughout the United States but also in France, Germany, Russia, and Japan. (Learn more about Frederick Taylor and scientific management in Details on a Management Classic.)

Who Else, Besides Taylor, Were Major Contributors to Scientific Management?

Taylor's ideas inspired others to study and develop methods of scientific management. His most prominent disciples were Frank and Lillian Gilbreth. A construction con-

DETAILS ON A MANAGEMENT CLASSIC

Frederick Taylor's Pig Iron Experiment

Probably the most widely cited example of scientific management is Taylor's pig iron experiment. Workers loaded "pigs" of iron weighing 92 pounds onto rail cars. Their average daily output was 12.5 tons. Taylor believed that by scientifically analysing the job to determine the one best way to load pig iron, the output could be increased to between 47 and 48 tons per day.

Taylor began his experiment by looking for a physically strong subject who placed a high value on the dollar. The individual Taylor chose was a big, strong Dutch immigrant, whom he called Schmidt. Schmidt, like the other loaders, earned $1.15 a day, which even at the turn of the century was barely enough for a person to survive on. As the following quotation from Taylor's book demonstrates, Taylor used money—the opportunity to make $1.85 a day—as the primary means to get workers like Schmidt to do exactly as they were told:

> "Schmidt, are you a high-priced man?" "Vell, I don't know vat you mean."
> "Oh, yes you do. What I want to know is whether you are a high-priced man
> or not." "Vell, I don't know vat you mean." "Oh, come now, you answer my
> questions. What I want to find out is whether you are a high-priced man or
> one of these cheap fellows here. What I want to know is whether you want to
> earn $1.85 a day or whether you are satisfied with $1.15, just the same as all
> those cheap fellows are getting." "Did I vant $1.85 a day? Vas dot a high-priced
> man? Vell, yes, I vas a high-priced man."[5]

Using money to motivate Schmidt, Taylor went about having him load the pig iron, alternating various job factors to see what impact the changes had on Schmidt's daily output. For instance, on some days Schmidt would lift the pig iron by bending his knees, whereas on other days he would keep his legs straight and use his back. He experimented with rest periods, walking speed, carrying positions, and other variables. After a long period of scientifically trying various combinations of procedures, techniques, and tools, Taylor succeeded in obtaining the level of productivity he thought possible. By putting the right person on the job with the correct tools and equipment, by having the worker follow his instructions exactly, and by motivating the worker through the economic incentive of a significantly higher daily wage, Taylor was able to reach his 48-ton objective. ▼

tractor by background, Frank Gilbreth gave up his contracting career in 1912 to study scientific management after hearing Taylor speak at a professional meeting. Along with his wife Lillian, a psychologist, he studied work arrangements to eliminate wasteful hand-and-body motions. The Gilbreths also experimented in the design and use of the proper tools and equipment for optimizing work performance.[6] Frank Gilbreth is probably best known for his experiments in reducing the number of motions in bricklaying.

The Gilbreths were among the first to use motion picture films to study hand-and-body motions. They devised a microchronometer that recorded time to 1/2,000 second, placed it in the field of study being photographed, and thus determined how long a worker spent enacting each motion. Wasted motions missed by the naked eye could be identified and eliminated. The Gilbreths also devised a classification scheme to label 17 basic hand motions—such as "search," "select," "grasp," "hold"—which they called **therbligs** ("Gilbreth" spelled backward with the "th" transposed). This allowed the Gilbreths a more precise way of analysing the exact elements of any worker's hand movements.

therbligs
A classification scheme for labelling 17 basic hand motions.

Another notable associate of Taylor at Midvale and Bethlehem Steel was a young engineer named Henry L. Gantt. Like Taylor and the Gilbreths, Gantt sought to increase worker efficiency through scientific investigation. But he extended some of Taylor's original ideas and added a few of his own. For instance, Gantt devised an incentive system that gave workers a bonus for completing their jobs in less time than the allowed standard. He also introduced a bonus for foremen to be paid for each worker who made the standard, plus an extra bonus if all the workers under the foreman made it. In so doing, Gantt expanded the scope of scientific management to encompass the work of managers as well as that of operatives.

However, Gantt is probably most noted for creating a graphic bar chart that could be used by managers as a scheduling device for planning and controlling work (see Chapter 4). The Gantt chart showed the relationship between work planned and completed on one axis, and time elapsed on the other.

Why Did Scientific Management Receive So Much Attention?

Many of the guidelines Taylor and others devised for improving production efficiency appear to us today to be common sense. For instance, one can say that it should have been obvious to managers in those days that workers should be carefully screened, selected, and trained before being put into a job.

To understand the importance of scientific management, you have to consider the times in which Taylor, the Gilbreths, and Gantt lived. The standard of living was low. Production was highly labour intensive. Midvale Steel, at the turn of the century, may have employed 20 or 30 workers who did nothing but load pig iron onto rail cars. Today, their entire daily tonnage could probably be done in several hours by one person with a hydraulic lift truck. But they didn't have such mechanical devices. Similarly, the breakthroughs the Gilbreths achieved in bricklaying are meaningful only when you recognize that most quality buildings at that time were constructed of brick, that land was cheap, and that the major cost of a plant or home was the cost of the materials (bricks) and the cost of the labour to lay them.

General Administrative Theorists

Another group of writers looked at the subject of management but focused on the entire organization. We call them the **general administrative theorists**. They are important for developing more general theories of what managers do and what constitutes good management practice. Because their writings set the framework for many of our contemporary ideas on management and organization, this group and the scientific management group are frequently referred to as the **classical theorists**. The most prominent of the general administrative theorists were Henri Fayol and Max Weber.

general administrative theorists
Writers who developed general theories of what managers do and what constitutes good management practice.

classical theorists
The term used to describe the scientific management theorists and general administrative theorists.

What Did Henri Fayol and Max Weber Contribute to Management Thought?

We mentioned Henri Fayol in Chapter 1 for having designated management as a universal set of functions—specifically planning, organizing, commanding, coordinating, and controlling. Because his writings are important, let's take a more careful look at what he had to say.[7]

Fayol wrote during the same time as Taylor. However, whereas Taylor was concerned with management at the shop level (or what we today would describe as the job of a supervisor) and used the scientific method, Fayol's attention was directed at the activities of all managers, and he wrote from personal experience. Taylor was a scientist. Fayol, the managing director of a large French coal-mining firm, was a practitioner.

Fayol described the practice of management as something distinct from accounting, finance, production, distribution, and other typical business functions. He argued that management was an activity common to all human undertakings in business, in government, and even in the home. He then proceeded to state 14 principles of management—fundamental or universal truths—that could be taught in schools and universities. These principles are shown in Exhibit A-2.

Max Weber (pronounced Vay-ber) was a German sociologist. Writing in the early part of this century, Weber developed a theory of authority structures and described organizational activity based on authority relations.[8] He described an ideal type of organization that he called a bureaucracy. It was a system characterized by division of labour, a clearly defined hierarchy, detailed rules and regulations, and impersonal relationships. Weber recognized that this "ideal bureaucracy" didn't exist in reality but, rather, represented a selective reconstruction of the real world. He meant it as a basis for theorizing about work and how work could be done in large groups. His theory became the design prototype for many of today's large organizations. The detailed features of Weber's ideal bureaucratic structure are outlined in Exhibit A-3.

What Were the General Administrative Theorists' Contributions to Management Practice?

A number of our current ideas and practices in management can be directly traced to the contributions of the general administrative theorists. For instance, the functional view of the manager's job owes its origin to Henri Fayol. Also, while many of his principles may not be universally applicable to the wide variety of organizations that exist today, they became a frame of reference against which many current concepts have evolved.

Weber's bureaucracy was an attempt to formulate an ideal model around which organizations could be designed. It was a response to the abuses that Weber saw going on within organizations. Weber believed that his model could remove the ambiguity, inefficiencies, and patronage that characterized most organizations at that time. While not as popular now as it was a decade ago, many of bureaucracy's components are still inherent in large organizations today.

Human Resource Approach

Managers get things done by working with people. This explains why some writers and researchers have chosen to look at management by focusing on the organization's

▶ **1. Division of Work** This principle is the same as Adam Smith's "division of labour." Specialization increases output by making employees more efficient.

▶ **2. Authority** Managers must be able to give orders. Authority gives them this right. Along with authority, however, goes responsibility. Wherever authority is exercised, responsibility arises.

▶ **3. Discipline** Employees must obey and respect the rules that govern the organization. Good discipline is the result of effective leadership, a clear understanding between management and workers regarding the organization's rules, and the judicious use of penalties for infractions of the rules.

▶ **4. Unity of Command** Every employee should receive orders from only one superior.

▶ **5. Unity of Direction** Each group of organizational activities that has the same objective should be directed by one manager using one plan.

▶ **6. Subordination of Individual Interests to the General Interest** The interests of any one employee or group of employees should not take precedence over the interests of the organization as a whole.

▶ **7. Remuneration** Workers must be paid a fair wage for their services.

▶ **8. Centralization** Centralization refers to the degree to which subordinates are involved in decision making. Whether decision making is centralized (to management) or decentralized (to subordinates) is a question of proper proportion. The task is to find the optimum degree of centralization for each situation.

▶ **9. Scalar Chain** The line of authority from top management to the lowest ranks represents the scalar chain. Communications should follow this chain. However, if following the chain creates delays, cross-communications can be allowed if agreed to by all parties and superiors are kept informed.

▶**10. Order** People and materials should be in the right place at the right time.

▶**11. Equity** Managers should be kind and fair to their subordinates.

▶**12. Stability of Tenure of Personnel** High employee turnover is inefficient. Management should provide orderly personnel planning and ensure that replacements are available to fill vacancies.

▶**13. Initiative** Employees who are allowed to originate and carry out plans will exert high levels of effort.

▶**14. Esprit de Corps** Promoting team spirit will build harmony and unity within the organization.

**Exhibit A-2
Fayol's 14 Principles
of Management**

human resources. Much of what currently makes up the field of personnel or human resource management, as well as contemporary views on motivation and leadership, has come out of the work of those we have categorized as being part of the **human resource approach** to management.

human resource approach
The study of management that focuses on human behaviour.

Who Were Some Early Advocates of the Human Resource Approach?

While there were undoubtedly a number of people in the nineteenth and early part of the twentieth century who recognized the importance of the human factor to an

**Exhibit A-3
Weber's Ideal
Bureaucracy**

▶ **1. Division of labour** Jobs are broken down into simple, routine, and well-defined tasks.

▶ **2. Authority Hierarchy** Offices or positions are organized in a hierarchy, each lower one being controlled and supervised by a higher one.

▶ **3. Formal Selection** All organizational members are to be selected on the basis of technical qualifications demonstrated by training, education, or formal examination.

▶ **4. Formal Rules and Regulations** To ensure uniformity and to regulate the actions of employees, managers must depend heavily on formal organizational rules.

▶ **5. Impersonality** Rules and controls are applied uniformly, avoiding involvement with personalities and personal preferences of employees.

▶ **6. Career Orientation** Managers are professional officials rather than owners of the units they manage. They work for fixed salaries and pursue their careers within the organization.

organization's success, four individuals stand out as early advocates of the human resource approach. They were Hugo Munsterberg, Mary Parker Follett, Chester Barnard, and Elton Mayo.

For What Is Hugo Munsterberg Best Known?

Hugo Munsterberg created the field of industrial psychology—the scientific study of individuals at work for the purpose of maximizing their productivity and adjustment. His text, *Psychology and Industrial Efficiency*, was published in 1913. In it, he argued for the scientific study of human behaviour to identify general patterns and to explain individual differences. Munsterberg suggested the use of psychological tests to improve employee selection, the value of learning theory in the development of training methods, and the study of human behaviour in order to understand what techniques are most effective for motivating workers. Interestingly, he saw a link between scientific management and industrial psychology. Both sought increased efficiency through scientific work analyses and through better alignment of individual skills and abilities with the demands of various jobs. Much of our current knowledge of selection techniques, employee training, job design, and motivation is built on the work of Munsterberg.

What Contributions Did Mary Parker Follett Make to Management?

One of the earliest writers to recognize that organizations could be viewed from the perspective of individual and group behaviour was Mary Parker Follett.[9] A transitionalist writing in the time of scientific management but proposing more people-oriented ideas, Follett was a social philosopher. However, her ideas had clear implications for management practice. Follett thought that organizations should be based on a group ethic rather than on individualism. Individual potential, she argued, remained only potential until released through group association. The manager's job was to harmonize and coordinate group efforts. Managers and workers should view themselves as partners—as part of a common group. As such, managers should rely more on their expertise and knowledge to lead subordinates than on the formal authority of their position. Her humanistic ideas influenced the way we look at motivation, leadership, power, and authority.

Who Was Chester Barnard?

A transitionalist like Follett, Chester Barnard's ideas bridged classical and human resource viewpoints. Like Fayol, Barnard was a practitioner—he was president of New Jersey Bell Telephone Company. He had read Weber and was influenced by his writings. But unlike Weber, who had an impersonal view of organizations, Barnard saw organizations as social systems that require human cooperation. He expressed his views in his book *The Functions of the Executive*,[10] published in 1938.

Barnard believed that organizations were made up of people who have interacting social relationships. The manager's major roles were to communicate and stimulate subordinates to high levels of effort. A major part of an organization's success, as Barnard saw it, depended on obtaining cooperation from its employees. Barnard also argued that success depended on maintaining good relations with people and institutions outside the organization with whom the organization regularly interacted. Barnard is also important for his enlightened ideas on authority. The dominant or **traditional view of authority** at the time he wrote was that a superior's right to exact compliance from subordinates develops at the top and moves down through an organization. Barnard offered a contrasting position, arguing that authority comes from below. The **acceptance view of authority** proposed that authority comes from the willingness of subordinates to accept it. According to Barnard, there can be no such thing as a person of authority, but only a person to whom authority is addressed.

What Were the Hawthorne Studies?

Without question, the most important contribution to the human resource approach to management came out of the **Hawthorne studies** undertaken at the Western Electric Company's Hawthorne Works in Cicero, Illinois. Scholars generally agree that the Hawthorne studies had a dramatic impact on the direction of management thought. Elton Mayo, a Harvard professor, concluded that behaviour and sentiments were closely related, that group influences significantly affected individual behaviour, that group standards established individual worker output, and that money was less a factor in determining output than were group standards, group sentiments, and security. These conclusions led to a new emphasis on the human factor in the functioning of organizations and the attainment of their goals. They also led to increased paternalism by management. (For further information on the Hawthorne studies, see Details on a Management Classic.)

Why Was the Human Relations Movement Important to Management History?

Another group within the human resource approach is important to management history for its unflinching commitment to making management practices more humane.

traditional view of authority
The view that authority comes from above.

acceptance view of authority
The theory that authority comes from the willingness of subordinates to accept it.

Hawthorne studies
A series of studies during the 1920s and 1930s that provided new insights into group norms and behaviour.

Members of the human relations movement uniformly believed in the importance of employee satisfaction—a satisfied worker was believed to be a productive worker. For the most part, names associated with this movement—Dale Carnegie, Abraham Maslow, and Douglas McGregor—were individuals whose views were shaped more by their personal philosophies than by substantive research evidence.

Dale Carnegie is often overlooked by management scholars, but his ideas and teachings have had an enormous effect on management practice. His book, *How to Win Friends and Influence People*,[11] was read by millions in the 1930s, 1940s, and 1950s. In addition, during this same period, tens of thousands of managers and aspiring managers attended his management speeches and seminars. What was the theme of Carnegie's book and lectures? Essentially, he said that the way to success was through winning the cooperation of others.[12]

Abraham Maslow, a humanistic psychologist, proposed a theoretical hierarchy of five needs: physiological, safety, social, esteem, and self-actualization.[13] In terms of motivation, Maslow argued that each step in the hierarchy must be satisfied before the next can be activated, and that once a need was substantially satisfied it no longer motivated behaviour.

Douglas McGregor is best known for his formulation of two sets of assumptions—Theory X and Theory Y—about human nature.[14] Briefly, Theory X presents an essentially negative view of people. It assumes that they have little ambition, dislike work, want to avoid responsibility, and need to be closely directed to work effectively. On the other hand, Theory Y offers a positive view. It assumes that people can exercise self-direction, accept responsibility, and consider work to be as natural as rest or play. McGregor believed that Theory Y assumptions best captured the true nature of workers and should guide management practice.

What Was the Common Thread that Linked Advocates of the Human Relations Movement?

The common thread that united human relations supporters, including Carnegie, Maslow, and McGregor, was an unshakable optimism about people's capabilities. They believed strongly in their cause and were inflexible in their beliefs, even when faced with contradictory evidence. No amount of contrary experience or research evidence would alter their views. Of course, in spite of this lack of objectivity, advocates of the human relations movement had a definite influence on management theory and practice.

Who Were the Behavioural Science Theorists?

behavioural science theorists
Psychologists and sociologists who relied on the scientific method for the study of organizational behaviour.

One final category within the human resource approach encompasses a group of psychologists and sociologists who relied on the scientific method for studying organizational behaviour. Unlike the theorists of the human relations movement, individuals such as Fred Fiedler, Victor Vroom, Frederick Herzberg, Edwin Locke, David McClelland, Richard Hackman, Jeffrey Pfeffer, Kenneth Thomas, and Charles Perrow engaged in objective research of human behaviour in organizations. They carefully attempted to keep their personal beliefs out of their work. They sought to develop rigorous research designs that could be replicated by other **behavioural scientists**. In so doing, they hoped to build a science of organizational behaviour.

DETAILS ON A MANAGEMENT CLASSIC

The Hawthorne Studies

These studies, originally begun in 1924 but eventually expanded and carried through the early 1930s, were initially devised by Western Electric industrial engineers to examine the effect of various illumination levels on worker productivity. Both control and experimental groups were established. The experimental group was presented with varying illumination intensities, while the control group worked under a constant intensity. The engineers had expected individual output to be directly related to the intensity of light. However, they found that as the light level was increased in the experimental group, output for both groups rose. To the surprise of the engineers, as the light level was dropped in the experimental group, productivity continued to increase in both groups. In fact, a productivity decrease was observed in the experimental group only when the light intensity had been reduced to that of moonlight. The engineers concluded that illumination intensity was not directly related to group productivity, but they could not explain the behaviour they had witnessed.

In 1927, the Western Electric engineers asked Elton Mayo and his associates to join the study as consultants. Thus began a relationship that would last through 1932 and encompass numerous experiments covering the redesign of jobs, changes in the lengths of the workday and workweek, the introduction of rest periods, and individual versus group wage plans.[15] For example, one experiment was designed to evaluate the effect of a group piecework-incentive-pay system on group productivity. The results indicated that the incentive plan had less effect on workers' output than did group pressure and acceptance and the concomitant security. Social norms or standards of the group, therefore, were concluded to be the key determinants of individual work behaviour.

The Hawthorne studies have not been without critics. Attacks have been made on procedures, analyses of the findings, and the conclusions drawn.[16] However, from a historical standpoint it is of little importance whether the studies were academically sound or their conclusions justified. What is important is that they stimulated an interest in human factors. The Hawthorne studies went a long way toward changing the dominant view at the time that people were no different than machines; that is, you put them on the shop floor, cranked in the inputs, and they produced a known quantity of outputs.▼

What Can Be Concluded from the Human Resource Contributors?

Both scientific management and the general administrative theorists viewed organizations as machines. Managers were the engineers. They ensured that the inputs were available and that the machine was properly maintained. Any failure by the employee to generate the desired output was viewed as an engineering problem: it was time to redesign the job or grease the machine by offering the employee an incentive wage plan. After all, who wouldn't work harder for a few more dollars? Apparently, a lot of people! UPS, which we earlier described as being a modern-day proponent of scientific management principles, has pushed a number of its drivers so hard that they quit. As one driver put it, "They squeeze every ounce out of you. You're always in a hurry, and you can't work relaxed."[17] Contributors to the human resources approach forced managers in many organizations to reassess the simplistic machine-model view.

The Quantitative Approach

We close our discussion of the period of diversity with a review of quantitative contributions to the study of management. This approach has also been labelled as operations research or management science.

quantitative approach
The use of quantitative techniques to improve decision making.

The **quantitative approach** to management evolved out of the development of mathematical and statistical solutions to military problems during World War II. For instance, when the British confronted the problem of how to get the maximum effectiveness from their limited aircraft capability against the massive forces of the Germans, they turned to their mathematicians to devise an optimum allocation model. Similarly, U.S. antisubmarine warfare teams used operations research techniques to improve the odds of survival for Allied convoys crossing the North Atlantic and for selecting the optimal depth-charge patterns for aircraft and surface vessel attacks on German U-boats.

After the war, many of the quantitative techniques that had been applied to military problems were moved into the business sector. One group of military officers, labelled the "Whiz Kids," joined Ford Motor Company in the mid-1940s and immediately began using statistical devices to improve decision making at Ford. Two of the most famous Whiz Kids were Robert McNamara and Charles "Tex" Thornton. McNamara rose to the presidency of Ford and then became U.S. Secretary of Defence. At the Department of Defence, he sought to quantify resource allocation decisions in the Pentagon through cost-benefit analyses. He concluded his career as head of the World Bank. Tex Thornton founded the billion-dollar conglomerate Litton Industries, again relying on quantitative techniques to make acquisition and allocation decisions.

What Are the Quantitative Techniques and How Have They Contributed to Current Management Practice?

The quantitative approach to management includes applications of statistics, optimization models, information models, and computer simulations. Linear programming, for instance, is a technique that managers can use to improve resource allocation choices. Work scheduling can be made more efficient as a result of critical-path scheduling analysis. Decisions on determining the optimum inventory levels a firm should maintain have been significantly influenced by the economic order quantity model.

How Has the Quantitative Approach Contributed to Management Practice?

The quantitative approach has contributed most directly to management decision making, particularly to planning and control decisions. Without denigrating the contribution of the quantitative approach, it should be noted that it has never gained the influence on management practice that the human resource approach has. This is undoubtedly due to a number of factors: many managers are unfamiliar with the quantitative tools; behavioural problems are more widespread and visible; and most students and managers can relate better to real, day-to-day people problems in organizations—such as motivating subordinates and reducing conflicts—than to the more abstract activity of constructing quantitative models.

Scoring Keys for Exercises

Chapter 1 • How Strong Is Your Motivation to Manage in a Large Organization?

Total your circled numbers. Your score will fall somewhere between 7 and 49. Arbitrary norms for comparison are as follows: Scores of 7–21 = relatively low motivation to manage; 22–34 = moderate; 35–49 = relatively high.

Chapter 2 • What Are Your Personal Value Preferences? (Self-Assessment)

These 18 values have been labelled as instrumental values, which means they represent beliefs about near-term modes of conduct. Research studies have found that different groups have different ranked preferences. The following represent the highest ranked and lowest ranked values from three groups: 345 graduates of a university's executive MBA program; a sample of 1,000 members from a steelworkers' union local; and a diverse set of 234 community activists.

		Executives	Unions	Activists
Top five responses:				
	1.	Honest	Responsible	Honest
	2.	Responsible	Honest	Helpful
	3.	Capable	Courageous	Courageous
	4.	Ambitious	Independent	Responsible
	5.	Independent	Capable	Capable

	Executives	**Unions**	**Activists**
Bottom five responses:			
14.	Helpful	Helpful	Ambitious
15.	Polite	Cheerful	Self-controlled
16.	Cheerful	Intellectual	Polite
17.	Clean	Forgiving	Clean
18.	Obedient	Imaginative	Obedient

What were your top five and bottom five responses? How do they compare with the three groups above?

Chapter 2 • The International Culture Quiz (Class Exercise)

The correct answers are:

> 1. a   2. b   3. e (Portuguese)   4. b   5. d
>
> 6. a   7. d   8. d   9. b   10. b

Scores of eight correct answers or more indicate that you are relatively knowledgeable about customs, practices, and facts regarding different countries. Scores of four correct answers or less suggest considerable room for expanding your knowledge of other people and lands.

Chapter 3 • Are You a Good Planner?

According to the author of this questionnaire, the "perfect" planner would have answered:

> 1. Yes   2. No   3. Yes   4. Yes
>
> 5. Yes   6. Yes   7. Yes   8. No

Chapter 4 • Are You an Entrepreneur?

Total your score for the 22 characteristics. Your score will fall between +44 and −44. The higher your positive score, the more you share traits common to highly successful entrepreneurs.

Chapter 5 • What's Your Intuitive Ability?

Total the number of "a" responses circled for questions 1, 3, 5, 6, 11; enter the score here [A =   ]. Total the number of "b" responses for questions 2, 4, 7, 8, 9, 10, 12; enter the score here [B =   ]. Add your "a" and "b" scores and enter the sum here [A + B =   ].

This is your intuitive score. The highest possible intuitive score is 12; the lowest is 0. The author of this scale states that traditional analytical techniques "are not as useful as they once were for guiding major decisions. . . . If you hope to be better prepared for tomorrow, then it only seems logical to pay some attention to the use and development of intuitive skills for decision making." (Source: Weston H. Agor, AIM Survey (El Paso, TX: ENFP Enterprises, 1989), Part I.)

Chapter 6 • How Power Oriented Are You?

This test is designed to compute your Machiavellian (Mach) score. To obtain your score, add the number you have checked on questions 1, 3, 4, 5, 9, and 10. For the other four questions, reverse the numbers you have checked: 5 becomes 1, 4 is 2, 2 is 4, 1 is 5. Total your 10 numbers to find your score. The National Opinion Research Center, which used this short form of the scale in a random sample of American adults, found that the national average was 25.

The results of research using the Mach test found that men are generally more Machiavellian than women; older adults tend to have lower Mach scores than younger adults; and high-Machs tend to be in professions that emphasize the control and manipulation of individuals—for example, managers, lawyers, psychiatrists, and behavioural scientists.

Chapter 7 • Is an Enriched Job for You? (Self-Assessment)

This exercise is designed to assess the degree to which you desire complex, challenging work. A high need for growth suggests that you are more likely to experience the desired psychological states in the job characteristics model when you have an enriched job. This 12-item questionnaire indicates the degree to which you have a strong versus weak desire to obtain growth satisfaction from your work. Each item on the questionnaire yields a score from 1 to 7 (that is, "Strongly prefer A" is scored 1; "Neutral" is scored 4; and "Strongly prefer B" is scored 7). To obtain your individual growth need strength score, average the 12 items as follows:

#1, #2, #7, #8, #11, #12 (direct scoring)
#3, #4, #5, #6, #9, #10 (reverse scoring)

Average scores for typical respondents are close to the midpoint of 4. Research indicates that if you score high on this measure, you will respond positively to an enriched job. Conversely, if you score low, you will tend not to find enriched jobs satisfying or motivating.

Chapter 7 • What Kind of Organization Design Do You Want to Work For? (Class Exercise)

For items 5, 6, 7, and 9, score as follows:

Strongly agree	= +2
Agree	= +1
Uncertain	= −0
Disagree	= −1
Strongly disagree	= −2

For items 1, 2, 3, 4, 8, and 10, reverse the score (Strongly agree = −2, and so on). Add up your total. Your score will fall somewhere between +20 and −20. What does your score mean? The higher your score (positive), the more comfortable you'll be in a formal, stable, rule-oriented, and structured culture. This is synonymous with large corporations in stable environments and with government agencies. Negative scores indicate a preference for small, innovative, flexible, team-oriented cultures that are more likely to be found in research units or small businesses.

Chapter 8 • How Do You Define Life Success?

This questionnaire taps six dimensions of life success. These are the achievement of status and wealth; contribution to society; good family relationships; personal fulfilment; professional fulfilment; and security.

Calculate your scores as follows:

The STATUS/WEALTH SCORE is found by adding responses to items:

									/8 =
1	7	12	16	24	26	34	36	Total	

The CONTRIBUTION TO SOCIETY SCORE is found by adding responses to items:

									/8 =
6	15	18	22	33	35	39	42	Total	

The FAMILY RELATIONSHIPS SCORE is found by adding responses to items:

									/8 =
3	8	10	11	20	25	31	41	Total	

The PERSONAL FULFILMENT SCORE is found by adding responses to items:

									/8 =
2	14	17	23	27	29	38	40	Total	

The PROFESSIONAL FULFILMENT SCORE is found by adding responses to items:

						/5 =
5	13	21	32	37	Total	

The SECURITY SCORE is found by adding responses to items:

						/5 =
4	9	19	28	30	Total	

You can compare your scores with the following norms based on surveys of managers:

	Females (n = 439)	Males (n = 317)
Status/Wealth	3.48	3.65
Social Contribution	4.04	4.07
Family Relationships	4.44	4.28
Personal Fulfilment	4.60	4.43
Professional Fulfilment	4.21	4.15
Security	4.30	4.21

Chapter 9 • How Ready Are You for Managing in a Turbulent World?

Score 4 points for each A, 3 for each B, 2 for each C, 1 for each D, and 0 for each E. Compute the total, divide by 24, and round to one decimal place. While the results are not intended to be more than suggestive, the higher your score, the more comfortable you seem to be with change. The test's author suggests analysing scores as if they were grade point averages. In this way, a 4.0 average is an A, a 2.0 is a C, and scores below 1.0 flunk. Using replies from nearly 500 MBA students and young managers, the range of scores was found to be narrow—between 1.0 and 2.2. The average score was between 1.5 and 1.6—a D+/C sort of grade!

Chapter 10 • Who Controls Your Life?

This exercise is designed to measure your locus of control. Give yourself 1 point for each of the following selections: 1B, 2A, 3A, 4B, 5B, 6A, 7A, 8A, 9B, and 10A. Scores can be interpreted as follows:

8–10	=	High internal locus of control
6–7	=	Moderate internal locus of control
5	=	Mixed
3–4	=	Moderate external locus of control
1–2	=	High external locus of control

The higher your internal score, the more you believe that you control your own destiny. The higher your external score, the more you believe that what happens to you in your life is due to luck or chance.

Chapter 11 • How Trustworthy Are You?

Add up your total score. It will be somewhere between 8 and 80. What does your score mean?

65–80	=	High trustworthiness
24–64	=	Moderate trustworthiness
8–23	=	Low trustworthiness

Chapter 12 • What Needs Are Most Important to You?

Place the values you gave A, B, C, D, and E for each question in the spaces provided in the scoring key. Notice that the letters are not always in the same place for each question. Then add up each column and obtain a total score for each of the motivation levels.

Scoring Key		A	C	B	E	D
	Question 1					
	Question 2	A	B	D	C	E
	Question 3	B	C	E	D	A
	Question 4	E	A	C	B	D
	Question 5	C	B	D	A	E
	Question 6	B	C	A	E	D
	Question 7	E	A	D	C	B
	Question 8	B	C	A	E	D
	Question 9	B	C	E	D	A
	Question 10	B	D	C	E	A
	TOTAL SCORE					
		I	II	III	IV	V
		MOTIVATION LEVELS				

The five motivation levels area as follows.

Level I:	Physiological needs
Level II:	Safety needs
Level III:	Social needs
Level IV:	Esteem needs
Level V:	Self-actualization needs

Levels that received the highest scores are the most important needs identified by you in your work. The lowest show those needs that have been relatively well satisfied or that have been deemphasized by you at this time.

Chapter 13 • What Kind of Leader Are You?

To find your leadership style,

1. Circle the item numbers for items 8, 12, 17, 18, 19, 30, 34, and 35.
2. Write a "1" in front of the circled items to which you responded S (seldom) or N (never).
3. Write a "1" in front of items not circled to which you responded A (always) or F (frequently).
4. Circle the "1s" which you have written in front of the following items: 3, 5, 8, 10, 15, 18, 19, 22, 24, 26, 28, 30, 32, 34, and 35.

5. Count the circled "1s." This is your score for concern for people. Record the score.
6. Count the uncircled "1s." This is your score for concern for task. Record this number.
7. Now refer to the diagram. Find your score on the concern-for-task dimension on the left-hand arrow. Next, move to the right-hand arrow and find your score on the concern-for-people dimension. Draw a straight line that intersects the two scores. The point at which that line crosses the shared leadership arrow indicates your score on that dimension.

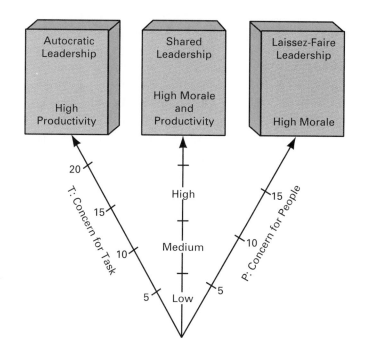

Chapter 14 • Conflict-Handling Style Questionnaire

Total your choices as follows: give yourself 5 points for "Often"; 3 points for "Sometimes"; and 1 point for "Never." Then total them for each set of statements, grouped as follows:

Set A:	items 13–16	Set B:	items 9–12
Set C:	items 5–8	Set D:	items 1–4

Treat each set separately. A score of 17 or above on any set is considered high; scores of 12 to 16 are moderately high; scores of 8 to 11 are moderately low; and scores of 7 or less are considered low. Sets A, B, C, and D represent different conflict-resolution strategies:

A = Force/domination: I win, you lose.
B = Accommodation: I lose, you win.
C = Compromise: Both you and I win some and lose some.
D = Collaboration: I win, you win.

Everyone has a basic underlying conflict-handling style. Your score on this exercise indicates the strategies you rely on most.

Chapter 15 • How Willing Are You to Give Up Control?

Add up your total score for the 18 items. Your score can be interpreted as follows:

72–90 points	=	Ineffective delegation
54–71 points	=	Delegation habits need substantial improvement
36–53 points	=	You still have room to improve
18–35 points	=	Superior delegation

Chapter 16 • Testing Your Understanding of Computers

The correct answers are as follows:

1. B	2. A	3. E	4. B	5. C	6. D
7. A	8. B	9. D	10. D	11. E	12. A
13. D	14. A	15. B	16. E	17. A	18. D
19. E	20. C	21. A	22. E	23. D	24. A
25. A	26. B	27. E	28. A	29. B	30. D

Arbitrary cutoffs suggest:

25–30 correct	=	High literacy
20–24 correct	=	Considerable computer knowledge
15–19 correct	=	Some computer knowledge
10–14 correct	=	Modest computer knowledge
0–9 correct	=	Very little computer knowledge

appendix 3

Answer Key for Testing Your Comprehension

Chapter 1:

p. 22

1. **b**	10. **a**
2. **a**	11. **c**
3. **c**	12. **d**
4. **b**	13. **c**
5. **b**	14. **c**
6. **d**	15. **b**
7. **c**	16. **b**
8. **b**	17. **c**
9. **d**	18. **d**

Chapter 2:

p. 52

1. **b**	10. **d**
2. **c**	11. **a**
3. **a**	12. **b**
4. **c**	13. **c**
5. **d**	14. **b**
6. **c**	15. **a**
7. **c**	
8. **d**	
9. **b**	

Chapter 3:

p. 83

1. **c**	10. **a**
2. **d**	11. **c**
3. **c**	12. **b**
4. **a**	13. **a**
5. **b**	14. **a**
6. **c**	15. **b**
7. **b**	16. **c**
8. **c**	
9. **d**	

Chapter 4:

p. 109

1. **c**	10. **c**
2. **d**	11. **b**
3. **c**	12. **c**
4. **b**	13. **d**
5. **a**	14. **b**
6. **d**	15. **d**
7. **a**	16. **a**
8. **b**	17. **c**
9. **c**	18. **d**

Chapter 5:

p. 136

1. **b**	10. **b**
2. **a**	11. **a**
3. **c**	12. **c**
4. **d**	13. **d**
5. **a**	14. **a**
6. **c**	15. **b**
7. **b**	16. **d**
8. **c**	17. **a**
9. **d**	

Chapter 6:

p. 167

1. **c**	10. **c**
2. **a**	11. **c**
3. **b**	12. **c**
4. **c**	13. **b**
5. **a**	
6. **b**	
7. **d**	
8. **a**	
9. **a**	

Chapter 7:

p. 202

1. **d**	10. **a**
2. **a**	11. **c**
3. **c**	12. **a**
4. **d**	13. **d**
5. **b**	14. **d**
6. **a**	15. **a**
7. **a**	16. **c**
8. **d**	17. **b**
9. **b**	18. **d**

Chapter 8:

p. 233

1. **d**	10. **c**
2. **c**	11. **d**
3. **c**	12. **b**
4. **a**	
5. **b**	
6. **c**	
7. **d**	
8. **a**	
9. **c**	

Chapter 9:
p. 257

1. c
2. a
3. a
4. c
5. d
6. b
7. a
8. c
9. c
10. b
11. c
12. d

Chapter 10:
p. 286

1. b
2. d
3. c
4. d
5. b
6. a
7. d
8. b
9. b
10. c
11. a
12. d
13. d
14. a

Chapter 11:
p.306

1. c
2. b
3. c
4. b
5. a
6. d
7. c
8. a
9. d
10. b
11. c
12. d
13. a
14. b

Chapter 12:
p. 330

1. d
2. b
3. a
4. c
5. a
6. d
7. b
8. a
9. d
10. c
11. d
12. b
13. d
14. c
15. d

Chapter 13:
p. 359

1. d
2. b
3. c
4. a
5. c
6. b
7. a
8. d
9. a
10. c
11. a
12. b

Chapter 14:
p. 385

1. b
2. c
3. d
4. c
5. a
6. d
7. d
8. c
9. a
10. a
11. c
12. a
13. b
14. d
15. b

Chapter 15:
p. 410

1. a
2. d
3. b
4. c
5. a
6. c
7. a
8. b
9. d
10. a
11. c
12. b
13. c
14. a
15. c
16. d

Chapter 16:
p. 442

1. c
2. d
3. a
4. b
5. c
6. c
7. b
8. c
9. d
10. a
11. b
12. c
13. d

Endnotes

Chapter 1

1. David Berman, "Car and Striver," *Canadian Business*, September 1996, pp. 92–101.
2. U.S. Bureau of the Census, *Statistical Abstracts of the United States: 1993*, 113th ed. (Washington, D.C.: Government Printing Office, 1993), p. 405.
3. Henri Fayol, *Industrial and General Administration* (Paris: Dunod, 1916).
4. Harold Koontz and Cyril O'Donnell, *Principles of Management: An Analysis of Managerial Functions* (New York: McGraw-Hill, 1955).
5. For a comprehensive review of this question, see Colin P. Hales, "What Do Managers Do? A Critical Review of the Evidence," *Journal of Management Studies*, January 1986, pp. 88–115.
6. Henry Mintzberg, *The Nature of Managerial Work* (New York: Harper & Row, 1973).
7. Fred Luthans, Stuart A. Rosenkrantz, and Harry W. Hennessey, "What Do Successful Managers Really Do? An Observation Study of Managerial Activities," *Journal of Applied Behavioral Science*, Vol. 21, No. 3 (1985), pp. 255–70; Fred Luthans, "Successful vs. Effective Real Managers," *Academy of Management Executive*, May 1988, pp. 127–32; Fred Luthans, Richard M. Hodgetts, and Stuart A. Rosenkrantz, Real Managers (Cambridge, Mass.: Ballinger Publishing, 1988); and Fred Luthans, Dianne H.B. Welsh, and Lewis A. Taylor III, "A Descriptive Model of Managerial Effectiveness," *Group & Organization Studies*, June 1988, pp. 148–62.
8. See, for example, Larry D. Alexander, "The Effect Level in the Hierarchy and Functional Area Have on the Extent Mintzberg's Roles Are Required by Managerial Jobs," *Academy of Management Proceedings*, 1979, pp. 186–89; Alan W. Lau and Cynthia M. Pavett, "The Nature of Managerial Work: A Comparison of Public and Private Sector Managers," *Group and Organization Studies*, December 1980, pp. 453–66; Morgan W. McCall, Jr. and C.A. Segrist, *In Pursuit of the Manager's Job: Building on Mintzberg*, Technical Report No. 14 (Greensboro, N.C.: Center for Creative Leadership, 1980); Cynthia M. Pavett and Alan W. Lau, "Managerial Work: The Influence of Hierarchical Level and Functional Specialty," *Academy of Management Journal*, March 1983, pp. 170–77; Hales, "What Do Managers Do? A Critical Review of the Evidence;" Allen I. Kraut, Patricia R. Pedigo, D. Douglas McKenna, and Marvin D. Dunnette, "The Role of the Manager: What's Really Important in Different Management Jobs," *Academy of Management Executive*, November 1989, pp. 286–93; and Mark J. Martinko and William L. Gardner, "Structured Observation of Managerial Work: A Replication and Synthesis," *Journal of Management Studies*, May 1990, pp. 330–57.
9. Pavett and Lau, "Managerial Work: The Influence of Hierarchical Level and Functional Specialty."
10. Stephen J. Carroll and Dennis A. Gillen, "Are the Classical Management Functions Useful in Describing Managerial Work?" *Academy of Management Review*, January 1987, p. 48.
11. See, for example, Harold Koontz, "Commentary on the Management Theory Jungle—Nearly Two Decades Later," in Harold Koontz, Cyril O'Donnell, and Heintz Weihrich, eds., *Management: A Book of Readings*, 6th ed. (New York: McGraw-Hill, 1984), pp. 10–14; and Carroll and Gillen, "Are the Classical Management Functions Useful in Describing Managerial Work?", pp. 38–51.
12. Harold Koontz, "Commentary on the Management Theory Jungle—Nearly Two Decades Later"; and Peter Allan, "Managers at Work: A Large–Scale Study of the Managerial Job in New York City Government," *Academy of Management Journal*, September 1981, pp. 613–19.
13. Robert L. Katz, "Skills of an Effective Administrator," *Harvard Business Review*, September–October, 1974, pp. 90–102.
14. See, for example, James W. Driscoll, Gary Cowger, and Robert Egan, "Private Managers and Public Myths—Public Managers and Private Myths," *Sloan Management Review*, Fall 1979, pp. 53–57; David Rogers, "Managing in the Public and Private Sectors: Similarities and Differences," *Management Review*, May 1981, pp. 48–54; Graham Allison, "Public and Private Management: Are They Fundamentally Alike in All Unimportant Respects?" in F.S. Lane, ed., *Current Issues in Public Administration*, 2nd ed. (New York: St. Martin's Press, 1982); Douglas Yates, Jr., *The Politics of Management* (San Francisco: Jossey-Bass, 1985), pp. 12–39; J. Norman Baldwin, "Public vs. Private: Not That Different, Not That Consequential," *Public Personnel Management*, Summer 1987, pp. 181–91; and Hal G. Rainey, "Public Management: Recent Research on the Political Context and Managerial

Roles, Structures, and Behaviors," *Journal of Management*, June 1989, pp. 229–50.

15. Joseph G.P. Paolillo, "The Manager's Self–Assessments of Managerial Roles: Small vs. Large Firms," *American Journal of Small Business*, January–March 1984, pp. 58–64.

16. See, for example, Gerald d'Amboise and Marie Muldowney, "Management Theory for Small Business: Attempts and Requirements," *Academy of Management Review*, April 1988, pp. 226–40.

17. Jennifer Hunter, "The Ultimate Mushroom Recipe," *Canadian Business*, October 10, 1997, pp. 98–99.

18. Harold Koontz, "The Management Theory Jungle," *Journal of the Academy of Management*, December 1961, pp. 174–88.

19. Harold Koontz, ed., *Toward a Unified Theory of Management* (New York: McGraw-Hill, 1964).

20. See, for example, Louis W. Fry and Deborah A. Smith, "Congruence, Contingency, and Theory Building," *Academy of Management Review*, January 1987, pp. 117–32.

21. Based on: "The Fan versus the Businessman," *Inc. 500*, 1995, pp. 34–35.

Chapter 2

1. Elizabeth Church and Gordon Pitts, "How Three Eaton's Suppliers are Coping," *The Globe and Mail*, April 1, 1997, p. B9.

2. Linda Gyulai, "Trumps In Suits," *Time*, April 28, 1997, p. 41.

3. Robert H. Miles, *Macro Organizational Behavior* (Santa Monica, Calif.: Goodyear Publishing, 1980), p. 195.

4. Robin Bates, "Exports, Eh?," *Canadian Business*, January 1997, p. 21; Geoffrey York, "Ski-Doos Latest Trendy Toy in Russia," *The Globe and Mail*, January 21, 1997, p. A1; Andrew Purvis, "Super Exporter," *Time*, April 28, 1997, p. 34; Janet McFarland, "Canada Shines in Global Ratings," *The Globe and Mail*, May 26, 1997, p. B1.

5. Dennis Bueckert, "Government, Industry, Hail Communications Agreement," *The Montreal Gazette*, February 16, 1997, p. A5.

6. Kenneth Kidd, "At Speedy, You're Quelqu'un," *Report on Business Magazine*, May 1997, p. 9.

7. Madelaine Drohan, "Canada 4th Best Competitor," *The Globe and Mail*, May 21, 1997, p. B1.

8. John Stackhouse, "Greed Can Mean Firing Squad in Vietnam," *The Globe and Mail*, March 26, 1997, p. A1.

9. Geert Hofstede, *Culture's Consequences: International Differences in Work–Related Values* (Beverly Hills, CA: Sage Publications, 1980), pp. 25–6; and Geert

Hofstede, "The Cultural Relativity of Organizational Practices and Theories," *Journal of International Business Studies*, Fall 1983, pp. 75–89.

10. Ibid.

11. Hofstede called this last dimension masculinity–femininity. We've changed it because of the strong sexist connotation in his choice of terms.

12 Robert D. Hisrich, "Entrepreneurship/Intrapreneurship," *American Psychologist*, February 1990, p. 218.

13. See, for instance, Thomas M. Begley and David P. Boyd, "A Comparison of Entrepreneurs and Managers of Small Business Firms," *Journal of Management*, Spring 1987, pp. 99–108.

14. Peter F. Drucker, *Innovation and Entrepreneurship* (New York: Harper & Row, 1985).

15. Karl H. Vesper, *New Venture Strategies* (Englewood Cliffs, N.J.: Prentice-Hall, 1980), p. 14.

16. Gary W. Loveman and John J. Gabarro, "The Managerial Implications of Changing Work Force Demographics: A Scoping Study," *Human Resource Management*, Spring 1991, pp. 7–29.

17. See, for example, Bob Krone, "Total Quality Management: An American Odyssey," *Bureaucrat*, Fall 1990, pp. 35–38; Andrea Gabor, *The Man Who Discovered Quality* (New York: Random House, 1990); Jim Clemmer, "How Total Is Your Quality Management?" *Canadian Business Review*, Spring 1991, pp. 38–41; and Marshall Sashkin and Kenneth J. Kiser, *Total Quality Management* (Seabrook, Md.: Ducochon Press, 1991).

18. Albert C. Hyde, "Rescuing Quality Management from TQM," *Bureaucrat*, Winter 1990–91, p. 16.

19. Archie B. Carroll, "A Three-Dimensional Conceptual Model of Corporate Performance," *Academy of Management Review*, October 1979, p. 499.

20. Mira Friedlander, "Corporations and the Public Good; Proud to Be Green," *Financial Post Magazine*, December 1996, pp. 9–10.

21. See, for example, Rogene A. Buchholz, *Essentials of Public Policy for Management*, 2nd. ed. (Englewood Cliffs, N.J.: Prentice-Hall, Inc., 1990).

22. See S. Prakash Sethi, "A Conceptual Framework for Environmental Analysis of Social Issues and Evaluation of Business Response Patterns," *Academy of Management Review*, January 1979, pp. 68–74.

23. See, for example, Donna J. Wood, "Corporate Social Performance Revisited," *Academy of Management Review*, October 1991, pp. 703–8.

24. Mike Gauthier, "Province to Phase in Waste Watch System," *The Guardian* (P.E.I.), April 23, 1997, p. A1.

25. See, for example, Michele Galen, "Out of the Shadows," *Business Week*, October 28, 1991, pp. 30–31; and Joann S. Lublin, "Sexual Harassment Is Topping Agenda in Many Executive Education Programs," *Wall Street Journal*, December 2, 1991, p. B1.

26. Alanna Mitchell, "Harassment Risk High, Study says," *The Globe & Mail*, December 15, 1994.

27. Ibid.

28. Katrina Onstad, "If You Have a Lemon, Make Lemonade," *Canadian Business*, September 1996, pp. 48–54.

29. Thomas A. Stewart, "Reengineering: The Hot New Managing Tool," *Fortune*, August 23, 1993, pp. 41–48.

30. Ibid., p. 42.

31. See Kenneth W. Thomas and Betty A. Velthouse, "Cognitive Elements of Empowerment: An 'Interpretive' Model of Intrinsic Task Motivation," *Academy of Management Review*, October 1990, pp. 666–81.

32. See S. Dentzer, "The Vanishing Dream," *U.S. News & World Report*, April 22, 1992, pp. 39–43; and Aaron Bernstein, "The Global Economy: Who Gets Hurt," *Business Week*, August 10, 1992, pp. 48–53.

33. Archie B. Carroll, *Social Responsibility of Management* (Chicago: Science Research Associates, 1984), p. 13.

34. Keith Davis and William C. Frederick, *Business and Society: Management, Public Policy*, Ethics, 5th. ed (New York: McGraw-Hill, 1984), p. 76.

35. Gerald F. Cavanagh, Dennis J. Moberg, and Manuel Valasquez, "The Ethics of Organizational Politics," *Academy of Management Journal*, June 1981, pp. 363–74. See F. Neil Brady, "Rules for Making Exceptions to Rules," *Academy of Management Review*, July 1987, pp. 436–44, for an argument that the theory of justice is redundant with the prior two theories.

36. Brian Dumaine, "Exporting Jobs and Ethics," *Fortune*, October 5, 1992, p. 10.

37. See, for example, M. Cash Mathews, "Codes of Ethics: Organizational Behavior and Misbehavior," in William C. Frederick and Lee E. Preston, eds., *Business Ethics: Research Issues and Empirical Studies* (Greenwich, Conn.: JAI Press, 1990), pp. 99–122.

38. John Heinzl, "Survey Finds Few Firms Act on Code of Conduct," *The Globe and Mail*, February 21, 1997, p. B11; Alan Toulin, "Canadian Firms Sign on to New Code of Ethics," *The Financial Post*.

39. Paul Richter, "Big Business Puts Ethics in Spotlight," *Los Angeles Times*, June 19, 1986, p. 29.

40. Case adapted from: "Jack Welch's Nightmare on Wall Street," *Fortune*, September 5, 1994, pp. 40–48.

Chapter 3

1. Lawrence Surtees, "The VP in Charge of Clean Business," *The Globe and Mail*, March 18, 1997, p. B12.

2. See, for example, John A. Pearce II, K. Keith Robbins, and Richard B. Robinson, Jr., "The Impact of Grand Strategy and Planning Formality on Financial Performance," *Strategic Management Journal*, March–April 1987, pp. 125–34; Lawrence C. Rhyne, "Contrasting Planning Systems in High, Medium, and Low Performance Companies," *Journal of Management Studies*, July 1987, pp. 363–85; Richard Brahm and Charles B. Brahm, "Formal Planning and Organizational Performance: Assessing Emerging Empirical Research Trends," paper presented at the National Academy of Management Conference, New Orleans, August 1987; John A. Pearce II, Elizabeth B. Freeman, and Richard B. Robinson, Jr., "The Tenuous Link between Formal Strategic Planning and Financial Performance," *Academy of Management Review*, October 1987, pp. 658–75; and Deepak K. Sinha, "The Contribution of Formal Planning to Decisions," *Strategic Management Journal*, October 1990, pp. 479–92.

3. Russell Ackoff, "A Concept of Corporate Planning," *Long Range Planning*, September 1970, p. 3.

4. Michael B. McCaskey, "A Contingency Approach to Planning: Planning With Goals and Planning Without Goals," *Academy of Management Journal*, June 1974, pp. 281–91.

5. Several of these factors were suggested by J. Scott Armstrong, "The Value of Formal Planning for Strategic Decisions: Review of Empirical Research," *Strategic Management Journal*, July–September 1982, pp. 197–211; and Rudi K. Bresser and Ronald C. Bishop, "Dysfunctional Effects of Formal Planning: Two Theoretical Explanations," *Academy of Management Review*, October 1983, pp. 588–99.

6. Richard F. Vancil, "The Accuracy of Long-Range Planning," *Harvard Business Review*, September–October 1970, p. 99.

7. The concept is generally attributed to Peter F. Drucker, *The Practice of Management* (New York: Harper & Row, 1954).

8. See, for example, Edwin A. Locke, "Toward a Theory of Task Motivation and Incentives," *Organizational Behavior and Human Performance*, May 1968, pp. 157–89; Edwin A. Locke, Karyl N. Shaw, Lise M. Saari, and Gary P. Latham, "Goal

Setting and Task Performance: 1969–1980," *Psychological Bulletin*, July 1981, pp. 125–52; Mark E. Tubbs, "Goal Setting: A Meta-Analytic Examination of the Empirical Evidence," *Journal of Applied Psychology*, August 1986, pp. 474–83; Anthony J. Mento, R. P. Steel, and R. J. Karren, "A Meta-Analytic Study of the Effects of Goal Setting on Task Performance: 1966–1984," *Organizational Behavior and Human Decision Processes*, February 1987, pp. 52–83; and Edwin A. Locke and Gary P. Latham, *A Theory of Goal Setting and Task Performance* (Englewood Cliffs, N.J.: Prentice-Hall, 1990).

9. See, for example, Gary P. Latham and Lise M. Saari, "The Effects of Holding Goal Difficulty Constant on Assigned and Participatively Set Goals," *Academy of Management Journal*, March 1979, pp. 163–68; Miriam Erez, P. Christopher Earley, and Charles L. Hulin, "The Impact of Participation on Goal Acceptance and Performance: A Two–Step Model," *Academy of Management Journal*, March 1985, pp. 50–66; and Gary P. Latham, Miriam Erez, and Edwin A. Locke, "Resolving Scientific Disputes by the Joint Design of Crucial Experiments by the Antagonists: Application to the Erez–Latham Dispute Regarding Participation in Goal Setting," *Journal of Applied Psychology*, November 1988, pp. 753–72.

10. Gary P. Latham, Terence R. Mitchell, and Dennis L. Dossett, "Importance of Participative Goal Setting and Anticipated Rewards on Goal Difficulty and Job Performance," *Journal of Applied Psychology*, April 1978, pp. 163–71.

11. Robert Rodgers and John E. Hunter, "Impact of Management by Objectives on Organizational Productivity," *Journal of Applied Psychology*, April 1991, pp. 322–36.

12. See for example, Larry J. Rosenberg and Charles D. Schewe, "Strategic Planning: Fulfilling the Promise," *Business Horizons*, July–August, 1985, pp. 54–62; and Walter Kiechel III, "Corporate Strategy for the 1990s," *Fortune*, February 29, 1989, pp. 34–42.

13. "A Solid Strategy Helps Companies' Growth," *Nation's Business*, October 1990, p. 10.

14. "Colleges Undergo Reassessment," *Time*, April 14, 1992, p. 81.

15. N. Venkatraman and John E. Prescott, "Environment–Strategy Coalignment: An Empirical Test of Its Performance Implications," *Strategic Management Journal*, January 1990, pp. 1–23.

16. See Susan E. Jackson and Jane E. Dutton, "Discerning Threats and Opportunities," *Administrative Science Quarterly*, September 1988, pp. 370–87.

17. See, for example, Jay B. Barney, "Organizational Culture: Can It Be a Source of Sustained Competitive Advantage?" *Academy of Management Review*, July 1986, pp. 656–65; Christian Scholz, "Corporate Culture and Strategy—The Problem of Strategic Fit," *Long Range Planning*, August 1987, pp. 78–87; Sebastian Green, "Understanding Corporate Culture and Its Relation to Strategy," *International Studies of Management and Organization*, Summer 1988, pp. 6–28; Toyohiro Kono, "Corporate Culture and Long–Range Planning," *Long Range Planning*, August 1990, pp. 9–19; and C. Marlene Fiol, "Managing Culture as a Competitive Resource: An Identity–Based View of Sustainable Competitive Advantage," *Journal of Management*, March 1991, pp. 191–211.

18. See, for example, Michael E. Porter, *Competitive Strategy: Techniques for Analyzing Industries and Competitors* (New York: Free Press, 1980); Michael E. Porter, *Competitive Advantage: Creating and Sustaining Superior Performance* (New York: Free Press, 1985); Gregory G. Dess and Peter S. Davis, "Porter's (1980) Generic Strategies as Determinants of Strategic Group Membership and Organizational Performance," *Academy of Management Journal*, September 1984, pp. 467–88; Gregory G. Dess and Peter S. Davis, "Porter's (1980) Generic Strategies and Performance: An Empirical Examination with American Data—Part I: Testing Porter," *Organization Studies*, No. 1, 1986, pp. 37–55; Gregory G. Dess and Peter S. Davis, "Porter's (1980) Generic Strategies and Performance: An Empirical Examination with American Data—Part II: Performance Implications," *Organization Studies*, No. 3, 1986, pp. 255–61; Michael E. Porter, "From Competitive Advantage to Corporate Strategy," Harvard Business Review, May–June 1987, pp. 43–59; Alan I. Murray, "A Contingency View of Porter's 'Generic Strategies,' <KC–6>," *Academy of Management Review*, July 1988, pp. 390–400; Charles W.L. Hill, "Differentiation versus Low Cost or Differentiation and Low Cost: A Contingency Framework," *Academy of Management Review*, July 1988, pp. 401–12; Ingolf Bamberger, "Developing Competitive Advantage in Small and Medium–Sized Firms," *Long Range Planning*, October 1989, pp. 80–88; and Michael E. Porter, "Know Your Place," *Inc.*, September 1991, pp. 90–93.

19. "Just a Few of the Best," The Branham Group, *Financial Post Magazine*, March 1997, p. 63.

20. Brian Hutchinson, "Merchants of Boom," *Canadian Business*, May 1997, p. 38.

21. Dean M. Schroeder and Alan G. Robinson, "America's Most Successful Export to Japan: Continuous Improvement Programs," *Sloan Management Review*, Spring 1991, pp. 67–81; and Richard J. Schonenberger, "Is Strategy Strategic? Impact of Total Quality Management on Strategy," *Academy of Management Executive*, August 1992, pp. 80–87.

22. Celine Bak, "Lessons From the Veterans of TQM," *Canadian Business Review*, Winter 1992. Reprinted with permission, The Conference Board of Canada.

23. Alan D. Gray, "Partnership Began in the Ladies' Room," *The Montreal Gazette*, January 20, 1997, p. F3.

24. David Berman, "Engineered For Success," *Canadian Business*, December 1996, p. 112.

25. Tamsen Tillson, "Wired Wellness," *Canadian Business*, September 1996, pp. 85–86.

26. Wendy Stueck, "The Making of a Screen Star," *The Globe & Mail*, January 23, 1995.

27. See, for example, J. Barton Cunningham and Joe Lischeron, "Defining Entrepreneurship," *Journal of Small Business Management*, January 1991, pp. 45–61.

28. Adapted from Howard H. Stevenson, M.J. Roberts, and H.I. Grousbeck, *New Business Ventures and the Entrepreneur* (Homewood, Ill.: Irwin, 1989).

29. See, for instance, Thomas M. Begley and David P. Boyd, "A Comparison of Entrepreneurs and Managers of Small Business Firms," *Journal of Management*, Spring 1987, pp. 99–108.

30. John A. Hornaday, "Research about Living Entrepreneurs," in Calvin A. Kent, Donald L. Sexton, and Karl H. Vesper, eds., *Encyclopedia of Entrepreneurship* (Englewood Cliffs, N.J.: Prentice-Hall, 1982), p. 28.

31. Robert H. Brockhaus, Sr., "The Psychology of the Entrepreneur," in Kent, Sexton, and Vesper (eds.), *Encyclopedia of Entrepreneurship*, pp. 41–49.

32. Based on B. G. Posner, "Targeting the Giant," *Inc.*, October 1993, pp. 92–100.

Chapter 4

1. Janet McFarland, "Philip Environmental Posts Revenue Gain," *The Globe and Mail*, May 22, 1997, p. B6; Janet McFarland, "Philip's Buying Binge Cleans Out Smaller Players," *The Globe and Mail*, March 25, 1997, p. B12; Janet McFarland, "Philip Snaps Up Two U.S. Firms," *The Globe and Mail*, March 7, 1997, p. B1; Deborah Thompson, "Scrappy Competitors," *Time*, April 28, 1997, pp. 40–41; Tim Falconer, "Retail Services Entrepreneur of the Year," *Canadian Business*, December 1994, p. 46; Mark Stevenson, "Waste Not," *Canadian Business*, January 1994, pp. 20–26; John Southherst, "Services Entrepreneur," *Profit*, December 1994, pp. 24–25.

2. John Diffenbach, "Corporate Environmental Analysis in Large U.S. Corporations," *Long Range Planning*, June 1983, pp. 107–16; Subhash C. Jain, "Environmental Scanning in U.S. Corporations," *Long Range Planning*, April 1984, pp. 117–28; Leonard M. Fuld, Monitoring the Competition (New York: John Wiley & Sons, 1988); and Elmer H. Burack and Nicholas J. Mathys, "Environmental Scanning Improves Strategic Planning," *Personnel Administrator*, April 1989, pp. 82–87.

3. William L. Renfro and James L. Morrison, "Detecting Signals of Change," *Futurist*, August 1984, p. 49.

4. Benjamin Gilad, "The Role of Organized Competitive Intelligence in Corporate Strategy," *Columbia Journal of World Business*, Winter 1989, pp. 29–35; Betsy D. Gelb, Mary Jane Saxton, George M. Zinkhan, and Nancy D. Albers, "Competitive Intelligence: Insights from Executives," *Business Horizons*, January–February 1991, pp. 43–47; Leonard Fuld, "A Recipe for Business Intelligence," *Journal of Business Strategy*, January–February 1991, pp. 12–17; Gary B. Roush, "A Program for Sharing Corporate Intelligence," *Journal of Business Strategy*, January–February 1991, pp. 4–7; and Richard S. Teitelbaum, "The New Role for Intelligence," *Fortune*, November 2, 1992, pp. 104–7.

5. John Greenwood, "Job One," *Financial Post Magazine*, June 1997, pp. 18–23; John Lorinc, "Now the Customer is Job One," *Canadian Business*, July 1997, pp. 22–28.

6. Robichaux, "'Competitor Intelligence': A Grapevine to Rivals' Secrets."

7. Robert Matas, "Fierce Contest has Retailers Using Guerilla Tactics," *The Globe & Mail*, December 30, 1994.

8. Hugh McBride, "They Snoop to Conquer," *Canadian Business*, July 1997, pp. 45–47.

9. This section is based on Bruce Brocka and M. Suzanne Brocka, *Quality Management* (Homewood, Ill.: Business One Irwin, 1992), pp. 231–36; George A. Weimer, "Benchmarking Maps the Route to Quality," *Industry Week*, July 20, 1992, pp. 54–55; Jeremy Main, "How to Steal the Best Ideas Around," *Fortune*, October 19, 1992, pp. 102–6; and Howard Rothman, "You Need

Not Be Big to Benchmark," *Nation's Business*, December 1992, pp. 64–65.

10. Linda J. Shinn and M. Sue Sturgeon, "Budgeting from Ground Zero," *Association Management*, September 1990, pp. 45–58.

11. John V. Pearson and Ray J. Michael, "Zero–Based Budgeting: A Technique for Planned Organizational Decline," *Long Range Planning*, June 1981, pp. 68–76.

12. Peter A. Pyhrr, "Zero–Based Budgeting," *Harvard Business Review*, November–December 1970, pp. 111–18.

13. Virendra S. Sherlekar and Burton V. Dean, "An Evaluation of the Initial Year of Zero–Based Budgeting in the Federal Government," *Management Science*, August 1980, pp. 750–72.

14. See Harold E. Fearon, William A. Ruch, Vincent G. Reuter, C. David Wieters, and Ross R. Reck, Fundamentals of Production/Operations Management, 3rd ed. (St. Paul, Minn.: West Publishing, 1986), p. 97.

15. See, for example, Sarah Stiansen, "Breaking Even," *Success*, November 1988, p. 16.

16. Stephen E. Barndt and Davis W. Carvey, *Essentials of Operations Management* (Englewood Cliffs, N.J.: Prentice-Hall, 1982), p. 134.

Chapter 5

1. Brian Hutchinson, "Merchants of Boom," *Canadian Business*, May 1997, pp. 30–48; Gina Mallet, "Book Store Wars," *Financial Post Magazine*, May 1997, pp. 42–49; "How Amazon.com Keeps Customers Loyal," *The Globe and Mail*, May 15, 1997, p. B10; Ann Gibbon, "Bollum's Books Grow Up Too Fast," *The Globe and Mail*, April 10, 1997, p. B17; Sean Eckford, "Ottawa's Independent Bookstores Join Forces," *Marketing Magazine*, January 27, 1997, p. 2; Paul Waldie, "Chapters Speeds Up Superstore Expansion," *The Globe and Mail*, p. B1; John Heinzl, "Books, Bach and Beer," *The Globe and Mail*, September 4, 1997, p. B1.

2. William Pounds, "The Process of Problem Finding," *Industrial Management Review*, Fall 1969, pp. 1–19.

3. Roger J. Volkema, "Problem Formulation: Its Portrayal in the Texts," *Organizational Behavior Teaching Review*, Vol. 11, No. 3 (1986–87), pp. 113–26.

4. See Herbert A. Simon, "Rationality in Psychology and Economics," *Journal of Business*, October 1986, pp. 209–24; and Ann Langley, "In Search of Rationality: The Purposes Behind the Use of Formal Analysis in Organizations," *Administrative Science Quarterly*, December 1989, pp. 598–631.

5. Fremont A. Shull, Jr., Andre L. Delbecq, and Larry L. Cummings, *Organizational Decision Making* (New York: McGraw-Hill, 1970), p. 151.

6. A few of the more enlightening of these would include Michael D. Cohen, James G. March, and Johan P. Olsen, "A Garbage Can Model of Organizational Choice," *Administrative Science Quarterly*, March 1972, pp. 1–25; Henry Mintzberg, Duru Raisinghani, and Andre Theoret, "The Structure of 'Unstructured' Decision Processes," *Administrative Science Quarterly*, June 1976, pp. 246–75; Karl E. Weick, *The Social Psychology of Organizing*, rev. ed. (Reading, Mass.: Addison-Wesley, 1979); Anna Grandori, "A Prescriptive Contingency View of Organizational Decision Making," *Administrative Science Quarterly*, June 1984, pp. 192–209; and Paul C. Nutt, "Types of Organizational Decision Processes," *Administrative Science Quarterly*, September 1984, pp. 414–50.

7. James G. March, "Decision-Making Perspective: Decisions in Organizations and Theories of Choice," in Andrew H. Van de Ven and William F. Joyce, eds., *Perspectives on Organization Design and Behavior* (New York: Wiley–Interscience, 1981), pp. 232–33.

8. See Neil McK. Agnew and John L. Brown, "Bounded Rationality: Fallible Decisions in Unbounded Decision Space," *Behavioral Science*, July 1986, pp. 148–61; Bruce E. Kaufman, "A New Theory of Satisficing," *Journal of Behavioral Economics*, Spring 1990, pp. 35–51; and David R.A. Skidd, "Revisiting Bounded Rationality," *Journal of Management Inquiry*, December 1992, pp. 343–47.

9. H.A. Simon, *Administrative Behavior*, 3rd ed. (New York: Free Press, 1976).

10. David Olive, "Tire on a Roll," *Report on Business Magazine*, July 1997, pp. 17–25; Stephen E. Bachand, "There's a Lot More to Canadian Tire," *Business Quarterly*, Spring 1995, pp. 31–39.

11. "This Meeting Will Come to Order," *Time*, December 6, 1985.

12. Irving L. Janis, *Victims of Groupthink* (Boston: Houghton Mifflin, 1972).

13. Irving L. Janis, *Groupthink* (Boston: Houghton Mifflin, 1982); C.R. Leana, "A Partial Test of Janis' Groupthink Model: Effects of Group Cohesiveness and Leader Behavior on Defective Decision Making," *Journal of Management*, Spring 1985, pp. 5–17; and G. Morehead and J.R. Montanari, "An Empirical Investigation of the Groupthink Phenomenon," *Human Relations*, May 1986, pp. 399–410.

14. Andre L. Delbecq, Andrew H. Van de Ven, and David H. Gustafson, *Group Techniques for Program*

Planning and A Guide to Nominal and Delphi Processes (Glenview, Ill.: Scott, Foresman, 1975).

15. See, for example, Timothy W. Costello and Sheldon S. Zalkind, eds., *Psychology in Administration: A Research Orientation* (Englewood Cliffs, N.J.: Prentice-Hall, 1963), pp. 429–30; Robert A. Cooke and John A. Kernaghan, "Estimating the Difference between Group versus Individual Performance on Problem–Solving Tasks," *Group and Organization Studies*, September 1987, pp. 319–42; and Larry K. Michaelsen, Warren E. Watson, and Robert H. Black, "A Realistic Test of Individual versus Group Consensus Decision Making," *Journal of Applied Psychology*, October 1989, pp. 834–39.

16. Shull, Delbecq, and Cummings, *Organizational Decision Making*, p. 151.

17. A.F. Osborn, *Applied Imagination: Principles and Procedures of Creative Thinking* (New York: Scribners, 1941).

18. The following discussion is based on Andre L. Delbecq, A.H. Van de Ven, and D.H. Gustafson, *Group Techniques for Program Planning: A Guide to Nominal and Delphi Processes* (Glenview, Ill.: Scott, Foresman, 1975).

19. See A.R. Dennis, J.F. George, L.M. Jessup, J.F. Nunamaker, Jr., and D.R. Vogel, "Information Technology to Support Group Work," *MIS Quarterly*, December 1988, pp. 591–619; D.W. Straub and R.A. Beauclair, "Current and Future Uses of Group Decision Support System Technology: Report on a Recent Empirical Study," *Journal of Management Information Systems*, Summer 1988, pp. 101–16; J. Bartimo, "At These Shouting Matches, No One Says a Word," *Business Week*, June 11, 1990, p. 78; and M.S. Poole, M. Holmes, and G. DeSanctis, "Conflict Management in a Computer–Supported Meeting Environment," *Management Science*, August 1991, pp. 926–53.

20. See William M. Bulkeley, "'Computerizing' Dull Meetings Is Touted As an Antidote to the Mouth That Bored," *Wall Street Journal*, January 28, 1992, p. B1.

21. This section is substantially based on Ellen P. Jackofsky, John W. Slocum, Jr., and Sara J. McQuaid, "Cultural Values and the CEO: Alluring Companions?" *Academy of Management Executive*, February 1988, pp. 39–49.

22. K. Labich, "Nike versus Reebok," *Fortune*, September 18, 1995, pp. 90–106.

Chapter 6

1. *Report on Business Magazine*, "The Top 1000," July 1997, p. 142; R. Karlgaard, "Percy Barnevik," *Forbes ASAP*, December 5, 1994, pp. 65–68; C. Rapoport, "A Tough Swede Invades the U.S.," *Fortune*, June 29, 1992, pp. 76–79.

2. Stephen P. Robbins, *Organization Theory: Structure, Design, and Applications*, 3rd ed. (Englewood Cliffs, N.J.: Prentice-Hall, 1990), Chapter 4.

3. Charles Perrow, *Complex Organizations: A Critical Essay* (Glenview, Ill.: Scott, Foresman, 1972), p. 59. See also Robbins, *Organization Theory: Structure, Design and Applications*, pp. 312–14.

4. See, for instance, Brian S. Moskal, "Supervisors, Begone!" *Industry Week*, June 20, 1988, p. 32; and Gregory A. Patterson, "Auto Assembly Lines Enter a New Era," *Wall Street Journal*, December 28, 1988, p. A-2.

5. The matrix organization is an obvious example of an organization design that breaks the unity of command. See, for instance, David I. Cleland, ed., *Matrix Management Systems Handbook* (New York: Van Nostrand Reinhold, 1984); and Erik W. Larson and David H. Gobeli, "Matrix Management: Contradictions and Insights," *California Management Review*, Summer 1987, pp. 126–38.

6. Stanley Milgram, *Obedience to Authority* (New York, NY: Harper & Row, 1974).

7. See, for instance, David Kipnis, *The Powerholders* (Chicago: University of Chicago Press, 1976); Jeffrey Pfeffer, *Power in Organizations* (Marshfield, Mass.: Pitman Publishing, 1981); Henry Mintzberg, *Power In and Around Organizations* (Englewood Cliffs, N.J.: Prentice-Hall, 1983); and David W. Ewing, "Do It My Way or You're Fired": *Employee Rights and the Changing Role of Management Prerogatives* (New York: John Wiley, 1983).

8. Steven N. Brenner and Early A. Molander, "Is the Ethics of Business Changing?" *Harvard Business Review*, January–February 1977, pp. 57–71.

9. Herbert C. Kelman and Lee H. Lawrence, "American Response to the Trial of Lt. William L. Calley," *Psychology Today*, June 1972, pp. 41–45, 78–81.

10. See John R.P. French, Jr. and Bertram Raven, "The Bases of Social Power," in Dorwin Cartwright and A.F. Zander, eds., *Group Dynamics: Research and Theory* (New York: Harper & Row, 1960), pp. 607–23; Philip M. Podsakoff and Chester A. Schreisheim, "Field Studies of French and Raven's Bases of Power: Critique, Reanalysis, and Suggestions for Future Research," *Psychological Bulletin*, May 1985, pp. 387–411; Ramesh K. Shukla, "Influence of Power Bases in Organizational Decision Making: A Contingency Model," *Decision Sciences*, July 1982, pp. 450–70;

Dean E. Frost and Anthony J. Stahelski, "The Systematic Measurement of French and Raven's Bases of Social Power in Workgroups," *Journal of Applied Social Psychology*, April 1988, pp. 375–89; and Timothy R. Hinkin and Chester A. Schriesheim, "Development and Application of New Scales to Measure the French and Raven (1959) Bases of Social Power," *Journal of Applied Psychology*, August 1989, pp. 561–67.

11. Lyndall Urwick, *The Elements of Administration* (New York: Harper & Row, 1944), pp. 52–53.

12. Quoted in Jim Braham, "Money Talks," *Industry Week*, April 17, 1989, p. 23.

13. John S. McClenahen, "Managing More People in the '90s," *Industry Week*, March 20, 1989, p. 30.

14. David Van Fleet, "Span of Management Research and Issues," *Academy of Management Journal*, September 1983, pp. 546–52.

15. John H. Sheridan, "Sizing Up Corporate Staffs," *Industry Week*, November 21, 1988, p. 47.

16. Tom Burns and G.M. Stalker, *The Management of Innovation* (London: Taristock, 1961).

17. Alfred D. Chandler, Jr., *Strategy and Structure: Chapters in the History of the Industrial Enterprise* (Cambridge, Mass.: MIT Press, 1962).

18. See, for instance, Raymond E. Miles and Charles C. Snow, *Organizational Strategy, Structure, and Process* (New York: McGraw-Hill, 1978); and Herman L. Boschken, "Strategy and Structure: Reconceiving the Relationship," *Journal of Management*, March 1990, pp. 135–50.

19. See, for instance, Peter M. Blau and Richard A. Schoenherr, *The Structure of Organizations* (New York: Basic Books, 1971); D.S. Pugh, "The Aston Program of Research: Retrospect and Prospect," in A.H. Van de Ven and W.F. Joyce, eds., *Perspectives on Organization Design and Behavior* (New York: John Wiley, 1981), pp. 135–66; and R.Z. Gooding and J. A. Wagner III, "A Meta-Analytic Review of the Relationship between Size and Performance: The Productivity and Efficiency of Organizations and Their Subunits," *Administrative Science Quarterly*, December 1985, pp. 462–81.

20. C. Chet Miller, William H. Glick, Yau–De Wang, and George Huber, "Understanding Technology–Structure Relationships: Theory Development and Meta-Analytic Theory Testing," *Academy of Management Journal*, June 1991, pp. 370–99.

21. Joan Woodward, *Industrial Organization: Theory and Practice* (London: Oxford University Press, 1965); and Charles Perrow, *Organizational Analysis: A Sociological Perspective* (Belmont, Calif.: Wadsworth, 1970).

22. Donald Gerwin, "Relationships between Structure and Technology," in P.C. Nystrom and W.H. Starbuck, eds., *Handbook of Organizational Design*, Vol. 2 (New York: Oxford University Press, 1981), pp. 3–38; and Denise M. Rousseau and R.A. Cooke, "Technology and Structure: The Concrete, Abstract, and Activity Systems of Organizations," *Journal of Management*, Fall–Winter 1984, pp. 345–61.

23. See Robbins, *Organization Theory: Structure, Design, and Applications*, pp. 210–32.

24. Nicholas Jennings, "Front and Centre Stage," *Maclean's*, July 28, 1997, pp. 48–51; Peter Waal, "The New Kid's Nettwerk," *B.C. Business*, March 1997, pp. 28–31.

25. Ilan Vertinsky, David K. Tse, Donald A. Wehrung, and Kam–hon Lee, "Organizational Design and Management Norms: A Comparative Study of Managers' Perceptions in the People's Republic of China, Hong Kong, and Canada," *Journal of Management*, December 1990, pp. 853–67.

26. Geert Hofstede, "Motivation, Leadership, and Organization: Do American Theories Apply Abroad?" *Organizational Dynamics*, Summer 1980, p. 60.

27. Peter Fitzpatrick, "This Dog Won't Fly," *The Financial Post*, September 6, 1997, p. 12.

Chapter 7

1. Brian Christmas, "Allied Forces," *The Globe & Mail*, March 6, 1995.

2. Robin Stuart-Kotze and Donald Rumball, *The State of Small Business and Entrepreneurship in Atlantic Canada—1993*, (Moncton, N.B.: ACOA, 1993).

3. U.S. Small Business Administration, *The State of Small Business: A Report of the President* (Washington, DC: GPO, 1986).

4. Henry Mintzberg, *Structure in Fives: Designing Effective Organizations* (Englewood Cliffs, N.J.: Prentice-Hall, 1983), p. 157.

5. See, for instance, Jay Galbraith, "Matrix Organization Designs: How to Combine Functional and Project Forms," *Business Horizons*, February 1971, pp. 29–40; and Lawton R. Burns, "Matrix Management in Hospitals: Testing Theories of Structure and Development," *Administrative Science Quarterly*, September 1989, pp. 349–68.

6. Philip DeMont, "The CEO in the Fast Lane," *The Financial Post*, October 11, 1997, p. 6; Bruce Livesey, "Tag Team," *Report on Business Magazine*, July 1997, pp. 39–48; Susan Bourette, "NorTel Wins German Deal," *The Globe and Mail*, August 7, 1997, p. B1.

7. See, for example, Neal E. Boudette, "Networks to Dismantle Old Structures," *Industry Week*, January 16, 1989, pp. 27–31; Walter W. Powell, "Neither Market Nor Hierarchy: Network Forms of Organization," in B.M. Staw and L.L. Cummings, eds., *Research in Organizational Behavior*, Vol. 12 (Greenwich, Conn.: JAI Press, 1990), pp. 295–336; and Michael Selz, "Small Companies Thrive by Taking Over Some Specialized Tasks for Big Concerns," *Wall Street Journal*, September 11, 1991, p. B1.

8. Barnard Wysocki, Jr., "Cross-Border Alliances Become Favorite Way to Crack New Markets," *Wall Street Journal*, March 26, 1990, p. A1.

9. Mel Duvall, "Applied Terravision Joins U.S. Giant," *Calgary Herald*, April 10, p. D1.

10. William J. Altier, "Task Forces: An Effective Management Tool," *Sloan Management Review*, Spring 1986, pp. 69–76.

11. Ronald Henkoff, "Getting Beyond Downsizing," *Fortune*, January 10, 1994, pp. 58–62.

12. Ibid.

13. John A. Byrne, "The Horizontal Corporation," *Business Week*, December 20, 1993, pp. 76–81.

14. Ibid.

15. Ibid.

16. Ibid.

17. Thomas A. Stewart. "Welcome to the Revolution," *Fortune*, December 13, 1993, p. 66; and Noel M. Tichey, "Revolutionize Your Company," *Fortune*, December 13, 1993, pp. 114–18.

18. "A Master Class of Radical Change," *Fortune*, December 13, 1993, p. 83; and Byrne, "The Horizontal Corporation," p. 78.

19. "A Master Class of Radical Change," p. 83.

20. Ibid., p. 88.

21. Byrne, "The Horizontal Corporation," p. 76.

22. Ibid.

23. Ibid., p. 80.

24. Ibid.

25. Ronald Henkoff, "Make Your Office More Productive," *Fortune*, February 25, 1991, p. 84.

26. Ibid.

27. Linda Smircich, "Concepts of Culture and Organizational Analysis," *Administrative Science Quarterly*, September 1983, p. 339.

28. Alice M. Sapienza, "Believing Is Seeing: How Culture Influences the Decisions Top Managers Make," in Ralph H. Kilmann et. al., eds., *Gaining Control of the Corporate Culture* (San Francisco: Jossey-Bass, 1985), p. 68.

29. Based on Geert Hofstede, B. Neuijen, D.D. Ohayv, and G. Sanders, "Measuring Organizational Culture: A Qualitative and Quantitative Study Across Twenty Cases," *Administrative Science Quarterly*, June 1990, pp. 286–316; and Charles A. O'Reilly III, J. Chatman, and D.F. Caldwell, "People and Organizational Culture: A Profile Comparison Approach to Assessing Person–Organization Fit," *Academy of Management Journal*, September 1991, pp. 487–516.

30. Donald C. Hambrick and Sidney Finkelstein, "Managerial Discretion: A Bridge between Polar Views of Organizational Outcomes," in L.L. Cummings and B.M. Staw, eds., *Research in Organizational Behavior*, Vol. 9 (Greenwich, Conn.: JAI Press, 1987), pp. 384–85.

31. N. Gross, "Why They Call Japan 'Robot Paradise,'" *Business Week*, August 20, 1990, p. 93.

32. "The Internet: Instant Access to Information," *Canadian Business*, May 1995, pp. 41–43.

33. R. Karlgaard, "ASAP Interview: Mike Hammer," *Forbes ASAP*, September 13, 1993, p. 70.

34. "IT Sector Growing Rapidly in the Province," *Nova Scotia Business Journal*," September 1997, p. 23.

35. R. Hotch, "Communications Revolution," *Nation's Business*, May 1993, pp. 21–22.

36. B. Ziegler, "Building a Wireless Future," *Business Week*, April 5, 1993, p. 57.

37. F.L. Luconi, T.W. Malone, and M.S.S. Morton, "Expert Systems: The Next Challenge for Managers," *Sloan Management Review*, Summer 1996, pp. 3–14.

38. Cited in T.A. Stewart, "Brainpower," *Fortune*, June 3, 1991, p. 44.

39. W.R. Pape, "Beyond E-Mail," *Inc. Technology*, Summer 1995, p. 28.

40. See, for example, Ricky W. Griffin, "Toward an Integrated Theory of Task Design," in Cummings and Staw, eds., *Research in Organizational Behavior*, pp. 79–120; and Michael Campion, "Interdisciplinary Approaches to Job Design: A Constructive Replication with Extensions," *Journal of Applied Psychology*, August 1988, pp. 467–81.

41. J. Richard Hackman and Greg R. Oldham, "Development of the Job Diagnostic Survey," *Journal of Applied Psychology*, April 1975, pp. 159–70.

42. J. Richard Hackman, "Work Design," pp. 136–40.

43. Ibid.

44. J. Richard Hackman, "Work Design," in J. Richard Hackman and J. Lloyd Suttle, eds., *Improving Life at Work* (Glenview, Ill.: Scott, Foresman, 1977), p. 129.

45. General support for the JCM is reported in Yitzhak Fried and Gerald R. Ferris, "The Validity

of the Job Characteristics Model: A Review and Meta-Analysis," *Personnel Psychology*, Summer 1987, pp. 287–322.

46. Ibid.

47. Based on L. Brokaw, "Thinking Flat," *Inc.*, October 1993, p. 86.

Chapter 8

1. Bruce Livesey, "Provide and Conquer," *Report on Business Magazine*, March 1997, pp. 32–42; Greg Keenan, "Husky and Healthy," *The Globe and Mail*, August 1, 1995, p. B8; David Menzies, "What Do You Mean There Are No More Donuts?," *Financial Post Magazine*, December 1996, p. 10.

2. Kenneth Kidd, "Cracks in the Glass Ceiling," *Report on Business Magazine*, May 1997, p. 9; Jennifer Wells, "Stuck on the Ladder," *Maclean's*, October 20, 1997, pp. 60–64.

3. Elmer H. Burack, "Corporate Business and Human Resource Planning Practices: Strategic Issues and Concerns," *Organizational Dynamics*, Summer 1986, pp. 73–87.

4. David A. De Cenzo and Stephen P. Robbins, *Human Resource Management: Concepts and Practices*, 4th ed. (New York: John Wiley and Sons, Inc., 1994), p. 136.

5. Thomas J. Bergmann and M. S. Taylor, "College Recruitment: What Attracts Students to Organizations?" *Personnel*, May–June 1984, pp. 34–46.

6. Judith R. Gordon, *Human Resource Management: A Practical Approach* (Boston: Allyn and Bacon, 1986), p. 170.

7. See, for example, Jean Powell Kirnan, John A. Farley, and Kurt F. Geisinger, "The Relationship between Recruiting Source, Applicant Quality, and Hire Performance: An Analysis by Sex, Ethnicity, and Age," *Personnel Psychology*, Summer 1989, pp. 293–308.

8. Joseph Spiers, "Upper Middle Class Woes," *Fortune*, December 27, 1993, p. 80.

9. See, for example, Leonard Greenhalgh, Anne T. Lawrence, and Robert I. Sutton, "Determinants of Work Force Reduction Strategies in Declining Organizations," *Academy of Management Review*, April 1988, pp. 241–54.

10. Shona McKay, "Wired for Growth," *Report on Business Magazine*, December 1996, pp. 57–58.

11. James J. Asher, "The Biographical Item: Can It Be Improved?" *Personnel Psychology*, Summer 1972, p. 266.

12. George W. England, *Development and Use of Weighted Application Blanks*, rev. ed. (Minneapolis: Industrial Relations Center, University of Minnesota, 1971).

13. John Aberth, "Pre-Employment Testing Is Losing Favor," *Personnel Journal*, September 1986, pp. 96–104.

14. Chris Lee, "Testing Makes a Comeback," *Training*, December 1988, pp. 49–59.

15. Ibid., p. 50.

16. See "Resume Falsehoods," *Boardroom Reports*, May 1, 1989, p. 15; and Joan E. Rigdon, "Deceptive Resumes Can Be Door-Openers But Can Become an Employee's Undoing," *Wall Street Journal*, June 17, 1992, p. B1.

17. Edwin E. Ghiselli, "The Validity of Aptitude Tests in Personnel Selection," *Personnel Psychology*, Winter 1973, p. 475.

18. G. Grimsley and H.F. Jarrett, "The Relation of Managerial Achievement to Test Measures Obtained in the Employment Situation: Methodology and Results," *Personnel Psychology*, Spring 1973, pp. 31–48; and Abraham K. Korman, "The Prediction of Managerial Performance: A Review," *Personnel Psychology*, Summer 1968, pp. 295–322.

19. Robert L. Dipboye, *Selection Interviews: Process Perspectives* (Cincinnati, Ohio: South–Western Publishing, 1992), p. 6.

20. See, for instance, Richard D. Arvey and James E. Campion, "The Employment Interview: A Summary and Review of Recent Research," *Personnel Psychology*, Summer 1982, pp. 281–322; and Michael M. Harris, "Reconsidering the Employment Interview: A Review of Recent Literature and Suggestions for Future Research," *Personnel Psychology*, Winter 1989, pp. 691–726.

21. Dipboye, *Selection Interviews*, p. 180.

22. See, for instance, Eugene C. Mayfield in Neal Schmitt, "Social and Situational Determinants of Interview Decisions: Implications for Employment Interview," *Personnel Psychology*, Spring 1976, p. 81; Arvey and Campion, "The Employment Interview"; Milton D. Hakel, "Employment Interview," in K.M. Rowland and G.R. Ferris, eds., *Personnel Management: New Perspectives* (Boston: Allyn and Bacon, 1982), pp. 129–55; Edward C. Webster, *The Employment Interview: A Social Judgment Process* (Schomberg, Ontario: S.I.P. Publications, 1982), Harris, "Reconsidering the Employment Interview"; and Amanda Peek Phillips and Robert L. Dipboye, "Correlational Tests of Predictions from a Process Model of the Interview," *Journal of Applied Psychology*, February 1989, pp. 41–52.

23. De Cenzo and Robbins, *Human Resource Management*, pp. 208–9.

24. See Irwin L. Goldstein, "The Application Blank: How Honest Are the Responses?" *Journal of Applied Psychology*, October 1971, pp. 491–92; and Winifred Yu, "Firms Tighten Resume Checks of Applicants," *Wall Street Journal*, August 20, 1985, p. 27.

25. Paul M. Muchinsky, "The Use of Reference Reports in Personnel Selection: A Review and Evaluation," *Journal of Occupational Psychology*, April 1979, pp. 287–97; and R.R. Reilly and G.T. Chao, "Validity and Fairness of Some Alternative Employee Selection Procedures," *Personnel Psychology*, Spring 1982, pp. 1–62.

26. Cited in "If You Can't Say Something Nice…," *Wall Street Journal*, March 4, 1988, p. 25.

27. Mayfield in Schmitt, "Social and Situational Determinants of Interview Decisions."

28. Mark E. Mendenhall, E. Dunbar, and Gary R. Oddou, "Expatriate Selection, *Training*, and Career-Pathing: A Review and Critique," *Human Resource Management*, Spring 1987, pp. 331–45.

29. Cited in "The Five Factors That Make for Airline Accidents," *Fortune*, May 22, 1989, p. 80.

30. "13th Annual Survey," *Training*, October 1994, p. 36.

31. Donald E. Super and Douglas T. Hall, "Career Development: Exploration and Planning," in Mark R. Rosenzweig and Lyman W. Porter, eds., *Annual Review of Psychology*, Vol. 29 (Palo Alto, Calif.: Annual Reviews, 1978), p. 334.

32. Alan White, "Spreading the Word about Literacy," *New Brunswick Telegraph Journal*, May 7, p. B1.

33. See, for instance, Elmer H. Burack, "The Sphinx's Riddle: Life and Career Cycles," *Training and Development Journal*, April 1984, pp. 53–61; and Douglas T. Hall and Associates, *Career Development in Organizations* (San Francisco: Jossey-Bass, 1986).

34. James A. Breaugh, "Realistic Job Previews: A Critical Appraisal and Future Research Directions," *Academy of Management Review*, October 1983, pp. 612–19; and Steven L. Premack and John P. Wanous, "A Meta-Analysis of Realistic Job Preview Experiments," *Journal of Applied Psychology*, November 1985, pp. 706–19.

35. See, for example, Michael A. Verespej, "Partnership in the Trenches," *Industry Week*, October 17, 1988, pp. 56–64; and "Unions and Management Are in a Family Way," *U.S. News & World Report*, June 12, 1989, p. 24.

36. See, for example, S.L. Premack and J.P. Wanous, "A Meta-Analysis of Realistic Job Preview Experiments," *Journal of Applied Psychology*, November 1985, pp. 706–20.

37. "Top 50 R&D Companies," *Report on Business Magazine*, July 1997, p. 100.

Chapter 9

1. Tamsen Tillson, "Corel Inside Out," *Canadian Business Technology*, Spring 1997, pp. 58–62; Jill Vardy, "Corel Fights for Time and a Jittery Market," *Financial Post*, March 8–10, 1997, p. 1; Bert Hill, "Business is Booming on the Internet," *Ottawa Citizen*, May 2, 1997, p. C3; Patrick Brethour, "Cowpland Bets the Company," *The Globe and Mail*, March 8, 1997, p. B1; Geoffrey Rowan, "Corel Sells CD-ROM Unit in $22-million Partner Deal," *The Globe and Mail*, April 7, 1997, p. B4; Lesley Daw, "Corel Fires First in New Battle With Microsoft," *Marketing Magazine*, January 27, 1997, p. 3; Patrick Brethour, "Corel Ditches Java Initiative," *The Globe and Mail*, August 19, 1997, p. B1.

2. Louise Gagnon, "Coffee Wars Perking up in Quebec Market," *Marketing Magazine*, January 20, 1997, p. 3.

3. Peter Morton, "Teleglobe Goes Head to Head with U.S. Giants," *The Financial Post*.

4. Karen Howlett, "Peso Plunge Hits Scotiabank," *The Globe and Mail*, March 24, 1997, p. 1.

5. Timothy Pritchard, "Peace Breaks Out on the Shop Floor," *The Globe & Mail*, July 6, 1993.

6. The idea for these metaphors came from Peter B. Vaill, *Managing as a Performing Art: New Ideas for a World of Chaotic Change* (San Francisco: Jossey-Bass, 1989).

7. Kurt Lewin, *Field Theory in Social Science* (New York: Harper & Row, 1951).

8. See, for instance, Tom Peters, *Thriving on Chaos* (New York: Alfred A. Knopf, 1987).

9. "Corporate Class," *Canadian Business*, April 1997, p. 3.

10. Jennifer Wells, "We Can Get It For You Wholesale," *Report on Business*, March 1995.

11. L. Coch and J.R.P French, Jr., "Overcoming Resistance to Change," *Human Relations*, Vol. 1, No. 4 (1948), pp. 512–32.

12. Peters, *Thriving on Chaos*, p. 3.

13 Ibid.

14. See, for example, Barry M. Staw, "Counterforces to Change," in Paul S. Goodman, and Associates, eds., *Change in Organizations* (San Francisco, Calif.: Jossey-Bass Publishers, 1982), pp. 87–121.

15. John P. Kotter and Leonard A. Schlesinger, "Choosing Strategies for Change," *Harvard Business Review*, March–April 1979, pp. 107–9.

16. Ibid., pp. 106–14.

17 Dan Ciampa, *Total Quality: A User's Guide for Implementation* (Reading, Mass.: Addison-Wesley, 1992), pp. 100–104.

18. Keith H. Hammonds, "Where Did We Go Wrong?," *Business Week*, Quality 1991 Special Issue, p. 38.

19. See, for example, K. Kelly, "3M Run Scared? Forget About It," *Business Week*, September 16, 1991, pp. 59–62; and R. Mitchell, "Masters of Innovation," *Business Week*, April 10, 1989, p. 58.

20. These definitions are based on Teresa M. Amabile, "A Model of Creativity and Innovation in Organizations," in B.M. Staw and L.L. Cummings, eds., *Research in Organizational Behavior*, Vol. 10 (Greenwich, Conn.: JAI Press, 1988), p. 126.

21. Jill Vardy, "Corel to Offer Java-based Software for testing April 2," *The Financial Post*, March 22, 1997, p. 10.

22. Fariborz Damanpour, "Organizational Innovation: A Meta-Analysis of Effects of Determinants and Moderators," *Academy of Management Journal*, September 1991, pp. 555–90.

23. Peter R. Monge, Michael D. Cozzens, and Noshir S. Contractor, "Communication and Motivational Predictors of the Dynamics of Organizational Innovation," *Organization Science*, May 1992, pp. 250–74.

24. See, for instance, Amabile, "A Model of Creativity and Innovation in Organizations," p. 147; Michael Tushman and David Nadler, "Organizing for Innovation," California Management Review, Spring 1986, pp. 74–92; Rosabeth Moss Kanter, "When a Thousand Flowers Bloom: Structural, Collective, and Social Conditions for Innovation in Organization," in Staw and Cummings, eds., *Research in Organizational Behavior*, Vol. 10, pp. 169–211; and Gareth Morgan, "Endangered Species: New Ideas," Business Month, April 1989, pp. 75–77.

25. This dilemma is based on Kevin Kelly, "When a Rival's Trade Secret Crosses Your Desk . . . ," *Business Week*, May 20, 1991, p. 48.

26. J.M. Howell and C.A. Higgins, "Champions of Change," *Business Quarterly*, Spring 1990, pp. 31–32.

Chapter 10

1. Andrew Nikiforuk, "Why Safeway Struck Out," *Canadian Business*, September 1997, p. 27.

2. S.J. Breckler, "Empirical Validation of Affect, Behavior, and Cognition as Distinct Components of Attitude," *Journal of Personality and Social Psychology*, May 1984, pp. 1191–1205.

3. Paul P. Brooke, Jr., Daniel W. Russell, and James L. Price, "Discriminant Validation of Measures of Job Satisfaction, Job Involvement, and Organizational Commitment," *Journal of Applied Psychology*, May 1988, pp. 139–45.

4. Icek Ajzen and Martin Fishbein, *Understanding Attitudes and Predicting Behavior* (Englewood Cliffs, N.J.: Prentice-Hall, 1980).

5. Leon Festinger, *A Theory of Cognitive Dissonance* (Stanford, Calif.: Stanford University Press, 1957).

6. Ibid.

7. Victor H. Vroom, *Work and Motivation* (New York: John Wiley, 1964); and M.T. Iaffaldano and P.M. Muchinsky, "Job Satisfaction and Job Performance: A Meta-Analysis," *Psychological Bulletin*, March 1985, pp. 251–73.

8. Julian B. Rotter, "Generalized Expectancies for Internal versus External Control of Reinforcement," *Psychological Monographs*, Vol. 80, No. 609 (1966).

9. See, for example, Jean B. Herman, "Are Situational Contingencies Limiting Job Attitude–Job Performance Relationship?" *Organizational Behavior and Human Performance*, October 1973, pp. 208–24; M.M. Petty, Gail W. McGee, and Jerry W. Cavender, "A Meta-Analysis of the Relationships between Individual Job Satisfaction and Individual Performance," *Academy of Management Review*, October 1984, pp. 712–21; Charles N. Greene, "The Satisfaction–Performance Controversy," *Business Horizons*, February 1972, pp. 31–41; Edward E. Lawler III, *Motivation and Organizations* (Monterey, Calif.: Brooks/Cole, 1973).

10. See, for instance, Dennis W. Organ and Charles N. Greene, "Role Ambiguity, Locus of Control, and Work Satisfaction," *Journal of Applied Psychology*, February 1974, pp. 101–02; and Terence R. Mitchell, Charles M. Smyser, and Stan E. Weed, "Locus of Control: Supervision and Work Satisfaction," *Academy of Management Journal*, September 1975, pp. 623–31.

11. T. Adorno et al., *The Authoritarian Personality* (New York: Harper & Brothers, 1950).

12. Harrison Gough, "Personality and Personality Assessment," in Marvin D. Dunnette, ed., *Handbook of Industrial and Organizational Psychology* (Skokie, Ill.: Rand McNally, 1976), p. 579.

13. R.G. Vleeming, "Machiavellianism: A Preliminary Review," *Psychological Reports*, February 1979, pp. 295–310.

14. Based on Joel Brockner, *Self–Esteem at Work* (Lexington, Mass.: Lexington Books, 1988), chapters 1-4.

15. See M. Snyder, *Public Appearances/Private Realities: The Psychology of Self-Monitoring* (New York: W.H. Freeman, 1987).

16. R.N. Taylor and M.D. Dunnette, "Influence of Dogmatism, Risk-Taking Propensity, and Intelligence on Decision-Making Strategies for a Sample of Industrial Managers," *Journal of Applied Psychology*, August 1974, pp. 420–23.

17. Ann J. Nelson, "Get a Life," *Working Woman*, November 1993, p. 57–58.

18. Irving L. Janis and Leon Mann, *Decision Making: A Psychological Analysis of Conflict, Choice, and Commitment* (New York: Free Press, 1977).

19. N. Kogan and M.A. Wallach, "Group Risk Taking as a Function of Members' Anxiety and Defensiveness," *Journal of Personality*, March 1967, pp. 50–63.

20. John L. Holland, *Making Vocational Choices: A Theory of Vocational Personalities and Work Environments*, 2nd ed. (Englewood Cliffs, N.J.: Prentice-Hall, 1985).

21. Rick Spence and Richard Wright, "Canada's Hottest Start-ups," *Profit*, September 1997, pp. 34–37.

22. See, for example, A.R. Spokane, "A Review of Research on Person–Environment Congruence in Holland's Theory of Careers," *Journal of Vocational Behavior*, June 1985, pp. 306–43; and D. Brown, "The Status of Holland's Theory of Career Choice," Career Development Journal, September 1987, pp. 13–23.

23. H.H. Kelley, "Attribution in Social Interaction," in E. Jones et al., eds., *Behavior* (Morristown, N.J.: General Learning Press, 1972).

24. See A.G. Miller and T. Lawson, "The Effect of an Informational Option on the Fundamental Attribution Error," *Personality and Social Psychology Bulletin*, June 1989, pp. 194–204.

25. B.F. Skinner, *Contingencies of Reinforcement* (East Norwalk, Conn.: Appleton-Century-Crofts, 1971).

26. Ibid.

27. A. Bandura, *Social Learning Theory* (Englewood Cliffs, N.J.: Prentice-Hall, 1977).

28. The idea for this exercise came from Jeffrey Gandz and Jane M. Howell, "Confronting Sex Role Stereotypes: The Janis/Jack Jerome Cases," *Organizational Behavior Teaching Review*, Vol. XIII, No. 4 (1988–1989), pp. 103–11.

29. Based on A.B. Fisher, "Japanese Working Women Strike Back," *Fortune*, May 31, 1997, p. 22.

Chapter 11

1. Mick Lowe, "Steel Resolve," *Financial Post Magazine*, April 1995, pp. 20–29; *Report on Business Magazine*, "The Top 1000," July 1997, p. 108.

2. Solomon E. Asch, "Effects of Group Pressure upon the Modification and Distortion of Judgments," in *Groups, Leadership and Men*, ed. Harold Guetzkow (Pittsburgh: Carnegie Press, 1951), pp. 177–90.

3. See, for instance, E.J. Thomas and C.F. Fink, "Effects of Group Size," *Psychological Bulletin*, July 1963, pp. 371–84; and Marvin E. Shaw, *Group Dynamics: The Psychology of Small Group Behavior*, 3rd ed. (New York: McGraw-Hill, 1981).

4. See Robert Albanese and David D. Van Fleet, "Rational Behavior in Groups: The Free-Riding Tendency," *Academy of Management Review*, April 1985, pp. 244–55.

5. See, for example, L. Berkowitz, "Group Standards, Cohesiveness, and Productivity," *Human Relations*, November 1954, pp. 509–19.

6. Stanley E. Seashore, *Group Cohesiveness in the Industrial Work Group* (Ann Arbor: University of Michigan, Survey Research Center, 1954).

7. Based on Eric Sundstrom, Kenneth P. DeMeuse, and David Futrell, "Work Teams," *American Psychologist*, February 1990, p. 120; and Carl E. Larson and Frank M.J. LaFasto, TeamWork (Newbury Park, Calif.: Sage Publications, 1992).

8. Brian Dumaine, "Payoff from the New Management," *Fortune*, December 13, 1993, pp. 103–110.

9. S. Sherman, "Secrets of HP's 'Muddled Team,'" *Fortune*, March 18, 1996, pp. 116–120.

10. See Sundstrom, DeMeuse, and Futrell, "Work Teams"; Larson and LaFasto, *TeamWork*; J. Richard Hackman, ed., *Groups That Work (and Those That Don't)* (San Francisco: Jossey-Bass, 1990); and Dean W. Tjosvold and Mary M. Tjosvold, *Leading the Team Organization* (New York: Lexington Books, 1991).

11. Adapted from Fernando Bartolome, "Nobody Trusts the Boss Completely—Now What?" *Harvard Business Review*, March–April 1989, pp. 135–42.

12. Larson and LaFasto, *TeamWork*, p. 75.

13. Bob Krone, "Total Quality Management: An American Odyssey," *Bureaucrat*, Fall 1990, p. 37.

Chapter 12

1. Deborah Jones, "The Master Builder," *Report On Business Magazine*, April 1997, pp. 58–67.

2. Ralph Katerberg and Gary J. Blau, "An Examination of Level and Direction of Effort and Job Performance," *Academy of Management Journal*, June 1983, pp. 249–57.

3. Abraham Maslow, *Motivation and Personality* (New York: Harper & Row, 1954).

4. See, for example, Edward E. Lawler, III, and J. Lloyd Suttle, "A Causal Correlational Test of the Need Hierarchy Concept," *Organizational Behavior and Human Performance*, April 1972, pp. 265–87; and Douglas T. Hall and Khalil E. Nongaim, "An Examination of Maslow's Need Hierarchy in an Organizational Setting," Organizational Behavior and Human Performance, February 1968, pp. 12–35.

5. Douglas McGregor, *The Human Side of Enterprise* (New York: McGraw-Hill, 1960).

6. Frederick Herzberg, Bernard Mausner, and Barbara Snyderman, *The Motivation to Work* (New York: John Wiley, 1959); and Frederick Herzberg, *The Managerial Choice: To Be Effective or To Be Human*, rev. ed. (Salt Lake City: Olympus, 1982).

7. See, for instance, Michael E. Gordon, Norman M. Pryor, and Bob V. Harris, "An Examination of Scaling Bias in Herzberg's Theory of Job Satisfaction," *Organizational Behavior and Human Performance*, February 1974, pp. 106–21; Edwin A. Locke and Roman J. Whiting, "Sources of Satisfaction and Dissatisfaction Among Solid Waste Management Employees," *Journal of Applied Psychology*, April 1974, pp. 145–56; and John B. Miner, *Theories of Organizational Behavior* (Hinsdale, Ill.: Dryden Press, 1980), pp. 76–105.

8. David C. McClelland, *The Achieving Society* (New York: Van Nostrand Reinhold, 1961); John W. Atkinson and Joel O. Raynor, *Motivation and Achievement* (Washington, D.C.: Winston, 1974); and David C. McClelland, *Power: The Inner Experience* (New York: Irvington, 1975).

9. McClelland, *The Achieving Society*.

10. David C. McClelland and David G. Winter, *Motivating Economic Achievement* (New York: Free Press, 1969).

11. McClelland, *Power: The Inner Experience*; David C. McClelland and David H. Burnham, "Power Is the Great Motivator," *Harvard Business Review*, March–April 1976, pp. 100–10.

12. "McClelland: An Advocate of Power," *International Management*, July 1975, pp. 27–29.

13. David Miron and David C. McClelland, "The Impact of Achievement Motivation Training on Small Businesses," *California Management Review*, Summer 1979, pp. 13–28.

14. J. Stacey Adams, "Inequity in Social Exchanges," in Leonard Berkowitz, ed., *Advances in Experimental Social Psychology*, Vol. 2 (New York: Academic Press, 1965), pp. 267–300.

15. Paul S. Goodman, "An Examination of Referents Used in the Evaluation of Pay," *Organizational Behavior and Human Performance*, October 1974,

pp. 170–95; Simcha Ronen, "Equity Perception in Multiple Comparisons: A Field Study," *Human Relations*, April 1986, pp. 333–46; R.W. Scholl, E.A. Cooper, and J.F. McKenna, "Referent Selection in Determining Equity Perception: Differential Effects on Behavioral and Attitudinal Outcomes," *Personnel Psychology*, Spring 1987, pp. 113–27; and Carol T. Kulik and Maureen L. Ambrose, "Personal and Situational Determinants of Referent Choice," *Academy of Management Review*, April 1992, pp. 212–37.

16. Paul S. Goodman and A. Friedman, "An Examination of Adams' Theory of Inequity," *Administrative Science Quarterly*, September 1971, pp. 271–88.

17. See, for example, Michael R. Carrell, "A Longitudinal Field Assessment of Employee Perceptions of Equitable Treatment," *Organizational Behavior and Human Performance*, February 1978, pp. 108–18; Robert G. Lord and Jeffrey A. Hohenfeld, "Longitudinal Field Assessment of Equity Effects on the Performance of Major League Baseball Players," *Journal of Applied Psychology*, February 1979, pp. 19–26; and John E. Dittrich and Michael R. Carrell, "Organizational Equity Perceptions, Employee Job Satisfaction, and Departmental Absence and Turnover Rates," *Organizational Behavior and Human Performance*, August 1979, pp. 29–40.

18. Paul S. Goodman, "Social Comparison Process in Organizations," in B.M. Staw and G.R. Salancik, eds., *New Directions in Organizational Behavior* (Chicago: St. Clair, 1977), pp. 97–132.

19. Victor H. Vroom, *Work and Motivation* (New York: John Wiley, 1964).

20. See, for example, Herbert G. Heneman, III, and Donald P. Schwab, "Evaluation of Research on Expectancy Theory Prediction of Employee Performance," *Psychological Bulletin*, July 1972, pp. 1–9; and Leon Reinharth and Mahmoud Wahba, "Expectancy Theory as a Predictor of Work Motivation, Effort Expenditure, and Job Performance," *Academy of Management Journal*, September 1975, pp. 502–37.

21. See, for example, Victor H. Vroom, "Organizational Choice: A Study of Pre-and-Postdecision Processes," *Organizational Behavior and Human Performance*, April 1966, pp. 212–25; and Lyman W. Porter and Edward E. Lawler, III, *Managerial Attitudes and Performance* (Homewood, Ill.: Richard D. Irwin, 1968).

22. Among academicians these three variables are typically referred to as valence, instrumentality, and expectancy, respectively.

23. This four-step discussion was adapted from K. F. Taylor, "A Valence–Expectancy Approach to Work Motivation," *Personnel Practice Bulletin*, June 1974, pp. 142–48.

24. See, for instance, Marc Siegall, "The Simplistic Five: An Integrative Framework For Teaching Motivation," *Organizational Behavior Teaching Review*, Vol. 12, No. 4 (1987–88), pp. 141–43.

25. Geert Hofstede, "Motivation, Leadership, and Organizations: Do American Theories Apply Abroad?" *Organizational Dynamics*, Summer 1980, p. 55; and cited in J. Greenwald, "Workers: Risks and Rewards," *Time*, April 15, 1991, p. 42.

26. Itzhak Harpaz, "The Importance of Work Goals: An International Perspective," *Journal of International Business Studies*, First Quarter 1990, pp. 75–93.

27. Shona McKay, "Betting on a Full House," *Report On Business Magazine*, December 1996, pp. 59–60.

Chapter 13

1. Konrad Yakabuski, "Bombardier Gets N.Y. Subway Deal Worth $1.3 Billion," *Globe and Mail*, May 1, 1997, p. B1; Bruce Livesey, "Ceiling Unlimited," *Report On Business Magazine*, April 1997, pp. 36–44; Linda Gyulai, "The Highest Flyer," *Time*, April 28, 1997, pp. 39–40.

2. See Shelly A. Kirkpatrick and Edwin A. Locke, "Leadership: Do Traits Matter?" *Academy of Management Executive*, May 1991, pp. 48–60.

3. Ralph M. Stogdill and Alvin E. Coons, eds., *Leader Behavior: Its Description and Measurement*, Research Monograph No. 88 (Columbus: Ohio State University, Bureau of Business Research, 1951). For an updated literature review of the Ohio State research, see Steven Kerr, Chester A. Schriesheim, Charles J. Murphy, and Ralph M. Stogdill, "Toward a Contingency Theory of Leadership Based upon the Consideration and Initiating Structure Literature," *Organizational Behavior and Human Performance*, August 1974, pp. 62–82; and Bruce M. Fisher, "Consideration and Initiating Structure and Their Relationships with Leader Effectiveness: A Meta-Analysis," in F. Hoy, ed., *Proceedings of the 48th Annual Academy of Management Conference*, Anaheim, Calif., 1988, pp. 201–5.

4. R. Kahn and D. Katz, "Leadership Practices in Relation to Productivity and Morale," in D. Cartwright and A. Zander, eds., *Group Dynamics: Research and Theory*, 2nd ed. (Elmsford, N.Y.: Row, Paterson, 1960).

5. Justin Smallbridge, "How I Quit the Government and Learned How to Ban the Bomb," *Canadian Business*, March 1997, pp. 88–92.

6. Robert R. Blake and Jane S. Mouton, *The Managerial Grid III* (Houston: Gulf Publishing, 1984).

7. L.L. Larson, J.G. Hunt, and R.N. Osborn, "The Great Hi-Hi Leader Behavior Myth: A Lesson from Occam's Razor," *Academy of Management Journal*, December 1976, pp. 628–41; and Paul C. Nystrom, "Managers and the Hi-Hi Leader Myth," *Academy of Management Journal*, June 1978, pp. 325–31.

8. See, for example, the three styles—autocratic, participative, and laissez–faire—proposed by Kurt Lewin and Ronald Lippitt, "An Experimental Approach to the Study of Autocracy and Democracy: A Preliminary Note," *Sociometry*, No. 1, (1938), 292–380; or the 3–D theory proposed by William J. Reddin, *Managerial Effectiveness* (New York: McGraw-Hill, 1970).

9. Fred E. Fiedler, *A Theory of Leadership Effectiveness* (New York: McGraw-Hill, 1967).

10. Lawrence H. Peters, D.D. Hartke, and J.T. Pholmann, "Fiedler's Contingency Theory of Leadership: An Application of the Meta-Analysis Procedures of Schmidt and Hunter," *Psychological Bulletin*, March 1985, pp. 274–85.

11. See, for instance, Robert W. Rice, "Psychometric Properties of the Esteem for the Least Preferred Co-worker (LPC) Scale," *Academy of Management Review*, January 1978, pp. 106–18; and Chester A. Schriesheim, B.D. Bannister, and W.H. Money, "Psychometric Properties of the LPC Scale: An Extension of Rice's Review," *Academy of Management Review*, April 1979, pp. 287–90.

12. Robert J. House, "A Path–Goal Theory of Leader Effectiveness," *Administrative Science Quarterly*, September 1971, pp. 321–38; Robert J. House and Terence R. Mitchell, "Path–Goal Theory of Leadership," *Journal of Contemporary Business*, Autumn 1974, p. 86; and Robert J. House, "Retrospective Comment," in Louis E. Boone and Donald D. Bowen, eds., *The Great Writings in Management and Organizational Behavior*, 2nd ed. (New York: Random House, 1987), pp. 354–64.

13. Victor H. Vroom and Phillip W. Yetton, *Leadership and Decision-Making* (Pittsburgh: University of Pittsburgh Press, 1973).

14. Victor H. Vroom and Arthur G. Jago, *The New Leadership: Managing Participation in Organizations* (Englewood Cliffs, N.J.: Prentice-Hall, 1988). See especially Chapter 8.

15. See, for example, R.H. George Field, "A Test of the Vroom-Yetton Normative Model of Leadership," *Journal of Applied Psychology*, October 1982, pp. 523–32; Carrie R. Leana, "Power Relinquishment

versus Power Sharing: Theoretical Clarification and Empirical Comparison of Delegation and Participation," *Journal of Applied Psychology*, May 1987, pp. 228–33; Jennifer T. Ettling and Arthur G. Jago, "Participation Under Conditions of Conflict: More on the Validity of the Vroom-Yetton Model," *Journal of Management Studies*, January 1988, pp. 73–83; and R.H. George Field and Robert J. House, "A Test of the Vroom-Yetton Model Using Manager and Subordinate Reports," *Journal of Applied Psychology*, June 1990, pp. 362–66.

16. Steven Kerr and John M. Jermier, "Substitutes for Leadership: Their Meaning and Measurement," *Organizational Behavior and Human Performance*, December 1978, pp. 375–403; Jon P. Howell and Peter W. Dorfman, "Substitutes for Leadership: Test of a Construct," *Academy of Management Journal*, December 1981, pp. 714–28; Peter W. Howard and William F. Joyce, "Substitutes for Leadership: A Statistical Refinement," paper presented at the 42nd Annual Academy of Management Conference, New York, August 1982; Jon P. Howell, Peter W. Dorfman, and Steven Kerr, "Leadership and Substitutes for Leadership," *Journal of Applied Behavioral Science*, Vol. 22, No. 1 (1986), pp. 29–46; and Jon P. Howell, D.E. Bowen, Peter W. Dorfman, Steven Kerr, and Philip M. Podsakoff, "Substitutes for Leadership: Effective Alternatives to Ineffective Leadership," *Organizational Dynamics*, Summer 1990, pp. 21–38.

17. W.J. Reddin, *Managerial Effectiveness*, (New York: McGraw-Hill, 1967).

18. Rick Roskin and Robin Stuart-Kotze, *Success Guide to Managerial Achievement*, (Reston, VA: Reston, 1983).

19. Jay C. Conger and R.N. Kanungo, "Behavioral Dimensions of Charismatic Leadership," in J.A. Conger, R.N. Kanungo and Associates, *Charismatic Leadership* (San Francisco: Jossey-Bass, 1988), p. 79.

20. Robert J. House, "A 1976 Theory of Charismatic Leadership," in J.G. Hunt and L.L. Larson, eds., *Leadership: The Cutting Edge* (Carbondale: Southern Illinois University Press, 1977), pp. 189–207.

21. Warren Bennis, "The 4 Competencies of Leadership," *Training and Development Journal*, August 1984, pp. 15–19.

22. Conger and Kanungo, "Behavioral Dimensions of Charismatic Leadership," pp. 78–97.

23. Robert J. House, J. Woycke, and E.M. Fodor, "Charismatic and Noncharismatic Leaders: Differences in Behavior and Effectiveness," in

Conger and Kanungo, *Charismatic Leadership*, pp. 103–04.

24. House, "A 1976 Theory of Charismatic Leadership."

25. D. Machan, "The Charisma Merchants," *Forbes*, January 23, 1989, pp. 100–101.

26. See James M. Burns, Leadership (New York: Harper & Row, 1978); B.M. Bass, *Leadership and Performance Beyond Expectations* (New York: Free Press, 1985); and B.M. Bass, "From Transactional to Transformational Leadership: Learning to Share the Vision," *Organizational Dynamics*, Winter 1990, pp. 19–31.

27. B.M. Bass, "Leadership: Good, Better, Best," *Organizational Dynamics*, Winter 1985, pp. 26–40; and J. Seltzer and B.M. Bass, "Transformational Leadership: Beyond Initiation and Consideration," *Journal of Management*, December 1990, pp. 693–703.

28. B.J. Avolio and B.M. Bass, "Transformational Leadership, Charisma and Beyond," working paper, School of Management, State University of New York, Binghamton, 1985, p. 14.

29. Cited in B.M. Bass and B.J. Avolio, "Developing Transformational Leadership: 1992 and Beyond," *Journal of European Industrial Training*, January 1990, p. 23.

30. J.J. Hater and B.M. Bass, "Supervisors' Evaluation and Subordinates' Perceptions of Transformational and Transactional Leadership," *Journal of Applied Psychology*, November 1988, pp. 695–702.

31. Bass and Avolio, "Developing Transformational Leadership."

32. Keith Davis, *Human Behavior at Work: Organizational Behavior*, 6th ed. (New York: McGraw-Hill, 1981), pp. 141–44.

33. Based on C.B.C. program: "Roger Gruben," *Venture* 466, December 12, 1993.

Chapter 14

1. Story based on J. Cusman, "Avianca Flight 52: The Delays That Ended in Disaster," New York Times, February 5, 1990, p. B-1; and E. Weiner, "Right Word Is Crucial in Air Control," New York Times (January 29, 1990), p. B-5.

2. Larry E. Penley, Elmore R. Alexander, I. Edward Jernigan, and Catherine I. Henwood, "Communication Abilities of Managers: The Relationship to Performance," *Journal of Management*, March 1991, pp. 57–76.

3. Charlotte Olmstead Kursh, "The Benefits of Poor Communication," *Psychoanalytic Review*, Summer–Fall 1971, pp. 189–208.

4. George Cohon and David MacFarlane, *To Russia With Fries*, McClelland and Stewart, 1997; "Canada's Corporate Elite," *Financial Post Magazine*, November 1996, p. 64.

5. David K. Berlo, *The Process of Communication* (New York: Holt, Rinehart, & Winston, 1960), pp. 30–32.

6. Ibid., p. 54.

7. Ibid., p. 103.

8. Albert Mehrabian, "Communication Without Words," *Psychology Today*, September 1968, pp. 53–55.

9. Robert J. Graham, "Understanding the Benefits of Poor Communication," *Interfaces*, June 1981, pp. 80–82.

10. T.D. Lewis and G. H. Graham, "Six Ways to Improve Your Communications Skills," *Internal Auditor*, May 1988, p. 25.

11. Based on Shoukry D. Saleh, "Relational Orientation and Organizational Functioning: A Cross-Cultural Perspective," *Canadian Journal of Administrative Sciences*, September 1987, pp. 276–93.

12. Kenneth W. Thomas and Warren H. Schmidt, "A Survey of Managerial Interests with Respect to Conflict," *Academy of Management Journal*, June 1976, pp. 315–18.

13. Ibid.

14. J. Graves, "Successful Management and Organizational Mugging," in J. Papp, ed., *New Directions in Human Resource Management* (Englewood Cliffs, N.J.: Prentice-Hall, 1978).

15. This section is adapted from Stephen P. Robbins, *Managing Organizational Conflict: A Nontraditional Approach* (Englewood Cliffs, N.J.: Prentice-Hall, 1974), pp. 11–14.

16. Ralph H. Kilmann and Kenneth W. Thomas, "Developing a Forced-Choice Measure of Conflict Handling Behavior: The MODE Instrument," *Educational and Psychological Measurement*, Summer 1977, pp. 309–25.

17. Leonard Greenhalgh, "Managing Conflict," *Sloan Management Review*, Summer 1986, pp. 45–51.

18. Robbins, *Managing Organizational Conflict*, pp. 31–55.

19. Charlotte O. Kursh, "The Benefits of Poor Communication," *The Psychoanalytic Review*, Summer–Fall 1971, pp. 189–208.

20. This section is drawn from K.W. Thomas, "Toward Multidimensional Values in Teaching: The Example of Conflict Behaviors," *Academy of Management Review*, July 1977, p. 487.

21. Kenneth W. Thomas, "Conflict and Conflict Management," in Marvin Dunnette, ed., *Handbook of Industrial and Organizational Psychology* (Chicago: Rand McNally, 1976), pp. 889–935.

22. See, for instance, Dean Tjosvold and David W. Johnson, *Productive Conflict Management Perspectives for Organizations* (New York: Irvington Publishers, 1983).

23. Robbins, *Managing Organizational Conflict*, pp. 78–89.

Chapter 15

1. John Southerst, "How MDS Cut Lab Costs," March 10, 1997, p. B6.

2. Kenneth A. Merchant, "The Control Function of Management," *Sloan Management Review*, Summer 1982, pp. 43–55.

3. Eric Flamholtz, "Organizational Control Systems as a Managerial Tool," *California Management Review*, Winter 1979, p. 55.

4. Steven Kerr, "On the Folly of Rewarding A, While Hoping for B," *Academy of Management Journal*, December 1975, pp. 769–83.

5. Harold Koontz and Robert W. Bradspies, "Managing Through Feedforward Control," *Business Horizons*, June 1972, pp. 25–36.

6. William H. Newman, *Constructive Control: Design and Use of Control Systems* (Englewood Cliffs, N.J.: Prentice-Hall, 1975), p. 33.

7. Ibid.

8. Neil A. Campbell, "Pizza Duo Find Dough in U.S. Hockey," *Globe and Mail*, April 8, 1997, p. A13.

9. Based on a tape recording made by the Dallas Fire Department and made available under the Texas Open Records Act.

10. Cited in Archie B. Carroll, "In Search of the Moral Manager," *Business Horizons*, March–April 1987, p. 7.

11. See, for instance, Bernard J. Jaworski and S. Mark Young, "Dysfunctional Behavior and Management Control: An Empirical Study of Marketing Managers," *Accounting, Organizations and Society*, January 1992, pp. 17–35.

12. Malcolm J. MacKillop, "How to Cope with Substance Abuse," *Globe and Mail*, March 18, 1997, p. B12.

13. Edward E. Lawler III and John Grant Rhode, *Information and Control in Organizations* (Santa Monica, Calif.: Goodyear, 1976), p. 108.

14. James D. Thompson, *Organizations in Action* (New York: McGraw-Hill, 1967), p. 124.

15. J. Rothfeder and J. Bartimo, "How Software Is Making Food Sales a Piece of Cake," *Business Week*, July 2, 1990, pp. 54–55.

Chapter 16

1. John T. Small and William B. Lee, "In Search of an MIS," *MSU Business Topics*, Autumn 1975, pp. 47–55.

2. Herbert A. Simon, *Administrative Behavior*, 3rd ed. (New York: Free Press, 1976), p. 294.

3. John C. Carter and Fred N. Silverman, "Establishing an MIS," *Journal of Systems Management*, January 1980, p. 15.

4. See W. David Gardner and Joseph Kelly, "Technology: A Price/Performance Game," *Dun's Review*, August 1981, pp. 66–68; "Computers: The New Look," *Business Week*, November 30, 1987, pp. 112–23; and William M. Bulkeley, "PC Networks Begin to Oust Mainframes in Some Companies," *Wall Street Journal*, May 23, 1990, pp. A1, A13.

5. See Steven A. Stanton, "End-User Computing: Power to the People," *Journal of Information Systems Management*, Summer 1988, pp. 79–81; and Glen L. Boyer and Dale McKinnon, "End-User Computing Is Here to Stay," *Supervisory Management*, October 1989, pp. 17–22.

6. See, for example, David Kirkpatrick, "Here Comes the Payoff from PCs," *Fortune*, March 23, 1992, pp. 93–102.

7. Justin Martin, "Freeze, It's the Cyber Fuzz!" *Fortune*, May 2, 1994, pp. 14–15.

8. See, for instance, John C. Henderson and Michael E. Treacy, "Managing End-User Computing for Competitive Advantage," *Sloan Management Review*, Winter 1986, pp. 2–14; Peter Coy, "The New Realism in Office Systems," *Business Week*, June 15, 1992, p. 128–33; and Myron Magnet, "Who's Winning the Information Revolution," Fortune, November 30, 1992, pp. 110–17.

9. Elizabeth Church, "How to Keep Customers," *Globe and Mail*, February 27, 1997, p. 14.

10. See, for instance, Stephen W. Quickel, "Management Joins the Computer Age," *Business Month*, May 1989, pp. 42–46; and George P. Huber, "A Theory of the Effects of Advanced Information Technology on Organizational Design, Intelligence, and Decision Making," *Academy of Management Review*, January 1990, pp. 47–71.

11. Lynda M. Applegate, James I. Cash, Jr., and D. Quinn Mills, "Information Technology and Tomorrow's Manager," *Harvard Business Review*, November–December 1988, pp. 128–36.

12. Joseph H. Boyett and Henry P. Conn, *Workplace 2000* (New York: Dutton, 1991), p. 25.

13. Ibid.

14. Bruce Little, "Stock Answers," *The Globe & Mail*, June 6, 1995.

15. This section is based on Richard C. Huseman and Edward W. Miles, "Organizational Communication in the Information Age: Implications of Computer-Based Systems," *Journal of Management*, Summer 1988, pp. 181–204.

16. Cited in *Fortune*, October 28, 1985, p. 47.

17. Stephen E. Barndt and Davis W. Carvey, *Essentials of Operations Management* (Englewood Cliffs, N.J.: Prentice-Hall, 1982), p. 112.

18. Joel Dreyfuss, "Shaping Up Your Suppliers," *Fortune*, April 10, 1989, pp. 116–22; and Thomas M. Rohan, "Supplier–Customer Links Multiplying," Industry Week, April 17, 1989, p. 20.

19. Rohan, "Supplier–Customer Links Multiplying."

20. Richard B. Chase and Nicholas J. Aquilano, *Production and Operations Management: A Life–Cycle Approach*, 3rd ed. (Homewood, Ill.: Irwin, 1981), pp. 551–52.

21. Kevin Marron, "It can Pay to Expect the Worst," *Globe and Mail*, March 18, 1997, p. C1.

22. "The Productivity Paradox," *Business Week*, June 6, 1988, p. 100.

23. Jim Thomas, "As Easy as ABC," *Chilton's Distribution*, January 1994, p. 40.

24. See, for example, David A. De Cenzo and Stephen P. Robbins, *Human Resource Management*, 4th ed. (New York: John Wiley and Sons, 1994), pp. 385–393.

25. BARS have not been without critics. See, for example, Luis R. Gomez–Mejia, "Evaluating Employee Performance: Does the Appraisal Instrument Make a Difference?" *Journal of Organizational Behavior Management*, Winter 1988, pp. 155–71.

26. Shaun Herron, "20-year Employee Wins Back Job Lost Over Aptitude Test," *The Montreal Gazette*, January 22, 1997, p. A9.

27. Robert D. Bretz, Jr., George T. Milkovich, and Walter Read, "The Current State of Performance Appraisal Research and Practice: Concerns, Directions, and Implications," *Journal of Management*, June 1992, p. 331.

28. Douglas McGregor, "Hot Stove Rules of Discipline," in George Strauss and Leonard Sayles, eds., *Personnel: The Human Problems of Management* (Englewood Cliffs, N.J.: Prentice-Hall, 1967).

29. It has been argued that indirect control mechanisms are most appropriate in organic structures. See Steven Kerr and John W. Slocum, Jr., "Controlling the Performance of People in Organizations," in Paul C. Nystrom and William H. Starbuck, eds., *Handbook of Organizational*

Design, Vol. 2 (New York, NY: Oxford University Press, 1981), pp. 128–30.

30. S. Oliver, "Virtual Retailer," Forbes, April 24, 1995, pp. 126–127; "Information Technology," *Fortune*, April 18, 1994, p. 106.

Appendix

1. Based on Daniel Machalaba, "United Parcel Service Gets Deliveries Done by Driving Its Workers," *Wall Street Journal*, April 22, 1986, pp. 1, 26; and Michael Skratulia, "Scientific Management: A Case Study of the United Parcel Service," a research paper prepared under the supervision of Professor Stephen P. Robbins, San Diego State University, 1990.

2. Claude S. George, Jr., *The History of Management Thought*, 2nd ed. (Englewood Cliffs, N.J.: Prentice-Hall, 1972), p. 4.

3. Frederick W. Taylor, *Principles of Scientific Management* (New York: Harper and Brothers, 1911).

4. Machalaba, "United Parcel Service Gets Deliveries Done by Driving Its Workers"; and Skratulia, "Scientific Management."

5. Taylor, *Principles of Scientific Management.*

6. See, for example, Frank B. Gilbreth, *Motion Study* (New York: D. Van Nostrand, 1911); and Frank B. Gilbreth and Lillian M. Gilbreth, *Fatigue Study* (New York: Sturgis and Walton Co., 1916).

7. Henri Fayol, *Industrial and General Administration* (Paris: Dunod, 1916).

8. Max Weber, *The Theory of Social and Economic Organizations*, ed. Talcott Parsons, trans. A.M Henderson and Talcott Parsons (New York: Free Press, 1947).

9. Mary Parker Follett, *The New State: Group Organization the Solution of Popular Government* (London: Longmans, Green and Co., 1918).

10. Chester Barnard, *The Functions of the Executive* (Cambridge, Mass.: Harvard University Press, 1938).

11. Dale Carnegie, *How to Win Friends and Influence People* (New York: Simon & Schuster, 1936).

12. Daniel A. Wren, *The Evolution of Management Thought*, 3rd ed. (New York: John Wiley & Sons, 1987), p. 422.

13. Abraham Maslow, *Motivation and Personality* (New York: Harper & Row, 1954).

14. Douglas McGregor, *The Human Side of Enterprise* (New York: McGraw-Hill, 1960).

15. Elton Mayo, *The Human Problems of an Industrial Civilization* (New York: Macmillan, 1933); and Fritz J. Roethlisberger and William J. Dickson, Management and the Worker (Cambridge, Mass.: Harvard University Press, 1939).

16. See, for example, Alex Carey, "The Hawthorne Studies: A Radical Criticism," *American Sociological Review*, June 1967, pp. 403–16; Richard H. Franke and James Kaul, "The Hawthorne Experiments: First Statistical Interpretations," *American Sociological Review*, October 1978, pp. 623–43; Berkeley Rice, "The Hawthorne Defect: Persistence of a Flawed Theory," *Psychology Today*, February 1982, pp. 70–74; Jeffrey A. Sonnenfeld, "Shedding Light on the Hawthorne Studies," *Journal of Occupational Behavior*, April 1985, pp. 111–30; and Stephen R. G. Jones, "Worker Interdependence and Output: The Hawthorne Studies Reevaluated," *American Sociological Review*, April 1990, pp. 176–90.

17. Machalaba, "United Parcel Service Gets Deliveries Done by Driving Its Workers," p. 1.

Name and Organization Index

Illustration Credits

CHAPTER 1
2 Courtesy Magna International
3 Reuters/Grigory Dukor/Archive
Photos **9** Andre Forget/Canadian
Press CP **12** Courtesy North Star
Navigation **13** Courtesy Cinar Films Inc.
16 Andrew Stawicki/Canadian Press
TRSTR **17** Pablo Rivera/Superstock

CHAPTER 2
28 Jean-Marc Carisse, Office of the
Prime Minister. Ch. Req # 14645
30 Courtesy The Thomson
Corporation **36** National Archives
of Canada/PA-48394 **37** Christopher
Newhook **39** Shonna Valeska
43 Courtesy Envirolutions Inc.
45 Teri Stratford **47** Lara Del Pino/
Federal Express **49** Koster Photography

CHAPTER 3
62 Courtesy Northern Telecom Limited
67 Jeff McIntosh/Canadian Press CP
70 Brownie Harris/Courtesy GE
71 Courtesy Corel Corporation
75 Courtesy of Shikatronics Inc.
75 Courtesy Big Rock Brewery Ltd.
81 "Jennifer Corson, M. Arch."

CHAPTER 4
89 Courtesy Philip Services
Corporation **90** Riclafe/Sipa Press
91 Courtesy Ford Canada **93** Courtesy
Great Adventure People **95** Courtesy
Volkswagen Canada **101** AP/Wide
World Photos **105** Courtesy John
Taggart

CHAPTER 5
115 Courtesy Chapters Book Stores
117 Courtesy Clearly Canadian
Beverage Corporation **118** Courtesy
Seanix Technology Inc. **126** Canadiean
Press TRSTR **127** Courtesy Neptec
132 Katherine Lambert

CHAPTER 6
Courtesy ABB Inc. 149 Stock
150 US Army **160** Mike
162 Courtesy Bombardier,
Press/EDMS **163** (top)
Samuel, Linda Lingerie
(bottom) Spar Aerospace
ated Press AP

CHAPTER 7
172 Neil Graham **176** Courtesy Buick
177 Courtesy of Northern Telecom
Limited **179** Brownie Harris/The Stock
Market, Bob Sacha **183** Ryder Truck
Rental Canada Inc. **186** Chris Reardon
Photography **188** Courtesy Husky
Injection Molding Systems Ltd.
190 Courtesy Fred Deeley Imports Ltd.
191 Celestica Inc. **192** Courtesy The
Shopping Channel **193** Standard Aero

CHAPTER 8
209 Courtesy of Husky Injection
Molding Systems Ltd. **214** Les
Produits Alimentaires Mondiv Inc.
217 Financial Post **224** Mr. Andrew
Badia, Iris Hosiery Inc., Honeywell
Limited **225** Mike Surowiak/Tony
Stone Images **196** Taro Yamasaki

CHAPTER 9
240 Courtesy Corel Corporation
241 Acadian Seaplants Limited
244 Courtesy British Columbia
Telephone **245** Courtesy Stentor
246 Dick Hemingway **248** Bob
Daemmrich/Stock Boston
252 Courtesy Ballard Power
Systems Inc. **253** Colin Patey/
The Waterford Hospital

CHAPTER 10
265 Al Harvey/The Slide Farm
272 Jen Holland/Sunnybrook Health
Science Centre **274** Courtesy YOUtv
Inc. **276** Courtesy Rubbish Boys
Disposal Service **278** Bob Carroll
281 Tim Brown/Tony Stone Images

CHAPTER 11
291 Courtesy Algoma Steel Corp. Ltd.
293 Courtesy Mr. Terry Hui, BurnCon
Properties Ltd **298** Andy Freeberg/
Andy Freeberg Photography
300 Kevin Horan

CHAPTER 12
311 Courtesy of PCl Construction
313 Bettmann **317** Ken Karp
323 Courtesy Antoine Paquin/
Andrew Balfour, Photographer,
Ottawa **328** Courtesy Teknion
Furniture Systems

CHAPTER 13
337 Studio Don Graetz **338** Kirdi/
Ponopresse **341** Patrick Fordham
344 Janet Gill/Tony Stone Images
349 Courtesy Jeff Spencer **354** David
Ximeno Tejada/Tony Stone Images
355 Canadian Press CP

CHAPTER 14
365 Harrington/Masterfile
367 Andrew Stawicki/Canadian Press
TRSTR **369** A. McNeill **372** Sharp
Electronics Corp **374** Courtesy Stria
Communications **378** Bryce
Flynn/Picture Group **383** PH Photo
Archives/CAW Canada

CHAPTER 15
393 Courtesy MDS Inc. **396** Courtesy
earls, Great Food, Great People; Author
Tilley/FPG International **399** Courtesy
Digital Renaissance Inc. **401** Courtesy
Metervision, Michael Abramson **403**
Goodyear Tire & Rubber Co. **405** CP
Archive Photo public

CHAPTER 16
418 Clearly Canadian Beverage
Corporation **419** Ed Kashi **420** John
Madere **423** Courtesy Robert Cullen/
Mount Sinai Hospital **426** Levenson/
Tony Stone Images **429** PHC Archives
430 Paul Chesley **433** Courtesy
Hospital for Sick Children

Illustration Credits

CHAPTER 1
2 Courtesy Magna International **3** Reuters/Grigory Dukor/Archive Photos **9** Andre Forget/Canadian Press CP **12** Courtesy North Star Navigation **13** Courtesy Cinar Films Inc. **16** Andrew Stawicki/Canadian Press TRSTR **17** Pablo Rivera/Superstock

CHAPTER 2
28 Jean-Marc Carisse, Office of the Prime Minister. Ch. Req # 14645 **30** Courtesy The Thomson Corporation **36** National Archives of Canada/PA-48394 **37** Christopher Newhook **39** Shonna Valeska **43** Courtesy Envirolutions Inc. **45** Teri Stratford **47** Lara Del Pino/Federal Express **49** Koster Photography

CHAPTER 3
62 Courtesy Northern Telecom Limited **67** Jeff McIntosh/Canadian Press CP **70** Brownie Harris/Courtesy GE **71** Courtesy Corel Corporation **75** Courtesy of Shikatronics Inc. **75** Courtesy Big Rock Brewery Ltd. **81** "Jennifer Corson, M. Arch."

CHAPTER 4
89 Courtesy Philip Services Corporation **90** Riclafe/Sipa Press **91** Courtesy Ford Canada **93** Courtesy Great Adventure People **95** Courtesy Volkswagen Canada **101** AP/Wide World Photos **105** Courtesy John Taggart

CHAPTER 5
115 Courtesy Chapters Book Stores **117** Courtesy Clearly Canadian Beverage Corporation **118** Courtesy Seanix Technology Inc. **126** Canadiean Press TRSTR **127** Courtesy Neptec **132** Katherine Lambert

CHAPTER 6
146 Courtesy ABB Inc. **149** Stock Boston **150** US Army **160** Mike Blackwell **162** Courtesy Bombardier, Canadian Press/EDMS **163** (top) Beborah Samuel, Linda Lingerie Archives; (bottom) Spar Aerospace **165** Associated Press AP

CHAPTER 7
172 Neil Graham **176** Courtesy Buick **177** Courtesy of Northern Telecom Limited **179** Brownie Harris/The Stock Market, Bob Sacha **183** Ryder Truck Rental Canada Inc. **186** Chris Reardon Photography **188** Courtesy Husky Injection Molding Systems Ltd. **190** Courtesy Fred Deeley Imports Ltd. **191** Celestica Inc. **192** Courtesy The Shopping Channel **193** Standard Aero

CHAPTER 8
209 Courtesy of Husky Injection Molding Systems Ltd. **214** Les Produits Alimentaires Mondiv Inc. **217** Financial Post **224** Mr. Andrew Badia, Iris Hosiery Inc., Honeywell Limited **225** Mike Surowiak/Tony Stone Images **196** Taro Yamasaki

CHAPTER 9
240 Courtesy Corel Corporation **241** Acadian Seaplants Limited **244** Courtesy British Columbia Telephone **245** Courtesy Stentor **246** Dick Hemingway **248** Bob Daemmrich/Stock Boston **252** Courtesy Ballard Power Systems Inc. **253** Colin Patey/The Waterford Hospital

CHAPTER 10
265 Al Harvey/The Slide Farm **272** Jen Holland/Sunnybrook Health Science Centre **274** Courtesy YOUtv Inc. **276** Courtesy Rubbish Boys Disposal Service **278** Bob Carroll **281** Tim Brown/Tony Stone Images

CHAPTER 11
291 Courtesy Algoma Steel Corp. Ltd. **293** Courtesy Mr. Terry Hui, BurnCon Properties Ltd **298** Andy Freeberg/Andy Freeberg Photography **300** Kevin Horan

CHAPTER 12
311 Courtesy of PCI Construction **313** Bettmann **317** Ken Karp **323** Courtesy Antoine Paquin/Andrew Balfour, Photographer, Ottawa **328** Courtesy Teknion Furniture Systems

CHAPTER 13
337 Studio Don Graetz **338** Kirdi/Ponopresse **341** Patrick Fordham **344** Janet Gill/Tony Stone Images **349** Courtesy Jeff Spencer **354** David Ximeno Tejada/Tony Stone Images **355** Canadian Press CP

CHAPTER 14
365 Harrington/Masterfile **367** Andrew Stawicki/Canadian Press TRSTR **369** A. McNeill **372** Sharp Electronics Corp **374** Courtesy Stria Communications **378** Bryce Flynn/Picture Group **383** PH Photo Archives/CAW Canada

CHAPTER 15
393 Courtesy MDS Inc. **396** Courtesy earls, Great Food, Great People; Author Tilley/FPG International **399** Courtesy Digital Renaissance Inc. **401** Courtesy Metervision, Michael Abramson **403** Goodyear Tire & Rubber Co. **405** CP Archive Photo public

CHAPTER 16
418 Clearly Canadian Beverage Corporation **419** Ed Kashi **420** John Madere **423** Courtesy Robert Cullen/Mount Sinai Hospital **426** Levenson/Tony Stone Images **429** PHC Archives **430** Paul Chesley **433** Courtesy Hospital for Sick Children